BOOK DESCRIPTION

The sweeping history of the Ojibwe and Three Fires People of Michigan includes all the tribes connected to the Great Lakes. This is the truth that has been scattered and hidden away by time, name changes, and complexity. The great black unknown, what we never learned about Indian history, the groundbreaking, in-depth research now made accessible. You can know the truth!

"Powerful," "I marvel at the extraordinary research," "a real history," "amazing," "chock full of information"... These are just some of the comments about the book.

The difficult history is presented, clarified, and revealed in one volume.

"Cheryl Morgan's passion for the history of the Native Americans in Southeast Michigan shines through her extensive research in *Ottissippi*. Her journey of understanding the nearly-forgotten lifeways of the Native peoples could not come at a more relevant time—readers and researchers will be impacted by the significance of such a rich culture, deeply challenged by a dominating race at every turn, yet continuing to find strength in the values of their own people."

— Sara Kenosha

OTTISSIPPI

OTTISSIPPI

THE TRUTH about GREAT LAKES INDIAN HISTORY
and The Gateway to the West

CHERYL MORGAN

Copyright © 2017 Cheryl L. Morgan
This book may not be reproduced, distributed, or reprinted in any printed or electronic form (except for review and educational use) without permission from the Author-Publisher. Please purchase authorized editions in support of the author's work. U.S. Copyright Act, 1976. International and Pan-American Copyright Conventions.

ISBN: 978-0-9993923-2-4 (Paperback)
ISBN: 978-0-9993923-0-0 (eBook, Amazon)
ASIN: Amazon, B075H1ZWR3
ISBN: 978-0-9993923-1-7 (eBook, Smashwords Edition)
LLOC: 2017914259
ISBN: 978-0-9993923-4-8 (eBook, Ingramspark)

OTTISSIPPI: The Truth about Great Lakes Indian History and The Gateway to the West
Cheryl Morgan 2017

TABLE OF CONTENTS

Book Description	i
Preface	viii
Prologue	x
Chapter 1: Origins	1
Chapter 2: A Sense Of Place–Waterways, Ste. Clare, Walpole, and Boundaries	8
Chapter 3: Early Indian Culture And History	32
Chapter 4: Explorers and Missionaries	66
Chapter 5: Disease And Epidemics	127
Chapter 6: Trade and Traders	132
Chapter 7: Part I: The French, British, English and Americans	191
Chapter 7: Part II: Forts, Indian Captives and American Biography	260
Chapter 8: Early Detroit and Canada	278
Chapter 9: Biographies of Indian Chiefs	306
Chapter 10: Reserves and Indian Lands	356
Chapter 11: Mounds and Treaties	379
Chapter 12: Northern Slavery	413
Chapter 13: Indian Culture And Lifeways, Part I – Religion, Tribal Structure, Roles, And Responsibilities	432
Chapter 14: Indian Culture And Lifeways, Part II – Hunting, Fishing, And War	485
Chapter 15: Blue Water Indians Then and Now	507
Chapter 16: Early St. Clair County Pioneers	542
Glossary: Indian Names and Places	572
Appendix: Peoples, Places, and Waterways	581
Afterword	592
End Notes	594
Recommended Reading	595
Bibliography	596
Acknowledgements	616
Author Biography	617
Index	618

PREFACE

After a three-month search, I realized the Southeast Michigan Indian History had not been written. It is buried, erased, forgotten, scattered, inaccessible, lost to time and change. I believe a person should be able to easily find this information at the library and on the Internet. It is now a very complex, difficult search and dissemination of information.

The Great Black Hole, the huge mess no one talks about is now recorded in one volume. This groundbreaking research and sweeping history creates understanding where there is none for the good of mankind.

Ottissippi is the collection and compilation of many early writers, historians, and others who recorded something about the Indians of Southeast Michigan and the Northwest Territory. It includes modern writers who added valuable contributions to the Indian History of Michigan and beyond.

This book will provide the full history and culture of the Old West and New for the Ojibwe and the Three Fires Confederacy Peoples of Michigan. It is a sweeping history that is interconnected with many tribes, states, territories, and governments.

The many name changes of waterways, places, and peoples recorded within the book will be an invaluable tool in understanding and researching older writings and documents. Without this information, one would not know they are reading about the Michigan Indians, lands, or waterways we now know by other names.

The amazing Indian Culture is explained—what we never knew, the answers to many questions. The real history, the truth about Indians made plain. The origins, prophecies, migration, religious beliefs, Midewiwin, medicine, totems, chiefs, native government, every nuance of their culture and lifeways, biographies—all explored in detail. The racism, corruption, and northern slavery and genocide are revealed.

This is the shocking truth we never knew. Shocking because we never had heard of or learned these hidden truths before now. It will be an emotional revelation, but also very rewarding to know and understand.

Cheryl Morgan, 2017

PROLOGUE

Who were they? Where did they go? Why do we rarely learn about the Indians? We saw the racism and stereotyping on TV. We know they have Pow Wows, casinos, and lawsuits. What is their history?

Discover the true history, hidden for centuries. The land, chiefs, peoples, culture, and lifeways!

The Anishinabe believe the East Coast Salt Ocean peoples came by land, either by foot or a short boat ride, and were here very early to inhabit it. Due to continental drift, the lands divided and—according to the Anishinabe—spontaneous man, they have always been here.

The great family of the Algonquin's extended right up through the centre of the continent (N. Plain).

Ottissippi, meaning Clear Water, was the Indian name for the strait- the Detroit, the St. Clair River, and the Detroit River.

Aamijiwnaang—where the people gather by the rapid waters, territory at the foot of Lake Huron- Karegnondi, and the Ottissippi – St. Clair - Detroit River, strait, was a natural trade center, a huge trading area of great commerce for the Native Americans. It was a strategic military position on the largest inland water transportation system in North America and the world. It was the natural gathering place that was easy to reach from all directions.

The rock weirs of the Ottissippi Delta, at the head of the Ottissippi - St. Clair River, at the foote of Lake Huron, were the great fishery of the tribes in the surrounding area. The Anishinabe—First People—gathered to spear and net large quantities of whitefish and sturgeon swarming in shallow waters and through the narrow channels (D. Plain).

The mouth of the St. Clair River once flowed more east of the present channel mouth, from Lake Huron into the St. Clair River. There were three channels which flowed into the St. Clair River. The river was much shallower, with sand bars throughout it. There were rocks and more islands.

The tribes were Traders, the whole continent traversed by Indian trails and trade routes. They traded copper, jade, obsidian, soapstone, mica, paint, stones, and shells for *wampum* and buffalo robes.

The Indians had a well-developed religious and social system. It made sense, was effective and comfortable. They had no reason, or desire, to change their customs or beliefs. Their way of life did change with new trade items, and their life decisions had complex ramifications.

"In the Early Days, in the Northeast, Norsemen Fishermen brought diseases, around 1001 A.D. There were very high death rates. The estimates are about 70 – 90%" (Tanner, "The Ojibwe").

Revenge, booty, and hatred were not the only motives for Indian raids. Often children and young men were taken as captives to replace a beloved warrior lost in the fighting. The captive became part of the family and was adopted.

The hidden history of northern slaves and plantations is ignored or forgotten. Detroit and the vicinity was a haven of slave trade with the Indians.

In 1761, Chief Minavavana said to the English at Fort Michilimackinac in his speech:

> *We, are not conquered. The Great Spirit provides for us, we will not be slaves. These lakes, woods, mountains, were left to us by our Ancestors. They are our Inheritance and we will part with them to none. Your Nation supposes that we, like the white people, cannot live without bread and pork and beef! But you ought to know, that He the Great Spirit and Master of Life, has provided food for us in these spacious lakes, and on these wooded mountains.*

Gradually it became known that the new race had a definite purpose: to chart and possess the whole country. Regardless of the rights of its earlier inhabitants. Still the old chiefs urged patience, for the land is vast—both races can live on it in their own way. "Let us befriend them and trust their friendship."
- Charles Eastman

The vast resources of the Michigan Indian lands became known. There was great pressure to exploit the country's riches. The land itself, fur, timber lands, and mineral lands were the major causes of wars to strip the Natives of their country. Fraud and manipulation were the actions used by the government and men who were in business as land speculators, timber barons, and fur traders. Most all were abusing the Indians and the people's trust. There was great corruption in the 1800s.

"In the 1819 Treaty of Saginaw we asked where will our children sleep, we will not sell our lands.

Underhanded ways were used to quell dissenters, and special land deals were made. A large quantity of liquor was used before, during, and after the Treaty, to convince a sale. This Treaty gave half of Michigan to the U.S. government, six million acres. (Diba Jimooyung, Ziibiwing)

There were great oil and coal reserves in this territory. There were 114 signers, chiefs and head chiefs of the Chippewa Nation. Their totems affixed to the Treaty, all friends to Jacob Smith, their generous friend and trader.

The European, American, colonialism, capitalist economic globalization had from its beginning a genocidal tendency. It was an ethnic cleansing. A game of divide and conquer, not only to extermination and removal, but also to the disappearing of the prior existence of Indigenous peoples (A Fake History); this continues to be perpetuated in local histories, writing Indians out of existence.

"Tell your people that, since we were promised, we should never be moved, we have moved five times."—An Indian Chief in 1876

The facts are that the Americas were occupied by millions of people who had achieved technological development, similar to contemporaries in Europe, Africa, and Asia. They had excelled in many specific areas. They did have weaknesses, like trust, honesty, and kindness, that were used to abuse, steal their land, life, and all. (Adapted from, BC OPEN TEXTBOOKS, opentexcbc.ca, Canadian History, Preconfederacion).

An Indian exodus from Detroit never occurred. Many bought land and homes to stay on the original Indigenous Homelands. They are our neighbors at work, school, college, and church and are living, loving, and raising families.

There were no tranquilizers, drugs, alcohol or ulcers. There was, thousands of years of peace before 1492. There are no taxes, borders or boundaries, no Insane asylums, jails or prisons, no orphanages. There was honest leadership selection, bravery and courage. There was no Religious Animosity, no poor and no rich.

—Will Antell, Ed McGaa, DSS Publication, St. Paul Minn.

There is not a need to challenge Indians Traditional beliefs. Appreciate their Spirituality and join them in coming nearer to God. Rev. Lewis Church, Chairman of Michigan's Commission on Indian Affairs, Lansing /Methodist Ministries in Michigan, Dorothy Reuter 1993.

The Anglo-American majority needs to be educated concerning the Native Americans, their cultural values and contributions they can and have made. The Indian has insights which can contribute to the renewal and, indeed, perhaps the survival of us all. Rev. Lewis Church.

CHAPTER 1
Origins

Origins of the Anishinabe of Ontario; Lake Superior, Michigan; Saginaw, Michigan; Black River and Swan Creek, Michigan; and the Ojibwe and Three Fires Peoples

ANISHINABE

The Anishinabe or Anishenahbek—First or Original men, or Spontaneous men—migration story tells of living on the Great Salt Water of the Eastern Seaboard. *Anishinabeg* means "from whence lowered the male of the species". They were part of a great confederacy of Algonquin-speaking peoples, tribes, and nations in about 600 to 900 A.D. The confederacy was called the *Waabinaki* Confederacy - "People from the Daybreak Land". The Daybreak people were *Waubun U Keeg - Abnake*. There were great gatherings and debates among them.

Their prophets of old received divine instructions from the Creator - "The Great Mystery", "The Great Spirit", "The Master of Life", "Gitchi Manito", or God. The divine revelation warned of a race of men with light skin, who would come to this land over the Great Salt Water and be the cause of great changes and threats to the Anishinabe. The people were to move west to a place where *manoomin* ("food") grows on water, to escape destruction.

THE SEVEN FIRES

The prophets—*nee gawn na kayg*—also gave seven fires—*neesh wa swi ish ko day kawn*—or prophecies, eras of time to the people which they had received

Ottissippi

from Gitchi Manito. The people believe the present era of time is the beginning of the Seventh Fire Time era, a time of new birth and great blessing.

The seven major prophets each gave a prediction about what the future would bring. Each prophecy was called a "Fire". Each Fire, is a period of time or era. It is also a place where the people lived.

The first Fire tells that the people would follow a Sacred Shell-a cloud. The people would follow the Megis Shell (cowrie shell) west to an island shaped like a turtle. This island would be linked to the purification of the earth. Such an island would be found at the beginning and the end of the journey. They would find a river connecting two large sweet seas. It would be narrow as though a knife had cut through the land. There would be seven stops, or Fires. The journey would be complete once they found the place where food grows on water. But if they did not leave to begin their journey, they would suffer and be destroyed.

The Second Fire told of stopping by a large body of water where they would lose their direction. At this time the dreams of a little boy would point the way back to the true path, the traditional ways, and the islands – Turtles, stepping stones to the future.

The Third Fire tells of continuing, on the path to the West, to the place where food grew on water.

The Fourth Fire was two who came as one. The first tells of the light-skinned men who would come over the Great Salt Water. The future would be known by the face, or intention, that the light-skinned people would wear. If they came in brotherhood, it would be a time of wonderful change. New knowledge would be joined with old and the two peoples would join- together to make a mighty nation.

The second being of the fourth prophet warned the light skin might wear the face of death that would look almost the same as the face of brotherhood. If they come carrying a weapon and if they seem to be suffering, beware. Behind this face is greed. You shall recognize the face of death if the rivers are poisoned and the fish unfit to eat. The face of this race remains uncertain.

The Fifth Fire tells of a great struggle that was to come. The way of the mind of the light skinned people and the natural path of spirit of the many nations. They are told of one who holds a promise of great Joy and salvation. If the people abandon the old teachings, the struggle of the Fifth Fire will scorch the people for many generations. It will nearly destroy the people.

The Sixth Fire tells about grandsons and granddaughters who would turn away from the teachings of the elders. The promise of the Fifth Fire was false. The spiritual ways of the people would almost disappear. Those who were deceived would take their children away from the teachings of the elders. The elders would lose their purpose in life, many will become sick and dying. A sickness will plague the people, many will be out of balance, and the cup of life will become the cup of grief.

The prophet of the Seventh Fire was younger and had a strange light in his eyes. He told of poisoned waters, forests gone, the air would begin to lose the power of life. The people of the whole earth would be in danger. A new people will emerge, from the clouds of illusion. A retracing of steps to find the treasures left beside the trail. A returning to find strength in the way of the circle, a searching for the Elders' teachings and guidance. But many of the elders have passed on, and many have forgotten their wisdom. The sacred fire will be relit, and there will be a rebirth and renewal. This fire would give the light-skinned people a choice to choose the right road.

The Seventh Fire would light the Eighth and final Fire. An eternal fire of peace, love, and brotherhood/sisterhood. The wrong road would bring suffering, death, and destruction".

The Seven Fires Prophecies are the Traditional Ojibwe Teaching, Adapted in part from Edward Benton Banai/The Mishomis Book.

The Seven Prophecies are also found in Chapter 13: Culture and Lifeways Part I.

THE GREAT MIGRATION

The great migration to the Great Lakes began about 900 A.D. (Joyce Reid, Papers, Timeline)

Each tribe of Indians has their own migration story of where they traveled on the route to the West. Their migration stories were precisely recorded on scrolls of birch bark, skins, wood, or copper sheets. The scrolls were handed down from generation to generation, showing all the prominent landmarks, stopping places, and events along the migration routes. The records were kept and preserved as sacred by the Mide, or Medicine Men. These were the Holy Men of the Tribe. The Mide were learned men who cared for the people's whole being. They knew medicines of every kind to bring health to the people. They were the spiritual leaders of the people. (Medicine means everything that is good.)

Fires were the stopping places where the people lived for a time. Fires were also long periods of Time - Eras.

The people were led by a Sacred Cloud, that looked like a Megis Shell (cowrie shell), that rose in the sky leading the Anishinabe in the Great Spiritual

Migration. There were 7 Fires or places where the migration stopped for a time over many generations. The Migration taking about 500 years.

MIGRATION SCROLLS – MZINIGAANSAN

The migration scrolls, or *mzinigaansan*, were made and kept by the Mide priests. A typical scroll—*wee gwas*—could be nine feet long and one or two feet wide. They were charts or maps showing locations, stops, and events along the way. The scrolls were often rubbed with red ochre dye or paint, a red vermillion color, to show their sacredness. Each tribe had their own chart to show the way they traveled from east to west. The records were also passed down through a very precise oral tradition.

"All things are bound together all things are connected". Chief Seattle

The Anishinabe grew in numbers and arrived at Sault Ste. Marie, Michigan and Lake Superior, where they flourished; it was decided to split into three groups or tribes: the Ojibwe—Chippewa, Pottawatomi—Bodawatomi, and the Ottawa—Odaawaa. They were known as the "Three Fires Confederacy". The Three Fires were established throughout Michigan in 1200 to 1300 A.D.

As the migration moved, some of the people stayed along the migration route to live, help others who came after, and maintain the lands. They grew crops, stored food, gathered, and hunted.

In 1525, after being led to Lake Superior by the Megis Shell Cloud over the water, the Three Fires peoples separated into three groups.

Some of the Indigenous people groups are believed to have arrived in the Americas by coming from the West along the Pacific.

The book of Genesis in the Bible tells of the lands dividing and the people being scattered. It also tells of the languages being confused so the people were dispersed to populate the whole earth as God commanded. Therefore, nations, tribes, and peoples were dispersed to populate the Earth.

The Anishinabe believe the East Coast Salt Ocean peoples came by land and were here very early to inhabit the Land, either by foot or a short boat ride. Due to continental drift, the lands divided and—according to the Anishinabe—spontaneous man, they have always been here.

"The Norsemen were in Newfoundland in 956 A.D. Other countries had been in the Americas very early also". (Metis History Timeline, Canadian History a Distinct Viewpoint)

"In the early days, in the Northeast, Norsemen Fishermen brought diseases, around 1001 A.D. There were very high death rates. The estimates are about 70 – 90%." (Tanner, "The Ojibwe")

"The Lennapi, Algonquin speaking Tribes have a tradition, that their ancestors coming from the Westward took possession of the whole Country from Missouri to the Atlantic, after driving away or destroying the original inhabitants of the land whom they termed Alligewi. In the Migration and contest, which endured for a series of years, the Mengue, or Iroquois kept pace with them, moving in a parallel but a more Northern Line and finally settling on the St. Lawrence, and the Great Lakes from which it flows." (The Penny Magazine, April 29, 1837)

America was known as "Turtle Island". For centuries, the Anishinabe traveled widely throughout the Great Lakes. The population at European contact in the 1600s numbered upwards of 500,000 in the Great Lakes.

When the people were living at Boweting (Sault Ste. Marie area), the people grew large and decided to divide into the "Three Fires". The Ottawa remained at Michilimackinac and became the Eastern Vanguard. The Pottawatomie (Oday Watomi) went south into lower Michigan, and the Northern Ojibwe settled around Lake Superior. There were five original clans of Ojibwe: Fish, Loon, Crane, Bear, and Marten. All were related within clans and were obligated to serve or assist brothers and sisters of extended kinship. There was an atmosphere of security and well-being, giving and sharing of personal wealth. Misfortune could befall any member; it was not manipulative, but rather a selfless sharing in time of need. They were super-families, a network of support.

The Crane and Loon clans represented the chieftainship, or leadership. Fish consisted of philosophers and mediators; Turtle were Chief of the Fish Clan and were also intellectuals. Bear were guardians, protectors, and healers— herbal medicine people. Marten were warriors, hunters, and providers and became the totem of the Metis, or mixed blood.

Other clan totems were added as the people grew in number. The Deer clan were reconcilers and negotiators, gentle people. The Bird clan were spiritualists and pursuers of knowledge. Chief of the Bird clan was called the Bald Eagle. They were knowledgeable of soil and seeds, growing and harvesting Seasons.

"All things were part of Creation, gifts given to men, they were thankful and respectful, they honored the earth, now called Conservation and Environmentalism. They were part of The Sacred Circle, the relatedness of all things. Open quarreling and bickering were unacceptable behaviors. Conflict and criticism of others was avoided. Self-discipline and control, were highly valued. Conflict and hostilities, detracting from wellbeing." (H.H. Tanner)

OTTISSIPPI

In the beginning, only Kitchie (Gitchie) Manido existed; he created the earth, stars, sun, moon, plants, animals, and man. The Great Flood came. The world was created when muskrat brought mud from the bottom of the flood to be placed on the turtle's back.

THE THREE FIRES

The Three Fires lived in all of Michigan and Western Ontario prior to the time of the Iroquois dispersion of the peoples to upper Michigan and Wisconsin, as well as other places north and west. During the Great Iroquois Purge that came about after the Iroquois acquired guns or "fire sticks", the people who had been moved to safe places far away and inland returned to their homeland.

They were called the "Fire People"—*Ish ko day wa tomi*. The waterways were teaming with life, wetlands were extensive, and the beaver (*castor*) was King. The area of the strait was called Tucsha Grondie, "Place of many beavers".

THE CALENDAR

The people gauged time by moons; every moon had a name. There are 13 moons in a calendar year, known as the lunar cycle. Each moon is named for a seasonal activity, influenced by natural phenomena, animal activity, and cultural practices and beliefs. In the vast area of North America, the same names are not used by all the peoples. The months of the year depend on the location, weather, and seasons.

The turtle shell was the original calendar. The turtle has 13 central plates or boxes, called scutes, surrounded by 28 smaller plates. The larger plate represents the 13-moon lunar cycle, and the smaller plate, the 28 days in each moon.

For the Ojibwe, the moons are as follows:

- January – Great Spirit Moon, Gitchi Manidoo Giizis
- February – Sucker Moon, Namebini – Giizis (OOG), also called Mullet Fish Moon and Bear Moon
- March – Snow Crest Moon, Bebookwaadaagame (OOG), also Wild Goose Moon
- April – Walk on the Lakes, Broken Snowshow Moon, Iskigamiziege – Giizis (OOG), Frog Moon, Sugar Moon
- May – Blossom Moon, Waaabigwani – Giizis, also Bloom Moon
- June – Strawberry Moon, Ode Imini – Giizis
- July – Raspberry Moon, Aabita – Niibino – Giizis

- August – Ricing Moon, Berry Moon, Miini – Giizis, also Huckleberry Moon
- September – Rice Moon, Manoominike – Giizis, also Falling Leaf Moon and Changing Leaves Moon
- October – Falling Leaves Moon, Binaakwe – Giizis
- November – Freezing Moon, Gashkadino – Giizis (OOG)
- December – Small Spirits Moon, Manidoo Gizsoons, or Spirit Moon

(Adapted from, Phil Konstantin), Ojibwe Calendar, www

Each tribe had their own name for the seasonal moons, and each season has a name.

- One Week – Ningo Anami'e Gizhig
- One Month – Ningo Giizis
- One Year – Ningo Biboon

A stick was used to record each day and month of the year, with a new stick for each year. Days were represented with a small notch, and months a large notch, for each new moon, or month. Years were called *biboon* and were counted by winters. For example, a person's age was counted by the number of winters that had passed since their birth.

This is the beginning of the Anishinabe Three Fires People history in the Great Lakes, Michigan, Ontario, and the Ottissippi – Strait of St. Clair and Detroit River area.

The light skinned people would become a very large part of the history of the Anishinabe throughout Turtle Island – North America, and forever change their lives.

The prophecies have been fulfilled, and it is the time of the Seventh Fire; the time of the Eighth Fire is near.

CHAPTER 2
A Sense Of Place-Waterways, Ste. Clare, Walpole, and Boundaries

MICHIGAN

Michigan was known by many other names, as were its waterways, places, and peoples. There is much confusion when reading historical maps and writings due to the name changes. Many were changed multiple times. The Ojibwe Indians were known by over 70 different names in the past. Thus, this chapter will help to understand other historical writings.

Michigan was called Mitchi Gami or Kitchi Gami, meaning "Great Lake" or "Big Lake" of the Ojibwe. "The name Michigan is derived from two Chippewa words, Mitchaw – Great, and Sagiegan – Lake. Great Lake" (Farmer). "Kietchi, means every kind of Greatness, in quality" (Chaput). *Mitchi* or *Missi* means "quantity" or refers to quantity.

Michigan has the longest coastline in the lower 48 states. There are 420 named Islands in the Great Lakes belonging to Michigan.

Mi shee kain means "turtle" in Ojibwe. "Mishiiken, is the Ojibwe word for Turtle" (Ziibiwing, Saginaw Chippewa). Michigan was the turtle; the USA was the turtle. There are many "turtle" islands in Ojibwe history. The turtle was very important from the beginning of Ojibwe history and at the end.

Mishikan means Snapping Turtle clan. Mike – Red Sky. Sarnia, 2017.

THE GREAT LAKES

The lands of the Northwest were called the "Pays De En Haut", or The Upper Country, the Great Lakes Basin.

The Great Lakes consist of five lakes: Lake Ontario, Lake Erie, Lake Huron, Lake Superior, and Lake Michigan.

> *"The waters of which unite to form the St. Lawrence River. Lake Superior, the true source of the St. Lawrence, is the greatest freshwater lake on the globe! Its waters are carried off into Lake Huron. Lake Huron also receives the waters of Lake Michigan. The River St. Clair carries off the waters of these Three Inland Seas; after running about 30 miles between moderately high banks, it expands into Lake St. Clair, which is only about 30 miles in diameter. Lake St. Clair is connected with Lake Erie by the River Detroit. Lake Erie is connected with Lake Ontario by the Niagra River on which are the celebrated Falls. From Lake Ontario, the river commences to Montreal Canada and on out to the St. Lawrence River and to the Atlantic Ocean. A distance only 600 or so miles shorter than the Mississippi".* (The Penny Magazine, April 29, 1837, "The River St. Clair and the Chippeway Indians")

Niagara Falls "Great Falls", Kitchi ka be kong and Animikee wa-bu - "Place of the Thunder Water" and "Crooked Place". On the Niagara River, Niagara Falls was known as St. Louis in Quebec, French Louisiana.

"The Indians had long ago called the Great Lakes 'Mitchi Asugyegan', meaning 'Lake Country'" (John T. Barnes). "The early Jesuits Missionaries called the Great Lakes, 'Sweet Water Seas' (Barnes, Honorary Chippewa Chief 1967).

Below are the names of the Lakes used throughout this history, as well as their locations.

- Lake Erie: "Okswego" or "Swege" (Jenks) "the White Waters Lake" (Plain, 1300 Moons). West of Lake Ontario above Ohio and Pennsylvania, and south of southwest Ontario, Canada

- Lake Huron, bounded by East Lower Michigan, Upper Michigan, Western Ontario, Canada: its bay, (Georgian Bay) in the northern part of Ontario, part of East Lake Huron, was called "Bay of Missisagues" (Lahonton II, 1603)
- Lake Superior: upper peninsula of Michigan, upper Wisconsin, and Minnesota and south of Canada
- Lake Michigan: west of Lower Michigan and East of Wisconsin and south of Michigan's Upper Peninsula
- Lake Ontario: lies above New York and below Ontario
- Georgian Bay, East Lake Huron in Southwest Ontario, Canada
- Lake Simcoe, east of Georgian Bay: "Lake Aux Claies" by early French families
- Lake St. Clair, Lake Nipigon, and Georgian Bay were sometimes called "the sixth lake".

See pages in appendix at the back of the book for more names of the lakes.

LAKE HURON

Lake Huron is 250 miles long, 120 miles wide, and 800 feet deep. It is 576 feet above sea level and 20,500 square miles. It is the third largest of the great freshwater lakes. Lake Huron rises and falls once every seven years.

Lake Huron was known by the following names:

- Lake Orleans by the early French
- Lake Ottawa or Ottawa Lake
- Lake Michigan, meaning Great Lake
- Canatara, an Iroquois name
- Karegnondi and Karegnon by the Missisaugas
- Mer Douce, French for "Sweet Seas" (not having salt)
- The Calm Sea
- Lake Mer Duce, meaning "Placid Sea" in French (Schoolcraft)

"The land on the Easternmost shore of Lake Huron was called Sahgeeny and Nohtooway or Nahtoowassee" (George (John) Copeway). Land to the west of Lake Huron was called "Conchradum" by the French. The southern Great Lakes were called "Wakashan" by the Iroquois.

LAKE HURON LAND BRIDGE

Beneath the waters of Lake Huron lies an ancient land bridge which separated Lake Huron into two smaller lakes. The land bridge once connected Northeast Michigan's Alpena area to Point Clark near Amberly in Southwest

Ontario. Amberly is due east from the tip of Michigan's thumb. The land bridge now lies 100 feet beneath the surface of Lake Huron.

John O'Shea and associates from the Museum of Anthropological Archaeology, University of Michigan, conducted research in 2009 which provided evidence to suggest that this ridge served as a seasonal migratory link (spring and fall) for mastadon and caribou. Because of its narrow width and limited escape opportunities, this crossing created exceptional hunting, which ended as the lakes rose to an elevation which submerged this bridge. New maps were released of the Lake Huron area by the U.S. government, clearly showing this land bridge.

A complex network of rock hunting blinds, drive lanes, and food cache sites were identified at a location which would have intersected the seasonal migration route of the caribou. The area is about 35 miles southeast of Alpena. It is identified as "The Drop 45 Drive Lane". The incredibly organized hunters clearly understood the migratory instincts of caribou, placing boulders in two parallel directions. Caribou followed such paths to the dead end of the human erected stone wall, thus providing great sustenance to the hunters. It is theorized that meat harvested during the fall migration was stored in these caches until winter and then retrieved by sled. Such pursuits were once a communal activity. It is assumed they dried the meat for storage. This story can only be told because of its underwater preservation (University of Michigan Museum of Anthropology, Memoir 57. Caribou Hunting in the Upper Great Lakes, Sonnenburg, Lemke and John O'Shea).

LAKE ST. CLAIR

Lake St. Clair is 430 square miles: 26 miles long and 24 miles wide. It is a heart shape with the world's largest freshwater river delta and one of the largest deltas in the world. The delta is on the northern end where the River St. Clair enters Lake St. Clair. Lake St. Clair is 10 to 19 feet deep; the shipping channel dredged through the center is 27 to 29 feet deep. It is often called the sixth Great Lake.

It is and has always been a sport fishing haven for both Americans and Canadians. It is in the major bird migration pathway called the Atlantic and Mississippi Flyways. "The Marshes were luxuriant, with Manoomin – Wild Rice, also called Wild Oats, A feast for the great variety of birds, waterfowl, and for the Native Americans" (Angel Fire).

In the late 1950s, a channel was created in Lake St. Clair to accommodate large freighters hauling products out of and into the Great Lakes. The swift current from Lake Huron carries sand and gravel to Lake St. Clair through the St. Clair River.

St. Claire was the name Pere Hennepin, an explorer, called the lake, naming it after the saint whose day it was when he arrived there. St. Clare was devoted to living simply; she was the founder of The Poor Clares. Ste. Claire was applied to the entire District of Ste. Claire.

Sinclair was the name of the British Captain Patrick Sinclair who built a post at what is now St. Clair. However, St. Clair, the town and city, was named after General and Governor Arthur St. Clair in 1828, ten years after he died.

Lake St. Clair was called the following names:

- Otsiketa and Otiketa, meaning "salt water" and the Indian name for "Round lake" – the lake has a heart shape
- Wahwehpyahtahnoong: "The Round Lake", "Missauga Ojibwe" (Jenks 1912)

SAINT CLARE

Saint Clare of Assisi was an Italian saint. She was one of the first followers of St. Francis of Assisi. She founded the Order of Poor Ladies. She wrote the Rule of Life, the first monastic rule written by a woman. Following her death, the order she founded was renamed "The Order of St. Clare", referred to today as Poor Clares (Poor Ladies of San Damiano).

She was devoted to prayer, and her mother and three sisters also entered Clare's monastery. She exchanged her rich gown for a plain robe and veil and lived with no possessions. The nuns went bare foot, slept on the ground, ate no meat, and observed almost complete silence.

She was titled after Franciscus and aided Francis, her lifelong friend. She took care of him during his old age. She endured a long period of poor health until her death. Her Theology of Joyous Poverty was in imitation of Christ.

In 1253, her last words were "Blessed be you, O God, for having created me". Her Influence was such that Popes, Cardinals, and Bishops came to consult her.

Lake St. Clare or St. Clair was named on August 11, 1679, her Feast Day (Saint Clare, www).

BOUNDARIES AND REGIONS

QUEBEC

Quebec is the name used for a very large part of New France, including the area of Michigan and Canada; it went south to the Ohio River and west to the Mississippi.

KENT COUNTY

Kent County – 1791 – "is to comprehend all the country, (not being territories of the Indians), not already included, in the several counties, herein described, including all the territory to the westward and southward of the said line, to the utmost extent of the country commonly called or known by the name of Canada" (Colonel John Graves Simcoe).

British Kent County included Michigan and Illinois, Lakes Michigan and Lake Superior extending to Hudson's Bay in the North, and seemingly to the North Pole; it was the largest county in Canada. In those days, Kent County was called Fairfield. (See Chapter 8: Detroit and Canada.)

THE DETROIT

The Strait, or Detroit as the French called it, the Strait that runs between Lake Huron and Lake Erie. The whole region was known as the Detroit. This has caused great confusion in reading historical writings because Detroit was used as the name for the city that arose at a much later date.

Le Detroit, "this strait", runs from Lake Huron to Lake Erie. "Detroit was the entire district between Lake Huron and Lake Erie. The Strait was the entire channel between Lake Huron and Lake Erie" (Jenks). The Detroit of Lake Huron and the Detroit of Lake Erie. The Detroit cuts through the lands like a knife; it is fairly straight running between Lake Huron and Lake Erie.

Detroit means "the Strait" in French, this also described the land and people who lived there, through the whole of the Strait. The Detroit Chippewas were the Black River and Swan Creek People from along the whole Strait. The Detroit of Lake Huron describes the Strait above Lake St. Clair, now the St. Clair River (Jenks, History of St. Clair County). The Detroit of Lake Erie describes the Strait below Lake St. Clair, now the Detroit River.

The word Detroit-strait at that time had no reference whatever to the locality of the present city of that name but covered the whole waterway from Lake Erie to Lake Huron (Jenks 1912). This generalization had led several modern authors into the error of locating events here (City of Detroit) that really occurred on the River Ste. Claire (Farmer 1884).

Ottissippi

TEUSCHA GRONDIE

From the earliest time, this region was noted for its beavers. The localities where the beaver flourished were the most valuable and coveted lands and waterways (Jenks).

This region included Windmill Point, on the Detroit River near Lake St. Clair; Sanguenaum - the west shore of Lake Huron; and Port Credit - the site of Fort Gratiot, the trading post (Map of Sarnia, Lambton Maps).

Teuscha Grondie was known by the following names:

- "Teuscha Grondie or "Teuchsa Grondie": The Strait region, "Place of many Beavers"; also, "Tysch Sarondia" and "Tosh Sagh Rondie" (Farmer 1884)
- "In 1620, the trading post of the French at the Old Indian Village on its site, Teuchsa Grondic" (Colden/Lanman, History of MI, pg. 6)
- "Tii Ux Son Runtie: the west side of the Detroit River, Lake St. Clair, and St. Clair River
- Tie ug sach rondio: the name for Fort Detroit or Fort St. Joseph at the foot of Lake Huron
- Tircksarondia or Tyscharondia: Fort St. Joseph (Jenks vol. 1, 1912 History of St. Clair County Michigan)
- Fort De Tret: Tieugsachrondio, "Place of Many Beavers", was in St. Clair County, Michigan, Fort Gratiot area

AAMJIWNAANG – THE GATHERING PLACE

"This is the name of the Territory that once covered a great area of Eastern Michigan and Western Ontario. It extended North to Goderich, Ontario, to Toronto, Ont., and North around Georgian Bay in Ontario. It reached South to Detroit, and West to Lansing, and to White Rock in Michigan. Today it is represented by one small reserve in Sarnia, Ontario" (Plain).

Aamjiwnaang is pronounced *am-jin-nun* and means "Place by the Rapid Water" or "at the Spawning Stream" (Sarnia Chippewa First Nations). According to the Ontario Encyclopedia, Aamjiwnaang also means "where the people meet by flowing waters". David Plain states, "Aamjiwnaang means, Contrary place water flowing, Place where water flows contrary, pooling back to the lake".

"The Port Huron area was a huge trading area of great commerce between tribes" (Joe Greaux, Woodlands Metis Peace Chief, 2014 interview). "It was called 'The Gathering Place'" (Anita, Ziibiwing, Saginaw Chippewa). This was one of their favorite camping places to visit family, hunt, fish, and rest while traveling along the great travel routes of the St. Clair River, Lake Huron,

Black River, and the Thumb of Michigan, to all parts in every direction as was the custom to travel throughout the Great Lakes region. It was also a place of great commerce between other tribes and the white and Metis (mixed breeds traders). There was plenty of food in the area, a large trading place, and a staging area for any wars that the Alliance Confederacy would be involved in.

Being at the foot of Lake Huron, having many sandbars and shallow channels on the St. Clair River made for an easy crossing to the other side on the east shores, now Canada. It was a stopping place to Warpole, or St. Mary's Island, now Walpole Island, and the many other islands near Lake St. Clair, Swan Creek, the Huron (Clinton River), Rouge River, and all points south and in every other direction.

Aumichoanaws is an Indian word for what is now the St. Clair County area and was the name of the village at Black River, consisting of more than 20 villages along the nearby waterways. "Aamjiwnaang, has always been a favorite resort of the Chippeway Indians, even while retreating in the advance of European Emigration" (The Penny Magazine, 1837).

THE FOSSIL TREES

In 1830, *The Detroit Gazette* printed this original poetry:

> *Just below Fort Gratiot at the Foot of Lake Huron, the bank of the River is 30 or 49 feet high, and nearly perpendicular. The force of the current washing constantly against detrition of the current has been opening to view a number of Fossil Trees. In other words;*
>
> *At Huron's Foot, there is a lofty bank, some 30 feet or more of elevation. Which worn away by chafing waves have rent the seal away which for Long Centuries has kept from view, the changeful freaks of Earths Primeval Day, when land and water other boundaries knew.*
>
> *Here where alluvial sands a bed have found, usurpers o'er the clay or yielding waves; Trees that in earliest ages, waved around, are slowly peeping from their Ancient Graves.*

Ottissippi

Where is the Record of this Hemisphere, its retrospect embraces but a span. What a Long sweep of Ages, lengthened were which has no History in the mind of Man. But strange developments many yet be made, Types of those buried Times, may yet arise. For Earths Deep Mysteries when all betrayed, may shed New Light on our Be-Nighted Eyes. (MI Room, SCC Library)

Cholera Point was where Pine Grove Park is now; the area of the Water Works building is where land once jutted out into the St. Clair River, below Fort Gratiot. Soldiers in 1832 were taken off the ship "Henry Clay" coming from Detroit and left at the Fort Grounds, where many died and were buried at the Fort Cemetery.

RIVERS AND THEIR ISLANDS

BLACK RIVER

Black River is 60 miles long with a watershed of 690 miles. It falls 200 feet from its source near Minden Bog, west of Palms in Sanilac County, Michigan. Black River was also known as River Delude, Duluth, Dulhut, Hauviere Deludes, Riviere Des Loutres, Noar, River Lowar, La Riviere Noire, and River Aux De Lu. Duluth for the famous French officer who in 1686 established a Post - Fort at the foot of Lake Huron called Fort Duluth, Fort Detret, and Fort St. Joseph.

There was a saying called "Black River Gold": this was not a metal, but the white pine and cork pine that made many millionaires and barons of lumber fame and fortune.

Blackwater River People, the people who lived on the Black River, were called Mekadewagamitigweyawinniwak – The Blackwater River People. Nancy Brakeman Papers

"Muck A Ta See Bing [is the] Indian name for Black River". (Nancy Brakeman)

Muck" means black, and "Noir" is French for black.

THE ST. CLAIR RIVER

The St. Clair River is 44 miles long and 833 feet wide at the Blue Water Bridge, widening to about 3,000 feet at some points.

"The St. Clair River had 3 Mouths in 1670" (Hennepin). "Two channels were open in the 1770s" (Farmer 1884).

"The St. Clair River was formerly known as: Huron River and Riviere Huron" (Charles Moore, "History of Michigan").

HURON RIVER

"The Clinton River, (Macomb County, MI) was also called Huron River" (Jenks).

Fairfield was a settlement for the Delaware Moravian Indians on the Huron River.

The St. Clair River at one time was called the Huron River.

The Huron River flows into Lake Superior in the upper peninsula, above L'Anse (Historic MI).

The now Cass River in Huron county (the thumb of Michigan) was called the Huron River and empties into the Saginaw River.

The Huron River was also the name of a river flowing through Ann Arbor and Ypsilanti, entering Lake Erie near Flat Rock, Michigan.

THE OTTISSIPPI

The Ottissippi was the Indian name for the St. Clair River/Detroit River, meaning "clear water" (Barnes/Plain).

Belle River, which is now Marine City, Michigan (called "She Ban Me To Go Sebing" by the Ojibwe) (Mitts), with Catholic Point to the south and Yankee Point to the north.

"Pointe Du Chene, was Algonac, MI. Also called, Point Aux Chenes – Nemitifomisking, Oak Point" (Chaput).

La Channel Du Bark was a branch of the St. Clair River (Map Library, U of M, Ann Arbor, Harlan Hatcher Grad Library).

Below is a letter to General Brown at Brownville by Samuel Storrow, 1817:

> *"Without reference to the map, a stranger is led into error from the different names given to the same Water. Since leaving Detroit, I had been on One Stream known in its various parts as Detroit River, Lake St. Clair, the River St. Clair, and the River Huron. Fort Gratiot is situated on the right bank of the latter which is the Rapid formed by Lake Huron in its first*

OTTISSIPPI

outlet to the water below. Its direction is from North to South, its width about 800 yards, its length about a mile and the rapidity of the current nearly five miles an hour". (Wisc. State Historical Society, "The Northwest in 1817", the St. Clair River)

In the late 1950s, a channel 28-feet deep (8.3 meters) was created in the St. Clair River. The St. Clair River Delta at the south end entering Lake St. Clair is the Largest Freshwater Delta in the World. It is a rich source of feed for the great variety of birds and waterfowl that live there and pass through on their annual migration. The swift current from Lake Huron carries sand and gravel to Lake St. Clair from Lake Huron. The St. Clair River is the world's highway!

"At one time, you could walk across the River, there was 150 feet of Shoreline. It wasn't nearly as deep, as it is now. Pine Grove Park extended 75 to 100 feet out into the river. The tree stumps are still there where they went over the original bank of the St. Clair River. Brian Hock, Black River Ojibwe, 2014

ISLANDS IN THE DETROIT RIVER

Isle La Peche, or Isle of the Fishes, was renamed Peach Island in 1810. It's located on the Canadian side of the Detroit River and was the home of Chief Pontiac during the summer months.

Belle Isle was also known as Isle Aux Cochons, Hog Island, Rattlesnake Island, and Ste. Marguerite.

Fighting Island was also Turkey Island in 1796. It was originally occupied by the Wyandots, then sold to the Canadian government. In 1810, Indian entrenchments were plainly visible on the northeast end of the island, and from these warlike appearances the island took its name. It lies across the river from Ecorse, south of Detroit Michigan.

Grosse or Great Island is the largest in the river. There was an extraordinary quantity of apple trees on this island in 1717.

Bois Blanc – We Go Bee Min Is – was known as Whitewood Island and Bass Island on the Canadian side. It was occupied in 1742 by the Huron, a village of several hundred people. In 1796, the British built a blockhouse there and later erected a fort at Malden. Tecumseh camped there before the 1813 Battle of the Thames where he died. The Patriots were in possession of the island in 1838.

Other islands in the Detroit River include Cartwright, Grassy, Little Turkey, Middle Island, Mud, Stoney, Sugar, Tawa, Celeron, Calf, Elba, Fox,

Hickory, Horse, and Humbug. Also, there was Mama Juda, named after an Indian woman who camped there during the fishing season.

For a complete list, see Farmers, History of Detroit and Michigan, 1884, pg. 7.

ISLANDS AND FLATS IN THE ST. CLAIR RIVER

The St. Clair Flats is the delta area from the St. Clair River, entering north of Lake St. Clair and made up of many Islands.

Walpole Island is Indian land and consists of five islands.

Dickinson Island was also known as Stromness Island, Thompson's Island, Laughton's Island, and St. Clair's Island.

The Eagle Channel runs between Harsens Island and Dickinson or Stromness Island.

Willow Island was near Port Huron at Pine Grove Park and had been dredged out.

Other islands include Harsens Island (formerly Jacobs Island, Jacob Island, James Island) and Russell Island.

CANADIAN ISLANDS IN THE ST. CLAIR RIVER

- Boise Blanc: Bob Lo Island, famous amusement park and island near Detroit
- Fawn: Woodtick Island, Eagle Island, or Belle Island
- Stag Island: Isle Au Serfs or Isle Aux Serfs Indian name is "Sawge Too Yawn"; was an ideal pasture for Nelson Mills of Marysville, Michigan to keep his horses with no fences, plentiful clean water, and shade; great hunting island

WALPOLE ISLAND

Walpole Island is Indian land and consists of five islands.

- Bassett Island: part of Walpole Indian lands
- Pottawatomi Island: in the middle of Walpole Island, where Pottawatomi came on removal from the USA in the 1840s
- St. Anne's: lies east of Walpole Island, a hunting paradise
- St. Mary's: Walpole Island
- Seaway Island
- Squirrel: south of Walpole, under the same Indian council as Walpole

Walpole Island, Bkajananj or Bakyewang ziibi, means "river flowing off", "where the water splits", or "where the waters divide". Was also known as St.

Ottissippi

Mary's Island, Warpole Island, for the Poles that edged the entrance to the island, having scalp locks of the enemy attached. The only native homeland never ceded to any government.

Walpole Island is part of the St. Clair River Delta above Lake St. Clair, one of the largest deltas in the world. Walpole is one of many islands in the delta.

There are five islands that make up Walpole Territory: these are Walpole, St. Anne's, Squirrel, Basset, and Pottawatomi. Pottawatomi Island is in the central south portion of Walpole Island. Walpole is the largest in the Archipelago, with seven other islands; Harsens Island and Russell Island are on the American side of the border. It has been a haven to many native peoples. The Pottawatomi came after being removed from the Western USA in 1837.

Tecumseh, the great leader of the Indians of the Northeast, is buried on the Island. His body and bones have been secretly kept safe from destruction and were moved a couple times previously.

Walpole New Hampshire was the home of Stanley Griswold, secretary of Michigan territory until 1808.

The Walpole Island Stewardship Environmental Legacy won a prestigious United Nations award in 1995 for Management of Resources.

The Biodiversity Atlas of Lake Huron to Lake Erie (Hudgins, 2002) is a wonderful resource; it covers every nuance of the waterways. It is available as a book and also on the www (See the Reservations Chapter 10).

- Chematagon: Jimmie Tagen; small channel separating Squirrel Island from Walpole Island; very winding; Indian for "stream that runs away from another"
- Chenel Escarte or Chenail Escarte River: called "Lost Channel" or "Lost River"; the Sny Carte, a common name for Chenal Es Carte in French, meaning "Blank Channel", separates Lambton County and Walpole Island, joining the Sydenham River near Wallaceburg, Ontario, then flowing into Lake St. Clair.
- "Chenail Escarte - the South side was Pakeitchewane, the North side Wappissejunkissy cawpowa" (Chenail Escarte Treaty, 1796, Sarnia # 7)
- In addition, the Turtle Channel and Squirrel Channel ran near Walpole Island.

PLACES IN SOUTHWEST ONTARIO

- Baby's Pointe: in South Sombra Township
- Bunyan: in Sarnia Township; named after John Bunyan, author of *Pilgrims Progress*

- Fairfield or New Fairfield: Delaware Moravian Indians moved here on the Thames; they had been in Pennsylvania and Ohio, and then on the Huron River in East Michigan
- Ipperwash: Upper Wash, between Kettle Point and Stoney Point, northeast of Sarnia, Ontario; reservation land that in 1942 was made a huge military camp (See Reservations Chapter, 10 for more on Ipperwash)
- Kettle Pointe: Indian reservation (See Reservations Chapter, 10)
- La Petite Cote; meaning "Little Coast", and La Cote de Misere means "Misery Coast"; Windsor Canada; opposite of Detroit, Michigan; now a dumping ground; the only stretch of natural Detroit River beach in the entire area
- "Maiden, British name for Detroit Post (fort)" (C. Moore, History of MI). Maiden was also the Post across the river when the British evacuated in 1796. (C. Moore, History of MI)
- Malden: now Amhersburg; the Canadian Base for many wars, directly across from Detroit; christened Molden, then Smugglingburg in 1796; 18 miles below Sandwich (Windsor)
- Perch: 12 miles north of Sarnia
- Petit Cote: a mile above the bridge at River Aux Canards
- Sandwich: now Windsor; in 1725, it was called Point De Montreal and the Parish of Assumption. "Sandwich was known as Faubourg Ste. Rosalie, on the Detroit River, now Windsor" (Askin 1, pg. 292).
- Stoney Pointe, named for its stony surface, was an Indian reservation made into a huge military camp in 1942 called Camp Ipperwash.
- Taranto: Lake Simcoe in Ontario, Canada
- York, now Toronto
- Windsor was known as Petite De Cote, directly opposite of Detroit, Michigan.

SARNIA, ONTARIO

Sarnia was called "The Rapids", the Roman name for the Island of Guernsey. It was also called Port Sarnia at an early date. The French described these rapids as second only to Niagara Falls.

POINT EDWARD ISLAND – PETWAGANO

Point Edward was an Island, and one of the original three channels of the St. Clair River ran east of it, carrying waters from the Upper Lakes through Lake Huron to the St. Clair River and beyond. A great storm filled the channel, and

Ottissippi

it became part of the mainland that is now Point Edward, Ontario. Point Edward was called Huron Village. It became Point Edward in 1879.

"There was a Delta at the Mouth of the St. Clair River" (Diba Jimooyung, Ziibiwing Saginaw Chippewa). The mouth of the St. Clair River once flowed more east of the present channel mouth, from Lake Huron into the St. Clair River. There were three channels which flowed into the St. Clair River. The river was much shallower with sand bars throughout. There were also more islands; one was called Willow island and was not far from Pine Grove Park, Port Huron, Michigan.

- A great storm blew for three days and made the present, new channel flowing from Lake Huron into the St. Clair River.
- Fort Edward: on Pointe Edward Island, Ontario (Point Edward is not an island now, but part of the mainland)

SARNIA BAY AND ST. CLAIR RIVER

"In the early days, the waters of Lake Huron flowed into Sarnia, called Odanonsing by the Ojibwe, meaning "Little Town", in several channels, none of which were very deep. In 1771, Captain Barr of Detroit said there were still two channels, one a league (three miles) wide, with a depth varying to 48 feet. Today there is only one, dredged to a depth of 70 feet, carrying the rush of waters through the land contours on the Canadian side where the other channels once were. The great storm of November 9, 1913 almost reopened the second channel; a few more hours and the topography of Point Edward would have gone back 140 years.

It was traditional for up-bound craft to lay over in Sarnia Bay at nightfall; Lake Huron was unpropitious. In 1926, the government dumped material from the elevator slip and winter harbor into the shoaling. Some 100 acres of made land were planted with Carolina poplars, and the outer edge of the Sarnia Yacht Club was established" (V. Lauristan, Lambton's 100 years).

In our own lifetime, we have seen the wetlands that were once a great part of the Sarnia area filled in more around the Blue Water Bridge on the Canadian side of the St. Clair River.

The village at the foot of Lake Huron on the Canadian side was known as "The Rapids", or Les Chutes by the French, and translated to "The Rapids", by the English-speaking settlers. It was then named the Village of Sarnia in 1836. Sarnia is the Roman name for Guernsey England, where Sir John Colburn had been a lieutenant governor.

THE RAPIDS

"Near the outlet of Lake Huron and the St. Clair River, the land was called Detroit, Fort Detroit, or Fort St. Joseph. This fort was destroyed in 1688" (Burton, Beginnings of Michigan, pg. 60. Hathi Trust, WWW). The Rapids between Black River and Fort Gratiot were strong. The Rapids were one half to one mile long.

> *A mile below the spot where the River St. Clair issues from Lake Huron, the River forms a Boundary between, Upper Canada and the Territory of the U.S. The Waters of Lake Superior, Michigan, and Huron, poured through this narrow Channel, flow with considerable velocity, but their force is partly broken, by the curves or bends of the River. (The Penny Magazine, April 29, 1837)*

> *There were great Rapids at the Mouth of the River. Huge rocks were along the entrance to the Channel, producing many sandbars. Below the Rapids the River grew very deep with a strong current. Along the banks of the River there were Back Currents flowing, North back toward the Lake. This created many eddies and whirlpools among the choppy waters, which seemed to braid it. It was said that if one looked closely and carefully enough one could catch glimpses of the, Mahnedoog or Spirits just beneath the surface. This is the meaning of the Name, Aamjiwnaang. (David D. Plain, The, Plains of Aamjiwnaag)*

Sarnia – Aazhoogayaming – means the "Crossing Waters Place". Also, O Dan Ong Sing – Little Town – was called "The Rapids" and Port Sarnia.

The Muneedo – Mannedog or Mahnedoog – or Spirits were not limited to "spirit" but can refer to the essence, characteristic, or power of a thing, such as a plant or river, meaning it is very powerful, or in this case, the rushing currents.

"The Rapids Tribe", the Kioscanee Tribe at Lake Huron, were named after the Otchipwes Chief of War, Kioscance ("Young Gull"), War Chief against the Wyandots – Huron – and the Six Nations Iroquois Confederacy.

Amjiwnaang means "Place of the Rapids". It (the rapids) has all been dredged out (Joe Greaux and Brian Hock, Black River Ojibwe).

"A Traditional Story relates, that long ago, the most easterly Channel of the St. Clair River, ran from Lake Huron through the eastern end of Canatara Park, flowing in a southerly direction, and emptying into the wetlands at Sarnia Bay. Lake Chipican in Canatarra Park, is the only vestige, of the eastern Channel of the River St. Clair" (Plain).

- Sault Ste. Marie (Skaernon or Boweting), or the Falls of Saint Marie, Ontario, is the ancient homeland of the Three Fires Peoples and was the great fur trading center for the upper Midwest, Northwest and northern Canada. It was on St. Mary's River, the great whitefish-catching place is in the swift, shallow waters. Sault Ste. Marie: ancient homeland of the Ojibwe.
- Bahwatig or Bahweting, also Baaitigong and Boweting: means "At the Place of Shallow Water, Pitching over Rocks" (Schoolcraft/Chaput)
- Boweting: homeland of the Ojibwa and Ottawa in Upper Michigan, now Canada; great fishing; the people were called Bawitigwakinini – Men of the Falls, now Sault Ste. Marie, Michigan and Canada. See Appendix.
- Today the locks raise ships up to Lake Superior.

OTHER MICHIGAN ISLANDS - MANISS

GULL ISLAND

Gull Island in the St. Clair River is a made island from dredging the shipping lanes located south of Harsens Island. It is the site of the annual "Jobbie Nooner" or "Bachanalia", the largest boat party in the midwest. Held in Muskamoot Bay since 1974, when it started, thousands gather for the day-long party held the Friday before the Fourth of July weekend. It is like a Mardi Gras party. The Jobbie Nooner II, is held on the second Saturday in September. The Army Corps manages the island.

MACKINAC ISLAND

St. Joseph, now Mackinac Island, was a British military fort. "Mackinac, The Ottawa and Chippewa, named the Island after a remnant race that had left, called Mii Shi Ne Macki Nawgo, as a Memorial to them. A great Chief was named, Mac Quiquio Vis" (Hotchkiss). Mackinac was the great trading place for the North Country and the Military Base of Operations for the British.

Below are other names for this island:

- "Michilimacina, was called, "Isle of Orleans" (WM. Clements Library, UOM/Mitts)
- Michilimackinac: Mish inim auk in ong
- Natives also called it "Michi Mac", meaning Great Turtle, and "Mich Iae Mauk I Onk", meaning "Place of the Great Fairies"
- Mackinac Island, Ancient Homeland of the Ojibwe: the great trading place for the North Country

OTHER ISLANDS OF THE EASTERN UPPER PENINSULA OF MICHIGAN:

- Sugar Island and Drummond Island
- St. Martins Island's source of plaster of Paris is in Lake Huron, near Mackinac Island.

MADELINE ISLAND

Madeline Island: Moning wunkaunig; ancient homeland of the Ojibwe in Lake Superior; trade and religion center.

- La Pointe, Wisconsin; Old Homeland and capital of the Chippewa's – Ojibwe, an extensive widespread race.
- "Mantoulin Island, formerly called Ottawa Land, Island in East Lake Huron, Ontario, Canada. Ancient Home of the Ojibwe" (Andrew Blackbird)

RIVERS

- "Au Vaseau – Riviere Aux Vases, flows into Lower Lake St. Clair, above the Clinton River, the Home of Chief Machonce, and Machonces Village, rises in Chesterfield twp., empties into Lake St. Clair through New Baltimore, Mi" (History of Macomb County, www).
- Belle River was called De Belle Chasse. It begins in Lapeer County; flows through Memphis, Michigan; receives the waters of Day Creek near Richmond, becoming a much larger flow; and then empties into the St. Clair river at Marine City.
- Bloody Run – Parents Creek: "2 miles north of Fort Detroit, where Pontiac's Warriors slew many soldiers from New York" (Losing)

Ottissippi

- Cass River, an extensive river system starting in the thumb of Michigan and flowing to the Saginaw River. It was the Huron River, and Indians called it "Nottawayseepee", "Mottaway", or "Nadoweg", meaning "adder" or "snake" enemies. The Cass River passes through a thickly populated Indian district, east of Saginaw into the thumb of Michigan.
- "Clinton River, was the Huron River, North of Detroit, MI, the Indian name was Nottawayseepee, Nottaway or Nadoweg, meaning Adder of Snake, Enemies. The North and Middle Branch's, are fed by numerous streams, from Armada, and Richmond, Ray and Shelby, The South Branch called Red Run, is fed by Bear, Beaver, Plum creeks, and other small streams, drawn from Sterling and Warren twps. To Clinton Twp. And empties into Lake St. Clair" (History of Macomb County, www)
- "Crapau, Headwaters in St. Clair County, flows into Macomb then into Lake St. Clair" (History of Macomb County, www).
- St. Denis – River Rouge
- Flint River, spreading into Lapeer County and southeast Michigan, empties into the Saginaw River. The Flint River nearly parallels the Cass River into the thumb of Michigan. It was used extensively for commerce.
- Huron, now the Clinton River, was an important transportation route. The Huron led to the Grand River and Lake Michigan.
- Huron, now the Black River and the St. Clair River.
- The Grand River – O Wash Ta Nong – meaning "Far Away Water", is the second largest drainage system in the state of Michigan. It is the longest, flowing from Grand Haven at Lake Michigan for 260 miles through Grand Rapids, Lansing, and Jackson. It is close to Lake Erie.
- Knaggs Creek: Riviere Au Jarvais, near Detroit
- The Looking Glass River and the Red Cedar River join the Grand at Lansing, Michigan.
- Macon River falls into the Raizin (Raisen), upstream 14 miles from the mouth of Lake Erie.
- Maumee or Miami River: from Lake Erie, it was the route of travel to the Mississippi and into Michigan.
- "Milk River – Reviere Du Lait, on Lake St. Clair's west shore in South Macomb county, was formerly in the now defunct Township of Erin" (History of Macomb County, www)
- Pine River: mouth is at the St. Clair River in what is now St. Clair
- Puces River

- "Rosine – Raisen, south of Detroit, Important route for transportation. The Raisen River led to Kalamazoo, and on to Lake Michigan. The Raisin, was called Sturgeon River by the Indians, an abundance of grapes grew on the borders of the River" (Tanner/Voegelin, Lossing)
- Rouge River: important for transportation routes
- Saginaw River – Saw Gee Nong: the river and its tributaries drain about half of lower Michigan, a rich river system; ancient home of the Saulk and Ojibwe
- "Salt Creek or River, known as Swan Creek. Rises near Richmond and flows through Lenox and Chesterfield, MI, it enters the Lake St. Clair, a few miles south of the Ancient Salt Springs" (History of Macomb County, www)
- "Springwells, The sand hills where springs gushed out pure water, the French called it Belle Fontaine, the 3 Hills were Indian Burial places" (Lossing)
- St. Joseph River: river of the Miami's in southwestern, lower Michigan; Pottawatomi homeland
- "Stoney Creek, empties into Lake Erie, also known as Rocky River, 10 miles west of Cuyahoga" (Voegelin/Tanner)
- Swan Creek: Riviere Des Sygnes, River Aux Ecors, and Salt River; was also at Toledo, Ohio and Saginaw Bay
- Tuckers Creek: Ventre De Boeuf, Ambrose or Tremble Creek, and La Socier; all flow into Lake St. Clair
- "Together with the Rivers named, there are numerous rivulets, coursing throughout every Section of the County" (History of Macomb County, www).
- The Portages in Hillsdale County were very important. Here one could transfer between the Raisen River, flowing into Lake Erie, and two important rivers flowing into Lake Michigan, the Kalamazoo and the St. Joseph. From this same Crossroad Portage, one could Travel south by access to the Little St. Joseph River, a tributary of the Wabash River. Pottawatomi villages were on all of these rivers, which cross part of Northern Ohio and Indiana, and Southern Michigan. (Voegelin/Tanner/Hindsdale, "Indians of Northern Ohio and Southeast Michigan" Ethnohistory series)
- Anchor Bay is on the northwest side of Lake St. Clair.

Other historic rivers include:

Ottissippi

- Allegheny River: Delaware name for the Ohio River, meaning "Fine or Fair River" (Beauchamp/Chaput)
- Maumee: Miami River at Toledo in Northern Ohio; from Lake Erie, it is the route west to the Mississippi.
- Miami: Mee Au Mee; in Northern Ohio; very important Native American homeland
- Ohio River: – oyo, means, Kiskepeelasepee – Eagle River. Ohio also means Beautiful. Ohionh – Iio, means River Beautiful.
- Sandusky: Sawn Dustee

This list is not all inclusive. The history of the historic waterways in the Northwest Territory and the Great Lakes is much greater than this volume can contain.

CANADIAN RIVERS

- "Aux Canards - Ta ron tee, 4 miles above Malden – Amherstburg (Ontario)" (Lossing)
- Aux Sable – Au Sable: The River of Sands flows into Lake Huron at Grand Bend, Ontario
- Bear Creek, or Bear River, became the Sydenham River (Ontario).
- Chenel Escarte or Chenail Escarte River: called "Lost Channel" or "Lost River"; the Sny Carte, a common name for Chenal Es Carte in French, meaning "Blank Channel", separates Lambton County and Walpole Island, it joins the Sydenham River near Wallaceburg, Ontario, then flowing into Lake St. Clair.
- "Chenail Escarte - the South side was Pakeitchewane, the North side Wappissejunkissy cawpowa" (Chenail Escarte Treaty, 1796, Sarnia # 7)
- Grand Bend, Aux Coches: means "riverbend", where the Aux Sable takes an abrupt turn from flowing north to flowing south. It lies on the southeast shore of Lake Huron, about 45 minutes north of Sarnia, Ontario. It was called Port Franks at one time.
- Grand River: in Ontario, North of Lake Erie and Lake Ontario
- La Tranche: The River Trench; The Thames River in Southern Ontario
- Mississauga River: near Georgian Bay, Ontario
- River Au Chaudiere: Catfish Creek, Northwest Lake Erie
- "Ruscom River, up from Sandwich – Windsor" (Lossing).
- Sahgeeng River: flows into southern Georgian Bay of Lake Huron

- Sydenham: commonly known as Bear Creek. It flows to and covers the greater part of the central and southern part of Lambton County, having two Branches: a northern and a southern. Then it forms the Parent River, emptying into Lake St. Clair, named after Lord Sydenham, Governor General of Canada in 1839.
- Teeswater River: branch of the Sahgeeng
- The Thames River: Riviere La Tranche; New River; also called the Horn River; flows in Southern Ontario, then into Lake St. Clair
- "Turkey Creek, 9 miles below Sandwich – Windsor" (Lossing)
- Lakes in Lambton County are found in the Appendix.

CREEKS

There are many historic creeks in St. Clair County, Michigan:

- "Bunce Creek – Baby's Creek, Beaver Creek" (Wisc. Hist. Co. pg. 144)
- Gervais Creek: Named after a Frenchman in the late 1700s, it flowed near Water Street on the south side of Black River, in what is now Port Huron, Michigan.
- Gorse Creek: Mill Creek; Morass's Mills were located in what is now Clyde Township.
- Indian Creek: once flowed through Port Huron, Michigan, south of Black River, and emptied into Black River near 7th Street.
- McNeils Creek: flows from Howe Brandymoore Drain in Clyde Township to Port Huron; it formerly flowed through Fort Gratiot Reserve, then entered the St. Clair River at the mouth of Lake Huron.

"Mill Creek, also called, Indian Creek, River A Jervais, and Gorse Creek (Clyde Twp.)" (Jenks). Mill Creek starts in Lapeer County and was home to many Indians. It was used to float logs to many Sawmills downstream in the Lumber Era.

OTHER PLACES

- Albany, New York: Dutch fur trading center
- Cataraqui: Fort Frontenac, now Kingston on the St. Lawrence
- Chilicothe: capital of the Shawnee nation; Old Chilicothe is now New Piqua, Ohio. The current Chilicothe is the New Chilicothe, Ohio.
- Cuyahoga Creek: now Cleveland, Ohio
- Forks of the Ohio: now Pittsburgh, Pennsylvania
- Fort Necessity, Penn.: now in northeast Ohio
- Fort Recovery: now Ohio

Ottissippi

- "The Glaize – Au Glaize or Auglaise River, La Glaize, now Defiance Ohio, 50 miles southwest of Toledo, Ohio. An old Buffalo Wallow. Where the Buffaloes are always found; they eat the clay and wallow in it. Called the Forks where it connects with the Miami – Maumee River and flows into Lake Erie near now Toledo, Ohio" (Voegelin/Tanner, Ethnohistory Northern Ohio and Southeast MI).
- Gnadenhutten, Penn.: now in northeast Ohio; where over 90 unarmed Christian Indians were killed
- "Grand Portage, at the Western end of Lake Superior, a 9 mile, Portage to a point above the Falls on Pigeon River. During the British Regime, Grand Portage was the great Interior Entrepot of the Fur Trade conducted by Montreal Merchants in the far Northwest" (Askin Papers vol. 1, 74).
- Great Falls, on the Ohio River, now Louisville, Kentucky
- Kekionga, (Fort Wayne, Indiana), Miamitown, Kiskakon, Miami Indian Capital, controlling the 3 rivers, St. Mary's, St. Joseph, and Miami, the shortest route to the Mississippi. Twightwee Village (Croghan).
- "Maguaga, Mongenaga, or Monguagon, 14 miles below Detroit, now Trenton" (Lossing)
- Montreal, Mount Royal: the great French fur trading and shipping center; the New France capital of government in Canada on the St. Lawrence; gateway to the Atlantic Ocean
- Nipigon: known as the Sixth Great Lake; located northeast of Lake Superior in Ontario, Canada
- Pewanagoing or Piwangoning, means Flinty Point
- Picawillany, now Picqua, Ohio.
- Pointe Au Cotoner or Cotton Point, near Lake St. Clair, was owned by Francis Marsac in 1797, Andrew Harrow bought this Land.
- Presque Isle, was at now, Erie Pennsylvania, in Lake Erie.
- Salem: Pettquotting, a high or round hill
- Sault Ste. Louis: Lachine Rapids, Ontario; Caughnawaga meaning "at the Rapids".
- Sandusky, Ohio: called "Canuta", meaning "cabin", by the Indians. Sandusky: Sawn Dustee
- Skull Island: Peguahkoondebaymenis; there were several Skull Islands around Lake Huron.
- Sombra: means shade; Sombra Ontario was a Shawnee or Shawanese refugee reserve on the St. Clair River, set aside by Alexander McKee,

British Indian Agent, for the Indians who were United Empire Loyalists, or loyal to the British.
- "Springwells, (Detroit) Large Copper smelting works were here, upon the River" (Lossing).
- "Stoney Point – Point Au Roche, in Frenchtown Twp. Monroe County (MI), about midway between the Mouths of the Huron and Raisen Rivers" (Askin II, pg. 722).
- Tippacanoe: was south of Cleveland, Ohio; Tecumeh's relatives were slaughtered by General Harrison here, starting the War of 1812.
- Wyoming: means "the Large Plains"; it is about 20 miles east of Sarnia, Ontario.

The booklet *Lambton County Ontario: Names and Places* was the best resource for Canadian places.

Farmer, *The History of Detroit and Michigan*, 1884 was used for many place name references.

The appendix at the back pages of this book lists more information on waterways, peoples, and places.

CHAPTER 3
Early Indian Culture And History

The aged Sachems of the Ojibwe nation tell the traditional teaching that Gitchi Manito – Keechemunedoo or Kezha-Munedoo – the Benevolent Spirit, or Master of Life, created the Indians and placed them on the continent of America, that every nation speaking a different language is a separate creation, but that all were made by the same Supreme Being. How they were created is not known. They say that when the Great Spirit made the different nations of the Earth and gave them various languages, complexions, and religions, as well as the divers customs, manners, and modes of living. When he gave the Ojebway's their religion, he told them how they were to act; and with this knowledge, they think it would be wrong and give great offense to their Creator to forsake the old ways of their forefathers.

The Anishinabeg is the race of all indigenous tribes. It means "Original Men" – Good Beings. They are of one blood, all the nations of the earth (Rev. Peter Jones, History of the Ojibwe Indian, 1861).

The Totem – Oten – was a village or clan naming system. The family name and identification, the symbol marked graves, and villages. Totem meant "village": family, people, not a location. Later, totem meant a mark or symbol or an arms or family mark. It was the means of identification, a link in the genealogical chain by which bands are held together. The totem was not a personal guardian spirit, powerful protector, or guiding spirit.

The system of totem names served to regulate exogamy or marriage to those who are not near relatives, and ensure the continuity of the people. As the people grew in numbers, new totems formed within larger groups. The village was the people, not the place, persons who live in the same lodge under the same chief (Schoolcraft/Schenk).

The people were egalitarian, or equals among equals—a consensual democracy.

A band is a group allied with another or a few. Bands averaged 100 people. Later in the 1800s, the bands were larger, having about 450 people. Bands were part of clans and clans were tribes. Each local band was independent and sovereign; no one chief could speak for or represent all the others (Schenk).

An egalitarian band society, no one chief had authority over any other. There was no first or principal chief. Government was run by consensus, including women, yet no one was bound to obey. When a single spokesperson was necessary, it was an orator who was selected, not a chief. Each chief and warrior had the right to speak for his own group. There were no degrees of leadership, nor was the office of chief hereditary for life. The chiefs are seldom so well lodged or well dressed as the others (Schenk).

The patrilineal (father's line) egalitarian band formerly matrilineal, seemingly without laws or organization, was the very foundation of Ojibwe society. Limited band size and mobility were essential to the survival of the group (Snow 1981/Schenk 1997).

The whole clan are kindred – related, descended from the same ancestor. The family traced by a Totem, a device which marked the division of tribes into clans.

In other tribes, those of the same totem were considered close kin. A person could expect help, and safety, and hospitality from any other tribe of the same totem; even strangers were considered brothers.

Nations are tribes or totems. The people never married within their own totem, always of a different Gens-Totem, creating a great network of intermarried bands and tribes. A great security, they helped one another and were quick to aid in any conflict with other nations. The great numbers of the same totem were called a Phratries group of the tribal nation. Phratries are large divisions consisting of many clans. The totem sign marked territories, villages, and wigwams.

The Clan system was 15 to 20 families, each with a different totem. Allied groups were part of the most important among them. Sauteur's and others included, the Ojibwe were enlarged.

Fifteen lodges were 250 to 300 people, and 70 warriors. The average family was seven members. There were five to seven families per lodge during fishing season. The clan was made up of men and women from different totems. All the men were of the same totem, the women from other totems.

Ottissippi

Originally there were five clans. The original totems were: Catfish (intellectuals), Crane (Ojeejok), Loon (Ahahwauk), Bear (Makwa-Nocke), Moose (Monsone). The Marten was designated for the "Mixed blood of the French Fathers" (Warren 1984, 44–45). Marten were warriors, hunters, and protectors. Marten was made with the totem of the mixed blood (Schenk, "The Voice of the Crane Echoes Afar", 1997).

The Crane and Loon clan were chiefs. Fish were intellectuals and intermediaries. Bear had the knowledge of medicine and were the "police force", or protectors and warriors. Moose or Deer were the peaceful artisans and poets (1988, Benton Bane).

The Crane was the government leadership and records totem. They were also protectors and hunters. The Cranes go back to the flood. The lofty crane of ancient bands (refers to) the ancient band of red men whose totem is the lofty crane. (They were) called "bus in aus e", echo maker or Crane (Warren 1984). The Crane called the tribes together for councils and ceremonies. Ojibwe means "the voice of the Crane". The Ojibwa or Sauteurs were the original Crane People of the Algonquin's. (They were the) spiritual leaders of the people.

There were many subdivisions made, and more totems added as the nation grew.

The traditional greeting is "What is your *dodem*?" to establish social conduct between two meeting parties, as family, friends, or enemies.

The people had a Great Migration from the Eastern Seaboard. They were led by a great cloud shaped like a megis shell (cowrie shell). When the people arrived at Boweeting (Sault Ste. Marie), they grew and flourished. It was decided to split into three great nations and spread out. They became the Three Fires Confederacy – Ishkodaywatomi. This was about 1525 A.D. The Ojibwe, Ottawa and Pottawatomi, some were left along the migration path and were in Southern Ontario and Michigan – Big Water.

Lapointe on Madeline Island in Wisconsin, was the ancient capital and center for spirituality, a key Ojibwe village - castle and trading center for the Northern Ojibwe. Chaqwamegon or Chequamenon in Wisconsin was the metropolis of the Ojibwe.

The Aztecs are believed to be the first occupants of this region. The meaning of their tribal name is "People of the Lakes".

Of the more modern Indian tribes of this region, the Algonquin race was the earliest. Among their numbers in the Northwest were the tribes of the Ottawa's, Menominee's, Sacs, Foxes, and the Chippewa (Ojibwe). In the vicinity were also the tribes of the Miami's, Pottowatomi's, Winnebagoe's, and the Ouendat's or Wyandotte's (Huron).

The Ojibwe were a widespread, extensive race. They were the most populous, and important, existing branch of the Algonquin Race. The Algonquins covered one quarter of North America, from Nova Scotia to the Carolinas, to the Rocky Mountains and into Northern Canada (Jenks, History of St. Clair County, 1912).

Ojibwe was the *court language*, the language used by all Algonquins. The universal language of the continent. They were the largest tribe in North America. There are only 17 letters required to write the language. It is a very expressive, beautiful language. You see it as you speak it.

The *oral histories* are passed down with very precise accuracy. The people repeat their history often, so it is not to be lost. It is handed down from generation to generation. The elders tell the history exactly, precisely the same, word for word (Tolatsga Whoa, www).

The Chippewa's, Ottawa's, Missisauga's, and Pottawatomi's inhabited the central area of the Great Lakes (N. Plain). The Pottawatomi, Mascouten, and Miami occupied the southern third of the Lower Peninsula. In 1519 to 1520, the Chippewa-Ojibwe took control of the Northwest Territory.

The Ojibwe were "The Turtle Nation." Sagaunaum was the thumb of the Michigan region, called Mount Pleasant – Isabella Territory. Islands are called "Turtles".

Every Turtle has 13 boxes or scutes on its back (Digger, Mike Leon Martin, Cherokee).

The Ozhibiiwe – Those who keep records. The Medewiwin Rites Society, Holy Men, are the keepers of detailed and complex scrolls of events, history, maps, memoirs, stories, geometry, mathematics, visions, music, and pictorial writings or pictographs. The *sacred scrolls* are kept hidden away until those who are worthy and respect them are given permission to see and interpret them properly.

The Huron were friendly Iroquois traders, brothers to the Eastern Iroquois. The Huron lived among the Ojibwe. They were comparatively wealthy people, engaged in extensive trade in tobacco and many other products with the Neutral Missisauga, and Petun - Tobacco Hurons), and other Iroquois Neutrals who lived south of them in Southern Ontario. The Huron traded at Montreal, Canada with the French. They traded with indigenous nations as far as the Lower Mississippi. The Ojibwe were called Neutrals" because they remained neutral in the conflict between the Huron and Iroquois. The Huron forcibly prevented the Neutrals from direct trade with the French and, as such, were able to command huge profits as middlemen.

Ottissippi

The Huron (Theonontaternons-Tionontati) were called the Tobacco Hurons, or Petuns. The whole peninsula between Georgian Bay and Lower Lake Huron was known as the "Country of the Ancient Hurons". Upon the Lake of Huron were the Outaouas – Ottawas, the Nockes, the Fies, the Missisagues – River Indians, the Attikamek, and the Outchipwes – Sauteurs (Ojibwe or Chippewas), good warriors". The Western Algonquin were destroyed by the Iroquois and small pox.

Saulteurs-Outchibouee, "People of the Rapids", was the French name for the entire Ojibwe nation at Sault Ste. Marie and elsewhere.

The Iroquois also appeared from time to time. This nation was originally the Onondagas, Cayugas, Senecas, Oneidas, and Mohawks. The Tuscaroroas of North Carolina united with them, and they became known as the six nations (Farmer, The History of Detroit and Michigan).

Black Hawk, a great Sauk leader tells the traditional story:

> *The Great Father of the Anishinabe people, Na Na Makee, was given dreams of the White man for four years. The Great Spirit gave divine wisdom to the prophet that men with pale skin would be coming across the Great Salt Water. At the same time, the White men across the salt water ocean had dreams. When the White man came, he brought many gifts for the people—guns, spears—and showed them how to use them. Large quantities of gifts and goods, cooking utensils, everything necessary for comfort. Na Na Makee was given a medal of honor by the Great White Father. He became a great chief and was given a great medicine bag.*
>
> *"Many countries from the European continent came to the Maritimes fishing at an early date.*
>
> *The sun was a symbol of divine intelligence. Fire was symbolical of purity.*
>
> *Blood memory is the emotional connection to our ancestors. Blood memory is described as our*

ancestral (genetic) connection to our language, songs, spirituality, and teachings. It is the good feeling that we experience when we are near these things. Blood memory has been crucial to the survival of our culture". (Ziibiiwing, Saginaw Chippewa)

The Neutral Nations and Huron Nations cultivated considerable land and had many villages in the St. Clair River region and Niagara. The Iroquois were in hostile conflict with the Hurons and were deadly enemies to all North and Western nations. They coveted the land and furs in the Northwest. Their own land in New York was depleted of fur to trade to the Dutch in Albany. They had a feud of long standing and were bitter enemies (Fowle).

The Huron Petun tobacco nation left the violence and went west, settling in Oklahoma and Arkansas.

The Iroquois Neutrals waged war on the Algonquins of Southeast Michigan in the 1640s, wanting the rich beaver grounds. In 1652 to 1653, the Neutrals fled to the west shore of Lake Huron and then dispersed (Adapted from Rogers/Smith, 1995, Aboriginal Ontario).

In 1649, the Eastern Iroquois wiped out the Huron with "firesticks" *(fusees)*—guns—supplied by the Dutch in Albany, New York. The Huron sought refuge with the Ojibwe in Michigan and were absorbed into the Ojibwe and Ottawa traders. They were called Wendat, Wyandotte, or Ouendat, meaning "dwellers on a peninsula". Some went to the north at Baawaating (Sault Ste. Marie) and Chequamenon Bay in Wisconsin, some to Detroit. Six hundred went to Montreal Quebec with the Jesuit (Black Robes) missionaries, and some were absorbed into the Seneca Iroquois in New York. The Michigan and Ontario tribes had no weaponry like the mighty guns that killed from a distance, unseen. All fled before the Iroquois. The Neutrals and the Erie (Cat People) were attacked and destroyed. The Iroquois sought captives to replace losses from epidemics and furs to buy more guns.

The displaced people moved to other areas away from the "firesticks" of the Iroquois. Some of the Fox and Sauk moved west of Lake Michigan, some to South Carolina along with the Kickapoo and Shawnee.

The Iroquois then commanded and monopolized all trade in Ontario and the waterways of the St. Lawrence and the Detroit. No one ventured into the southeast of Michigan and Southern Ontario. The land was without occupants. No one was allowed through the Strait (The Detroit) to trade with the Northern and Western tribes. The Three Fires and their allies went through the northern route at the Ottawa River route to trade in Montreal, the headquarters for the French Fur Trade.

The other tribes—Fox, Mascouten, Kickapoo, Pottawatomi, and Illinois—were forced to go west across and around Lake Michigan into other lands east and west of the Mississippi.

The Odawa (Ottawa) were the traders or middlemen between the people and the Huron traders, who were the main suppliers in trade. The Ottawa worked with many tribes.

The Ottawa's original totems are Bear, Deer, Wolfe, and Turtle. The whole race was interwoven into one great family. The Ottawa traveled hundreds of miles to exchange goods with tribes. They traded corn and other goods for furs. The Ottawa then traded furs for Huron goods. They had a monopoly over the trade routes and trade partnerships by marriage, charging tolls to use the trade routes.

The Ottawa tribes wore a pierced nose with a stone attached that comes down to the mouth which was a charm against medicine spells. The Ottawa and Huron slept with whoever they choose. "Cadillac"

The Pottawatomi were the Keepers of the Fire, responsible for ceremonial fires and the gatherings for the four seasons. They were hospitable and friendly with all the tribes.

EARLY HISTORY

The land of the Saulk's (also, Sauk or Sac) occupied a large area extending to Detroit, Thunder Bay at Alpena, Michigan, and to Lake Michigan. The Saginaw River and its tributaries reached in every direction like a web. The land was a rich hunting and fishing land. It was much coveted by other tribes, traders, and powers. The Sauk and Fox occupied the eastern lower half of Michigan between Saginaw Bay and Detroit.

The Sauk were always at war with their neighbors, the Pottawatomi, to the south; the Ojibwe to the north and in Canada, along with The Ottawa, Huron, and other nations in Canada. www, History of Saginaw County, James Cooke Mills). They were a fierce, warlike people. Their hunting territory extended into Southern Ontario. The Saulk fought with the tribes who were moving west before the Iroquois, who were seeking furs in Ontario and Southeast Michigan.

A well-known Indian trader, Peter Gruett of the American Fur Company, found the old Indian Puttaguasamine, who was well over 100 years old in 1834. He told the history of the Sauk's nation. The Sauk's occupied the country to Detroit, Thunder Bay, and Lake Michigan to the headwaters of the Shiawasee to the south. The balance of Michigan was Potawatomie's.

In the Lake Superior country were the Chippewa and Ottawa; the Menominee's in Green Bay, Wisconsin, and the Sioux west of the Mississippi.

In 1519, there was a council of the Northern Confederacy where the tribes, Three Fires, and their allies decided to join forces at Mackinaw to exterminate the Sauk (Reid, Joyce). A great massacre was made on them at Saginaw River and at Flint. They were caught by surprise by a mighty army of warriors, and the Sauk nation was wiped out (Chief Puttamasine, Ojibwe, The Indian and Pioneer History of Saginaw County, www). The Sauk's were driven from the bank of the Saganaw about the close of the 1500s or beginning of the 1600s (Henry Schoolcraft letter to C.A. Harris, Office Indian Affairs Michilimackinac, 1838. NAM M1R 37:547 – 564). David Plain in his book, *From Quisconsin to Caughnowaga*, dates the Sauk War as 1618.

One group came from the south, the other from the north, to attack and destroy the enemy near Saginaw River at the Bay City area and its tributaries, and at Flint. At the mouth of the Saginaw River, the Sauk's retreated to Skull Island. Through the night, the water froze over and the allies were able to cross over and destroy the Sauk. There are many mounds, Skull Island in the Saginaw River, was littered with the dead of the Sauk. They were found all along the tributary rivers and exterminated. There were taken prisoner twelve female survivors, who were sent west of the Mississippi to the Sioux.

The Sauk who managed to escape retreated to Lake Michigan near Green Bay and lived on the Door County Peninsula of Wisconsin for a short time before their aggressiveness drove them to the Fox River and southward. They lived among the Fox (Mesquackie), west of Lake Michigan.

A few warriors escaped the slaughter and lay hidden in the woods, living in No Man's Land. The land was divided among them all as a common hunting ground. A great many who came to hunt never returned or were heard of again. A few Socks, had lingered around, watching for hunters and killing them at every opportunity. The land was believed to be haunted. No one came to hunt, though game was abundant. The tribes were terrified of the area. If they were passing through and thought a Sauk was near, they left everything and fled for their lives. The land was a place of exile, a Penile Colony; criminals would flee to escape punishment or be banished to the "Haunted Hunting Grounds" for serious crimes. However, there were few serious crimes; the people were peaceable most of the time, unless threatened by harm (Reid).

The Fox were driven out of Michigan in the 1640s to Greenbay, Wisconsin. The Saulk were friendly to the Fox (Masquackie) and were allies in wars with other tribes. The Saulk - Sauk - Sac, became the Osage, who moved to Kansas. The southern tribes are the Osaugee.

Neutral Indians of Western Ontario related that, in the ancient days, a great chief and magician lived at Petegwano (Pointe Edward), where the waters of Lake Huron flowed into the Ottissippi (St. Clair-Detroit River). Ottissippi means "Clear Waters". He was known as "The Keeper of the Gates". There were then three channels and a delta more east and a mile north of the present mouth. There were great rocks and sandbars among these shallow channels. The water was very swift and turbulent; as the waters entered the Ottissippi, they made a deep pool from the churning current. This was the main thoroughfare of water travel: the best and main way. It was known as "The Rapids". There were many streams, sandbars, hills, and islands in the delta.

Another great magician, Great Bear from Boweeting (Sault Ste. Marie), had a beautiful daughter who was kidnapped from Boweeting. The father came to Petagwano to search for her, suspecting "The Keeper of the Gates", and in his great wrath, he made "Great Magic so "Keewahdin – North Wind", filled up the waters of Lake Karegnondi – Lake Huron, and drove the waters over Pointe Edward, washing away the delta at the mouth of the St. Clair River which went downstream to form Stag Island and Fawn Island (John T. Barnes, Ontario).

The St. Clair River had three mouths in 1670 (Hennepin, Explorer, and Missionary). Two channels of the delta at the foot of Lake Huron were open in 1770.

The Ottissippi was much narrower and shallower with islands and sandbars throughout its length. There were many rocks, streams, hills, and stones. Poles were used to cross the river in certain places; the people were known to pole vault across. They also swam and used canoes, rafts, and horses were swam across. The shallow waters were an easy crossing. The land was very wet and swampy. Land on the east side was called *O Dan Non Sing*. There were several lakes in the area near the rapids of the Ottissippi. Below the rapids, the river grew very deep with a strong current, the same as it is today.

The Gathering Place of the waterways of now western Ontario and Eastern Michigan were one of the favorite camping, fishing, hunting, and resting places, along the great travel routes of the St. Clair River Lake Huron, Black River, and the Thumb. It was a beautiful place; there was plenty of food and a large trading and staging area for any wars the alliance would be involved in. It was the great stopping place on the way to St. Mary's (Walpole) and other islands near the Strait (The Detroit), the Huron, River Rouge, and all points south and in every direction.

Port Huron (Aamjiwnaang) was the resort of the Indians from time immemorial. They indulged in games of athletic sports and skill. It was a ground of neutrality, and common assemblage (hence the name "The Gathering Place") for various tribes over a large section of the country. There was easy access by way of the Black River and St. Clair River. They came from near and far to enter the games with rival tribes (History of St. Clair County Andreas 1883).

Pine Grove Park was the trading place. The original riverbank can still be seen; it is about 30 feet below and 70 feet out from the present bank. The stumps of trees that lined the shore are still preserved under water.

The islands in the Ottissippi were spiritual places; councils, Pow Wows, and dances were held on these islands.

The foot of Lake Huron was a great fishery. Many tribes gathered there during spring, summer, and fall for the great catch of whitefish, sturgeon, salmon, and more. The Anishinabe dried great quantities of fish for the winter months. The drying racks were stacked eight feet high at the foot of Lake Huron during the seasonal gathering.

Thousands of Anishinabe kin groups met here to renew friendships, meet future spouses, celebrate with dancing, Religious ceremonies, play games, trade from near and far. To make future plans, share ideas, discuss concerns and share information.

The Sun Dance was the culmination of brotherhood and worship of the God of Creation and sustainer of the people. It was the highlight of the religious ceremonies, held in July when the sun was at its highest of all seasons. The preparation for the Sun Dance took several days, and the Dance lasted three to four days. The *Buffalo Dance* celebrates the buffalo, which gave it's all and supplied every need of the people: food, shelter, clothing, and many others. Many other dances were performed. Spiritual renewal and balance were reaffirmed.

Kinship speaks of the philosophy of interconnectedness and balance between all living generations, as well as all generations of the past and future.

Lake Chipican in Canatarra Park, north of Point Edward, Ontario was part of the original east channel, which was part of the delta of the Ottissippi at Lake Huron (Karegnondi).

Black River, Elk River, and Cass (Huron) River were popular places, waterways, and were the Indian highways. Canoes the vehicle of transportation.

In the thumb of Michigan, there were numerous villages and camps every few miles along the shore of Saginaw Bay and the islands. The Huron lived in palisaded villages. The Ojibwe did not use palisades.

The fishing was superb, and there were maples along the shoreline that supplied sugar. The stone quarries at Bayport and Grindstone were used for tool and weapon making. Many clans lived here, artifacts by the truckload were found (Al and Dave Eicher, The Indian History of Michigan's Thumb).

Pipes were made of stone found along the Cass River (Joyce Reed, Deckerville).

A legend tells of a lead mine along the Cass River. The Indians died with the secret of its location.

Runners delivered messages to tribes everywhere. They were endurance runners who quickly conveyed important news (Reid).

The Indians were very spiritual people; they knew that all life in the whole universe is sustained by God (Gitchi Manito), and it was given by him to the human race for sustenance, and the Indian was never known to kill wantonly. All the days were God's. The people worked for the good of the tribe as a whole and held that land belonged to the tribe and not to the individual. If a member of the tribe was in want, it was because the whole tribe was also. "All for one and one for all" was the motto (Nicholas Plain).

Heaven was *ponemah*: "perfection". A beautiful sunset was the headdress of the Keeper of the Land of Souls. The splendor of this headdress was most beautiful.

Mitchi Manito was the evil spirit or Snake. Pauguk was the Spirit of Death (Fragments of the Ojibwe of the Great Lakes, Ralph E. McCarry, SCC library MI Room).

There were no written laws that bound the liberties of individuals. All were in common, shared freely, and helped one another. Indians were kind, honest, and truthful. Children were taught by example and encouragement.

Annual festivals, harvest time, and thanksgivings, were times of ceremonies and public games. The prizes: an eagle wing, a sash of braided grass, a belt of wampum, the bark of mountain ash, a polished oar of Mtn. Ash, or a bark canoe (Hathi Trust, adapted from, Teucsha Gronde, 1870, A legendary Poem).

There were no borders to separate states and provinces. Waterways were the boundary lines of the many indigenous people. (Peter Schmaltz, "The Ojibwe of Southern Ontario").

THE IROQUOIS WARS

The Assisternonon – Three Fires nation and allies living in Southeast Michigan – were attacked by the Huron, Ottawa (Neutrals), and Tionontati

(Petun Iroquois). The Iroquois nation drove them all out. The Algonquin tribes fled to the north and west.

The great number of refugees created chaos in Wisconsin, Northern Michigan, and other places. Many tribes were starving, sick, and at war with the neighboring peoples. The refugees began a new era of intermixed tribes from this point. Disease had spread and the now smaller groups intermarried.

The Allies of the Assisternonon – Three Fires Nation were the Fox, Sauk, Mascoutin, Kickapoo, and Piankeshaw (Kaskaskias).

When the French came, they claimed much of the Eastern, now United States and Canada, though the French were very small in number. The country was called New France. The southern portion of their territorial claim was to the Ohio River and the Mississippi to the west, called Quebec (We were Quebec, Louisiana Territory).

The lands of the Northwest, were called, the "Pays De En Haut", or The Upper Country, the Great Lakes Basin.

The Huron were Iroquois but allied with the Ojibwe. There was a great rift with the New York Iroquois. The Huron were the French connection to the Ojibwe for furs and trading. The Huron had huge agricultural lands in Southern Ontario, growing 15 varieties of corn, 60 types of beans, six kinds of squash, tobacco, and more for trade (Ojibwa, Whoa, www). They had warehouse space and protection. They supplied two-thirds of the Fur Trade at Montreal in 1685.

The principal Huron village was Carhagouha, which was west of Lake Simcoe. There were 200 bark lodges with a palisade 35 feet high. The men used huge wooden shields for protection (Hathi Trust, The story of the Great Lakes, 1909, Edward Chemins, Marion Florence Lansing).

Ohio is Iroquois for "beautiful" and was known as "The Ohio Country". Lake Huron was called "Canatarra" by the Iroquois.

The Iroquois were peaceful trading partners of the Ojibwe; they were allowed into Ontario for hunting. They made villages in many areas. The flint beds at Albino Point were kept secret by the Attawandron (Erie) who were manufacturers of flint arrowheads, tomahawks, and knives. The Neutrals at Kettle Point shared their flint beds with other tribes. The Mohawk – Iroquois, became jealous, greedy, and contentious when their own territory was hunted out. They expanded west to hunt fur for tradeestroying the Neutrals in 1632. The Iroquois were sometimes called Mohawks.

In 1641, the Ottawa and Neutrals battled with the Assistaeronon - The Fire People, in Michigan. There was a 10-day siege; 2,000 Ottawa and Neutral captured a fortified Assistaeronon village. At a large Indian fort on Black River near Wadhams (4 miles west of Port Huron, MI), the Sauk took refuge in it. The

Ottissippi

fierce fighting went on for 10 days; in the end, 800 women and children were captured and taken prisoner. Seventy of the finest warriors were burned alive at the stake. They put out the eyes of the old men and cut away (girdled) their lips, leaving them to wonder and die in agony or drag out a miserable life (Ojibwa Whoa, www. /Reid; Jenks, 1912). The Iroquois were the cannibals of America!

The Iroquois were of many nations. They were enemies of the Huron and other tribes living at or near Detroit, warfare was frequent. In 1649, the Iroquois, having obtained Dutch guns from trade, drove the Algonquin nations from this region and the, Huron - Petun, and Neutrals out of Southern Ontario. Farmer 1884

The other tribes having no weapons to meet the Fuzee's – guns. The Iroquois Wars pushed the people who were living in Southern Ontario into Michigan, as they fled, before the "fire sticks" or unseen bullets started killing everyone in their path. The Huron were driven everywhere. They were scattered, slaughtered, and adopted; many were pushed into Michigan among the Three Fires Peoples. The Fox living here were pushed out and fled west to the Sauk, whom they were in close alliance with.

The Ontario and Missisauga Ojibwe were pushed into Michigan by the Huron and Wyandotte, finding refuge with the Three Fires peoples and, in the Upper Peninsula, among the Northern Three Fires Confederacy. A small group fled to Arkansas, called the Osagee (John T. Barnes, Ontario).

There was a large fortified village called *Mitchigami*. The Fur Trade turned the Great Lakes into a war zone (Ojibwe Whoa, www).

In 1650, the Iroquois destroyed the Erie people, having only their bows and arrows. Those warriors not burned at the stake were adopted and made to fight with the Five Nations Iroquois. The Iroquois became the overlords of Southern Ontario and the Teucsha Grondie or "Place of many beavers" (the Detroit Strait). From the earliest times, the region was noted for its beavers (Jenks, 1812).

The French in Montreal and the Maritimes had been feuding with the British for a very long time in the Upper St. Lawrence. The Iroquois were being squeezed from every direction in the east.

The "Rat" was a general and chief councilor of the Huron (Lahonton).

The Mission of St. Joseph was attacked by the Iroquois in 1648. Seven hundred Hurons were massacred at St. Joseph. Others fled to St. Marie. There were eight missions in Huron country. They endured relentless attacks from the New York Iroquois. There were 6,000 refugees. The Huron had 20 towns or castles, with a population of about 30,000 people in 1637.

The Huron survivors were split up, and the Ouendat became Wyandotte, living from south of Detroit to Cleveland, Ohio. Large numbers were taken captive and absorbed into the Iroquois five nations peoples. Some went to Quebec with the Jesuits, and some to the Upper Peninsula to live among the Ottawa traders who assumed the Huron trade of those lost to the Great Battle. They were the business men, the sales force, and were indispensable.

The Iroquois claimed a great extent of territory around the Great Lakes (Jenks 1912). The Iroquois continued to push the Three Fires from their homes. They raided, attacked, and ravaged our people for twenty years. We rejoined our northern families at Boowaating and Chequamenon Bay; (Bayfield Wisconsin). The Boowaating suffered greatly from warfare, starvation, and disease" (Diba Jimooyung, Telling our story, Ziibiwing, Saginaw Chippewa).

The Iroquois were a menace to the people: invading villages, stealing their crops, and kidnapping their children. They followed the Huron enemies.

In 1662, the Iroquois with 1,200 well-armed men came to St. Ignace to continue the destruction. Many captives were tortured and burned. The Iroquois went in all directions to control the trade. The Tuscarora Indians of now North Carolina used many slaves growing tobacco for trade. They joined the five nations Iroquois in the Great Wars (Canadian Indian History, www).

The Missisauga and Saginaw were displaced by the Huron – Neutrals and Tiontonti in 1652. The Iroquois continued attacking for 20 years. The Shawnee in Ohio and Southern Michigan Algonquin's were also displaced from every direction.

The Black River was inhabited by Hurons, and WeMekeuns was a chief. The Huron, Ouendat – Wyandotte lived throughout the eastern lower Michigan shoreline. The Huron's trade empire collapsed, and the people scattered.

At Boweeting, the weakened people gathered together to plan and carry out a counterattack to drive the Naadawe (Snakes) back to New York.

There were 20,000 battered refugees crowded into the north country. During the time between 1640 and 1690, the refugees' traditional culture was transformed by war, disease, European teachings, and the Fur Trade. They became dependent on the French traders for firearms and ammunition.

A peace conference was called at a major Mohawk town at the mouth of the Saugeen River. A delegation from Superior country was attacked at an Ojibwe village. The young son of an Ojibwe chief had been kidnapped. When the delegation arrived for the conference, they were given the royal treatment. A huge feast was given. A new agreement was quickly reached. The delegates left for home, not realizing their hosts had cooked and fed the flesh of the captive son to his own father!

The Iroquois also interfered with the French and Indian traders delivering furs to Montreal. They were pirating the loads of furs and the trade goods coming back to the northern Indians throughout the Ottawa River route connecting through Lake Huron to the St. Lawrence at Sault Ste. Marie and beyond.

The Ojibwe were outraged, and the news spread.

The Chippewa's, Ottawa's, Missisauga's, and Pottawatomi's took council together at Boweeting (Sault Ste. Marie) to plan a stratagem of extermination of the Iroquois from the area. This plan called for four divisions to leave in the spring and surround the Iroquois. This movement was timed by so many moons, and at a certain moon they were to attack simultaneously. They would travel at night and attack on the new moon. Thus, with this stratagem, they succeeded in surrounding the Iroquois.

The Chippewa (Ojibwe) the Amikouai (Beaver Tail tribe from Sault Ste Marie-Boweeting) were led by "White Cloud" from the north. They would attack at Saugeen, Bruce Peninsula, lying in wait for the new moon. The Ottawa would attack from the north, led by their great War Chief, Sahgimah. They arrived at the Penetanguishen Peninsula, and lay in wait. The Missisaugas, the largest Ojibwe tribe, were led by "Bald Eagle" from the east and south and the Pottawatomi from the west and south.

"Young Gull" or Kioscance, a major Ojibwe war chief, led the western division. They came down the east side of Lake Michigan through the St. Joseph River to the Detroit Strait. He led 3,200 warriors.

His warriors were made up of Ojibwe, Pottawatomi, and Wyandotte warriors, the protectors, Policemen. They gathered at Round Lake (Lake St. Clair) to attack from the west. The western division, according to the oral record of Animekeence – "Little Thunder", consisted of 400 war canoes, manned by eight warriors, with their weapons and supplies. They filled the Ottissippi's (St. Clair River), entire length from the mouth at Karegnondi (Lake Huron) to Bkejwanong (Walpole Island).

When the new moon arrived, they all attacked simultaneously. Though the Iroquois were well-equipped with guns from the traders. Our great population of warriors of the Three Fires and our allies outnumbered the Iroquois four to one (3,200 warriors represented about 16,000 to 20,000 people).

Near Chatham, Ontario, the Seneca were destroyed, their warriors decapitated, and the skulls piled into a large pyramid to warn off further intrusions into the Ojibwe territory.

The slain of the Ojibwe were buried in a mass grave, a huge burial mound with full burial rites, their weapons and daily utensils buried with them to make the four-day journey to the Land of Souls as easy as possible.

At the Saugeen River, the Battle of Skull Mound left a Great Burial Mound. This was a large Mohawk town. Saugeeng means the "coming out place", the river mouth. The same at Skull Island in Georgian Bay, then at White Cloud Island, then at Owen Sound, and Nottawasaga River.

Sahgimah was victorious at Orilla.

Bald Eagle was victorious at Mattawa River, Otonabee River, Moira River, Rice Lake, and the Rouge and Humber Rivers.

Surrounded, surprised, and outnumbered, the Mohawk – Iroquois, were defeated utterly and driven back to New York across the Niagara River in 1670 (D. Plain).

The final battle was fought on the south shore of Lake Huron. Only one boy and a girl were saved. They kept them until they grew into man and woman, then took them across the Lakes to send them home to their own country with a warning message to the Iroquois race: to stay in their own territory, and if they in the future made another attempt to invade the Algonquin territory, the whole Algonquin race would invade their territory (Nicholas Plain, the History of the Chippewa of Sarnia. 1950/ David Plain, "Plains of Aamijiwnaang").

These wars were called "The Beaver Wars" or the Iroquois Wars. In 1690, there were massive battles on Lake St. Clair and Lake Erie. And from 1628 in the St. Lawrence to 1700 in Ontario and west.

After the Iroquois were pushed back to New York, the land once again became Anishinabe villages in Southern Ontario. The people flourished and grew to become a widespread nation, covering a great area. To the Ausable River in Michigan and the great Saginaw Watershed to Lansing, to Detroit, and to Toronto, Canada, and Georgian Bay (Diba Jimooyung. Ziibiiwing, Saginaw Chippewa).

The Iroquois reported the establishment of sixteen new castles (towns) of the three Ojibwa nations, including the Saulteur, Mississauga, and the Ottawa. They spread as far as Toronto and Frontenac, near Niagara and well into Michigan (Schmaltz, The Ojibwa of Southern Ontario, pg. 32).

The major war chief in the Iroquois wars was Ojibwe Chief Kioskance "Young Gull", who led the Western division of Anishinabek warriors. Kioskance was the major war chief of Bawatinwakinini at Sault Ste. Marie. He

Ottissippi

had moved his people from LaPointe, Wisconsin to Sault Ste. Marie. *Kiosckance* was the chief of the Otchipwes in the wars against the six nations – Iroquois and some of the Wyandotte's. Young Gull had recurring dreams of the place at the foot of Lake Huron and Black River, before and after the Iroquois Wars. He and his extensive fleet of warriors had camped at what is now Fort Gratiot on their return from the lower lake wars. He afterwards made the district his home. Aamjiwnaang, "at the spawning stream", was a beautiful place with a temperate climate, plenty of game, fish, and every plant and material needed to live comfortably (David D. Plain, "The Plains of Aamjiwnaang").

Half of the people at Boweting (Sault St. Marie) moved down to the foot of Lake Huron at Black River (Port Huron, Michigan) and (Ontario, Canada) and south of Algonac, Michigan at Swan Creek. The two large groups would meet in the summer for a large gathering. When the people grew large and the village grew to 1,000 people, they would split off into two groups and begin a new village (Plain). The book *1300 Moons* is the life story of Young Gull by his descendent, David D. Plain. This book gives much greater detail of the Iroquois Wars.

Aamijiwnaang ("where the people gather by the rapid waters"), the territory at the foot of Lake Huron – Karegnondi and the Ottissippi (St. Clair/Detroit River), was a natural trade center, a Huge Trading Area, of great commerce for the Native Americans. It was a strategic military position on the largest inland water transportation system in North America and the world. It was the natural gathering place that was easy to reach from all directions. The Detroit – Strait, is The Ottissippi, it means Clear Waters.

The rock weirs of the Ottissippi Delta, at the head of the St. Clair River, at the foote of Lake Huron, were the great fishery of the tribes in the surrounding area. The Anishinabe gathered to spear and net large quantities of whitefish and sturgeon swarming in shallow waters and through the narrow channels.

The Ojibwe occupied both sides of the river. They spent much time on the east side in what is now Canada, or in the Saginaw Valley near Bay City, Michigan. They were master canoe builders and handlers. This was the great highway connecting with all the country. The Ojibwe then enjoyed a "Golden Age". This Golden Age was to become a nightmare (David Plain).

Young Gull's people settled at Lake Huron, St. Clair River, Black River, Swan Creek, Michigan, and east of the Ottissippi (St. Clair River), in Canada and spread far and wide to the north and west. They did not live in long houses (Plain).

The Ojibwe – Chippewa spread from Lake Huron to the Saginaw Watershed and Lake St. Clair. Where the Saginaw grew large and were clearly the military and political leaders in the Upper Great Lakes.

The Mississauga were back in Southern Ontario in 1696. They reoccupied lower Michigan and Ontario lands. They flourished and became the largest, most powerful Indian nation in North America.

The Anishinabe groups inhabited the islands at the delta area around and above Round Lake (Lake St. Clair). There were very large villages in this beautiful area, including all the rivers, streams, and creeks.

Aamijiwnaang territory stretched from Georgian Bay, Ontario, east to Toronto; south to Detroit, Michigan; and west of Lansing, Michigan; and north to Alpena, Michigan. Territories were separated by watersheds and waterways.

The Ojibwe held the richest trapping grounds and largest military power on the continent (David Plain).

When the beavers were plentiful, the waterways extended much farther, connecting a thorough network of all the waterways. Travel was mostly by water to near and far. The people traveled frequently within 100 miles in every direction of the main villages, or castles.

They were known as the Lakes Indians, the Lakes People, the Rapids Tribe, and the Detret – Detroit – Strait Indians.

The Indians were very hospitable people, sharing everything they had if needed, including food, shelter, medical care, and any other necessity. Hospitality was an Indian virtue. Everyone was expected to practice it. When an Indian arrived at the wigwam of another Indian, he expected to be hospitably received. He would enter without a sign. If guests were hungry, they would receive whatever happened to be in the house, even if it happened to be intended for seed corn. The frontier families became accustomed to arising in the morning to several Indians lying on the floor rolled up in their blankets with their feet stretched toward the fireplace. This practice was common along the well-traveled trails. (Emmert, MHC vol. 47).

Democracy and freedom were the Native American Indian ideals (Canadian Indian History, www). They were masters of the Great Lakes region, and determined to destroy any who entered the Country, their territory.

At the Great Peace Treaty of 1701 in Montreal, many of the first nations Iroquois and other Indians made peace and shared the waterways and lands.

THE BLACK RIVER OJIBWE

The Mekadewagmitigweyawininiwak – "People of the Blackwater River" – lived along the Black River in the Michigan thumb on Mill Creek and all other streams and creeks that existed at that time in the area.

Amchoanews Village was the main castle or center of government for the people. The Black River people were part of the *Missisauga Ojibwe*, living on both sides of the Strait (The Detroit) that cut like a knife between Lake Huron and Lake Erie. The hunting grounds and winter camps were throughout the Thumb of Michigan, known as Saginaw, named after the great chief over this section of the territory. The Thumb from Detroit to Saginaw and into Ontario were covered in huge forests. Towering trees made a wonderful home. The hunting was superb.

Mekadewagamitigweyawininiwak is the longest word in the Ojibwe language, having 30 characters.

Makade Ziibii means "the Original People of the Black River", The Black River Band. The Black River Band were of the Bear (*Makwa*) clan totem (*dodem*). They were the protectors and keepers of records.

THE SWAN CREEK OJIBWE

The Wabisiwisibiwiiniwak – "Men of Swan Creek" – lived in a huge, beautiful village at the north side of Lake St. Clair (Round Lake). It is now Anchorville, Michigan. Waabziin Ziibii means "Swan Creek Band". The Swan Creek men had extensive corn fields and tool factories.

THE SAGINAW OJIBWE – CHIPPEWA

The Zaagiinaa Ziibii means "The Saginaw Band". They occupied a large area covering the Saginaw River Watershed around Saginaw Bay and into the thumb of Michigan. This was a rich country; the natural resources were envied by many. Foot trails and roads led into all directions. They have become the roads and highways of today.

The thumb of Michigan was a great gathering place. Truckloads of artifacts have been collected in this area. Koylton Highland Pass a high point in the thumb of Michigan. The ancient pass in Highland Township was at the top of the mound. The Thumb was farmland and forest, at Indian Fields (town), large crops of Indian corn were grown of every kind, squash, beans, potatoes, sunflowers, and many other vegetables.

THE PETROGLYPHS

The only, rock carvings – *Muz I Nee Bi Ah Sin* – in Michigan are the petroglyphs. Ezhibiigaadek – written on stone, in the Anishinabemowin language. The Huron (Cass) River runs near this special place where Indians gathered for ceremonies and meetings. A sacred place on the high land in the Thumb of Michigan. The Black River and Cass River were an easy portage; they could be reached from all directions. It is a historic ceremonial site.

Here there is a great rock of sandstone, 40 feet long and 15 feet wide. Having many carvings upon it, flying birds, other animals, a man with a bow and arrows, swirl lines, and handprints. The spiral pattern is the symbol of life. There are over a hundred figures of men, birds, mythology animals, spirals, tracks, weapons, etc.

The fires of 1871 and 1881 cleared vegetation that had protected it for centuries. Much study has been done at this site.

The park is a special place for indigenous people, even today. It is a spiritual gathering place, used for religious ceremonies, weddings, and special meetings. It is against the law to take, disturb, or dig artifacts from Indian sites (Joyce Reid, Deckerville Papers),

WATERWAYS AND TRAILS

The whole country was a great network of connecting trails (Farmer, 1884, History of Detroit and Michigan). Trails and great roadways, hundreds of miles in length, extended across the whole country. A thoroughfare of roads went in every direction. Some roads were 165 feet wide. Our highways and bridges are the same thoroughfares made by the Indians, and followed in their transportation. The best routes and crossings were chosen.

One a 2,000-mile thoroughfare from Montreal Canada to the Mississippi on U.S. Highway 12 follows this route. Copper and shells were traded for many other treasures from far-away places. Horses arrived in 1730. The Assiniboine Ojibwe had many horses; they were expert horsemen and breeders, trading horses for goods.

The Huron Trail led from Detroit to Black River and around the Thumb to Saginaw, Michigan. A trail from Anchor Bay led to Bay City, Michigan. There were trails along all the waterways having villages and camps every few miles apart.

The Old Black River Trail started near 10th and Water Street, now at Port Huron, and led out to the John Riley Settlement in now Riley Township, northwest of Memphis, Michigan near the Belle River.

Ottissippi

The trails were used as war paths, in trade, in the hunt, and every other purpose in life. Some were specifically used for hunting and war to conceal the men. Often the wildlife left trails, selecting the best routes (Wm. Hindsdale, "Trade and lines of travel of the MI Indians", The Archaeological Atlas of Michigan, 1928, U of M).

The west shores of Lake Huron were called Sanguenaum.

The Saginaw Watershed, *O Sagenon* or *Saginawe*, meaning "to flow out", contains 175 inland lakes and about 7,000 miles of rivers and streams. It is America's largest freshwater coastal wetland system! It is like a large web reaching in all directions. Restoration of the degraded and polluted environmental conditions is progressing. In 1813, Louis Campau erected an Indian trading post along the Saginaw River. This led to the development of Saginaw.

The Great Lakes are the largest inland water transportation system in the world! They always have been. Copper, bark, skins, feathers, corn, quills of porcupine, pipestone, mica, flint and other stone and rocks, and scores of other items found and made. All these trade items required travel.

The rivers were great highways, used for quick travel and transportation; portages were short between other waterways. In the winter, dog sleds and snow shoes were used to travel.

Shells from the gulf have been found in a great many Michigan burial grounds. They were made into ornaments and implements. Articles obtained by trade, raids, or brought by travelers, from a great distance. Indians were familiar with places hundreds of miles away.

Canoes were the ultimate in vehicles of travel. They could speed along to faraway places, they could navigate far up streams, and they had very little draw in depth. They were used for storage, they were a shelter, to sleep under or stay dry during storms.

The Ojibwe were expert craftsmen in building canoes, having the precise techniques to build the best models for any use. They built large and small. They traded canoes for other goods. Each family typically had four canoes for their needs. Canoes traveled all the Great Lakes, staying nearby the shoreline for safety.

The beavers made great dams, backing up the waters to create a much greater distance for travel on all the waterways than we have today. The rivers and streams were also deeper. However, the lumber industry caused them to be filled in. The beavers created natural dams to back up water and create canoe travel far up streams, that are now but drains (Wm. B. Hindsdale). The water table of the southern part of Michigan has been lowered four to five feet, and the beaver dams have been removed and are yet being removed.

The waterways were the place of a great many villages – towns or castles and camps – on lakes and navigable rivers and streams. In fact, most of the towns and cities of today are on the same grounds that once were occupied by the Native Americans. Government buildings, schools, and parks are mostly on Indian sites.

Large stepping stones were in the water to cross streams; bridges, now are where these trail crossings once were, and the trails became highways.

Waterway travel was the highway of great importance, in the early history of America, when the Indian alone dominated the land (Hindsdale).

CUSTOMS

NANABOZOO

Nanabozoo was an Adam Type a Great Spirit who was Co–Creator of the world, the inventor of fishing and hieroglyphs (word pictures), and teacher of all things. Who lived through the Great Flood on a raft with animals.

The Mide Medewiwin Society – Healers were revered, visions and dreams held Great Importance. Offerings of Tobacco were made in gratitude and respect to the Heavenly Spirit. The people, were thankful and worshipped the creator always.

The Grand Medicine Society – Mide Medewiwin – was made up of holy men or healers. Midewiwin learned hunting medicine to find game. Midewiwin prayers were for abundant game, fish, and other food, as well as for health, long life, fair weather, and community ethics, the concerns of traditional Ojibwas.

Mides made tobacco and dog sacrifices to the Manitos (God's messengers) as part of their official acts. They took sweat baths before entering the medicine lodges. Mide members used ritual pictographs in greatly expanded form. Ceremonies were requested for the help and blessings of the powerful Manitos. The Mide called on the Manitos for pity and charity. Offerings of tobacco were made in gratitude and respect to the Heavenly Spirit. The people were thankful and worshipped the Creator always.

Mide initiates were often required to receive visions of the Manitos before approaching Mides for instruction. The first step toward society membership.

The Society devoted much of its instruction to the knowledge of medicinal herbs and other curing devices. Midewiwin's major concern was the maintenance of health and the combating of diseases. Midewiwin taught its members ways of gaining power over sickness, just as the Manitos taught traditional Ojibwes to avoid illness. In addition, Mides viewed ill health as punishment for sins against Manitos and encouraged Ojibwas to lead ethical and ritually responsible lives. In keeping with traditional morality, the society encouraged respect for all the living persons of the universe.

Midewiwin taught that every plant had a pharmaceutical use, and each member cultivated his or her own medicinal knowledge beyond the more elementary recipes (Densmore). Midewiwin initiation gave them the powers to heal and destroy, but they used those powers on their own, as though received from Guardian Manitos in private visions. The Society taught that the religious leader's role was to heal the sick.

Nanabozho was recognized as the founder of Midewiwin. His role was intercessor between Kitchie Manito and the Indians. The Supreme Being was the ultimate source of medicine in many of the Society's myths.

Midiwiwin kept pictograph records, ceremonial speeches, and ethical doctrines in scriptural scrolls. Their Birchbark Records were the Indian equivalent of the Christian Bible. They used them as representations of the origin myths, charts of the movement of Ojibwas and Midiwiwin, maps to heaven, guides to moral life, instructional catechisms, ceremonial guides, and sacred manifestations of Kitchie Manito's message. The Ojibwe passed down these scrolls from teachers to students, from community to community, as embodiments of God's teachings.

A Secret Society was developed within the structure of Society. The specialists went beyond a secret language, a depth of understanding, and ceremonial knowledge, separate from those of the common Ojibwa. The Master Mides of the highest degree's activities were veiled from the lower degrees. They opposed the activities of the Djessakids and other religious specialists. A very exclusive and secretive priestly group. The exclusiveness of Midewiwin leadership was fostered by the high cost of instruction and initiation.

Mide worshipped the Supreme God. Midewiwin fostered Ojibwa unity, organized religious leadership, maintained curing, and morality. The Midewiwin teaching lodge means, from the heart, prayers are offered, along with songs and stories and counseling. Medicine is anything good.

The Indians had few diseases; their medicines were quick to cure and generally infallible (Canadian Indian History, www).

The Medicine Bundle is a collection of objects which symbolize a spiritual path, symbols of power.

Ojibwes associated health with correct morality. Mide taught that proper conduct determined one's length of healthy life. Generosity, honesty, strength of character, endurance, and wisdom were the admired qualities of the Indian. To the Indian, the land was the source of life for everything alive on earth, the creation of the Great Spirit. The land was priceless and holy and useful. It was the sustainer and nurturer, "Mother Earth". Everything belong to the world and its people. The universe is built of a grand design by Gitchi Manito, the Great Spirit. Gitchi Manito had many helping spirits that are the animals and otherwise around us. Evil spirits were rattlesnakes and big storms.

There was unfailing respect for the established place and possessions of every other member of the family circle. There was habitual, quiet order and decorum in behavior. Family was the social unit, also the unit of government. The Native is not demonstrative in affection at any time. Two who should be in love, should be united in secret, before public acknowledgement of their union. (C. Eastman, The Soul of the Indian).

The position of women was secure. All property was held by her. Modesty was her chief adornment; she ruled undisputed within her own domain, a tower of moral and spiritual strength. Young women were usually silent and retiring (C. Eastman).

The Indian is an individualist in religion as in war. There was no national army, nor an organized church, no priest to assume responsibility for another's soul. This was the supreme duty of the parent, in some degree, since the children were of his creation and protecting power, who alone approaches the solemn function of deity – God.

Indian people do not choose which religious tradition they will practice. They are born into a community and its particular ceremonial life (Eastman). A religious man from his mother's womb, taught silence, love, and reverence: the trinity of first lessons. She later adds generosity, courage, chastity, she learns from Mother, and Grandmother Nature.

The love of possessions is a weakness to be overcome. Children must learn early the beauty of generosity. Taught to give what they prize most, taste the happiness of giving. To give away all that they have, above all to the poor and aged, and hope for no return.

Indian etiquette was very strict. We always avoid, a direct address. The title of a person was used to show respect. Children were not allowed to speak in adult presence, unless requested. Children are taught generosity to the poor and reverence for the Great Mystery. Religion was the basis for all Indian training.

The Indian was a blood brother to all living creatures; the storm wind, a messenger of the Great Mystery.

Grandparents teach our history, repeating the time-hallowed tales with dignity and authority, to lead into his inheritance in the stored-up wisdom and experiences of the race. Old were dedicated to the service of the young. They were the teachers and advisors. The young regard them with love and reverence. Old age gave much freedom (C. Eastman).

Some words have different meanings for men and women.

Boozhoo is a greeting. *Migwetch* is "thank you." *Chi Migwetch* is a big "Thank You".

The Ojibwe are not boisterous; they speak in a low tone. They never interrupt. They have a natural politeness. They are gentle, obliging in manners and bashfulness.

The Indian is very superstitious (Eastman).

The land was a pristine Eden. The vegetation was magnificent; rich clusters of grapes hung from the trees (Lanman, History of MI). The soil was rich and produced immense crops of corn, beans, pumpkins, squash, and other vegetables. The virgin soil was extremely fertile with luxuriant growth. The pigeons were thick like a cloud and easily caught with a net. They and the abundant other fowl and waterfowl left abundant natural fertilizer.

The Indians rotated their town sites every 10 years and let the land lay fallow. Being enriched with vegetation and natural fertilizer from the many animals and birds. Indians built the first corn cribs.

Wildlife and game abounded, fish were abundant, there was plenty. The Indians shared the excess among them. This was called *daawed* – "sharing" (D. Plain).

Great numbers of moose and elk, having huge horns that rivaled the branches of trees, were thriving. Wild beeves (buffalo) were among the wildlife (Lanman, 1855). Bison – buffalo, were in Canada, the Southeast, and prairies of Michigan. At an early day, the buffalo roamed from Canada to Mexico. Tens of millions of buffalo fed on the prairies. One way of hunting the buffalo was to surround them with a fire circle; they were then easily captured for sustenance.

The marshes were luxuriant with wild rice, a feast for a great variety of birds and waterfowl, and for the Indians. The area is a major migration flyway. Marsh hay was abundant (Hudgins, "The Biodiversity Atlas of Lake Huron to Lake Erie". Sec 2, 1936, "The Walpole Indian").

In the spring of the year, the hunters would set fire to the marsh grasses to cause flight and the appearance of game, beaver, deer, muskrat, and otter. Then the prairie would be a sea of flame. After the fires, May, brought forth the sweet grass, and nature again restored her bright carpet (Marantette Papers, Michigan Archives).

Wild geese collected around small interior lakes after the winter migration, where they obtained their food from the wild rice, which was the peculiar product of this region. Lanman, 1855). Wild rice was at Saginaw Bay and in many lakes and ponds, along with other waterways in Michigan, Wisconsin, Minnesota, and throughout North America. The rice season, lasted 10 days to three weeks in early autumn.

The game was much tamer, the deer fed at deer parks. Clearings were made to supply fresh grasses and draw them, elk, and caribou, to certain areas for hunting. Moose fed along the swampy places. Trees were girdled and burnt to clear the trees for game and fields crops. Bears and wolves were many.

When the need was established and the Great Spirit worshipped, it was fitting for the earthly relatives to make the supreme sacrifice to aid man. As a token of gratitude, the Indians always placed a bit of tobacco in the hole where he gathered roots for medicinal use.

Wild rice was gathered from shallow waters, maple sugar was made from the many groves. Maple syrup was poured over snow to make candy and into molds. The duck bills filled with maple sugar were a favorite for infants. Brushes were made from the tail of a porcupine. Wild fruits of many kinds and berries were gathered and dried. Choke cherries were pounded pit and all; mixed with pounded jerked meat and fat to form a much-prized Indian delicacy. Pemmican was travel food; warriors took it in a pouch for the hunt and war. The Indians drank teas boiled from plants and herbs and sweetened with maple sugar. They carried water in bags made of tripe or pericardium.

Every flower had a wise purpose; every blade of grass, every plant, herb, root, and tree, and was to be used to please God – Gitchi Manito (Canadian Indian History, www).

There was scarcity of food in the spring. Everything was free: food, lodging, everything. All were rich alike in summer.

The trade of the Indians was more a social and political trade than an economic. The giving of trade goods was not economic, for profit or wealth.

The Indian hardly ever cried. This was very necessary: we rise early, silent and reticent – the foundation of patience and self-control. There are times of mirth, but the rule is gravity and decorum.

The wise man believes profoundly in silence and absolute poise or balance of body, mind, and spirit. The man who preserves his selfhood ever calm and unshaken by the storms of existence. Silence is the cornerstone of character. Truthful and brave, hard exercise was kept up. Fasting and two meals a day. It is an honor to be selected for difficult or dangerous service (C. Eastman).

A first birth name was given, honor name, nicknames. A child is named after they are able to walk, a distinguishing character or a famous deed to live up to, unstained. Like giving away property to those in want, love and goodwill toward fellow man. If they grow up and fail to live up to the name chosen, they are no longer called by it.

Bear, wolf, and eagle are masculine. Fire is the symbol of enthusiasm, energy, devotion.

The doe, mink, ermine, and otter are feminine. Sky, wind, and water are either (Charles Eastman).

SEASONS AND THE INDIAN CAMP

The maple camp and fishing was early spring, the time of new beginnings and renewal. The garden camp was early summer, the beach for summer gatherings and fishing. It was the time for socializing with the greater family who would gather in great numbers for religious ceremonies, games, storytelling, council meetings, planning and preparation for winter. The rice field or fishing camp in the fall. Winter camp, hunting and trapping; it was the camp in the woods, where the forest protected the people from fierce winds and winters. It was a time for oral history and storytelling on long winter nights. It was singing, repairing tools, sewing new clothing, tanning hides, gathering wood, and making furniture of small limbs tied with gut.

Charles Eastman in his "Indian Boyhood" relates;

> *The Indian exercised much ingenuity in selecting a suitable campsite. There must be water and fuel. Next, sanitation and drainage and protection from the elements and ready discovery by foes. Finally, beauty of situation.*
>
> *In midsummer in a great number, they choose an extensive plateau on a secondary bank of a river or lake or upon the level bottomlands of some large stream.*
>
> *For a winter camp, they prefer a protected site in the deep woods, near a large river or lake. A small party concealment is the first principle to be observed. Seclusion gives a sense of security, but a beautiful spot, which commands all approaches, or a hidden cave, guarded by curving shores but very near a long-distance view, is used for a lookout.*

In summer, he pitches his tepees upon a high rocky point to get away from mosquitoes but is protected to the approach of others, concealed at the back and sides that afford a retreat in case of danger and also shortcuts for return from hunting and trapping. Teepoles are left when they move. They build small fires, as the smoke may be seen a long way off if the wind is right. Only in cold weather or a special purpose is a huge fire built. In no case does he leave it without it being entirely extinguished. It is built on rocks if possible, so the ashes are removed by wind and rain, and the ground shown no disfigurement.

Tents are pitched in a circle with the entrance always toward the watering place. Council lodges are opposite the entrance. There are more than one circle for large parties with each band or clan having its own.

Camp breakup is announced the day before, and the next site is already explored and selected. The people are guided by the men to the chosen spot. The start is before daybreak; the packing is done quickly with a well-understood system. Wagons, ponies, dogs, canoes, or men and women are used to transport the belongings from place to place. There is nothing messy or haphazard. A carrying strap, with a head and chest piece of two strings four to five feet and two inches wide, long enough to encircle the head and shoulders, is used. Goods are secured in a well-balanced roll or bundle that is not carried too low to suit their strength and comfort. They do not let it sway or swing. The *travois* is the primitive vehicle used for many years. It is two tent poles and a basket with the end of the poles bound to a saddle. It contains all the household goods, and sometimes young children.

The temporary shack is six- or eight-sided with six poles that are 10 feet long, a fork branch that is set two feet deep in the ground and eight to twelve inches apart, with other poles resting on the forked ends. Four more poles are in the center, forming a square, and are also connected at the top. In the middle, a hole is dug for a fireplace and lined with stones.

For the bark house, the outer wall is of split poles driven into the ground, close together, and neatly overlaid with bark of the birch, elm, or basswood in strips eight feet long by four to six inches wide. Outside posts hold light saplings which hold the bark in position. Crosspieces are also tied to the split poles with strips of tough cedar bark; the roof is made the same way. The overlapping bark is waterproof with an adjustable opening over the fireplace. The door opens to the south side, three by six feet, and is closed by a movable door of bark or rawhide. The home may be thatched with coarse meadow grass instead of bark. Some are partly underground for warmth in winter and covered with sod or earth; then it becomes a round house. The *wickiup* was a brush shelter.

Beds are built with poles and bark; robes are spread and blankets for beds by night and a lounging place by day. Grass of rushes are braided into mats and used for coverings and carpets. The Plains Indians used buffalo hides, nicely tanned and sewed together in a semicircular shape. If nothing better, a quantity of grass will make a warm bed.

Winter stores are stored overhead and roundabout in every space. Weapons of war and of the chase (Hathi Trust, Levi Bishop 1870). Mounds were made for lookouts or signal stations.

Time was told by the sun's shadow hunger was a good guide, and the distance traveled. (Eastman)

THE TEACHING STICK

Teaching sticks were used to tell the truths of our people. At a council, the person holding the stick is the only one allowed to speak. The answering feather is passed to someone who is asked a question. The stick is passed from person to person. Everyone is allowed their own, sacred point of view and are respected in their viewpoint.

People responsible for holding any council meeting make their own talking stick. It is used when teaching children, holding council, settling disputes, at Pow Wow's, storytelling circles, or a ceremony where more than one person will speak.

It is the medicine stick of the owner, and each stick is different. White pine is the peace tree, birch symbolizes truth, evergreen is growth, cedar is cleansing, aspen is for seeing clearly, as there are many eye shapes on the truth. Maple represents gentleness, elm is used for wisdom, mountain ash is for protection, oak is for strength, cherry is for expression, high emotion, or love. Fruit woods are for abundance, walnut or pecan for gathering energy or beginning new projects. Each must decide which type of standing tree will assist their needs and add needed "medicine" to the councils held.

The ornamentation on the stick all have meaning. Red is for life, yellow knowledge, blue for prayer and wisdom, white is for spirit, purple is for healing, orange for feeling kinship with all living things, and black is for clarity and focus.

The feathers and hide are very important as well. The answering feather is usually an eagle feather, which represents high ideals, truth from sight on high, and the freedom that comes from speaking the truth to the best of one's ability. It can also be a turkey feather, the peace eagle of the south, which brings peaceful attitudes and the give and take to solve problems. The owl feather may stop deception.

The skins, hair, or hides bring the ways of the creature. The buffalo brings abundance, elk fitness and stamina, deer gentleness, rabbit listening, horse hair perseverance and connection to the earth and wind spirits. If there is a sickness of heart, mind, body, or spirit, a snake skin may be wrapped around the stick so healing of those persons may occur.

The talking stick teaches each one to honor the sacred point of view of every living creature.

BURIAL CUSTOMS

The Indian looks forward to a happy return to a Land of Plenty and Great Joy – not literally, but in spirit. And this desire and hope fills his soul with exultation when he sees the glorious orb of day sinking near the abode of departed spirits (Jones).

They hold nothing, so precious as the bones of their dead. They do not have a Hell.

When a man is at the point of death, he is decked with all the ornaments owned by the family. They dress his hair with red paint mixed with grease and paint his body and face red with vermillion; he is dressed as richly as possible. Red means life, thus the color. They adorn the place where he is lying with necklaces of porcelain and glass beads, or other trinkets. His weapons beside him and at his feet, all articles that he used in war during his life. All his relatives and, above all, the Jugglers – Holy Men – are near him.

When he seems to struggle to give up his last breath, the women and girls begin mourning. They sing doleful songs, cries and lamentations, and weeping. The men do not weep.

When he is dead, or a moment before, they raise him to a sitting position, his back supported as if he were alive. The corpse remains thus sitting until the next day and is kept in this position.

Death is the test and background of life. It holds no terrors for him but is met with simplicity and perfect calm, seeking an honorable end as his last gift to his family and descendants. He courts death in battle; it is disgraceful to be killed in a private quarrel.

Ottissippi

We cut our hair, sacrificing all personal beauty and adornment, the dress was trimmed off the fringe and ornaments, cut it short or cut robe or blankets in half. Men blacken their face, widow women or bereaved parents sometimes gash their arms and legs till they are covered with blood. They give away all that they have, not caring about any earthly possession, even beds and home, wailing day and night unto voicelessness. Some are put on a scaffold or platform, sometimes the body is placed against a tree or rock in a sitting position facing the enemy.

A lock of hair in pretty cloth is rolled up, a spirit bundle is suspended from a tripod and occupied a place of honor in the lodge; at every meal, a dish of food placed under it. A person of the same sex and age is invited to eat the food. At the end of a year, a feast and gift giveaway are given. The lock of hair is buried with ceremonies. The spirit returns to God after it is freed from the body. It is everywhere and pervades all nature. Yet lingers near friends to comfort and hear prayers. There is so much reverence for the spirit, we didn't even speak the name aloud.

The head was always buried facing west. Offerings of food and other valuable items for travel were placed, in the grave house. The deceased person was buried with their most valuable possessions: guns, jewelry, their best clothing. Men were buried with their tobacco pouch, a bowl of fish stew or other food, a jar of water, gun, shot and ball, tomahawk, knife, and blanket. Sometimes corn, pelts, trade goods, and other gifts were placed all around the casket (Plain, 1300 Moons).

A spirit house was built over the grave of many dead. It was made of branches and was like a small log or bark house with a hole in one end to place food and other necessities. The hole also allowed the spirit to leave for the spirit journey of four days to the Land of Souls.

Scaffold burials also were used, the scaffold erected seven or eight feet high. After one year, the bones were cleaned and buried. Sometimes the bodies were burned on six poles, the bones cleaned, polished, or blanched for travel (Plain, 1300 Moons).

After burial, the family make liberal payment to those who took part therein. For a year food was placed often in the grave house for the departed.

In the home, a place was set and food placed for the person who died. If a child was taken, the mother carried a baby bundle with her for a year, in mourning. Near relatives wore their most ragged clothes for a year in mourning (Eastman).

A feast of the dead is held every three years. They bring the bones of their relatives. They set them out and heap gifts upon them of all their finest and best possessions. The cooking pots are constantly on the fire, full of meat for anyone to eat who likes. They make a continual song night and day with drums or pots or bark and sticks. They go out and fire muskets, and begin howling until the air quivers, they reenter daubed with black. This goes on for 3 days and nights. Toward the end, they make presents to those invited to the feast of all that belongs to the dead. They go out uttering great howls and, with heavy blows, break the ceremony hut to pieces. The women, lay fir branches on the ground where the hut was. They kill a large number of dogs which are to them as sheep are to us and are valued more than any other animal, and make a feast of them. Prayers are made for pity on the souls of their relations, to light them on their journeys and to guide them to the dwelling place of their ancestors. Then each takes the bones of their relations; and bury them in stony, unfrequented places. After that, the dead are never spoken of again in any way.

The Feast of the Dead was a mingling of bones in a common grave, dance, games, contests, election, and feast. Presents were distributed by the families of the dead, marriage alliances made and plans. (Schenk).

In the following, Cadillac gives much insight into Anishinabe life:

> *White men came and found the continent: everywhere was occupied by Indians. Scores of tribes scattered over the continent. They were highly hospitable, sharing their cabins, food, and women. Sagamity is different foods mixed together to be eaten.*
>
> *They eat fish cooked in all sorts of ways, fried, roasted, boiled, smoked, and stewed.*
>
> *They have no butter or oil. They have grease or marrow, from elk, moose, or buffalo, which is brought to Michilimackinac from the Illinois, or Chicago.*
>
> *The Miami bring huge bears into their village they have captured and tamed, driving them before with switches, like sheep.*
>
> *Their cabins are weatherproof; no rain gets in them. Poles are thick as one's leg and very long. Entwined between are cross pieces as thick as*

one's arm. An opening about two feet wide runs along the peak. They are 100 to 300 feet long and 20 to 24 feet high. (Pierre Margry, volume, French North America)

Every tribe has its doctors, surgeons, and apothecaries, called Jugglers. *Dogs are sacrificed. The Medicine Men are highly rewarded. Experience shows they can cure a wounded man in a week; better than our surgeons can in a month. (Cadillac)*

They anoint and perfume the hair in oil and grease. They fight to the death for liberty; nothing is so shameful to a man as slavery.

They marry several wives and put (them) away whenever they are pleased. The brother marries the widow.

They observe the 40-day purification after birth. They speak in parables and metaphysically. They tell of the Flood Deluge. Their manners, customs, and ceremonies resemble the Jews.

All Indians are naturally intelligent; they have great faculty for drawing, painting, and sculpture, and God had given them a very good memory (Cadillac).

Lahonton in "Travels in Louisiana" wrote:

At a feast, there was two hours of singing and dancing. After that the slaves came to serve. Four platters were set before me. One had two whitefish, only boiled in water, another the tongue and breast of a roe buck boiled; the third two wood hens, the hind feet or trotters of a bear, and the tail of a beaver all roasted; the fourth contained a large quantity of broth made of several sorts.

For the drink, a very pleasant liquor; a syrup of maple beat up with water.

The most curious thing I saw in the villages was 10 to 12 tame beavers that went and came like dogs from the river to the cottages.

They know how to make great sloops that will hold 30 or 40 men.

Large quantities of tobacco are grown in New France. In addition, much was imported, this being preferred, by the Indians.

Slavery among Indians was entirely due to prisoners taken in war, a mild form, being treated as members of the family, in the hope of exchange or ransom by their own tribe.

See chapters 13 and 14 on customs and lifeways for a more complete picture of the Indian customs, hunting, chiefs, religion, and lifeways.

CHAPTER 4
Explorers and Missionaries

"Before the Europeans arrived in the Americas, more than 500 tribes or collective groups of 22 million people inhabited what is now the United States" (Red Road, "365 Days of Walking the Red Road, Terri Jean 2002).

Many countries were coming to the Maritimes and along the East Coast, fishing and whaling at a very early date, including the Norsemen and many others.

In 1453, the trade routes from Western Europe to India and China were cut off by Sultan Mehmet II when he captured Constantinople. The European nations were searching for a new trade route to India and China and sent many explorers: French, English, and Spanish.

In 1520, Portuguese fishermen were drying cod for the trade.

In the early 1600s, ships from many nations were coming on a regular basis; the Basques, Biscaynes, Bretons, Portuguese, and English came for the fishing and whaling and capturing Indians for the slavery and fur trades. Trading ships came, and the East Coast experienced contact. White Men began pushing the indigenous people out of their happy and fertile homes.

At one time, the Europeans recognized that land could not be claimed as others already lived there. In 1493, during the Renaissance, the Pope of the Roman Catholic Church stated that inhabited lands could be claimed in the name of God: "Imperialist Colonial European Nations were competing for wealth, power, and the control of resources around the Globe. Pope Nicolai allowed the subjugation of Indigenous peoples around the world. To take over and make them slaves, to use and profit by any means necessary to convert

Aborigines of discovered Lands to Christianity" (Papal Bulls). Exploitation was often veiled by religious and political illusions.

The Anishinabe believe use of the land is a birth right to all human beings. For the Europeans, land could be owned and exploited for profit: this is basic to their system. "The Western World has limited truths, and cannot see what we see" (Anishinabe).

The French were the first to explore the interior to the Great Lakes. They became part of the Indian culture, marrying the indigenous women. The women were guides and interpreters for the fur traders. This also created a *trading relationship* with the Indian peoples. The women knew all the intricacies of Indian life and did much work to help their husband in his trade.

The Iroquois in New York were being squeezed from all sides.

White Rock was a prominent feature of the Michigan Thumb region; it was a huge limestone boulder in Lake Huron, three miles north of Forestville at White Rock Park on M-25. It is much smaller today due to theft and bombing. It was venerated by the Indians as a manitou and inscribed with petroglyphs – writings known as pictographs. At one time, it was large enough for six to eight sets of dancers.

"Because the Indian tribes gathered at the White Rock, so did the earliest explorers and trappers. The White Stone became the Eastern Boundary of the Treaty of the Northwest Territory in 1807

The great Indian village at the Detroit was called Teuchsa Grondie – Place of Many Beavers. The whole Strait was teeming with shallow waters in which beavers created their dams, backing up the waters, creating a haven for all wildlife. The backed-up waters also made the streams, rivers, brooks, and drains accessible to canoe traffic. The canoes needed only a few inches of draft in the shallow waters. As a result, canoe travel was very extensive.

Many French missionaries came to New France with a desire to teach the indigenous peoples their religion. While some were sincere and helpful, many were looking for riches and brought the evils of European dominance with them. It was a very dangerous undertaking; the Natives were not always friendly to the "Black Robes" and explorers. The force of nature in the wilderness and in water travel could be very dangerous.

The Europeans changed forever the Native Americans' lives, introducing them to communicable disease, which they had no immunity against, remedy for, or knowledge of. Hundreds of thousands died from disease, creating much suffering for the people and wiping out whole villages. The loss of many great leaders was severely endured. The people consolidated into new groups and became even more mixed.

Ottissippi

New ideas and technologies were introduced in the form of firearms, manufactured metal products, woven cloth, and alcoholic beverages. The Indians welcomed the French, married them, and loved them.

The Catholic Church had a monopoly of the missions to New France. The French Huguenots – Protestants – were refused entry to America. The Catholic religious leaders having much power with the French king and in the Americas. The Jesuits were the dominant political force in the New World.

The Indians knew all the trails and waterways – every inlet and stream, every Island, rock, and shoal. They were the guides, canoe men, carriers, interpreters, and traders.

The missionaries were eager to save the souls of the savages (Bald, Michigan in Four centuries). The missionaries followed the Indians in their migrations. There were great rivalries among the missionaries. The Catholic Priests, or Black Robes, were from many orders: the Sulpicians, the Recollects, and the Jesuits.

The first Norse explorer, Leif Ericsson, made the voyages to the East Coast in 1000 A.D., 500 years before Columbus. Leif was the son of Erick the Red of Iceland.

John Cabot, an Italian, visited in 1497 for cod, whaling, and fur. He claimed the region for England. There was contact and conflict.

New France was established from 1524 to 1763.

"In the mid 1500's, the Iroquois, Huron Petun, and Neutrals inhabiting Southern Ontario numbered 65,000" (Rogers/Smith).

Cartier visited the St. Lawrence Valley in 1534 and 1535, searching for riches and the passage to Asia. The men in his party were dying of scurvy; the Natives gave them the cure of cedar leaves tea.

In 1600, King Henry IV of France awarded a fur trading monopoly to a group of French merchants. In 1604, he gave De Monts exclusive trading rights to bring 60 colonists a year to New France. He founded the first French colony in North America.

The Company of 100 Associates founded by Cardinal Ricelieu were to establish a French Empire in North America.

The governor over the colonies had almost absolute power, being accountable to the King of France. The intendant was over finance and justice, and he worked with the governor.

Cartier then went on to establish Quebec in 1608. He brought two nephews and had a fur monopoly. Fighting broke out between the French and English for control of the Canadian fur market between the Colonies. Champlain surrendered Quebec to England. This went on back and forth between France and England. From this small settlement, the French began to explore the Great Lakes region, establishing a cooperative relationship with the Algonquin's and fur trading posts in North America.

In 1600, Chauvin and Dupont established a trading post at Tadoussac on the St. Lawrence River.

Father Le Caron, a Franciscan Recollect priest, and his 12 companions started a mission to the Hurons in Southern Ontario near Lake Huron in 1615.

Saint Marie among the Hurons was the first French outpost, near Midland Ontario. The head Jesuits were at Saint Marie, near the mouth of Wye River. The Huron were destroyed in 1649 by the Iroquois.

There was a Recollect Mission near Fort Gratiot (Port Huron, Michigan) or directly across from it. It was called Saint Marie. Bell's History of Canada says it was an important one.

The Franciscan Order was a small group who were replaced by the Jesuit missionaries. The Recollects then served as parish priests and chaplains to the troops in Canada. The Sulpicians were also headquartered in Montreal, providing village priests and chaplains.

CHAMPLAIN

"Samuel De Champlain was the Governor of New France in 1603. De Champlain had already journeyed afar, when in 1603 he was sent to direct and stimulate the development of New France. Filled with religious zeal and enthusiasm, rare executive ability, and a keen vision of the requirements of the gigantic task before him, he discharged his difficult duties so faithfully and well that he was honored with the name *Founder of New France*" (Fowle).

When Champlain arrived with his 79 men, they knew nothing of the country; his men were starving and dying of scurvy. He lost 35 men before the Indians gave him the cure of cedar tea.

In 1603, Champlain was working with Dupont, his uncle. In 1605, Champlain established Port Royal in Nova Scotia.

"French documents in 1603 report Saulteaux Ojibwe and Missisauga villages on Harsens Island and the North Shore of Lake St. Clair. There was a steady presence from the 1640's onwards" (Adapted from, Karen Jean Travers 2015, York University, Toronto, Canada).

In 1608, he founded Quebec City. The British destroyed Port Royal in 1613. This began the French settlement on the St. Lawrence.

In 1609, Champlain, with Algonquin allies and firearms, attacked the two Mohawk Iroquois chiefs on the Richlieu River; he was the first European to use firearms against Indians.

Ottissippi

The French had been trading in the north above Montreal for many years before they explored the Southern Ontario lands. There had been many fights with the British, Dutch, and Iroquois. The Iroquois were being pushed West due to colonial New York expansion. The Upper St. Lawrence was in turmoil and was carried on to the Lower St. Lawrence; this pushed the French West, having been introduced to the Algonquins and Hurons through the trade network.

LA CARON

Father La Caron, a Franciscan friar, arrived in 1615, establishing a Recollect Catholic Mission.

"When Champlain entered the country of the Hurons near the Mission of Father La Caron, at the Towns of the Hurons called *Carhagouna*, he recognized this community as different from all the others he had come upon. The Hurons lived by agriculture rather than the chase and they hunted as well. He had come upon one of the most remarkable savage settlements on the continent. All about were cleared fields in which were raised Indian corn, squashes, pumpkins, and sunflowers. Here they had permanent homes, protected by high and strong Palisades" (Fowle).

"The Priest Sagard classed the Hurons as the Nobility, the Algonquin's, the Burghers of the Forest, and the Montagnais, *Mountain People*, and the rabble of the woods" (Fowle). The Montagnais were from Newfoundland, which was North of Montreal.

The priests were pioneers and explorers, as well led the trading and commercial development.

The Jesuit Fathers in their volumes, "Relations", give the most interesting and illuminating accounts of this Huron tribe.

They call themselves *Attigonetans*. Their principal hamlet was *Cahiague*.

> *The women wear their hair in a single braid, the men in various ways. Some shave all the head, leaving only some tufts of hair here and there, others half of the head; others allow their hair to grow very long which is the most common. Others leave it only in the middle, or on the forehead, straight as bristles. From this the first Frenchmen gave our Barbarians the name* Hurens, *because of the Hure, the straight locks they wore on the middle of the*

head. Hure in French signifies the bristles of the Wild Boar.

From Lower St. Lawrence, Champlain had followed a Waterway to Lake Huron which was the one-time outlet of Great Lake Nipissing, the immediate predecessor of the present Great Lakes. Now returning, he was following the outlet of a still more ancient lake, Glacial Lake Algonquin, belonging to a very old Epoch, before Lake Nipissing. This route was the outlet of this Great Glacial Lake. (Fowle)

In 1627, there were 100 French inhabitants. The Company of 100 Associates sent 400 colonists, who were sent back to France, because of the war with the English in the Upper St. Lawrence. In 1635, there were 200 French people in New France.

The (Niagara) Falls were called St. Louis. The Island of Orleans became Quebec in 1638.

"During the 40 years following the founding of Quebec, a dozen mission posts were built in the Huron Country, south of Georgian Bay. Explorers and Interpreters were to live among the Natives, make friendships, and gain confidence of them. Experience must teach them to learn the language and customs because they must live among them" (Fowle).

The turbulent Ottawa River led to Lake Huron from the St. Lawrence Valley. The Rapids along the Ottawa River were grueling, having 36 portages. This led to Lake Nipissing, the French River, Georgian Bay, and Lake Huron.

The Lower Peninsula of Michigan was unknown to the explorers, due to the hostility of the Iroquois to the French. The Iroquois controlled Lake Ontario and the route through Lake Erie and the Ottissippi (St. Clair River) to Lake Huron.

The only route open to explorers was pointed out by the friendly Huron.

BRULE

Brule at age 16 was sent to live among the Indians to learn their language and culture and to explore and discover the *Lake Country*, and search for a route to the Pacific. In 1610, he was the first European to see Lakes Ontario, Huron, and Superior. Brule told the story of his explorations to Sagard, who reported to the Governor Champlain at Quebec. Brule betrayed Champlain by leading the English up the St. Lawrence River; he was charged with treason and other indiscretions. Brule was killed and eaten in 1632 by Hurons.

Native copper was transported from Lake Superior to the St. Lawrence. It was a great trade item used to make tools and many other items.

The first Jesuits arrived in 1611. In 1615, the Recollect Priests from Rouan, France sent missionaries to New France.

NICOLET

In 1618, Champlain, the French governor of New France, sent Jean Nicolet to live among the Algonquins as a boy, to learn all about them.

He found the Algonquins occupied Lake Huron and as far as Lake Superior. The Huron, the Nipissings in 1618, the Amikouai, the Oumisagia or Missisaga, the Pahuoitingwach Irini (People of the Falls – The Falls of St. Mary's River), the Saulteaur. Of the Ojibwe around Lake Superior and Lake Michigan, were the Marameg – Catfish People, the Mikinac – Turtle People, and the Noquet – Bear People (Ancestors of the Ojibwa – Chippewa).

In 1634, he was sent by Champlain and the Company of 100 Associates of France as a spy to search for a passage to the Pacific, leading to China. Dressed in Chinese garb, he found only naked savages who were in large numbers at Green Bay and who had never seen a White man. They were very impressed by his colorful robe and his pistols, which he fired into the air. This man who carried "thunder" in both hands appeared as God. These were the Winnebago people who spoke Siouan. The Moniminee – Wild Rice People, were in Eastern Wisconsin.

His Native nickname was Achirra, meaning "Superman". He was a spy, explorer, interpreter, and fur trade ambassador.

He did not reach the Pacific but went as far as Green Bay, Wisconsin, exploring the northern expanse of Lake Superior whereby the French learned more of the country. He died in 1642 in Quebec by drowning.

The Lower Peninsula of Michigan was not known for another 35 years. The Iroquois were very dangerous to passersby on the southern route. It was not explored.

"The Dutch raped and tortured. Setting an example for the Mohawks, they used scalped head as kick balls, European practices" (Metis History, www).

In 1625, the Jesuits began missionary work among the Indians. "The Jesuits impressed the Huron with technological superiority and superior knowledge, including predicting eclipses" (Rogers/Smith, 1995, Aboriginal Ontario).

Gabrial Sagard, of the Franciscan missionaries, lived with the Hurons. He recorded and reported to the Governor at Quebec the doings of the explorers and missions. His *Histoire Du Canada* was published in 1636.

"The Jesuit Order initiate the Cast System, by the color of the skin, religion or value system" (Metis History, info/metis.aspx, www).

In 1634, the Jesuits came among the Huron. The Huron were ravaged by smallpox in 1639; fully one half of their number died.

St. Joseph Mission, northwest of Lake Simcoe, had about 2,000 people. They were the first to be attacked by the Iroquois. The Iroquois took 700 prisoners.

In 1639, the Jesuits founded Sainte Marie among the Hurons. The Mission was burned in 1649. St. Joseph II and Saint Michel (mission), were near Hillsdale, Ontario, Southwest of Lake Simcoe.

"At the mouth of the Detroit River was a Jesuit Mission on Bois Blanc – Bob lo Island. A new Mission Station was made at La Pointe de Montreal, opposite Detroit" (Rogers/Smith, 1995, Aboriginal Ontario).

Brebeuf and Chaumont visited several Neutral villages in Southwest Ontario in 1640 and 1641.

"Father Isaac Jogues, and Charles Raymbault, went to Lake Superior and preached to the Chippewa. The Great Fishing Place of Whitefish, they named the place of the rapids, "Sault De Sainte Marie". The Chippewa were called Saulteurs, because they frequented the Sault" (Michigan in Four Centuries, Bald). These men were martyred by the Iroquois at St. Ignace. The Iroquois continued raids on New France.

MENARD

Menard was a missionary in the Georgian Bay Country in Southwest Ontario from 1640 until the destruction of the Hurons in 1649.

Father René Mendard was sent to find the Christian Hurons who had been displaced and some were at Chaquamenon Bay, Wisconsin with the other Algonquins, gathered there after the Iroquois had terrorized their territory in Southern Ontario and Michigan. He joined a party of Ottawas and was the first missionary among these people. He established the Mission of the Holy Spirit in 1660. On a missionary journey in Northern Wisconsin, he was lost and perished. His assistant Jean Guerin continued the Mission.

In 1663, the contract with the Company of 100 Associates was cancelled by the King. The fur trade then came under direct Royal control. This marked the end of monopoly control and the emergence of the Free Trader and the

Coureur De Bois. The Company of 100 Associates surrendered their franchise in 1663.

In 1665, the first intendant, Marquis De Tracey, came to run the Colony as a representative of the King and Council of France. The population was then 3,215 French people. De Tracey was the Lt. General of all Canada and brought the first considerable body of French troops to New France.

Women were sent for to marry the men. Siegnor lands were rented to the inhabitants. The feudal system of France was brought across the ocean.

"Father Claude Allouez went through Michigan in 1665, to reestablish the Mission of the Holy Spirit at the West end of Lake Superior. Other missionaries soon followed. Allouez supplemented earlier reports of copper deposits and was the first to speak of a River, 'Messipi'" (Fuller).

FATHER MARQUETTE

In 1669, Father Marquette was sent to Cheguamenon Bay. There he heard from the Illinois Algonquins about the Great Mississippi River that lead to the Gulf of Mexico. He determined to go to the savages along its banks and carry the gospel to them, when the Sioux Indians were to extract vengeance for the murder of several Sioux. The Hurons fled East to the Straits of Mackinaw. Father Marquette followed them Huron and Ottawa) back there (Michilimackinac), establishing the Mission of St. Ignace in 1671. He, with Dablon, had established the mission at Sault Ste. Marie. They were courteous and entertained traveling missionaries. However, they made it clear to Father Galinee and Dollier of the Sulpician Order that there was no place in the West for any other than the Jesuit missionaries.

Father Galinee wrote of the mission: they had accomplished little. Not one Indian was permitted to attend the Mass, which was only for the 25 to 30 Frenchmen there at the time.

Father Marquette was a great explorer, the oldest founder of Michigan. He was the discoverer of the Upper Mississippi and the first White navigator of the Great River.

Traders also settled here; it was the great jumping off place to the Northwest fur market. It also became the great trading center of the North Country.

Galinee, a priest, constructed a Mission in 1670 near the River on Lake Huron, sometimes called The River Lyon, where the village of Port Dover is now situated. In a small ravine, he built a cabin strong enough for the resistance against the savages. It was their home, their chapel, their storehouse, and their fortress.

Galinee describes their surroundings:

> *beautiful woods, where they gather stores of nuts, acorns; the luxurient vines loaded with excellent grapes, from which they made an abundance of wine. Clear swift streams, plentifully stocked with fish and beaver, the forests teeming with deer, moose, and bear. A hundred bucks were seen in a single band, and nearly as many does. The bears were fatter and more succulent, than the most, savory pigs of France. After the cabin was constructed, all hands labored to gather an abundance of food supplies for the winter.*

Galinee describes the method of curing meat:

> the mode of curing it in the woods, is to slice it very thin, and spread it on a gridiron, raised from the ground covered with small wooden branches on which you spread your meat. A fire is made beneath and the meat is dried in the fire until there is no moisture in it and it is as dry as a piece of wood. It is put up in packages of 30 to 40 lbs. rolled up in pieces of bark and thus wrapped up. It will keep 5 or 6 years without spoiling. When you wish it, you reduce it to powder between two stones and make a broth by boiling *it with Indian corn.*

Dollier, a priest with Galinee, in 1670 passed through the Detroit and, not far from the site of Detroit, destroyed a stone idol which the Indians made sacrifices of skins and food. When about to embark on the lake, now St. Clair, they broke a hatchet, in breaking the stone to pieces, and threw them into the River.

In 1674, a new office was established: a bishop would be Head of the Clergy in New France. Montmorency was the first.

Ottissippi

HENNEPIN

Louis Hennepin – Father Hennepin – was a Belgian (Spanish Netherland), Franciscan Recollect. He was kicked out of the Catholic Church and forbidden to preach his book *Description of Louisiana*, which in 1683, had 46 editions. In his book *A New Discovery*, he records the ship "Griffon" sailing into the Detroit – The Strait.

He wrote, "the Country is stocked with stags, wild goats, and bears, which are good for food. Turkeys and swans are very common, and several other beasts, and bird's unknown to us, but they are extremely relishing".

Father Hennepin earned his place in history, for his exploration and as a historian.

In 1680, Hennepin was taken prisoner by the Sioux and carried up the Missouri. He and his two companions were rescued by, Dulhut, the Great Trader.

Hennepin wrote of the Great Lakes: "It were easy to build on the sides, of these Great Lakes, an infinite number of considerable towns, which might have communication one with another by, navigation for five hundred leagues together, and by an inconceivable commerce which would establish itself among Em."

JOLIET

Adrien Joliet was the first White man known to visit the Lower Peninsula. Joliet – Sieur Pierre Joliet – was the first explorer to take the Detroit Route in 1670. He was a seasoned trader, sent to find the copper the Indians told about. Louis Joliet also came. The Ottawa River from Montreal was impractical, having 36 portages.

> *At the Sault Ste. Marie, Joliet spent the winter. An act of humanity furnished him with a solution. The Saulteurs were about to burn at the stake, an Iroquois prisoner, whom Joliet rescued. The Indian out of gratitude, gave him the secret to a direct route to the Land of his People. A fine waterway, without portage, or dangerous rapids, unknown to the French, an easy passage to Montreal. He offered to conduct Joliet over this route.*

Down the Lake of the Hurons, to its outlet they proceeded. Down the beautiful river and across the placid Lake, through the Detroit – Strait, to Lake Erie. How charming the forest on either hand and silent, the former inhabitants driven away from their homes many years ago. Not a soul around, only the otter and beaver playing on the water, a deer drinking, the moose feeding at the water's edge. The Kingfisher flitting overhead. The cacophony of myriad wild fowl, flying about. (Fowle)

"Joliet in 1674 reported to Governor Frontenac in Montreal that 'A person can go from Lake Ontario, and Fort Frontenac, in a bark to the Gulf of Mexico. There being only one carrying place half way where Lake Ontario communicates with Lake Erie'. Joliet and Lasalle were sent to find a new route to carry Ore from the Upper Peninsula" (Fowle).

"Father Allouez arrived at Kachkachria, in 1677, on the Mississippi, (near Utica Ill), where there were 351 cabins of eight tribes. They lived on corn, 14 kinds of roots, 42 kinds of fruit, 25 types of fish, 40 kinds of game and birds, bison, turkey, wildcats and 22 other species of animals. They processed salt, had several wives. The Miami were reported as a consecrated people, since they had no canoes to travel and no contact with commerce to learn secrets" (Metis History, Canadian History a Distinct Viewpoint, info.pagesstudy.com, www).

"The 'Griffon' was built at the mouth of Cayuga Creek on Lake Erie, in 1677" (Metis History Timeline, Canadian History, a Distinct Viewpoint, info.metis.aspx, www). "Chevalier De La Salle, who sailed the famous Griffon through the Strait of the Detroit in 1680, was also known as Rene Robert Cavalier, Sieur De. Lasalle.

"The first ship to sail the Upper Lakes (built by white men) with 45 tons burden about 60 feet long. A small vessel, but a marvel achievement. The Iroquois upon seeing her on this side of Niagra, exclaimed, *Gannorum* meaning 'that is wonderful.

In 1679, thirty-four men, including two Recollects, sailed West with a favorable wind. Nothing unfavorable had occurred in Lake Erie, which had been described as full of dangerous rocks and sands which rendered navigation impracticable. They entered the Detroit – The Strait. Hennepin was charmed by the landscape, and wrote: this is 'One of the finest prospects in the World! This Strait is finer, than that of Niagra, being 30 leagues long (90 miles), and everywhere one league broad, except in the middle, which is wider, forming the Lake we have called St. Claire.

In describing the country above Lake St. Clair, he said: "hills covered with vineyards; trees bearing good fruit, groves and forests so well bestowed, that one would think that Nature alone could not have made, without the help of art, so charming a prospect".

They had a hard time finding the main channel to the river entering the flats above Lake St. Clair, but finally located it and sailed into the swifter water above. They encountered a swift headwind which compelled them to send men ashore and towed the ship into Lake Huron.

They entered Lake Huron and found the storm of Lake Huron severe and thought they were lost. La Salle recommended the men to make peace with their Creator. The captain openly cursed La Salle, "Who had brought them hither to perish in a nasty Lake, and lose the glory he had acquired by his long and happy navigations on the ocean". They weathered the storm and found harbor on the point of St. Ignace, which Hennepin calls Missilmackinack. The Griffon was lost in the northern part of Lake Huron. On the return trip to Niagra, the men went back to Detroit by land in 1680, then crossed the Detroit River on a raft and proceeded to Niagra" (Fowle).

"In 1680 Lasalle came to Ville Detroit, New France, the Village at the Straits – Fort Detroit, after the Griffon sank in Lake Ontario in the storm" (Canadian History, A Distinct Viewpoint, Metis Timeline, info/metis.aspx, www).

"Sieur De Lasalle – Rene Robert Cavalier – was given a patent from the King Louis XIV – The Sun King, of France, for a monopoly of the Buffalo hide trading south of Montreal. Henri De Tonti was his Lieutenant. They built Fort St. Louis in 1683, at Starved Rock on the Mississippi River in Illiniwek Land.

"La Salle and Father Hennepin took possession of the West Louisiana Territory and the Northwest for France in 1682. In 1682, he followed the Mississippi to the Gulf of Mexico with 23 Frenchmen including his friend Tonti and 31 Indians. He (Lasalle) was killed by mutiny of his men in 1687 in Texas, after searching for months for the channel to the Gulf of Mexico.

"The French eliminated the middlemen when they moved to Michilimackinac, intercepting furs from the far North and West being traded to the Huron" (Rogers/Smith).

DULUTH – SIEUR GREYSELON DELUD

"Duluth, a French Soldier, spent 12 years exploring and trading, securing the Indians in the French interest. He was a Fur Trader on a large scale. A celebrated Scout, and Courier De Boise, companion of Joliet, and Commander at Michilimackinac. Duluth had an intimate relationship with the Indians of the Lake Region, his associations with them were most amicable for many years" (Utley, 1906).

He was so powerful, his services were sought by the successive governor, Lemoyne. He was wanted as Interpreter of the Colony at Montreal.

In 1685, Dulhut was relieved of the Post of Michilimackinac and asked to build a post at the foot of Lake Huron where he had to garrison and provision it at his own expense. This post, called St. Joseph, was established to prevent a junction of the English traders of the South with those of the Hudson Bay. Dulhut was successful in this object for the two years his post existed.

Duluth supervised the building of Fort St. Joseph for trading with the Indians of the area in 1686. La Honton burned the fort in 1688, fearing Iroquois invasion.

Duluth made peace between the Sioux Indians and their Michigan and Wisconsin Indian neighbors, opening trade to the West beyond Lake Superior.

Father Stephen De Carheil had been laboring among the Indians near the Detroit before 1687, but it was in 1702 that a Mission was established at Detroit itself.

"The French came to trade directly with us, we married them. All children born were of Metis – Mixed Blood. They were given the Totem of the Martin Clan, by Decree of our Spiritual Leaders. Our ancestors foresaw this Mix. We respected the choices of our women and provided for our children. The French built Fur Trading Posts and laid claim to the vast territory, continuing the booming Fur Trade" (Diba Jimooyung, Saginaw Chippewa).

> *Forts were trading places for skins and goods, not military soldiers.*
>
> *"Fathers Brebeauf and Chaumont attempted a mission to the Huron's in 1640 and 1641, but they abandoned it. The Hurons called them Demons.*
>
> *The Neutrals refused the trade of the Black Robes, knowing the consequences and danger put to the country. The Echon were forced to withdraw. Echon was called 'Agwa', their greatest enemy, and was considered a great*

sorcerer who carried death and misfortune everywhere he went.

In Native culture, women were revered as equals; the Jesuits believed women were Evil Incarnate. The Huron women were warned they must obey their husbands. Women were blamed for all the evils and only the Jesuits were to be obeyed.

The Great Spirit was loved by the Indians; no one was in fear. They were slow to anger and tolerant of other's opinions. There was no concept of the Devil or Hell. They loved freedom and independence; there was horror of restraint and bondage." Metis History, www

In 1640, they built a Mission, St. Michael of Khioeta, on the Detroit. They built a second Mission, St. Francoise, on the shores of Lake Huron between Sarnia and Grand Bend. They brought European diseases and sickness among the people. Their teachings were very different from the Anishinabe and created great dissension among the tribe.

The women were not allowed to vote. Women's values and dignity were changed to that of the Roman Church. Women were the chattel (property) of man, subordinate to man, every evil Church tradition. The Black Robes, they forced Baptism on the dead and dying children without the parents' permission at times. Feasts were banished, medicine banned, 'They forget how we saved the early French Colony'. Sharing was rejected by the Jesuits.

In the 1600's the French targeted spiritual beliefs as the need to explore. They were tolerated for the most part. False religions of the Jesuits, beating babies and people. Native people consider it sorcery, perverted European practice, work of the Devil, or walk in darkness.

The Jesuits humiliated the Algonquin religious beliefs, calling it superstitious, they say our dance is paying homage to the Devil, possessed by the Devil and the drum is banned.

The Jesuits teach that faith is to Love God, work hard, suffer much, and consider oneself as very useless. They say to be a Christian is to give up all the Peoples medicine, that has been given to them by God. The same medical knowledge that saved the Early French Colony. (Metis History, www)

The Black Robes forbade any traditional rituals to be practiced; the converts were not allowed to fight alongside non-Christians, even against a common enemy. The converts were paid higher prices for furs and could buy muskets in 1641; this encouraged baptism.

Antisocial behavior, was seen as a form of witchcraft that threatened the well-being of the community, creating division and turmoil among the people.

Many refused baptism, believing their souls might join relatives who had died without baptism in the traditional Village of Souls. (Rogers/Smith)

Nuns in 2002 in Canada received 8 months in prison for doing the same, beating children. Indians never raised a hand to any child. Moral decay spread, dividing the nation against itself.

Lawsuits, ambition, avarice, lust, and the desire for revenge were rarely seen in New France, yet the people are called Savage and Barbarian.

The Mission Village of St. Joseph (Teanaustaye) was established.

The most easterly village was at "Round Point", a bay also called French Aunce Bay, known as Kewaonon, near Detroit.

In 1663, John Eliot translated and published the Bible into Algonquin.

"The White man does not obey the *Great Spirit*, that is why the people could never agree with him" (Flying Hawk, Ogala Sioux).

"Manliness is demonstrated by abstaining from sex; this is self-control, and strength. It was common to abstain for two years after a child" (Metis History, Canadian History, a Distinct Viewpoint. www).

"In time, missionary power grew and fur trade posts saturated Anishinabe Country. The *Black Coats'* intense effort divided the people, encouraging rejection of traditional teachings of the Mide Lodge" (Flocken UMN 2013).

"Traditional medicine extensively linked to spirituality failed against epidemics that continuously ravished the populations. Missionaries remained healthy, appearing to have a more powerful religion. Hunting success became depleted which was closely related with Spirits, hunting, and medical failure, and a newly impoverished society caused many to abandon Midewiwin and spirits and convert to Christianity" (Vecsey, 1983/Flocken UMN 2013).

"American missionaries failed because they wanted to change every aspect of Anishinabe society to reflect theirs" (Flocken).

"In the later 1600's, we reclaimed our homeland in Southern Lower Michigan and Ontario. The Ontario Anihinabe were named Missisaugas – "River Indians". Quebec included all of the Great Lakes. The Missisauga are "The Lakes People" (Diba Jimooyung, Saginaw Chippewa).

"The Huron Confederacy was one of the largest and most enlightened bodies of North American Indians. When first encountered by the French, they numbered about 16,000 and had villages between Lake Simcoe and Georgian Bay. The Jesuit Mission of Huronia was destroyed, and the Hurons dispersed by the Iroquois War raids in 1648 to '49" (Lahonton).

"Jacques and Roymboult, Jesuits from the Huron villages at South Eastern Lake Huron, preached at the Sault in 1641" (Cleaver Bald, "Michigan in 4 Centuries").

"Grossilliers, an explorer and fur trader, came in 1654. He and Radison worked together and took a huge amount of furs from the North Country to Montreal in 1669 without a license. They were imprisoned and their furs confiscated. Upon release, they made a trip to England and received the support of the King, and established the Hudson's Bay Co. This gave them complete control over one-fourth of North America. An Empire, an Imperial Domain. The most gigantic monopoly in history. The French went to stop them" (Utley).

Radison was an explorer and fur trader who came to the Northwest and returned to Montreal in 1660.

"The Hudson's Bay slave rolls had many 'Hospital Boys', raised in residential schools. The poor orphans, young, were used in the slavery trade. There was cruelty, bullying, and flogging" (Canadian History, A Distinct Viewpoint, Metis History Timeline - 1677, info.pagesstudy.com, www).

In 1657, the Sulpicians and Recollects were sent out to Canada with support of the King of France.

In 1664, copper was known to be at a Lake Superior island.

Father Peter Francis Xavier Charlevoix arrived in 1721 and stayed 12 days.

"The priests protested the Liquor Trade to no avail" (Jesuits Relations Volumes). The restrictions placed upon the sale of liquor to the Savage, which restrictions are by no means observed. When drunk, the Indians were quarrelsome and dangerous among themselves and the town. They gladly exchanged furs for trinkets, which they thought of enormous wealth. Thus, the Indian was cheated outrageously.

When it became known that there were such enormous profits, the authorities sought to control and restrict it by regulations, which diverted a part of the profit to the officers at the head of Affairs. A license was required to trade. The owners shared all the way down the line, and so the matter soon became little short of scandalous. Traders were forbid to engage in the traffic without a license under penalty of law.

"The Frenchmen found the Indian women were good partners. The Indian custom was to offer a woman as a gift to someone they wanted to be more than a casual friend. A number of Frenchmen had a traditional Christian wedding blessed by a priest. The Indian woman perceived herself as privileged when chosen for gift giving. Lack of guilt and a genuine desire to give a good friend a precious gift was a practice abhorrent to strict Christians" (Kah Wam Da Meh, Jean Frazier/ Herman E. Cameron, 1988).

"In 1756, Fort Detroit was on the d'Etroit (the strait), near Lake Huron" (Metis History, info/metis.aspx, www).

The Iroquois destroyed the Hurons and continued to wreak havoc into the Ohio and Michigan Algonquin tribes. They reached as far as the Sault Ste. Marie in 1662.

Ottissippi

SAULT STE. MARIE

"Sault Ste. Marie was the Central Mart of the whole Northwest" (Fowle).

"Corn, tobacco, and sugar were available for trade with the natives for furs. The Huron – Ottawa – were the Great Traders, having the monopoly over the Northern trade areas. In 1812, the total White population of the territory was under 4,000" (Fowle).

"The Old Copper Culture of the Great Lakes made this region the home of the oldest metal workers in the world" (K. Porterfield, "10 Lies about Indigenous Science").

FORT ST. JOSEPH

Fort St. Joseph was built by Duluth in 1782. The little fort was a bastioned block house of logs at the strait of Lakes Huron and Erie. The fort or the trading house was used by the Huron and Ottawa of Lake Huron to retreat to against the Iroquois invaders.

"I am to go along with Mr. Dulhut, a Lion's Gentleman, a person of great merit and who has done his King and his country very considerable services. M. De Tonti is another of our company" (Lahonton).

The Recollects priests brand the savages for stupid, gross and rustik persons incapable of thought or reflection. But the Jesuits priests give them other sort of language. For they entitle them to good sense, to a tenacious memory, and to a quick apprehension seasoned with a solid judgment. That these savages take pleasure in hearing the word of God and readily apprehend the meaning of scripture.

The Recollects and Jesuits content themselves with glancing at things without taking notice of the (almost) invincible aversion of the savages to the truth of Christianity.

They are indefatigable and inured to hardships, their whole time being spent in the way of exercise, running up and down, at hunting, and fishing, or in dancing and playing at football or such games as require the motion of the legs.

The women never cut their hair, whereas men cut theirs every month. Sometimes hair is cut as a punishment for adultery, though very rare. (Lahonton)

Their villages are fortified with double pallissadoes of very hard wood, which are as thick as one's thigh and fifteen feet high, with little squares about the middle of the courtines. Commonly their huts, or cottages, are 80 feet long, 25 to 30 feet deep, and 20 feet high. They are covered with the bark of young elms and have two alcoves, one on the right and one on the left, being a foot high and 9 feet broad, between which they make their fires, there being vents made in the roof for the smoak. Upon the sides of the two alcoves are little closets, or apartments, in which the young women or married persons lye upon little beds raised about a foot from the ground. One hut contains three or four families.

They are very healthy and have no European diseases, but are liable to smallpox and to pleurisies. They commonly live to 80 or 100. But there are some who do not live too long because they voluntarily poison themselves. 'We payson (poisen) ourselves in order to accompany our relations to the Country of Souls'.

Money is in use with none but those that are Christian who live in the suburbs of our towns. They will not touch silver or look upon it, but call it the Odioes, name of the French Serpent.

Ottissippi

They'll tell you that amongst us the people murther (murder), plunder, defame, and betray one another for money. That the husbands make merchandise of their wives, and the mothers their daughters for the lucre of that metal. They think it unaccountable that one man should have more than another, and that the rich would have more respect than the poor. In short, they say the name of savages, which we bestow on them, would fit ourselves better since there is nothing in our actions that bears an appearance of wisdom.

They neither quarrel nor fight, nor slander one another. They brand us for slaves, alleging we degrade ourselves in subjecting to one man, who possess the whole power and is bound by no law but his own will. That we have continued jars among ourselves: that our children rebel against their parents, that we imprison one another and publickly promote our own destruction. They pretend that their contented way of living far surpasses our riches. That all our sciences are not valuable as the art of leading a peaceful, calm life.

They are as ignorant of geography as of other sciences, and yet they draw the most exacting map imaginable of the countries their acquainted with. For their nothing wanting in them but the longitude and latitude of places: they set down the true North, according to the pole stars, the ports, harbours, rivers, creeks, and coasts of the Lake, the roads, mountain, woods, marshes, meadows, accounting the distance by journeys, and half journeys, of the warriors. These choro-graphical maps are drawn upon the rind of your birch tree, and when the old men hold a council, about war or hunting, there always sure to consult them.

They have a wonderful idea of anything that depends upon the attention of the mind and attain to an exact knowledge of many things by long experiences: To follow the tract of a man or beast upon the grass of leaves; so, they know the hour of the day and night exactly, even when it is so cloudy that neither sun nor stars appear. I impute this talent to a steady command of mind which is not natural to any but those whose thoughts are little distracted as these men are. They pay an infinite deference to old age. They take the ancient men for oracles.

They have no set hours for meals; they eat when their hungry, and commonly do it in a large company feasting here and there by turns.

Their game of counters is purely numerical: add, subtract, multiply, and divide the best by these counters is the winner.

The Savages are a very sensible people and perfectly well-acquainted with the interest of their nation.

All Savages are convinced there is a God by the frame of the universe which naturally leads us to a higher and omnipotent being. Man is the work of a Being superior in wisdom and knowledge, whom they call the Great Spirit *or* Master of Life, *and which they adore in the most abstract and spiritual manner.*

Ottissippi

The existence of God being inseparable from his essence; it contains everything, it appears in everything, and gives motion to everything. In all that you see, all that you can conceive, is the Divinity. They adore Him in everything they see and believe nothing comes to pass but by the decree of that infinitely perfect Being. They believe that God, for reasons above our reach, makes use of the sufferings of good people to display his justice.

The Christians they say make jest of God's precepts for they counteract his orders without intermission and rob him of the worship, which he claims as his due, by paying it to silver, beavers, and to their own interest. They murmer against Heaven and him when things go cross with them. They go about their business on days set apart for works of piety and devotion. Spend their time in gaming, drinking in excess, fighting, and scolding. In the nighttime, they debauch, the women savages. They murther one another, every day, for theft, or affronts or women, pillage and rob one another, without regard to tyes of blood or friendship.

They bespatter and defame one another with outrageous calumnies and make no scruple to lye when it will serve their interest. Debauch other men's wives. They incessantly transgress. I should never come to the end, if I entered into the particulars of their savage ways of reasoning. (Lahonton, "Voyages to New France, Voyages to North America" II)

The young men marry at 30 years old, they abstain from women to keep their strength, for enemie's attacks. They are a stranger to blind fury, which we call love. They content themselves with a tender friendship. They are very careful in preserving the liberty and freedom of their heart, which they look upon as the most valuable treasure upon earth. From whence I conclude, that they are not altogether so savage as we are. They never quarrel, reproach, or affront one another. All are as good as another, all upon the same level. Adultery is abhorred. Their huts are open day and night. No robbers or secret enemies apprehensioned.

The young women drink the juice of certain root which prevents conception or kills the fruit of the womb. Venereal distemper is common.

Tis allowable for married men and women to part when they please, giving eight days warning. The children are the treasure of the savages and are split evenly.

When a woman is with child, there is abstinence, until 30 days after birth. They suckle as long as they have milk; they are not jealous.

There is no wound or dislocation they cannot cure with the simples or plants whose vertue's they are well-acquainted with, and their wounds never run to a gangrene.

Upon the death of a savage, his slaves marry and live by themselves free. The children are adopted and are as children of the nation. (Lahonton)

In 1687, Fort St. Joseph was the mobilization center for a French and Indian War party to New York.

FRANCE CLAIMS THE REGION

In the spring of 1687, the Marquis De Denonville, Governor of Canada, determined on an expedition against the Seneca – Iroquois of New York, enemies of the Canadian Colonies. M. De Tonty, Commander at St. Louis – Niagara, was called to meet up with Duluth and his allies, and Sieurs, LaForest (subordinate to Tonti), and La Durante all joined at Detroit (Port Huron – Fort Gratiot). They took formal possession of the Strait as far down as the River St. Denis (probably the Rouge).

Durantaye had with him 30 Englishmen, whom he had captured on Lake Huron while on his way down from Mackinaw. They had been sent by Colonel Dongan, Governor of New York, to take possession of Mackinaw and the region and to open up trade with the Indians.

The party consisted of 150 Frenchmen, 400 Indians, and the 30 Englishmen. They captured a second party of Major McGregor, 16 Englishmen, and 13 Allied Indians, who were also on their way to Mackinaw. They proceeded to Niagra. (Fowle)

"La Durante had halted his Savage forces from the far Indians (Mackinac) at the head of the Strait leading from Lake Huron to Lake St. Clair. There on June 7, 1687 had erected the Arms of France and taken formal possession of the vast region in the name of the King" (Lahonton).

"It is a fearful passage through Iroquois Country. To die is nothing, but to live in the midst of fire is too much" (Lahonton).

You cannot imagine the pleasant prospect, he (Lahonton) assures. The banks are covered with all sorts of wild fruit trees. Charmed with the beauty and free life of St. Joseph, the Country. The youthful Commandment, passed the autumn with the chase to which he had become passionately devoted, and dallying with parties of tribesmen that passed up and down, bent on war, plunder, and hunting. The restless commander sought an excuse in lack of provisions, to set out with the majority of his force. A small garrison was left at the fort. He left for Mackinac, the little French military and trading station, to buy up corn from the Huron and Ottawa's. He joined a Chippewa party from the northwest in a raid into Iroquois Country, east of Lake Huron, stopping at his fort only long enough to land a few sacks of corn. He was accompanied by the Huron chief, the Rat, whom he calls Adario *in his voyages.*

Parties of Indians at the fort in the summer brought news of disease, destitution, probable abandonment, and a peace with the Iroquois at Niagra. At his own discretion, he burned the fort and left for Mackinac with all his men.

Lahonton was to return to France, but at Montreal, Frontenac wanted him to stay as a companion on his journeying's because of his experience with the outposts, the aborigines, and took counsel of him for the desperate condition of New France. After a time, Lahonton did go to France to his ruined estate. Then he was sent to Canada again with a plan for the destruction of the Iroquois and a defeat of five English ships, who battered the fort with 2,000 cannon shots and some fishing villages.

He became Lieutenant of the King for Newfoundland and Acadia. In Maritime New France, which was a fiasco, when he returned to Europe in exile and wrote his journals.

The Natives he describes as a creature of rare beauty of form, a rational being, thinking deep thoughts on great subjects. But freed from the trammels and frets of civilization. Bound by none of its restrictions. No court, law, police, ministers of an American State, or other paraphernalia of government Arcady. A natural, sweetly reasonable religion.

Here no vulgar love of money pursued the Native in his leafy home. Without distinction of property, the rich man was he who might give most generously. Man, innocent and unadorned, passed his life in the pleasure of the chase, warring only in the cause of the Nation. Scorning the supposititious benefactors of civilization and free from its disease, misery, sycophancy and oppression.

The American wilderness was the seat of serenity and noble philosophy. A delightful representation, arousing the keenest curiosity, regarding the New World. A land so enormous, undiscovered by half. Great rivers, cataracts, inland lakes like oceans. Vast unknown land, wherein mysterious beasts of prey, clad in furs to be envied by a Monarch.

Lahonton was a precursor of the Great Thinkers of the Revolutionary period in France. Passionately just and fair.

Cheryl Morgan

I wish I could spend the rest of my life in his hut to be no longer exposed to bending the knee to a set of men that sacrifice the public good to their private interest and are born to plague Honest Men.

Whores were brought from France to Canada to wife the men.

I have been at hunting with 30 to 40 young Algonins, who were well-made, clever fellows. I was to learn the language of the Country, for all the Nations for a thousand leagues round understand it perfectly well all over North America. The Huron and Iroquois were aliens in their midst". (Lahonton/Powell 1885)

Of the Five Nations Iroquois village, each village contains 1,400 souls, though some will tell you that each village has not above 1,000 souls. They look upon themselves as sovereigns accountable to none but God alone. They were harassed by the French. In 1696, Frontenac crushed the Iroquois.

The canoes are four and a half feet wide and 28 feet long. Crack open upon stone or sand, and spoil the provisions and merchandise. Every day there is some new shink, or seam, to be gummed over. At night, they are always unloaded and carried on shore, pegged lest the wind should blow 'em away. When the season serves, they carry little sails. There are no keels, nails, or pegs in the whole structure. They last five to six years.

The Iroquois at Montreal, asking for a missionary at Quinte, threw in upon us harts, roebucks, turkeys, and fish in exchange for needles, knives, powder, and several cayugas.

Fevers raged among the militia, being unacquainted with the way of setting their boats. With poles. They were faced at every turn to get into the water and drag 'em up against the rapid stream. (Lahonton, "New Voyages to America")

"The Iroquois robbed the French who supplied their enemies, the Ojibwe, with guns, powder, and ball. They raided Huron villages, taking furs and trade items, needing more furs to pay for guns, powder, and shot. The farmer (not agricultural) formed a Company collecting duties on skins at Montreal. There was a 700% clear profit" (Lahonton).

CADILLAC

Monsieur Antoine De La Motte Cadillac, Commandant at Fort Michimilimackinac, understood the Indian customs and respected them. The French in Paris made judgments about Michigan by the reports sent by the priests. The priests complained about the warriors sent to fight wearing no clothing, and selling them liquor in trade was withholding Christianity from the Savage. An order came to Cadillac to clothe the Indians and prohibit liquor at the settlement.

Cadillac answered to a friend,

it is a great mistake if people think this place is deserted. There is a fine fort of pickets and 60 houses that form a street in a straight line. There is a garrison of well-disciplined, chosen soldiers consisting of about 200 men. This place should not be deprived of the privilege of furnishing the necessary drinks for their men. Houses are arranged along the shore of this Great Lake Huron, and fish and smoked meat constitute the principal food.

The villages of the Indians, in which there are six or seven thousand souls, are about a pistol-

shot distance from ours. All the lands are cleared for about three leagues or nine miles around their village and perfectly well cultivated. They produce a sufficient quantity of Indian corn for the use of both the French and Indian inhabitants. Now what reason can one assign that the Indians should not drink brandy bought with their own money, as well as we?

The law strictly forbids anyone to trade with the Indians for their arms. As for their clothing, can anyone assert that clothing is necessary for them to go to war? It is the custom when the moment comes for their departure on warlike expeditions, for the warrior to dispose of all his clothing, making presents of the different articles to those who remain at home; and on their return, it is permitted to each of them to gather all that belongs to him.

It is bad faith to represent to the count that the sale of brandy reduces the Indian to a state of nudity and by that means places it out of his power to make war; since he never goes to war in any other condition.

Prohibiting the transportation of brandy had much discouraged the Frenchmen who are here from trading in future. Ceasing to sell liquor has caused a universal commotion among all the Nations.

The Indians would not exchange their life or wigwams for the Louvre.

In his 1695 meeting with the Chippewa, the Indians affirmed they wanted to be friends with the French, and brothers. But if the French treat them as enemies or slaves and withhold brandy for beaver pelts, the Indians would take their furs to the English, who would give them liquor.

In 1696, Frontenac gathered 2,000 men and Indian allies to raid the Iroquois and permanently end their harassment in New France. Duluth was among them with 500 Ojibwe warriors, gathered from the post around Fort St. Joseph. This number represented about 3,000 people.

A Peace Treaty was agreed upon with the Iroquois for safe passage of the fur traders.

The French returned to Michigan in 1701 to establish only one fort that would be manned. Cadillac convinced the King that the Strait would stop the English from trading furs to the northern and western country. Cadillac would build Fort Ponchetrain at Detroit, named after the Colonial Minister Count Ponchetrain. Fur trading continued. In 1715, Cadillac and his son Jacque, made an expedition to the North, Illinois Land and discovered vast mineral deposits.

St. Anne's Church was built in Detroit in 1701, the first structure in Detroit named after the Virgin Mary, the Mother of Christ. It was burned in 1703. It is now the second oldest Roman Catholic Church in the nation. The church was again burned in 1714 by the people to avoid it being used as cover by the Fox Native Americans during the great battle with them.

The French Catholic fathers who established missions wanted Indians to renounce what they perceived as pagan idolatry and to embrace Christ through baptism. They expected total conformity to ridged Catholic edicts. The Indian had a well-developed religious and social system. It made sense, was effective, and comfortable. They had no reason or desire to change their customs or beliefs. Their way of life did change with new trade items. Their life decisions had complex ramifications.

The French were interested in trade and the Indians' goods and services, as well as spreading the message of Christianity. The French were glad to have guides, hunters, trappers, and warriors as allies and friends. They traded for furs, corn, wild rice, meat, fish, sugar, clothing, moccasins, and many other Indian products.

GUIDES AND INTERPRETERS

Guides and interpreters were indispensable to any North American expedition. They knew the country, the people, any possible dangers. They knew friends and enemies, how to make friends, and appease the enemy, when to follow their employers' whims, and when to assert authority, born of superior knowledge. Very often they were Metis – mixed blood, French and Native, always longtime friends with the indigenous people or married into the tribe. They knew the ways and thoughts of the natives.

For the most part, the French were not here to change the customs or occupy Indian lands; they were a very small number of people among hundreds of thousands of indigenous people. The Fur Trade was very lucrative.

The missionaries endured great hardship in carrying the gospel to the savages, enduring the dangers of the Indians and the unfriendly traders.

The missionaries, "Black Robes", also brought disease, and the Indians were fearful of their presence. The missionaries' work was very difficult; the Indians moved frequently, were absent in the winter for hunting, and were well-established in worshipping the Great Spirit.

Throughout the time of the exploration of North America, South America and Central America were also part of the New World of riches to be found; slaves, sugar, salt, and rum trades was also emerging, and gold was found. The Spanish had claimed most of these lands. They were eager to exploit the natural resources and peoples of these New World countries.

The missionaries were also explorers searching for the riches of the New World. They were very influential in politics and economics. In Montreal, the Catholic Church received one-eighth of all land sales. Clergy reserves were 200 acres.

There were great numbers of Anishinabe in Michigan, Ontario, and the Northwest before explorers and missionaries arrived. The country was well-settled.

The Hurons were the first Natives in Southern Ontario to be penetrated by the Black Robes. They called them sorcerers and imposters come to take possession of their country: "The Huron said, when the Black Robes, 'Echon' ('Demon') Jean De Brebeauf, the Jesuit, set foot in the Huron country, he had said, 'I shall be here so many years, I shall cause many to die, then go elsewhere to do the same, until I have ruined the whole land'. A genocide policy, or biological warfare" (Metis History, www).

"Smallpox raged fiercely; the pretext of trade opened doors for the trade and disease" (Metis History, www).

> *Women of the Ojibwe and Anishinabek were revered and treated as equals. The Jesuits changed that.*
>
> *The Jesuits were given to flogging and slavery.*

Ottissippi

The people loved their freedom and independence. They were slow to anger and tolerant of others' opinions. They were in horror of restraint and bondage.

The Jesuits in 1644 had the gift of cures, the gift of tongues, the gift of prophesy, everything that can astonish. The people believe it is jiggery and pokier, based on sorcery. The priests call for flagellation and whipping even children at the breast. The perverted practice called Holy Ceremony. The Indians never raised a hand to any child for any reason. We were not to participate in any religious services.

The Jesuits were destroying family harmony and breaking up families. Our Giving Away was called not Christian but a Pagan practice; they rejected the sharing of our culture in everything. (Metis History, www)

"In 1728, the Jesuit mission to the Hurons included, a Catholic School, for Indian children. Religion was the first area of Indian culture with which the White Man interfered. Here the White Man actively sought to change the Indians' way of life. Other Indian customs and behavior patterns became points of conflict as they obstructed the White Man's desires, which centered around full and undisputed possession of the best farm land" (Emmert, MHC vol. 47).

From 1687 to 1688, Father Aveneau was the resident priest at Fort St. Joseph, at the foot of Lake Huron, the first on the west side of the St. Clair River.

"The St. Joseph Mission, at the foot of Lake Huron, was destroyed and Father Daniel slain" (History of Oakland County).

The first French and Iroquois war was in 1641.

When the Huron Wendat were slaughtered, the *Petun*, Tobacco Huron People, moved to the West to leave the violence. They settled in Oklahoma. The Huron Wendat joined the Ojibwe and settled at the Huron River. Some went to Montreal with the Jesuits, others were captives, adopted into the Iroquois in New York. Some went North and lived with the Ottawa and Ojibwe.

The Huron River was the St. Clair River, the Strait. Between Lake Huron and Lake St. Clair, there was also a Huron River at what is now the Clinton

River, at Mt. Clemons, Michigan, and a Huron River at what is now called the Cass River in Michigan's Thumb.

"There was a Mission village of St. Joseph, Northwest of Lake Simcoe" (Lahonton II, Voyages to America).

Lahonton wrote of the Indians:

> *The Oucabipoues, called Sauteurs, of the Eagle Tribe – Missisaugas – say the Great Spirit has given us an understanding of good and evil, and we religiously observe the true measure of justice and wisdom. That the tranquility and serenity of the soul pleases the Great Master of Life. That he abhors trouble and anxiety of the mind, because it renders men wicked. That Life is a dream and death the season of awakening, in which the Soul sees and knows the nature and quality of all things, visible and invisible. That the utmost reach of our minds can't go one inch above the surface of the earth so we ought not corrupt and spoil it, by trying to pry into invisible and improvable things. We believe we will go to the Country of Souls after death. If your religion differs from ours it does not mean that we have none at all. My belief to such things as are visible and probable. The Great Spirit is wise, all his Works are Perfect, tis He that made us and He knows perfectly well what will become of us.*
>
> *Tis our part to act freely, without perplexing our thoughts about future things.*
>
> *Your Worship consists only in words and seem to be calculated to cheat us. Make pretentions to faith but are downright infidels, pass for wise but are fools. You think yourselves men of sense, but the Truth is ignorance and presumption is your true character.*

Ottissippi

Man is full of corruption. Passions, interest, and corruption are not known among us. The French have no regard to the laws of their religion. The Jesuits send us to Hell for a trifle.

Our young men do not marry till he has made some campaigns against the Iroquois and taken slaves to serve him. He will not use his energy by venery, when his strength is needed to serve his nation in war. And he will not expose a wife and child to the affliction of seeing him killed or taken prisoner.

The French rob our Girlies, deflowering 'em. French have such an itch to gather for themselves. Our men when they marry, they marry as a valuable treasure. It is a crime of the highest demerit.

For my part I shall not think it strange if there be not one Ecclestiek in the Paradise of the Great Spirit.

The innocence of our Lives, the love we tender to our brethren, and the tranquility of mind we enjoy, the Great Spirit requires of all men. We do these naturally in our villages. Are not laws the same as just and reasonable things?

Man is not entitled to that character by walking on two legs, reading and writing and shewing a thousand instances of his industry.

I call that creature a man that hath a natural inclination to do good. And never entertains the thought of doing evil. You see that we have no Judge. We neither quarrel or sue one another. We are resolved to neither receive or know silver. Why? Because we are resolved to have no laws, since the World was a world where our ancestors lived happily without 'em. We have no lawsuits. The word Law does not signifie Just and Reasonable things as you use it.

The Black Devils are not in the regions where souls burn in flames, but in Quebec and in France where they keep company with the Laws, the False Witnesses, the conveniences of life, the Cities, the Fortresses and the pleasure you spoke of.

We have no laws, no prisons, pass our life in a state of sweetness and tranquility. We live quietly under the laws of instinct and innocent conduct. Money is the Father of all the mischief in the World. A Man is of Wisdom, Reason, Equity.

Our Happiness is Liberty and Tranquility of Mind. We fear no robbers, assassins or false witnesses. (Lahonton II)

John Eliot, a Puritan, printed the first Bible in America. He printed the New Testament in 1661 and the Old Testament in 1663. John Eliot wrote and published the First Indian Bible; it was written in Algonquin.

"Charlevoix visited New France – Detroit, and wrote that game was abundant, and herds of buffalo were then ranging upon the prairies about River Raisen" (Cass/Wells and Whitney, Detroit, 1834).

Buffaloes – *pisikious* – were called "oxen" or "wild cattle" by the French.

"In 1750, Father Vivier says the Jesuits error in saying the Indians are savage. They are gentle and sociable by nature, have wit, and seem to have no more than our peasants, as much at least as most Frenchmen. Neither rank nor dignity among them, all Men seem equal to them. Never interrupt in conversation. Speak as boldly to a king as to the lowest subject. Do not get angry while conversing. Many qualities are not found in civilized people. They live in great peace" (Canadian History, a Distinct Viewpoint, Timeline, Metis, www).

The Copper Country was well used in the trade with the Nations tribes and for tools, weapons, jewelry, and many other items. The Mascoutins were said

Ottissippi

to be the mine workers. There were hundreds of mines and ancient mining pits. The copper was used in many ways. The Indians used large quantities of hammers, ancient hammers, tools, wedges, baskets, and scaffolding. Ten cartloads of ancient hammers, one weighing 39 ½ pounds having double handles, were found near Ontonagon River in Upper Michigan.

The Sault was the gateway to the rich northern country. There were over 1,100 canoes to support the huge business of the Fur Trade. The Christina Huron alone acquired firearms from the traders.

When the Indians were first exposed to the wondrous trade goods of the French, objects of metal, cloth, and glass, they believed they were in the possession of Diety. Here were beautiful beads, time saving pots and tools, and the woven fabric was much easier to work with. The metal knives and hatchets were highly appreciated.

Early trade was conducted as if the French were members of another tribe. The exchange of trade goods.

The Indian traders, Huron and Ottawa, blocked the French from the direct trade route, with the other tribes initially. They had the monopoly on Indian trade.

NEW FRANCE

Colonial France was along the St. Lawrence. The Isle of Orleans was Montreal. New Orleans, Quebec, was founded in 1718, named after the King's son, "The Duke of Orleans". The New Country was called Quebec.

"The Jesuit Mission at Montreal was called 'Sault Saint Louis', or 'Saint Louis Rabids'" (Global Genealogy, Ontario, Upper Canada, Canada West, Resources. www).

In 1632, a man named Hebert a Physician, was the first settler and received the first slave of the French Colony, a Black boy from the West Indies. Slavery was common. The Indians also had slaves taken from enemy raids. Slavery was actively practiced in New France, in the St. Lawrence Valley and in Louisiana Territory, for two centuries.

In the late 1600s, the French took captives from the British Colonies, brought from Louisiana Territory and the Caribbean.

The majority of Native American slaves were given to the French as tokens of friendship. By early 1700, the buying and selling of captives like merchandise was common.

The Pawnees of the Missouri River Basin who were taken captive were called 'Panis', or Pawnee became the generic name for any aboriginal slave. *Esckave Panis* means 'Panis slave' in French.

Cheryl Morgan

In 1719, the Louisiana's large area of American slave trade came from Africa.

In 1807, slavery was abolished in the British Colonies. (C. Moore, The History of MI)

The Catholic Church was said to be the largest slaveholder in New France. The French kept their slaves until death.

See "Chapter 12: Northern Slavery".

In 1682, LaSalle had the honor of claiming Louisiana for the French, held by the Spanish at the time. The French had named the Territory La Louisiana in honor of King Louis XIV. Upper Louisiana included the Great Lakes, Canada, and the Rocky Mountains. Lower Louisiana Territory reaching the Gulf of Mexico. France ceded the Eastern Territory in 1763 to Britain and the Western Territory to Spain.

In 1685, the French Huguenots left France; they were leaving because they were Protestants of the Catholic Church corruption of France. They wanted equal rights and tax reform. The Catholic Seigniorial Feudal System had made everyone – the Common People – slaves to masters.

At Stadaconia, an Iroquois Village on the St. Lawrence, where Cartier and his men were saved by the people who cured the scurvy with rich cedar broth. He took ten Natives back to France with him and who died there of disease. Champlain later established the Colony of L'Habitation, the beginning of Quebec at this place.

By 1700, Acadia changed between French and English rule many times.

Kanata – Canada, means "village". Hochelaga was Mount Royal in Montreal. Ville D' Etroit were the few French who settled along the Strait.

In 1776 in Montreal, the French Fur Traders banded together to form the Northwest Company in order to compete with the Hudson's Bay Company of the Grossieliers Empire, of English support.

By 1803, every person of eminence and prominence was engaged in trade. 1803 was also the year of the Louisiana Purchase from Napoleon Bonaparte of Spain, who also held most of North America.

Whiskey was a necessary commodity. Tens of thousands of gallons were transported to the trading posts. There were Forest Salons for the men. The Ojibwe and allies' women and girls were beautiful and in demand. Polygamy was common, as the men were killed at times in war. Wife stealing and adultery among the Pottawatomi was common.

The Jesuits claim that the Courieurs De Bois and French soldiers were ruining the Indians with brandy and debauching their women by turning them into trade goods. The Jesuits teach that people are a dog and less than a flea before God. They destroyed the belief of God's help in the environment and against enemies.

> *The progress of population at present is obstructed, not only by the wet, unhealthy state of the Country, but also by other circumstances: One-seventh of the whole Country is reserved for the Crown, and one seventh for the Episcopal Clergy: also by an existing law of Old Canada, all real estates, though sold seven times in seven years, must be sold at the Chapel door, mostly on the first day afternoon, one ninth of whereof goes to the Roman Catholic Church. By this means some congregations, especially in Montreal and Quebec, have become immensely rich and enabled to carry on their idolatrous pomp and parade of worship so as to make the world wonder. But as light is rising, a necessary reform is apprehended to be not far distant.*
>
> *Had a solid interview with Elliott, Deputy Agent of Indian Affairs for the British. He is preparing to return to the Indian Council at the Rapids. We proposed to him whether there would be any impropriety in our going with him. To which he replied as his sentiment, that where the Indians were now assembled was their own Council Ground and on a path, that was not to be trod in but by warriors: and therefore, it was his opinion it would not be advisable. (MPHC, vol. 17, Expedition to Detroit, Friends Miscellany, 1793)*

"In 1812, the total White population of the Territory was under 4,000, and mostly French. The Fur Trade was the leading industry" (Fowle).

The XY Company became the new Northwest Company, absorbed by it in 1804.

Leadership power shifted to warriors in the 1850s.

MISSIONARIES

"The Church wanted to concentrate Anishinabe on Reservations to more effectively proselytise them. The State wanted them removed for settlers and corporate interests. The traders, to cheat and grow rich" (Flocken).

"The churches were given absolute control and power over reservations. They were given power to appoint the Indian Agents who manipulated and controlled resources, favoring Christians and withholding services to those who refused to convert. They were extremely powerful to Indians, totally dependent on annuities confined under Church Rule. The Indian Agent had a dictatorship" (Flocken).

Preachers gained further power from traditional religious leaders, by the authority granted them by Canadian and U. S. governments, as distributors of government rations, food, and clothing, making all decisions of importance. They mediated between Indian factions, which they helped create, and selected Christian Indians as their representatives in community councils.

The Methodist Church was a very important part of the Indian Missions.

In 1804, Nathan Bangs was appointed to a circuit in Western Ontario, which included "The Detroit Country". He made three visits to the settlement and was thoroughly discouraged at the results. He made no converts and could find only a few who even wanted to attend the services. Detroit was abandoned by Protestant preachers for a while.

Some Moravian preachers who visited previous to Bangs have written that they found Detroit to be the most immoral and Godless place they have ever seen.

Five years later, the picture changed more settlers were coming to the peninsula. Exploration was making known the nature and fertility of the soil. The government of the territory had made treaties with the Indians, and gave a greater sense of security.

In 1809, William Case was appointed by Bishop Asbury of the New York Conference, to Detroit, and it first appeared in the records of the Methodist Church. He rode on horseback through the forests in a one-month circuit. There were no church members to receive him. With the conversion of Robert Abbott, Auditor Treasurer of the new Michigan Government, his home became the hostel for Methodism.

Ottissippi

In a report to Asbury, Case portrays the conditions he found at Detroit in 1809 and 1810:

> *this country is perhaps the most wicked and dissipated of any part of America. There is no preaching except the Roman Catholic and some of the Church of England.*
>
> *The Holy Sabbath had no preference over any other day except they make choice of it as a day of wicked amusements. Visiting in parties, dancing, hunting, fishing, etc. For drunkenness and fornication, I suppose no place is more noted; and that with the savages, which are very common on the Indian lines, have made a strange and motley mixture here among the offspring. Many of the people know little of the Bible, having never learned to read. And some of those who can read have no Bible in their families, nor do they think they need any, for some have openly blasphemed the Name of the Lord Jesus and spoken of the Lord Jesus in a manner too shocking to repeat.*

Reverend William Case crossed the river and attended the Circuit of the Thames. He was the first Protestant Minister in that region. Every three weeks, he had to pass a wilderness of fifty-seven miles without habitation and swim his horse five times across rivers each trip. In the winter when the ferry boats stopped, he had to leave his horse on the Canadian side and walk up and down the river, seeking the strongest ice to leap over wide fissures in order to get to Detroit. His sincere faith and work, regardless of personal danger. He considered it a privilege, to share the knowledge of the Faith to the multitudes who were perishing in the chaotic state of the country". (William R. Prescott).

In the fall of 1810, William Mitchell organized the first Methodist Society in Michigan at Detroit, having seven members: Robert Abbot and wife, William McCarty and wife, William Stacey and wife, and Sarah Macoomb. This was the first Protestant church in the territory.

Reverend David Bacon was the Protestant minister who first made a sustained effort to bring the gospel to Michigan before the War of 1812. During the period from 1801 to 1804, he and his son worked in Detroit. There were a couple Catholic priests there since the early 1700s, when Cadillac came to plant a settlement on the Strait to keep the English from the rich Fur Trade of the northwest. The people spoke French, and the highways were the waters.

Reverend Nonian Holmes came to Detroit and served on the Canadian side of the river, known as "The Upper Canadian District of the Genesee Conference".

In 1846, the Conference at Detroit reported 1,733 members. The Church took the high ground on slavery and temperance.

Several German Methodist churches arose in Southeast Michigan.

THE CATHOLIC CHURCH

The Jesuits were men of great intelligence and purity of life. The majority of them, tried faithfully to instruct the Indians in the ways of righteous living. Their religious system emphasized the outward expression, rather than the inward life, and to place before their converts the necessity of a high standard of morals. The only opportunities for education came by the priests.

As early as 1670, two Sulpicians, Dollier and Galinee, visited the Indian villages along the Ottissippi (St. Clair) River and are supposed to have made a stay at the Champlain Mission at the head of the River St. Clair, opposite, Fort Gratiot. Nelson Roberts reported to his father when he passed this way about 1780, en route to Red River, that he had seen a priest with the Indians at Black River. After the war of 1812, the visits of the missionary Fathers to this district became more regular.

In 1817, twelve Catholic families moved northward from Swan Creek and located along the North Bank of Black River. Reverend Father Badiu visited the settlement that year when Mass was celebrated at the house of Louis Tremble.

Rev. Besrinquet arrived from Quebec in 1820, and erected a little church on Walpole Island, and visited the Black River Mission in 1820 or 1821, staying at Louis Tremble's house, baptizing children, and performed a few marriage ceremonies. This priest went on to Lake Superior and became a great Indian missionary.

Rev. Father Sagelle came in 1825 and made regular visits to the Mission Stations at La Riviers Aux Pins – St. Clair City, La Belle Riviere – Marine City, La Riviere Aux Cignes – Swan Creek, and New Baltimore, Michigan, making his home at Louis Tremble's house. Rev. Gabrial Richard had visited all these stations before the coming of Father Sagelle.

Ottissippi

Rev. Andrew Vizoiski made frequent visits to St. Clair, Michigan. Rev. Frederick Baraga came to Cottrellville, Michigan in 1834 and later moved to the North and was a great man, helping the Indians there and at Lake Superior. He was made Bishop of Sault De Ste. Marie, Michigan.

Many other priests visited the Missions of St. Clair County, Michigan.

Rev. Lawrence Kilroy came in 1850 and established churches throughout St. Clair County, Michigan, at Marine City, St. Clair, Port Huron, Columbus, Burtchville, and Kenokee. He laid the cornerstone of St. Stephen's Church of Port Huron, Michigan, and Rev. Edward E. Van Lauwe finished the work in 1868, then built the parsonage and school.

At Detroit, Father Simple Bocquet began serving in 1755, and served St. Anne's Church until 1782.

Father Gabriel Richard served St. Anne's as its pastor from 1802 to 1832. He founded churches and schools, cofounded the University of Michigan, and was a politician and member of Congress. He was also a printer, publishing Michigan's first newspaper, *The Observer*. He imported carding looms and spinning wheels. He died tirelessly tending the sick of the cholera in 1832.

Father Gabriel Richards of the Order of the French Sulpicians came to Detroit in 1798. He was a very good man as a missionary and teacher. He died helping others during the Cholera Epidemic of 1832 in Detroit. Father Gabriel was a Michigan delegate to Congress, the only Catholic priest to sit in the U.S. House of Representatives until 1871. He, with John Monteith and Judge Augustus Woodward, organized the University School, which became the University of Michigan.

In 1824, Father Richard purchased land at Catholic Point – Marine City – for a Mission. In 1826, Rev. Pierre Dejean built Saint Felicite here, the first Catholic Church in the county (St. Clair).

THE METHODIST CHURCH

William Prescott wrote *The Fathers Still Speak: A History of Michigan Methodism* in 1941. The following is from this work.

> The itinerant system was peculiarly suited to the needs of pioneer life. The early preachers made their way from settlement to settlement, over roads and through trails [. . .] they were looked upon as messengers, bearing news from

> *other worlds. With but meager education, and dealing with people even less fortunate than themselves, [...they] answered the needs of the day and that was by far of the greatest importance.*
>
> *William Case, who visited [...] both sides of the river, during the years of 1809 and 1810, [wrote]: 'Their amusements are racing, dancing, gambling, which, together with the destructive practice of excessive drinking, have prevented the prosperity of this country.'*

Case preached in all the places within 100 miles of Detroit, and magistrates ordered heavy fines upon those who permitted him to hold services in their homes. Some received him kindly. At Malden, he preached to a large crowd. His labors were necessary on the Canadian shore.

At Detroit, he requested the use of the Council House to hold meetings. The governor approved, and he preached to large and listening crowds during the time he stayed in the country. A few were awakened to the fact that they were living in deplorable conditions.

Case was an energetic Irishman from Canada, and one of the sturdiest pioneers of his day. He was known as "The Apostle to the American Indians". His greatest usefulness was among them. He became the Father of Methodism in Michigan and Canada. His converts John Sunday and Peter Jones had great success winning converts to Methodism.

The early Northwest suffered from the lack of religious supervision and high ideals.

Reverend Mr. Hickcox was a preacher on the Michigan side.

In 1819, Truman Dixon was the last of the Michigan Methodist preachers to be appointed from the Genesee New York Conference. In 1820, Michigan became part of the Ohio Conference.

> *The Indians were very religious, with primitive conceptions and ideas about God. He acknowledged but one Great Spirit, who lived in the Heavens and most of the time in the Sun. He was the author and giver of all that was good in life and had lesser Spirits under his*

control who took special care of the various parts of nature. He carried with him his special Medicines of Feitch, a bird or beast as a patron saint.

All things in nature had a spirit, and he made propitiations – offerings – as often as he had to deal with it. He believed that the Lake had the power to destroy his canoe and would sacrifice a dog or a handful of tobacco to the Spirit of the Water. The earth, water, and sky teemed with Spirits. W. Prescott

"Curing sick people with the power that came through me. Not I who cured. It was the power from on high – the outer world. I was only a vessel, like a hole through which the power could come to man" (Black Elk, Holy man).

"Many were systematically imprisoned in mental hospitals for practicing their religion in the 1800s, late nineteenth century, and early twentieth century by the U.S. Government.

The most difficult and discouraging of all the early charges was the St. Clair Circuit. It extended along the St. Clair River and included, Algonac, Marine City, St. Clair, Port Huron, and several small settlements which were located back from the river. Its isolation, and the character of the inhabitants who showed little regard for religious teachings, made the work doubly difficult.

The itinerant preachers on these circuits were of an unusual type, but not of unusual ability. Their success was due to deep-seated sincerity and uncompromising determination which seldom allowed defeat. Their work was connected, with great danger and toil. Men thoroughly acquainted with the Bible, men of great faith and prayer. He went into every nook and corner of the Country.

Camp meetings were held in the summer with great crowds, like a religious holiday. Some came and stayed the whole week. The services were conducted by visiting preachers. A time of renewing friendships and laboring in the cause". (Wm. Prescott, 1941)

The Indian hymnbook contained "The Ten Commandments", "The Creed", "The Lord's Prayer", and "Prayers from the Common Book of Prayers" (Anglican).

See "Chapter 10: Reserves" for more on camp meetings.

In 1832 at the Huron Mission at Flat Rock, a school was begun and William Brockway was the teacher. Indian and White both went to church and school there. They learned to read and write. The Indians would pray and sing in their own language.

In 1835, he (Brockway) came to Saginaw Mission where there were about 20 houses at the time. When he arrived, there were 1,000 Indians camped to receive their land payment from the Government Annuity. He was greatly disturbed by the scenes of traders selling liquor to get the money from the Indians and leaving them drunk and in general debauchery. This was a four-week circuit. (Reuter, History of Methodism in Michigan)

In, *The History of Methodism in Canada* (1962), George F. Playter writes:

From St. Clair Mission, James Evans writes in 1835, 'I baptized 16 last sabbath. We believe the net is cast on the right side and that the lord will give us the "one hundred fifty and three". A seeker from Lake Huron told us of a band of Indians waiting for instruction, some of them determined to be Christians. Tomorrow we

Ottissippi

start to see them. Pray for us! There are sixty or seventy on Walpole Island, others at Bear Creek, anxiously waiting. The Black River Indians have visited us and are coming again. Bro. Sunday (John Sunday) should, if possible, visit us in April or May. My interpreter being absent, I endeavored last Sunday to preach in Indian.'

The Rev. William Case reports an expedition to the North: '1835, today our Indian friends went aboard the steamboat "Holland Landing" to cross Lake Simcoe. These brethren will cross Lake Huron in the Penetanguishene for St. Marie. The Rev. Mons. Gavin from Switzerland had taken passage for the North West on a Mission to the pagan Indians.

'At Holland Landing in 1827, the writer Peter Jones delivered the first messages of salvation to these tribes of Simcoe and Huron. There were about 600 of them exhibiting the most disgusting and appalling scenes of drunkenness and poverty. In one year after, 150 were baptized on the same ground; and now that whole body is comfortably settled on the North bank of Lake Simcoe, a sober religious and useful people.'

The Rev. James Evans sent an interesting account of the St. Clair Mission, March 1835: 'This river is a link in the mighty chain of waters connecting the inland seas, Huron and Superior, with the Atlantic Ocean. Most of the settlers have been in the British Army or Navy and the Back Townships are mostly taken by actual settlers. A direct road is open from London to Lake Huron, passing through five or six townships of excellent land, dotted with substantial houses and rising villages.

'On the reserve, many of the Indians have as yet, made little improvement, but prospects are brightening. Most of them are away much of the time and are now about to leave for the Sugar Bush.

'About 15 with Wawanosh, the Head Chief of about 500 souls, were striving for the Faith of the Gospel. The chief's wife is an amiable woman, whose equal I have not found among the Pagans. Noticing the plainness in dress of some Indian women from the Credit, she at once brought down her headdress, a beautiful beaver decorated with silver bands and seven elegant ostrich plumes, to the required standard, declaring whatever is required by the word of God, she will strive to do.

'The faithfulness of those who have embraced the truth astonishes those who expected to see them drunk again. In addition to the White settlements, there are Indians by thousands scattered through the wilds, north and west, ready to stretch out their hands unto God. May the God of Missions crown our efforts.'

REVEREND PETER JONES – KAH KE WA QUO NA BY – "SACRED WAVING FEATHERS"

Peter Jones was an Indian missionary. He wrote *A History of the Ojebway Indians* in 1861. He wrote an Ojibwe Christian hymnbook, translating the great Church hymns from English to the Chippewa tongue, which was of incalculable value. Born in 1802, he was half-Ojibwe, he was educated in the English schools. In 1823, at a camp meeting conducted by Reverend William Case, he became a believer in the Christian message. He was an Indian preacher with the Methodist Church that was in this area – East Michigan and Ontario. He was a preacher in Sarnia, Ontario. He did much to help his people adapt to the White Man's ways.

Peter lived near Toronto, Ontario, he began preaching in the Anishinabek, their own language, translating the new Christian religion into Ojibwe, making the Christian message alive and vital for those who accepted it, who were many.

Peter Jones became an important missionary to the Native Americans. He translated hymns and the Bible to their own language. He wrote that the Indian was "Born Free"; he wrote of his conversion to Christianity. He wrote:

> *that slaves carried the skins to the Merchant Houses (the farmers' office) of the Fur Trader.*
>
> *That Pontiac was King of the Country. Of large canoes with 10 men and 65 packages of furs at 50 pounds each. In 1793, slaves belonging to American citizens were taken by the British and not restored.*
>
> *The British kept the Indians as friends, by their gifts. To take advantage for preventing this broad fertile region from passing out of their hands, there was a Great Confederacy of Indians to stop the Americans from taking their lands. Detroit was the principle depot for the Fur Trade. Frenchtown was the depot for the Northwest Company, a British Company, the Northwest Co. wanted the Fur Trade and excited the Indians to fight the Americans to hold land borders.*
>
> *There were three great Indian Confederacies: the first was under Pontiac – Boondiac, the second was under Little Turtle, and the third was under Tecumseh, the Great Champion of Indian Rights.*
>
> *The blighting effects of the French Feudal System, it was a ranging ground for Jesuits and Fur Traders. That the White men encroach on*

long cultivated soil. That they rudely disturb the graves of the dead. The Americans drove the people from the land to occupy it themselves. The Indians were deceived by treaties.

There was war; the British were impressing American seamen for service, pirating American vessels, and enforcing illegal blockades. Indian fighters were in the tops of trees.

Detroit was given up by Hull without a shot. The American troops were 5,000; the British-Canadian were 100,000 including the Savages. The soldiers dashed their muskets upon the ground in agony, shame, and indignation.

The usurpers overran and exploited the land. The European Legacy is one of racism, imperialism, and nationalism.

In the United States, Grant's peace policy brought the Christian clergy into almost total control of Ojibwe destinies. To many Ojibwas, religious leadership had come to mean religious tyranny.

The heritage of conflicting associations and movements of religious leaderships has been the increase of witchcraft accusations. Every religious association has been accused by nonmembers of fomenting witchcraft. In former times, the religious leaders fought witches. Now they are powerless to do so and are accused of being the very witches that in traditional times they were expected to combat.

The Ojibwas have lost much of their religious heritage. They no longer trust the traditional Manitos, as their ancestors did. They do not believe the truthfulness of their once sacred myths. Isolated from their meaningful past, Ojibwas turn to their surviving religious leaders in order to regain contact with the sources of existence. In traditional times, any Ojibwa could have performed religious acts. The average Ojibwa has been stripped of much religious knowledge through the centuries and needs a specialist to perform the most basic religious acts. He still feels a need for those acts because Christianity has not adequately replaced the traditional religion.

The nineteenth century Methodists and Episcopalians made the greatest efforts to train Native Ojibwe for ministry. The early Methodist Ojibwe clergymen included John Sunday-Shahwundais or "Sultry Heat", Peter Marksman, Peter Jones, Peter Jacobs, and George Copway. (Peter Jones)

WILLIAM CASE

William Case was the Father of Methodism in Michigan and Canada. He was the founder of Protestantism in Michigan and called the Father of Missionary Work in the Northwest. He was the man who worked with Indians and taught them missionary work and ministry as Methodists.

John Sunday was a very effective Methodist minister. A Mississauga Ojibway chief, he served in the war of 1812. He was a missionary in Upper Canada and Michigan.

Reverend James Evans taught many to read and write and converted many to the Methodist faith. Evans developed the first written language for the Ojibwe.

George Copway translated the Christian Gospels into Ojibwe in 1851. Peter Jones also translated hymns and the New Testament into Ojibwe.

"Peter Jones was very effective in showing the Ojibwas could approach the Christian God just like Whites. Rev. Peter Jacobs stated that his conversion resulted from seeing Jones in a position of Christian leadership, praying directly to God. He saw a chance that he too could become a Christian and still be an Ojibwa religious leader" (Kienietz).

Peter Jones, "Sacred Feathers" or "Sacred Waving Feathers", was a Missauga Ojibwe chief of the Eagle totem, a Methodist minister, author, and translator. He was born in Hamilton, Upper Canada, and raised by his Ojibwe Missisauga mother until age 14. He learned brickmaking to support himself while at school. He had a Welch father who was a provincial land surveyor, who educated him. Peter became a Methodist minister under William Case, the Father of Methodist Missions. He taught and helped his people learn to farm and live on the reservations. He ministered to both Ontario and Michigan natives. Peter married an English wife and was at home in both worlds. He went to Britain and raised large amounts of money to build Indian schools in Southern Ontario.

The Wesleyan Methodist camp meetings were held on the Sarnia Reserve. A clearing was prepared and a temporary pulpit erected, with tents, wigwams, and booths nearby, the latter two of tree branches. The congregation of converted Indians on this reserve, and from Monketown on the Thames. Many coming on foot, the dress very orderly and with great deportment, to the meeting, the singing parts of which they all joined in, in a very beautiful manner, the timing and music of their combined voices pleasing.

The clear sky, the rude seats of fresh felled trees split and raised. Pillars were erected in different places, eight to ten feet high for burning fires on, to give light at night, and warm the atmosphere.

The service was conducted by Rev. James Evans, the resident missionary, assisted by several of his reverend brethren. He was perfectly acquainted with their language, with a good knowledge of their manners and customs, and having a very mild easy and pleasing conciliatory address. A most devoted man, highly beloved and respected by the Indians, both converted and unconverted, and the White settlers as well. He had done an immense good among them. There is scarcely a thing as drunkenness.

In now Port Huron, Kimball, Wadhams, and Ruby, Michigan, on the Mill Creek and Black River, were Indian villages. Mr. Evans has been indefatigable in his labors, having translated a considerable portion of the Holy Scripture, principally the Gospels, into their language and printed for the use of their school. Mr. Evans prayed and sang in the Indian language, he addressed the congregation in English, for the benefit of the English in the audience. An

Ottissippi

Ojibwe interpreter made known the words. But now he preaches to them in their own Language.

The Black River Society Methodist Church at Mill Creek, was for the mill workers and loggers. It was attended by the Indians. The Indian preachers came here to minister to the area. The Black River Mission had 246 members.

The Methodists were opposed to alcohol, not just because of its effects on the Indians, but because it seemed to be threatening the foundation of White society in Upper Canada. It was the enemy of thrift, industry, discipline, and punctuality. Many Europeans considered alcohol indispensable to the enjoyment of life.

Uprooted like the Ojibwa and forced into a grim struggle, with a new and unfamiliar environment, the immigrant population of Upper Canada had...relied on intoxicants as an all pervasive necessity. The use of liquor was, therefore, the symptom of broader environmental problems, that both groups were attempting to solve. (Schmaltz)

The first Minister of the Gospel to visit this county, St. Clair, was Mr. Dixon, who came to the residence of Harvey Stewart on Harsen's Island in the winter of 1818. There were three families on the Island at that time, all assembled to hear the first sermon preached by a Protestant minister in St. Clair County.

Ministers occasionally visited from that time forward from both Canada and the Ohio Conference. Some who visited were Williams, Jones, Huston, Demorest, Slater, Parker, Case, Griffes, Jackson, and Adams. John K. Smith's home was always a refuge for the weary itinerant.

CHERYL MORGAN

St. Andrews Episcopal Church in Algonac, Michigan was organized in 1807 by Rev. Joseph Prichard, he was succeeded by Rev. Andrew Jamieson of Canada, who for 31 years labored among the Indians of Walpole Island [in the St. Clair River, above Lake St. Clair]. (Western Historical Co.)

When Peter Jones went to Walpole Island in 1829, he told of his visit:

About noon all the principal men of this vicinity came, and the women fixed a large shade on the green grass with coarse linen cloth. The men sat in a ring under the shade, their Principal Chief Pazhehezhiquasnkum at the head.

The chief arose and said:

'Brothers and friends, I will tell you what happened to some of our Forefathers once they became Christians. . .They threw away all their medicines, pouches, and everything they used in their arts into the River. They had no sooner done this than a Great Sickness came among them, and but few escaped death. . . How can I, who have grown old in sins and in drunkenness, break off from these things, when the white people are as bad and wicked as the Indians? Strong drink has made us poor. I am poor and barely able to buy enough cloth for a pair of leggings, wherewith would I be able to buy cloth for a pair of pantaloons, to dress like the White man, if I should become a Christian or live like a White man?'

See "Chapter 10: Reservations" for more on Peter Jones, James Evans, and William Case.

Ottissippi

In 1833, the Rev. Henry P. Chase – Pahtakquahong, or "Coming Thunder" – was sent hither by the British Government to make a treaty with the Indians. He was the hereditary chief of the Ojibwe nation. He was to distribute supplies among them. At that time, there was only one framed house at the Rapids – Sarnia – that of the French Voyageur LaForge. There were a few log huts and wigwams.

The Sarnia Indian Reserve was then five miles square and home to several Indian bands. The Indians hunted and fished. Furs were sent to England by way of Montreal. There were 500 Indians living in bark wigwams. He found a few log houses. The only framed dwellings were the Agency House, Council House, and the Mission House. Henry served on both banks of the River St. Clair.

"In 1833, the Methodist Missions among the Ojibwe transferred to the Wesleyan Missionary Society, covering both the United States and Canadian Territories" (Schoolcraft, vol. 6, pg. 739/Vecsey, Traditional Ojibwe Religion).

> *In 1838, the Methodists had a Mission here, Sarnia, Ontario, and built a Mission House on land owned by the Grand Trunk R.R. James Evans was the first Missionary in 1836. James Evans had made a written Ojibwe language, which was a great help to all.*
>
> *At a camp meeting, their noted conjurer and medicine man was converted, and "See We Taug Un" became Peter Salt and remained a good Christian man. (Mrs. B.C. Farrand 1888, Lambton Archives, Wyoming, Ont. Canada)*

Agent J.W. Keating in 1842 wrote a report of the Walpole Indians:

> *They are cheerful in the extreme; joke and merry talk go-round the wigwam fire. They are sociable and friendly toward one another. They are generally intemperate and will part with everything for ardent spirits once they taste them. Their generosity is unbounded; in time of need, all is divided.*

After coming to the Island and left without assistance, they became prey to their rapacious White neighbors, and in a moment of intoxication, signed papers that turned out to be leases for the best and most fertile lands, which forcible and instant possession was taken. I was enabled to expel many of the most audacious intruders and place their farms at the disposal of the Indians.

Although they have but two meals a day, they frequently when in the house dip into the kettle of corn soup, always kept filled to give to any visitors or poor hungry Indians, and there are many who in their escape from military pursuit in Michigan are compelled to abandon all their property.

They are exceedingly fond of liberty and hate the slightest restraint upon their motions.

Nicholas Aylmer Plain was Chief of the Chippewa at Sarnia and also a minister of the Methodist Church on the reservation. He had an Indian songbook of hymns printed and distributed it to many reserves in Ontario and in Michigan Indian communities. He spread 3,000 English and Indian songbooks among the people.

"The U.S. and Canada used to hunt down and murder those who were part of the Tent Shaking Religious Ceremony. It was said to be occult practice, speaking with the spirits. These men were called 'Conjurers'" (Turtle Nation Indians, www).

Classes at Albion Wesleyan Seminary opened in 1843. This seminary educated Indian preachers, interpreters, and teachers from all over Michigan.

"Government workers were shareholders in mining companies. The government turned a blind eye, ignoring treaty rights and obligations, while opening the way for speculators, prospectors, business men, and companies" (Smith, Mississauga Portraits).

Dams raised lake water and made them too deep for rice beds, eroding plant and wildlife habitat.

There was genocide, ethnic cleansing, human rights violations. Institutionalized poverty. The European imperial thinking was to exploit all people but their own elite.

The Indians artificial identity makes them scapegoats and political hockey pucks to keep their lily-white hands clean in their fraudulent claim to this bloodied land. While they speak of justice and with flowery words dripping with honey, the people live in slums. There is destruction of the ecosystem, pollution, and institutionalized exploitation of people, snake oil salesmen obscuring the truth of the human rights violations they perpetuate on everyone else. Medieval thinking, European Capitalism, Feudalism, and Constitutional Monarchy. Pseudo-legalized theft, sno jobs, rip off, philosophies which do not belong on this land. There are schemes and cover ups, Roman law, anarchy, and lawlessness at the top.

Racism obscures the social and genetic engineering that is being done to American Society. It prevents dialogue, discussions, unity, and getting together to make this a better world. This works to the advantage of policy makers at the top of the social hierarchy. (Smith, "Ojibwe Bibliography", part 9 Missisauga Portraits, "Sacred Feathers")

"French Missionary Louis Baroux in 1833 wrote, 'It is necessary to understand the history of their persecutions, to see face to face the victims of the White Man's double dealing, to consider well their patience and their saintly resignation in order to comprehend the sublimity and nobility of these newly made Christian Souls'" (Students on Site, Native American Missions and Schools, www).

"They regard the White Man as fulfilling prophecies of their own priests" (Schoolcraft, 1821).

"An old, battle-scarred warrior said to a preacher, 'Why we have followed this law you speak of for untold ages'".

Everything held sacred is called Medicine and receives no payment. Then greed led to the demoralizing practice" (Charles Eastwood, "The Soul of the Indian").

THE CAMP MEETINGS

"The camp meeting of the Frontier Methodist Church was fascinating to Indians". The following is from Prescott/Emmert, MPHC Vol. 47:

> *At the bend of the Cass River in Saginaw County in 1850, there were from 800 to 1000 Indians encamped at the meeting: From two to three hundred of them were Pagans. They came from many surrounding counties and some from Canada. Among the number were 16 chiefs.*
>
> *A more detailed description of an Indian camp was given by Lucius Gould; both White families and Christian Indians attended the meetings. The meetings combined the familiar Protestant Church doctrines and bits of Indian Ceremony. They were held under primitive pioneer conditions.*
>
> *The meeting was held in a large wigwam or tent, built of poles covered with bark. In the center of the tent under a hole in the roof, burned a great fire over which a kettle of corn and beans – succotash – was cooking. The preacher stood in the center of the tent by the fire, while the people both White and Indian were seated around him in a circle. Those who did not care to look upon the fiery Indian preacher could watch the pot boil over the fire.*

The singing of the congregation was fine. The Indians were well-provided with singing books. The arrangement of these books was after the plan of Henry R. Schoolcraft. On one page of the books, the hymns were printed in English, while on the opposite page they were set forth in the language of the Indians. The singing of the mixed congregation when once heard was never to be forgotten. The deep mellow voice of the Indian gave forth low sweet music. To this at times, character was added by the clear ringing voices of the French girls who were present and could sing as if they were birds in the Indian tongue. The meetings were attended by Indians, French, English, and Americans. And while it is true that all present did not understand the words of the Indian preacher, yet when the voice of song arose, the hearts of those who had come to worship were touched as if by fire.

At the close of the meeting, the preacher announced that, at the service to be held the following Sunday, an interpreter would be present in order that all might enjoy the sermon. The preacher was Ick-Wa-Co-Mick. He was well-known throughout the region of Shiawassee, Michigan. He was fiery and eloquent; the people loved to hear him. Wa-Ba-Tang was his assistant, also another Indian preacher. He preached the doctrines and conducted his services according to the simple form of the Methodist Church, which was so dear to many pioneers in those early days.

METHODIST MISSIONS

The Methodist Work in Saginaw was begun in 1848. The Saginaw Watershed was filled with Indians, known as the Indian District. At Taymouth township, Michigan, on the west bank of the Flint River, was a large band of Ojibwe in an ancient village. This became the Taymouth Methodist Indian Mission at Pe-won-go-*wink, Taymouth Township*.

Young Ash a tah ne qua beh – "Almost Touches the Clouds" – became Daniel Wheedon (Wheaton); upon hearing the gospel, he became a great Methodist missionary.

Early Methodist preachers had a great response when preaching the gospel where it had not been heard. Daniel C. Jacokes and Joseph Bushy (Bushag) also preached at Saginaw, the Indians singing and praying as though piercing the heavens. Jacokes preached to the Indians on Black River near Port Huron, Michigan. In the Saginaw area, he traveled 350 miles every three weeks, sleeping outdoors many times.

Peter Marksman, a great Ojibwe preacher, was at Lakeville Mission, northeast of Oakland County, Michigan, thirty miles southeast of Flint. He also preached in the Upper Peninsula and at Nebeseeng (Nepessing) near Flint, and all declared their faith in Christianity, destroying their images and bad medicine. Lakeville Mission was changed to the name Flint River Mission, a four-week circuit of 450 miles. The Indians had moved to the Flint River at Nebissing, seven miles west of Lapeer. Nebissing was later called "Bradleys Chapel". Canadian John Kahbeige (Kabbeige), a Chippewa Methodist interpreter, worked here. This was the former Lakeville Mission, now renamed the Flint River Mission.

George Bradley reported that the Missions were poor and needed clothing for the children and some needed food. They also needed books to teach from, hymnbooks, Bibles, and Testaments. In 1845, Rev. George Bradley came to Saginaw and was in charge of the Flint River Mission. Rev. Hickey and others held camp meetings. The traders were very hostile to missionaries, who they were afraid would destroy their lucrative trade. All the Missions were along the Flint River and the Saginaw Valley. Nebissing and the Black River Society were nearby.

Ottissippi

There were 42 Indian churches at one time that later closed. Some were held in a wigwam or home. The Indians moved onto reservations or other places by the mid and later 1850s.

The preachers ate with their people as they traveled. One tells us a story: "One evening an Indian squaw tried to feed me fried snake for supper, and I said, 'Oh, no! I have eaten your raccoon, porcupine, squirrels, and your sweet muskrat meat, but I will not eat your snake!' She replied, 'You had him for dinner soup.' By the way, if you run out of food in the woods, just dig up some cattail roots, boil them, and you will have pretty good potatoes, and the tender tops of the cattails make splendid greens."

Many of the Missions bought land to live on. Home economics were taught, including sewing and knitting. Most families farmed to some extent.

George Bradley wrote, "we received some opposition from the Indian party, but the influence exerted by Indian traders and some Government Officers – White Men – are much worse than any found among the Indians. We want hymnbooks, Peter Jones translation, with the English on one side and the Ojibway on the other. We need 500 copies. We want a quantity of primary English books for the use of the schools".

The Lutherans also had Missions at Frankenmuth, Sebewaing, and St. Louis. This was the founding of Frankenmuth in 1845. There were many villages here.

The Methodist Episcopal Church worked with the Methodist Church in the Indian Mission District. Most of the people moved in 1857 to the Isabella Reservation lands and Saginaw Bay – Pe-sah-gen-ing – 50 miles north of Saginaw.

"There is not a need to challenge Indians' traditional beliefs. Appreciate their spirituality and join them in coming nearer to God" (Rev. Lewis Church, Chairman of Michigan's Commission on Indian Affairs Lansing /Methodist Ministries in Michigan, Dorothy Reuter 1993). The Anglo-American majority needs to be educated concerning the Native Americans, their cultural values, and contributions they can and have made. The Indian has insights which can contribute to the renewal and, indeed, perhaps the survival of us all.

Chief Seattle in 1854 said, "One thing we know, which the White Man may one day discover – our God is the same God. You may think now that you own him as you wish to own our land; but you cannot. He is the God of man and his compassion is equal for the Red man and the White. This Earth is precious to him, and to harm the Earth is to heap contempt on its creator. The Whites too shall pass; perhaps sooner than all other tribes..."

CHAPTER 5
Disease And Epidemics

The indigenous peoples were mostly very healthy and had long lives. When the Norsemen came to the eastern shores, they brought their germs with them. The Norsemen who fished the Atlantic Maritimes brought disease in 1001 A.D. The death rate was very high, and 70 to 90% of the people died. The explorers and missionaries also brought disease and, through their contact with the native peoples, caused great devastation among the Native Americans.

Immigration brought much illness, famine, and hardship, along with the grieving of the loss of their loved ones. The Europeans also suffered from disease and epidemics. In the Lakes region of Michigan in the heat of summer, myriads of mosquitos and poisonous insects, miasmatic vapors of decaying soil, and fetid bogs caused a malarial fever and dysentery.

The Eastern Seaboard and the Maritimes were the first areas to suffer the consequences. Through their contact with other indigenous peoples and the White Man. The Anishinabe people of the Northwest at the time were greatly affected. Whole villages and peoples were wiped out. So many died, and the people rushed away from outbreaks that the dead were not buried at times. A once very numerous people were reduced time and again in very large numbers. Many of their great leaders and many, many family members were lost, causing untold suffering.

The native peoples had no immunity to these diseases and germs brought amongst them. The medicines and the Medicine Men had no effect for the curing of any of these new plagues and epidemics. Smallpox, cholera, diphtheria, scarlet fever, chicken pox, whooping cough, measles, mumps, consumption (tuberculosis), scarletina, typhoid, and dysentery wreaked havoc and ravaged through the land.

Cholera is an acute infectious disease characterized by watery diarrhea and vomiting. It is spread by eating or drinking water contaminated with the bacterium. People can die within hours of infection from dehydration. It usually occurs when human feces from a person who has the disease seeps into a community water supply. It also lives in warm, brackish waters.

Smallpox is an infectious disease known as pox or red plague. It causes a huge rash and blisters. It also causes blindness. It had a very high rate of death in Native Americans, as there was no immunity. The incubation period is around 12 days. Once inhaled, it invades the body like a viral disease, bringing muscle pain, malaise, headache, and prostration. The digestive tract is often involved; fever, nausea, vomiting, and backache often occur, lasting two to four days. By the twelfth to fifteenth day, lesions looking like red spots appear in the mouth and throat. These lesions rapidly enlarge and rupture, releasing large amounts of the virus into the saliva. A rash develops over the body, and some forms bleed into the skin.

Trachoma blindness was among the Indian diseases; it is caused by the bacterium chlamydia trachomatis. It is an infection of the eye and, left untreated, can lead to blindness.

Following is nearly every instance of these epidemics that affected the Great Lakes Indians, though this will not cover all the sickness that the people suffered.

1617: The Great Plague falls on the Ohio Valley tribes.

1634: European diseases killed half of the Hurons. They had no immunity to these new biological weapons.

1635-1640: "smallpox, influenza, and measles brought misery to the Huron traders and Wyandot Middlemen; half of the peoples were lost to the diseases" (Turtle Mountain Band of Chippewa, Ojibwe History, www).

1639: Smallpox ravaged the Hurons.

1677: "an epidemic hit the Great Lakes tribes thought to be a flu virus" (Tanner).

1681: "smallpox again strikes Sault Saint Marie, New France" (Metis Timeline, Canadian History a Distinct Viewpoint, info/metis.aspx, www).

1751: "smallpox swept the Great Lakes and Ohio Valley" (Dickshovel, Huron History).

1752: M. De Longueuil wrote of the smallpox commits ravages; it begins to reach Detroit. Over eighty Indians died of the disease at adjacent villages, including Chief Kinousaki, who was much attached to the French.

1757-1758: "smallpox came among the people and many were lost. It was brought back from the New York, Iroquois Peace Treaty to the villages. It swept through the Great Lakes in the winter" (Tanner).

1764: At Fort Pitt, the Indians were given blankets infested with smallpox. As a result, it raged through the Delaware, Ottawa, and Ojibwe camps all summer into 1764.

1766: "smallpox again brought devastation to the Great Lakes peoples" (Tanner).

1780: Smallpox ravaged the whole of New France.

1793: A smallpox epidemic swept through the Lake Simcoe communities. After the American Revolution, mass immigration began. Ten thousand refugees (United Empire Loyalists) and soldiers came to upper Canada of which Michigan was a part at that time.

1813: An epidemic of whooping cough and typhoid attacked the Great Lakes people.

1832: A great cholera epidemic started at Detroit and moved with the soldiers sent to the Black Hawk War.

1834: "cholera was brought among the People" (Tanner).

1836 and 1837: "in the Saginaw Basin Country, smallpox ravaged the people. Two-thirds of the Ojibwe numbers were lost" (Tanner).

B.O. Williams describes the results of the 1837 smallpox as follows:

> *Thus, whole villages and bands were decimated, and during the summer and fall many were left without a burial at the camps in the woods, and were devoured by the wolves. I visited the village of Cheassining (Big Rock Village) now called Chesaning, and saw in the summer camps, several bodies, only partially covered up and not a living soul could I find except one Old Squaw that was convalescent. We afterwards sent some flour and other provisions to the few that remained. Judge Dexter, of the Village of Dexter, gave me ten dollars to assist them to flour. Most of the adults attacked died and it is a remarkable fact that no White person ever took the disease from them, although in many instances the poor,*

emaciated creatures, visited White families while covered with pustules and scabs. (Emmert/Williams, Shiawasee County, MHC, vol. 47)

The disease broke up the bands, some fled to Canada and others to the West. Some remained in the area living on what they could find in their wanderings or begging. A number of Indians, remained in the villages in South Saginaw County and occasionally came into Shiawassee County. (Emmert, MHC, vol. 47)

1870: "Smallpox again struck the tribes" (Tanner).
1870s and 1880s: The Indians living at Lake Nepessing, near Lapeer, were struck, and most of them died, wiping out the whole village. These were the Black River peoples.
1880s: More disease claimed the people through smallpox and diphtheria.
1889 and 1890: "an epidemic of influenza or La Grippe was common in the country and in Michigan in the winter and spring months of the years 1890-1891 and 1891-1892. Over a thousand deaths occurred from the influenza in 1890, 1891, and 1892" (25th annual report, MI, Secretary of State, Lansing, Robert Smith & Co. 1893).
1903: "smallpox struck near Detroit" (Farmer).
1918 and 1919: "influenza killed thousands worldwide" (Farmer), and "the Spanish Flu took its toll on the Reservation at Sarnia, Ontario" (Canada West Last Frontier).

"Death and Warfare became a major part of Anishinabe life in the woods and lakes of our land" (Diba Jimooyung, Zibiiwang, Saginaw Chippewa). In *Metis History*, www it is said that smallpox raged fiercely. The pretext of trade was used to open doors for trade and disease.

The Black Robes at Huron, when "Echon", Jean De Brebeauf, the Jesuit, set foot in the Huron Country. he said, "I shall be here, so many years, I shall cause many to die. And then go elsewhere to do the same, until I have ruined, the whole land". Echon is the most famous Black Robe sorcerer or Demon, it was a Genocide Policy of Biological Warfare.

The Huron informed the Neutrals, that the Black Robes were sorcerers and imposters come to take possession of their country". Metis History, www

For Europeans, any illness also befell them. The most common was the ague and fever of a swampy country. Whiskey was the great medicinal element of backwoods life, a sovereign remedy for all prevailing ills. Malaria, ague, and bilious fever were common ailments.

The practice of bleeding was common; the priests shared this with the Indians. All physicians used bleeding at times. Some Native Americans were given vaccines for smallpox, but most were not.

"Flint blades were surgical instruments. The blades were so thin that the incisions made could not be duplicated until the advent of laser surgery. The indigenous peoples performed surgery and kept wounds sterile with botanical antiseptics. Syringes of bird bones and animal bladders were used to administer plant medicine. The indigenous people were the pioneers of using plant breeding genetics. Many pharmaceuticals came from traditional medicine of the indigenous peoples" (K. Porterfield, "10 Lies about Indigenous Science"). "More than two hundred drugs derived from plants for pharmacological uses were discovered by American Indians" (James W. Loewen, Lies My Teacher Told me).

"Syringes and hypodermic needles from bird bones were attached to small bladders to inject medicines. There were large and small syringes for enemas, to irrigate wounds and clean ears. The bird bones – Nanandawi iwe winini – used for tube sucking were small hollowed bones two inches long" (Plain, 1300 Moons).

"There were over 2,500 uses for medicinal plant species. There were oral contraceptive plants.

"Pest controls were made from tobacco and other plants. Petroleum collection and extraction pits were used for ceremonial fires and lotion on skin. For baby bottles and formula, [the] washed, dried, and oiled intestines [were used, to contain milk] with a bird quill for a nipple" (10 inventions that changed the world. Indian Country Today, Media Network www).

"In 1682, (and before), Spruce Sap Beer was used for scurvy" (Metis Timeline, Canadian History, A Distinct Viewpoint, metis-history.info/metis.aspx, www).

John Wesley noted that "the Indians had exceedingly few diseases; their medicines are quick and generally infallible". Furthermore, "Cotton Mathers wrote, Indian healers produce many cures that are truly stupendous" (Canadian History, a Distinct Viewpoint, www). "The Mediwiwin, native physicians, were very effective in their treatments of any ills. But the European diseases, they had no remedy for."

CHAPTER 6
Trade and Traders

"The Ojibwe of Sault Saint Marie (Michigan) and LaPoint (Wisconsin) had formed the merchant center of the Midwest trading network, reaching far and wide from about, 1400 A.D.

The European Fur Trade led to new lands and exploration. It created much friction between competing governments for the riches being found in the New Territory. It also created greed and war among Natives and traders.

The Spanish voyages to the New World in the 1400s were the beginning of transatlantic exploration and trading. The defeat of the Spanish Armada in 1588 opened the Atlantic Trade to European nations and England as a power. It was also the beginning of colonization on the Atlantic Seaboard, the Caribbean, and Central and South America. The fishing grounds in the North Atlantic, the furs, salt, rum, slaves, sugar, rice, natural resources, and their exploitation were of great wealth to Europe.

The European nations and Russia had a declining fur population due to the great demand. The high price of the luxury furs created the market in North America. The Native Americans doing the work of gathering and processing of the furs. They were possessed of the knowledge and skills and played the central role in the Fur Trade. They became entwined with the European world economy and its political designs for expansion. Charter companies with monopoly rights to trade began the colonization of America.

The French Company of 100 Associates in 1632 passed to the Company of the Indies, John Law's company, in 1665. The French were world traders in the slave and Indian trade of tobacco. They had 10,000 indentured slaves, a total monopoly in Louisiana between 1717 and 1731" (Lanman, Redbook).

"When the Indians were first exposed to objects made of metal, glass, and woven fabric, they assumed these to be wondrous possessions of manitous or deities. The trade goods made their lives much easier. The French had been trading in the Maritimes with the Montagnais Natives, along with the British and the Dutch, who traded with the Iroquois. The Iroquois became cornered by all.

The French were introduced to the Algonquins, who lived west and north of Montreal, Canada. Their new center of operations, for New France, the Fur Trade was booming in Europe. The French met the Saulteurs in 1623 at Sault Ste. Marie. France sent out explorers to find the passage to the Pacific and an easy trade route to China and Asia. The Natives led the explorers to all the natural resources in the New France. The French Monarchy used the feudal system with the expense of settlement on a seigniorial officer. The seignior had limited independence, power, and wealth. This system did not attract a large amount of immigration. It did attract fur traders, adventurers, and explorers, who sought freedom from the authorities. The great distance from official government made it difficult for the authorities to manage the Fur Trade and traders. In 1627, French merchants founded Compagne De La Novelle France, and the Seigneurial Regime began.

The Natives were essential to the production of furs; they were trappers, traders, processors, and marriage partners. The Native women were a great asset to the fur traders. They were guides, interpreters, working alongside in the trade, as well as nurturers, cooking, making clothing, and all other necessary chores in the wilderness life. The children who resulted from these unions were of mixed heritage and were called the Metis; they were also known as the *coureurs de bois*, woods runners, and half-breeds. They were the link between both worlds, knowing the Indian ways and the European. They were essential to the governments of both worlds. The life of the fur trader was wild, free, full of peril and hardships. Free from the bonds of civilized society. Once they had a taste of it, most did not return to the authority of living in towns." (Parker)

COUREURS DE BOIS

Coureurs de bois -Bush Rangers: unlicensed, lawless traders who knew the Natives and land intimately. They were mostly French or the Metis – Half-Breeds – who believed the fur-bearing animals belonged to neither the monopoly of the king, nor a company, but were the spoils of all. They defied the so-called laws put upon the land and furs. They made the barters with the Natives, lived with them and like them in perfect contentment, marrying their daughters. These men could paddle, hunt, trap, speak the native tongue, and understood the Indians. They were gay, singing songs on their journeys, lighthearted, carefree. They were of great endurance and very strong: "the rovers of the woods". The Frenchmen could paddle sixty strokes a minute, fifteen hours a day. He would decorate his long hair with eagle feathers, paint his face with vermillion, ochre, and soot, and adorn his greasy hunting frock with horsehair fringes.

Ramsay Crooks of the American Fur Company wrote, "the Canadian had a temper of mind to render him patient, docile, and persevering; in short, he is [...] harmless in himself, with habits of submission which fit him peculiarly for our business." Americans were considered too independent to submit quietly to proper control. This control was exercised by the employers, or Bourgeois (Parkman).

"When the number of traders increased, specialty classes began. The bourgeois, the voyageur, the *mangeurs de lard*, the clerks, engages (indentured servants), hivernans – winterers, and artisans. Many others were employed in the Fur Trade at posts and in the woods. The bourgeois was head commander at the permanent post, who ruled the army of traders in military fashion. He supplied and sent out traders to various areas, saw to the packing and shipping of the furs, and kept in touch with the representatives at outposts: a man of great responsibilities. The partisan was similar to the duties of the bourgeois.

The Voyageur: The life of a voyageur was a dangerous one. He was always on the water, the lakes, and rivers. He was usually a man of powerful physique, of a rough, coarse way, illiterate, and cowardly. Often called the slave of the Fur Trade, laboring under heavy loads, furs, supplies, and trade goods over portages. The Northern route to Montreal required 26 portages in the early days. They were amazingly fit and energetic. In spite of his labor, he made music with his boat songs.

The *mangeurs de lard* were the pork-eaters who were not eating the provisions of nature. No bear grease, lard, or lyed corn for them. These were the Greenhorns, who had much to learn about living in the wilderness. He was not able to endure the rigorous life of *coureurs de bois*. They did menial services around the posts and were paid low wages. They were always in debt to the post and were forced to stay at work, paying their debt.

The clerk was next to the bourgeois in responsibility and social life, often filling in when the bourgeois was absent. He frequently commanded posts and was a trusted servant of the company, often a shareholder.

The engages were laborers and boatmen.

The hivernans were winterers who spent several winters in the forests among the Natives and were experienced in the fur trade.

The artisans were a large group who were skilled in various trades: boat builders, masons, tailors, interpreters, clerks, traders, blacksmiths, carpenters, and hunters. These men were at all the post villages.

The free trapper or hunter was very essential. He was his own master, going where and doing what he pleased. Keeping all the fruit of his labor. Sometimes these men hunted together for protection. They would live at the Indian camps and villages, marry the maidens, and live there the greater part of the year, occasionally bringing his peltries to market" (Adapted from, Ida Johnson, The Michigan Fur Trade, 1919).

"Fur traders were known as the ruffians of the coarsest stamp. Fierce, bold, and truculent" (Parkman). "They were often the outcasts of all Nations, and the refuse of mankind" (Bassett).

"These were men who cheated, plundered, and cursed the savage. The French most often ill-treated the Indians, pillaging and carrying away their merchandise, heaping upon them insults and indignities. We often think of the French as friendly fur traders.

Father Carheil paints a vivid picture of the trader's life at Michilimackinac; it was one of lawlessness, drunkenness, debauchery, and vice. The Jesuits give similar reports. They were illiterate and men who seemed to have no other purpose in life but to roam the forest and secure a few peltries. Though they were not all this way. Others were educated and intelligent men. Finding satisfaction in the rich returns of the trade and having freedom from rules, etiquette, and where social ceremony held sway. There were many who were sincere in their trade to the Indians and were great friends and brothers to them.

A bushel of corn and two pounds of fat were the month's allowance. The trader was to consume one-fourth of corn and one-half pint of bear's grease each meal. At times, they lived on wild rice and were at times in starvation, if lost. Eating moss or, in desperation, a dead companion's flesh. When there was plenty, a common saying was that they could devour the whole side of a buffalo. At night, the men camped by a stream, often sleeping on the ground or pine boughs, or under their canoe, a small fire and a knife for protection from predators and enemies. Sometimes on horseback or on foot, over swamps, through impenetrable forest, day after day, journeying mile after mile. The traders and Indians ran up debts at the trading posts, from year to year being indebted. Until they brought in their furs. Sometimes the furs profits were 700%. The goods in the canoes usually amounted to four canoes of furs traded for each in trade items. This was about 160 packs of skins, with forty skins in each pack. Each pack worth 50 crowns, or eight thousand crowns in a load. The merchant took six hundred crowns for the license. A thousand for the goods granted on credit for trade. Leaving 6,400 crowns of which he deducted 40%, or 2,500 crowns. The balance was divided among the six men of the canoe party, each receiving 600 crowns.

At portages, the packs were carried on their backs, with a strap from their foreheads called a tumpline to even the load. Often two at a time. The packs weighed from 80 to 100 pounds, the latter being seldom. Other writings say the packs weighed from 50 to 80 pounds. Sometimes the portage was two or three miles. The canoes were carried on the shoulders of the men, stopping only for a quick meal or a pipe. The pork-eaters could only carry one package. Some of the men carried two or three occasionally.

Johnson said that the men could undergo and become so inured to hardships and see them rush and splash through the mud and water like so many cattle is astonishing. The men in the employ of merchants or companies could not grow rich on their trade; several independent traders amassed fortunes. The Fur Trade was the main business of the Northwest, every man and family connected to the pursuit of fur. Fur was used as the money for trade. Weaklings were weeded out; the old, experienced trader was sought out" (Adapted from, Ida Amanda Johnson, The Michigan Fur Trade, 1919).

"The trading centers were a huge annual affair in spring and summer. When the traders, *coureurs de bois*, Indians, and voyagers arrived in these towns, they brought all, of the license of the forest with him. They received the money for their furs, then proceeded to trade, buy supplies or go on a drunken debauch, on the town. A ritual practiced each fur season. The whole town would come out to meet them and welcome them. They filled the marketplace. Thousands gathered for the Grand Trade Fair.

The Mission fathers wrote, 'Our Missions are reduced to such extremity that we can no longer maintain them against the infinity of disorder. Brutality, violence, injustice, impiety, insolence, scorn, and injury which the deplorable and infamous traffic in brandy, has spread universally among the Indians of these parts.'

Smuggling and pirating were a huge problem in the Trade. Every dirty trick was used to gain an advantage by many traders and governments. The voyageurs were openhearted, jovial, and friendly, singing their boat songs as they paddled the waterways of the Great Lakes, St. Lawrence, and beyond. Fur trapper, trader, explorer, and Indian fighter, the *coureur de bois* was a most important factor in making the Great Lakes country known to Europeans, opening trade with the Western Indians – meaning Michigan. They were experts in managing canoes or finding his way in the primeval forest. A man of strength absolutely necessary to conquer a Wilderness. Braving danger, enduring hardships, and adapting to Indian life. He was often an outlaw to the peculiar system of government in New France and faced severe penalties when he was in reach of the authorities. He could not see the justice in monopolistic government and trading companies taking the lion's share of the profits, he by toil and danger secured over a thousand-mile trip beyond their sphere of influence.

He intercepted the Indians on their way to the French Market and sent the peltries to their rivals, the English and Dutch in New York. Where he received better prices and better goods and escaped the confiscation of a part of his goods. The young men who indulged in the illicit trade were forbid, to return to their farms or take part in the work of the colony. They stayed away from the law and lived with the Indians. Once they had tasted the sweet freedom they never wished to return to the limited life of the Habitant". Fowle

"The French population remained very small, the fur trade men married Indian women. The profits and pursuit, robbed Canada of its young men while supplying it with wealth". Lahonton

"If the intendant could have controlled them, he would have them settle down, raise a family, and work. His attempts drove them into the wilderness to run their own life. The authorities were thwarted in his effort to collect taxes. The Courieur did help in explorations, and in times of danger, they would help the threatened settlements" (Winsor/Fowle).

"An official reported in 1680 that 800 of 10,000 men had vanished from sight into the wilderness and that there was not a family of any condition or quality that had not children, brothers, uncles, or nephews among the traders" (Lahonton).

"The Frenchmen loved the freedom of the Indian country; they preferred Indian religion and culture" (Metis History). "The *coureur des bois* – Mixed blood – discovered the savages lived Christian principals rather than preaching its platitudes, and they converted to savage ideology" (Canadian History, A Distinct Viewpoint, Metis timeline – 1677, info/metis.aspx, www).

"Not all *coureurs de bois* were outlaws; many openly took their furs to the official French market places and submitted to the outrageous taxes and duties placed on the trade. In times of peace, industry and management filled the fur traders' stores. In time of war, it was his control and authority and friendship with the Indians that gave the French success. They were soldiers, sailors, gentle and common, the White men roaming the wild country. The freedom and excitement of the life were ever sufficient to render all punishment and persuasion ineffectual to prevent the evil" (Mclennon/Fowle).

Ottissippi

"The *coureur de bois*, when not a fully-fledged Indian adoptee, wore a distinctive and picturesque clothing: a blanket coat, moccasins of elk or moose, leggings of deer skin, with a cap and sash of bright red. These men were experts in the science of the woods and in diplomacy. They became important and influential leaders to whom the most difficult negotiations depended upon. The sash worn by the *coureurs des bois* was called the Assomption Sash; it was attractive, practical, and versatile, a temporary tumpline for carrying furs with the sash about the forehead, a covering, rope, emergency bridle, and saddle blanket. The traders, *coureurs de bois* and voyagers, flaunted the laws, often in collusion with authorities for mutual profit. There was much corruption in the Trade. The voyagers traveled light: moccasins, rough leggings, a blanket coat, a woolen cap, a cotton shirt, a fabric belt holding a large knife, a tobacco pouch, fire material, a robe blanket, and a spare shirt. With them, he (*coureur des bois*) challenged a continent. The French created a great empire with the help of guides, interpreters, friendly Indians, and the Metis" (Gordon Speck, Breeds and Half Breeds).

"In 1631, beaver pelts sold to traders at one livre each, who sold them to merchants at 15 livres each. This brought tremendous wealth to the French Empire. The Huron were trade middlemen, a buffer between Ojibwe and Iroquois. When smallpox ravaged the Huron, the Iroquois took advantage of this desolation and displaced the Huron in 1649. The Iroquois in New York allowing passage through the waters of the lower and upper gateways to trade at Montreal. The English at New York and the Dutch at Albany contended for the furs of the Northwest. Trying to lure the Natives away from the French with cheaper and better trade goods.

The Algonquins were paid tolls from the Huron traders for safe passage through their country. The French came to Sault Ste. Marie, usurping the Huron traders to obtain large quantities of prime pelts at cheaper prices. They became the middleman, earning great profits.

The Huron in the North encroached on the Dakota Sioux. This caused warfare between the Northern tribes" (Adapted from Rogers/Smith, 1995).

"The traditional territory of the Ojibwas-Chippewa's stretched northward from the eastern shore of Georgian Bay. Displaced by the Iroquois, they scattered, some going to Michigan, others to the St. Lawrence. They then spread northwestward, along the Northern shores of Lake Huron and Lake Superior. They migrated in the later 1600s, into Eastern Michigan once again, and settled around Saginaw, Detroit, and Southern Ontario. They occupied lands west to the Grand River drainage, around what is now Lansing" (West to Far MI).

"The Pottawatomie's, Huron, and Ottawa also returned to Lower Michigan and Southern Ontario. The Natives were allies of the French in the Great Beaver Wars. Between the English and French and other tribes who were competing for the rich fur-bearing lands. The Ottawa and Huron acted as the middlemen for the fur trade, procuring from the, back country Natives and transporting the furs to Montreal, Canada. They were the rulers of the Michigan Fur Trade. The Ojibwe were trade middlemen to the Assiniboine and Cree, North of the Great Lakes, until the Hudson's Bay Company was created in 1680 by Grossilliers and Radison.

The Iroquois went North and West to rob furs.

The Indians loved the alcohol, rum, brandy, high wine, and whiskey that the traders brought into the forests. Tens of thousands of gallons of alcohol were brought into the interior trading posts each year. It became the most sought-after trade item; this was the most essential item for trading. Trading season was a time of gift-giving, information exchange, celebration, and then trade. Trading was an exchange, more social and political than economic. The Black French were from trade. The Indians giving of trade was not economic, for profit or wealth, but of sharing. Lack of trade meant greed, hostility, and war.

To the Anishinabe, credit was an extension of gift-giving. The work shifted to the women as contact changed the traditional leadership balance. The women were fishing, hunting, tanning more hides.

One of the most successful traders was Medard Chouart, Sieur De Grossilliers. In 1654, he made his way to Lake Superior. He proceeded to work the Fur Trade for two years and, in 1656, brought his canoes loaded with rich furs to Montreal to trade the fur to the farmer at French Headquarters. The great trading center was established at Montreal. He went back for 1658, beaver season, with his brother-in-law, Pierre Espirit Radison, refusing to take government agents or missionaries, keeping his secrets for the trade. The men left without a license from the governor's agents. When they returned in 1660 with the great prize of furs, they were arrested and their furs confiscated. The governor would not stand for their ignoring his edicts. He would not listen as they advised that the best furs were obtained in the far North above Hudson's Bay.

Grosseillers and Radisson were thoroughly upset with the French authority. They made a trip to England and persuaded the king to see their plan, which he approved. The Hudson's Bay Company was born in 1670. It grew to be an amazing empire of great wealth. In the Fur Trade, at times the profits were enormous, and other times the market became saturated and the prices fell to ruin. After Grosilliers and Radissons' success became known at Montreal, many traders set out to the Northwest in search of furs.

The superior of the Jesuits sent Father Rene' Manard with the fur traders to establish a Mission among the Christian Hurons at Chequamenon Bay, Wisconsin. He was lost in the woods there and perished.

Canoes were the mode of travel; they came in any size for many uses. The average freight canoe had a capacity of four tons and six people. There were canoes made of skin, bark, and dugout. Snowshoes and toboggans in winter. All were astonishingly effective in moving people and goods long distances" (Ontario History in Maps). (some have written of 5,000 lbs. capacity for freight canoes)

"The ever-present canoe was at the door and ready for use. Canoes made a shelter for stormy weather and a place for sleeping under. The birch bark canoe was sometimes six feet wide and 35 feet long, the carrying capacity was enormous. Sixty packs of furs weighing up to 100 pounds, a half-ton of provisions for a crew of eight men. Gum pitch and bark were carried along for any necessary repairs. The canoes used thick bark from birch and elm trees, about a thumb's thickness. They were durable and lasted five to six years.

The Griffon, sailed by La Salle and Hennepin, was the first sailing ship to pass the Strait – The Detroit. She was built near Niagara in 1679. With thirty-two men onboard, when passing through the Little Round Lake above Detroit, they named her Lake Sainte Clare, after the Franciscan Nun whose day it was. On the return trip, she was lost, the men survived, returning on foot to Detroit. After, *The Griffon* voyage, no ships passed through the Detroit for nearly a century" (Farmer).

There was fierce competition between the French fur traders. And much conflict between indigenous groups due to French control. The French required a license to trade in furs. This was often ignored.

Michilimackinac was the French Indian trade connection. The Jesuits were against the trade in alcohol and complained to the king and governor about all the evils it created among the savages. It was a resort for gamblers and drunkards, a den of lawlessness and fraud of wickedness and vice. The missionaries having no influence on the traders no matter what they do, the soldiers and commandments wreak havoc. They impair both the advancement of the faith and the trade of the voyageurs. Though they had come to uphold the law, they themselves violated it on every hand. Forbidden to trade, yet they traded. The soldiers roamed the forest selling merchandise and brandy to the Indians, sharing the profits with the commandment. At the post, open liquor ships were maintained, where drunken Indians, soldiers, and *coureur de bois*, commandants, and licensed traders gambled and made merry, day and night. The latter at times surpassing the savagery, coarseness, and barbarism of their Indian allies" (Travels through Louisiana, John Reinhold Forster).

"Cloth was a luxury. Glass beads were highly valued" (Rogers/Smith).

"Father Carheil recommended a return to the pelts being brought to Montreal. The Indians had had it with the French Jesuits. They began trading with the English who had good whiskey, better prices, and better goods.

The great Indian village at the Detroit was called Teuchsa Grondie – 'Place of Many Beavers'. The whole Strait was teeming with shallow waters, and beavers created their dams, which backed the waters up, creating a haven for all wildlife. The waters being backed up also made the streams, rivers, brooks, and drains accessible to canoe traffic. The canoes needed only a few inches of draft in the shallow waters. Travel was very extensive by water.

Cadillac went to France and convinced the king to let him occupy Detroit, to stop the English from the Northwest trade route. In 1701, he established Fort Ponchetrain as a Seignorial, who rented lands to French immigrants. He was the law of the land. Illicit trade continued and Michilimackinac continued to be a Fur Trade center. The French have African Slaves in New Orleans – Quebec; they work the soil and plant the crops. The missionaries get the richest land through intrigues" (Travels through Louisiana, John Reinhold Forster).

"When the British claimed all the French Territory in 1763, with the Fall of Quebec, the policy was to encourage the Fur Trade and to discourage all monopolies by making it free to all. Only a license was required, without fee and a promise to observe all trade regulations.

Thomas Gage's letter (March 20, 1762) says, "Immediately after we became masters of this country, all monopolies were abolished and all incumbrances removed (MI Historical Collection, XIX 17).

Thomas Gage, also in 1761, recommended that the small posts be closed and the five largest be maintained with proper troops. Strong garrisons were built to protect the posts – forts, for respect to the British.

The Indians preferred their fun-loving, happy-go-lucky, ease-loving Frenchmen to the reserved, practical-minded British.

Ottissippi

The French Aristocracy, with decree upon decree, aimed to control trade and limit it and preserve it, resulting in illegal trade and defiance of unjust laws. The French were kind and treated the Indians as equals, respecting their lands, living with and marrying them.

The English treated the indigenous peoples as inferiors that could be bought with presents. Severity and harshness, were his attitude, not acknowledging the Indians' rights to the land and themselves as the invaders. Insolence and haughty British with their ill-treatment upset the Indians. The English made it free for the taking, another disaster, greed and war among traders. Eventually the Indians did accept the British as the better of two evils, with the American- British claiming their lands.

This freedom led to such competition as scheming and underselling in trade, which brought on lawlessness and bitter feuds. The wiser traders combined their interest to protect the Trade. This was the beginning of the great fur trading companies, the Northwest Company, the Mackinac Company, and the XY Company. These companies absorbed more and more of the commerce of the Fur Trade, scattering fur trading posts, agents, and clerks to every Indian hunting ground and coming into conflict with independent traders. The giving of presents to the Indians was continued from the French custom, which was an Indian custom the French adapted to. By giving presents, the traders aimed to entice them from other traders. The presents always returned furs or other goods in return" (Adapted from, Amanda Johnson, The Fur Trade, 1919).

In Utley's history of 1906, *Michigan as a Province and Territory*, he related that,"great abuses exist, for lack of regulation in the trade, in weights and measures used by the traders. Silver is so debased by copper in trinkets as to open a large field for complaint. Many traders have no principle of honesty and impose upon these poor people in a thousand ways. The distrust and disgust for the traders occasions many disputes, which frequently end in murder.

The traders being lucrative engages, with no capital to procure credit, sometimes to large amounts. Their ignorance or dishonesty occasioned failures. The adventurers decamp to some other part, where they recommence the same traffic, improving in the art of villainy.

Scottish merchants, the lords of trade, set their faces against the encouragement of any enterprise.

The Indians gladly exchanged furs for trinkets, which they thought of enormous worth. Thus, the Indian was cheated outrageously.

With a license to trade, the owners shared all the way down the line. The matter soon became little short of scandalous, the traders being forbid, to engage in traffic without a license under penalty of death. At the Office of the Farmer

General (French Montreal, New France Headquarters), The Company of 100 Associates, who were organized to handle the affairs of the colony in Quebec. They would take advantage of possession of peltries when the trader could not show a clear title to them. A vast amount of intriguing political and otherwise went on".

The woods of Michigan were literally alive with animals whose furs were of the highest value in the market. Beavers were very abundant. The choicest of all. Some of the most highly prized of the fur-bearing animals, such as the beaver, otter, fisher, and mink, who lived upon fish. The lakes and streams of both (Michigan) peninsulas swarmed with their food supply (Fish). The fox, wolverine, lynx, and black bear, in vast numbers, roamed the forests. These facts account for the early establishment at SS Marie and Michilimackinac of depots for the traffic in peltries. These points were conveniently accessible from all directions by canoe, as well as overland.

The Key of the Northwest and to it from every side, adventurous travelers gathered. A great rendezvous and of great importance to the common interest of the country, as it intercepts all trade of the Indians of the Upper Country from Hudson's Bay to Lake Superior. It affords protection to various tribes who constantly resort to it to receive presents from the commandments office. And which traders take their departure to the waters of the Northwest. They disliked the British, who had given substantial aid and encouragement to their hereditary enemies, the Iroquois.

There were great annual fairs at Montreal. Men called farmers collected duty on skins. The company of the colony in 1700 were paying a quarter of the fur prices to the farmers of the western domain.

Other trades misused the monopoly. There was great competition between the French and British traders and couriers and various Indian tribes; it was a mess.

The exchange of furs was common in every household of Detroit during the French Regime" (Ida Amanda Johnson, 1919, The Michigan Fur Trade).

"Lake Huron was called the Great Fish Lake. Fort St. Joseph was on the Detroit – the Strait – of Lake Huron and Erie. Horses, were swam across holding the bridle from a canoe, or with the horse's feet tied or hobbled together, the forefeet in one canoe and the hind in another, and transported across. These were the early ferries crossing the St. Clair River and other rivers.

The King of France granted titles of nobility and conferred seigniories upon almost any who would consent to go out to New France and undertake to occupy and improve the land, the French feudal system modified. In the days of its greatest power, every man was a lord or vassal. The fief dominant, vassals owing taxes and dues, military service, homage, and fidelity. Land ownership bestowed political, legislative, and judicial power. The feudal lord was both proprietor and absolute sovereign over his vassals, and might be a vassal himself of a superior suzerain under dukes, counts, viscounts, barons, marquises, etc., down a very long line of nobles of rank and authority of mutual support and fidelity. A mutual obligation and a transgression upon either side, worked a forfeiture of land or signatory. The system was founded on ancient custom and friendly attachment, gratitude, and honor. The sanctions of religion were employed to strengthen those ties and render them equally powerful with the relations of nature and far more so than those of political society. The slaves of peasants were subject to caprice, ambition, and avarice of their overlords. The feudal aristocracy threatened the prerogatives of the king himself. So, he asserted his authority for protection of the royal domain from unrest. Canadian feudalism produced a faint and harmless reflection of French aristocracy, simply and practically to distribute land among settlers – granted directly by the crown, answered directly to the crown, the government's only power. The people were to clear the land; it was overrun with young noblesse, who could not work and their families were starving.

Cadillac could not get a title as a noble but was a simple sieur with his signatory and all its responsibilities and appurtenances to look after. He had large expenses he paid himself. The Company was to have exclusive trading rights, hampering him until after three or four years when he was given these privileges. The king annulled his rights to property in 1716; he was treated shamefully and died a few years later.

Grossilliers and Radison had their huge load of furs confiscated at Montreal; they were arrested for not having a license. These Frenchmen went to the English King and were awarded Prince Rupert's land, a quarter of North America from Hudson's Bay North. They became the Hudson's Bay Company, having absolute sovereignty over laws, justice, war, and peace treaties. An empire, an imperial domain of absolute monarchy, the most gigantic monopoly in history. The French and other men went to stop them forming the Northern Company. Many other companies tried to gain the market.

The French and English Trade wars in Europe and border raids in the Northwest and St. Lawrence made peace and harmony impossible. The French occupying land into Ohio and Pennsylvania and to the Mississippi, English soil by charter of the king. French traders were sending peltry from along the Mississippi and the Northwest to Montreal via the Upper Ottawa River route. When the Iroquois heard this, their wrath was fired. They went on the attack into the Illinois country. The Illinois refused to send furs to Albany, passing through the Iroquois to Fort Orange – Albany – and down the Hudson to the Dutch.

There were several practicable routes for the traders to reach this section - East Michigan and Western Ontario. The original and most noted one was the Ottawa River, Lake Nipissing, and Georgian Bay, Ontario. It was the main route between Huron Country and the trading interests on the Lower St. Lawrence. It was separated from the predatory tribes near Lake Ontario. The second route was by the St. Lawrence and Lake Ontario to the Trent River, Lake Simcoe, and Georgian Bay. The Iroquois used this route in forays against the Hurons; this was one of the best routes. The third was from present Toronto and thence to Lake Simcoe and Georgian Bay. The fourth was by the head of Lake Ontario, the Grand River to Lake Erie and Thames Rivers, and Lake St. Clair. This became a very important line of traffic except during the time of open hostilities with the Iroquois. It was the safest and easiest route to reach the Great Saginon – Saginaw – fur-producing region. The fifth was by the Niagara River but was seldom used for valuable goods because of the proximity to the Iroquois in Western New York" (Western Historical Co.).

"Sault Saint Marie was the grand thoroughfare of Indian commerce for the Upper countries as far as the Arctic Circle. All the fur trade of the Northwest was compelled to pass through it. The Hurons were also bypassing the Iroquois, the furs being taken to Montreal on the Northern Ottawa River route until 1649, when the Iroquois decimated the Hurons.

THE METIS

The Metis were the children born of White men to Native maidens. They were social outcasts and considered outlaws, though the Native communities loved and cared for all their children. The sons of French settlers who built shanties in the Upper Detroit, the St. Clair and Black River region, married Natives and Metis who trace both to early Detroit trade and also to the Michilimackinac Fur Trade circa 1752. The Upper Detroit Metis families are recorded as trading across the river in Canada at the Southern Sauble River, Port Franks area, and Goderich area prior to 1820. In 1822 at Bayfield, Ontario, these were described as being mixed-blood traders, from Detroit and the Northwest.

The Little Red River at Goderich was a frequent calling place for fur traders. The Hudson's Bay service had huts upon it of a few half-breeds, as well as Chippewa wigwams. The names of these traders are Belhmeurs, Deschamps, Duchenes, Caselets - Cosley, Andres, Cameron, Tranchemontagnes, Cadottes, Beausoleil - Bosley, De Lamorandiere, Gonneville - Granville, Lange - Longe, Martin, Normandin, Sayer, and others. At Goderich, a log house beautifully situated on a bold hill overlooking the harbour, called the Castle, and a dozen or so log cabins inhabited by French and half-breeds. Customs were adopted from both cultures, but neither was fully embraced" (Historic Saugeen Metis, Patsy McArthur/B.C. Farrand. Upper Detroit to Saugeen, Lower Lake Huron's Metis and Trade, Upper Region of the Detroit River, Lake Huron Watersheds, Bruce Peninsula. Inver Huron Learning Center, Southampton, Ontario. 2013).

"These men became important to governments and negotiations. In 1767 alone, over 700 men in 121 canoes entered the Great Lakes with over 38,964 sterling in merchandise. There were considerably more illegal traders, such as Ramsay, who had no permission at all to trade.

Ojibwe came to the post naked and destitute of everything, having sold their skins at Toronto for rum. Regulations and licensing was ill-suited to the circumstances, clogging the trade with useless and vexatious restrictions rather than to remove the evils of which complaint had been made. The regulations were ineffective, and illegal trade practices continued beyond the canon of the Forts" (Schmaltz).

In 1763, the Indians under Pontiac attacked all 11 British posts within their country. Mackinaw was the resort of the European fur traders.

"Johnson was in charge, of the Indian relations, in the Great Lakes area. His hands were often tied by colonial governors who were petitioned by the Fur Trade lobby" (Schmaltz).

"Liquor was killing off the young men more effectively than war, with no expense to the government in loss of soldiers and money. Violent acts were common, including murder and the Indians killing their own people in a drunken state. The vast majority of cases involving even Whites, never saw the courts. The highest officials in the Indian Department made their fortunes through trade in spirits. Trade goods consisting almost entirely of rum were common. A gallon of rum was traded for one beaver skin. There was great fraud. Each band of Indians and each trader determined the law or lawlessness among themselves. Crimes and retaliation went unchecked" (Schmaltz).

"In the eighteenth century, cloth and ready-made clothing were the most important trade item" (D. Anderson, 1991/Cleland). "Hundreds of tons of maple sugar were exported in trade" (Cleland).

"The British thought it best to leave the country to the Indians alone, and the fur-bearing animals who made their profits" (Utley).

See "The Quebec Act" below.

"Two hundred thousand skins annually were traded under the British at Detroit. There were numerous gaudily decorated canoes" (Burton, The City of Detroit, 1922).

"The methods used to trap and hunt these animals was determined by their varying habits. The otter, which fished at night, was speared by the Indians. The muskrat was dug out of its nest and shot. The mink, were stabbed or clubbed to death. The fox was trapped and the deer hunted. In exchange for his pelts, the Indian received many necessities of life such as guns, powder, metal traps, knives, brass rings, silver arm bands, crosses, beads, wampum – shells, cloth, dyes, shirts, blankets, needles, tools etc. and the staple whiskey and rum. Skins are sold for wares which are fearfully expensive, reported the Moravians. Furs and skins were in abundance and were used for household purposes. Beds made of them, clothing. Thousands and thousands of skins were held in warehouses and in dwelling houses in Detroit, and the people used them for all sorts of purposes. When the Fur Market flooded in the old world, social laws were enacted in France to force the greater use of furs, hats, clothes, and muffs were worn on the streets of Paris.

Madame Framboise, half-Ottawa, became a great trader taking over her husband's trading posts in the Grand River Valley. The post in Grand Rapids was the first building in Kent County, (Michigan). She was very successful and later retired to Michiliimackinac. Other Indian women collected furs. The women also worked in the trade in many ways, including trapping, hunting, guiding, tanning, etc.

TRADERS

"British Captain Patrick Sinclair built Fort Sinclair at now St. Clair in 1763 to 1764. He traded with the Indians and supplied the other forts in the Upper Great Lakes. He built a sawmill, supplying lumber to Detroit. He also protected the waterways for the safe travel of the fur traders. Some of the items for sale and traded at the Fort Sinclair Trading Post were; lots of rum, tobacco, powder and shot, flint, fabric, sugar, salt, corn, nuts, wheat, bread, turnips, tallow for candles, shingles, horse shoes, pork, wheels for carts, canoes, trunks, barrels, needles, combs, thread, silver broaches, earbobs, scissors, looking glasses, axe, fire steels, knives, shoes, moccasins, stocking, socks, ribbon, blankets, Jew Harps - Jaw Harps, buffalo shoes, gift paper, quills, leggings, soap, nails, putty, and boards. The fur and animal trades were elk, bear, doeskins, fox, raccoons, mink, wolf, muskrats, beavers, caribou, porcupine, martin, otter, fisher, cats, ducks, and fish. Other items that were traded for goods were apples, pumpkins, lard, beans, eggs, cranberries, geese, salt pork, and maple sugar" (Adapted from, Mayhew. A complete list is found in the book, Fort Sinclair, Mayhew, 2003).

"Some of the goods available for trade at Fort Sinclair Trading Post in 1783 were fabric, tobacco, rum, canoes, powder, shot, sugar, salt, mittens, shirts, bed lace, ribbon, blankets, fishing equipment, cod lines, chain, nets, trunks, barrels, bridles, potatoes, venison, pipes, twine, and chalk.

In 1785, Antoine Morass bought sundries at the St. Clair Trading Post. He began operating Baby's mill in 1784.

"Louis Bonvien was a large trader" (Mayhew 2003).

"The Negro Baptiste Point Du Sable from Haiti managed the Pinery at Fort Sinclair. He replaced Francis Bellcour and was fair to the Indians. He was educated in France and a farmer, carpenter, and business man. He became the founder of Chicago in 1779" (Mayhew, 2003).

Daniel Boone in 1769 stated that the herds of buffalo – *bizhiki* – were larger than the cattle, and most of the roads and trails followed the beaten buffalo paths. He also sold large quantities of buffalo meat for the trade. He was a land speculator and surveyor, at one time owning most of Kentucky and Tennessee with Henderson.

The Trade was mutually profitable and mutually destructive. Traders were sources of trouble between the English and Indians. Unscrupulous, without principles, they aroused hatred and the ire of savages" (Burton, City of Detroit, 1701 – 1922, 1922).

Francis Parkman stated, "The European lost his refinements, but gained independence, self-sustaining energy, and power of action. The Indian in turn gained material advantage but lost his own independence by becoming dependent on the White man's goods.

Trading posts were built throughout the country of the Northwest along major waterways. The population in Southeast Michigan in 1773 was 1285, with half living around the fort. In 1796, the population was 2,215.

Great company gains killed the competition, there were endless difficulties. They would crush those they could not buy. Underselling by the best traders created hostile relations with the Indians to destroy the others' trade.

Rix Robinson, was a sutler, to the U.S. troops. He was a great friend and politician and friend of the Indians. He married an Ottawa woman. He was respected, fair and honest to all. The Indians named him Wavaohase - Marten, known for cunning and resourcefulness.

Rix Robinson and Madame Framboise, an Indian woman, were large traders with the American Fur Co. Rix Robinson was agent and sales manager, he assumed and managed at Madam La Framboise retirement, her 21 trading posts along the Grand River. He was a judge, senator, and member of the State Constitutional Convention, as well as a friend of the Indians, a peacemaker, and negotiator with the Government. The traders paved the way for future settlers.

The St. Martins were an old, respectable trading family at Quebec. John Baptiste St. Martin came to Detroit in 1740 and served as an interpreter of the Huron language, his services highly desired during the Pontiac Conspiracy of 1763. He married Marianne Navarre; De Tonty and De Bellestre were his uncles.

James Abbott at Detroit was an independent and large trader in the Northwest.

Judge James Abbott – The Earl of May – at Detroit was the superintendent for the American Fur Company. He came to Detroit in 1768. His business name was Abbott Fur and Mercantile. He had a substantial household including two slaves. He died in 1800.

James Abbott was one of the most active merchants in Detroit, being the first English trader to open a post at Detroit after 1760 when the British Americans won the French War. In 1778, his trade goods were confiscated for violating the regulations restricting the sale of liquor to the Indians. In 1780, he was given a grant of land by the Pottawatomi and Chippewa Indians on the Detroit River and on Lake St. Clair. Abbott traveled to Micilimackinac, Green Bay, Prarie Duchien, Ft. Wayne, Ouitanon, and Vincennes. Abbott's sons, Robert and James Jr., both were leading merchants in Detroit after James Abbott Sr.'s death in 1800.

Robert Abbott, son of James Abbott Jr. of Dublin, Ireland, was born at Detroit. He is said to be the first English-speaking man who opened business at the old post of Detroit. Father and son both were early fur traders and were known from Detroit to Mackinaw, and then to Chicago. His business connections came next in importance to the Campeau's" (Western Historical Co.).

James Abbott Jr. and Robert Abbott, sons of James Abbott, were also agents for the American Fur Company.

Edward Campau a trader of this district, Southeast Michigan. Henry Conner, a trader and faithful interpreter at treaty negotiations. Gabriel Godfroy was a well-known extensive trader. Mr. Jacob Harson in 1778 received 3,000 acres from the Chippewa Indians. He was a gunsmith and fur trader from Holland. He owned 47 books.

In 1780, Duperon Baby, British Indian agent and fur trader, owned a sawmill at now Marysville, Michigan on Baby Creek, now Bunce Creek. He was granted 57,600 acres of land by the Indians, from Sinclair's Trading Post and Fort to Lake Huron and up Black River for 15 miles. He also owned land on the now Canadian Side of the St. Clair River.

Ottissippi

At the end of the Revolution to the Jay's Treaty in 1783, which marked the end of the English control of Detroit. The English monopoly of the fur trade, continued in the area, of Detroit and stretched through the Lower Peninsula to Wisconsin and Illinois through Western Ohio, Indiana, and beyond, was being challenged by the Americans. The English in 1796 left Detroit after exploiting the trade as looters.

Larger ships began to be used to transport goods and supplies. Ships ranging from 12 to 96 tons were used on the Montreal to Detroit trips before and after the Revolution in 1776. Private vessels were banned from the lakes during the war. The English drastically reduced the amount of goods being shipped. Only government shipping was allowed, which proved to be insufficient. Shipping was necessary for importation of supplies, trade goods, and the exportation of the furs collected and was also important in supplying the far western posts.

The fur trade was moving West to Lake Superior country. Detroit became an important supply depot for corn, pork, and flour. Sloops had been built in Detroit in 1769 and 1770. The prospect of a thriving ship-building industry was being impeded by the English restrictions.

The merchants at Detroit, sent letters attacking the policy and urging the use of private vessels for trade. John Askin, a prominent Detroit trader who later became important in Canadian government, stated the difficulty in fulfilling contracts. That year Colonel Arent DePeyster took Askin's ship into service of the king. Objections were made to favoritism on the official's part and that everyone was suffering for abuses of a few traders. There was a great deal of opposition during the war, but the loudest objections came when the restrictions continued afterward. In 1784, the merchants expected a return to the use of private vessels. There was no relaxation in the wartime rules until 1789 for the Upper Lakes.

James McGill, one of the wealthiest merchants in Canada and founder of McGill University, in 1785 urged the necessity of rapid transportation of goods to Detroit before winter set in. He also warned that the traders would lose interest in the English merchants and seek other markets for their goods and services. In 1786, Todd and McGill in Montreal wrote to John Askin, saying they believed Governor Carleton would soon allow private vessels back on the lakes. The pressure finally effected change: In 1785, private vessels were allowed from Montreal to Niagara. In 1787, they were permitted on Lake Ontario. By 1789, private ships reappeared throughout the Great Lakes.

The Treaty of Paris in 1783 allowed Americans to enter the waterways without hostilities from the Mississippi East and through the Great Lakes.

Detroit and the other Western posts were now in American hands, though the British did not cede Detroit until 1796. The merchants reacted immediately. Since 1760, the merchant group had acquired and kept enormous influence in Canadian affairs; they became the most self-conscious and assertive of all social classes. Why, they argued, had England granted so large a cession of land? Why had the English negotiators failed to consult the merchants before making such an illegal move, and how were the diplomats now going to correct their mistake?

Lord Shelbourne justified the treaty as necessary to gain the friendship and gratitude of the Americans. He also thought the English were not losing a great deal in ceding the Northwest. There was great ignorance of the vastness of the lands and boundaries. The merchants were hardly willing to give up this territory. They believed that two-thirds of the furs from Canada came from the region now in American hands and predicted the end of the Canadian Fur Trade.

One historian wrote; there are times when catastrophes in life are so great they cannot be possibly duplicated. This seemed one such time. The merchants realized that the Americans would be unable to compete with them favorably, even if the posts were evacuated; they were still shocked at what they felt was a sellout.

Henry Hamilton, Lt. Governor of Canada, urged that the wilds were to be looted of furs before the Americans can take possession. Shelbourne talked to the merchants of free trade, saying there was nothing to hinder the English from passing goods over all or part of America. The merchants were not impressed; they remained advocates of mercantilism, opposing the loss of valuable fur trading area and hesitating to anger the Indians. Fearing reprisals, as in 1763, for the betrayal of their allies who had not been informed of the final boundary of the Treaty of Paris in 1783. The English had not only ceded their claims to the Ohio Valley, but had ceded those of the Indians as well.

Cession of the territory proved to be entirely different than actual abandonment of it. The English continued to occupy Detroit and insured control of the trade south of the lakes as well. The Spanish were unable to bring goods cheaply enough to compete to procure trade goods, and they were forced to barter furs with the English traders.

The Treaty of Paris in 1783 called for the evacuation of Detroit by the English. Article 7 stated that the posts were to be evacuated at all convenient speed. This, to the English, meant 13 years. The nature of the fur trade with vast distances to cover meant two or three years for a return on an original investment from Montreal; goods were shipped to Detroit, then sent out to the traders wintering with the Indians. The traders returning in the spring to Detroit with furs. The furs were then sent to Montreal and on to London.

During the war, the whole procedure had been interrupted, causing transportation to be impeded and causing an accumulation of delays and debts. Due to these factors, there was confusion as to a convenient time for evacuation. The Americans offered a grace period of three years to evacuate the posts but allowed for reciprocal use of the waterways into the Indian country. This offer was ignored by the English.

For the next 13 years, the English troops held control of Detroit and other posts Northwest of the Ohio River to the Mississippi. Americans moving into the area were stopped and turned back. The English and Indian Alliance prevented American entrance into the area ceded by the English at the 1783 Treaty of Paris. English traders continued to hold absolute monopoly of the fur trade and benefited from a prosperous era of trade until the outbreak of war on the frontier and in Europe disrupted trading again. The English took advantage of the Ohio country for profit and mischief.

The English claiming there had been no orders for evacuation received from London. The main legal point for the English retention of the posts was the Americans failure to repay the Loyalists who had evacuated to Canada and the repayment of British merchants after the War. The merchants of London, Montreal, and Detroit pressured the government to retain the posts and exploit the Fur Trade of Detroit. In addition, they feared the anger of the Indians which may have been turned against the English with their departure to the Canadian side.

The Americans under George Washington in 1784 were extremely eager and anxious to gain Detroit and the Indian Trade. Detroit was the key to the trade of the Great Lakes area, including the trade south of the lakes.

Detroit traders who had been stymied by years of warfare and Indian unrest began to reestablish trade connections weakened by the turmoil of the past decade. The leading Detroit traders were Alexander and William Macomb, William Robertson, and John Askin. The merchants felt they would need at least five years to prepare their withdrawal and to wind up their affairs.

Saginaw Bay and all along the Coast were numerous rivers and inlets which ships could use for shelter and the means of exploring and carrying commerce into the interior. The Canadian Coast had few such advantages. The loss of Michigan would also force the English into competition with American manufacturers. American goods could easily be smuggled into Canada, eliminating the British Market there. To forestall the American attempts to seize Detroit, British Crown Loyalists settled there, seeking an asylum from the persecution they are subjected to in the States.

The English created two great trading firms: The Northwest Company and the Mackinaw Company. The members were mostly British Scotchmen. These companies were chartered in 1808.

Archibald Lyons, trapper in Macomb and St. Clair County, moved to Saginaw.

John Riley was a Metis or half-breed. His father from New York married an Indian princess from Saginaw. John was a great spirit for the Ojibwe Indians; he was Chief of the Black River bands, his group known as the Riley band. He kept a trading post at Black River and St. Clair River in now Port Huron, Michigan, near the corner of Water St. and Military St. His home was a great meeting place for the Indians. John served the U.S. government as a scout, interpreter, and special assignment man. His services were essential to negotiating treaties with the Indians and keeping the peace. See "Chapter 9: Biographies of Indian Chiefs".

Louis Beaufait was a friend to all and a great peacemaker, in the trader's circle.

Ver Hoeff and Jasperson had the largest general store on the St. Clair River, Peter Brakeman later bought the mercantile firm. Peter Brakeman was a fur trader who had a trading post at Algonac, Michigan. Peter arrived at Detroit with seven cents in his pockets in 1824. He worked harvesting for General Cass and then came up river to Point Du Chien, now Algonac. He taught school on Harsens Island and worked in the first store opened there. He became a partner and then bought out the partner. He married Nancy Brown of Cottrellville, daughter of William Brown and Martha Thorn Brown. Peter was a colonel of the Michigan militia, justice of the peace, and township clerk. He carried on a large trade with the Indians on Walpole Island; he spoke their language and was a great friend of them. He went on to live at Port Huron, building the first dock and warehouse on the river there. He then moved to Willow Creek and started Huron City in 1845 in the Thumb of Michigan on the east Michigan Lake Shore as a lumberman and held offices in Port Huron, Michigan and Sanilac County, which was later Huron County.

William Brown kept a public house on the St. Clair River; he was called Uncle Billy Brown. He came in 1816 and was about the first settler in the county. His place was on the river below Marine City.

Malcolm Cameron's store east of the St. Clair River was the great trading center at the north part of the Strait on the Canadian side.

Joseph Campau, a trader in real estate at Detroit and many commercial enterprises, was among the Michigan men of greatness, having much influence in all business affairs. His French military ancestors came with Cadillac to establish Detroit. Marquis J. Campeau may be the first White settler of Michigan. He built a home beyond the fort. He erected the Catholic church near his home. Joseph Campau's great grandfather was Jaques Campau; they were part of the Family Compact, French government. Joseph Campau is Michigan's first millionaire.

Barney Campau, nephew of Joseph and Jacques Campau, was an honest and trusted trader.

Louis DeQuindre, a trader, lived in St. Clair County for many years.

"Jacob Graveraet lived at Harsens Island. He was a silversmith and gunsmith trader, a son-in-law of Jacob Harsen, who married a daughter of Kiskawko" (Western Historical Co.).

"The Miami Company was a Fur Trade conglomerate that traded from the Hudson River to Iowa.

Henry Nelson, Indian trader of St. Clair, moved to the Saginaw District in 1820 and then to Isabella County.

The Hudson's Bay Company was also in the region with posts for trade in Georgian Bay.

Saginaw had many traders.

Edward Petit was a fur trader in the area on both sides of the St. Clair River. At 15 years old, he was well equipped to trade in furs. Being the first White child born in now Port Huron, Michigan, he was raised hunting and fishing with the Indians and learned their language as well as his parents' French and the English of the new settlers. He took supplies of shot, powder, calicoes, and blue broadcloth, one and three-fourths yards of which was called a blanket. The Indians gave for them maple sugar and furs – otter, beaver, mink, marten, and bear skins" (History of SCC, Western Historical Co.).

"Edward was employed with G. and W. Williams and had a post on the bend of the Cass River in the Thumb of Michigan.

Patrice Reaume, trader among the Huron, St. Clair, and Raisen districts, was appointed factor of the American Fur Company near Pontiac and then the Tittabawasee and Saginaw" (Western Historical Co.).

"Leon St. George was a trader among the Hurons and Chippewas.

Francois Tremble was a well-known fur trader from Montreal to Detroit and Saginaw.

Whittemore and James Knaggs were among the first White men, North of the Huron. Captain Knaggs was an unflinching patriot. During the War of 1812, he was one of the Indian interpreters, spoke freely six or seven of their languages, together with French and English, and exercised great influence over many warrior tribes. Guide to General Winchester at the Raisen, he was present at the death of Tecumseh" (Western Historical Co.).

"Peter Gruette, Francois Corbin, John Harsen, Michael Medor, Joseph Benoit, Leon and Louis Tremble, with other traders, hunters, trappers, and interpreters, who established temporary posts on the Clinton, Flint, Shiawasee, and Black River in Michigan. Made this country a rendezvous and won the respect of the American pioneers.

Christian Clemons, John Stockton, and General Brown are early pioneers of the State. James May came in 1778. He was Chief Justice, Marshall of Michigan Territory. Angus McIntosh was a factor of the Northwest Company.

Albany firms set up in Detroit. James Henry operated the Point Tannery, selling to Jacob Astor in New York.

The English created two great trading firms: The Northwest Company and the Mackinaw Company. The members were mostly British Scotchmen. These companies were chartered in 1808.

In 1808, a whole swarm of Yankee traders arrived at Detroit, mainly from Boston. Many fur buyers were bankrupt. The traders going into the wilderness and the Detroit merchants were deeply in debt. The traditional hunting grounds were systematically destroyed, and the merchants turned to the Christian Trade: the sale of goods to settlers. The Fur Trade was moving further West, and Detroit became increasingly important as a supply depot. At Malden during the War of 1812, the British destroyed trade goods of the United States Government, and there was no trade in furs for a time.

Suspicion and hostility stemming from technological and cultural differences, as well as feelings of superiority, have permeated relations between Native American and Non-Indian in North America.

John Askin was the most active of the traders, supplying traders, collecting furs, operating a shipping company on the Great Lakes, growing and marketing agricultural products for supply of the fur trade, and land speculation. He had first settled at Mackinac in the Indian trade and land speculation. He moved to Detroit in 1780 and remained until 1802, when he moved to Canada. His contacts and business dealings extended throughout the old Northwest. He also had contracts with Montreal, London, and Pittsburgh. Many chief traders and clerks were former British subjects, now Americanized.

Askin contracted to supply 600 bushels of corn to the Northwest Company in 1789 for three years at two dollars per bushel. This was later raised to 1,200 bushels per year. In 1786, when the Moravian missionaries left their location near Mt. Clemons, Askin purchased the land and grew corn and potatoes there. John Cornwell was sent by him to ship lumber, flour, and pork to Askin. Askin traded at Albany, Michilimackinac, and Detroit and across the river in Petite Cote. He supplied everything, having a diverse commercial enterprise. He also traded Native slaves, including women and children.

The practice of forming partnerships was common among traders. Many formed small and large companies to overcome transportation and credit difficulties. These small companies usually met with little or no success. Some larger trading companies were active in the area. The largest and most influential was the Northwest Company. In 1783, several private Montreal traders combined forces to more easily exploit the far western trade and formally established the company four years later. This company controlled over half of the Canadian Market. The company operated mainly north of Lake Superior, and furs were sent to Mackinac and Detroit for repacking, inspection, and transportation to Montreal. At Detroit, Angus McIntosh, a prominent trader, acted as agent for the company operations. The Michilimackinac Company organized about the same time as the Northwest Company and had many of the same partners. Its focus was within the United States. Detroit supplying the agricultural products for the trade: corn, flour, pork, rum, etc. After the Americans arrived in 1796, the company declined due to competition, mainly from John Jacob Astor. Astor buying the company in 1811, and forming the Southwest Company.

MacIntosh was the Chief Representative of the Northwest Company in this area. He owned large buildings on the Canadian side of the Detroit River. This was the center for distribution of trade goods and a distillery for whiskey.

The Northwest Company had 23 shareholders and 2,000 clerks, guides, interpreters, and boatmen or voyageurs. Their headquarters were at Montreal, Canada" (Fuller).

"In 1779, Major A. S. Depeyster bought 600 bushels of corn from the Indians at Saguina. The lands were very fertile; there were wetlands and swampy muck areas.

Trade follows the line of low cost and profitable markets. A trader would outfit himself with a Montreal merchant's trade goods and had no compunction about selling his furs on the Mississippi or at Albany, New York. There was cutthroat competition. Traders began organizing large groups of trusted partners" (Fuller).

"In the early 1800s, Detroit had three tanneries at Point Industry. Hides of deer, calf, sheep, hogs, horse, bear, and dog, were being tanned for the trade.

Pirates were very active throughout the waterways, stealing furs and other goods being transferred.

The American Fur Company was established in 1808 by John Jacob Astor. Seven-eighths of the traders were absorbed by the American Fur Co. Robert Stuart and Ramsay Crooks were representatives of the American Fur Co. at Mackinac. The traders gathered in July to trade with the Indians. Furs of beaver, martin – sable, mink, otter, fox, moose, elk, bear, buffalo, wolverine, badger, and wildcat were traded. The American Fur Co. had 400 clerks and traders and 2,000 voyageurs. At these summer trading fairs, there was dancing, drinking, gaming, fighting, bullies, and truculent men from the north with feathers" (Charles Moore, History of MI).

"In 1834, Astor sold the American Fur Co. to Ramsay Crooks and his associates Robert Stuart and Rix Robinson.

The Indians were the White man's dupes, exchanging costly furs for mere trifles, had undergone an education. Articles of inferior quality were contemptuously called American. The best quality was from the British at Michilimackinac. In July and August, thousands of people gathered there to trade" (Farrel).

"At Sandusky and the Maumee River in now Ohio, the Indians traded with the colony of Pennsylvania traders" (Rogers/Smith, 1995, Aboriginal Ontario).

"The Miami's Co. was a group of six leading Detroit trading firms, organized in 1786 to control the Wabash and Maumee Rivers. James Abbott, John Askin, Angus McIntosh, and the firms of Meldrum and Park, Leith and Shepherd, Sharp and Wallace. Traders were hired by the company to go into the Miami country to exploit trade. Gabriel Hunot was hired in 1788 to go to the Huron River and its dependencies. For this he received 750 livres in wages, board, and lodging. The amount of credit to be extended was not to exceed 100 beavers. The Detroit merchants, traders, and clerks traveled west to Chicago, Milwaukee, Kaskaskia, and Cahokia on the Mississippi, East of St. Louis, Missouri, in search of furs. The competition from Detroit traders coming into the country belonging to the United States created more problems.

The trader endured untold toil and privation, his life was constantly in danger. The weather was the most frustrating with rain, sleet, snow, and cold. The credit system often caused great problems. The trade goods were sent from London to Montreal to Detroit and into the wilderness, all on credit. The reliance on credit opened the door to much abuse. Some resorted to collecting their own debts.

The merchants also used arbitration boards set up among themselves to solve disputes. Often the most prominent Detroit merchants decided local affairs. In a district with little legal jurisdiction, the role of the more prominent members of the community in deciding justice was quite important. This problem was solved when Detroit was incorporated into the Government of Canada in 1788, with the creation of the District of Hesse. A Court of Common Pleas was established at Detroit. Henry Hay summed up the unpredictable nature of the fur trade from Detroit saying, 'In short, I cannot term it in a better manner than calling it a rascally scrambling trade.'

Friendly relations with the Indian tribes was essential to the profit and safe conduct of the fur trade. The Miami's, Wyandot's, Ottawa, Chippewa-Ojibwe, Wea – Ouiatanon, Shawnee, Piankashaw, Pottawatomi, and Delaware were some of the Indians in contact with the forest runners – traders.

The French were often the link between the English trader from Detroit and the Indian of the forest. The French maintained a close working relationship and were the middlemen, along with the Ottawa and Wyandott – Huron – traders.

In times of war, stopping the trade as the Indians were on the 'war path', and not in the forest hunting, the traders often lost everything, including their lives. There was great competition and debauch in the trade, fighting among themselves and slanderous conduct. The Indians complained of James Abbott's tactics and disrespect for English officials. This was an accepted part of the trade, and the traders held no grudge against Abbott.

William Robertson was a prominent trader who came to Detroit in 1782. Employed as John Askin's secretary, he soon became a partner and then a prominent trader in Detroit and Canada.

The Macomb brothers, William and Alexander, prospered during the Revolution, supplying the military. William Edgar was also a partner. They engaged in real estate, banking, and selling general merchandise and the Indian trade. At one time in 1781, the firm brought 12,132 deer; 9,483 raccoon; 413 bear; 682 cats and fox; 16 elk; and 3 wolf pelts to Detroit. In August of 1784, they reported having 1,000 packs of furs after shipping out many. William Macomb at one time owned 26 slaves.

Meldrum and Park began in 1783 and was still in operation on the arrival of the Americans in 1796. Park then moved across the Detroit River to Petite Cote, below Sandwich – Windsor, Ontario, refusing to become an American citizen, although the firm continued its operations until 1803. Park had a great deal of influence as justice of the peace at Detroit and captain of the militia at Sandwich. Meldrum was commissioner of the District of Hesse, this included East Michigan, and was created in 1788 under British Canada. Meldrum remained in Detroit after the American occupation in 1796 and lived until 1827. The firm sold to all the French, British, American, and Natives.

Leith and Shepherd were leading traders at Detroit during the 1780s and 1790s. George Leith was at Miami Town, Fort Wayne, Indiana, where he carried on extensive trade with Detroit. The firm became Leith, William Shepherd, and William Duff, after Thomas Shepherd drowned on a return trip to England. The firm continued trading in the Maumee country as late as 1796.

John Porteus, from Scotland, came to Detroit in 1762 and later traded between Albany and Mackinac.

George Ironside was a prominent Detroit merchant from Scotland. He traded on the Auglaize River near now Defiance, Ohio during the late 1780s and early 1790s. A member of the British Indian Service, he was forced to leave the Miami country by American military advances and settled at Amherstburg, across the river from Detroit.

Other traders were Richard Pollard, Sharp and Wallace, Graverat and Visger, Mark and Conant, Forsyth and Co., Joseph Campau, and James McGregor.

Financial success was not a prerequisite for social, political, or economic influence. The fluctuation of fortunes of the fur trade were ever known. Many traders lost their fortune to aiding the American Government for control of the country. The social companionship of the trade between Leith, Henry Hay, George Ironside, James Abbott, and others was celebrated with drinking wine.

Sites on the English side of the river, in Canada, had already been selected as early as 1782. There were plans to build a town opposite Detroit. Amherstburg was selected as the name, and it was guarded on the North by Fort Malden. This post was near the mouth of the Detroit River at Lake Erie, and such was able, to command the entrance to the river. Many Detroit merchants desired to move to the town, and by 1798, fifty lots were granted. Many prominent Detroiters crossed the river.

The towns of Assumption, the original seat of government for the Western District since 1783, and Sandwich, newly purchased land from the Indians, became towns. Peter Russel, Governor of Canada, stated the British merchants of Detroit, having asked him to give them a town where they may reside and carry on trade: Ere, we lost a very extensive commerce. The merchants acquired several lots to allow trading with the Indians, who were crossing the river to the Canadian side. Many traders also kept connections in Detroit and continued to live there but maintained their English citizenship.

The American citizens complained of the large number of British citizens at Detroit. Leading American merchants, such as James Abbott Jr., James May, Patrick McNiff, and Antoine Beaubien, expressed fear at placing too much confidence in Detroit's militia. Trade became sporadic due to constant warfare.

The transfer of the posts to the Americans seemed very peaceful, the new government taking control of an area populated by foreign residents and unfriendly Indians. There was a group in the city who were friendly to the American cause; among these were George McDougal and William Macomb. MacDougal being accused of planning to kill Matthew Elliot, English Indian agent, and Macomb, condemned by the English for his pro-American feelings.

Others were not content with the arrival of the Americans. 'The appearance is not agreeable to many who have long breathed under the British government,' declared William Park. No British, were allowed, to hold a position of trust in Wayne County, which then covered a great area. The Americans felt that the Indians were their enemy, and the English made him so.

One of the most able American traders was William Burnett, the first American trader in the Northwest. Burnett came from New Jersey after the Revolution, settled at St. Joseph near Niles, Michigan, and married Kawkenee, the daughter of a Pottawatomi chief, assuring his trade in the area.

John R. Williams was one of the most important American traders. A member of the Detroit Board of Trustees and captain of the artillery during the War of 1812. He later became associate judge of the court, adjutant general of

Michigan Territory, author of the city charter, and the first mayor of Detroit. Williams first came to Detroit at age 14 to work in the store of his uncle, Joseph Campau. John R. Street in Detroit, Michigan is named for this man.

The Williams brothers were successful and forbade ill treatment of the Indians. Their company was called the Shiawasee Exchange, or the Williams Exchange.

The population of Detroit in 1820 was 1,442. By 1821, all Detroit trade was in America". The above paragraphs of Detroit fur trade were adapted from David Farrel's 1865 dissertation on The Detroit Fur Trade, Master's Thesis, U O Wisc., Milwaukee/Michigan Archives, Lansing, MI.

"The Le Claires were on the St. Joseph River about 1780.

The Navarres and Baptistes were in Monroe County, where Frenchtown was founded in about 1784.

There were, still earlier trading camps (French) in St. Clair County" (Fuller).

"The average trading post consisted of two buildings. One story in height, each were 16 by 18 feet with a covered hall measuring 16 by 19 feet. Located between them as a meeting place for the Indians. In the rear was a place for the reception of furs, about 30 feet in length. The Indians held some of their wildest festivities near the posts on the banks of the waterways" (Marantette papers, Michigan Archives).

"One of the early Yankees was William Burnett, who married a daughter of a Pottawatomi chief. He was regarded as a trespasser in the territory, but the British respected his marriage.

The British – English – employed the French agents when they gained the country of the Northwest. The Indians were plundered without mercy. The lawless White men ruined the Natives' women with whiskey, his physical and spiritual wellbeing. The Indians were irritated by the English aggressiveness on their lands.

Traders boasted that whiskey is legal tender for the Red Men. Some traded furs for a small drink. Pokagon, 1899, Harpers Magazine vol. 98

Pontiac's rebellion was from the Atlantic to the Mississippi, taking 9 of 12 British fort-posts in one day. Detroit was under siege for 18 months. The French pioneers fled to the forts for protection.

The Treaty of Paris in 1783 resulted from these raids on the English. All the lands north of the Ohio Valley and west of the Allegheny's to the Mississippi were the exclusive possession and control of the Indians, reserved as his domain.

THE QUEBEC ACT

The outcome was the Quebec Act of 1774. The British now exacerbated the colonists. The Northwest was annexed to Quebec. It guaranteed the French inhabitants religion, the Roman Catholic Church tithes, and set up a civil administration, rather than the arbitrary rule of the military commanders. The main purpose of the Quebec Act, says Alvord, was the alleviation of the wrongs of the Alien population to Indians of the North, a last effort to protect a part of the Mississippi Valley to prevent the disorders of the region.

The territory was divided into districts, with a lieutenant government in each: Henry Hamilton for Detroit, and Patrick Sinclair for Michilimackinac. The purpose was to exclude all further settlements therein and establish uniform regulations for the Indian trade. The outbreak of the Revolution partly suspending the Quebec Act.

The British merchants now had the Fur Trade in their hands. The prolonged hostilities cut off American traders to the Indian country beyond the Ohio. When the war ended, the Great Lakes were awarded to the Americans. With the trade went the formal allegiance of the Indian tribes. For an entire generation, the strange situation existed wherein the land was American, and the economic activities were British. This situation is the key to understanding the history of Michigan until after the War of 1812" (Fuller).

"The British believed that ample room was allotted for settlement east of the line along the crest of the Appalachian Mountains. To the west, a vast country was assigned to the Indians and fur trader. Speculators and pioneers were transgressing the line, pouring through Cumberland Gap into Tennessee and through the Fort Pitt gateway to the fertile lands of Kentucky. The Ohio River was the barrier between the farmers and the Indian hunting grounds.

The Quebec Act stopped westward expansion. The French yet ruled British Quebec, north of the Ohio River. The colonies had no representation or claim from the king's charters. The region was the chief arena for the collection and transport of furs. The fur provinces were dependent upon British goods, shipping, and merchants.

When it became evident that the colonies invading Indian land were trying to set up an independent nation, the Indians recognized their self-interest was on the side (British) upholding the integrity of the hunting grounds of the West" (Fuller).

"The British backing the Indian in attacking the invaders crossing the Ohio. Detroit was the British and Indian capital of the Northwest, supplying the troops of warriors in defense of the British fur trade.

Pressure from Americans increased, but there was little fear from the English traders, as long as the English held Detroit. James McGill wrote in 1786, It would be a very long time before the Americans could venture on the smallest part of our trade.

British Crown Loyalists settled in Detroit after 1783, seeking an asylum from the persecution they are subjected to in the States. There was, however, a great deal of concern for the fate of Detroit. Detroit was the key to the trade of the Great Lakes and Northwest. The Americans were extremely anxious to gain Detroit and its Indian trade. The British delayed giving up the Michigan Fur Trade and retained the posts and exploited the Fur Trade of Detroit. The British, also fearing the anger from the Indians with their departure, continued giving presents to their Indian allies in Michigan and the Northwest.

In 1784, George Washington examined routes to the West in a plan to bring the trade of Detroit and the Northwest to Virginia. The Potomac Company was formed to achieve this goal with George Washington as the president. Washington was eager to gain the Northwest trade for America, saying 'I am not for discouraging the exertions of any state to draw the commerce of the western country'.

American militia troops crossed the Ohio River in 1790 and 1791, ending in the defeat of St. Clair and Harmar. A series of forts were built along the western boundary, stretching north from Fort Washington to Cincinnati, Ohio" (Farrel).

"Lt. Gov. Henry Hamilton at Detroit called the traders the most worthless vagabonds imaginable: 'they are fugitives in general from Lower Canada or the Colonies, who fly from their debtors or the law and, being proficient in all sorts of vice and debauchery, corrupt the morals of the Savages, without the family connections of the French traders or knowledge of the Indian customs'. The English were often brutal in their dealings and especially in the use of intoxicants, in the trade. Although the strong water was not new, it reached unprecedented proportions during the latter quarter of the eighteenth century (1700's). The traders justified its use by citing strong competition between traders and Indian demand. In rum, they found the perfect trade good: cheap, addictive, and immediately consumed. Rum was consumed in large amounts by men and women, young and old. Violence and mayhem always accompanied the liquor; they were accepted parts of the trade" (Cleland, Rights of Conquest, pg. 132).

"Cheated by the traders, ravaged by the violence brought about by the use, of intoxicants, unfairly treated in the restriction of firearms in trade, and humiliated by the contempt of English soldiers and administrators, the Great Lakes Indians seethed in growing anger" (Cleland, Rites of Conquest, pg. 133).

"Whites with strong drink overthrew the honor of the Red man, and power over a worthless husband purchased the virtue of his wife or daughter. When she fell, the whole race fell with her. Before this calamity, a happier home could not be found than that created by the Indian women. There was nothing artificial about her person, a strength and poise not to be overcome by any ordinary misfortune" (C. Eastman, Soul of the Indian).

"The Jay Treaty of 1795 provided free trade in the United States and Canada, subject to only the uniform customs, duties, and regulations. The actual forts and trading establishments of the British were moved to their side of the boundary, but the privileges of the treaty enabled them to maintain uninterrupted contact with the Indians and the sources of supply on the American side. British agents remained in Michigan. Complete freedom of trade existed, though technically the movement of British goods over the border amounted to smuggling.

A revenue district was established in 1799, with Michilimackinac as the headquarters. This was only a minor obstacle to the powerful British companies that dominated the trade on both sides of the border. It was only by a narrow margin that the British failed to retain all the fur trading areas of North America within their jurisdiction. It is true, commercial relations were dominantly British for twenty years after the international boundary was proclaimed by treaty.

The French diverted trade to New Orleans. The Albany traders diverted trade to New York. The Philadelphia traders sent merchandise to Kaskaskia, Illinois to compete with the French at St. Louis. The English merchants attempted to monopolize the Indian trade. This was a sore grievance for the colonies on the Atlantic Seaboard" (Fuller).

"John Jacob Astor arrived in this country a penniless emigrant boy, son of a butcher. He was born in the Duchy of Baden, village of Waldorf. He bought and sold furs in New York, early acquainted him with the business. His early financial success was as a ship owner in the oriental trade. A fortune was made in the sandalwood trade with China alone, the possibilities of which Astor discovered by accident, which made him a rich man before his competitors knew anything about his operations in that line. His ships circumnavigated the globe and called at every Occidental port where a lucrative trade could be obtained. When John Jacob Astor entered the Western field to compete in the Fur Trade, he was equipped with a ripe experience, ample means, and remarkably shrewd business instincts and methods" (Fowle, Sault Ste. Marie and MI).

Peter Grewett was an Indian trader for the American Fur Co. He was well known from Detroit to Sault St. Marie. He wrote the history of the Ojibwe of Michigan, as told to him by Puttaguasamine, then 100 years old in 1834.

"The Ogima – Forest King traded food for whiskey; it was the great means of drawing from him, his furs and skins to obtain. He made a beast of himself and allows his family to go hungry and half-naked. And how feeble is the force of law where all are leagued in the golden bands of interest to break it! The fur traders were petty dealers of all sorts, though they profess to obey the laws" (Schoolcraft, 30 years among the Indians).

"The American Fur Co. proceeded to strip the land of every furred animal to be found, and some to the verge of extinct and rare. It crushed any trader it could not buy, pitching a tent near the enemy and undersell him; and there was often violence. To create hostile relations between him and the Indians was the most potent means to destroy his trade, by giving presents, denouncing, cursing, and sabotage.

When the Indians were paid for their furs, before they set out for their winter hunting grounds, the agents usually paid at one of the warehouses. In a large room would be a long table or counter upon which were seated the agents, clerks, and interpreters. The Indians would enter the front door, one by one, sign their receipts or make their marks thereon, receive their money, from there and walk out the back door, where stood a crowd of hungry traders, who would quickly transfer most of the money from the hands of the Indians to their own pockets for the payment of old debts. The traders commonly claimed all they could see, and the Indians, as a rule, gave it up without protest. They were generally in debt but were always ready to pay when they had any money. The traders never hesitated to give credit to an Indian. The Indians left the next day, except for the drunkards and those who stayed behind for a debauch" (C. Moore, History of MI).

"Rogues were few among the Aboriginals; they were usually the victim of baseness, rather than its author" (Calvin J. Thorpe, MPHC vol. 28).

The Hudson's Bay Co. in the Ojibwe trade included venison, rice, fish, maple sugar, canoes, sleds, snowshoes, tents, fur pack wrappers, fat for candles, sturgeon oil for lamps, goose and duck feathers for mattresses and blankets, quills for pens, birch bark shingles, spruce gum to seal roof cracks and patch canoes, show shoe netting, making, and mending and cleaning of cloth, nets from twine for fishing, guiding, and freighting.

"A large number, of Mohawk near Montreal went as free traders with the Northwest Co., Hudson's Bay Co., and Pacific Fur Co. Their contribution to opening the west is understated" (Metis Timeline, www).

Joseph Campau of Detroit, whose great grandfather was Jacques Campau, was a great trader. Joseph sold the British military alcohol, firearms, ammunition, pork, and other necessities. The market played to certain readily available commodities and outstripped even the Fur Trade, as the most lucrative endeavor, of the Eighteenth Century Frontier. Merchants would outfit expeditions, swapping merchandise for furs. Some of the items for trade were looking glasses, blankets, stockings, padlocks, scalping knives, mustard, spices, silk handkerchiefs, beads, bread, shoes, bowls, butter, buttons, hinges, etc. Trading stores were packed with merchandise, every square inch was crammed with a bewildering array of commodities. This was one-stop shopping. Detroit was crucial to the American economy, the metropolis of the Midwest, the inland seaport reaching all parts of the world.

In 1793, Don McKay reported, "the only thing necessary for trade is a good supply of rum" (Metis Timeline, www).

"Fort Gratiot was the natural point of destination for the products of the county surrounding it. It was also the key to the three Upper Lakes, Huron, Michigan, and Superior. A port of transportation, shipment, and original export, it was the central point for various diverging routes by water and rail. The first great landing and distribution point for all Western emigration, the natural depot for commodities intended for shipment" (Jenks II, 1912, Biographical History of St. Clair County).

Daniel and Jeremiah Harrington were on a fur trading trip to Saginaw country in 1819, with several other men. They were in an open batteau they had built in Fremont, Ohio, named the *Saginaw Hunter*. In passing Crow Island, they were met by a fleet of canoes led by Kishkaukau, who yelled, "*Puckachee*, go, go." After some time, they were allowed, to go before the tribal chiefs and negotiate a permission to enter the country. They eventually settled 10 miles south of the mouth of the Saginaw River and built a trading house to pass the winter. They had great success using their dogs to hunt fur-bearing animals. Kishkaukau tried every means to drive them away. With diplomacy and making a great feast, they were accepted. At that time, there were only two houses in the Saginaw River area: one of Louis Campau, where his brother, Antoine, worked the Fur Trade post, the other Peter Riley, brother of John Riley.

The Harrington's later settled in St. Clair County on Black River.

Judge Jewitt was at Saginaw. "By 1816, British traders were cut off from Michigan forests.

In 1816, Abbottsford, Michigan was settled around a sawmill on Mill Creek, also called Fairfield. Abbottsford had a post office from 1892 to 1942. Ruby, Michigan was just east of Abbottsford. Ruby later moved to the former

Abbottsford location. Abbottsford was named after Judge James Abbott, a very large and influential fur and timber trader in Detroit, who sold many other goods. The mill site at Abbottsford was the same place that Ignass Morass had built on in 1786, having first choice of the vast timber surrounding the mill. Ignass Morass supplied spars and other timber for ships being built on the River Rouge and other locations for the coming war between Britain and America in 1812. This timber was hauled on horse trains over the ice down Black River, the St. Clair River, and over Lake St. Clair to the Detroit River. The axe and oxen the only tools to accomplish such a great feat in the woods.

Abbott was Chicago's first bridegroom. In 1804, Abbott rode on horseback to Chicago from Detroit to marry Sarah Whistler, daughter of Captain John Whistler, builder and commandment of Fort Dearborn. John Whistler also served at Fort Gratiot at the foot of Lake Huron. Sarah was aunt to the famous American artist James A. McNeil Whistler. The couple spent their honeymoon on the return to Detroit, traveling by horseback 300 miles on the Indian trail. Abbott was postmaster at Detroit for over 25 years and a slaveholder. Abbott also owned vessels, bringing salt to Detroit from New York. Captain William Brown sailed for him.

This land at Mill Creek was originally deeded to Duperon Baby in 1780 by the Indians; he was the British Indian agent who abandoned his claim and mill to American Territory in 1796. Abbott's mill was formerly owned by Ignass Morass, who built the mill in 1786. Abbott sold his mill to Judge Z.W. Bunce.

Many other sawmills were in the area along Black River and Mill Creek. Black River was the place of early lumbering in Michigan, having tremendous growth of white pine and pumpkin pine – fully mature pine. Shingles and staves were made also. Many of the lumber barons of Michigan and the nation had their start in St. Clair County, Michigan. There was heavy growth of timber.

The Beards and Glyshaws were lumbermen who called Ruby "Abbottsford Home". There were two stages daily coming through Ruby and Abbottsford in the 1800s and early 1900s. In 1837, there were 339 residents in Ruby (Abbottsford). The Black River Valley reached its peak production in 1871, the first valley in Michigan to do so" (Hudgins, 1953, pg. 63). Some lumber trails which later became roads. The hills have been shaved down; they were at one time, steeper.

Abbottsford and Ruby were huge lumbering villages, eventually having eight or more hotels and numerous boarding houses in the area to accommodate the men who came to work in the woods and those passing through to other places. It was once a thriving town with many businesses, machine shops, stores, etc. Other small hamlets were nearby: Fargo, Hardscrabble, Atkins, Zion, Avoca,

Brockway, Brockway Center, Merrillville, Kenockee, and Jeddo. Many more small towns were nearby. They all had their favorite bar, hotel, or boarding house. The Hardscrabble Hotel had a famous history in its day; it was on Beard Road and Kilgore Road. On Saturday nights in these small towns, musicians delighted the people at the dance halls.

"The Liquor Trade at Ruby – Abbottsford – caused many problems in the town. One fine establishment was burned to the ground by the women of the town who had had enough" (Jackie Praeter).

Fairfield appears to be a holdover from the British settlement in the area west of Ruby, Michigan. The Fairfield militia was commanded by James Abbot, who was a large trader in Detroit. In the book, *West to Far Michigan*, Kenneth E. Lewis (2002) lists Fairfield as having two retail places, 25 production activities, and 9 service activities.

The Dorsey House was a famous stop for travelers going in every direction Northwest of the St. Clair River and Black River. It was located on Wildcat Road and now M-136 Highway, east of Ruby Michigan.

"Usury - charging interest on credit, was a European tradition, unknown in America. Indian corn, wheat and rye were grown, nearly all were distilled into whiskey, the principle drink. Wine is hardly known here. Rye was also prepared to be used as a coffee substitute. Oats, flax, potatoes, and garden vegetables were also grown for the trade. A bushel of corn was traded for a gallon of whiskey, five quarts for a bushel of wheat or rye.

There was no money, no shoes, no school, barely clothed a ragged state. Clothing was worn out, everything was scarce, there was one pot to do all. Home spun was worn. There was no church and no cellar. A hollow sycamore was used as a smoke house.

The Mack and Miller Distillery was at Harsens Island, Michigan" (MPHC vol. 4).

The New Vandalia Co., Indiana Co., Walpole Co., and Venice of America were land speculation companies in the Northwest Territory.

In the 1820s and 1830s, the Indians were forced to kill off their main source of meat for the trade. Deer and muskrats became the main furs when the beavers were decimated. The Indians began to starve.

FIRE WATER

Fire Water – *Ish kuday wa bu* – was the name for the alcoholic mixture made up for the Indian trade, it was often diluted. Brandy, rum, and whiskey – *scoota wah boo* – were indispensable trade items.

"Traders' Whiskey: 2 gallons of unrectified spirits, 30 gallons of river water, ½ oz. of cayenne pepper, 2 oz. tobacco plug for color.

Ten Rod Whiskey: high wine to which brown sugar and tobacco were added to give it its color.

Indian Whiskey: one barrel, river water, 2 oz. strychnine, 3 plugs of chewing tobacco, 5 bars of soap, 1 lb. of red pepper, sagebrush leaves. Boil until the liquid turns brown, then bottle. Strychnine for its stimulating qualities, the soap gave it a bead, the tobacco gave the necessary nausea, for no Indian thought he was drinking whiskey unless it made him violently ill" (Robert Murphy, Saturday Evening Post 1947).

"Whiskey was a main trade item, sometimes the main trade item. The Indians also wanted blankets, tools, weapons, butcher knives, scalping knives, tomahawks, cloth, beads, mirrors, combs, needles, thread, fishing hooks, silver jewelry, ammunition, ball and shot, gunpowder, flint, steel, gun screws, kettles, flour, and other items. The Indians came to trade. They feasted and treated until incapable of business, and then they were induced to sign agreements they knew nothing of and of which they had no recollection.

Liquor – Devil's Spittle – undermined tribal interests and destroyed their personal powers and social safety. They knew the danger but could not shun it. During the high time, all deadly weapons were removed. There were noise and demons of darkness and hate, broken property, bruised, maimed, and suffering people. The Indians borrowed and repaid with interest" (MPHC, 28, Calvin Thorpe).

Whiskey was an essential element of the backwoods life, a sovereign remedy for all prevailing ills, fever, and ague of a swampy country. It was the medicinal for pioneers.

MONEY

"A major problem for merchants was the aggravating lack of cash. Until 1775 and later, trade had been in the form of barter and value in terms of beaver pelts. Bills of exchange were often issued; these were only used in and around the city, their value and reliability depended upon the reputation of the issuer. Chief Pontiac had issued bills of exchange on pieces of bark, the value of each determined by the number and type of animals represented. These were faithfully redeemed.

French, Spanish, Portuguese, and English money were used, since silver and gold were scarce. As there were few small coins, the larger ones were cut into pieces, called hobnail currency. There were several types of English currency

Ottissippi

including Halifax, New York, and sterling, sterling being the standard of value" (Farrell, MI Archives).

"Trading was almost wholly by barter of furs, shingles, and labor; shinplasters, local made coinage, were used in the making of small change. The principal coins of the early century were foreign silver.

In 1837, the Saganaw's sold to two traders the furs of 40 bears, 65 deers, 35 otters, 33 pounds of beaver, 570 muskrats, 140 minks, 55 fishers, 40 foxes, 17 elk, 4 moose, 890 raccoons, and 19 cats" (Letter from Henry Schoolcraft to C.A. Harris, Office Indian Affairs, 1838, NAM MI R.37:547 – 564).

In the later 1800s, the price of furs or skins were recorded in Judge Bunce's records in American currency (McKay):

"Bear skin, well-furred and fine, 32/each; bear of a common quality, 16/ poor bear, 20/-, poor bear, or such as were killed in the fall, 6-8/. To 8/., cub bear, large size and well-furred, 16/; cub bear, small size and well-furred, 8-12/; cub bear about the size of a raccoon are worth 2/each, and some of them are worth nothing.

Deer: grey deer, well-furred, 4-5/at 1/PH; grey deer, 2-3/ at .6 cents/PH; blue deer or such are more – killed in September, 15 cents/PH; red deer, 1/6 PH. Elk skins, 12/. For each skin. Fisher: prime no. 1, 16/; fisher, prime male, 12/each; fisher, not prime, 4/.6/.8/. Fox: red fox, 4/.6/.8/. grey fox, 2/. Martin: prime no. 1, 10/ male prime, 8/; martin not prime, 4/. To 6/. Mink: mink, full grown prime, 4/., mink, female prime, 3/ female no. 2, 4/ inferior mink, .6 cents/ 1 B. Muskrat: prime, .11 cents; muskrat, fall, 8 cents; muskrat killed November & December, 6 cents; kitten muskrats, 2 cents. Otter: full grown, prime no. 1, 28/ otter small but prime, 20/; otter no. 2, 12-16/no. 3, 8-10/cub, 4-6/. Raccoons: full grown, prime no. 1, 5/; raccoons, small but prime skins, 3/ to 3/B; raccoons, no. 2 – that is fall skins but well-furred, 2/ to 2/6 according to size, raccoons, no. 3, 1/; raccoons, no. 4, 5 cents; some raccoons no. 4 are worthless. Wild cat, prime, same price as raccoon".

Edward Petit, born at now Port Huron, was a very early inhabitant, a fur trader for Gordon and Ephraim Williams. He had a post and traded on the bend of the Cass River in the thumb of Michigan. The Indians were numerous and usually intelligent; the traders had plenty to eat and plenty to do, looking them up and bartering with them.

In 1831, he found Chief Tawas and his band, after others could not, after a long winter, knowing they must have a great quantity of furs. Young Petit resolved to secure this prize and started out with a week's provisions on his back, taking as guide an Indian with one arm. The other arm sacrificed to the revenge of the Indians who had shot him because he murdered his own wife at La Riviere

Delude – Black River. They found Tawas near White Rock with only one loaf of bread remaining. Tawas was preparing to make sugar. They had brass kettles of all sizes. This spot was chosen for its fishing facilities. They were almost starving, having only moose tallow scraps. Petit divided with them his loaf and shared in their tallow scraps for several days. He purchased at this time 500 martin skins at 1.00 each, which were selling for 2.00 each. Only the finest could be taken away. He returned to camp rejoicing, his wages were quadrupled by his employers. Petit also traded in Ontario on the Sable about 40 miles northeast from Sarnia. He was the first White settler in Huron County, Michigan. He opened a trading post on Shebeon Creek and later moved the post to White Rock at White Rock City.

"Large canoes carried 10 men and 65 packages of furs, weighing from 50 to 80 pounds" (Lanmar, Red Book).

"The steamer *Winslow* carried 70 Negros from Virginia and Kentucky aboard, bound for Ste. Saint Marie to quarry stone. The rapids were difficult to ascend into Lake Huron with watercraft; the channel was shallow and the current very swift. Vessels waited for a favorable south wind to push them through; sometimes it was a long wait. Vessels were also towed through, by a long line, with Indians pulling it through. The tow ropes were made of boiled basswood bark. Later yokes of oxen were used to tow the vessels through the rapids and channel, upon the waterline. Often the line was chopped by an axe to prevent the oxen from being dragged into the resistance of the current" (OGS Hodgins).

SLAVERY

Native Americans are color blind; all men are equal. Though Native Americans did have captive enemy slaves, they were treated more like family. Children born to slaves were born free. If a slave's spouse died, they were then free and lived among the Indians as family or left to do as they pleased.

The practice of brutal slavery came from the Europeans, who brought the old ways with them. Blacks were captured in wars and raids into enemy territory. They were sold as war booty back at the forts – trading posts. Native slaves were also traded at the posts, women and young girls included. The East Coast Traders were heavily involved in slave trading from Africa to the Caribbean Islands of the West Indies. Where they worked in the salt trade and sugar cane, rum, silver, and other mines for trading with Europe. Most slaves were worked to death, and more brought to replace them. England, Spain, and France were also slave holders in South America and Mexico.

Participation in this lucrative trade generated enormous sums. Mercantile capitalism was a fundamental part of the Northwest economy. 11.8 million slaves were taken from Africa. The West India Co. had the largest slavery owners, monopoly. The British also had tobacco plantations for trading in Virginia and the South which also included Kentucky, Tennessee, and surrounding areas. There were many Indian slaves in South Carolina: 1,400. The Church was the largest holder of slaves. They were used to do the work in trading and agricultural pursuits and other domestic work for the priests. The French kept their slaves until death.

At Montreal, the Catholic Church received one-eighth of all land sales. In New France, slavery was common. In Canadian history, there are recorded 4,092 slaves. Of the total, 2,692 were Indians and 1,400 were Blacks. Indentured slavery was also common: those wishing to cross to the New World would pay their crossing by working off the cost.

Escaped slaves came to Canada. This part of Southeast Michigan was part of Canada and under British occupancy until 1796. Even though the Americans had won the War of Independence in 1783, the slaves knew there was safety and freedom in Canada. Many crossed over the river to the mainland Canada and lived in Black settlements and villages. Canada's main Black settlements are Owen Sound, Amherstburg – Sandwich, Windsor, Chatham, Elgin, Dawn, Dresden, Niagara Peninsula, Toronto, and Hamilton. Many Blacks were United Empire Loyalists.

Many earned their freedom fighting in the wars for the British. Many came with their British Loyalist masters. Many ship captains were abolitionists and carried slaves to freedom. Many free slaves worked loading ships with goods and, later, with ore and other resources. Slavery was abolished in the North in 1834 with a gradual emancipation.

See "Chapter 12: Northern Slavery".

LUMBER

St. Clair County was very rich in pine and oak, the two most important species of timber, the most valuable a new county could furnish. St. Clair County was famous for its extensive groves of the best pumpkin pine, and Black River and Mill Creek carried fortunes to market in logs, timber, lumber, shingles, etc.

Pumpkin pine was the grade of pinus strobus, known as cork pine or pumpkin, a fully ripe timber of large proportions, cutting up with a freedom from knots and other defects and of a softness of texture which rendered it highly desirable in the building arts and in the commerce of the continent.

It was said that Black River gold, the valuable timber of this area, was the making of many men. The very finest of the white pine, in all of North America, was found in St. Clair County, along Black River and Mill Creek.

The white oak in many parts of the county was the finest known (and) was ruthlessly slaughtered. Using less than half the tree, it was used for pipe staves and butts, the balance left to rot. The same for shingle bolts, only the best of a straight-grained tree being used.

A total of three trillion feet of timber, being a conservative estimate, of lumber, shingles, and log products from Streams tributary to the St. Clair River were harvested. Grant and Burtchville Townships had the finest stand of cork pine ever found. It grew in profusion.

The following is a partial list of lumber men. Many became barons and are worthy of much more detailed biographies.

Eber Ward became the wealthiest man in the State. David Ward was the Timber King or "Pine King". He was a teacher as a young man and a land looker for others.

The Rust Brothers, Ezra and Amasa William, were huge lumber operators. They were raised in Marine City, Michigan, and their father died at an early age. They were involved in shipping, salt mining, iron ore, and the lumber industry.

Alfred Dwight was a man of affairs throughout the Northwest. He was in the mercantile business and operated saw mills in Huron County and lumbering on Mill Creek and Black River. He went on to build dams on the Ausable River, near Ostego, and Traverse Bay, a pioneer of the timber industry. He was a partner with Smith. He improved Mill Creek and Belle River for floating timber opening up the Imlay City area.

Henry Howard, a great lumberman in Michigan, was also a supplier of long sticks to Detroit and Lake Erie. He owned Howard Towing Assoc., a tug business. Henry held many offices at Port Huron, Michigan, was a banker and hotel owner, and was involved in every major interest of commerce: the railroad, Gas Light Co., and newspaper, *The Port Huron Times*. He was Vice President of Port Huron Engine and Thresher Company and Michigan Sulphite and Fibre Company and was a member of the state legislature. He was known for his integrity and honest business principles.

Henry Howard was the Michigan Director of the Grand Trunk R.R. Lines west of the St. Clair River, as well as President of the Northern Transit Co. of Port Sarnia. He cut timber in Sanilac, Huron, Saginaw, Presque Isle, and Sheboygan, cutting long timber and rafting it east as far as Buffalo, New York.

He invested in pine in Chippewa County in the Upper Peninsula. Henry was President of the Port Huron Driving Park Assoc.

A.D. Bennet, son-in-law of Henry Howard, continued the estate of Henry Howard Business.

Francis Palms was a very large lumber baron in Michigan and other States.

In the Haynes Family, Jacob P. was at the forefront of the lumber industry at Port Huron, Michigan and went on to the Upper Peninsula. He purchased large tracts of pine lands, making the St. Clair River famous, and for many years had extensive operations on Black River and other streams emptying into the St. Clair River. With his son, he operated a cedar business at Cedarville in Mackinaw County, supplying posts, poles, railroad ties, etc. Maintaining a yard at Port Huron in wholesale and retail.

David Jerome became Governor of Michigan after amassing great wealth. He did office work, then went into the lumber trade. He as a lake pilot conceived the idea to tow vessels through the serious obstruction at the St. Clair Flats. Eventually influencing Congress to remove the obstruction, making tremendous improvements to shipping. He went on to discover the Live Yankee Tunnel Mine in California, then went into the lumber business at Saginaw. He was a charter member of the Republican Party, becoming a State Senator. He became a military aid and was on the State Military Board as president for eight years. He was chairman of the Committee on Finance and was appointed to prepare a new state constitution. He was thereafter appointed a member of the Indian Commissioners. He was chairman of a commission to visit Chief Joseph of the Nez Perce Indians.

The following is a short list of lumbermen, though there were many, many more:

Burtch, Jonathon: lumbered at Lakeport, went on to Alpena in 1836 and Cheboygan

Cornell, Extra: the largest private pine land owner in the nation

Bartlett, Allen Luce: a huge lumberman

Charles Merrill: a famed lumberman

Miller, an early lumberman

Nelson Mills: shipbuilder at Marine City, sawmill operator at Marysville – Vicksburg. He owned land on Black River and a lumber yard at Toledo, Ohio. He entered the vessel business as Mills Transportation Company with 20 or more steam and tow barges and sailing craft. He was a partner with Williams and Reeves at Vickery and with Caleb Jewett at Cleveland, in the lumber business. At St. Clair, he had an extensive planning mill, making sashes, doors, etc. He was also interested in banking, the Ferry Company, Port Huron Engine and Thresher Company, and a resort on Stag Island in the St. Clair River. He invested in timber in West Virginia and was a postmaster, school inspector, and justice of the peace.

Smart, Robert: built a sawmill at Wadhams in 1827, which he sold to Ralph Wadhams and Henry Howard.

Cameron: large lumberman and politician; owner of a large trading center at Sarnia, Ontario, and Point Edward, Ontario. Canada.

William A. Burt and John Allen: built many sawmills in the new territory of Michigan. Burt was also a surveyor, legislator, and Commissioner of Internal Improvement. He invented the solar compass, used in mining operations. They built the mill of Alphaeus Wadhams. He invented the typewriter in 1828 and, he became Deputy U.S. Surveyor, for all, of the Northwest; his five sons, and many others that he trained, surveyed much of the Northwest Territory. He was also judge of the Circuit Court in Macomb County. He discovered iron ore in the Upper Peninsula of Michigan. The U.S. Government had exclusive use of the solar compass for 50 years; Burt was never compensated for it. He invented the equatorial sextant used to navigate ocean crossings. He was associate with Douglas Houghton. He was a pioneer in canal building, locks, shipping ore, railroads, and was a prolific inventor for industry.

Alpheus Wadhams – Ralph Wadhams – came to Detroit in 1823 from Goshen, Connecticut. He operated Reese and Wadhams, a general merchandise firm, selling lumber in Detroit. He began lumbering operations on Black River at Clyde Mills, now Wadhams, Michigan. About 1829, he moved to St. Clair County. By 1830, he built the first grist mill at Clyde Mills. In 1832, Wadhams was elected supervisor of the town of Desmond – Port Huron, Michigan. He was also a delegate to the Constitutional Convention where Michigan was admitted to the Union. He was postmaster at Clyde Mills – Wadhams – for 36 years. He raised champion cattle. He died in 1877.

Stephen Moore came from Maine to carry on the lumber business. He made shingles and worked for Daniel B. Harrington and Alfred Dwight of Detroit. He was boom master on the Black River. He was foreman for Avery and Murphy on Mill Creek for 12 years, running camps in winter and as a looker in the summer. He bought some choice locations for himself. He was superintendent for Sanborn and Rust on the Muskegon River and worked for himself there.

All the Detroit lumber firms depended on Black River log stock. The lumber industry caused irreparable harm to the waterways, clogging streams with silt, the removed trees, caused the temperature to rise in the waterways, and fish populations declined. There was massive pilferage; the government had no control over the Frontier. Justice seldom prevailed over controlled votes. The government, was often corrupt and poorly managed. Pinery owners bought newspapers to control public opinion.

Port Huron had 26 saloons devoted solely to the sale of intoxicating drinks. There were also eight hotels with bars in 1867. "In 1867, on the East Shore of Michigan, there were 212 sawmills, 5,209 mills men, and 10,250 woodsmen" (Lanmar, Redbook).

Saginaw had 366 saloons. There were underground tunnels, and saloons were many stories high. Here were the vilest and most depraved tastes and moral corruption. Prohibition had no effect here; saloons and drunkenness flourished. Thieves and pickpockets descended when the drive was in. There were 800 camps and 25,000 loggers working the wilderness region. The Saginaw tributaries could float logs for 864 miles. Night and day, the lake ships and rafts moved down the river in a scum of sawdust.

The corruption at Saginaw was unbelievable. Ezra Rust, Charles Rodd, Andrew Campau, Henry Peters, Fred Hall, George Bradley, Timothy Jerome, and George Williams were involved in great land fraud of the best timber at Isabella Reserve. Rodd and Campau, mixed-breed Saginaw Chippewa, made a purchase of 10,000 acres, then selling to others. The Rust purchase was declared invalid in 1870.

Federal agents worked in league with persons in lumber concessions, using unknown Indian names and dead Indian names.

Clyde Township, St. Clair County, and the thumb of Michigan were on the forefront of the lumbering era, and then Saginaw, Alpena, Cheboygan, and Michigan's Upper Peninsula, and into Wisconsin.

Loggers and lumbermen who became rich moved on to the Northern States or the Pacific Northwest. Many of the men who worked for them also went on.

"European axes were used primarily for making firewood" (Metis History, www).

In 1837, Michigan had 433 sawmills, 114 gristmills, and 16 distilleries.

The following paragraphs on lumber are from Hotchkiss, *History of the Lumber and Forest Industry of the Northwest*, 1898.

"Black River flows from just west of Palms, Michigan in Sanilac County. It is 56 miles long. The Black River was always important; it served the Indians, lumberman, hunters, and settlers. In 1875, the largest raft of oak supported by cork pine floated downriver. It was 1,000 feet long.

The following are lumberman terms:

A *mill pond* held the logs until needed for the cutting mill. It was a deep pond; the river had to be dammed up. The river will widen and deepen into a small lake or pond behind the dam.

Each log received a *timber mark*, claiming ownership. Sawdust was used as insulation and a source of heat. Two horses could pull a load of 50 logs piled high and chained. *River pigs* or *river hogs* kept the logs moving, a very hazardous occupation.

A *wanigan* is a shanty for cooking and sleeping. It sat atop the rafts floated down and nudged by, *cant hooks* and *pike poles*. These rafts were huge; fires were burned on a *combuse fireplace*, a log frame filled with a bed of sand. The log rafts had shanty's, on them, and there were floating stores for the loggers.

Cribs were logs that were tied together, the cribs were then tied together to make a raft. The rafts were steered by long oars called *sweeps*. Jams often occurred; they were very dangerous to dislodge. Many drownings occurred.

River hogs were experts at undoing log jams. In the spring, they could convert a creek into a stream big enough to carry 16-foot logs to mills. Sometimes a series of dams were used to float the logs. Canadians and Indians were the premier river men, surefooted and daring.

A *peavy* was the most useful tool, its pointed end a prod and an adjustable hook used to roll a log to one side.

A *widow maker* was a branch heavy enough to destroy an ox. The Indian name for sawmill is *Kau Goosh Kaw Nick*. There were many Indian and Black lumbermen. Frank May was a hardwood dealer in Detroit. He was a colored man who went from being a slave to a business man. He sold furniture stock in Michigan and Ohio".

PAUL BUNYAN

"Paulette Cicero, a French Canadian, was a land looker who was a cook at Wadhams, now Kimball Township, Michigan. He is said to be the real Paul Bunyan. Bunyan was a real man, said to come from Canada to Black River. His shoulders were two axe handles and three plugs of spearhead in width.

Black River was called Little River and St. Clair River, the Big River. The settlement at the mouth was called Down at the Mouth. He was very clever his skills were only used when necessary. Paul's ox babe was white, and his color changed to blue after spending so much time outdoors in the winter (Mitts, That Noble Country, 1968, Dorrance & Co.).

Paul was from New Brunswick, Canada; he was Paul Bonhomme. His legend grew to the whole Northwest. Paul's cook was Big Joe. The stories were made up in camps in the lake states, the tellers made up the stories as they went along, using fantastic exaggeration. It helped while away dull evenings and impress greenhorns, who were persuaded to believe almost anything. Old timers would nod in agreement. When one man's lie was finished, another would try to top it. Rafting crews had Whiskey Jack, a mere seven feet tall. But he could lick any man on the river" (Mitts, Dorrance).

MILL HISTORY

"About a week was consumed in sending grain to the grist mills. Many packed grain, to the mill, on their backs, a long distance.

Whipsaws were used to make planks before sawmills were built; it was long, slow work. The men who built the sawmills were called the millers or sawyers.

By 1690, a sawmill was built at the mouth of what was later known as Bunce Creek in St. Clair County, then in the Western Province of Canada in New France. The mill was built by a Frenchman from Montreal, and 90 years later in 1780, a mill was built at the same place by Enos Morass. His son, Ignace Morass, erected a mill on Mill Creek at Abbottsford in 1816. This mill was purchased in 1831 by James Abbott, who rebuilt the mill and added a grist mill. Judge Bunce erected a third mill near this site in 1817.

In 1749, Chaussegros De Lery, an engineer, owned a large wooded tract on Black River, he built the earliest sawmill on Black River – River Du lhut. Gervais operated the mill and sent lumber to Detroit.

A sawmill was reported for Black River in the 1740s" (Lowrie and Clark, 1832:379).

"St. Clair County and the tributaries leading to the St. Clair River were among the earliest lumbering and logging areas in the state and the Northwest. Men came and built fortunes of the forest products.

The pine was the best the world has ever seen. The White pine was much in demand, and it was easy to work with in building. The pumpkin pine was abundant here. The pine belt soil is of a lighter and more sandy nature. The hardwoods of a rich alluvial character soil affording excellent farms. The finest timber was found in sections where the soil was favorable to both pine and hardwood growth. Where pine was found mixed with hardwood, its quality was vastly superior in the production of the finer grades of lumber and in freedom from defects.

In the early history of the state, before settlement had gone beyond the almost exclusively hardwood-producing South. The mills used whitewood and basswood, which were found in great abundance and were easy to work with, found favor of the settler. The Indians had used this wood for eons in their canoes and homes. The settler burning up all the other varieties of timber in clearing the land many times.

The pressing immigration of 1835 to 1836 pushed settlement into the pine regions, and the value of that timber was demonstrated. The white oak was ruthlessly slaughtered, often less than half a tree was used for pipe staves and butts, the balance being left to rot. Only the best of a straight-grained tree being used for shingle bolts, and the rest for the worms and to rot on the ground" (Hotchkiss).

The Black River Valley was where the early commercial logging industry began in 1805 and 1806. Limited logging had taken place here very early. White oak in many parts of the county was the finest known. "Every brooklet was forced to do a river's work in mills and factories" (C. Eastman).

Some time, previous to 1809, Meldrum and Park built a mill at the mouth of a creek below Marysville on Pine River.

Enos Morass contracted with the U.S. Government to supply spars, masts, and ship timber at Detroit during the winter of 1811 to 1812, hauling over the ice of Black River, St. Clair Lake, and Detroit River. At that time, it was considered a most extraordinary and hazardous undertaking.

A water mill was built on Mays Creek, just below Detroit, in or around 1734, and in 1790, Jean Baptiste Beaubien built a house and sawmill on the north shore of Lake St. Clair near Grosse Point, believed to be the mill later owned by Meldrum and Park. There was a mill at Mackinaw in 1780. Other mills were on Conner's Creek and on Bloody Run at Detroit.

"Ralph Wadhams was for many years the head lumberman in Clyde Township. He employed a large crew of men and realized handsomely from lumbering operations. He was a partner with Henry Howard in the firm of Howard and Wadhams. He built two sawmills and one grist mill and kept a general store of general merchandise. His large dining room served many purposes for the community, as a meeting room, dance hall with musicians, and the Methodist Episcopal Church quarterly meeting. Friends from Port Huron coming to partake. Indians brought sugar and cranberries down the river, often in birch bark canoes. The sugar and cranberries were sold to the inhabitants along the banks of the river" (Jenks Papers/Wadhams, Burton Historical Library, Detroit, MI).

"William R. Goodwin was the minister and blacksmith for the lumber camp for 40 years.

Black River Steam Mill was built prior to 1834. It was built by F.P. Browning and managed by Captain John Brown, and then it was owned by a Detroit company. It ran two upright saws and cut about 10,000 feet in 12 hours. This mill was burned twice and rebuilt and had three upright saws and one circular, siding mill. The first steam mill of the county was built at Port Huron in 1832 by Dr. Justin Rice, under supervision of Captain John Clark for Detroit Parties, and was known as the Black River Steam Mill Co. Mill. Dr. Rice's mill was the first mill known to use saw dust under the boilers for fuel.

D.B. Harrington, built a mill, one half mile below Port Huron, a mill was built by John Howard three miles above Port Huron. Jonathan Burtch had a mill on Black River and at Lakeport, as did Farrand, Sanborn's, and Switzer. Burtch took a contract to furnish some of the building materials for the Indian homes built at Sarnia Reserve.

Ai Beard came to Ruby in now Clyde Township in 1830. At that time, it was in Desmond Township. Ai built the Beard Mill. In 1839, his sons, John and James Beard, commenced lumbering on their own. The capital of the firm of J. and J. Beard consisted of a yoke of oxen and an old sled, a tea kettle, a frying pan, and an iron pot. They had no money and did not own an acre of land. Their first venture was a contract to get out logs for a Mr. Cameron of Sarnia. In 1841, they bought their father's interest in the mill and lands adjoining on time.

Great sticks for vessel spars, were drawn, by six span, of horses. Eventually, the spars marked the skyline on finished ships, launched

Cheryl Morgan

with colorful ceremony and great civic pride" (Hudgins). "One spar from the Beard Mill at Ruby measured 22 feet in diameter at the bottom and was 105 feet from the butt" (Fred A. Beard, Reminiscences in, St. Clair County Pioneer Society scrapbook and minutes, pg. 211 Jenks Collection/Fred Landon, Lake Huron, pg. 86).

"In 1869, more than sixty-four million feet of logs floated the Black River alone. The forests were worked until they were depleted, the lumbering era reaching its peak in the St. Clair River area in the late 1870s" (Fred Landon, Lake Huron, pg. 86).

There were several heavy pine land owners at Port Huron; some bought early and to great advantage. The greatest curse to the country for many years was the extensive entries of the choicest pine lands by a large company from Maine, who brought their surveyors and traversed the whole region, selecting the very choicest (cream) of the timber, entering vast quantities with soldiers' warrants, fighting taxes and opposing improvements, thus throwing heavy burdens upon the poor settlers and preventing advancement. They made mints out of their sales in later years. Another outrage was perpetrated by men who bought school lands, making perhaps a quarter payment and stripping the lands during the first year, abandoning them, refusing to make further payment. The school lands of the whole state were in this manner, robbed of millions of dollars before stringent laws and careful supervision were established.

In the Lewis and Hadley Annual for 1869, it says, "the production of St. Clair County is stated at 51 million feet; Lapeer, 22 million; Huron, 40 million; Sanilac, 14 million; and Wayne – Detroit, at 55.5 million. In 1873, the *Lumberman's Gazette* gives production at Port Huron: Batchelor & Sons, 8,500,000 feet of lumber and 4,500,000, lath; W.B. Hibbard, 5,700,000 feet lumber and 3,000,000, lath; William Sanborn & Bros., 6,000,000, lumber and 2,7500,000 lath; and A. & H. Fish, 10,000,000, lumber".

In 1847, there were 22 water mills and 12 steam mills. Black River before 1840 was navigable as far as Wadhams Mill. The steamer *General Gratiot*, running between Detroit and Port Huron, extended her trip to the sawmill, six miles from the mouth of Black River" (Andreas).

In 1827, Ralph Wadhams had a water mill about eight miles up Black River, which ran about half the year operating two sash saws. The cut of this mill was some two and a half to three thousand feet to each saw in the usual 12-hour run. The place was called Clyde Mills, now Wadhams, in Kimball Township, St. Clair County, Michigan. The schooner *Emily*, built in 1828 and owned by Howard and Wadham's, was used to carry lumber from Clyde Mills on Black River, now at Wadhams, and carry supplies back.

Fifteen miles up Black River, Ai Beard, before 1833, had two sawmills run by water power. Logs were floated to the slides above each dam. The appliances for handling logs and holding them on the carriage were rude, bungling affairs.

Half a mile up Mill Creek from Beard's Mill was Zephaniah W. Bunce's Mill. Mr. Bunce settled three miles below Port Huron in 1817 and built a water mill there on Beaver Creek – Baby Creek, later named Bunce Creek, afterward building the mill up Mill Creek. Which he operated until 1850, running one sash saw, the logs being floated down the river in times of flood, as was the lumber of other mills, and reached the mouth of the river bruised, split, and loaded with sand and muck, and then sold at ruinous prices.

Half a mile above Bunce was a small mill built by Westbrook.

Some years later, there were mills at Vickery – Marysville – six miles below Port Huron, run by steam using upright and circular saws. There were also two steam sawmills at St. Clair Village. These were well-handled and cut large amounts for those days. Truesdell owned one. Some miles below near Clarks Point was a small steam mill, and at what was then Newport, now Marine City, there were two good mills. At Algonac was a good mill doing custom work. All, of these mills, had good docks, at which any vessel then upon the lakes could load. Some of the products of these mills went East, some to Chicago and Milwaukee.

Willard Parker, Brooks, and St. Clair were among the manufacturers of an early day at St. Clair. In 1837, M. Folger built a mill with two muley saws at Marine City. Comstock operated on the Black River above Port Huron. In 1842, E.B. Ward and Rust erected mills, and in 1850, Dr. L.B. Parker erected a mill.

At St. Clair and below, logs were floated out of Pine River. In 1835, the Throop brothers took a large contract to get spars, booms, bowsprits, etc. They banked some 85 or 90 sticks, some of the large spars required 25 yokes of cattle – oxen or horses – to move them. The Throop brothers took a big bill of timber for a large Catholic church at Windsor. You can imagine what a time we had scoring, hewing, and back-breaking on trees 30 or more inches at the top, all the work being done with our axes. On stormy days, we made shaved shingles, always keeping bolts on hand at rough sheds under which we could work. We supplied logs for mills at Detroit and on the St. Clair, those for down the river being rafted with boom poles around a strongly-built crib of timber, eight or ten feet deep, on which were built houses for the men, who were supplied with anchors and chains, tow lines, and boats. The cribs were floated down and anchored or tied up near Lake St. Clair and towed across the Lake on still nights by small steamers, which took them to the mill booms of Detroit.

In the 1850s, mills were built at Port Huron by Wells, Davis, Fish, and Hibbard and Chase.

The Saginaw Valley Watershed area became the boom area. Many corrupt lumbermen went there and stripped the land of its wealth. The Isabella Land Ring was involved in criminal activities; there was outrageous fraud, leaving the Natives destitute. The wealthy influential in civil, religious, and political circles suppressed investigations. The lumbermen went on to Alpena, Tawas, Cheboygan, the Upper Peninsula of Michigan, Georgian Bay, Ontario, and Wisconsin. Most of this lumber was floated down to Detroit and Cleveland for shipment East and beyond.

In 1837, a State Census reports there were no less than 433 sawmills scattered throughout the young State, of which not more than a half-dozen, were cutting pine timber. Reports of lumber statistics could easily be doubled, as they must be taken with a large grain of allowance. There was a great demand for wood used to power steam ships. Thousands of men, many Natives, hauled timber to the docks at the storekeepers on the St. Clair River; there was day and night service. Hundreds of teams worked, hauling cordwood to the riverfront to fuel wood-burning steamers. The men often worked until 10:00 p.m.

"A cord in those days was eight feet long, four feet wide, and four feet high. Steamboat fire boxes were built to take the standard four-foot length. The Indians and farmers stacked wood so high, it was impossible to see the river from the road" (Lauriston).

Staves and shingles were another side business of the lumber industry. Staves were used to make barrels, which were used to transport various products. The tradesman was called a cooper. Two types of barrels were made: stack cooperage, were used for non-liquids, such as nails, and the tight cooperage was used for liquids, and only white oak, was used for alcoholic beverages. An expert shingle-maker could rive, shave, and pace 1,000 shingles in a day, for which he received $1.00. The shingle weaver would load his sleigh with shingles and drive to the mouth with them, where he would exchange them for pork, flour, tobacco, whiskey, boots, shoes, etc. There were no plastics in the 1800s, wooden barrels, trunks, pails, boxes, and baskets were used to package and store many useful items. Pottery, glass, and woven bags were also used.

"Many roads were built by the lumbermen to extract the timber. Roads were impassable except in winter. Horses were crossing the river in canoes tied together, their forefeet in one and the hind feet in another. The Indians would swim the horses across the river by the lighthouse, one paddling a canoe and one holding the horse's head" (Shirley Brownlee, 1857, Sarnia Observer). Canoes were tied together, and lumber was brought from Port Huron this way also.

In about 1840, the commercial value of black walnut, walnut, oak, and cherry wood became recognized. From an almost valueless product of the forest, and in 1870, even the stumps of the trees, cut many years before, were eagerly sought. Furniture manufacturing became a huge business in Michigan.

Michigan was a very important part of the Western expansion. Many federal land agents shared in the land and timber theft, going along with schemes to cheat the government, people and Natives. Honest agents were driven off in many corrupt ways. By about 1865 or 1870, the timber tributary to the streams in SCC was gone, and the mill industry obtained its log stock from Saginaw Bay and Canada by raft.

Railroads opened up regions, too far from streams. The railroads were huge land owners and there was much corruption. By 1870 to 1890, the huge forests of Michigan now were mostly cut, the last stand of pine cut in 1894. Fires in 1871, 1881, and 1891 caused much damage, many did not rebuild.

LUMBER CAMPS

The lumbermen were called woodsmen, piney boys, and shanty boys. After 1870, they were called lumberjacks.

Timber cruisers, or land lookers, would select the best land available and reserve it at the land office for their employers. Later, under the Homesteading Act of 1862, men were hired to claim a plot of 160 acres and stay on it until the timber was cut.

Crews would come in and build a camp, bunkhouse, cook shanty, dining room, and kitchen, the most important part of the camp. A grainery and barn were built. The first party of shanty men usually went out in November and located a site near the center of where the winters labors were to be carried on, always choosing a dry knoll in the immediate vicinity of a spring, lake, or brook. They constructed a log house and cut a road to the nearest stream on which the logs were to be floated down. The log house was sufficiently large enough to accommodate ten to twenty men. In the center, a raised place was built under the apex of the roof which apex let out smoke and let in the sunlight and the rain. Logs were used for seating, grass, evergreen boughs, sawdust, and straw were used for mattress ticking. Bunks were around the outside of the building. The log-cutting usually began in early December and continued until the ice broke up in the spring. Traders were never allowed to bring intoxicating drinks like whiskey, the men having no money to pay for it, as their contract was to be paid at the close of their engagement, the employer supplying food and other necessities in the interim. Whiskey was an essential element of backwoods life, a sovereign remedy for all prevailing ills. It also caused many fights and much damage in the little towns when payday finally came.

Many of the men were young bachelors. Lumber workers often joined volunteer regiments. The men were used to a rugged life and made good soldiers. There were a few women who worked as cooks or clerical workers. Lumber camps became hideouts for deserters and draft dodgers. It was a winter, cold weather job, many farmers went to the woods for the winter. Food was plentiful, if boring. Bread, potatoes, flour, rice, tea, beans, salt meat, pork, and game were the menu. Sugar, jam, fresh vegetables, and fruit were a luxury.

The men were up at 4 AM and worked until dusk. Their teams of horses and oxen were used to haul logs to the river. The horses were often kept in the same building. The loggers made ice-covered roads, the logs were pulled on sleds; they were extremely large loads. There were contests between rival camps to see who could stack the highest loads. The logs were taken to the banks of the rivers and piled 20 to 30 feet high to await the spring thaw, when the flooded rivers, streams, and brooks could float the logs to towns and markets. Many times, dams were built to create enough water to float timber. When the rivers melted, the logs were pushed into the swollen rivers and floated to the mills. At the mills, the logs were sorted into boom areas, each log identified the owner by a log mark on the end of it. The logs were sorted so each company's logs were together.

The forest was so thick with white pine, there was no underbrush, and the sky couldn't be seen overhead. Some trees were over 100 feet tall; a tree, less than three feet in diameter was too small to cut. Some trees were so large it took only four to build a good-sized house.

The growth of towns and cities were around mills. The settlers quickly spread, the land was easier to clear and farm. Timber theft was wide spread.

The work was dangerous and risky. Safety failures and accidents were common. Many were injured and killed. Many were killed by being crushed or drowned in raging rivers by huge sleds and falling trees. Nevertheless, the men were very skillful, contests, and burling contests, were performed. Lumberjack shows were great fun.

The company store had all the necessities for the men: socks, gloves, heavy woolen Mackinaw coats and blankets, tobacco, and a few other items. The men often worked all winter to pay for their clothes and blankets. An old Jack supplied wood for the stoves, hauled water, did washing, etc.

In 1870, the men began to use saws to cut trees down, instead of chopping with an axe. They continued to use the axe to lop off branches and cut a wedge to direct the tree's fall.

Many Indians worked in the lumber industry and boat building trade. Many would cross over from Canada to work on the American side. Judge Bunce had a group who lived nearby and worked for him. They were called Bunce's Indians. Judge Bunce operated a trading post and sawmill business. He had Indians working for him at Bunce Creek and in Abbottsford, where he had two mills in now Ruby, Michigan.

Joe Greaux, Peace Chief of the Woodland Metis Ojibwe Indians, shared how "the Indians worked in the logging camp on Black River and were located at what is now the Clyde Township Hall land on Vincent Road in St. Clair County, Michigan". Many Indians and Black men worked in the lumber camps in Michigan.

BLACKSMITH

The blacksmith was the local toolmaker and engineer, the dentist, doctor, undertaker, veterinarian, and surgeon. He was a horse dealer and usually held important offices in a village, camp, church, or magistrate. The blacksmith was at the heart of every country village, the Jack of all trades. Charcoal was used in the forge; it was homemade of elm and soft maple. Metal was heated to cherry red to white, and the fires were very hot. He would roll his tool, always turning to keep the soft bead on the tip. Sometimes the metal was dipped into water to cool it. Metals were mixed to make tools or other items with special properties. Hammers were used to form products of the forge. These items were made by hand and were called wrought iron.

Blacksmiths kept the horses healthy and made shoes, some having cleats or spikes for the icy roads. Blacksmiths were required to do almost anything. They made wagon wheels of split white oak and hickory and spikes for the wagon wheels. Aside from axes and saws, everything was made on the spot. Pans, nails, armor, chain, swords, every kind of tool, and other items of metal were the blacksmith's craft, made, repaired, and invented. They were the forerunners of today's modern engineering business.

Boom towns sprung up. Preachers were often ignored. The North was the Wild West, the Old West.

Sporting houses were at the edge of towns. They were an accepted part of life in the lake states, necessary to keep respectable females, safe from lustful men. Word of mouth was the advertising, and saloon fights were normal recreation in the woods towns. Many had their pay stolen when drunk. The loggers set their own rules.

There were practical jokes, brawling, brash towns, and lumberjacks. Some men followed a pattern of alternate toil and indolence, hardship and debauch. Some simmered down to start respectability. There were makeshift bars, a board across two stumps, a sawhorse, or barrel. There was a melting pot from all over the world. There was unspeakable whoredom, drunkenness and lawlessness were common. Many met an early death in an, unmarked grave.

The lumbermen left the piney a wasteland. The requirements of sawmill operators encouraged the rise of many machine shops and foundries. These men and shops were used to fuel the farm implement explosion, and fuel the auto industry. Blacksmiths, grist millers, saw millers, potash makers, woolen millers, shingle makers, carpenters, and cobblers were all part of the new settlements. The village store was a trading center for farm products. Barter was the way of buying goods.

TRADER BIOGRAPHIES

"Z. W. Bunce was an early pioneer in St. Clair County, Michigan: a lumberman and Trader, and territorial judge.

Daniel B. Harrington, a gifted natural American, was here in 1819, soon after the territory was organized. He was always in the front of business and intellectual pursuits and did many great things to improve St. Clair County,

Michigan. He was a land surveyor, fur trader, and lumberman. He well knew the forests". MPHC, vol. 28

"Daniel B. Harrington's sawmill was near the now west end of Holland Avenue on the Black River. He cut the timber to build a road north of the fort, now Pine Grove Avenue. He dug a ditch through the swampy lowlands of McNeil's Creek, the forerunner of the canal later built in 1912, between Lake Huron and Black River. Jeremiah Harrington came to Michigan with his brother, Daniel, as fur traders. He worked for the government as a mail carrier in Ohio during the War of 1812. He and Daniel engaged in the lumbering business. His son, Henry, played with the Indian boys and learned their language. His farm was supreme for raising crops of potatoes and corn.

Ralph Wadhams was a lumberman, politician, raised prizewinning cattle, and was a business man and postmaster at Wadhams on the Black River. Ralph and Henry Howard bought the mill of Robert Smart in 1827 at Clyde Mills. Ralph was a delegate to the State Constitutional Convention. He was a supervisor of Desmond Township in 1835, then a large portion of St. Clair County.

David Ward, son of Nathan Ward, was the Timber King, a cousin of Eber Ward. He was a schoolteacher, then a surveyor for Joseph Campau and pine land cruiser, or looker, with his father Nathan. He became an expert, and it became his chief interest. He received a quarter of the lands he surveyed and explored, selecting the best lands. He was a Saginaw land looker. He was involved in bringing the railroad to Saginaw opening up the forests, of Ostego, Manistee, AuSable, Oscoda, and Northwest of Frederick. He also became a physician and surgeon. He was a cousin of Amasa Rust. He had a lifelong feud with his cousin, Eber Brock Ward. David Ward platted the villages of Ruby, Lakeport, and Brockway, and added to Port Huron.

Eber Ward, nephew of Sam Ward, was the Pine King and manager for Sam Ward, who later gave him a large inheritance. Eber built ships at Detroit and Marine City. Eber owned immense mills at Ludington, Michigan and Toledo, Ohio. Eber was involved in lumbering, banking, plate glass making, steel making, and railroad building. He owned land in Ohio and other Northern States.

He owned an island in Lake Superior and had a huge silver mining and smelting business. For fifteen years, the island was the world's greatest silver mine. He then went into the ore business and was a chief promoter of the canal at St. Mary's Falls at the Sault Ste. Marie. He entered the steel making business, making railroad rails and sheet metal, having plants at Wyandotte, Michigan and Chicago, Illinois. He owned controlling interest in six of the greatest iron companies.

He was a pioneer in the iron and steel industry, and the giant of industrialists of the Northwest. Eber died of apoplexy – stroke, or heart attack – on a Detroit street in 1875. Eber's daughter Clara married a Prince Joseph De Caramen-Chimay of Belgium. Eber Ward was once the wealthiest man in the United States" (D. Mitts, 1968, That Noble Country, pg. 122).

"Emily Ward was the sister of Eber Brock Ward, and she was endowed with a great ability in business principles and management of money. She was responsible for much of his phenomenal success. She ran a school to educate young women at Marine City, now the Library. She was a kind, generous, courageous woman, one of the most notable pioneers of the St. Clair River District" (Mitts).

"Sam Ward was a great trader, bringing supplies into the wilderness. His floating bazaar of merchandise was a welcome sight. He owned a sawmill, was a farmer, and owned a large fleet of both passenger and cargo ships. He was also a ship builder at Marine City – Newport. Sam platted the village of Newport and was postmaster, and also operated a trading post and general store at Belle River, now Marine City.

Marine City was the center of shipbuilding, by 1910, 210 vessels had been built there" (Mitts, That Noble Country, pg. 197). "There were many other shipbuilding yards all along the St. Clair River, from Swan Creek to Lakeport on Lake Huron.

Heavy duties on import and export and a monopoly of trade promoted smuggling. There was much pirating and smuggling on the waterways" (MPHC, vol. 28, D.C. Walker).

Black River is 73 miles of main stream, and there are 118 miles of major tributaries. Dams were built at Ruby on the Black River and at Croswell. These dams block fish migration, keeping walleye and sturgeon from prime spawning grounds. The river is yet cleansing itself of debris. Bald eagles are once again frequenting the area above the valley. There are 89 species of fish in the Black River. There are 96 dams on the Huron River, 79 on the Clinton River, and 63 on the Rouge River.

The Strait of the St. Clair River, the Detroit River, and the St. Lawrence Seaway are the busiest waterways on earth. Steamers and sail vessels pass through the Strait of the St. Clair River every four minutes, day and night.

There are 6,000 shipwrecks in the Great Lakes.

"Pirouges (large dugouts), Mackinaw Barges (Batteaus), and Durham boats which had flat bottoms and a running board along the whole length of each side, the crew walked on while poling the boat. These were used in early trade. Sails were used when the winds were fair. Petiager was a boat made from a tree trunk hollowed out, often provided with a plank bottom, the trunk being split in two halves, each of which was made to serve as one side of the boat" (Askin 1, pg. 238).

"During the British occupation, boats were built at Detroit. Between 1774 and 1782, nine vessels were built and launched at Detroit boatyards for defense and trade. They were from 18 to 136 tons burden" (Parkins).

"The first boat other than the Indians' vessels, canoes of all sizes, was the *Griffon* in 1680, with LaSalle and Hennepin aboard. LaSalle was granted a monopoly on trade of the Mississippi for five years; the Jesuits incite war and try to ruin him" (Metis Timeline, info/metis.aspx).

"The Miller salt well was a great source of wealth. Mack and Miller had a distillery on Harsens Island" (MPHC vol. 4). Aura Stewart was a distiller on Harsens Island.

"100 million acres of land was given to the railroad companies in the U.S. for free. Much swindling, scheming, and profiteering was involved. Wild fraud and monopolies bled the people" (The Peoples History).

"In 1878, on the St. Clair River, 37,188 vessels of all kinds passed through. The Strait of St. Clair and Detroit Rivers were the only route of travel for the immense commerce of the great chain of Lakes. The St. Clair River is one of the finest and safest harbors in the world" (Jenks).

CHAPTER 7
Part I: The French, British, English and Americans

"War was the royal pastime – the hunting game of Princes for spoil and dominion. [. . .] for the purposes of violence and devastation, of lust, rapine, and insatiate ambition, long drenched the earth with blood and tears, and rent the sky with cries of anguish" (Macomb Memoir, www).

Wampum and the calumet pipe of peace, or truth pipe, were used in Council Assemblies as the Bible is used in taking an oath. It was a, Thank or Grace, oath of loyalty and good faith, ascending to the Father of Spirits.

The Dutch introduced the practice of scalping and expanded it to include bounty for Natives fit to be sold into slavery. The Dutch and Puritans joined forces to exterminate all Native Savages. Slicing open innocents' heads and using them as kickballs and decorations, they raped and tortured all night as entertainment, doing this as an example for the Mohawk Iroquois. The horrific European practice was often attributed to Aboriginal people (Metis Canadian History, A Distinct Point of View, www).

THE FRENCH

Fish, furs, and French jealousy were all factors in the efforts of France to possess the New World. Political and religious ambitions that knew no bounds incarnated in men who feared nothing and would dare everything to further the interests of France and the Jesuit Order. They went everywhere and marked the route, claiming the land as its own. It was designated New France, Louisiana, or Canada.

Ottissippi

Four kings have ruled this region: Henry IV, until he died. Then Louis XIII, at age 16, with Cardinal Richlieu as his Prime Minister. Louis XIV, at age 14, became King. The Duke of Orleans served as Regent, when Louis XV, at 13, was crowned King. Then King George of England became Sovereign of Detroit, in 1763 and the Treaty of Paris.

Under the French Government, a governor general appointed by the king commanded at Quebec. Local commandants were appointed for Detroit and other posts. They were held responsible to the governor general to whom they reported from 1603 to 1760.

Cadillac's description of Detroit: The Detroit is but a channel or river of medium breadth and 25 leagues, through flows the waters of the Sweet Seas to the ocean. Its borders are so many vast prairies, and the freshness of the beautiful waters keeps the banks always green. The prairies are bordered by long and broad rows of fruit trees which have never felt the hand of the vigilant gardener. Here also orchards, young and old, bend their branches under the weight and quantity of their fruit towards the Mother Earth which has produced them. It is in this land, so fertile, that the ambitious vine builds a thick roof with its large leaves and heavy clusters.

Under these broad walks one sees assembled by hundreds the timid deer and faun, also the squirrel bounding in his eagerness to collect the apples and plums with which the earth is covered. Here the turkey gathers the grapes. Golden pheasants, the quail, the partridge, woodcock, and numerous doves swarm in the woods and cover the country, which is dotted and broken with thickets and high forests of full grown trees, forming a charming perspective. The hand of the pitiless reaper has never mown the luxuriant grass upon which fatten the wooly buffaloes of magnificent size and proportion.

The fish are here in great abundance. Swans are so numerous that one would take for lilies the reeds in which they are crowded together. The gabbling goose, the duck, the widgeon, and the bustard are so abundant that they draw up in lines to let the boats pass through. The climate temperate, the air purified by a gentle breeze, the sky's always serene.

The situation is agreeable, and it opens and closes the door of passage to the most distant nations situated on the borders of the vast seas of sweet water.

None but the Enemies of Truth could be enemies to this establishment so necessary to the increase of the glory of the King, to the progress of religion, and the destruction of the throne of Baal (Cadillac).

So numerous and large, indeed, were the wild bison that the making of garments from their wool was seriously considered. In addition to the animals named, elk, moose, wolves, bears, rabbits, otters, lynxes, wildcats, beavers, and muskrats were very numerous in the vicinity, of Detroit. There was a three or four dollar, bounty paid for killing wolves. Myriads of wild pigeons made their roosts in the forests of the country, being so numerous that hundreds could easily be killed with a walking stick (Western Historical Co. 1883).

Canada was surrendered to the British in 1760. The Quebec Act of 1774 called for a civil government of the territory, including Detroit. None of the governor generals exercised any authority over this region, except as military officers. The resident commandant exercised both a civil and a military rule, subject to the orders of his commanding general. All posts West of Detroit were governed from this establishment (Farmer, 1884).

Throughout its history, the Port Huron, Michigan area and the Strait lands of Canada and Detroit, as the strategic gateway to the Upper Lakes, was an area that a succession of Indian, French, British, and American leaders sought to control (Adapted from Mitts, The Times Herald, "As the Wild Goose flies", SCC library MI Room).

The Ojibwe were a major power; a variety of names and divisions of population masked their true size. The Grand Saulteur was an important Ojibwe chief. There were 150 bands of 35,000 Ojibwe living at Sault St. Marie River in Southern Ontario (Chippewa History, EHow, www).

The King made grants to seigneurs, giving him complete control of large estates, which were parceled out to purchasers or cultivated by his own people or were farmed out to lessees on terms agreed upon. The terms of sale were by decree of the King. When an officer was allowed to build a fort in a new place, he was often made proprietor of the fort and certain adjacent lands, which he could lease or sell (Farmer).

EARLY FRENCH HISTORY

Jean Talon, the Intendant of New France, was determined to expand the territory of King Louis XIV. The Hudson's Bay Co. was in the far North, and he thought it may come South also. He sent Nicolas Perrot, an intrepid explorer and interpreter, to call an assembly of the tribes of the Northern Lakes at Sault Ste. Marie. Francois Daumont, Seiur De St. Lusson, was sent as the King's representative.

On June 14, 1671, beside the St. Mary River Rapids, a great crowd gathered and a ceremony made. A procession of French missionaries in black robes, the interpreter, Nicolas Perrot, and St. Lusson, wearing an army uniform, were followed by the traders and voyagers with bright sashes about their waists. The cross was then planted and the territory claimed for French dominion.

Ottissippi

The Iroquois attacked Grand Kaskaskia, Illinois in 1680, then attacked Fort St. Louis, where they were beaten in battle and retreated (Metis Timeline, info/metis.aspx).

The first Indian scalps were cut off during King Phillip's War in 1675. In 1683, New France began taking Iroquois slaves by the King's order (Metis History, www).

In 1684, slaves flee the British for the Spanish colony of La Florida; thousands flee for freedom and establish St. Augustine, Florida.

DULHUT - DULUTH

The most famous of the *coureur de bois*, "the King of the *Coureurs De Bois*", was Daniel Do Grosollon, Sieur Du L'Hut. Born at St. Germain En Laye, France. A member of the Royal Guard for Louis XIV. At 20 years old, he obtained a captain's commission in the Marines in Canada. He returned to France in 1674 and fought with Cond'e, the Prince of Orange. The Recollect Louis Hennepin was also there as a noncombatant, aiding the wounded and confessing the dying. Hennepin was a companion to LaSalle on his voyage in New France. Returning to Montreal, Duluth sold his quiet home to embark on a life of adventure.

In 1678, he and his brother, Claude Grossalon De La Tourette, six Frenchmen, and three Indian slaves, presented to him by friendly Indians to serve as guides, set out. His object was to enter the Sioux country west of Lake Superior. In 1679, he reached the village of Kathio, the main castle of the Sioux. He planted the French Royal Arms, taking possession of the country in his liege's name. He made peace between the Ojibwe and the Sioux with treaties to take their furs to Montreal. This act opened the West to French trade.

When Dulhut heard about prisoners in the Sioux camp, he went to find them. One was Pierre Hennepin, his friend from France and explorer with LaSalle. He commanded their release, and they were released.

Dulhut was condemned as going against the French policy of non-traffic with the Natives during this time. He was condemned as being the captain of the *coureur de bois*, which he denied, spending all his time persuading the Western Indians to trade with the French at Montreal, defeating the designs of the English from the South and the North at Hudson's Bay. He went to France and was entirely restored. On return, he was appointed to a council to decide on the course of action regarding the Iroquois.

In 1683, he was sent to Michilimackinac to direct the important Indian Trade of the North. He built a new fort, Kaministiqua, three miles from Fort William, the main fort in use. LaSalle from St. Louis was sent to

Michilimackinac to answer to La Durantaye, commander at Michilimackinac, for his lawless misdemeanors. He passed the charge to Dulhut, claiming he was "King of the *Coureurs De Bois*" and to blame.

When Dulhut was left in command of the fort while La Durantaye was away as envoy to LaSalle, he was brought news of two Frenchmen being murdered by Indians near Keweenaw. He deemed for the safety of all that the offenders be apprehended, tried, and punished. He went to the Folle Avoine, "Rice People", who told him it was Achiganaga and his son who murdered and pillaged the traders. They were found and acknowledged their fault. The Indians normally paid restitution for a death. After a great council, the father, and a Folle Avoinee, were released, and the two sons accused one another. They were convicted and must die as the Frenchmen had. The men were taken to a hill, shot, and buried upon their own testimony. Dulhut was the first to exhibit the French Code. Some condemned the act as harsh and impolite, yet as the Enforcer of Life, he was upheld.

Dulhut was a leader of the Indians. His services were sought in dealing with the Indians. He was a friend of Governor Frontenac engaged in the Fur Trade on a large scale. He became the commandant of Michilimackinac and the trade of the North and West.

In 1685, Dulhut was asked to build a post (fort) at the foot of Lake Huron – or Fort Detroit, Fort Duluth, or Fort St. Joseph, as it was called. A military trading post to protect the Allies when fighting the English and Iroquois invaders. The forts were a haven of protection. He was promised a garrison of 50 men. Instead, he had to garrison and provision the post at his own expense.

Fort Saint Joseph was built by Duluth, the little bastioned block house of logs. M. De Beauvis was lieutenant of Fort St. Joseph at the Strait of Lakes Huron and Erie. Fort St. Joseph was elevated, commanding the rapids. The fort at St. Joseph is called "Tirkarondia" or "Tyscharondia", meaning the "Place of Many Beavers" (Jenks, vol. 1, 1912).

In 1686, Duluth was called to gather allies for an attack on the Seneca Iroquois in New York, who had smuggled trade items to Michilimackinac for the Albany Dutch traders.

The fort complex was the staging area for military actions. Governor Denonville planned a great campaign against the Iroquois. Fort St. Joseph became the mobilization center of 200 *coureur de bois* and 500 Indians of the Three Fires Alliances. Henry De Tonti, Nicholas Perrot, and LaForest each brought a contingent from their posts. La Durantaye had caught 30 prisoners and an English party, with a load of goods, on a second trip to Michilimackinac.

Ottissippi

The Indians celebrated with wild demonstration and were hurried away by Duluth to rendezvous with Governor Denonville. Another party of English traders were captured on Lake Erie. The expedition did not accomplish much but was a show of force in defense of Canada.

Louis Arnand De Lom D'arce, Baron Lahonton, was then the commandment of Fort St. Joseph. He had a keen sense of humor and unusual ability as a writer. His writings of the savages and New France are enlightening. He was a great hunter with his Indian companions. The long winter gave him time to write. He wished for a more exciting place, and being short on supplies and hearing of the French failure in New York, he abandoned the post to transfer the forces and supplies to Michilimackinac and burned the post in 1688, the only barrier against the English and Iroquois.

LAHONTON

Lahonton was sent to man the post at Fort St. Joseph, being accompanied from Niagra by Dulhut.

In 1687 to 1688, we killed deer and roebucks of the islands in the water. We arrived at the mouth of the Lake of Huron's.

From Lahonton's *Travels through Louisiana*, he tells of life at Ft. St. Joseph: the men of my detachment are brisk, proper fellows, and my canoes are both new and large. The Iroquois canoe was made of elm bark and very thick and heavy. Thirty men row in them, they are so long and broad; they are two abreast. I am to go along with M. Dulhut, a Lion's Gentleman, who is a person of great merit and has done his king and his country very considerable service.

Mr. Delhut's *coureur de bois* had planted in the fort, bushels of turkey wheat (maize or Indian corn), which afforded a plentiful crop that proved of great use to me. Our fort covers a square of one arpent (French about .8445 acre) in extent, without the bastions, and is very advantageously situated on an eminence (hill), separated from the river by a gentle slope of about 40 paces – 120 feet. Mr. Delhut has presented me with a great roll of tobacco to trade for corn at Mackinac. The Indians raised summer squash extensively.

Fort St. Joseph is used by the Huron and Ottawa of Lake Huron to retreat to against the Iroquois.

Sault Ste Marie was visited by traders as early as 1616. After the discovery of the Mississippi, Michilimackinaw became the most important, and SS Marie became a station on the trade route to the far Northwest.

Lahonton saw the English as taking over the Fur Trade, the Fish Trade, and more. Their prices were lower for better goods. Birch leaves as fine as paper are here, and I frequently made use of 'em, for want of paper, in writing the journal of my voyages.

Henry De Tonty was a Neopolitan whose Father invented the insurance system (Lahonton).

To die is nothing, but to live, in the midst of fire is too much.

La Durantaye had halted his savage forces from the far Indians (Mackinac) at the head of the Strait, leading from Lake Huron to Lake St. Clair, and there on June 7, 1687 had erected the Arms of France and taken formal possession of this vast region in the name of the King. Fevers raged among the militia who, being unacquainted with the way of setting boats with poles, were faced at every turn to get into the water and drag 'em up against the rapid stream.

Fort Debaude, the French fort in Sault Sainte Marie, was the headquarters of the French Fur Trade in the Northwest of New France. With the government in Montreal and Quebec City, the country was of two parts: Quebec in the North, and Louisiana below.

Due to increasing hostility of the English and their allied Indians, Governor Denonville was unable to cope, and Louis XIV appointed Frontenac again, now 70, as Governor of New France. He returned to Quebec in the momentous year of 1690.

He immediately sent 150 Canadians with Louvigny to build Fort De Baude at Michilmackinac, named for Count Frontenac. The English would receive a warm welcome if they dared to come trading. Charles Lemoyne, Sieur De Longueuill, led the expedition which founded Louisiana in 1699. In 1692, he served against the English in Acadia. He also attacked the English Fleet in the West Indies in 1706.

Frontenac beat off an attack on Quebec by an English Squadron in 1690. In 1691, he had built a fort on the St. Joseph River, near Niles, Michigan, to stop the English traders going West near Lake Michigan and the Mississippi. It was called Fort St. Joseph (Fowle). The fort was on the main trade route and the war routes in Southern Michigan.

Father Claude Allouez was at the Mission to the Miami and the Pottawatomi. There the Iroquois attacked in 1694 and were vigorously beaten, withdrawing their plan to war with the Illinois Indians, allied with the French.

Chief Kondiaronk, of much ability, played a prominent role in Frontenac's War, his skill in diplomatic and confederating the tribes. He was a precursor to Pontiac and Tecumseh. He was strongly attached to Frontenac and accepted his council. He was a Christian convert who preached at Mackinac. He died at Montreal during an important Peace Conference in 1701. He was interred with elaborate rites.

Ottissippi

CADILLAC

Antoine De La Mothe Cadillac, a captain in the troops of the colony. The governor praised Cadillac for his valor, wisdom, experience, and good conduct.

Cadillac was born in the Province of Gascony, France. In 1658, he went out to Canada and, around 1683, to Nova Scotia. He married Marie Therese Guyon, daughter of a sea captain he had explored the New England Coast with. For a time, he was a seigneur at Bar Harbor Maine, granted to him by the King.

Cadillac was called on in 1689, after the outbreak of war, to return to France and relay his knowledge of the New England Coast. He returned to Canada with orders for Governor Frontenac to reward him for his services. The governor soon discovered his great capabilities. A true Gascon, proud, energetic, sharp-tongued, quick to draw his sword, and facile with a pen. His vigorous administration and ability to control the Indians, his loyalty, won the support of Count Frontenac and of Count Ponchetrain, the Minister of Colonies, and Louis XIV himself.

Michilimackinac was the most important place in the West, the commandant of Fort Debaude having the supervision over all the forts. Father Nouvel, the superior over all Western Missions, was also headquartered in the Mission at Sainte Ignace. A small French village was nearby, and the Huron and Ottawas had large towns close by.

During the trading season, the towns swelled to 5,000 Indians camping, and the *courieur de bois* added another hundred. The sale of brandy soon caused a feud between Cadillac and the Jesuits, which had disastrous consequences for him. The region had become safe again for voyagers to bring furs to Montreal; the Jesuits demanded that the Indians be protected from traders selling whiskey in the villages.

In 1686, Louis XIV decreed that the West would be closed to all Frenchmen, except the missionaries. The Indians would have to carry their furs to Montreal. The French population remained small, the King allowing only Roman Catholics entry. Many French Huguenots – Protestants who rejected the Catholic system of feudalism – came to America and went to English lands.

The English Colonies were growing very large. The religious groups being persecuted in Europe found freedom to worship as they pleased. Thousands of French Huguenots fled to Germany, England, and the American Colonies, where they became valuable members of communities.

Fort Debaude and Fort St. Joseph were abandoned in 1698.

Cadillac had done well in the trade at Michilimackinac and worked with the Indians. He went to the King with a plan to establish a post on the Strait between Lake Huron and Erie to keep the English from the rich fur country of the Northwest. Cadillac would bear the costs with his trade to the area. The strategic position of the fort was superior to the Michilimackinac Post.

Cadillac was one of the few French military who understood the Indians and demanded they be respected.

It was not uncommon for the same person to be designated two or more names, entirely different from each other (Farmer 1884). This adds great confusion to history, as does changing names of places, waterways, and landmarks.

CADILLAC AND THE DETROIT

Antoine De La Mothe Cadillac, also Lamothe Launay or Laumet, was a close observer. He thought out his work and planned like a general. He exhibited rare commercial foresight; he would neither yield his right of judgement nor his prerogatives as commandant.

He was opposed in many of his plans by trading companies and by the Jesuits, who were the dominant political force in the New World and the strongest religious power. While yielding the Jesuit Fathers all deference in religious matters, Cadillac would not yield to their dictation in matters pertaining to the Civil State. He knew his rights, and was able, to maintain them even against large odds, with spirit and determination. Nothing escaped his observation; he discerned motives and plans.

In 1701, Cadillac was granted a seigniory, a domain of 15 arpents square, or 15 acres square, equal to 225 acres, to encourage settlement of the French in the new region and block the English from trading to the North and West. Cadillac's grant would now be bounded by the Detroit River, Brush Street, and Cass and Grand River Avenue. Documents in Quebec show he claimed all of the land on both sides of the River Detroit from Lake Erie to Lake Huron. He claimed the entire Strait because of the great expense he incurred in establishing the first colony and also because of the general benefits accruing to New France from the peace he secured with the Iroquois and for establishment of the fort at Detroit, which prevented the English from reaching the Western Indians.

In pursuance of his claim, he made a concession to his eldest son of a tract of land on the river, beginning at the entrance into Lake Erie, with a frontage of six leagues (18 miles), and extending back five leagues (15 miles) from the river. This concession included Grosse Isle and all the adjacent islands. He made grants to Guion and Witherell.

He praised the Strait extravagantly to Count Ponchetrain: The earthly paradise, beautiful streams, broad avenues of fruit trees, never having a watchful

Ottissippi

gardener, drooping under the weight of their fruit. So temperate, so fertile, and so beautiful. It may justly be called the Earthly Paradise of North America.

The Wyandotte – Ouendats – were already here doing the business of trading with the tribes. The Ojibwe, Miami, Pottawatomi, Winebagoe's, Ottawa, and Huron were Algonquin and Allies. Trading was more a social and political exchange of goodwill than economic. The ancient Huron village was across from Detroit. The Illinois, Osage, and Missouri also sent some families to Detroit.

The Wyandots were the leading tribe in the territory of the Northwest. To them was entrusted the Great Calumet, which united all the tribes in that territory in a confederacy for mutual protection and gave them the right to assemble the tribes in council and to kindle the Council Fire (Taylor 1898).

The main Ottawa village was at Gibralter, Michigan and about Amherstburg on the main land (Ontario), where they erected their Council House. In this village was kept their archives and international Council Fire. They occupied a great territory from the Detroit River to Cleveland, and South to the Shawnee towns (in southern Ohio). (Taylor 1898).

A large rock (Gibralter) in the Detroit River marked the turn on the river to the Wyandotte council area for many far away tribes coming to the councils.

The calumet was the great token of peace (the Truth Pipe). A large pipe made of marble with a two and a half-foot long reed or cane adorned with feathers, women's hair, and bird wings. A pipe for peace and for war. Councils were to be true and honest before God (Ohio History Central Connection).

Cadillac invited the friendly Indians to settle nearby for trade and for protection against the English Allies. The Huron and Miami settled below the fort, the Ojibwe and Ottawa above, The Pottawatomi to the West.

So many of the Northern Indians left Michilimackinac that Father Carheil burned the Chapel of St. Ignace and left for Quebec.

The Indians who come to trade at Detroit are the Hurons, the Ottawas, the Sauteurs, and the Pottawatomie's, who are of all the Indians most faithful and the most attached to our interests. They never murdered any Frenchmen and have often warned us of the plots of other tribes.

Cadillac was denied schools and military training for the Natives. After buying out the Company of the Colony at Quebec, Cadillac had full command.

In 1705, about 200 Indians had settled nearby. The numerous Indians were overcrowded, taxing the resources and quarreling with each other.

Cadillac always received the visiting Indians chiefs with great courtesy. They dined with him, and he lavished presents upon them. Vermillion was given, red coats, white ruffled shirts, silver bangles, tobacco, and brandy. The

Indians returned furs in appreciation. Wampum was always used to record transactions, and he smoked the Red Calumet of Peace with them.

As a seignior, Cadillac would pledge fealty to the King, file the lands granted to tenants, and built a mill for the villagers, and was to perform military service as needed. The habitants owed the seignior fealty and homage. They would raise their hats to him, grind their grain at his mill, paying one-fourteenth for the grinding, work a certain number of days each year on the seignior's farm, and pay rent in produce or goods. The tenants paid rent in fun (pleasure) or cash, though most traded produce. They paid a fee to work at a skilled craft. They were required to erect a maypole at his residence. A celebration was made for all.

The habitants had the privilege of trading, hunting, and fishing, but were not to kill hares, partridge, or pheasants. He could not sell or give his land as security without consent, and if it was sold, Cadillac was to have the first right of purchase. One De Lorme's grant of 32 acres also stipulated he was also to furnish timber for vessels and fortifications when desired, and further promised not to work as a blacksmith, cutler, armorer, or brewer without a special permit. He might import goods but could employ no clerks unless they lived in Detroit. And he was not to sell liquor to Indians.

Under Cadillac, a windmill was built on the river. He was reported to the governor for charging one-eighth and was ordered to reduce it to the usual rate. Cadillac brought horses and cattle from Montreal, and pigs were kept on Isle Aux Cochons, Hog Island – Belle Isle. The fort was equipped with the best armament available.

Cadillac called a great council of the chiefs for four days, August 6 to August 10, 1707. The following is from a Colonial Memoir written in 1707 and preserved at Paris.

The village of the Pottawatomie's adjoins the fort, they lodge partly under apaquois, which are made of mat grass. The women do all this work. The men are well clothed. Their entire occupation is hunting and dress. They make use of a great deal of vermillion and, in winter, wear buffalo robes richly painted and, in summer, either blue or red cloth.

They play a good deal at Lacrosse in summer. Twenty or more on each side. Their bat is a sort of little racket, and the ball with which they play is made of very heavy wood, somewhat larger than the balls used at tennis. When playing, they are entirely naked except a breech cloth and moccasins on their feet. Their body is painted with all sorts of colors. Some, with white clay, trace white lace on their bodies, as if on all the seams of a coat, and at a distance, it would appear to be taken for silver lace. They play deep bets, and often village against village. (This letter is continued in "Chapter 4: Explorers and Missionaries".)

Ottissippi

The face of nature, fresh in luxuriance of virgin soil, was everywhere clothed in magnificent vegetation, Indian trails wound through the forest, extensive tracts of oak lands that seemed like cultivated parks, studded with little crystal lakes and streams covered with flowers.

Herds of buffalo – beeves – great numbers of moose and elk, rich clusters of grapes, apples and plums.

A large number of half-breed children were around their posts, the offspring of their licentiousness (Lanman, Red Book).

There was a vast mart of trade of commercial preeminence. The Ottawa first felt the repercussions of the permanent invasion. Indian tribes and White traders were dealing directly with the French or British for foreign-made goods. The French trusted the Indians; no seals or locks were placed on the storehouses, and the Indians came and went when they pleased.

Cadillac's enemies in New France used their influence against him. The Montreal Merchants, "The Company of the Colony of Canada", feared injury, and the missionaries opposed the liquor trading and debauching of the Indians. Many attempts were made to remove him. Because of frequent complaints, he was removed in 1710 and appointed Governor of Louisiana, the Southern French lands.

THE FOX WAR

The Fox Indians from the West were invited to Detroit, who created unending disturbance. The quarrels at Detroit in 1706 were over resources; large numbers of people caused shortages, some villages were being plundered.

France and England tampered with the Indians. English intrigue with the Iroquois of New York planned to attack Detroit and capture it, using Fox and Mascoutin warriors from Green Bay, Wisconsin, enemies of the Huron's who controlled trade. The Fox who were pushed West from Michigan were invaders at Detroit, by English and Iroquois designs.

A Mascouten village on the St. Joseph River in Southwest Michigan had been attacked by Saguina, an Ottawa war chief, and his Pottawatomi allie, Makisabe. Over 150 people were killed in the attack. Outraged, the Fox and Mascouten took hostages and threatened to kill Ottawa and Potawatommi and their French allies (Cleland, Rites of Conquest, pg. 115, 116).

They came in May of 1712, an unexpected arrival. While the Huron and Ottawa were away hunting, 30 men burnt the church and storehouse. Commandant DuBusson called for reinforcements of Indian allies. Many came to destroy the Fox and Mascouten: they were Huron, Miami, Illinois, Missouri's, Osages, and other far nations. The Ottawa, Pottawatomi, Sacs, and

Menominie's were all nations against the Fox and Mascoutens. Their armies marched in good order with as many flags as there were different nations. They went directly to the fort of the Huron's and immediately went to fight.

There were 400 to 500 who made a blockade at their village and fort, fighting for 19 days. At Windmill Point, the Fox, having 1,000 people, were overtaken, few Fox escaped. Women and children were taken as slaves. The men shot and tortured four of five every day (Utley).

The Fox dug in and built a fort for defense, sending blazing arrows to burn the town. The fight lasted 19 days. On a stormy night, they escaped in retreat; they were overtaken in pursuit by the allied warriors at Windmill Point – Grosse Pointe. The majority of the Fox were destroyed, and many captives were tortured. The few who returned to Wisconsin created bitter enemies to the French, blocking further Westward fur trading on the Fox River route to the West. There was almost constant turmoil, quarrels, and jealousies among themselves (Utley).

In the Fox War in 1712 at Detroit, the Fox were trying to burn up the town. Their method of firing the place was to shoot large arrows mounted with combustible material in flame, in a rainbow form track through the sky. The bows and arrows being very large and stout, the Indians lay with their backs on the ground, putting both feet against the central portion of the inner side of the bow and pulled the strings with all the might of their hands. A ball of blazing material would thus be sent arching over nearly a quarter of a mile, which would come down perpendicularly upon the dry shingle roofs of the houses and set them on fire. The French then covered the roofs with wet skins (Western Historical Co. History of St. Clair County).

The Northern Fox Wars were over the rice lakes and furs. The English continued fighting for the French Country on both sides of the Atlantic. Pent up millions in semi bondage, select ones claiming divine origin came to pluck the wealth of the new world. The art of the printing press was soon to emancipate – free the mind – and cast broadly the seeds of universal liberty; the rich soil was to germinate the great truths of science – knowledge.

There were French and English trade wars in Europe and border raids in America; peace and harmony was an impossibility. The French were occupying land into Ohio and Pennsylvania, the Ohio and the Mississippi, English soil.

A new fort was established at Mackinaw in 1715, called "Michilimackinac". Fort St. Joseph was built in Southwest Michigan near Niles on the St. Joseph River, and Fort Ponchetrain was maintained to stop the English from passing to the Upper Lakes and obtaining furs.

Border raids continued in the East, and the English continually crossed the Allegheny Mountains into the Ohio Country. English traders encroached into the territory, selling cheaper and better goods to the Indians. The Indians became lukewarm to their French brothers.

In 1736, there were 500 Indian warriors at Detroit, 200 from the Huron and Ottawa tribes and 100 from the Pottawatomie's. This represented over 2,500 people. Sometimes the number of people gathered at Detroit was about 6,000, representing many tribes.

In 1749, at Pickawillany, the great Miami Indian village of Chief La Demoiselle – Old Britain at Piqua Ohio – the Indians favored the English traders, refusing to obey the French order to remove to the Maumee River under the French Trade. Celeron, the commander at Detroit, went to Quebec to report the state of affairs in the Ohio country. He was sent back with orders to punish La Demoiselle and drive the English out of the region.

In 1752, a great flotilla of canoes carrying 250 Ottawa and Ojibwa – Chippewa warriors – came to Detroit from the North. The commander, Charles Michel Mouet, Sieur De Langlade, a half-breed from the North, who gathered his war party at Sault Ste. Marie and Michilimackinac for the purpose of destroying Pickawillany. Reinforcements from Detroit joined and went to visit Pickawillany. The fierce attack was successful. LaDamoiselle was boiled and eaten, six English traders captured.

The traders from the North began avoiding Michilimackinac and trading to the English for better and cheaper goods.

The French built a fort at Sault Ste. Marie to capture the trade. Repentigny, a capable trader from New York, was co-seignory with Debonne, whose uncle was Governor La Johnquiere.

France and Britain were officially at peace. Events were moving to a collision. New forts were ordered by Marquis Dusquense, a line from Lake Erie to the forks of the Ohio, to exclude the English – British – from the West. In 1751 and 1752, Celeron, the French commandant, wrote to the King that wives for the men was the greatest want.

The French built Fort Dusquense, now Pittsburgh, at the forks of the Ohio. British General Braddock crossed the Allegheny to attack Fort Dusquense; Charles Langlade and his allied warriors led the French defense.

George Washington at 21 years old was sent to give a message to the French at Fort Leboeuf at Erie Penn to leave the British Territory. He was treated well and went back to Virginia to relay information that the French intended to take the country.

The English Governor Robert Dinwiddie of Virginia in 1753 to 1754 sent Major George Washington to warn the French to leave the Allegheny River Line to the Ohio River Forks. He was informed they would not remove from their posts and intended to control the Ohio River.

The Iroquois began selling land belonging to the Shawnee and Delaware people, forcing them to withdraw to new territory west of the Appalachian Mountains (Adapted from, page 47, Tanner, The Ojibwa). Then the Iroquois granted British land speculators rights to land in the Ohio River country, and settlers started coming across the mountains in 1754. The Delaware and the Shawnee attacked them (Tanner, page 47, The Ojibwa).

In 1754, the Council of the St. Clair Saulteaux sent 10 warriors to the Ohio to survey the situation. They would have been led by their War Chief, "Little Thunder" (David Plain). Washington was sent to build a fort there at the forks of the Ohio. At the Ohio River where the forks to the Monongahela and Allegheny Rivers meet, Washington built a small fort. The French ousted Washington, then went to now Pittsburgh, Pennsylvania and built Fort Dusquense.

THE FRENCH AND INDIAN WAR

A courier was sent to Washington, ordering them to vacate French lands. Washington attacked and killed him – a great mistake. The French and Indian Allies were taken by surprise and bested, the British killed 10 Frenchmen and taking French prisoners. This is what started the French and Indian War. The Indians treated messengers with utmost respect and safety. It was the Indian way to never injure a messenger. Washington was routed by the French and compelled to surrender his whole force on July 4, 1754. This was the beginning of the French and Indian War.

Colonel Stephen wrote Colonel Washington that his men needed shoepacks or moccasins: "The Indians discover our parties by the track of their shoes. It would be a good thing to have shoepacks, or moccasins, for the scouts" (Col. Adam Stephen to Col. Washington, 27, Sept. 1755).

In 1755, Charles Langlade and the French and 400 Indian Allies from Canada, including 11 Lake Indians from the St. Clair, gathered with 500 Frenchmen who went to Pittsburgh and fought General Braddock and General Washington, Braddock's Aide De Camp. Pontiac was there, Henry Gladwin was there. Daniel Boone was there and escaped on a horse to his father's farm. There was a great defeat of the British. Braddock had four horses shot out from under him, and Washington had two horses shot from under him and four bullet holes in his coat. The Indians carried away much war booty in horses and other goods.

The Americans had no clue to the Indians' forest warfare tactics. The British hardly saw the enemy hiding among the trees, thickets, rocks, gullies, and logs. The Americans were in total disarray and retreated. General Braddock was killed, and 977 of his forces were killed or wounded. The Indians lost 23.

In 1755, scalp bounties were offered for Indian scalps by the English. During the 1700s, the French bounty was 40 pounds for each English scalp (Metis History, www).

In 1756, the Ojibwes and Allies went to New York to a Peace Treaty with the Iroquois to create a stable trade route. They were given silver boxes as gifts to take home to their villages. These boxes were infected with smallpox. It was brought back to the villages and swept through the Great Lakes in 1757 and 1758, killing many with biological warfare. In 1757, at Pittsburgh, silver boxes contaminated with smallpox were given to the Ottawa by Americans who brought them to the villages in the Great Lakes and Ontario. Smallpox raged through the land.

The French intermarried with the Indians, they were surrounded by thousands of savages. The British and English also married the Indian maidens (Farmer, 1884 pg. 326).

THE BRITISH

French Quebec fell to the British in 1758. The French title to Louisiana at the Gulf was turned over to Spain. The new British Governor Lord Jeffrey Amhurst, a British Army General and Royal Governor of Virginia from 1759 to 1768. Born in Kent County, England, Amhurst served as Commander General of British Forces in North America in 1758.

Major Rogers was sent to receive the surrender of Detroit. 600 people lived within the palisades. The settlement was on both sides of the river, having 2,500 inhabitants in 80 houses with 300 families (Parkins, Historical Geography of Detroit). In 1760, with the surrender of Fort Ponchetrain at Detroit, the French were defeated, and the British came in to rule the new Frontier. The British established posts on the border. They made annual gifts to their Indian allies. Rum was plentiful.

British traders moved into the Ohio Valley. The Ohio River was called Belle Riviere (David Plain). The Treaty of Utrecht was their reason. This was a treaty with the Iroquois Indians who had long since lost this territory. Though the French had claimed it, the Ohio Territory belonged to the Miami, Delaware, and Shawnee.

In 1761, Chief Minavavana said to the English at Fort Michilimackinac in his speech, "We are not conquered. The Great Spirit provides for us; we will not be slaves. These lakes, woods, mountains were left to us by our ancestors. They are our inheritance, and we will part with them to none. Your nation supposes that we, like the White people, cannot live without bread and pork and beef! But you ought to know that He, the Great Spirit and Master of Life, had provided food for us in these spacious lakes and on these wooded mountains.

Englishman, our Father the King of France, employed our young men to make war upon your nation. In this warfare, many of them have been killed, and it is our custom to retaliate until such times as the spirits of the slain are satisfied. But the spirits of the slain are to be satisfied in either of two ways: The first is by the spilling of blood of the nations by which they fell; the other, by covering the bodies of the dead, and thus allowing the resentment of their relations. This is done by making presents.

Englishman, your King has never sent us any presents, nor entered into any treaty with us, wherefore he and we are still at war; until he does these things, we must consider that we have no other Father, nor friend, among the White men than the King of France, but for you we have taken into consideration that you ventured your life among us in the expectation that we should not molest you. You do not come armed with an intention to make war; you come in peace, to trade with us and supply us with necessaries of which we are in much want. We shall regard you, therefore, as a Brother; and you may sleep tranquilly without fear of the Chippeway's. As a token of our friendship, we present you with this pipe to smoke."

In tribal tradition, peace could have soon been concluded with the payment of reparations as gifts. The British, being ignorant of this fact, regarrisoned the Western posts but did not supply the Indians with presents. This greatly angered the Indians, who viewed the same arrangement with the French as a form of rent on the land where the forts were erected, and as a toll for passage through their country. British trade policy and attitude of the colonial administrators toward Indians, and bad traders, along with communications on language, gave the British Fur Trade a shaky start and led to armed hostilities.

Cheated by the traders, ravaged by the violence brought about by the use of intoxicants, unfairly treated in the restriction of firearms in trade, and humiliated by the contempt of English soldiers and administrators, the Great Lakes Indians seethed in growing anger. Finally, in the spring of 1763, the resentment resulted in open war to kill and remove all British from the land (Cleland, Rites of Conquest, pg. 133).

The line between New France – Canada, and the French and the English colonies was always vague and indefinite and was the subject of many battles.

Ottissippi

The French Jesuits were the dominant political force in the New World. There was much jealousy and distrust.

The 1762 Peace Treaty allowed the English to occupy Detroit and Mackinac and to establish Fort St. Clair (MPHC vol. 8, Wm. T. Mitchell, SCC History). When France ceded to British England her territories east of the Mississippi and ceding to Spain the land west of the Mississippi, many colonists left the country in disgust.

Britain obtained Canada in 1763. The Royal Proclamation made peace and preserved Anishinabe lands in Michigan from being seized by unscrupulous traders and land agents. There would be no public land sales. It also limited the number of guns, shot, and powder available to the Natives, believed to be a potential threat. This did not stop the settlers from squatting on Indian lands or the land companies from surveying. They ignored this law from the King and Crown of England. The King's proclamation that all the territory not included within any of the New Provinces, or within the lands of the Hudson's Bay Co. lying west of the Alleghenies, be reserved for the Indians until further consideration.

The English were just beginning to realize the Indians disliked and feared the English continually encroaching and moving onto their lands. The government ordered the colonists to stop this. The land was not to be sold or granted. The Indian lands not ceded to or purchased by the English King were reserved to the Indians for hunting grounds. And further that if any sales were to be made, they were to be only for the King at a public meeting held for that purpose by the governor or commander in chief. These prohibitions continued in effect so long as the English Crown controlled the situation, but were not always obeyed (Jenks, 1912).

The Iroquois ceded lands in Ohio and Pennsylvania belonging to other tribes. This started 50 years of war in 1768 over these treaties with the Indians and the Kentucky and Virginia militia.

The Iroquois were again driven from Ojibwe lands into Canada in 1778.

From 1760 to 1796, the English governed the land of Ontario Canada and the Northwest, including Michigan.

The English employed French agents in the trade. The Indians were plundered without mercy. The lawless traders ruined the Natives and their women, with whiskey, his physical and spiritual well-being. They were rude, repulsive, and they gave no gifts as was the Indian custom for sharing the land. The White men encroaching of his livelihood (Utley). The Indians were treated with arrogance, not humility, and the British did not give annual gifts as the French. The prices of goods were double at the posts. The Indians were not pleased with the new regime and their lack of respect for the Natives and their land.

General Jeffrey Amhurst was hostile to the Natives, disrespectful to the former enemy. The English cast system began, which is highly effective in destroying civilization and corrupting the moral fabric of other nations (Ojibway History/Migration to the Great Lakes, www).

The French had lost their claim to the country, not the Anishinabe, who controlled the territory.

William Smith Jr.'s letter to Ms. Gage in 1763 New York: "Heaven preserve you, my friend, from a war conducted by a spirit of murder rather than of brave and generous offense" (Parkman, The Conspiracy of Pontiac 1763).

In England, slavery was outlawed; the colonists feared the Crown would stop slavery in the New World also. This was not what the Virginia planters wanted to hear, as they were ready to expand plantation slavery to the Ohio country and the Northwest.

The English did not give ammunition to the Indians, causing great problems in finding food. Some starved for lack of bullets. The Indians saw that they were being deprived of their livelihood and subsistence and brought to perpetual bondage and slavery (Jenks 1912, History of SCC MI).

When surveyors with Captain Charles Robertson and his survey party came up the St. Clair River taking soundings, his party were ambushed by the Ojibwe at now Pine Grove Park, Port Huron, and most were killed. This was the beginning of the Pontiac War in 1762.

PONTIAC

A young Ottawa emerged who rebuffed all the White Man's ways, teaching that the Indian must return to his ancient values. He was Chief Pontiac – Boondiac. His home was on Peche Island about eight miles above Detroit which looks out on the Lake St. Clair. He was a well-informed man with a high degree of intelligence. In 1746, he had defended the Detroit Village against the Northern tribes.

Pontiac, an Ojibwe chief, was the "Grand Sauteur". He commanded the Indians around Detroit, the Ottawa and Ojibwe. As early as 1747, he commanded the warriors against the Northern tribes. Pontiac at the Maumee was chosen as their commander by the 18 nations who united (Parkman). Pontiac was dictator of the Northwest area, from the Alleghenies to the Ohio River and to the Mississippi, until 1766 (Fuller, SCC History).

Ottissippi

In 1762, he called a general council of the tribes, sending out ambassadors in all directions with wampum belts and the tomahawk. A grand Council was held near Detroit, and Pontiac gave his great speech to the tribes:

"It is important for us, my brothers, that we exterminate from our lands this nation which seeks only to destroy us. You see as well as I do that we can no longer supply our needs, as we have done from our brothers, the French. The English sell us goods twice as dear as the French do, and their goods do not last. Scarcely have we bought a blanket or something else to cover ourselves with before we must think of getting another, and when we wish to set out for our Winter Camp, they do not want to give us any credit as our brothers, the French, do.

When I go to the English Commander and say to him that some of our comrades are dead, instead of bewailing their death, as our French brothers do, he laughs at me and at you. If I ask for anything for our sick, he refuses with the reply that he does not want us, from which it is apparent that they are seeking our death. We must destroy them without delay. They are few; we will defeat them and stop the way, so that no more shall return upon our lands.

All the Nations who are our brothers attack them – why should we not strike too? Are we not men like them? Have I now shown you the wampum belts which I received from our Great Father, the Frenchman? He tells us to strike them. Why do we not listen to his words? What do we fear? It is time" (Chief Pontiac, May 5, 1763. Detroit).

In 1763, Pontiac united the Anishinabe to remove the British from their lands and to return to the Old Ways. These men were overbearing. The forts were open during the day. The plan was to overthrow all the forts on the same day, of the Northwest Territory. Surprise and siege were the chief tactics. The Great Uprising of 1763 was to return to the old ways and values. Neolin the Prophet counseled the tribes to give up the liquor and White ways.

Pontiac's Rebellion was from 1763 to 1766. The Allied Indians at the designated time destroyed all the forts of the Northwest Territory, taking 8 of 11. Detroit and Pittsburgh were under siege, the other not taken was Niagra. The eight forts taken by the Indians were St. Joseph, Miami, Michilimackinac, Green Bay, Presque Isle, Le Boeuf, Sandusky, and Venango. The areas west of the Alleghenies had been purged of their inhabitants. The frontiersman had suffered greatly and wanted vengeance. They began attacking peaceful Indians.

In 1763, the Chief Pontiac Rebellion was from the Atlantic to the Mississippi. The people irritated by the English arrogance and aggressiveness on Indian lands. The Indian Allies successfully took 9 of 12 British posts – forts. Three were in Michigan. The fort at Detroit was under siege for 18 months. At

Fort Michilimackinac, the men were invited to watch a game of lacrosse, and the Indian Allies attacked the unguarded men.

At Detroit, the Indian Allies sawed off their shotguns to hide them under their blanket coverings and asked to council. A young girl told the secret to the Americans of the plan, which saved them. Pontiac found and beat her with a racket used for ball play. All British outside the fort were murdered, and the French were not molested.

Their supplies being short, they were being starved out. They received French assistance, especially from Mr. Baby and others on the other side of the river who at night brought over in boats beef, pork, and other supplies. The siege lasted 18 months.

The Indians made use of fire rafts to destroy supply vessels bringing supplies to Fort Detroit. These were made of two dugout canoes tied together and filled with combustibles like pine pitch, birch bark, and other materials. Fireballs of pitch and flaming arrows were used on the forts and housing structures. Kee No Cha Meek, Great Chief of the Chippewa's, had a very long raft, taking 12 days to build it to go across the river and set fire to every part of it to burn British vessels (Parkman 1763).

Pontiac visited farms and wrote promissory notes upon birch bark for supplies for his warriors, and signed his totem, the Otter.

The Indians captured supply boats. They feasted, and the prisoners were butchered and tortured. 3,000 Natives were there with 820 warriors. They massacred many in the surrounding area. Parents Creek was renamed "Bloody Run".

The American British wrote, "we must use every stratagem to reduce them, sending smallpox blankets, kerchiefs to them, using dogs to search them out." Parkman

The schooner *Gladwin* from Niagara fought her way through and succeeded in reaching the fort with much needed supplies of ammunition, provisions, and reinforcements. Then barges with 280 men cannon and supplies came. There was no room in the fort. They immediately attacked the Indians and killed many.

Major Gladwin wrote to British General Amherst in 1763: "They have lost 89 or 90 of their best warriors: but if your excellency still intends to punish them further for their barbarities, it may be easily done without any expense to the Crown, by permitting the free sale of rum which will destroy them more effectively than fire and sword."

Chief Wabbicommivot, or Wapocomoguth, Great Chief of the Mississiauga of Upper Canada, living in the Toronto area, wanted to accommodate the English, their only trading partner. It was he and others like him, who prevented, the total destruction of all the forts, in the Great Lakes. Wapocomoguth came to Detroit seeking peace, Pontiac also sought peace (Parkman). This resulted in the Peace Agreement of 1764 between the British and the Anishinabe.

Indian independence was a lost cause, the Indian way of life doomed. Steadily and relentlessly they would be pushed from place to place, generation by generation. The object was not to defeat civilized man, but to come to some working relationship with him (Schmaltz).

In 1764, Pontiac and the Allied tribes made an agreement between the British and the Anishinabe. Johnson and Crogan made a treaty with the Indians for their land. The Indians made peace with the English – British. Gouin, a trader, acted as mediator between the Indians and the English. Pontiac often came to him for advice. Treaty terms were misunderstood by all.

2,000 warriors met at Niagra with Sir William Johnson. The wampum belt was an indispensable pledge, in a treaty, as the seals and signatures in a Convention of European Sovereigns. Every article must be confirmed by a belt of wampum, otherwise it is void. Major Monte, the British Historian of the French War. Parkman

Sir William Johnson, as superintendent of the Northern Indians under the King, was the most influential European man in contact with the Indians. Johnson was the man most responsible for preventing the useless attempt at retribution for the near 2,500 deaths resulting from the Indian uprising. George Crogan was his deputy and Indian agent. George Crogan was a trader among the Indians for many years, he was a trusted interpreter.

Sir William Bart Johnson served the Crown at Albany. He became superintendent of Indian Affairs for New York in 1755. He was very influential with the Indian Allies and worked to make peace between the American – British – and the Indians of Ohio, Pennsylvania, and Michigan.

In 1764, Johnson wrote to commander Gage to clarify the Indian point of view regarding the misconception among British officials that the Ojibwe and other Indians were subjects of the Crown:

"You may be assured that none of the Indians, Six Nations, Western, etc. ever declared themselves to be subjects, or will ever consider themselves in that light while they have any men, or an open country to retire to, the very idea of subjection would fill them with horror – indeed, I have looked into the Indian record of 1751; of those who made entry say that nine different Nations acknowledged themselves to be his Majesty's subjects, although I sat at that conference, made all entrys of all transactions, in which there was not a word mentioned which could imply a subjection. However, these matters seem to be not well known at home (in Britain), and therefore, it may prove of dangerous consequence to persuade them that the Indians have agreed to things which are so repugnant to their principles, that the attempting to enforce it, must lay the foundation of greater calamities than as yet been experienced in this country. It is necessary to observe that no Six Nation of Indians have any word which can express or convey the idea of subjection. Johnson admitted that greater calamities could occur if the indigenous people were treated as subjects by traders, settlers, soldiers, and government officials."

The Indian had no comprehension of what the Crown had written down. In the eyes of the Indian, they had given little in these Grand Councils, but in the eyes of the British, they had given a great deal. These misunderstandings would continue for generations.

The farmers and settlers east of the Alleghenies were not pleased and wanted vengeance.

Gladwin was honored in England, having inestimable influence, fixing for all time the sovereignty of the White race in the Lake region, a brave and wise commander (Utley).

Many chiefs listened to Pontiac, and his influence and following grew until he changed his allegiance to the British. Pontiac explained his change of loyalty, saying his loyalty was to the foreigner who would be best for the Indians. He predicted the French would be defeated and wanted his people to be on the winning side for the future negotiations.

Pontiac – Boondiac – was an Ottawa with an Ojibwe mother. He lived on Peach – Peche Island (*Peche* means "Fish") – at the mouth of the Detroit River above the fort. His sons were Shegenaba and Otussa.

There was no retaliation against them, and abundant presents were distributed to them by the British, and a Royal Proclamation was issued, protecting their lands and hunting grounds.

Major Bouquet was Amherst's successor. In 1764, he wrote to General Gage: "Many desert; there are no medicines, no surgeons. The men are denied discharge when their time of service is expired, keeping us seven years in the woods, the reason for this unprecedented desertion."

After the Pontiac Conspiracy, the British began taking more interest in the needs of the Indians of the Northwest. Indian departments were established, and gifts were liberally given. Fur traders were only allowed to trade with the Indians by license. These policies were followed by the British at Detroit until 1776.

Ottissippi

Patrick Sinclair, after serving in the British Navy in the Indies, established a post at St. Clair River and Pine River – Cabelle Chase. In 1763 to 1764, the Indians helped in building the fort. The Fort was used in transporting supplies between Detroit and Michilimackinac. He obtained a deed from the Indians for a large tract of land containing over 24,000 acres. He called the land "The Pinery". His farm was 4,000 acres along the St. Clair River at the south bank of the Pine River. The Indian burial mound was opposite on the north bank of the Pine River. His mill supplied lumber to Detroit. There were numerous Indians who helped in maintaining and provisioning the boats, the garrison, Indian traders, and merchants. Goods were traded for furs, the fort protecting the business of the fur traders and security for British vessels and forts on the Upper Great Lakes (Jenks/Mayhew 2003 Fort Sinclair). Fort St. Clair was a fur depot and supply station for the Northwest Territory forts and posts.

Sinclair gave power of attorney to Nicholas Boilvin, or Boulvin, to take charge of his farm in 1783, his stock, houses, barns, orchards, gardens, timber, and every other article thereto appertaining (Jenks 1912).

Along the Detroit Frontier, rules were bent to fit existing or desired conditions. From 1763 to 1796, the British Era, land was claimed on both sides of the Strait and in Southern Ontario, with the consent of the Indians.

Germ and chemical warfare were used against the Indians. Smallpox-infested blankets were given as presents to the Indians. Infested handkerchiefs in silver boxes were given. The free flow and sale of alcohol was used to conquer the Indians, causing great social disintegration among the tribes. Bouquet, in 1763, calculated the expense of 375 pack horses to carry 18,000 gallons of liquor to Fort Pitt.

In 1765, Sir Guy Carleton, the first British Governor General of Canada, made new laws to govern the now British lands. The inhabitants were mainly French, Quebec included Michigan. The new laws, usages, and religion were so different from the new rulers as to be wholly incomprehensible.

The British were honest and sincere; they had not learned the art of plundering their subjects as had the officers of the French.

Pontiac was assassinated in 1769 near St. Louis, Missouri. A Kaskaskia Illinois killed him at Cahokia, Illinois, the huge Indian castle near the Mississippi. This brought great vengeance to the tribe, nearly destroying them. The Allied tribes of the Northwest went to Cahokia and made war with the Illinois Indians.

In the Treaty of Paris in 1763, France ceded North American territory to England. The Quebec Act was made to stop the White invaders encroaching into the Ohio Valley and adjacent lands. The treaty forbid entry into reserved land of the Northwest Territory, the Indian domain, where he was to have exclusive possession and control. There were many attacks on squatters and many Whites captured in raids.

The Quebec Act of 1774 aroused New England, charging that the Quebec Act had substituted an Arbitrary Government for the "Free System of English Laws". The Allegheny Line was defied and broken through by speculative and land-hungry pioneers who poured through the Cumberland Gap into Tennessee country and through the Fort Pitt gateway to the fertile lands of Kentucky. So, at the beginning of the Revolution, the Ohio River, and not, the "Allegheny Hills", represented the barrier, between the farm settlements, and the Indian hunting grounds (Fuller).

George Washington was a surveyor for his uncle, Thomas Lord Fairfax, Baron Cameron. Fairfax owned five million acres in Virginia, which he had received from the Crown to make plantations producing tobacco for trade. There were many slaves in Virginia. Virginia land claimed to cross the U.S. to the Pacific, from Sea to Shining Sea. The other Colonial States also claimed the lands west of them to the Pacific.

George Washington was a prolific surveyor and received a share of all he surveyed in land for his payment. He was surveying lands for the Virginia Colony well into the Ohio Valley when the Seven Years War started.

Colonel George Washington fought in 1763 with Braddock against the French at Pittsburgh to oust the French from their new Fort Duquense, east of the Ohio. Washington collaborated with his friend, William Crawford.

Detroit was a post of some importance; the English Government was in deep ignorance when Quebec was established in 1763. The Western line was so drawn that no part of this region was included. For some years, Detroit to Mackinac was under no government. In 1774, the situation was corrected, the lines of Quebec were extended to take in this section (Jenks, 1912, vol. 1, History of SCC).

The Frenchmen still tried to create problems for the British, having influence on their former allies.

The Metis children born to the Indian maidens with the White men of all nations were racial outcasts, though most bands were loving and understanding of all their children.

Washington wrote, "my plan is to secure a good deal of land under the guise of hunting game". The surveying of Indian lands proceeded, surveying for soldiers' bounty lands, the cream of the country, the first choice.

George Washington inherited his half-brother Lawrence's interest in the Ohio Land Company in 1752. The Ohio Land Co. was pursuing its claim to land by the King's early grants, which extended to the West to the Mississippi and beyond. When Washington died, he owned 63,000 acres, mostly in the Ohio Valley. The Proclamation of 1763 made his titles worthless. This was unacceptable to many land speculators. The Revolutionary War was a war between the elite of the old regime and the elite of the new Regime.

The British Americans operated under organized debauchery. They engaged by fair or foul to get the possessions of those who really labor. The Indians came in contact, with this class and suffered the consequences. The English and Heathen were to be exterminated (Fuller, History of MI).

The British discouraged settlement for the benefit of the Mother Country, wanting to keep the land as Fur Trade. They also feared manufactured goods would be made and the losing of these markets. Parkins

Detroit was the most important commerce. Detroit, commanded all, of the Upper Lakes, the whole of the Northwest Trade, coming through these waters. Detroit was visited by and communicated with most of the Indians of the Lakes region (Parkins).

Many presents for the Indians were appropriated by dishonest officials and sold to the Natives. The English traders did mischief, greedy unscrupulous adventurers cheated and deceived the Indians. John Johnson, Indian agent, came in 1761 to correct these abuses (Parkins, Historical Geography of Detroit).

The Proclamation of 1763, stopping settlement West of the Allegheny Mountains, did not apply to influential people with interests in the American West. It was modified to suit many high British officials and colonial leaders. This led to the Revolutionary War of 1776, in which the U.S. fought the Crown British troops for the land in the Northwest, Ohio, and Michigan Territory.

Following the French and Indian War, the Treaty of 1768 between the British Government and representatives of the Six Nations, whereby Kentucky was ceded to the British Crown, Kentucky was the principal hunting ground of the Shawnee who did not consent to the cession and caused warfare against the White hunters and settlers entering the area. This led to Dunsmore's War in 1774, where Virginia militiamen began raids of destruction against the Indian towns across the Ohio River. Kentucky was a county of Virginia (Ohio History Central connection). www

There was confusion about the Southern boundary of Canada for many years. Michigan was claimed by Canada, yet the treaty papers did not show it. It was a French city ruled by British military without formal government for many years (Palmer, Friend, The City of Detroit, 1701 – 1922, 1922, Burton is a great Historian explaining the situation. www).

THE QUEBEC ACT

In 1774, the Quebec Act, Michigan became part of British Canada to the Mississippi and Ohio Rivers. This Act also confirmed the Roman Catholic Church had the right to collect tithes and laws were established. The 13 Colonies rebelled in 1775 at Montreal (The History of Canada and Canada West, www). The Quebec Act of 1774 made the Ohio Valley and Great Lakes part of Canada and brought Virginia and Pennsylvania to the point of revolution. Who had claim of the land by charters of the King.

Lord Dunsmore, the last British Royal Governor of Virginia, made a treaty in 1774 with the Shawnee to recognize the Ohio River borderline to separate lands for European settlement and the lands permanently to be retained by the Indians. The Revolutionary War began when the English Governor Dunsmore of Virginia led an expedition out of Virginia in 1774 to chastise the Ohio tribes who had banded together to defend their hunting grounds (Ohio History Central connection).

This treaty near Circleville, Ohio and the Treaty of Pittsburgh in 1775, reaffirmed by the new American Government, are the basis for Indian claims of the Ohio River as the boundary between the area of White occupancy and Indian lands. After this treaty, Major William Crawford, authorized by Lord Dunsmore, a British Governor organized an expedition against the Mingo towns near present Columbus, Ohio, that had refused to join the treaty. The booty taken was sold for 305 pounds 15 shillings, the proceeds divided among Crawford's men (Ohio History Central connection). Friendly, free, self-sufficient, happy Anishinabeg became distrustful, angry Indians of the late 1700s. Laws were useless; settlers had their own laws, the laws of the Frontier (Frazier/Cameron, Kahwamdameh).

The American Revolution began in 1775. The land companies could not abide the Proclamation and went ahead with their plans, surveying and making plans to buy up the Northwest. The American British organized militia and Indian allies to take the British Crown lands and organize a new government. The Anishinabe became neutral; they wanted to stay in their homelands and not offend the winner.

The British Army recruited soldiers from all over the world (Reibel, Lion in the Wilderness, 1960, Detroit Historical Museum, Hathi Trust, www). Hessians, Auxiliary regulars from Germany, were engaged by the British to fight the Americans during the Revolutionary War. These Germans settled Upper Canada.

Camp followers were women and children who were laundresses, nurses, cooks, and prostitutes.

Grief, madness, and despair was the life of the warlike Frontier (Parkman).

The British Governor Hamilton had unlimited authority over all the Western posts. The Indians were encouraged to take American scalps in Ohio, Pennsylvania, and Boonsboro, Kentucky. Hamilton was called "the Hair Buyer". He sent 15 Indian raiding parties into the Ohio Frontier. He paid cash for scalps and American prisoners. One of these was Daniel Boone, and 26 of his men, (salt makers), who were ransomed at Detroit in 1778.

The origin of scalping was from Europe. The American Colonials offered bounties for scalps. In 1724, Massachusetts offered 100 pounds sterling for Indian scalps, $500.00 and why associate this heathen practice to the Indians, who were of a pure nature. Wampum and calumet – Pipe of Peace – were used in Council Assemblies as the Bible is used in taking an oath (Nicholas Plain, Sarnia Reserve, 1950). "We were not a violent and quarrelsome people" (C. Eastman, "The Soul of the Indian").

The British urged attacks on Americans. The Detroit tribes were sent throughout the Ohio Valley to take scalps. The Iroquois remained neutral, the League of the Six Nations was destroyed in 1779.

Henry Hamilton said, "the traders cheated the Indians by false weights and measures. Powder, brandy, beads and fancy dress goods, were popular trade items" (Moore).

When it became evident that the Colonies from which this invasion came were trying to set up an Independent Nation, the Indians recognized their self-interest was on the side, doing its utmost to uphold the integrity of the hunting grounds of the West. Fuller

The tribes in this vast region north of the Ohio River and to the Mississippi, and the shores of Lake Superior, had a potential fighting force of about 8,000 warriors. Never at any time were the whole number mustered under one command, nor for a single campaign. But as typical Indian war and raiding parties moving swiftly and secretly to an objective, avoiding fortified places and organized resistance, relying on surprise and treachery and massacre, withdrawing as quickly as they came, they constituted a terrible menace to every outlying settlement to the Eastern foothill of the Alleghenies. Not only was their alliance with the power that dominated the wilderness for trade, but the British were able to supply abundantly the manufactured goods, which as presents or in exchange for peltries, were the sure guarantee of loyalty.

The tribes for two generations had met with the French and then the English at their grounds on the Detroit River. Detroit became the chief source of supplies for the British and Indian War. Great stores of weaponry were here distributed, and here were held the "talks" or plans to stop the intruders. Here British Governor Hamilton sent Indians on the warpath to worry the Frontiers. They left a trail of destruction. The Girty's, Alexander McKee and Matthew Eliott, were among the cruel forays against men and property along the American Frontier. They were much hated by Americans.

Lieutenant Governor Hamilton, writing from Detroit in August 1776, says, "The Canadians are mostly so illiterate that few can read; very few, sign their own name. Backwardness in improving farming is owing (to) the easy and lazy method of procuring the bare necessities. Wood is at hand, the Strait so plentifully stocked with a variety of fine fish that a few hours amusement may furnish several families. Yet not one French family has a seine net. Hunting and fowling affords food to numbers" (Utley).

In 1776, Alexander Sr. and William Macomb (brothers) purchased Grosse Isle from 18 Pottawatomie chiefs. Alexander Jr. had been born in Detroit in 1782. His father was a fur trader, and supplying a huge volume to the post and Indian Department, and then moved the young family to New York and purchased the Macomb lands in Northern New York at 3.6 million acres, which he ended up losing. William owned 26 slaves.

Detroit was not only a military stronghold; it was the British and Indian Capital of the Northwest.

THE AMERICANS

George Washington wrote, "I have ever been of the opinion the reduction of the Post of Detroit would be the only certainty of giving peace and security to the whole Western Frontier". Fort Washington was at Cincinnati, Ohio. The Indians grouped as barriers on all sides. Nearly all the defense of Detroit was done by these Indian pawns under the leadership of the renegade Tories – British Crown Loyalists.

George Rogers Clark was a surveyor in Kentucky in 1772. In 1779, when George Rogers took Vincennes, called Sackville, in Illinois County Virginia (now Indiana), the British at Detroit became nervous lest their Indian Allies become misled by the Americans. Beginning in 1780, Councils were held at Detroit among the Pottawatomi, Chippewa, Hurons, and Ottawa to guarantee their allegiance to the British Crown. To prove their allegiance, the Pottawatomi gave large pieces of their hunting grounds along the River Rouge to officers, Indian agents, and interpreters stationed at Fort Lernoult. They in turn parceled out this land and sold it to French Canadian and British families of Detroit (Woolworth, Dearborn HS).

Ottissippi

Duperon Baby owned 57,000 acres of land deeded from the Indians in 1780. This land was on both sides of the St. Clair River and Black River. James Abbott, in 1780, received extensive grants of land along the Detroit River and Lake St. Clair made by the Pottawatomi and Chippewa tribes. Many grants of land were given to trusted friends who were to protect the land from speculators. The Indians were to have free access to the land and resources.

Colonel Clark led in the expedition and claimed the Northwest for the Americans at Vincennes, Illinois. He wanted to take Detroit, but Congress lacked cooperation. A dearth of men, provisions, equipment, and transportation, the settlers were more intent on establishing homes than joining dangerous treks through savage wilderness to the North (Fuller). Clark counseled with the Indians in Illinois and others: "The English wouldn't let our women spin or men make powder, not let us trade with anyone. They said we must buy everything from them, then made us pay double for blankets. Said we must do as they pleased and killed some of us (Americans). This is the truth and cause of the war between us." Clark had also taken Kaskaskia and Cahokia (Adapted, Thom, Long Knife).

British Colonel Hamilton with allies came from Detroit and took Vincennes (Indiana), which was lightly guarded by Helms the American under George Rogers Clark. In mid-winter, Clark came with 150 heroic men from Cahokia and Kaskaskia, Illinois, through flooded plains and icy rivers. Hamilton was taken by surprise and sent to Williamsburg, Virginia, where he was jailed and placed in chains by Governor Thomas Jefferson (Thom, Long Knife). He was released and returned to England. He later returned to Canada, becoming Lieutenant Governor at Quebec. He went on to serve as Governor General of Bermuda and Dominica.

British Brevet Major General Depeyster came to Detroit in 1779 as Governor of Detroit and Agent for Indian Affairs, after Hamilton was captured at Vincennes, now in Indiana. Detroit was a depot for arming Indians to battle the Americans. Fort Detroit was a stockade town. Fort Lernault was built in 1778. Fort Maiden was across the river at now Amherstburg, Ontario.

The shield of one of the Count Depeyster, also De Pester or Peijster, displays the same effigy, the Turtle, as the Ojibwe Indian word for Michilimackinac and totem, "Big Turtle", shape of the Island.

The American Revolution began in 1775 and continued to 1783. The Indians were leaning toward the British, who claimed they were holding back pioneers and who had distributed presents for years among them.

Duperon Baby was the British Indian agent from 1778 to 1780 and had control over a very large portion of the Strait – the Detroit – now called the St.

Clair River. He was granted control of lands from the Indians. He was paid 10 shillings, sterling, a day for services as Indian agent.

Under the leadership of Chaminitawas, the British shared in distributing 17,520 gallons of rum in 1779 at Detroit alone.

Forty Indian towns were burned. George Washington was called "the Town Destroyer". The Iroquois were moved to Ontario, and their land grabbed up by rich and powerful New Yorkers. At Chillicothe, the Shawnee Capital near now Piqua, Ohio, five villages and 10,000 bushels of corn were destroyed. The Delaware Indian towns and Moravian village near Coshocton, (Ohio), in 1781 were destroyed, the plunder sold for over 80,000 pounds. In 1782 at Gnadenhutten, 90 unarmed Christian Lenape Delaware were beaten to death with mallets. The people had gone back to their fields to get crops for winter. After they were ordered to move north on Sand Creek too late to plant crops. The peaceful unarmed Indians were mistaken for Indians who made recent raids in Pennsylvania. Militia men attacked and brutally murdered them (Ohio History Central connection).

In 1781, George Rogers Clark gathered Pottawatomi allies, of the French and Spanish allies at St. Louis and, convincing the local Pottawatomie to remain neutral, attacked and captured the British garrison at Fort St. Joseph in Southwest Michigan. The next day, the Spanish returned to the Mississippi (Cleland, Rites of Conquest, pg. 151).

In 1781, there were a few English posts with small cultivated settlements around them. The entire territory was in occupancy of the roaming Indians. While the title was claimed by several colonies under grants from the English Kings, stretching to the Western extreme. Made in ignorance of the character and extent of land West of the Appalachians.

The Americans, nevertheless, were more skillful in fabricating Indian atrocity stories to gain support in the 13 Colonies against the British. Such inflamed propaganda and unjust American retaliation influenced the Southern Ojibwe to join the British (Schmaltz).

At the Battle of Sandusky in 1782, near the end of the American Revolution, Colonel Crawford, surveyor Western land agent, friend and companion of George Washington, fell into the hands of the Delaware Indians and was tortured in a horrible death – slowly roasted to death. This was Indian retaliation for the Gnadenhuttan Massacre in West Pennsylvania, where 90 unarmed Christian Indians were massacred. The Americans had ruthlessly killed 90 Moravian Indians in West Pennsylvania (now Ohio). The survivors fled to Detroit and lived on the Huron River for a time before moving to Canada on the Thames.

Ottissippi

Forty-four of the Lake Indians, 150 Wyandot of Sandusky and McKee's, 140 Shawanese, and British Captain Caldwell with 70 rangers went to Sandusky where the Americans were intending to continue their attacks on the Indians. They were able, to kill, 200, of the 500, mounted riflemen. This is where Okemos was severely injured. (See "Okemos" in "Chapter 9: Biographies of Indian Chiefs".)

Captain Alexander McKee, a most successful British Indian agent, in 1782 led 300 Huron and Lake Indians into Kentucky at Bryant's Station and Blue Licks. They defeated the rebel enemy. Colonel Daniel Boone was there, along with Colonel Todd and Trigg.

Boats on the Great Lakes were impressed for British Government use, transporting military supplies. There were restrictions on trade vessels, the British halting any smuggling to American traders in New York (Fuller). There was a huge amount of smuggling and pirating of vessels, many illicit traders.

Ben Franklin was the commissioner to the British Canadians.

The American Revolutionary War ended in 1782, Britain acknowledging the independence of the United States. Lower Michigan was then part of Pennsylvania from 1782 to 1786. In 1783, the 13 Colonies were then independent. The extension of the U.S. "from sea to shining sea" was the intention and design of the country's founders. Free land was the magnet, many slave owners wanting limitless land for cash crops. It is said that all the signers of the Declaration of Independence were smugglers.

The Treaty of 1783 drew an international boundary; all the Great Lakes except Lake Michigan were a part. The 1783 Treaty of Paris between Great Britain and the United States, and the United Colonies obtained from England a cession of its rights to this region. There were many claims by charter, from the English Crown, to all of the Northwest Territory, northwest of the Ohio River, by Pennsylvania, Virginia, and Massachusetts from 1628 to 1691, Connecticut from 1662, and New York. These claims were surrendered to create a common fund to aid in the payment of the National War debt. A law was passed in October 1780 that the territory ceded would be disposed of for the common benefit of the whole Union; that states erected therein should be between 100 and 150 miles square, and expenses incurred in recovering posts then in the hands of the British should be reimbursed. This meant the Indian lands would be confiscated and sold if necessary by war with Britain and the Indians.

Dodge was made Indian agent for this region in 1780, under an Act of Virginia (Farmer). We were Illinois County, Virginia under the old charter claim from 1779 until 1784.

Massachusetts claimed Southern Michigan until 1785. We were part of Massachusetts until it ceded the old charter claim to the U.S. Government in 1785.

The Virginians claimed their original charter covered the Ohio Territory. The Ohio Company was given a grant of 500,000 acres in the Ohio Valley, which included Western Pennsylvania. The British Crown gave this charter, providing they establish 100 families, and build a fort, and maintain a garrison there within seven years.

Virginia military lands were four million acres. There were overlapping and conflicting claims up to the Mississippi River. This resulted in the Virginia Declaration of Independence from British England. The Northwest Territory became the Virginia Military District.

In 1776, Kentucky became a county of Virginia; in 1779, a law passed which enormously increased immigration. Depeyster wrote, "But it happens, unfortunately for them, to be the Indians' best hunting ground, which they will never give up" (Riddell, 1924, notes Ch. ILL, 161. Life of Wm Dummer Powell).

The old colonial charters were relinquished. These claims were ceded to the United States. New York ceded in 1781, and Virginia in 1784 ceded their claim to land Northwest of the Ohio River, with some exceptions. Massachusetts ceded in 1785, and Connecticut in 1786, called the Connecticut Western Reserve until 1795.

Governed until 1800 by Connecticut Land Company, the west end of the Firelands or Sufferer's Land in Ohio was for the United Empire Loyalists – Tories – loyal to the British Crown.

The old Northwest became British North America, or the United States, with the Treaty of Paris in 1783, which concluded the American Revolution. Peace was established.

The new government was in great debt from fighting the war. Two alternatives were presented to the American people: restoration of credit or the downfall of the Infant Republic, for future exigencies of war. Duties and taxes would become permanent and adequate (Lossing).

Many thousands of Crown Loyalists or Tories left the newly created United States. The Tories were being persecuted; the Americans were bloodthirsty, vindictive – they burnt out, raped, and plundered the British Loyalists, who were forced out of their homes. The British Loyalists (UEL) were given free land, rations, farm stock, and implements, by the British Crown. Many other Americans emigrated to British North America – Canada – the free lands offered by Governor Simcoe called. November 25, 1783 was Evacuation Day; the cry was "Banish! Attain! Confiscate!" Michigan yet remained a British and Indian stronghold and would remain in British hands until they evacuated in 1796.

Britain held Fort Detroit as security for the proper treatment of the Crown Loyalists – Tories. Many had given their all for loyalty to the Motherland. Many of whom flocked to Detroit after the Peace of Paris Treaty in 1783. This was a temporary refuge.

The United Empire Loyalists -UEL began leaving the United States in 1783 in large numbers to join the British in Canada, Detroit, Southern Ontario, and Nova Scotia. Bringing their slaves with them, 62,000 UEL relocated to Canada. When the country was turned over to the USA, 80% stayed and became U.S. citizens. Some of the exiles later returned to the U.S. They also went to North Carolina and Kentucky, killing Indians as in the East. Many Black families fought for the British during the Revolution and gained freedom. Many other slaves fought for the Americans who promised freedom, some were returned to their masters.

In 1780, Negroes were brought to Montreal by the Indians and sold. They were valuable, and there were many Negro slaves in Canada. The Indians also had Panis, or Pawnee, slaves. There were also White slaves (The Slave in Canada, Journal of Negro History, 1920).

In 1781, the name of the United States of America was used by Canada and Congress (Lossing).

In 1783, the U.S. Congress ordered George Washington to retrieve the American's property – slaves – whom the British had brought North and set free in Canada. Michigan was yet Upper Canada until 1796. Slave owners went North to take back their slaves. Loyalists left the South, 9,000 in number, and took with them thousands of Blacks as slaves to the British West Indies.

The Native American Loyalists had their villages and crops burned. Chiefs were murdered, councils were divided. There were Civil Wars, migrations, and towns and forts were choked with refugees. There was economic disruption, breaking ancient traditions, losses in battle, disease and hunger, betrayal to their enemies. The American Revolution was one of the darkest times in Indian history. The 5,000 Iroquois Loyalists refugees moved to Canada along the Grand River, where land was given for them to live. Others came from Michigan to settle in Ontario, Canada.

Captain Robinson in 1782 said, "Sagana is the greatest corn post in this country."

The British policy coming from Quebec was to leave the Indian to their country. The wilder the country, the better for the Fur Trade.

The Eastern boundary of what is now Michigan was part of New France or Canada. The military commandment exercised a civil jurisdiction over the settlements surrounding the posts.

After 1783, the war in Ohio continued with few interruptions until 1795. The Treaty of Fort Harmar was a peace treaty that failed. The Americans did not seriously consider the Indians.

In 1783, nineteen Indian nations in the Great Lakes area and to the south united in a defensive alliance – confederacy – so that if one were attacked, all would come to its aid (Schmaltz, pg. 103). Most Indians preferred to remain neutral, and some delighted in the fact that the English enemies were killing each other. Both British and Americans put great pressure on the Indians to join their respective sides in the war (Schmaltz). Their unerring rifles and means of approaching the enemy unseen and unheard were coveted. They were admirable scouts, defending outposts and reconnoiters. They were intelligent, amiable, dignified, and firm (Parkman).

The Territorial Ordinance of 1784, by Thomas Jefferson, became the Northwest Ordinance written by Nathan Dane in 1787 under President James Monroe. The Northwest Territory was established in 1787; the motto was "He has planted one better than the one fallen". The Northwest Territory governed until 1803. Thomas Jefferson's son was a Loyalist to the British Crown.

The plan of Congress was to take over the Northwest Territory by The Ohio Co. with inducements to immigrants and post-Revolution veterans. A large tract of land was purchased above Marietta, Ohio and into Pennsylvania. Shawnee lands which were sold to the Americans by false treaties with the Iroquois, the Americans making repeated efforts to claim the land north of the Ohio River.

The National Constitution was formed in 1787 (Lossing).

The British introduced sound money, long-horned cattle, sheep, and better breeds of swine. They built larger ships for the trade and brought in trades people (Lion in the Wilderness, 1960 Hathi Trust, www).

Indian fisheries were threatened by the settlers. No Indian location was held sacred near a Loyalist settlement. In 1797, a proclamation was made to protect the fishing places and burying grounds of the Mississauga's. It was ineffective; pollution was a problem, and the people did not respect the Indians. Prejudice against the Indians came with the settlers. Loyalists recently forced from the American territories "avowed the opinion that a White man ought not in justice suffer for killing an Indian; and many of them...thought it a virtuous act to shoot an Indian on sight." The court's protective laws were not effective for Indians.

Ottissippi

Because of the bias against Indians in general, conflict began the moment the Loyalists arrived to reestablish farms lost in the Revolution. The Ojibwe were misled by Indian agents and early pioneer Loyalists. They were told that the farmers would help them; instead, they shot their dogs and never assisted the Indians, calling them dogs and threatening to shoot them too (Schmaltz).

In 1785, the train sled was horse-drawn and used on the ice, pulled by Indian ponies.

Americans flooded into Ohio. There were 12,000 Whites north of the Ohio River in 1785. Ojibwa numbers continued to decline, mainly a result of liquor and the "White Man's disease", smallpox (Adapted from Schmaltz, The Ojibwa of Southern Ontario). The contagious diseases were likely spread by numerous United Empire Loyalists who entered Southern Ontario after the American Revolution (Schmaltz).

The Onondaga Nation Chief Canassatego advised the new American Government on how to unite the American Colonists. The Five Nations Confederacy was greatly admired by America's founding fathers, including Benjamin Franklin. The United States Government is based on a Haudenosausee-Iroquois model of government.

The Northwest Ordinance created in 1785 was a land ordinance and declared that no White men would trespass or encroach on lands of the Indians across the Allegheny Mountains. It also reserved the American Government the right to buy land from the Indians by treaty. The British outposts remained on the Northwest Lakes. But treaties were meaningless documents to Frontier inhabitants and military. Kentucky was ceded to the British by the Six Nations, who did not have legal claim to the Shawnee hunting grounds.

After the American Revolution, George Rogers Clark and Kentuckians with allies, burned seven Shawnee towns on the Great Miami River in 1786, (natives killed 10 chiefs against Clarks orders), and did great damage to crops and cattle. Clark began building boats at Louisville, for the offensive to take Detroit. (Adapted, Thom, Long Knife)

Surveyors began work across the Ohio River. Leading Indian chiefs entreated the American Government to prevent this, yet the American Congress continued organizing the Northwest Territory and began military attacks to take the territory to Detroit.

The Ordinance of 1787 created the Northwest Territory, the first colony of the United States. General Arthur St. Clair was appointed governor. It was governed from Cincinnati, Ohio on the Ohio River from Fort Washington.

Michigan was yet under British control until 1796, part of British Canada.

In a district with few courts or official means of administering justice, the role of the more prominent members of the community in deciding justice was quite important. This problem was not solved until Detroit was incorporated into the Government of Canada with the creation of the District of Hesse in 1788. A Court of Common Pleas was established with Jacques Baby, Alexander McKee, and William Robertson appointed as judges. In 1789, a professional judge, William Dummer Powell, was appointed control of the Court (David Farrell, 1965 UWI, MI Archives).

Deputy surveyors received 20 to 50% of the acres for payment for their services. The Indians sent many letters asking the British at Detroit and Michilimackinac to help them drive out the intruders.

In December 1786, the Grand Confederate Council of the Indians, Northwest of the Ohio, was held near Huron Village at the mouth of the Detroit River. It was attended by the Huron, Ottawa, Miami, Shawnee, Chippewa, Cherokee, Delaware, Pottawatomi, and the Confederates of the Wabash (Powers, History of Northern MI).

In 1788, 80 chiefs of different tribes met at the Detroit River, waiting for Colonel Brandt (St. Clair Papers).

The Indian spokesman for the tribes said, "why do you complain that we fired at your soldiers and killed your cattle and horses? You yourselves are the cause of this. You marched your armies into our country and built forts here, though we told you, again and again, that we wished you to remove. My brothers, this land is Ours and not Yours". There was a shallow pretense that the forts were built for supplying the Indians with clothes and ammunition (Parkman 1870).

The Indian Confederation of United Indian Nations were led by War Chief Blue Jacket, a Shawnee; Little Turtle, a Miami; and Turkeyfoot, an Ottawa, the British supplying arms to the Indian conference. Washington charged Britain was seducing tribes that "we have hitherto been keeping at peace at a heavy expense, and who have no cause for complaint".

Governor Arthur St. Clair was president of Congress and governor of the Northwest Territory. His Treaty of Fort Harmar in 1789 was signed by a few Indians who were giving up much of their land in Ohio to White settlement. Many important Indian leaders were not invited or refused to participate. Those who did sign often did not represent the entire tribe. Rather than establishing peace with the Ohio country Indians, the treaty incited them to resist White settlement of their land.

George Washington was inaugurated President in 1789, the first President of the United States. The U.S. Treasury Department was established

Ottissippi

in 1789. As President from 1789 to 1797, George Washington began an Annihilation Program, burning settlements, crops, orchards, and immense quantities of stored corn in the country West of the Alleghenies.

In 1790, President Washington orders the Army to resolve the Indian Question once for all. There were Indian wars, land stealing, liquor, disease, and false treaties. Washington sent General Harmar and an army of 1,500 troops to conquer Indians living in the Northwest Territory, to take possession of their country for the Americans. Harmar destroyed 20,000 bushels of corn, girdled most of the fruit trees, and burned the principle village of the Shawnee.

The Indians in 1790 defeated, General Harmar who was trying, to take possession of their country for the Americans. Many men were deserting the American Forces. Little Turtle was a principal commander of the Native Americans. Luring the American Army deeper into Indian country, he led the Miami Indians with 1,100 men. In 1791, General St. Clair was then sent with 2,000 men and was also soundly defeated in trying to take Indian country. Blue Jacket led the Native Americans in the most severe defeat ever inflicted upon the U.S. by the Native Americans: 800 of 2,000 men were killed or wounded, the Indians having a small number of casualties. "St. Clair had three horses killed under him, and eight balls passed through his clothes" (Lossing). There were many desperate acts by Indians, massacres without number, and a hostile combination of different tribes.

George Washington called out for militia to meet force with force. The Whiskey Rebellion of 1791 came under the Presidency of George Washington. The cause was the first tax was made on the people of the U.S. The country needed revenue to pay for the war costs incurred from the American Revolutionary War.

Robert Hamilton, in a letter to Governor Simcoe in 1792, wrote, "The Americans seem possessed with a species of mania, for getting lands, which has no bounds. Their Congress, President, reasonable and wise in other matters, in this seem as much infected as the people, completely ignoring their own cavalier contempt for boundary treaties, solemnly signed by their leaders and sachems."

General Anthony Wayne, "Mad Anthony Wayne" or "Big Wind", trained his troops for two years and then came North to take the country for General Washington and the United States in 1795.

The surveys in Ohio were made under cover of troops, to survey the lines of Cutler and Sargent's purchase. The Ohio Co. was chiefly officers and soldiers of the Revolution; they purchased tracts of land called "The Ohio Purchase".

Kentucky was ceded by Virginia in 1792 to the United States, as part of the Virginia Military Lands. The Federal Southeast Territory included Kentucky and Tennessee.

The reorganized Army was termed, The Legion of the United States and was divided into four sub-legions, each under a Brigadier General: General James Wilkinson, Thomas Posey, and Charles Scott. The remnants of the regular Army were very small, and many deserted for fear of an expedition into Indian country. Some were caught and received 100 lashes; others were shot to death.

After the Revolutionary War, there were two reserves: the Virginia Military District and the Connecticut Western Reserve. The Connecticut Land Company bought the Fire lands of Ohio for those who lost lands in prior wars, in 1795. The Connecticut Western Reserve was purchased by the Connecticut Land Co.

In 1793, the U.S. Representatives were allowed, to meet the Indians, at the mouth of the Detroit River. The Indians' answer to selling their land was "We hope we may be allowed to point out a mode by which your settlers may be easily removed, and peace thereby obtained. We know that these settlers are poor, or they would never have ventured to live in a country which has been in continual trouble ever since they crossed the Ohio. Divide, therefore, this large sum which you have offered us among these people; give to each also a proportion of what you say you would give to us annually, over and above this very large sum of money, and we are persuaded they would most readily accept of it, in lieu of the lands you sold them. If you add the sums you must expend in raising and paying armies with a view to force us to yield you our country, you will certainly have more than sufficient for the purposes of repaying these settlers for all their labors and their improvements. You have talked to us about concessions. It appears strange that you should expect any from us, who have only been defending our just rights against your invasions. We want peace. Restore to us our country, and we shall be enemies no longer." These councils were held in Canada at Captain Elliott's, near the mouth of the Detroit River, in 1793.

At the Grand Glaize, Ohio in 1794, the Commander in Chief congratulated the Federal Army upon taking possession of the Grand Emporium of the hostile Indians of the West. The extensive and highly cultivated fields and gardens on the margin of these beautiful rivers show that they were the work of many hands and afford a pleasing prospect of bountiful supplies of grain on the troops progress toward the Lakes. Vegetables of all kinds were in abundance. For miles, they marched through great fields of corn, along the river. The Army was permitted unmolested to take or destroy such portions of these fine fields as might be desired (Fuller, Historic MI).

In 1794, after training for two years in Indian tactics and creating a regular Army, General Anthony Wayne came in and secured the American governance of the Northwest Territory. In General Wayne's campaign at Greenville, the Choctaw and Chickasaws were to be kept safe from shooting by his men by a yellow ribbon tied to the topknot or tuft of hair left on the crown of the head (Fuller).

Turkeyfoot led the Ottawa's at the Battle of Fallen Timbers. Roche de Bout is a rocky point on the Maumee River a mile above now Waterville, Lucas County, Ohio. Nearby was fought the Battle of Fallen Timbers in 1794 (Ethnohistory; Indians of Northern Ohio and Southeastern MI. Voegelein/Tanner). The British furnished only a small quantity of food and ammunition, no soldiers, and refused them shelter in the fort nearby.

Numerous garrisons, well supplied with artillery, have been compelled to remain tacit spectators of the general conflagrations round them, and their flag displayed to the disgrace of the British (Fuller, Historic MI).

The Treaty of Greenville followed in 1795, near Toledo, Ohio at Swan Creek. Land sales began.

The Jay Treaty of 1794 allowed safe passage through the waters of the Great Lakes and rivers to American traders. The British were to withdraw from Detroit and Michilimackinac in 1796. The U.S. did not have uncontested control of the Upper Peninsula until 1818, and Drummond Island in 1847. The treaty allowed British settlers and traders to remain. The Indians moved freely about between the U.S. and Canada borders (Flocken, UMN 2013).

The Americans were desperately trying to take possession of the Northwest Territory. Their funds were depleted and their Army without pay. They offered double pay and land for soldiers and garnered supplies. They waited until 1796 to take possession of the British forts.

There were great problems with desertion in the troops and militia for many reasons. Many times, the men did not receive pay. There were dire punishments for deserters, including flogging and death. "One punishment was to ride the Wooden Horse, a two-by-four or log placed between a man's legs with two men shaking it violently" (D. Plain). This was also the method used for riding a man out of town on a rail.

General Wayne concluded, the Treaty of Greenville in 1795 relinquished all United States claims to Michigan lands. The 1795 Treaty of Greenville was a peace treaty with the U.S. Government. Land was ceded around the forts, but by coercion. The Chippewa, Ottawa, and Wyandot's held the State; they never accepted English assumption of control.

Hunters, trappers, renegades, outlaws, and traders began their invasion of Indian country. Footpaths extending thickly in many directions, from all important points, were numerous and in constant use; they led to the easiest fords over streams and to the best fishing and hunting districts.

The Indians were skillful pontoonists and bridge builders. They set an X form a few inches below the surface of the water; this was a base for bare or moccasined feet with the support of a pole for balancing, or water canes, to cross creeks and rivers (Calvin J. Thorpe, MPHC, vol. 28).

Many Indians removed to Canada after the Treaty of Greenville in 1795. Many moved to Walpole Island in the St. Clair River Delta, north of Lake St. Clair, near a long-standing Missisauga Ojibwe community. The British Indian agent, McKee, set up a refugee camp on an Eastern Channel of the St. Clair River, called Le Chenail Escarte, later the "Sny". There were up to 3,000 temporary refugees: Ottawa from the Maumee and Missisauga Ojibwe. Most drifted back to the Maumee River region, now south of Toledo, Ohio. Bluejacket's family relocated on the Detroit River at Brownstown. The country north of Detroit belonged to the Mississauga Ojibwe bands of the Saginaw Valley to the headwaters of the Grand River near Lansing, Michigan.

Land was to be acquired for the United Empire Loyalists to settle in Canada, east of the Strait or Detroit, the St. Clair River, and the Detroit River. Alexander McKee, Indian agent for British Canada, in the Western District, negotiated for land with the Missisaugas along Lake Erie to Detroit, Lake St. Clair, and the Thames. Twenty-seven chiefs of the Ottawa, Chippewa, Pottawatomi, and Hurons retaining Huron Reserve and Huron Church Reserve on the east bank of the Detroit River. The land sold was a 1,200-acre tract.

The Americans claimed Detroit in 1796. The British evacuated to Malden across the river in Ontario, Canada. The British burned Detroit when they left in 1796. The United States claimed Mackinaw in 1796. The entire White population of Michigan was about 4,800: four-fifths were French and the remainder Americans. The settlement of Detroit and northward had about 2,200; Mackinaw about 1,000; the lower villages at Maumee, the Raisen, and the Huron of Lake Erie about 1,300.

The counties of now Huron and Erie in Ohio were owned by John Askin and associates. The Connecticut Legislature granted this land in 1792. Captain McKee would become a partner for free because of his influence with the Indians, to get them to deed the Fire Lands Tract of 500,000 acres of land near

Cayahaga to the U.S. in 1805. For the troubles, the inhabitants of New London who suffered from fire in the late troubles. (Askin II, pg. 453).

Governor St. Clair was now in charge of the New Territory of the Northwest. His secretary and acting governor was Winthrop Sargent. The American Government was impoverished and in debt. The plan was to take the Indian lands and sell them to pay for war debts.

Western Expansion continued. There was pressure to cede land along the rivers and lakes, the Indians being coerced and forced to sign treaties with the Federal Government. Though some thought the treaties honorable, protecting the Indians, they were in fact disastrous for the Indian.

The British Canadians stubbornly resisted the invasion of their domain from the South. The masters of the Fur Trade controlled the Michigan country, even after the British flags were hauled down at Detroit and Michilimackinac in 1796.

The British kept their militia men. Fairfield was a British militia. Abbott was a colonel of the British militia.

Haldimand, the Governor of Canada, refused to surrender the posts of the Upper Country, which Michigan was a part of (Haldimand Diary, Canadian Archives, 1889, vol. 38).

The economic rivalry ignored the international boundary. Most of the commerce went through British gates and ports on the Lower St. Lawrence. Canadians complained that much of the Western Territory business was getting into the hands of the Spanish and American merchants at St. Louis and New York (Fuller). Merchants with investments in land speculation, local sheriffs, and the justice of the peace hindered government efforts to secure just treatment for the Ojibwe.

The highest officials in the Indian Department made their fortunes through the trade in spirits, even though they knew the damage caused to the Indians. Presents with too much liquor and too little ammunition almost resulted in the disintegration of the Ojibwa as a people (Schmaltz).

There was Indian rum and good rum. See "Chapter 6: Trade and Traders".

A squad or team of scouts and rangers attached to an army or reported to military officers was called "a company of spies".

LAND TITLES

Ownership by Indians was a tribal or national ownership to be exercised in common, the land being occupied and claimed from time immemorial. The Europeans didn't recognize that the Indians had any title to any territory they occupied and treated them as occupants without real rights, and claimed absolute ownership and sovereignty.

The English king gave to individuals or companies vast tracts of land in the newly-discovered country, without any thought that the title rested anywhere else except in him. The French king had the same view. They both regarded the Indians as having no rights, but as privileges, which might be taken away if their conduct was not entirely satisfactory.

Land deeds were defined in the vaguest terms. Many times, blank papers were used as treaties, and no reference to the lands were used.

Fort Detret had great plenty of all manor, of wild beasts and boar hunting and growing land. The land was owned by Indian nations, states, territories, local bands, and tribes. Gradually it became known that the new race had a definite purpose, to chart and possess the whole country, regardless of the rights of its earlier inhabitants. Still the old chiefs urged patience, "for the land is vast; both races can live on it in their own way. Let us befriend them and trust their friendship" (Charles Eastman).

The tribes were traders, the whole continent traversed by Indian trails and trade routes. They traded copper, jade, obsidian, soapstone, mica, paint, stones, and shells for wampum and buffalo robes.

Revenge, booty, and hatred were not the only motives for Indian raids. Often children and young men were taken as captives to replace a beloved warrior lost in the fighting. The captive became part of the family and was adopted.

The viscous barbarian, surplus of over-populated Europe, are far behind the Wild Man in delicacy of feeling or natural courtesy (Metis History, www).

Fort Malden was at Amherstburg, east of the Detroit River, directly opposite Fort Maiden at Detroit (Farmer 1884).

Medals were given to the chiefs for their service to the Crown in bloody American wars. The medals given were usually large and handsome. A magnificent silver medal, nearly four inches in diameter and massive. Some were given much later by the Prince of Wales on a visit to Canada to the last surviving family member. As a rule, the Indians prize their medals beyond anything. They are cherished as priceless heirlooms of their forefathers.

After the War of 1776, when the United States began in 1783, the Pennsylvania Germans, Plain Folk, migrated to Canada. They included Mennonites, Dunkards, Moravians, Amish, and Huiterites. The Irish Palatines also came. The English and Dutch traders flocked in from Albany. 20,000 men, women, and children went down the Ohio River in boats to settle its banks.

Joseph Brandt, a Mohawk chief, said the British had sold the Indians to Congress. Britain readily agreed the Native warriors bled freely for the King. Britain sacrificed the Native Allies' interests to accommodate White America.

American government agents made fraudulent deals with renegade representatives of the tribes, or bribed chiefs with money and drink to get their mark on official documents. The official records from the Post of Detroit were removed and not recovered until a half century later.

Often land speculators claimed aboriginal lands before negotiations were complete and provoked the Aboriginals to do something about it. When warriors responded with force to protect what was theirs, the Army was called to "rescue" the American interlopers. Defeat followed, and chiefs were forced with punitive treaties to sign away their lands. This pathetic pattern was repeated throughout the American Westward Expansion. Half-hearted negotiations preceded force to convince the public opinion.

Jefferson said; Peace was unattainable on the terms the Indians would agree to. He said; If we are constrained to lift the hatchet, we will never lay it down till that tribe is exterminated, or driven beyond the Mississippi". He asked for and pledged friendship but stressed: those who turned violent would pay. "In war, they will kill some of Us; we shall destroy all of Them," Jefferson vowed (Early Canadian History Narrative, Upper Canada History, www).

In 1803, the Louisiana Purchase from the French under Napoleon Bonaparte greatly enlarged the lands of the U.S. The Continental Congress operating posts until after 1812.

Arthur St. Clair was the 9th U.S. President in Congress Assembled. He was the first Territorial Governor in U.S. history. Scottish born in 1736, who served with Colonel Jeffrey Amhurst in Canada. In 1775, he became a Brigadier General, serving with George Washington.

The Americans came and never stopped coming.

Elias Wallen, acting sheriff of Wayne County in 1800, came to Detroit in 1799. In 1802, when the town of Detroit was incorporated by the Legislative Council of the Northwest Territory, Wallen was appointed Marshal (Askin, vol. II, pg. 276).

The Connecticut Land Co. secured government cooperation in "extinguishing the Indian claim" to a large area of Ohio, south of Lake Erie from Sandusky to Toledo and south for a great distance. William Dean and Indian Agent Charles Jouett, hastily made arrangements for the Treaty of Fort Industry, which took place, near modern Toledo, Ohio on July 4, 1805. The Indians who signed were members of the Wyandot, Ottawa, Chippewa, Delaware, Shawnee, and Pottawatomi nations. The Indians who parted with these lands did so with much reluctance, and after the treaty was signed, many of them wept (Tappan/Ethno History; Indians of Northern Ohio and Southeaster MI, Voegelein/Tanner).

Under the Act in 1805, organizing the territory of Michigan, the governor was made the superintendent of Indian Affairs. Since 1836, persons have been appointed to act as Indian agents (Farmer).

In 1805, Governor Hull was in charge, Stanley Griswold was secretary of the territory and was acting governor (Jenks 1912). In the same year, U.S. Secretary of War Henry Dearborn instructed Hull to negotiate a land cession for two cents an acre. This became the Treaty of Detroit, ceding a quarter of Southeast Lower Michigan, the Indians retaining four reserves.

Traders at treaties falsified debts and inflated their trade prices, which were recovered from treaty annuities. Debt and reliance on credit and annuities pushed the Indians further into dependency. Government employees and traders pocketed a shocking amount from land treaties. There was much corruption in all the trade, military, and government (Flocken, UMN 2013).

Britain yet controlled the area, Jefferson argued. Great Britain, was not justified in exercising jurisdiction over the country and its inhabitants in the vicinity of the posts and excluding citizens of the U.S. from navigation, thus intercepting us entirely from the commerce of furs with Indian nations to the Northward, a commerce which has ever been of great importance to the U.S. not only for its value, but a means of cherishing peace with those Indians and of superseding expensive war. We have been obliged to carry on with them during the time those posts have been in other hands (C. Moore).

The Americans did not respect the Ojibwe and Aborigines as equal partners. Their interest was purely possession of the Indian land.

Stone Ground spoke: "Yes, we hate them. Because wherever they establish military posts to protect the Natives, they keep them like dogs. Because for the slightest folly we commit, they drive us under the ground, whip us with ropes, tie cords around our necks and hang us. We long for the French that they may prevent our young ones from exterminating the Americans" (Flocken, UMN 2013).

Whitmore Knaggs was acting Indian agent in 1801. Gabriel Godfroy was sub-agent and an interpreter of the Pottawatomi. Charles Jouett, or Joweet, was American Indian agent and surveyor for the Detroit at Fort Sinclair, about 1803.

The ruins of Fort St. Clair were yet visible in 1817.

The Americans usually limited annuity payments to 10 to 20 years, under the assumption that Indians as a distinctive people would no longer exist at the end of the period (Tanner).

THE WAR OF 1812

The chief cause of the war was Britain's insistence on its right to search American vessels for deserters from its own Navy. During the war in Europe against Napoleon, England had interfered with American trade with Europe; about 10,000 Americans, including Natives, were impressed for service to the British in Europe. The other cause was the British inciting Indians against American settlers along the Northwest Frontier. The British were trying to retain the great Fur Trade commerce they had enjoyed since 1760 and stop the Americans from taking over Canada. They blockaded all American trade to Europe; the customs revenue lost left the Administration of America bankrupt.

The British stopped the American invasion at Lundy's Lane near Niagara Falls. There were 1,700 casualties. The British burned the White House in 1814 and several other government buildings. The war had been won and a new treaty at Ghent, Belgium would make final agreements.

"The War of 1812 was the second and final struggle for the independence of the United States. It has four different viewpoints: the American, British, Canadian, and Native.

For the Americans, it was a glorious second War for Independence, the birth of American freedom and the founding of the Union" (Amanda Foreman, 2014 Smithsonian). "A precondition for entrenchment of slavery, the goal of man was to destroy the Red Race for industrial capitalist supremacy, the goal of Manifest Destiny" (Henry Adams/Foreman). "Thomas Jefferson, coveted all of North America, including Canada, for the U.S. Washington's willingness to war was proof that the Americans paid lip service to the ideals of freedom, civil rights, and constitutional government.

For Canadians, the war was the cornerstone of nationhood, brought about by unbridled U.S. aggression. There were two theaters of war: sea and land. The successful repulse of 10 U.S. incursions between 1812 and 1814 receive the most attention.

For the Indians, it was a short victory and then the end of freedom when Tecumseh was killed on the Thames near Lake St. Clair" (Foreman).

"For the British, America was a side issue to the war in Europe. 20,000 men died fighting the War of 1812. England hardly knows of the 1812 War. The British dismiss the U.S. as a haven for blackguards and hypocrites. The Napoleon War in Europe was between France and Britain was about survival and annihilation. 10,000 men were impressed" (Foreman).

MRS. JOHN HOWARD DIARY: WAR OF 1812

"Mother moved to Detroit and put herself under the protection of the government.

Many a day have I been to the storehouse to draw our rations. But when General Hull surrendered the fort to the British, we were alone again at the mercy of the Indians, all the American forces having become prisoners of war. All the public buildings were burned by the orders of the British General Proctor. There was a guard placed around General Hull's house until he could be escorted to Canada. The commandant's house stood where the Biddle house now stands. The English General Proctor occupied it after Hull left it, and he offered five dollars for every American scalp that the Indians would bring to him.

After Proctor had burned all he could in the way of public buildings and left for Canada, the few Americans would gather into a house, and the men would stand guard all through the night, their weapons, clubs – for they had no guns. What young men there were, secured boats and went down the river by night, to rejoin the Army in Ohio, in order, to come back with it, to retake Detroit. My oldest brother was one of these. We have never heard of him since. He was the one I leaned upon as a father, and the sad fortunes of war took him. Upon God, therefore have I leaned."

At Mackinaw, Colonel Crogan, nephew of George Rogers Clark and Commodore St. Clair, failed to take Mackinaw. Major Holmes was killed, and the Winnebago from Green Bay cut out the hearts and liver from the American slain, the British holding the post until the Treaty of Peace the following winter.

George Croghan, a prominent Indian fur trader, was the Indian interpreter and agent for General George Washington with Braddock's Army. He came to Detroit with Rogers Rangers, U.S. Army. George was deputy Indian Suprintendent, under Sir William Johnson, being very influential in Indian negotiations, amassing very large holdings in the Ohio country, called the Illinois country by the French, of Western Pennsylvania, New York, and Eastern Kentucky, a rival of George Washington in lands.

James Abbott was lieutenant colonel and commandant for the Ohio Co.

TECUMSEH – "SHOOTING STAR"

Tecumseh saw tribal chiefs swindled into selling millions of acres of land to Americans. The great Shawnee statesman and protector of his people and their lands knew the American's plan to take the land and exploit it, to remove and destroy his people.

Tecumseh had his town burned 6 times in Ohio moving west to live a peaceful life. He said; In our hearts, we can be pure and peaceful and sober and depend upon ourselves and each other and leave white men alone.

Ottissippi

"The Prophet - Tenskwatawas" Tecumseh's brothers divine message was of unity, and resistance to alcohol which was destroying the people dependence on trade goods, and return to our own traditions and practices. And to treat each other well, and respect the aged, infirm, diseased, children, and women, and eat traditional food. A very large group of Anishinabe from the Northwest gathered here to live and worship together.

Governor General William Henry Harrison without permission, massacred the Anishinabe settlement at Prophetstown on the Tippacanoe River in Indiana, in 1811. This act caused many tribes in Indiana, Ohio, and Michigan to fight many battles between the Allies and the U.S. Army. A year later in 1812, the U.S. and Great Britain declared war; the Anishinabek and Tecumseh fought for the British, warriors came from Wisconsin and many other places.

Tecumseh had been traveling to the tribes east of the Mississippi for over a year to gather support to stop the invaders from taking the Indian homelands. As he had received the prophecy from the Great Spirit, the time to meet him in the North would be the great shaking of the earth, at this sign it would be time to fight.

The earth shook for 2 days, with great rumbles like thunder of a hundred canons. Hard jolting shook homes to pieces, big trees were tossed about, the air darkened, the sun grew dull. Creeks went dry and streams flowed where none had been. The Mississippi changed its chanel, some places water stopped and flowed upstream. The terrain near the mouth of the Ohio River crumpled and changed shape. At New Madrid the Old Spanish town on the Mississippi, the land dropped, making a lake, 5-10 miles across. Dust blew making the sun red. On the Frontier, game ran and buffalo herds were thrown off their feet, then stampeded. All the warrior that Tecumseh had visited, remembered his words. Tecumseh felt greater strength and resolve. (Adapted from, Thom, Panther in the Sky)

As the prophet and visionary Tecumseh said that when he reached Detroit, he would stamp his feet three times. There were three earthquakes. Named the New Madrid earthquakes for New Madrid Missouri (the epicenter) The U.S. Geologic Survey writes that the earthquake was close to 10 times stronger than the one that destroyed San Francisco in the late 1800s. The major quake caused such a major shift of seismic plates that it was said church bells rang out in Boston, sidewalks cracked in Washi9ngton D.C., forests disappeared, lakes were created, villages were swallowed and for a few hours even the Mississippi River ran backwards. Chrisitina Rose, Native History: The Day Tecumseh's Prophecy Rocked the World, Indian Country Today, 2013, 2017

The British General Proctor was to help the Indian allies in Ohio to defeat the Americans. Tecumseh did not respect this man's judgement or leadership. At Fort Miami after a great victory, the prisoners were being killed, and Proctor did nothing to stop it. Tecumseh came, and took control saying; Begone Proctor! You are not fit to command! Go and put on petticoats". (Thom, Panther in the Sky)

The Iroquois from the Grand River and Caughnawaga in Ontario helped to defend British Canada. At the Battle of the Thames, the British fled, leaving Tecumseh to fight. Tecumseh died in the great Battle of the Thames, near now Chatham, Ontario, in 1813, after the British had given the Northwest to the Americans in 1796.

Tecumseh received an arm wound from the American artillery in the 1813 retreat up the Thames. Proctor kept moving the place they were to stand and fight and did not prepare for a battle. As Proctor retreated to Fairfield and fled, Tecumseh stayed to fight. Out-numbered four to one, he and his warriors were keeping the Americans from overtaking the Shawnee refugees who were going to Moravian Town (Jesus Town) for safety. Tecumseh said, we will fight the Americans large Army, it is strong hearts and being right that help us win. Tecumseh chose a swamp. He sang, "Gay goo awni zhee tungain – nee waynigoyawn." (Do not give up should I fall.) Colonel Richard M. Johnson, wearing a tall hat on the huge white bloody horse crashing through the brush (Thom), shot Tecumseh, point blank, after Tecumseh had shot and wounded Johnson with his rifle and emptied it (Wilson). Tecumseh had his leg shot off. His last words were "Leave me one or two loaded guns. I am going to have a last shot. Be quick and go."

Victories of Tecumseh are the following: Hull, Winchester, Mackinac (surrendered), Detroit, Chicago, and Harrison at Fort Meigs. (The battles in the Shawnee lands of Pennsylvania, Ohio, Kentucky, Indiana, and Illinois are not included in this history). See Tecumseh in the Biography chapter 9, for more on his life.

European contact often led the Anishinabeg to war. As a result, American mythology and history often casts these Indians as a race of warriors. This is a false image in the context of the prehistoric Anishinabeg; warfare did exist well before the arrival of Europeans. In the case of most tribal peoples, war seldom had territorial objectives and was almost never sustained. Anishinabeg war was in the form of periodic raids by small war parties. It was rare to war with neighbors, and never was total annihilation of enemies an objective. Glory, adventure, honor, and prestige were the rewards of war, and revenge its objective.

Ottissippi

While the threat of war was a reality as a practical matter, they lived mostly in peace (Cleland, Rites of Conquest, pg. 63).

All of the tribes, known to the Americans, north of the Ohio and east of the Mississippi, had their Council Fire, at the village of the Wyandott's near the mouth of the Detroit River. The Wyandott's alone had the power to convene the tribes, and when a Council was to be held, application was made to them, and it was held at their village. This fact gave the locality a peculiar importance and made it familiar to all the Indians. At various times, nearly all the noted Indian leaders visited this post. Pontiac, Tecumseh, and his brother, the Prophet, were frequent visitors. John Logan, the Cayuga Chief, was here in 1774, and after the Treaty of Chilicothe, he resided for many years in this vicinity.

Fort St. Joseph was the launching point for the War of 1812.

Andrew Westbrook purchased cattle in Ohio to meet the need of people for safety. He worked in the Commissary Department, collecting supplies for the troops. He was a valuable U.S. Army guide to his former home on the Thames in Canada. There was game of every description on the river, lake, and shore. Howling wolves, hooting of owls, and other voices of the night.

Mr. Harsen was a gunsmith, Mr. Graveraet a silver smith (Brakeman Papers, SCC library, MI Room).

The British hated the Yankees; the French liked the Yankees. The Indians also hated the Yankees (Jenks 1912).

In 1812, the British captured an American naval ship carrying General Hull's papers pertaining to the war efforts. The ship *Cuyahoga* was captured near Grosse Isle in the Detroit River. The Indian Allies blockaded the road from the River Raisen to Detroit, killed messengers, and captured the mail. Tribes west of the lakes came for reinforcements. Chicago and the mouth of the St. Joseph River were used by the British to supply Indians during the War of 1812. A secret village of the Pottawatomi was constructed. 500 people lived here away from the main route of travel. A blacksmith was supplied to repair weapons for the Indians serving in the war.

Indians clashed with the Americans at the mouth of the Raisen River and at Frenchtown, south of Detroit. A massacre followed the surrender of American General James Winchester and his Kentucky troops.

During the War of 1812, the British captured Detroit and Mackinac from the Americans. America reclaimed Detroit in 1813, and Fort Mackinac was returned to the Americans in 1815.

Lewis Cass became the Michigan Territorial Governor in 1815. He sought to obtain the fertile Saginaw Valley lands by treaty and to protect settlers from the threat of an Indian uprising along the St. Clair River – Detroit River – boundary. The government wanted to move the Indians West of the Mississippi and take over their settlements – villages.

The Indians were constantly attacking and looting the White settlements. Governor Cass had the Riley's lead and guide forays to put a stop to the atrocities and drive out the Indians. The Riley brothers were half-Ojibwe and half-White. (See "Chapter 9: Biographies of Indian Chiefs".) A posse was formed, including the Moran's, Dequindre's, Larned's, and Baubien's, to pursue them. Many Indians were killed, and many fled to Saginaw. The Indians taken prisoner were held under heavy guard in the Detroit Jail. The whole Riley family was friendly to the U.S. and a great help to them in many ways, as interpreters and carrying out diplomatic missions, especially during the War of 1812 to 1814 and in treaty sessions. James Riley was seized by the British and taken to Halifax during the war (Palmer, Friend, 1906).

There were many sufferings endured and dangers encountered in those days, which no mortal tongue will ever utter and no pen record (Palmer, Friend).

John Baptiste Askin, the Indian interpreter, believed that "Without the Indians, we never could keep this country, and that with them the Americans never will take the upper posts...for if we employ the Indians, we can have equal number, which is more than is wanted, for in the woods where the Americans must pass, one Indian is equal to three White men" (adapted).

One problem is the deep cultural significance the interior Ojibwe always have the weapons of their diseased relations deposited in their graves, which deprives the rising generation from benefitting by them (Schmaltz). This did not prevent the impressive victory at Detroit. It was not fear of Brock's Regular troops but the Indians that caused the commander at Detroit to capitulate with his superior force. In Brock's demand for the surrender of Detroit, he stated, "It is far from my intention to join in a War of Extermination, but you must be aware that the numerous body of Indians who have attached themselves to my troops will be beyond my control the moment the contest commences". The commander was led to believe that Brock had 5,000 Indians with him. Tecumseh circled the camp three times, the Americans thought the Indian Allies were an endless foe, many arriving after the surrender.

Proctor had sent a letter to Captain Roberts which was meant to be intercepted by Hull to alarm him. The letter telling Roberts that his force was considerable, and he need not send down more than 5,000 Indians. The British fired on the town of Detroit, the fort and camp. Americans were ordered into the fort. Balls sent into the fort killed 17. Hull had visions of overwhelming forces coming upon his rear and the superior army attacking on his front. Hull believed the population of Upper Canada was 20 times that of the territory of Michigan, and the collected force of all the Native Nations of Indians and the wealth and influence of the Northwest and other trading establishments, which have more than 2,000 White men, was overwhelming. This caused the truce flag, a white tablecloth, to be waved. Soldiers shed tears of mortification and disappointment (Lossing).

Tecumseh told his warriors: In my eyes, it is the act of a coward to hurt the helpless. Hurt no prisoners, women and children, nor steal and destroy. Two thousand five hundred prisoners were taken at Detroit. (Thom, Panther in the Sky))

The Indians were mild and hospitable in peace time, and merciless in war.

AURA STEWART

Aura Stewart recalls his father's word of the surrender of Detroit to the British:

My father witnessed the shameful surrender by Governor Hull. He gave a description of that scene: at that time, there was a lawyer by the name of Brush residing in Detroit, who was believed to be a traitor and unfriendly to the American cause, and who had a controlling interest over Governor Hull. It was believed that the British had secretly consorted with General Brock and advised the manner of attack. It was known that Brush had advised the surrender of Detroit and argued the impossibility of successfully defending it; that he was Hull's advisor and his influence over him great. The best men of Detroit gave the opinion that the cause of the surrender was cowardice on the part of Hull and treachery on the part of Brush.

The British treated the citizens kindly.

The Indian Shamans had dreamed of huge ships with wings and men in the branch's. The ships were full of powerful medicine. (Adapted from, Thom, Panther in the Sky, pg. 623)

The British at Fort Maiden, in the District of Maiden, later called Malden, near Amherstburg, Ontario, and Americans at Erie were pushing forward, with all possible dispatch, the building of vessels of war intended by each government to command our lakes, both fleets being in readiness by September 1, 1813. The American's fleet and Commodore Perry were the victors; now followed great confusion at the fort and in the town of Detroit. The British were in a hurry to evacuate the town and seized every boat and canoe to convey them and their baggage across the Detroit River.

In 1813, General Hull surrendered the Post of Detroit and all of Michigan to the British. Colonel Lewis Cass broke his sword rather than deliver it up to the English commander. Hull was a brigadier general who had never been in regular service and never commanded regulars in the field. General Brock, Lieutenant Governor of Canada, took 2,500 prisoners, the ammunitions, and stores. General Cass went to Washington to seek a court martial of Hull for cowardice. He was found not guilty of treason but was incompetent for the work assigned to him. General Cass then became Governor Cass (Moore).

The British obtained a large amount, of arms (2,500), 40 barrels of gunpowder, a great quantity and variety of military stores and ordinance, a stand of colors, and 25, iron, and 8 brass cannons, greatly needed in Upper Canada. General Hull and 350 regulars were held prisoners of war and sent to Montreal.

Brock placed his rich crimson silk sash publicly around the waist of Brigadier General Chief Tecumtha, who then placed it upon the body of Roundhead, celebrated and remarkable Wyandot warrior (Lossing). He also gave Tecumseh 2 silver trimmed pistols, and a gold compass with both their names engraved on it as he was leaving for service in Niagara. Tecumseh gave to Brock his respected friend a 6' wampum belt with an oak leaf design in green and white beads made by the women of Prophetstown saying, for one strong like the oak. (Thom, Panther in the Sky)

Governor Hull's surrender to the British in 1813 was due to his being outnumbered; his battle plans were captured from a ship carrying his papers, his medical staff was cut in half, his medical supplies were lost, and more than 400 of his garrison fell ill. His supply route from Ohio was cut off by Indian Allies and British soldiers. In addition, he faced a possible mutiny. His officers talked of putting Hull under arrest.

Brock left General Proctor in charge of Detroit during the short time of British reoccupation (Palmer).

Tecumseh told proctor his men serving the British cause, would eat beef like the other soldiers and not the horsemeat they had been sending. Tecumseh was always busy at council with the war chiefs, Elliott or British Officers. (Thom, Panther in the Sky)

MRS. JOHN HOWARD DIARY

"I have seen twelve Indians at a time go into his yard with scalps, where they made a large circle on the ground. They would then form themselves in this ring and dance while one of their number sat drumming on a small drum. The Indians would hold the scalps extended in the air on a long stick. There they would dance and cry the war whoop and raise the scalps higher and higher into the air.

Ottissippi

Commodore Perry's victory over the British gave the Americans command of the Lake Erie.

Amid the confusion of the British, and their hurry to leave Detroit, the Americans collected and had a secret consultation, having great anxiety about 600 Indian Allies at the River Ecorse, fearing they would rush into town and rob, and perhaps murder, citizens. It was thought to send a messenger to Commodore Perry, requesting him to send them succor as soon as possible.

The persons selected to bear the message were William Macomb, William Conner, Henry Graveraet, Knaggs, Charles Stewart, and Harvey Stewart – eight in all. These men were hired as guides to the army up the River Thames.

After Harrison's army had crossed over at Maiden, Perry's fleet weighed anchor, and all sails were spread, and the army being in line for marching, both proceeded up the river, the army keeping abreast of the fleet, which my father said was the most beautiful sight he ever witnessed" (Howard).

General Harrison with General Perry came by land and sea and drove General Proctor and the British and Indian Allies back into Canada (Tanner). Proctor knowing the British ships would no longer bring food or ammunition. His supply was cut off and the American soldiers would come on ships. Proctor began packing up his belongings, family. The fort, kitchen, armories, and offices were loaded on wagons, readying to flee. Tecumseh sent Elliott to Proctor for the Truth. The British set fire to the Fort and shipyard at Malden, fleeing without an enemy in sight. The Shawnee women and children and elders following the British to safety. (Adapted from, Thom, Panther in the Sky)

Colonel Proctor had marched to the Thames to avoid the fire of the American fleet at Fort Maiden. The American troops had followed the British into Canada. Tecumseh told Proctor, "You may go, as for us our lives are in the hands of the Great Spirit. He gave our ancestors the lands which we possess. We are determined to defend them, and if it be his will our bones shall whiten on them, but we will never give them up! Some of the officers applauded. At the Thames, Proctor had retreated, as Tecumseh and his men, stood ground fighting, for the Peoples homeland. Tecumseh had told his warriors at the fire, "If I am dead and we have lost, it will be the end of what we have tried to do. Then our warriors should leave the field and not waste their lives for the British. This was the prophecy given to him, he had seen the battle and that he would fall.

Tecumseh's death at the Thames near Chatham, Ontario on Lake St. Clair was the end of the War of 1812 and Indian resistance to the Americans. The Ojibwe never admitted losing any sustained war (Tolatsga Whoa, www).

General Harrison's command eventually took possession of Detroit for the Americans again. Colonel Lewis Cass was commissioned governor. Michigan then entered upon that political, social, and commercial course which led to her present greatness (Wisc. Historical Co.).

Two million acres were set aside for the soldiers of 1812 as their pay for the war effort (Moore). The Indians fought for free in the war, the Detroit bands fought for the British.

A letter from Forsyth to Clark, on September 12, 1812, "The Natives are very numerous on both sides of the Lake Huron, all the way to Mackinac and on both sides of Lake Superior".

After the War of 1812, the British Government helped 3,500 Black people resettle in Canada as United Empire Loyalists. Some of the Native Americans also moved to Canadian lands. Upper Canada – Western Ontario – was a refuge for United Empire Loyalists.

The government did not restrain lawless subjects who hesitated at no means to possess the land, furs, and other property of the Indians (Blackhawk). The government thought the Indians were in the way of progress, and good citizens could take possession. There was great corruption in business and political lawlessness.

Lewis Cass went on to be governor of the Northwest Territory, negotiating important treaties and establishing and organizing the territory. He became the Secretary of War in 1831 under President Andrew Jackson, and then a member of the U.S. Senate and more. His contributions to the nation cannot be overestimated (Western Historical Co.).

The Indians received many uniforms and medals for their service to the military of both the British and Americans. Many received pensions for their service at the Moravian towns on the Thames, near Lake St. Clair's northeast side, above Detroit.

Following Tecumseh's defeat at the Battle of the Thames, the Indian tribes stopped trying to prevent the encroachment of the White man by warfare and confined themselves to minor depredations, such as killing horses or oxen. Although the Western tribes urged the Eastern Indians to fight, the latter realized the hopelessness of battle and tried, unsuccessfully, to hold their ground by treaty (Emmert, MPHC vol. 47).

A large number, of Indians, camped in the area in 1813 and threatened to massacre the inhabitants. Most fled to Detroit for the duration of the war (Andreas 1883, pg. 260).

MRS. JOHN HOWARD PAPERS: 1813

Ottissippi

"When the Americans came back and took Detroit, it was a day of great rejoicing. All the people went out to meet them. It was a splendid scene, their guns glistening in the sunshine, and will ever be remembered by me.

Soon alas! Sickness came among the soldiers, and dysentery swept them like a scythe over the new mown grass. Governor Hull's house was used for their hospital. I have often been in when two or three would be laid out in the hall, and many others would be lying sick in the rooms, while still others would be going to the graves with their fellow soldiers.

As I lived but a short distance from the hospital, I would go in every day and take the soldiers something to relieve their wants, but it was very little in comparison to their needs. I was a child, but time can never erase these scenes from my memory."

In 1814, Fort Gratiot was built, and people returned, the settlement was small and French. The French provided fish to the fort (Andreas 1883, pg. 610).

Francis Bonhomme became captain of a company of local militia during the unrest (Andreas 1883, Pg. 260).

In June 1816, the British Indian agent at Fort Malden ceased issuing special rations to more than 1,000 Indians, signifying an end to the wartime basis for provisioning and dispersal of the last contingent of Indians receiving British military support. Great Lakes Indians from American Territory received annual presents at Fort Malden and the British posts on Lake Huron until 1842 (Tanner, page 121, Atlas of Great Lakes Indian History). Thousands of Indians came through St. Clair County annually to cross over the St. Clair River and receive British presents for their service to the Crown.

Even after this region was surrendered, the English Government sought the favor of the Indians by annual gifts; and year by year up to 1836, thousands from various tribes gathered at Detroit, Sandwich, or Malden to receive the presents of their Great Father, the King. The American Government was compelled to follow this precedent (Farmer, 1884).

The Dulhut Massacre took place in 1816 (Tanner). The same year, part of Michigan Territory was given to the State of Indiana.

In 1817, Lieutenant Colonel John McNeil purchased the claim 244 from the estate of F. Bonhomme and the LaSalle claim (SCC record of deeds liber, E 353-355, and lieber A: 173 – 175). This tract of land, called the McNeil Tract, was 1,200 acres. McNeil was the commandant at Fort Gratiot from 1817 to 1818.

THE ENGLISH

British America began in 1756 at the Dumfries Colony of Virginia. Virginia's claim to the Northwest Territory was established by George Rogers Clark at Kaskaskia, Cahokia and Vincennes (Fort Sackville), near the Mississippi River (now Indiana), in 1778, without a shot. Rocheblave the British Commander, was taken prisoner to Williamsburg, there was no harm or theft to the French and British at these posts. Clark was a very honorable and He would command the fort at the mouth of the Ohio river. This would stop the British from using the Mississippi and western water routes to bring in supplies, from the Spanish in New Orleans, like scalping knives, guns and ammunition, for war in Ohio and Kentucky. This would prevent the blood of the women and children by Indians through the British. Clarks Officers were, Simon Kenton (Butler), the best guide and hunter in the West. John Bowman, Harrod, Montgomery and Helms. He wanted to then take Detroit the base of British operations and the Northwest for Virginia. The Commonwealth of Virginia had not sent any funds or supplies, Clark depended on credit from Spanish Government and traders at St. Louis and New Orleans, the Catholic Majesty and French people, for supplies to fight the British and Their allies. The Spanish depended on Clark for safety against the British. The Spanish and traders lost fortunes aiding Clarks Military presence. Clarks wisdom and affability made him loved by all. Skins and Tobacco were used as currency. (Adapted from Thom, Long Knife).

The American Revolution was a war of the American British against the Crown British who ruled the Colonies from England. The main reason for the war was the 1773 proclamation called "The Quebec Act" of 1774 that blocked Virginia's claims over the chartered lands. The boundary for the Indian lands was the Allegany Mountain Chain. The settlers were not to cross the mountains to the West. This law was blatantly ignored; the transfer of government rule to Quebec, which stayed loyal to King George IV, was never obeyed or enforced. The White settlers continued to encroach onto the Indian lands, claiming the Virginia Charter as their authority, having no fixed Western boundary line. The Loyal Land Co., the Ohio Co., Manassas Cutler, Grand Ohio Company, and others were speculating on the Ohio country.

The Ohio Co. formed in 1747, for the purpose, of extending Virginia settlements. The tobacco trade was doing very well with slave labor.

In 1748, King George III granted the Ohio Co. of Virginia, a group of wealthy Virginians, 200,000 acres West of the Allegheny Mountains in Maryland, Pennsylvania, and Virginia, on both sides of the Ohio River.

Ottissippi

Surveyors began surveying these lands and land in Southern Ohio and Northeast Kentucky.

George Washington built Fort Necessity and killed a French Indian messenger, which started the French and Indian War. This war started in 1750, ending in 1763 with the British winning the war and then issuing a Proclamation, stopping White encroachment on Indian lands west of the Allegheny Mountains. Fort Necessity was in West Pennsylvania, now Ohio.

The French and Allied tribes went to the Ohio Valley to clear out the English traders.

General Braddock led the British. George Washington was his Aide De Camp. Braddock was a seasoned man, but Ben Franklin warned him that the Indian forest warfare was not to be trifled with. Charles Langlade with a war party of First Nations Ojibwe, 637 men, joined the French. The British were defeated, the soldiers in flight. Daniel Boone fled on horseback to his father's farm in Kentucky. Over 800 British were killed, many French and 23 warriors were killed or wounded. The Indians were well paid in booty: supplies, horses and cattle, artillery and coin (D. Plain).

As early as 1785, the White Loyalists possibly equaled the Ojibwa population in the Province of Canada (Schmaltz). The Loyalists treated the Indians as they had in the U.S.; they were taking all the game and fish, which the Indian depended on for their living.

One Southern Mississauga chief in 1820 told the English, "You came as a wind blowing across the great lake. The wind wafted you to our shores. We...planted and nursed you. We protected you till you became a mighty tree that spread thru our hunting land. With its branches, you now lash us".

British Ontario was a haven for Loyalists and immigrants from Britain. The settlers were shooting deer, bear, and game birds by the thousands, and the fisheries were threatened.

The Upper Canada Land Boards were established in 1765 to 1804. There were four districts; the District of Hesse, which later became the Western District, included Detroit and Michilimackinac (Riddell, Criminal Courts & Law in Early Upper Canada, www). East Michigan was included in Upper Canada until 1796 when the British evacuated and relinquished the country to the U.S. in the Northwest Territory. The other districts were Nassau, Luneberg, and Mekelenburg. Many Germans who had fought for Crown Britain settled here after the war. These districts became Upper Canada in 1791.

Some of the claims for land in the British Territory to the District of Hesse and the Western District dated to the 1730s. These were lands granted by the King, lands given without authority by commandants of old Fort

Ponchetrain, gifts from the Huron and Ottawa chiefs, claims granted by English commanders, after 1760, and land bought and sold in speculation, after 1760.

The militia of Virginia was the military power in Upper Canada. Abbott, Allen, and Cameron were officers. There was no fear of reprisals from the defeated French and British on behalf of the Indians.

The Europeans brought great change to the Indians' mode of living. Bows and arrows gave way to guns, animal skins gave way to blanket and fabric. Many other articles of fancy or practical use were made known, and new desires created. A means of satisfying these desires and obtaining articles was supplied by trading with the White Man to purchase with skins, leather, and fur of all kinds. The beaver was the most important, the localities where it flourished the most valuable. The beaver was a strong motive for causing infighting to kill, steal, and destroy by Europeans (Jenks 1912, vol. 1 History of SCC MI).

Washington had an enlarged plan to reach the Ohio as a means of conveyance of the extensive and valuable trade of a rising empire. He rode 700 miles to find a shorter route to the Potomac, fearing loss of trade to the West down the Mississippi. Washington's method was to draw trade, produce, and furs to our posts, adding immense increase to our exports and binding these people to us by a chain which can never be broken.

Dr. Manassa Cutler's Scioto Purchase of Ohio land was the Southern half of Ohio, 1,500,000 acres, half for the Ohio Co. and half for a Private Speculation. The Ohio Co. was organized to claim land under the Virginia Charter of the King of England.

A letter to Secretary Madison by Chief Justice Woodward (Michigan Territory, 1807):

"These settlements are pleasant, fertile, opulent. They present along the whole line an activity little realized in the U.S. The commerce in furs, which has been carried on in one channel for two centuries, is the cause of this phenomenon. This commerce belongs to another Nation. The Americans have never been able to succeed in it, though the most desirable post of it belongs to their own territory and the whole of it passes along their lines" (C. Moore, 1913).

Major Gladwin's proposal of free trade in rum, "more effective than fire and sword," was proving to be the final solution. Major Henry Basset at Detroit in 1773 reported that the chiefs complain much of the intention of the English to kill all their young men [with liquor], it prevents their hunting. . .and hurts the trade very much, for instead of that poison when they return from their winter, they would purchase blankets, shrowdings, etc. The chiefs declare that they lose more of their young men by rum than they used to by war. The free supply of rum by unscrupulous traders destroyed the power of the Ojibwa and their allies, without creating any great expense on the part of the government in loss of soldiers and money.

Alcohol was used by British and American traders to break the will and resistance of the Anishinabe and see their inevitable demise. Violent acts, including murder, were common in the Great Lakes. They were more likely to involve Indians killing their own people while in a drunken state. The vast, majority of cases involving even Whites, never saw the courts (Schmaltz, 1991).

Alcohol was cheap and plentiful (Riddell). The traders gave deep credit to the Indians, who depended on American goods. Alcohol was a large part of the trade, and Indians would run up huge debts with traders who sold at inflated prices for diluted trade goods. The traders knew they would eventually collect the debts in land or when treaties were signed.

At St. Joseph Station in 1757 to 1759, the Pottawatomi traded 400 packs of furs a year.

The early men of government were of considerable ability but were profoundly ignorant of the conditions in frontier life and problems of Michigan.

In the Treaty of Detroit in 1807, the Ojibwe and other tribes deeded all claim to the southeast portion of the territory of Michigan, including Detroit and the St. Clair Rivers. For many years, the Indians were yet numerous (Jenks 1912).

Detroit was the scene of one surrender, more than 50 pitched battles, and 12 horrid massacres (Hotchkiss).

Since 1810, buffalo were exterminated East of the Mississippi River.

In 1813, there was a large group meeting of the Indians on the St. Clair River. They determined to exterminate all the settlers who fled to Detroit for the safety of the fort. They stayed in Detroit for the duration of the war. The settlers were mostly French.

The Treaty of Ghent in 1814 returned the Michigan Territory to American authority. In the Treaty of Ghent, the War of 1812 was treated as a stalemate between the Americans and the British, but in actual fact the Ojibwe and Indian Allies had lost.

The Moravian Delaware were living on the Huron River north of Detroit temporarily. They were to move to Canada. Captain Thomas McKee, Indian agent, suggested the Fairfield location to the Moravian Delaware missionaries and made arrangements with the local Ojibwe. They soon seem to have replaced the Ojibwe in supplying Detroit with maple sugar and berries and were most generous to local Ojibwe.

Cheryl Morgan

For 200 years, Indians remained a vital force in the area's development, hunting furs and as allies in French, British, and American wars. After 1812, the value of Indians and their contributions to the Nations diminished (City Data, Michigan History, www).

Judge Abbott was Superintendent of the American Fur Co. at Detroit and a very influential man in the southeast of Michigan and Southern Ontario. Judge Jewitt was at Saginaw.

At Point Edward Ontario, the British had built Fort Edward. It was on 1,000 acres. It became the Grand Trunk RR Co. Town (John Munson, MI Historical Commission. MI Room, SCC Library).

In 1805, the governor acted as Superintendent of Indian Affairs, first Governor Hull, then Governor Cass from 1813 until 1834.

Governor Cass, was amazed to discover that the French were ignorant of the spinning wheel, and the loom, that they drew their manure over the ice in the winter, in order, to dump it into the lake, in the spring, that they threw away their sheep wool, and that they, looked on soap making as an experiment from which few cared to profit. He felt that Good Old Yankee stock was the tonic Michigan needed to grow and prosper (John Anthony Caruso, The Great Lakes Frontier).

The land had been described as an endless swamp and sterile land. Governor Cass read the official report sent from Meigs, Superintendent of the General Land Office, to President Madison. He sent a protest to Meigs: "The quality of the land in this territory has been grossly misrepresented". Tiffin's description was based on incorrect information, reminding Meigs that the surveyors had come to Michigan in the wettest season the territory had ever known. Two of the surveyors had praised the territory and had described the Territory, in glowing terms. He instructed Meigs on the proper method of conducting surveys and predicted that the territory would be quickly settled. New surveys were ordered.

After 1812, there were about 2,000 French Canadians living in Detroit. The Indian population of the hinterland in the Lower Peninsula of Michigan was probably between 10,000 and 15,000 (Tanner, page 69, The Ojibwa 1992). Four men made the decisions of government, making laws the citizens knew nothing of for many months (Palmer).

The Treaty of Saginaw in 1817 ceded much of Michigan and Indiana to the United States. (See "Chapter 11: Mounds and Treaties".) Governor Cass upon the Treaty of Saginaw set out in 1820 with a large group of men to explore the mineral wealth of the Northwest Territory in Upper Michigan, carrying the flag to remote regions. Cass and a distinguished entourage made a discovery tour of the newly acquired territory. As a geologist, he sought out the rich resources of the land. Those who joined him were, Major Robert Forsyth, his private secretary; James D. Doty, secretary to the expedition; Dr. Alexander Wolcott, physician; Captain David Douglass, topographer; Charles Trowbridge, his assistant, and Alexander Chase; Henry Schoolcraft, mineralogist and geologist; Lieutenant Aeneas Mackay, commanding the soldiers; James Riley, interpreter; and a number of engages (indentured servants), soldiers and Indians. 12 French Canadian voyageurs manning the canoes: 40 men in all. They left Detroit on May 24 and returned on September 23 after traveling 4,000 miles in 122 days. They made a stop at Fort Gratiot; a welcome salute of the cannon greeted them. Camping in a field above the fort, they observed the 40 acres of kitchen gardens and acreage of grain and beans north of the fort and back to Black River. He then organized and advertised for the sale of Michigan lands to immigrants.

In 1818, the bitterness of the Indians was expressed by Head Chief Ocaita on Drummond Island:

"Though many of our young men were mixed with the earth (killed in battle), we were happy and took your Chiefs (the British officers), the hair of a great many of the heads of your enemies; and though we were enjoying ourselves and everything was going on well, we were astonished one morning to hear by a little bird (messenger), that you had buried the hatchet and taken our enemies by the hand...my heart now fails me; I can hardly speak. We are now slaves and treated worse than dogs. Those bad spirits (the Americans) take possession of our lands without consulting us. They deprive us of our English traders. They even tie us up and torture us (flog them) almost to death. Our Chiefs did not consent to have our lands given to the Americans (in the treaty), but you did it without consulting us; and in doing that you delivered us up to their mercy. They are enraged at us for having joined you in the play (war), and they treat us worse than dogs. We implore you to open up your ears, to listen to our grievances, fulfill your promises that we may be released from slavery and enjoy the happiness we did previous to the war."

In 1819, U.S. Secretary of War Calhoun instructed Governor Cass to make a treaty at the most favorable terms he could with the Saginaw Ojibwe. This treaty is the Treaty of Saginaw, where about half of Lower Michigan and part of Ohio and Indiana were ceded, the Indians retaining reserves to live upon.

In 1824, Thanksgiving Day was observed for the first time.

In 1825, the Erie Canal was completed to Buffalo, New York. This brought much change as thousands of immigrants flooded into the territory. Many passenger ships were arriving daily, wagons and horses and families, carrying their all, most of whom were in a very deplorable condition.

In 1828, the first Capital Building was built in Detroit, the Capital of Michigan Territory.

The Indians who fled to Canada and were at Aamjiwnaang – Sarnia Reserve – fell into a deplorable condition. Our population was ravaged by wars and disease, smallpox and cholera epidemics. Our hunting grounds were being ruined. We were expected to stay on our reserves and take up farming. The dominant culture was overwhelming, and we were suffering from severe culture shock.

Reverend W. Scott, our missionary in 1841, wrote, "the propensity to roving and hunting is almost incredible in respect to the older Indians, and the younger ones are led to follow their example. Most try to find solace in alcohol. They were previously in a very wretched and miserable condition. Wicked, drunken licentious.

In 1832, during this distressing time, the Methodist Mission began on our reserve" (D. Plain, the Plains of Aamjiwnaang).

See "Chapter 11: Mounds and Treaties" and "Chapter 10: Reserves and Indian Lands".

In 1832, the Black Hawk War was fought over Chief Black Hawk planting corn on the east side of the Mississippi, his old homelands. He was falsely accused, beaten severely, villages were burned, crops destroyed, the people beaten. A son of Black Hawk was taken prisoner and received 500 lashes. This was the last of a series of outrages that induced his father to flee. He was taking his people to Canada, they were slaughtered, trying to escape to Canada and refuge.

Black Hawk had long been a visitor at Malden each year and received liberal presents.

"We have witnessed outrages committed upon the Indians until they gnashed their teeth and wept because they dared not make any resistance, for their wives and children's sake, well knowing upon the slightest pretext they would be overrun in a moment. Goaded into open hostility. Subjects of intolerable oppression, barbarities inflicted to which the flogging of the son of Black Hawk was most merciful" (Collection of Wisc. Historical Society, vol. 10).

The Indians had offered their services to the British in fighting the Americans. Each year they were rewarded for their service. After the War of 1812, most returned to their homes in the U.S. Territory, journeying back to Canada, Amherstberg, Port Sarnia, and Mantoulin Island, east of Mackinaw, annually for gifts distributed by the British Government for their service. After this region, The Northwest Territory, was surrendered to the U.S., the English

Government sought the favor of the Indians by annual gifts; and year by year up to 1836, thousands from various tribes gathered at Detroit, Sandwich, or Malden to receive presents of their Great Father, the King.

The American Government was compelled to follow this precedent. All year round, they came and went. The government blacksmith repaired, free of charge, their guns and traps. After receiving their payments, hundreds would lie about the city, drunken. In 1840, the U.S. Government protested to the British against this practice, on the grounds, that it made the Indians dissatisfied. In 1842, the American Indians were notified that if they wished to participate in future distributions of presents, they must reside in Canada (Lauriston, Lambton's 100 Years, 1971).

In 1835, the first state election and first Constitution in Michigan were adopted by vote of the people. In the same year, the Toledo War was a dispute over a reserved strip of land between Ohio and Michigan. Michigan eventually gave Ohio the strip and gained the whole Upper Peninsula.

In 1836, at the Treaty of Washington, the Black River and Swan Creek bands sold their reserves to the U.S. Government. This was the southeast quarter of Michigan, including half of the Thumb of Michigan. In 1836, enormous sales of public lands were made in Michigan, Wisconsin was created out of Michigan Territory, and Michigan participated in the first Presidential election of the United States. Since 1836, persons other that the governor, were appointed as Indian agents.

The Patriot War in Canada was from 1836 to 1838. The UEL from the U.S. protested the French seignorial system and the Catholic Church as the government. The government men were appointed for life, and there was no representation against the French Family Compact groups who ruled over all. The others were treated as peasants. This war was all along the Canadian border with the U.S., many farmers and others were killed and taken prisoner trying to take over the corrupt Canadian Government. Many men from the U.S. were involved, trying to help their Canadian friends.

After 1800, officials prohibited late Loyalists, Americans who immigrated after 1783 and not British subjects or loyalists the right to vote, hold office, or own land. They were only allowed to lease or squat land (Travers 2015). This led to the Patriot War in 1838.

In the rebellions through the 1838 Patriot War, the Anishinabe Allies were mustered in Sombra with 550 Kent County militiamen (Travers 2015). It was also called the Pirate War. The cry of "Freedom" was revived along the whole length of the Frontier. The steamer *Niagara* was captured in the Niagara River by British Forces and sent her over the Falls, with part of the Patriot crew aboard.

The Patriots had a considerable force on Navy Island; a Rocket Brigade was stationed at Windsor, Ontario. The Patriots had an encampment at Gibralter, Michigan.

Colonel Slingerland issued orders for duty, but so strong was the sympathy in favor of the Patriots and against the English that not over 30 men of 600 obeyed the order. Colonel Smith made a similar report, and the encampment remained undisturbed. Forts were looted of ammunitions and cannon to aid the cause, including one from Fort Gratiot. The sloop *Ann* was taken and General Theller and Colonel Dodge and crew were taken prisoner, as they with two other ships were about to capture Fort Maiden. A battle was fought at Windsor, the Patriots losing, and at Point Au Pelee, Ontario, where the Patriots were victors. All along the border, Patriots were creating havoc.

The Patriot War was an effort to drive the British from North America, once and for all. The Partisans were organized through secret societies, known as Hunters lodges – anti-British. They labeled themselves as Patriots. One group met at Fort Gratiot. Their object was to seize the Canadian Peninsula at Windsor and add this land to the U.S. The Battle of Windsor took place in 1837.

In 1838, a Patriot group, seized a number of ships from Detroit and attacked Amherstburg. The men marched across the ice to Fighting Island to attack at Sandwich – Windsor. The British had built three fortifications on Bois Blanc – Bob Lo – Island.

The Detroit Patriots attempted to seize Fort Gratiot and the U.S. arsenal at Dearborn and were fended off by Michigan militia groups. There was support all along the U.S. Canada border. The war was over in 1838. The hunter lodges closed in 1841 (The Rebellion of 1837, Mystic Detroit, www).

During the Patriot War, over a thousand men were killed, shot, hanged, or sent to slave labor camps in New Zealand and the Caribbean. The laws were finally changed after the Durham Report was made, and reforms were made, to the old French siegnors' ruling government.

In 1837, Michigan became the 26th State in the Union. In 1837, the U.S. Government began removing the Indians West of the Mississippi. In the same year, the first train to Michigan arrived at Toledo, and the Detroit Antislavery Society was organized.

In 1847, the Potato Famine in Ireland sent starving Irish to American shores. Until this year, Detroit was the Capital of Michigan. The Bill locating the State Capital at Lansing passed, and Lansing became the Capital of Michigan.

In 1854, the Republican Party was organized at Jackson, Michigan under a large oak tree. The republicans controlled the State until the 1930s.

Abraham Lincoln became the President of the United States in 1860.

In 1864, the Michigan Colored Infantry was 1,673 men who were sent to fight in the Civil War in the South. In the Civil War, Michigan sent 90,000 troops total. More Native Americans have served in the U.S. Armed Forces than any other ethnic group.

The Granger Movement was founded in 1867; it was a social, educational group in farming communities. It was also a political group, fighting abuses including the corruption of railroads crossing their land.

The District of Huron Custom House was erected for a bond warehouse for valuable imports for the benefit of all the importers of the Northwest who petitioned Congress to provide for its erection. The now Federal Building on Water Street in Port Huron was built in 1870 and is now the oldest Federal Courthouse in the Midwest. It was also used as a court house and a post office. It was used for the reception and distribution of all the mails of a hundred post offices and mail routes of Eastern Michigan and the Upper Lakes, so this building, though local in situation, is national in its objects and usefulness.

It is the Great Eastern Gate of Commerce through which pass a wealth of commerce unrivaled in the land. Duties and fees were collected here.

The District of Huron extends from Lake St. Clair to Mackinaw, with a shoreline of over 550 miles, embracing 22 counties. Port Huron is the port of entry, organized in 1866. From 1866 to 1872, 316,419 immigrants arrived at this port, second only to New York. Records were not kept of the large volume of early immigrant crossings. Port Huron was a bustling Frontier outpost in 1878.

Until 1871, Congress extinguished the Indian title only with the consent of tribes, recognized as having claim to the soil by occupancy (Jenks, 1912).

"Tell your people that, since we were promised we should never be moved, we have moved five times" (An Indian Chief in 1876).

There are no political solutions to spiritual problems (Ziibiiwing, Saginaw Chippewa).

INDIANS IN THE MILITARY

Indians have fought in every war of the United States; they love their country. Their people are loyal and patriotic.

18 tribes supplied "Code Talkers" in WWII. The Navajo are the best known. These men were revered upon return from the war. Their language could never be cracked. They were very instrumental to the Armed Forces. They

were scouts, two miles ahead of the troops in dangerous conditions. They were to be killed if captured, keeping the secret code. In 2000, the Navajo Code Talkers were given honors for their service.

COMPANY K MICHIGAN SHARPSHOOTERS

Company K was an all-Indian company known as the "Indian Company". When the Civil War broke out in 1863, the Union Army, the North, needed sharpshooters when the White men failed the tests. They went to the Native Americans, who were hunters and farmers and loggers. The "river hogs", experienced log handlers, became the Co. K 2nd Michigan Calvary.

147 men came to be tested, and 147 men were welcomed. Not one was a warrior. These men were indispensable to the cause. The company was mostly Native Americans from Michigan, a few from Ontario.

In order to be a sharpshooter, you had to be able to hit an eight-inch pie plate, four out of five times at a distance of 220 yards. This was with open sights and a musket rifle.

Company K fought in the Civil War under General Grant. They were mustered out into service on January 12, 1863. They were ordered to the front at the Battle of the Wilderness. Their captain was Archibald Campbell. They were of Boonville and Chattanooga fame, "The Black River Boys".

These men have seen hard service. They had volunteered several times, they had fought gallantly beside Black and White men. 25% gave the ultimate sacrifice. Fifteen were at Andersonville, Hell Prison, 9 died. They were promptly forgotten.

Captain Campbell's commandmant was, General Phillip Sheridan, who made his famous 20-mile ride on October 19, 1864 from Winchester to Cedar Creek, to rally his demoralized troops. Sheridan's war horse, "Riemzi", a black charger, was raised in Burtchville Township, near Lakeport, Michigan. The citizens purchased the jet-black colt from William Leonard and presented him fully-equipped to Captain Campbell. The colt was noted for his coolness and intelligence under fire. Campbell presented him to General Sheridan, who had admired the superb qualities of the fiery colt.

Russel Leonard bought the colt from A.P. Sexton for $90.00, who sold him to his son, William Leonard, who lived in Burtchville on Comstock Road. He broke him to harness and hauled cordwood 17 miles to Port Huron. He was known as the Leonard Colt, at three years old with three white feet and 16 hands high. A hand is four inches from ground to withers – top of shoulders – at the base of the neck. He was of Morgan Stock. He rode like eagle flight. The people of Port Huron paid $175.00 for this prize colt.

Ottissippi

He died at 20 years old after all the battles of Sheridan. His remains were stuffed and given to the Smithsonian Institute in Washington D.C. The saddle was in the Museum at Port Huron.

Letters received home from the superior officers stated that these Co. K men were among the best soldiers in service, gallantly charging in direct assault, as well as doing effective sharpshooting and picket duty. They fought valiantly under the Stars and Stripes as their ancestors did under the plumes of the Wild American Eagle. They cast a glamour over the annals of the North that shall not be easily effaced.

Lieutenant Garrett A. Graveraet recruited Indians and organized the Company. He brilliantly led his men in a daring charge at Spottsylvania, after seeing his father fall at his side. Graveraet was a talented young man. He was one of the first government teachers at L'Arbre Croache and had great influence among the Natives. Always honorable and straightforward in his dealings, his confidence was never betrayed. And, "My Indians", as he loved to call them, proved true and lasting friends. The remnants were among the first to enter Richmond and share the great victory of the North. William Gravaeratte, in 1944, spoke for the Ojibwe saying, "We've done our hitch in Hell".

In the Civil War, Native Americans had the largest number of deaths, fighting this war on both sides, Union and Confederate. In WWI, 12,000 Native Americans served. In WWII, 99% of eligible American Indians registered for the draft, the highest percentage of any ethnic group. 44,500 served in uniform; 46,000 served in the Defense Industry. In the Vietnam War, over 41,000 Native Americans served. In Operation Desert Storm, more than 24,000 Native Americans served.

Native Americans fought in the Korean War, Vietnam War, Gulf War, and Persian Gulf War, and 9,000 are still serving. There are 189,800 Native American veterans still living. The warriors dedicate their lives to preserve and protect the people.

Indigenous government decision making was adopted by Benjamin Franklin, as well as the founding of a democratic U.S. Government and the U. S. Constitution.

The last battle of the Old Indian Wars was fought in Nevada in 1911 (Steiner). In 1924, the Indian Citizen Act was passed. In 1937, the Saginaw Chippewa created their Tribal Constitution. In 1978, the Indian Religious Freedom Act was passed. In 1989, the Native American Grave and Repatriation Act was passed into law to bring home to the people thousands of Native American ancestors' bones and religious artifacts. This is ongoing, returning remains and artifacts from institutions across the country to the ancestral homelands at government expense.

CHIEF OKEMOS

When the Indians were fighting for their Lands. George Washington was the Leader of the American Forces. He was, in the forefront, to push into the Northwest, and claim land for his uncle, who was like a father to him. Which needed to be surveyed, before the charter claim was valid, by the Crown of British England. He made great headway. Surveying for soldiers Bounty Lands, first choice, The cream of the country

The Indians, were in agreement to stop him. They chose their best marksman for his accuracy and skill with the bow and arrow to go and find him and kill him.

This man was Chief Okemos, who, as a young man, became a great chief. Okemos was so accurate, that he was able to bring any bird he chose out of the air. He was a great warrior and leader in the British Revolutionary War. He was honored to be chosen and followed Washington around for days, waiting for the opportunity. His chance finally came, he saw Washington at his camp with his men. Early one morning, when the camp was quiet, Okemos found his opportunity. Washington had left his camp and had gone out alone into an open field near his encampment and was kneeling in prayer to God. He was very absorbed, he poured out his heart to the Great Spirit, unaware of the danger to him.

Okemos crept to a closer range for a perfect view; he was not heard or noticed. Washington kept on with his praying, oblivious to the sound of arrows whizzing by his head and body in front, at his feet, over close to each side.

All nine shots missed. Okemos was deeply moved, believing the Great Spirit, the White man's God, was protecting him and had saved the life of the White leader and had a special purpose for his life, he vowed never again to offend the White man's God. He left quietly as Washington was still kneeling.

Okemos lived to be very old and lived near Lansing, Michigan on the Looking Glass River. He was well admired and beloved by the Red and the White Man. He was the Head Chief over Southeast Michigan and Southwest Ontario.

CHAPTER 7
Part II: Forts, Indian Captives and American Biography

Forts were used as trading houses at the Indian fishing sites. The Indians gathered there seasonally to trade. The Indians believed them to be the first steps to enslave them and invade their properties.

M. Dole, a trader, said, "It is no crime to cheat and gull an Indian. There are a thousand opportunities present to take advantage of their ignorance. I employ rum".

Fort Washington was at Cincinnati, Ohio.

FORT ST. JOSEPH – FORT DETROIT OR FORT DULUTH

Fort St. Joseph was built in 1686 at the foot of Lake Huron near the rapids by the Frenchman Duluth and the *coureurs des bois*. Sieur Daniel Graysolon Du Luth, or Du Lhut, in 1686, using his own funds to establish a trading post. He was also a French military official who used the fort to gather men for military excursions. The fort was used by Allied Indians to retreat while hunting or marching against Iroquois. DuLuth was also called Delude; he was a cousin of Hennepin, the explorer priest (Jenks).

Farming was commenced within the fort grounds, planting "Turkey Wheat" (Indian corn). The harvest was winter sustenance.

The first priest was Father Claude Aveneau, a Jesuit, who was a resident for one winter.

Lahonton first commanded the post for two years and burned it upon transfer to the Fort at Mackinac in 1688.

"He, Duluth, chose a spot where the St. Clair River was the narrowest and established Fort St. Joseph. That site is located, in what is now, Pine Grove Park in downtown Port Huron, Michigan" (David Plain, "From Quisconsin to Caughnowaga")

"This Fort St. Joseph and the Fort St. Joseph on the river of the same name in Southwest Michigan are the oldest forts in the Lower Peninsula. They preceded Fort Ponchetrain built at Detroit River by Lamotte Cadillac by 15 years.

De Nonvile, governor general of Canada after Frontenac, says, "It was maintained eight years and exercised a powerful influence on the English. Possibly it was in use as a trading post before use as a military establishment" (Western Historical Co., History of SCC, MI).

There were four nations belonging to his post: the Ojibwe, Pottawatomi, Ottawa, and Huron.

Fort Duluth was soon destroyed. Fort Niagra had been abandoned to the Iroquois and, as a precaution, Baron Lahonton burned the fort and removed the garrison to Machinac in August of 1688, under order of Marquis De Deononville, the governor general of Canada (Lanman, 1839, pg. 36, History of MI).

"Mons. De Beauvois was lieutenant of Fort St. Joseph on the Strait (the Detroit) between Lake Huron and Erie. The Shawnees and Miami's visited the post" (Schoolcraft).

Baron De Lahonton's map and description places the fort on the American shore (La Honton, 1903 pg. 138-139). It has traditionally been placed by historians at the upper end of the Strait, near the site of later Fort Gratiot. Henri De Tonti states that the fort was at the head of the Strait (DeLanglez, 1944 pg. 279

The Franquelin map of 1688 locates the fort at the head of the Strait on the Canadian shore. Franquelin is said to have obtained firsthand information from Perrot, Du Luth, and Tonti. (Kellogg, 1925 pg. 236-237).

The British also had a St. Joseph Trading Post on Drummond Island. It was evacuated to the Americans in 1828. The 160 voyageurs, 30 Regular British, 75 families, and half-breeds – Metis – from Quebec for the Northwest Fur Co. migrated to Penetanguishene in Simcoe County, Ontario.

DuLuth went on to greatness as a trader, Indian agent, and government military officer. See "Duluth" in "Chapter 4: Explorers and Missionaries".

From this point, some of the French settlers stayed, living with the Indians. Sawmills and fisheries began.

FORT SINCLAIR

British Fort Sinclair was built after the Pontiac uprising in 1764, at the mouth of the Pine River in present St. Clair City. Fort Sinclair was built by British Officer Patrick Sinclair in 1764. Sinclair had bought land from the Indians for the fort and for himself. He built houses and barns and planted crops. Sinclair built a large military and trading post on the Pine River. This was a regular fortification, consisting of earthworks, mounting artillery with a stockade, rally post, etc. in the most complete order; and he occupied it for about seventeen years, acquiring from the Natives a title to about 4,000 acres of land bordering the river. He was the first permanent English settler and the only one along the river until 1782, when Major Rodgers took formal possession of the country in behalf of the British Crown. Both the river and the lake had the appellation of Sinclair rather than the original one given by LaSalle and Father Hennepin (Western Historical Co.).

The grounds of the fort were along the river for two and a half miles and were two and a half miles deep. This land was bought by Meldrum and Park, along with an additional 5,000 acres. They then owned 10 miles along the St. Clair River.

Jean Baptiste Point De Sable, a free Negro mulatto, kept the Pinery at St. Clair. He went on to build the first fort at Chicago, Fort Dearborn (Adapted from Mitts, The Times Herald, As the wild Goose Flies column, SCC library, MI Room).

On the east side of the St. Clair River was the British Fort Baby.

FORT EDWARD

Fort Edward at Sarnia, Ontario, a British fort, was directly across from Fort Gratiot, the American fort at the foot of Lake Huron and the St. Clair River in now Port Huron.

FORT GRATIOT

A letter sent to Brownville:

"Without reference to the map, a stranger is led into error from the different names given to the same body of water. Since leaving Detroit, I had been on one stream, known in its various parts as Detroit River, Lake St. Clair, the River St. Clair, and the River Huron.

Fort Gratiot is situated on the right bank of the latter, which is the rapid formed by Lake Huron in its first outlet to the water below. Its direction is from north to south, its width 800 yards, its length about a mile, and the rapidity of the current nearly five miles an hour. With Fort Gratiot, you are already acquainted. The site of it is within three hundred yards of the lake, on a slight eminence about 150 yards distant from the water's edge; so that the guns of a well-constructed work may command the Strait and its opposite bank which, for more than the range of common shot, is elevated by a few feet above the water."

Samuel Storrow's Letter to Major Brown (1817) (The Northwest in 1817, State Historical Society of Wisc. 6:154):

"I embarked in a barge from Detroit to proceed to the River and Lake St. Clair to Fort Gratiot. The country bordering the two waters I found level and fertile. It is scantily peopled by French Canadians who reside on the margin and make no improvements in the interior. The small surplus of their produce is purchased by vessels coasting between the Lakes. In the rear settlements is a growth of substantial timber and an abundant supply of natural grass. At the upper parts of the river, the soil meliorates; the banks are high and often picturesque.

Considering the River Huron as the natural avenue from the Upper to the Lower Lakes, it is surprising that no efforts were made to ensure the command of it previously to the year 1814, being held by the American Government since 1796. To ourselves, under the existing mode of communicating with the, North Western Frontier, it affords the only means of commercial or military conveyance. The position is less important towards any White neighbor than towards the Indians. To them it is the only thoroughfare. The possession of it engenders new dependence during peace and might become a most important barrier against invasion. Had the pass been defended in 1812, few would have gone beyond it to the siege of Detroit.

Within the range of the guns of the fort, there is a fishery which for many years, perhaps ages, has given sustenance to the tribes inhabiting the lower parts of Lake Huron. From this and other causes they have ascribed to it a moral value even beyond its due, and rarely pass without making it, as much from superstition as convenience, a resting place on their way below" (Storrow).

Fort Gratiot was built in 1814 after the War of 1812. In 1817 and 1818, the fort was garrisoned by Maine State troops, attracted by the pineries of the vicinity, who after discharge scattered, and many located in the vicinity. Captain Charles Gratiot, U.S. Government engineer, built the fort at the foot of Lake Huron, called, the most beautiful log fort in all, of the Northwest. His men also helped build the military road to supply the fort from Detroit, now Gratiot Road and Gratiot Avenue. He went on to greatness, becoming the chief engineer of the Army Corps of Engineers. He then went to Chicago and built Fort

Dearborn, teaching at West Point and later served as Lieutenant Colonel of Engineers in 1819 in Washington.

On arriving, they found the old French post occupied by a Canadian Frenchman with a small house and about two acres in cultivation. Major Forsyth took possession of the grounds and commenced the erection of a stockade and earthworks for artillery the next day.

The fort was garrisoned by a company under command of Colonel McNeil, Major Burbank, and Captain Whistler. McNeil went on to buy much of the fort grounds, called McNeil's Tract, and who McNeil's Creek, which flowed through north Port Huron and into Black River was named. McNeil went into real estate development with other Eastern capitalists, called the Huron Land Co.

The fort proper covered a large area, two acres, this being enclosed and was between Scott Avenue and Mansfield Street from Suffern – now Glenwood Avenue – to State Street. The northwest corner of the fort was at St. Clair Street. The fort grounds stretched from the St. Clair River at Pine Grove Park on the east to Black River on the west, it included the now Thomas Edison Inn and Parkway near the Blue Water Bridge. The fort is believed to be about 400 feet wide and 600 feet long, with two portals, one facing south and one facing the river.

There were many hills in the city near the river on Stone Street and Pine Grove Avenue. There were many mounds along the river and lake used for Indian burials in the past. See "Chapter 11: Mounds and Treaties".

A strong bulwark of earth was constructed of logs laid up to reinforce the east, facing the St. Clair River. From this raised position was a clear shot to the other shore, and the Lake and River to the British Fort there, Fort Edward. The canon, firing a 6 pound, shot, was used for salutes. The Americans feared a British invasion, this never happened.

An earth embankment surrounded the North, South, and West sides of the fort, which was surrounded by a large ditch. The fort was about 1,000 feet south of Lake Huron on an embankment. The parade grounds included Pine Gove Park and the cemetery grounds. The fort had 40 acres of gardens and acreages of grain and beans. This land was north of the fort and west to Black River.

The banks of the River St. Clair – Huron – at Fort Gratiot were 30 to 40 feet high and near perpendicular.

The fort was garrisoned in 1821. Abandoned in 1822, it was repaired and used for an Indian school of the Indian Department of the Presbyterian Missionaries Board. Hart and Hudson were the teachers, a few white children also attended. Hart and Hudson moved to Sault Ste. Marie in 1825. Some of the Indian families went with them, being attached to the teachers.

The fort was rebuilt and back in use in 1828. It was regarrisoned as a prevention of large foreign goods being brought in without paying duties and Indian trouble in the West. Orders came to palisade the fort and raise a flagpole. Soldiers were sent to the woods for logs, each log was 30 feet long when trimmed. Lookers found trees for the flagstaff, sufficient for a 77-foot mainmast and a 60-foot topmast. It took 61 men to carry it to the garrison. It was set about 15 feet into the ground and soared 122 feet above ground. The flag was of 24 stars and 15 stripes.

The fort was abandoned in 1831 and used sporadically by the military until 1879. The fort was the life of the little village outpost at what is now Port Huron.

"Judge Bunce was instrumental in building the first wagon road in the district, the road from Bunce's place to the fort. Bunce brought in supplies to the fort from the Detroit area. In its glory, the fort was under strict military discipline. The area of the fort grounds was 477.5 acres" (W.L. Jenks, History of St. Clair County, 1912).

"At the foot of Lake Huron stands Fort Gratiot. This battery commands the entrance into the Upper Lakes and would be of great military importance in case of war, in furnishing a bulwark against the encroachments of the savages and controlling the commerce of these waters.

The advantages of this position as a trading and military establishment were fully appreciated from an early period, and here the early French traders had erected a fort, which was subsequently occupied by the French Government, by the name of St. Joseph. The present fort consisting of a stockade, magazine, and two barracks" (History of MI, 1839, James H. Lanman, pg. 267).

When the fort grew, there was a hospital, commissary, and large field for crops. A barn, parade grounds, officer quarters, guardhouse, ice house, laundry, bakery, blacksmith shop, and carpentry shop.

Some time was spent on military drills. Much of the time was spent, in non-military activities: carpentry, agriculture, wood cutting for fuel or salvaging ship remains, and hunting and fishing.

Fort Gratiot was a recruiting center for many wars, including the Patriot War, Black Hawks War, the Mexican War, and the Civil War. It was rebuilt and remodeled as needed. Fort Gratiot was defended by one field piece, transported by a small sloop in 1814 (Western Historical Co.).

Colonel George Croghan, with 600 American soldiers and 500 Ohio militia, rendezvoused at Fort Gratiot to reclaim Fort Mackinac after the 1812 defeat to the British. Soon after this, several communities sprung up in the neighborhood, of Fort Gratiot.

Under Lieutenant Samuel P. Heintzelman and Major Alex Thompson in 1828, a suitable "stick" was placed for the fort's flagstaff. It was recorded as "The tallest and handsomest in the United States". Lt. Heitzelman later became a major general during the Civil War.

The fort's population varied from about 80 to 200 men.

The soldiers' pay in 1816 was $5.00 per month for a private; musicians $6.00 per month; corporals $7.00 per month; and sergeants $8.00 per month. Each man received a daily ration of one and a half pounds of beef or three-quarter pounds of pork, 18 ounces of bread or flour, and one gul (1/4 pint) of rum, whiskey, or brandy.

The soldiers visited the numerous saloons on Butler Street – Grand River Avenue – to drink and gamble. Fights were common among the soldiers, sailors, and river men working in the Lumber Industry. In 1869, there was a mammoth brawl between soldiers and citizens, known as The Riot.

The Blackhawk War brought many to the fort on their way to Chicago in 1832.

The Cholera Epidemic of 1832 raging in Detroit, and General Scott and his West Point cadets, 9 military companies, were enroute on the steamer *Henry Clay* to the Black Hawk War near Chicago. The cholera suddenly attacked, they landed the troops as the men were taken ill on board of their transport vessel. These men were taken off and the dead buried nearby at Cholera Point. Many died nearby along the banks of the St. Clair River. Under panic to escape the scourge and seeking help, the men dispersed, wandering for miles along the countryside, dying along the roadside, the fort inadequate for such a number. Most townspeople ignored the men staying locked in their homes. A few tried to relieve the suffering. Some handing our coffee through windows were rewarded for their compassion.

They were first buried in the old Fort Cemetery, near where Thomas Edison's boyhood home was. In 1884, the remains were moved and buried in Lakeside Cemetery, many of the 184 were unnamed graves. There is a marker on the south entrance to Lakeside Cemetery honoring these men; the monument was erected by the U.S. Congress.

The site where they were let off the ship was called Cholera Pointe, which is now the site of the City of Port Huron Water Works at the southeast corner of Pine Grove Park, Port Huron. There was at the time a point of land jutting out into the river.

The fort was abandoned in 1837. During the Patriot War, a detachment of the Brady Guards from Detroit came and removed the military supplies of ammunition to Detroit, remaining there until all danger was gone.

Dr. Charles W. Keeny was fort physician in 1844, followed by Dr. C. S. Tripler.

From 1846 to 1848, the fort was unoccupied, the men were sent to the Mexican War. From 1848 to 1852, the fort was repaired and garrisoned. From 1853 to 1861, the fort was not garrisoned. From 1852 to 1866, the fort was mostly unoccupied but was used as a recruiting center for the Civil War with several regiments organized.

In 1854, Mrs. Montgomery, widowed, was in charge, of the fort, and quite capable, going on to Washington.

Governor Cass was a frequent visitor on his many journeys to the Northern Lakes. On one visit, the fort officers were absent, and upon passing the Black River, they met a boat with a few soldiers under Lieutenant Webb returning with a load of watermelons obtained up Black River. Webb later became U.S. Minister to Brazil and was a friend of Napoleon, the French explorer, who persuaded the French removal of troops from Mexico.

The only town clocks for many years were the morning gun at Revile, the evening gun, the military music of "Strike your Tents", the bugler calls, the trumpeter, and the timed cannon.

In 1870, some of the reserve was sold. From 1874 to 1878, the fort was occupied most of the time. It was closed in 1878 and abandoned in 1879. In 1880 and 1881, the last of the reserve was sold at auction.

A splendid scale model replication of the fort as it was before 1879 is on display at the Port Huron Museum of Arts and History. It was built by Allen T. Carlisle.

The Old Fort! It has sheltered in its time many a gallant soldier and been the home of men whose names became eminent in the nation's history. Dear old memories cluster around it. Within its walls many a hopeful career began, and brave young hearts swelled with the first glory of martial life.

In recent years, it has served as a pleasant station for soldiers weary of the exposure to danger of life on the Western Frontier. The time came when its usefulness was over (Western Historical Co., 1883).

Many distinguished men served at Fort Gratiot, including Robert E. Lee (not the famous General), Captain William Whistler, uncle of American Painter James Abbott McNeil Whistler. Captain Whistler signed the earliest report on file in 1815 in the War Department relating to the fort" (Adapted

Ottissippi

from; Mitts, As the Wild Goose Flies, The Times Herald, SCC Library, MI Room).

Dr. Zina Pilcher, a post surgeon, became well-known in medical, educational, and political arenas. He became the founder of the University of Michigan School of Medicine. Another notable post surgeon was Alfred E. Fetchet, later a resident physician in Port Huron.

The Grand Trunk Depot was on the grounds of the old fort.

The old garrison buildings were torn down, the hill cut down to the present level, and the place it stood on covered by railroad tracks (Dorothy Mitts, Fort Gratiot. Adapted from; As the Wild Goose Flies Columns, The Times Herald, SCC Library, MI Room).

In 1671, Fort Mackinaw was built at St. Ignace to block the further passage of the English and as a trading center. It also served as a refuge for the French and Indian Allies against the hostile Iroquois.

Fort Dubade was built in 1679 at Sault Ste. Marie by LaSalle. This was the first French fort built by LaSalle. LaSalle also built Fort Miami in 1679 at the mouth of the St. Joseph River, near now Niles, Michigan. The second fort built by him, after he passed up the St. Clair River in the first sailing vessel, *The Griffon*.

Fort Ponchetrain was built at Detroit in 1701 by Cadillac. The fort occupied four blocks of the city, and there were 70 to 80 houses in the fort. A road inside the palisades, called Chemin de Ronde, went around the village. Burton, City of Detroit, 1701-1922, 1922

Fort Frontenac a French Fort, was built east of Detroit and the Detroit River, in now Ontario.

British Forts were across the river from Detroit, Fort Amherstburg, Fort Malden, Fort Maiden, Fort Edward, and Fort Baby were some of the nearby forts.

Fort Gratiot Lighthouse was built in 1829 and rebuilt in 1861. Fort Gratiot Lighthouse was the first lighthouse on Lake Huron, now the second oldest lighthouse in Michigan. George McDougal was the keeper of the lighthouse. He was a Lieutenant Colonel and second Aid De Camp to General Hull, Governor of Michigan, in the Legionary Corps. He then became adjutant general of the territorial militia (Western Historical Co.).

Fort St. Louis, a French post commanded by Tonti, is supposed to be located somewhere on the Detroit River (Western Historical Co., History of SCC MI).

Fort Maiden was a British fort above Malden, across from Detroit. Detroit had previously been called "Maiden".

INDIAN CAPTIVES

Many captives were freed, but many were unhappy and returned to Indian life, some being forced to abandon the wild license of the forest for the irksome restraints of society. To him who has once tasted the reckless independence, the haughty self-reliance, and the sense of irresponsible freedom which the forest life engenders, civilization thenceforth seems flat and stale. The wilderness has charms more potent in their seductive influence than all the lures of luxury and sloth. After it has cast its magic, one often finds no heart to dissolve the spell and remains a wanderer to his death. The voice of nature's melody and power, a theatre of boundless life, brimming with pleasure (Parkman).

Often Indians took captives in raids and war. Some were sold for slaves, some were returned to their families, being bought from them. Some were adopted into their families. Some were given as gifts to friends. Some were killed and tortured in horrible ways.

When the Indians lost family members to war or other death, they often adopted another to replace the dead. Adoption was very common.

In 1778, Daniel Boone was captured as a surveyor and scout soldier by the Shawnee. They brought him to Detroit to show him off and took him to their castle at Chilicothe and adopted him into the tribe as a brother to Tecumseh. He later escaped (Metis Timeline, www).

John Tanner was taken captive from his family farm on the Ohio River and taken to Saginaw by Kiskauko (The Crow) to replace a younger brother who had died, his mother was suffering cruelly from her loss. He was an eleven-year-old boy playing behind the cabin when he was taken. Negigwodkitchmeqa, on seeing the frightened boy, began to cry and hug and kiss him. The next day, an adoption or replacement ceremony was held at the grave of the dead son. Presents were given to unrelated families of the village.

Tanner, like many captives who survived the trauma of kidnapping and mistreatment, was eventually socialized into the tribal society. Tanner, was able to function in both Indian and American Frontier society, though he never seemed successful, in either place. He developed a terrific temper and was an angry man. He was filled with hatred and revenge and spent time in jail. He shot James Schoolcraft, brother of Henry Schoolcraft, the Indian agent in Michigan's Upper Peninsula Mines District, called "Uncle Sam's Pet".

Louis Campau stated, "The first Americans, as distinguished from the French farmers, were mostly prisoners taken by the Indians during the War of the Revolution and who remained after the Peace, and Englishmen who came in during the English Government and remained as Americans after the War".

Ottissippi

William Tucker and Richard Connor on the Clinton River (a part of Macomb County, Michigan), being in the original boundaries of St. Clair County, were Indian captives. George Cottrell, Captain William Thorn, and Mrs. Alexander Harrow on the St. Clair River were also captives.

William Tucker and his younger brother, Joseph, were taken from Virginia. Their father was killed, and they were brought to Detroit. Joseph drowned on a hunting trip with two Indians. William, at 18, escaped and returned to Virginia. He married and returned to Michigan, settling on the Clinton River. He was an important Indian interpreter.

George Cottrell was an Indian captive from the Mohawk Valley in New York. He was the only survivor of a massacre, an infant. The boy was redeemed from the Indians by a man named Cottrell. George Cottrell settled on the St. Clair River, and the town of Cottrellville took his name.

Captain Thorn was a political prisoner of the Indians. While piloting for the British, he was arrested as a spy and imprisoned, despite the 20 years he had been engaged in sailing the British ships. For a year, he was held mostly a captive of the Indians, and the charges dropped.

Mrs. Alexander Harrow was a captive from Kentucky and 15 years old, intelligent, and handsome. Captain Harrow ransomed the girl for a barrel of rum and took her for his wife.

Both Mr. and Mrs. Richard Conner were Indian prisoners. She was four when taken and brought up as a servant. When she was 17, she was bought by Richard for $200 and married him. In the contract, the Connors had promised the Indians their firstborn child. The mother was to keep the baby for one year and then was taken by the Shawnees until he was five years old, when they bought him back for $400, some time, later.

John Rutherford at 17 years old was taken prisoner when the others in his party were killed when surveying the St. Clair River off Pine Grove Park. Three were scalped, another trying to escape was decapitated, Robertson's body was cut up, and roasted, and eaten. A great celebration commenced.

He was seized by the hair and dragged off, his head was shaved, and he was stripped of most of his clothing and made a slave. Late that night some came to Perwash's hut and tried to seize Rutherford, "The English Dog", but the Chief's wife hid and protected him until he could be taken to another hut for safety. At night, he was tied hand and foot to a tree, alternately honoring him and treating him in inhumane ways. He was kept at the camp on the north side of Black River. In 1763, Chief Perwash, a Chippewa, was his captor. He was taken to Detroit to rendezvous with Pontiac's warriors after a four-day journey to Fort Wayne, Detroit. There he planted maize, pumpkins, and other vegetables. Pontiac also claimed him as his Little White Man. While there hidden in a house by his master, Rutherford crawled to a window and witnessed the execution of eight prisoners. One was a boy about 12 years old, a drummer of the rangers. All were shot, tomahawked, or shot with an arrow, and scalped. Some of the Indians removed skin from the arms of the victims to make tobacco pouches, leaving the finger joint as tassels. The bodies were then thrown into the river to float down to the fort where the Englishmen would see their fate. Two of the prisoners were kept as adoptees.

After unbelievable adventures, Rutherford escaped on the sloop *Michigan* and was sent back East to his relatives.

Andrew Westbrook had two of his children taken captive. He later found them, and they were returned home.

"There must be in the Indians' social bond something singularly captivating, and far superior to be boasted of among us; for thousands of Europeans are Indians, and we have no examples of even one of those Aborigines having from choice become Europeans" (Michel Guillaume Jean De Crevecoeur, Letters from an American Farmer/James W. Loewen, Lies My Teacher Told Me).

"No European who has tasted savage life can afterwards bear to live in our societies" (Benjamin Franklin).

AMERICAN BIOGRAPHIES

There were 14 American Presidents before George Washington. The Continental Congress first met in 1774. Its first order of business was to elect a president, who would function as Head of State and even preside over its deliberations. These 14 Presidents were the giants of their time, men of wealth and power, with experience to lead the nation through very difficult and treacherous days on the strength of their character.

GEORGE WASHINGTON

George Washington was the wealthiest man in America. He was a slaveholder, owning a large number of slaves to work in his plantations. He was a foster son of Old Lord Fairfax, Thomas Lord Fairfax, Baron Cameron of Cameron England, the very wealthy landholder of Virginia under grants of the King of England, Charles II. As a surveyor for Lord Fairfax to the immense estates, Washington received land in payment for surveying great parcels of land. Eventually, he owned 63,000 acres.

Lord Fairfax arrived in 1735 and claimed a vast inheritance in the Northern neck of Virginia, five million acres in 35 counties. He was the land agent and collected rent. Fairfax also owned lands in Barbados, West Indies. He had inherited his wealth. He was a relative of George Washington and was like a father to him, employing him to survey west of the Blue Ridge Mountains.

Washington was a skillful hunter and became the famous general leading the United States in the expulsion of the French from the Ohio country and in taking lands from the Indians and the British. He was the Commander in Chief of all Forces in the Colony of Virginia. The Commander in Chief of the Colonial Forces for the War of 1776, calling for a New Government of separation and strict constructionists.

At Trenton, New Jersey in 1776 on Christmas Eve, the Delaware Indians reported British troops and guided George Washington to safety (C. Eastman, The Indian Today). He was certainly under God's protection, for he was exposed to smallpox in the Caribbean and built an immunity to it. There were many instances when he could have had his life cut short but was preserved for God's design and plan.

Washington wrote to his brother, "By the all-powerful dispensations of Providence, I have been protected beyond all human probability and expectation: For I had four bullets through my coat, and two horses shot out from under me, yet I escaped unhurt, although death was leveling my companions on every side. Many said God has preserved Washington for some important service to his country."

He rose to honor, loyal to the British cause. He was also saved from drowning and freezing.

When the Indians were fighting for their lands, Washington was the leader of the American Forces. He was in the forefront to push into the Northwest and claim land for his uncle, who was like a father to him. Which (land) needed to be surveyed before the charter claim was valid by the Crown of British England. He made great headway, surveying for soldiers' bounty lands, first choice, the cream of the country.

George Washington visited Abbottsford, Scotland. His father-in-law, William Fairfax, was the President of the Executive Council of the Colony of Virginia.

George Washington was the President of the United States from 1789 to 1797.

GENERAL ARTHUR ST. CLAIR

Arthur St. Clair was born in 1734 and entered the Army, then came to America in 1758. He was at the capture of Louisburg and Quebec. He distinguished himself at Quebec catching up the flag dropped by Wolfe. He settled in Ligonier Valley, Western Pennsylvania. He served through the Revolutionary War as one of Washington's most trusted subordinates, and at the close of the war, was a delegate in the Old Confederation Congress, serving as the Thirteenth President of that Body in 1787. In 1788, he was appointed governor of the vast country called the Northwestern Territory, which now covers five States, and held the office until 1802, when he was removed by President Jefferson. His term covered the period of organization, of Indian troubles, and of the intrigues incident to settlement and struggles for political mastery. St. Clair was a pronounced federalist, elitist, and a steadfast friend of Washington and Hamilton. He early came into conflict with adherents of Jefferson and Madison. The bitterness of the political contest, incident to the formation of New States, blinded the people to his worth, his character, and the importance of his work. He died in poverty in 1818 at 84 years of age.

Later a measure of justice was done the man who made so courageous a fight against slavery and who played so conspicuous a part, of the formative period following the Revolution.

St. Clair gave his all to support the new country as a military leader and financier.

He wrote resolutions at the first meeting of the Patriotic Pennsylvanians, pledging support to the Colonists at Massachusetts Bay, declaring, "It is therefore become the indispensable duty of every American, of every man who has any public virtue or love for his Country, or any bowels for posterity, by every means which God has put in his power, to resist and oppose the execution of it (the system of tyranny and oppression): that for us we will be ready to oppose it with our lives and our fortunes".

He marched to Canada and, by his council, saved the Army in Canada. In Delaware, he was sent to reinforce General Washington; they became lifelong friends. St. Clair was brilliant, suggesting strategic movement by which the American Army escaped Trenton and won the victory at Princeton. His moves checked the enemy. He wrote, "by abandoning a post, I have saved a State". In time, he won a place in popular favor next to Washington and Greene.

In all the subsequent campaigns of the Revolution, St. Clair's plans and campaigns were submitted to Washington at his request.

In 1786, St. Clair was elected to the Congress Assembled and, in 1787, was made president of that body. It was this Congress that passed the Northwest Ordinance of 1787, which secured to freedom the vast territory Northwest of the River Ohio. This Congress also produced the U.S. Constitution. This was also the last Continental Congress.

St. Clair was made governor of the vast Northwest Territory. He was from first to last the opponent of slavery (Western Historical Society, History of St. Clair County, Michigan).

THE BABY FAMILY

Baby is also spelled as Baubee and Beebe.

As early as 1665, Jacques James Baby, Baby Deranville, had come to Quebec with a French Regiment. He entered the 1st Kent Militia. When Cadillac founded Detroit, Raymond Baby went West to found a family intimately associated with the Detroit Frontier, through more than two centuries.

There were three brothers who were with the French military: Francois, Jacques, and Duperon.

Jacques James Baby was an employee of the British Indian Department, a public servant, judge, landowner, captain, and interpreter.

In 1794, after the Jay Treaty, the Baby family abandoned considerable property in the Detroit region and moved to Sandwich, Ontario – Windsor. There they built a residence and a store and bought Canadian land.

Duperon Baby owned a large tract of land on Black River, property deeded to him by the Indians in 1780. A British Loyalist and Indian agent, he owned Baby Creek, now Bunce Creek, in Marysville, Michigan. He was a storekeeper, he abandoned his mill and claim to the American Territory (MPHC, vol. 11, 1887, Wm. L. Bancroft). His land was later claimed by Ignass Morass in 1786, and his son Victor Morass, who in 1820 claimed 640 acres at Bunce Creek (Jenks).

Jacques Baby was of the Family Compact brotherhood, a small closed group of men who had political, economic, and judicial power in Upper Canada, which included Detroit and the East Shore of Michigan. They were conservative and in opposition of democracy. They were resistant to responsible government, petty, corrupt, insolent, and a Tori clique (Fuller, History of Michigan).

A descendant, Francis Baby Jr., was among the earliest settlers in Sombra, Ontario, in about 1815. He owned land from the Chenail Escarte to the present Port Lambton, including the locality known as Baby's Point. A brother, James, came before 1829 and located to the North.

In 1852, James Jr. built a sawmill on the river bank. In 1853, he added a gristmill. So extensive was his timber business that the River Road would often be piled with white oak logs for a great distance. Vessels would be tied up at the dock, three deep waiting to be loaded, with timber, staves, cordwood, and the products of the gristmill (Lauriston).

The elder James Baby built a log house, which later he kept as a store and post office. He also farmed, exporting grain, hogs, and farm produce to Detroit. He engaged in the Lumber Business, having a dock and warehouse.

ANDREW WESTBROOK

Andrew Westbrook was offered a captain commission in the British militia but refused. He then came to Detroit in 1812 and offered his service to American Governor Hull.

Andrew Westbrook was born in Massachusetts in 1771. He moved to Nova Scotia, then to Delaware on the Thames, at Toronto, where he became wealthy, owning 9,000 acres. He was from a large family in Canada (The Westbrooks of Ontario, www).

He performed many and valuable services as captain of a company of scouts. He was well-acquainted with the Southern Ontario land of the British. The British called him the Traitor Westbrook; his merchandise was destroyed by the British, he went into Canada and set fire to his buildings and property to prevent it being used by the British. His land holdings were confiscated by the British.

He came from a large family of 12 children. He was called Baron Von Steuben. At this time there were no roads, no mills, no stores and no schools. The family used an Indian mortar for making flour and corn samp. The first milling, was done at a windmill, fifty miles downriver, opposite Detroit, and the trip was by canoe.

He purchased two claims up the St. Clair River, in East China Township, and soon became the largest and most prosperous farmer in the district. He bought much land, part of which became Fort Gratiot Military Reservation, which he sold to the government.

Andrew exchanged provisions, dry goods, hardware, oxen, horses, etc. for shingles and lumber.

In 1828, Congress granted him two sections of land for his war service. He chose the largest part from public lands in Clay Township.

While this country was still part of Macomb County, he was appointed by Governor Cass as supervisor of highways.

His first wife died in 1815; he then married Nancy Thorn. After her death, he married Margaret Ann Crawford and divorced her in 1834, marrying a fourth time. He had red hair. He lived to 65 years old and died in 1835.

GOVERNOR LEWIS CASS

Ottissippi

General Cass served Michigan as its Chief Executive for 18 years. He was appointed Secretary of War under President Jackson from 1831 to 1836. He was appointed six times without any opposing candidate or a single vote against him in the senate. He faithfully discharged his duties as Indian Commissioner and concluded 19 treaties with the Indians, acquiring large cessions of territory in Ohio, Indiana, Illinois, Wisconsin, and Michigan.

General Cass was the Father of Michigan. He was also an ambassador to France from 1837 to 1842. His father, Jonathan Cass, was a U.S. Marshal.

Governor Cass was a lawyer in the Ohio Legislature. He was a mason, the Third Grand Master of Masons in Ohio. He became a general in the U.S. Army, then Governor of Michigan Territory. He was the first Masonic Grand Master of the Grand Lodge of Michigan. He then became Governor of Michigan. He was also a senator and Secretary of State to President Buchannan in 1856. He ran for President of the United States in 1848.

Governor Cass went on a discovery tour after the 1819 Treaty of Saginaw to the Upper Peninsula and Lake Superior country. He had a 40-man expedition to explore and find the riches of the country. He made treaties to take the land for the government.

Governor Cass was nationally famous for the "Doctrine of Popular Sovereignty", which allowed voters to decide if slavery would be legal in their territory, rather than Congress deciding.

Cass became Secretary of War in 1831. As Secretary of War, he negotiated many Indian treaties to obtain the rich lands of the Native Americans. He was the main organizer in charge of the Indian Removal Process whereby the Native Americans East of the Mississippi were to be removed to West of the Mississippi. This process included the Trail of Tears in Georgia and Tennessee, where over 8,000 people died during this mass removal and walk of over 46,000 people to Oklahoma Indian Territory. The Northern removal of Indians to West of the Mississippi was called the Trail of Death.

Cass was a central figure in formulating and implementing the Indian Removal Policy of the Jackson Presidential Administration. He, with Henry Clary of Kentucky, wrote the Compromise of 1850, after the U.S. acquired territory during the Mexican American War, to avert a crisis between the North and South over free and slavery States and the Fugitive Slave Law.

While Governor of Michigan, Cass preferred to travel in his great colorful white birch bark canoe in his travels. He had a girl boatman as his guide and interpreter. The canoe was 36 feet long and 5 feet wide, in the middle, being painted with red stripes, and having a crimson canopy trimmed in green and white, and green trimming. He had French Canadian voyageurs as oarsman, wearing red wool caps, blue capotes belted with bright sashes, singing gay boat songs. The canoe was made at Fon Du Lac (Wisconsin) after the treaty there. The canoe was named "The Ark". On each side of the bow was an Indian chief smoking a pipe.

He usually dressed in full Indian regatta and had with him his interpreter, James Conner, who spoke the Indian language. James Conner spoke seven languages fluently.

HENRY SCHOOLCRAFT

Henry Schoolcraft was an Indian trader who worked with the Hudson's Bay Co. At Mackinaw, he became the Indian agent over the Upper Peninsula. He worked to gain land from the Indians for mining and the natural resources of Michigan.

He was an educated geologist from the East. He went on the discovery tour with Governor Cass in 1820. He married an Indian woman, Jane Schoolcraft, who was educated in Europe. Henry was a prolific writer and recorded much about Indian life.

CHAPTER 8
Early Detroit and Canada

The Detroit Indians or Chippewas were the Black River and Swan Creek people from along the Strait, the Detroit or Detret.

"Detroit was the home of many Indians. The Wyandotte (Huron) had large villages in the now Detroit area and West Lake Erie. The islands were all inhabited as were all the waterways.

The Hurons and Ottawas were excellent farmers and raised large quantities of corn. In 1714, twenty-four hundred bushels were sent from Detroit. Other years the provisions were very scarce due to the numbers of people gathered here" (Farmer).

"They play very deep (*gros jeu*), and often the bets sometimes amount to more than eight hundred livres. They set up two poles and commenced the game – lacrosse. From the center, one party propels the ball from one side and the other from the opposite and which ever, reaches the goal, wins (each man or woman having a racket). This is fine recreation and worth seeing. They often play village against village, the Poux – Pottawatomi against the Outaoues – Ottawas or the Hurons and lay heavy stakes. Sometimes Frenchmen join in the game with them.

The women cultivate Indian corn, beans, peas, squashes, and melons which come up fine. The women and girls dance at night, adorn themselves considerably, grease their hair, put on a white shift, paint their cheeks with vermillion, and wear whatever wampum they possess and are very tidy in their way.

The old men often dance the *Medelinne* (Medicine Dance). The young men often dance in a circle (*le tour*) and strike posts; it is then they recount their achievements and dance at the same time the War Dance (*Des Decouvertes*), and whenever they act thus they are highly ornamented. The dancing lasts almost the entire night. In the winter, they go hunting; they carry their *apaquois* (mat grass) rolled up for their shelter with them to hut under at night. Everybody follows: men, women and children, and winter in the forest and return in the spring.

THE FRENCH

Cadillac established the French Detroit in 1701, building Fort Ponchartrain in 1703. "When first settled, the location was named Fort Ponchartrain in honor of Count Ponchetrain, the colonial French minister of Marine. As the number of inhabitants grew into a village, it received its present name from the word Detroit or Strait. Its popular cognomen, the City of the Straits was thence derived. The early French colonists applied the name Detroit to the settlements on both sides of the river, calling one North Detroit and the other South Detroit" (Farmer 1884).

"In 1702, there were 6,000 people in the Detroit region (this would have included the Indians)" (Cadillac/C.M. Burton 1896).

"Farms were laid out along the River Detroit and St. Clair River in long strips called ribbon farms. This gave all the farms access to the river for water and transportation. Several *cotes* – settlements – were separated by creeks, swamps, or Indian villages. The farms were usually only four acres wide.

The soil is so good that great crops are raised by careless and very ignorant farmers. There is no such thing as a meadow, and last winter cattle perished for want of fodder. There are very extensive prairies in the settlement but so many natural advantages appear to encourage sloth, than excite industry. Bees are in great number and the woods full of blossoming shrubs, wild flowers, and aromatic herbs. The inhabitants may thank the bountiful Land of Providence for melons, peaches, pears, apples, mulberries, and grapes grew besides several sorts of smaller fruits. Several of these grow wild in the woods.

So numerous and large indeed in the vicinity of Detroit, were the wild bison's, that the making of garments from their wool was seriously considered" (Farmer, pg. 11).

Canoeing on the river was a favorite pastime; there were barbecues and pony racing on the ice. Crowds gathered along the channel; there was tremendous excitement and betting.

"The French were happy go lucky; he satisfied his stomach and let the world take care of itself. He had no ambition beyond his modest sphere of life. There was luxuriant virgin soil and cattle starved in winter. He drove a shaggy pony who was exceedingly tough and hardy and able to pick up its living year-round.

There were little gardens in front of the houses, kitchen gardens in back. Under windows flourished hollyhocks, bachelor buttons, and other gaudy flowers. Everything which drew its sustenance from the earth grew vigorously. The Detroit French were educated Noblesse.

There were several hundred French residents in 1760 when the settlement was ceded to the British, who did not leave until 1796. The English policy discouraged western settlement. The Indians were to be left alone to work the fur trade, without molestation. The American British did not agree and began surveying the land they had received as charters of the King.

In 1755, when the English banished the Acadians of Nova Scotia, many fugitives found a home in Detroit.

In 1757, Bougainville describes the foot races of the day: 'there are in Detroit some foot races between Indians and Canadians and they are as celebrated as those of horses in England; they take place in the spring. From 500 to 1,500 Indians are generally present at them. The length of the race is one mile and a half (go and return) from Detroit to the village of the Pottawatomi's. The road is broad and beautiful; there are some posts fixed in the ground at both extremities. The bets are very high on each side and consist of furs on one part and French merchandise on the other for the use of the Indians. The most celebrated racer is a Frenchman named Campau; his superiority is so well recognized that he is no more admitted into the races.'

M. Bouganville in 1757 says, 'there are two hundred habitations abundantly supplied with cattle, grain, and flour. The farmers can raise as many cattle as they want, as there is abundant pasture. They gather, in ordinary years, 2,500 measures of wheat and much corn and oats.'

The stores contained finery of all sorts. Corn was ground at the windmill" (Utley).

Bancroft, the historian, related the Detroit and St. Clair Districts previous to 1763: "of all the inland settlements, Detroit was the largest and most esteemed. The deep majestic river [...] imparted a grandeur to a country whose rising grounds and meadows [...] woodlands, brooks and fountains were so mingled together that nothing was left to be desired. The climate was mild and the air salubrious. Good land abounded yielding maize, wheat, and every vegetable".

"The forests were natural parks stocked with buffalo, deer, quail, partridge, wild turkey, and water fowl of delicious flavor hovered along its streams, which streams also yielded to the angler a large quantity of fish particularly white fish. There every luxury of the table might be enjoyed at the sole expense of labor" (Farmer).

THE BRITISH

"The area was no longer legally French, in 1763; much of the waterfront lands had been claimed. The Indians were still dominant in their lands.

"The British claimed the Northwest in 1764 from the French. The French Loyalists moved to French-held lands in Louisiana Territory. "The Illinois Indians had a very large empire at Cahokia, east of St. Louis in Illinois. There were 120 mounds and 30,000 people; it was a great trading center. There were plazas and a woodhenge for astrological observances, the calendar and town clock in the square. Monks mound is 10 stories high and 5.6 hectares at the base, about 14 acres" (Canadian History, Open Textbooks, Pays d'en Haut, www).

In 1764, when Laclede founded St. Louis, many went from Detroit, reducing the town population and vicinity from two thousand five hundred to eight hundred including Indians. In 1765, there were about 350 families at Detroit and in the immediate neighborhood" (Farmer 1884).

In 1764, Captain Patrick Sinclair, the Detroit Commandment, obtained title to over four thousand acres of land on the St. Clair River and Lake St. Clair.

Individuals were not allowed to purchase land directly from the Indians, tribal grants could only be received if the Indians would first cede their land to the Crown. Then the settler could request a grant from the King represented by the superintendent of Indian Affairs or the Governor of Quebec. While this policy was geared to protect the Indians, loopholes allowed clever individuals to acquire almost any land.

In spite, of official policy, settlement along the straits, had increased by the 1780s. The official grants were not all settled. Some grants were poor or swamp and, although recorded, had been vacated for other lands. Many soldiers, artisans, and voyageurs were not farmers but were involved in the fur trade.

In 1771, General Thomas Gage had declared all previous grants issued by the previous English commandments were null and void for not conforming to official regulations. French grants were approved only if they had been recognized by the Governor of Canada and registered. Grants issued by the last commandment, Bellestre, were invalid. Gage emphasized that the French nor the English allowed private purchases from the Indians and the tribes were told that the King as tender of their property was protecting them by these practices. The Indians persisted in giving gifts of land to reward their friends.

Many soldiers who wanted to come to the Detroit region were not able to be accommodated, as land grants were not available. 'Who must fly the place if land is not granted to them'.

The wild and reckless Coureurs De Bois' – traders' – fondness for ardent spirits were in common with their Indian friends. They were addicted to a plurality of wives" (Utley). In 1773, the population was 1,285, with half in the immediate area of the Fort. The settlement across the river had 465 people at Windsor – Sandwich and Amherstburg, Ontario.

In 1778, a census was taken of the settlement of Detroit by Governor Hamilton. It showed 172 male servants, 39 female servants, and 127 slaves, a total population of 2,144. There were 478 oxen, 885 cows, 650 heifers and steers, 470 sheep, and 1,312 hogs.

A survey of the Detroit settlement in 1779 was 239 in garrison and navy, 500 prisoners and extras, 1,810 population, 138 slaves, 413 oxen, 779 cows, 361 steers, 1076 hogs, 664 horses, and 313 sheep.

In 1780, there was 12,083 acres of land under cultivation, 175 slaves, 1,922 population with 100 absent in Indian country, 772 horses, 474 oxen, 793 cows, 361 steers, 279 sheep, and 1016 hogs.

In 1780, the people were near starvation in the winter and Lieutenant Governor Sinclair asked for assistance from the King's stores. The same year, however, 12,883 acres of land were reported as under cultivation. Detroit was a settlement of 2,000 people in 1780.

Immense pear trees were abundant, a hundred feet and more in height and one to three feet thick. Almost every farmer had from one to a half dozen, of these trees, producing from 30 to 50 bushels each" (Farmer 1884).

In 1782, the settlement at Detroit census was 179 slaves, 2,012 population, 1112 horses, 413 oxen, 453 heifers, 447 sheep, 1370 hogs, 4075 bushels of wheat sown last fall, 521 acres, Indian corn, 1,849 acres in oats, and 13,770 acres under cultivation. 3,000 bushels of potatoes was supposed to be in the ground and 1,000 barrels of cider was supposed to be made" (Lewis, West to far Michigan).

"In 1783, Governor Haldimand was to investigate the land granting system at Detroit. It was suspected that regulations forbidding individual purchases of land were being ignored.

After 1783, settlement in Canada was encouraged, land, religion and education were expected to benefit from land sales. Grants were offered to the Loyalists and disbanded troops as rewards for faithful service. Fees were dropped and provisions made for immigrants.

Along the Detroit frontier, the rules were bent to fit the existing or desired conditions. One of the most flagrant violations concerned individual purchases. One estimate claims that from 1763 to 1796, over four hundred families settled on land granted from the Indians.

The lack of knowledge concerning the region is afforded in the address of Mr. Lymbruner, agent of the Province of Canada, read in 1793 before the House of Commons. It contained this passage:

> *Although there is a small settlement at Detroit, which is, and must be considered, of great importance as a post to trade with the Indians, yet it must appear to this honorable house that from its situation, it can never become of any great importance as a settlement. The Falls of Niagara are an insurmountable obstacle to the transportation of such rude materials as the produce of the land. As the farmers about Detroit, therefore, will have only their own settlement for consumption of their produce, such a confined market must greatly impede the progress of settlement and cultivation for ages to come.*

During the war, a stronger fort had been built on a hill behind the town, Fort Lernoult. A palisade fence ten to fifteen feet high, ran from the fort, and entirely, surrounded the town largely as protection from Indians. No Indians, were allowed, to bring weapons, into town or permitted to stay after dark.

The danger of fire was real. The town of 109 buildings. The only stone structure the commandants house. Most buildings were used as both shop and home by English merchants. Within the stockade were two wharves at the river.

Several creeks running through the settlement were used as open sewers. The area was so filthy, Colonel Depuyster offered the land to any who would clean it up. The Detroit River ran at two miles an hour; the river carried pure water and wells were not needed until 1800.

The British encouraged immigration to Detroit, hoping to retain the area by right of possession. The loyalists could raise crops along with the Indian allies and guard the community. The king's ships offered free transportation to disbanded troops and loyalists.

Detroit and across the river were one settlement before 1796 when British Canada relinquished Michigan to the United States. Malden – Amherstburg was the British headquarters for the wars against the American United States. It was christened Molden or Smugglesburg in 1796. It lay directly across from Detroit.

THE AMERICANS

Even though the Americans had won the war of Independence in 1783, they did not occupy the land until 1796, when the British evacuated Detroit.

"In 1802, Detroit was incorporated and had its first post office. In 1815, a report from Edward Tiffin, Surveyor General, said there is not one acre in a hundred, if there would be in a thousand for cultivation. It is all swampy and sandy. The region as a whole was said to be extremely sterile and barren. Such representations must have been founded on unpardonable ignorance or knavery. No state in the Union has a larger proportion of excellent farming lands. The wheat crop in 1886 amounted to 26 million bushels and the productions of our garden fields and orchards are unexcelled. Beets weighing 18 pounds and watermelon weighing 40 pounds were common. In 1828, one hundred hogshead of Michigan tobacco was shipped to Baltimore. A pear weighing 38 ounces was grown by Judge Sibley; it was seven and a half inches long and fourteen and a half inches in circumference.

Large numbers of fish were taken from the waters, the whitefish the most numerous and highly prized. In 1822 at Hog Island – Belle Island, there were taken 1,200 barrels, worth four to five dollars a barrel. Thousands of barrels were sent to Ohio and New York. In 1836 to 1840, the catch in the Detroit River averaged about 3,500 barrels per year, worth eight dollars a barrel."(Farmer).

"Detroit was the real Capital of the Northwest" (C. Moore).

Father Gabriel Richard, General of the Catholic Church, arrived in 1796. He did much to help the fledgling town, helping to establish a road between Detroit and Chicago, brought the first printing press, and became a territorial representative in the U.S. Congress. In many other ways, he helped establish the new American Country. During the 1832 cholera epidemic, he worked untiringly, ministering to the sick at Springwells. He also died after two months of the same disease. He was a good, devoted, self-sacrificing man. There was another cholera epidemic in 1834.

By Act in 1802, it was designated the 'Town of Detroit'. By Act in 1815, it was called the 'City of Detroit'. In 1827, it was enacted that the name should be 'The Mayor, Recorder, and Alderman of the City of Detroit'. In 1857, it was enacted that the name should be 'City of Detroit'" (Farmer 1884).

The Great Fire of 1805 in Detroit leveled the village. The fire department was a Bucket Brigade. No one died.

THE DETROIT RIVER

"The city is located near the head of the river on its northerly and westerly banks. The Eastern boundary is about four miles from Lake Ste. Claire.

The river is usually tranquil and never dangerously rough. The water is of a bluish tinge, and in transparency and purity is unrivaled.

The breadth, general safety, and smoothness of the river make it especially inviting for boating and yachting; and in later years, many persons have availed themselves of the facilities afforded. Several noteworthy regattas have been held here, and boatman all concede that no finer location can be found for a trial of skill. During the summer season, excursions up and down the river and to different islands are of almost hourly occurrence. The islands vary in size from one to several thousand acres.

Within the city limits of Detroit, three streams of water once flowed. The Savoyard Creek branch of the Huron became practically an open sewer. Then it was converted to a deep and covered sewer, a Grand Sewer it became.

Mays Creek was also Campaus River, and Cabaciers Creek. It is claimed that Jacques Peltier erected the first grist mill on this stream just north of what is now Fort Street.

Parent's Creek, or Bloody Run, is the real historic stream. It was first named after Joseph Parent, a gunsmith whose name appears in St. Ann's records in 1707. It is now filled in. The name was changed to Bloody Run after the defeat of Captain Dalyell and slaughter of a large part of his company by the Indians in 1763.

Knagg's Creek was just outside the western limits of the city; it flowed into the Detroit River in Springwells on the Bela Hubbard Farm. Knagg's built a windmill in 1810, and it was used until 1840" (Farmer 1884).

In 1805, there were very few people in the Northwest Territory, and there were 180 White people in South Michigan.

Scores of canoes were hauled up on the riverside, while others flashed along the current or plied to either shore. Later on windmills stretched their broad arms to the breeze and, with fish nets hung on reels, formed the hallmarks of their day.

Ottissippi

In the 1800s, the winter season furnished many a scene of gay festivity. The little French or Canadian ponies were so plentiful as to be had for almost nothing, and box runners, then much in vogue, were so easily constructed that everyone could procure a 'turn out', and not only the river, but the grand marsh on the east and the River Rouge on the west became the race courses for the whole community. This last locality, the Red River as the English always called it, was the favorite place for this sport, and fast pacers were in special demand on these occasions.

The men who began the American regime in Detroit and Michigan were Governor Hull, Augustus Woodward, Fred Bates, James Witherell, John Griffin, Solomon Sibley, and Elijah Brush, confidant, attorney, and mayor.

In 1810, under Governor Cass the Michigan legislature passed a law repealing all laws pertaining to Michigan that had been passed by the legislature of the Northwest Territory.

Windmills were used to grind grain along the Detroit River and Lake St. Clair. People would travel long journeys to grind the grain to flour, some carrying the sack on their back up to 20 miles away. Skins were scraped as thin as possible and were used for windows on the log homes.

Women made coarse cotton and woolen clothes for the Indian Trade. Flax was grown for weaving linen cloth.

It was a luxury to have a look at things. Calico was used for wedding dresses. The people asked not for great things; they were inured of want. To have enough to eat and to be warmly clad and
housed from winters cold was their longing and hopes of plenty for the little ones in the future.

The first stage line in the territory was established in 1822; it ran from the county seat of Macomb County to Detroit.

Books and papers were practically unknown for very many years. News came from the outside world in the form of letters few and far between. Personal and family plans and adventures were the usual subjects of conversation and these with numerous Indian alarms and changes made by succeeding commandments filled up the measure of the passing years.

The tables were well-supplied, beaver tails, wild ducks, turkeys, partridges, quails, bear steaks, venison, whitefish, hulled corn, succotash, and baked French pears were common articles of diet. Later on many of the best families cured their own pork and beef and hams and shoulders were smoked at the smoke house of some enterprising grocer. A family of bovines (cattle) and eight chickens were sent from Montreal in 1701; they soon multiplied and the lowing of cows and the cackling of hens helped to make the wilderness seem a home. There was never more crops raised than was needed for home consumption, and after the War of 1812, a large share of the provisions was brought from Ohio and New York for nearly twenty years.

In July of 1817, more than 1,700 head of cattle were brought from Ohio. Prior to 1830, maple sugar was the only sugar in common use; it was finely grained by stirring. The Indians cooked their fish in the boiling sap.

Governor Cass in 1816 wrote a graphic picture of Detroit to the Secretary of War:

> *The Indian Trade originally furnished the only employment of the people of this country and their only resource against want. As traders, engagees, and voyageurs, they spent*

one half of the year in labor, want, and exposure, and the other in indolence and amusements.

Associated with the Indians, they contracted their manners and gained their confidence. As a necessary consequence, their farms were neglected, and the agricultural products

of the country formed a small portion of the subsistence of the inhabitants. When the failure of game reduced the profits of this trade, the people were driven to other pursuits and the fatal mistake of educating a whole community for a single and temporary business is now deeply felt and acknowledged. Driven to toil the soil, the state of the farms shows the extreme defect of agricultural knowledge.

The spinning wheel and loom are unknown in the country. The farmers are in the practice of drawing their manure upon the ice of the river during the winter, that it might be carried into the lake in the spring. The wool of the sheep was thrown away, and a pound of wool is not manufactured in the territory by any person of Canadian descent; and four-fifths of its inhabitants are of this class of population.

There can be no question that it is a remarkably desirable place for those who wish while making money to enjoy life as well. The population of the entire state, both Detroit and Michigan, stand for the New England of the West. (Farmer)

In 1827, only 39 unnaturalized foreigners lived in Detroit".

An 1831 report of Detroit:
The Society of Detroit is kind, hospitable, and excellent. A strong sense of equality and independence prevails in it. A citizen whose conduct is respectable and decorous is respected by all and associates with all. Very little etiquette is practiced here; genuine friendliness and cordiality are the agreeable substitutes. A frank, cordial, and general civility, at once peculiarly gratifying and indicative of the character of the Michiganians, has been extended to us.

"The Detroit River is undoubtedly one of the most remarkable in the world. It was declared a public highway in 1819. Its average width one mile, it offers one of the largest and safest harbors in the world. It is the natural drain or channel for the passage of waters from 82,000 square miles of lake surface, 125,000 square miles of land. The velocity is around 2 miles an hour. The water was pure in 1884.

"The price of food stuffs was high in Detroit before it was a settled country. As long as the influx of settlers continued the seller's market was good and prices high. In Detroit, consistent scarcity kept demand and prices high. "Nothing surprises a stranger in Detroit as the high price of everything that is brought to its market by the farmer" (Detroit Gazette, 1829). The provisions market was making great profit. The intensity of immigration caused great demand of the farmers, who found it difficult to reserve sufficient produce for their own families" (Democratic Free Press/Lewis, West to Far Michigan).

"Water was drawn from the river in pails and barrels. The water was not defiled by sewers and refuse from shops and factories at first; it was as clear as a diamond. The supply was as free as the air, and whosoever would might draw a drink. Buckets were carried on a wooden yoke borne upon the shoulders. Barrels were hauled in the old two-wheeled French carts and sold at sixpence per barrel. Two barrels was considered a load" (Farmer).

"It is truly discouraging to the emigrant, after having transported his goods safely for three or 400 miles, to have them dashed to pieces on our broken causeways within 10 miles of this place" (1825 Detroit Gazette/Lewis).

"Difficulty of access remained the greatest obstacle in the territory. In 1828, the 30, mile trip from Detroit to Ypsilanti took 3 days. In 1830, a trip from Detroit to Ann Arbor via Plymouth involved a week's travel. Mills attracted people from up to 40 miles away, and the trip was long and arduous.

In 1831, Chicago had a population of 200 people. The early settlers and pioneers found their way to Michigan's interior by following Indian trails. There was, no more awful and horrid roads to be found than all those leading out from Detroit in 1833 to 1837. Enoch Chase likened the poorly-drained roads of the eastern shore as almost a continuous mud hole" (Lewis, West to Far Michigan).

In 1832, Detroit was the Western limit of the established lines of Western transportation. Only a mail coach went to Niles once a week, then on horseback by Indians to Chicago

Detroit was devastated by cholera in 1832 and 1834. The people were panic-stricken. The city was quarantined and business suspended. Many fled to the country to escape the scourge. The death rate was 700 in a population of 3,500" (Hotchkiss).

"In 1833, there were 5,000 temperance societies in the U.S. with 1.25 million members. Liquor was a great problem.

Before 1835, not a street in Detroit was paved. The first streets were cobblestones, then the wood block roads in sand (corduroy roads). Then brick and stones. In 1849, Detroit was little more than a village; Woodward Avenue was surrounded by primeval forests.

Detroit was a place of fancy balls and proper luxury. It was a gay place of great parties. Music, liquor, and dance were all important. All the fancy of Europe was transplanted here. Intemperance was prevalent. Schools were scarce, the youth too fond of foolish amusements.

In 1853, prohibition was voted in for Michigan. To most people, this was a big joke and created the illicit trade of rum running. Bootleggers and kitchen operators were too numerous to mention. The waterways between Canada and the United States were heavily used to traffic Canadian whiskey to the United States, Michigan being the main source of the trade. Many people brewed their own beer and wine. Speakeasies were set up with special codes and rooms, and the people carried on as they had before. There were many arrests and confiscated bottles taken and dumped. There were secret hiding places, even in church basements, crawl spaces, haystacks, barns, holes in the ground, and in the river in crates. The government. gave up and changed the law.

Farmer in 1884 wrote of the Detroit River:

> *A lighthouse on what is known as Windmill Point marks the entrance of the river into the Lake St. Clair and is the chief landmark of the vicinity. The township of Greenfield adjoins the city on the north. Here is the immense seed farm of D. M. Ferry & Co. embracing 300 acres.*
>
> *Then as now islands like emeralds were strung along its way, and myriads of wild fowl then fed upon its shores; the waters were so calm and clear that the smoke of wigwams nestled on their banks was mirrored on their smooth surface.*

IMMIGRATION

Previous to 1853, persons and teams crossed over on the ice; since then the daily trips of the railroad ferry boats have broke it up.

A considerable amount of Irish came in 1833. The Germans began coming in the spring of 1832 and the Poles in 1870.

In 1870, the various nationalities in the city were as follows: France 760; Germany 12,647; England 3,282; Ireland 6,970; Scotland 1,637; Holland 310; Hungary 310; Norway 523; and Poland 325. Out of a total of 79,577 people, 44,196 were born in America.

Every State and Territory in the Union, except Montana, has contributed to our population. New York heads the list with 7,722. In 1880, there were 116,340 of which 70,695 were born in America and of these 2,300 were colored.

In 1860, copper smelting was the leading industry.

"Detroit was the first major city to use rock salt for snow and ice control" (Salt Mining, MSU).

"In 1917, hundreds of small craft of every description hastened hither and yon on business and pleasure. The great passenger ferries carrying tens of thousands to and from Windsor the Sister City across the stream; the towering, many-decked excursion steamers filled with pleasure seekers, bands playing and pennants streaming in the wind; noisy tugs towing great scows up and down and across the stream; car ferries cooperating with the tunnel in transporting freight to and from the foreign shore. In the 1917 season, a total of 24,673 vessels carrying 88,885,520 tons of freight, more than the combined freight tonnage in and out of all the principal maritime cities of the United States, Atlantic, Pacific, and Gulf for that year. Detroit has since become the industrial center of the richest country on the globe" (Fowle).

The Ku Klux Klan, a violent racist group, was a hotbed in Southern Lower Michigan in the 1920s. A very large number of the population were members. The headquarters were near Howell, Michigan, where rallies gathered. The KKK was anti-Catholic, anti-Black, anti-immigrant, and for Prohibition, wearing white hooded gowns to cover their identity. Scandal and illegal activity caused the decline of the KKK. It is still recruiting members to self-preservation and the advancement of White Christian America, a new law-abiding group with a nonviolent way. The National Office North is in Chicago, Illinois and in Fraser, Michigan.

CANADA

St. Clair County and Michigan were once part of Canada under the British. Earlier, we were part of Louisiana and Quebec under the French. Quebec was a very large part of Canada, reaching to the Ohio and the Mississippi Rivers.

QUEBEC

"Quebec was the name of the region of Michigan, Southern Ontario, and more. This name signifies a strait, as does Detroit. Quebec was also the oldest city in the Canadian dominion and first Capital of that region, the place from which Cadillac and the first settlers came hither. It is derived from the Algonquin word Quebeis or Quelibec, signifying a strait.

Lasalle built a stockade called Fort St. Joseph at Point Edward. Cadillac viewed the ruins of Lasalle's fortification in 1701.

In the early days, the waters of Lake Huron flowed into Sarnia in several channels, none very deep. In 1771, Captain Barr of Detroit said there were still two channels, one a league wide with a depth up to 48 feet. Today there is only one, dredged to a depth of 70 feet. The land contours on the Canadian side where the other channels once were. The Great Storm of 1913 almost reopened the second channel; a few more hours and the topography of Point Edward would have gone back 140 years.

A short distance below Sarnia was the storage boom for logs sent from the North. Now and then the rafts would be caught and twisted by the current, breaking them up, causing panic to steamers and delight to Indians who retrieved them for the sawmill at 25 cents salvage.

The gas buoy later marking the middle ground between Port Huron and Sarnia was on the site of what was once a willow-clad island rising several feet above the river. Different Indian tribes occupied the east and west banks of the St. Clair; and the Indians wishing to cross came to this island and made smoke signals. Erosion reduced the island to a mere spit, this was dredged out by the U.S. government.

Port Huron once had a history intertwined with Sarnia. The roads on the west side linking Fort Gratiot to Detroit were better than any on the Canadian side; so even the Canadians traveled on the west side, and the population on the American side grew rapidly after 1828" (Lauriston, Lambton's 100 years, 1971).

THE BRITISH

"John Askin was the leading fur trader, merchant, and government official. He was instrumental in establishing British rule in Upper Canada which is Southwest Ontario.

In 1781, the British Crown purchased land from the Missasauga-Ojibwe tribe in a series of treaties that encompassed much of Southern Ontario and parts of Southeast Michigan. They made land grants to United Empire Loyalists (UEL) who left property in the 13 colonies to reward them for loyalty to the Crown and bring more British people to the lands of Canada. The UEL-United Empire Loyalists called "Tories", started migrating to Canada and Detroit in support of the British Crown in 1776 during the Revolutionary War. The majority came after the Treaty of Paris in 1783, when the U.S. was given the land to the South in America. American settlers also came in large numbers to Canada for cheap land.

Patronage was strong with the British Tories; they were favored in all dealings, especially for military service" (History of Canada and Canada West, www).

THE FAMILY COMPACT

When Quebec was split in 1791, St. Clair County (Michigan) was in Upper Canada, part of British Canada from 1763 to 1796 when Britain evacuated the premises. It was governed by a legislative council, appointed for life, and a legislative assembly, elected by the people. Representative government was not responsible government (History of Canada and Canada West, www).

The appointed legislative council was called **The Family Compact**, a group of families who controlled the government. The elected legislative assembly had no real power, their bills were defeated. This led to rebellion and change. The 1837 Durham Report called for more freedom and a united Upper and Lower Canada.

Upper Canada was from 1791 to 1841. Michigan was a part of Upper Canada until the British removed in 1796. Lower Canada consisted of the Northeastern part of Ontario.

"The French and Indians were without representation in government."

EARLY BOUNDARIES

KENT COUNTY

Lambton County Ontario was Kent County under British rule in Upper Canada. St. Clair County, Michigan was also Kent County under British rule in Upper Canada.

Lambton County in 1842 was part of Kent County; in 1849, Kent County became Lambton County.

UPPER CANADA

Upper Canada was from 1791 to 1841. It was Southwestern Ontario and Michigan. Lower Canada was the Northeastern Canada lands, bordering New York and Maine along the St. Lawrence River.

Upper Canada was created in 1791 when the Colony of Quebec was divided into two parts. Lower Canada consisted of Northeastern Ontario reaching to the Maritimes.

Kent Township in 1792 included Michigan, Illinois, and Lakes Michigan and Superior" (Farmer 1884).

"In 1792, now St. Clair County, Michigan was part of Kent County Upper Canada, under control of the British. Kent County was also called Fairfield.

The Township of Zone was New Fairfield. The British formed the Fairfield militia.

York is now Toronto.

THE WESTERN DISTRICT

The District of Hesse was created in 1788 and renamed the Western District in 1792. The Western District of Upper Canada was created in 1792. The District of Hesse was then to the South and included part of Southeastern Michigan and Southwest Ontario.

The District of Hesse – The British, in 1788, comprehended all of the inland parts of the Western Provence, from the south to the northern boundaries, including East Michigan.

In 1798, the British of Upper Canada divided Kent County into Essex and Kent Counties. In 1849, the Western District became the United Counties of Essex and Kent.

The District of Kent – In 1847, Kent County was changed to the District of Kent and was not part of the Western District.

Slavery was abolished in Canada in 1807.

Lambton's first great wave of settlers came from Britain in the early 1830s. Many were tenant farmers kept poor by high rents, others were artisans whose work was being taken over by machines. Numerous weavers and a few military men who were granted free land" (Canada West Last Frontier).

From 1815 to 1850, the Great Migration came. Over 800,000 people came to Canada.

CANADA WEST

In 1841 to 1867, Ontario, Canada was called Canada West. Canada West at one time included Michigan, Wisconsin, Minnesota, and Manitoba.

St. Clair Township became Sarnia Township.

Sarnia – Aazhoogayaming – The Crossing Waters Place.

THE PATRIOTS WAR

"The Family Compact was the ruling government in early Ontario; they did not represent the people but the elite who controlled all decisions. They muzzled the press, ignored petitions of grievances, and discouraged education.

In 1837, MacKenzie called for independence, as did Louis Papineau. Both fled to the United States and later received amnesty.

This led to rebellion and revolt against domination from without and privilege within. In the Patriot War of 1836 to 1838, there were over a thousand, citizen militia, killed and deported to slave lands. Many men from Michigan and New York were involved, and government troops were sent to put them down all along the border of the St. Lawrence Seaway and the Strait of the Detroit and St. Clair River.

Ottissippi

The UEL invasion of Ojibwa lands came after the English traders. Promises were made that, if the Loyalists were permitted into Southern Ontario, they would improve the well-being of the Ojibwa. The peaceful acceptance of the rapid settlement of Indian and White Loyalists along the north shore of Lakes Erie and Ontario was typical of the way the Ojibwa comforted their defeated allies (adapted). The Loyalists did not appreciate and respect the generosity of the Ojibwa. The Loyalist promises of cooperation and peaceful coexistence were soon broken. The British government demonstrated some support and gave many promises, on the other hand, they took their lands. The death of Tecumseh in 1813 and the disintegration of the confederacy sealed the fate of the Southern Ojibwa. The hunting grounds that remained in their territory would be taken from them, radically changing their lives forever" (Schmaltz).

The Patriots' War began after years of failed efforts at peaceful change to a corrupt government, finally coming to rebellion. Over 1,000 farmers rebelled. Many were killed and sent to work camps in other countries owned by the British. The war was due to undemocratic, unworkable colonial systems of the imperial government who were out of touch with and unsympathetic to reform" (History of Canada West, www).

"On the U.S. side, Hunters' lodges (anti-British) were organized for Patriots, who were in sympathy with the Canadians. Many U.S. Patriots helped the farmers who were organizing to try to take over the country, as America had done to be independent from the Crown.

At the Battle of Windsor, hundreds of Patriots stormed the Canadian Frontier of the Detroit River. Some experienced death by flogging and hanging. Some leaders and supporters were arrested or sent as convicts to Tazmania, Australia.

Raids were made from the U.S. for nearly a year. Three hundred and twenty-five men died, all Rebels except 27 British soldiers. One hundred Rebels were captured and many were executed by the government.

The Durham Report of 1837 was the report on the affairs of British North America. It was written by John Lambton - Lord Durham, who was appointed Governor General of British North America. It called for more freedom and a united Upper and Lower Canada. It encouraged immigration to Canada from Britain to overwhelm existing numbers of French Canadians and French culture. It called for more progressive British culture. The Durham Report was the catalyst to change in Canada.

The Family Compact and the Chateau Clique eventually lost their power to reign supreme over the country of Canada. Upper and Lower Canada became united into the Province of Canada. The Durham Report was not accepted, and Canada would not get responsible government for another decade.

Land grants favored British settlers from Britain, as opposed to those with ties to the United States. Many were denied political rights. The Province of Canada began in 1841, uniting the Upper and Lower Canadas. This led to responsible government, democratic reform, and self-government" (History of Canada and Canada West, www).

"Sombra was the Shawnee refugee reserve. When the Indians were being removed in the United States, many natives were British Loyalists and were welcomed into Canada.

The Ojibwa Chief Shinguaconse reflected: 'When your white children first came into this country, they did not come shouting the war cry and seeking to wrest this land from us. They told us they came as friends to smoke the Pipe of Peace; they sought our friendship, we became brothers. Their enemies were ours. At the time, we were strong and powerful, while they were weak and few. But We did not oppress them or wrong them? No! and they did not attempt to do what is now done...Father. Time wore on and you have become a Great People, while we have melted away like snow beneath an April sun; our strength is wasted, our countless Warriors dead" (Schmaltz).

Great coal beds were found at Corunna. The east side of the St. Clair River was very swampy, having many small lakes and marshes.

In 1800, John Courtney became the first White settler on the east side of the St. Clair River. His farm was half a mile north of the Town of Moore.

"Louis and Joseph LaForge settled at now Sarnia prior to 1807. Tradition says he was the first permanent White settler on the east bank of the St. Clair River. Early records show him as a fur trader who came from Mt. Clemons. His father-in-law, Jean Baptiste Pare, and another Frenchman, Ignace Cazelet, came in 1808. They chose the site of now Sarnia for the swamps and marshes nearby that were swarming with animals, and the tribes of Indians in the vicinity were friendly and were partly Christianized. Louis returned to Detroit. Joseph and his brothers set out to trap and hunt and trade with the Indians" (OGS/Hodgins).

"James Baby came in 1815 and set up a store and did lumbering. The first post office was established here south of Sombra and in Sarnia in 1837. M. Pare Cosson was employed by the government for 30 years as a messenger and mail carrier from Kingston to York (Toronto) and between Detroit, and Sandwich (Windsor), Chatham, Malden (Amherstburg), Ontario, Canada.

No one was yet settled on the Port Huron side.

After a while, the Brandimores settled on the Port Huron side but soon moved to the Sarnia side and built a house where the shipyard was later built. The Indians were friendly, the fur, timber, and other trades that sprung up were profitable. It is said these French settlers used to carry little bags of gold".

PIRATES

Parties of Indians were accustomed to rove about the river and lakes as pirates, plundering the trading Indians and the settlers of their furs and other goods. They were finally caught up with by a large fleet of Indian canoes from Mantoulin Island. Along with other tribes, they joined battle in the St. Clair River above Stag Island.

The pirates and their allies were driven onto the head of the Island opposite Corunna, where a fierce battle took place. Many were killed and the pirates were vanquished; the Island and its shores were strewn with the slain. For many years, skulls and bones could be seen protruding from the sand, until recent years when the ghastly remains were at last buried.

SARNIA AND POINT EDWARD

John Courtney, an Englishman, is said to be the real pioneer settler on the east bank of the St. Clair River. John sailed in on a Batteaux and landed about 1800 and cleared land owned by Neil Simpson in Moore Township.

Many Old Country gentlemen and war veterans came to the St. Clair about 1830.

Some of the early settlers were Captain Vidal of the Royal Navy, who built a log house in the heart of Sarnia on Front Street. The only other houses were LaForge's and the houses built for the Indians who used them for stables for their ponies while they lived in wigwams.

William Jones, the Indian agent, had a home near the Indian reservation. He came in 1831, and he later became the head of Methodist Missions in the Canadian West and invented the Cree syllabic characters which gave these Natives a means of writing for the first time.

George Durand came to Sarnia in 1833. He purchased 25 acres from Captain Vidal. He built and occupied the first store on Front Street. Coming through the forests on an ox cart, Durand did much to advance Sarnia and amassed a fortune there. A post office was established at Port Sarnia with George Durand as the first postmaster.

Peter McGlashan arrived a few days after Durand. He was clerk of the first court. He was later the inland revenue collector.

Malcolm Cameron came in 1833; he was the real founder of Sarnia. He laid out Sarnia Town site on 200 acres. He operated the largest trading place on the east shore of the St. Clair River. Sarnia is the largest city on Lake Huron in Lambton County. It is a natural harbor. At the Rapids in the early days, men and horses pulled ships through the shallow waters.

Roman Catholic clergymen from Windsor were the first to hold religious services in Lambton. They worked among the French and Indians along the St. Clair River.

The first Protestant clergyman on record is Reverend William Griffis, who was appointed in 1824 to the Indian Mission at Sarnia under the Conference of the Methodist Episcopalian Church of the United States. The British Wesleyan Methodists took over the mission in 1832 and had a mission house built.

In 1835, Sarnia, or the Rapids, had 44 taxpayers. Sarnia was the Roman name for the Island of Guernsey.

St. Clair Township in Ontario became Sarnia Township in 1839.

Lambton County was formed in 1849, named after John Lambton – Lord Durham – who brought reform to the corrupt government.

The British North America Act in 1867 unified the Dominion of Canada.

An annual agricultural fair was held from 1846 to 1940.

"Point Edward, where Fort Edward was on 1,000 acres, became the Grand Trunk Railroad Company Town" (MI Historical Commission, John M. Munson, MI Room SCC Library).

"The Huron Company obtained and sold much land in Lambton County.

Transacting business and voting in the early days required a long journey and involved many days. There were many ferries operating between Canada and the U.S. side of the River St. Clair.

Moore Township was named for Sir John Moore, a military hero. For many years, Mooretown was the most important settlement below Sarnia. It was established by James Baby Jr., who built a store, and business places were established. Most articles were handmade, and shops manufactured as well as sold the goods.

James Baby came from the Sandwich/Detroit area in 1815. He inherited land from his grandfather, from Chenail Escarte to Port Lambton. They built the first Catholic church, Eglise De Sacre Couer, in Lambton County in 1827. Baby's timber business loaded many vessels at Baby's Point in South Sombra Township.

Ottissippi

At Port Lambton, Duncan McDonald from Ohio came in 1820; his son erected a steam mill and was a leading business man. Port Lambton was described as 'the liveliest little river town South of Sarnia.' There were many mills here. All were steam operated. A continuous dock, 45 feet long, fronted the village. There was a customs house and storehouses and warehouses.

In 1821, Abraham Smith and Samuel H. Burnham located on the site of Sombra. Two French families had been there for years, Beauchamp and Matavie. Angus McDonald was south of them, and Alex Kerby was north of the settlement.

Alexander McKenzie was Canada's second prime minister. He was a Reform Party leader. He became the leader of the Liberal Party. He went from being a stonemason to Prime Minister; he was also Minister of Public Works. He created many changes in the government of Canada, making fair laws for the people.

Point Edward was named for Prince Edward, Queen Victoria's father. One thousand acres was a military reserve. Land was leased here. It became Grand Trunk Railroad land.

Rum running was a large business during the U.S. Prohibition of 1919 to 1933. Bootlegging and rum running was the major pastime along the St. Clair and Detroit Rivers. Canadian liquor supplied many large cities in the U.S.A. Boat houses, marshes, and haystacks along the river provided bases to smuggle Canadian whiskey to America. It was impossible to control the easy access, and many officials were involved in the illegal activity. Hardened criminals and major crime organizations came to transport liquor to Chicago and other large cities. This was dangerous business.

The Canada Company formed in 1826; it had purchased a million acres in Bosanquet, Huron County, and Perth County, known as the Huron Tract, plus clerical land throughout the Colonies.

In the twenty-first century, the Canadian government awarded the Mississauga First Nation nearly 145 million in settlement of a land claim because of the Crown's underpayment in the 1700s.

Cheryl Morgan

SARNIA AND LAMBTON COUNTY INDUSTRY

Salt wells were found in Ontario and the Michigan Basin; they became a large industry. There are 70 caverns in Ontario used for storing hydrocarbons, oil, gas, benzene, methane, and natural gas. There are 112 salt wells in Ontario. Benzene is a petroleum derivative used in making plastic. It is a very toxic chemical. Hydrocarbons are liquid petroleum products.

Salt layers were deposited on the floor of the ancient sea. The Michigan Basin was a great salt lake, a Salt Basin" (Terry Carter, Petroleum Resource Center, London, Ont).

Natural gas is also a large industry in Ontario.

"James Miller Williams dug the first successful oil well in North America in 1858. The Enniskillen County Ontario lands contained gum beds. Williams was searching for a source of fresh water, and he struck oil. The oil industry began in Ontario during the 1860s. There were no automobiles, and plastic had not been invented. What was needed was a new source for lighting oil lamps. Whale oil was becoming scarce and expensive. In 1854, Abraham Geesner discovered a way to make lamp oil from petroleum and called it kerosene. Crude oil was used for making asphalt. James Miller Williams Inc. began his refining company called The Canadian Oil Company (the world's first integrated oil company) which operated in Hamilton. This market would change the lives of millions. He was the pioneer of oil refining, the Father of the Petroleum Industry in Canada.

This was the first place in Canada and North America to drill commercially for oil. The knowledge acquired here led to oil drillers from Sarnia traveling the world, teaching other nations how to drill for oil" (Sarnia, Wickipedia, www). Massive growth of the petrol industry followed.

The first refinery in Sarnia was called the Liverpool Oil Company. In the 1860s, a plank road was used to haul crude oil to the refineries.

Imperial Oil started in 1880 when sixteen oil producers formed a corporation. A majority interest was sold to Standard Oil in the U.S.A. J.D. Rockefeller, an American business man, purchased the company in 1891 and moved it from London to Sarnia. The original commodity was kerosene for lighting. Since then, 328 other products were made from oil. They had 650 patents awarded. In the 1950s, the first petrochemical plant in Sarnia produced polyethylene for making plastic.

A smaller oil company began in Petrolia, Ontario in 1901 and produced gasoline called "White Rose".

The IP pipeline reached Sarnia in 1953. Oil flows into Sarnia from Alberta, Canada.

Ottissippi

Sunoco and Shell built a large pipeline to bring oil to Sarnia for refining.

Polymer was a synthetic product used to make rubber and plastic. The natural supply for rubber had been cut off when the Japanese bombed Pearl Harbor in 1942. All the necessary products for making it were available here, including petroleum and benzene. The St. Clair River provided the transportation, cooling water, and brine. Polymer was built almost overnight and was incorporated in 1942. It was considered an engineering miracle due to its complexity. The company put out 5,000 tons of rubber a month. It was a Crown Company until 1971. It was sold to the Canadian Development Company and renamed "Polysar" in 1976.

Nova Chemical, Bayer, Cabot Corp., Ethyl Corp., Lanxess, and Dow Chemical came to Sarnia. Dow ceased operations at Sarnia in 2009. They decommissioned the land and sold it to neighboring Trans Alta Energy Corporation to produce power and steam for industry, the largest natural gas generation plant in Canada. The Blue Water Energy Park was created on the former Dow site. Lanxess produced 150,000 tons of butyl rubber annually, the sole producer of regulatory approved food grade butyl rubber for chewing gum. They also created the Bio Industrial Park at Sarnia.

The complex of refining and chemical companies is called Chemical Valley. It has the highest level of air pollution of any Canadian city. The area east of Chemical Valley has no vegetation. Families nearby the plants have had health issues from being exposed to various chemicals being released into the atmosphere and the water, causing significant air and water pollution. The Ojibwe reservation people have had reproductive problems and are the only place in the world where girl children are born at a three to one ratio over boys.

Enbridge Solar Power is the largest in the world.

Research Park is the Canadian center of commercial and biotechnology. It was known as the hub of the Great Lakes, the center of trade and culture.

The First Nations Three Fires Confederacy Council controlled much of the area. Farming was the major occupation until 1921.

The first paved highway in Lambton was in 1929 from Sarnia to London, having a concrete surface.

The Bluewater Bridge was built in 1937 to 1938 and opened in 1938. The second span of the Blue Water Bridge construction began in 1995 and opened in 1997. It was part of the great highway system between Montreal and Chicago, Illinois. It is 1,883 meters or 6,178 feet in length. Thousands attended the grand opening.

The Sarnia-Port Huron border crossing is the fourth busiest border crossing in Ontario, Canada.

In 1841, there were 610 people in Sarnia. In 1871, there were 2,929 people in Sarnia. Port Sarnia expanded throughout the nineteenth century. The name was changed to Sarnia.

Timber and the discovery of oil, along with the Grand Trunk Railroad in 1859, stimulated growth.

In 1890, the tunnel was built between Sarnia and Port Huron, Michigan. This was the marvel of the world at the time. It created much better routing of trains. The work was done by men and mules. It was the first railroad tunnel ever constructed under a river, through developing original technology for execution in a compressed air environment. The Excalibur Boring Machine was used to bore the tunnel under the St. Clair River.

In 1914, an act was passed to incorporate the city of Sarnia. The population was 10,985 in six wards.

The grain elevators at Sarnia ship all over the world.

Holmes Foundry was established in 1919. It was a major producer of cast products for automobiles, agricultural equipment, and defense. The main customer was Ford Motor Company.

Muellers was a brass plumbing and goods plant in Sarnia. The owner, Hieronymus Mueller, was from Germany. It was the second industry to be built in Chemical Valley.

Prestolite/Autolite began operations in Point Edward in 1930, one of 30 plants, producing starting motors and generators for the auto industries.

"Historically there were high incidences of chemical spills to the River St. Clair; those have been greatly reduced. However, spills still occur. Monitoring equipment was installed in many water intake plants. The Huron to Erie drinking water monitoring network has greatly improved notification to the public. Undesirable surface scum, suspended solids, and other unsightly flotsam are no longer a problem in the St. Clair River. Dredge spoils of the shipping channel since 1992 show no contamination that requires hazardous material disposal. Due to historical industrial contamination of sediments near the Canadian shoreline, navigational dredging is still restricted in Canada" (Friends of the St. Clair River Watershed).

In 1940, women get to vote.

The TransCanada pipeline crosses Canada in 1958, carrying natural gas. In 1982, the TransCanada highway opens.

NATIVES

"Land was acquired as it was needed for new settlers.

Ottissippi

In 1790, the McKee Treaty ceded a large portion of Western Ontario for the United Empire Loyalists. Most of Lambton County was yet Indian land.

After the American Revolution, the British government faced the problem of finding homes for the United Empire Loyalists; many of them had given their all for loyalty to the motherland. The Mississauga's of the territory, including most of the present counties of Essex, Kent, Elgin, West Middlesex, and the southern fringe of Lambton Counties, were the landowners. The treaty was signed by the chiefs of the Ottawa, Chippewa-Ojibwa, Potawatomi, and Hurons.

The price of $1,200 was paid in trade goods, including blankets, scarlet cloth, ribbons, thread, black silk handkerchiefs, guns and ammunition, looking glasses, fish hooks, brass kettles, scissors, horn and ivory combs, fire steels, 39 gallons of rum, a bullock, 400 pounds of tobacco, 24 lace hats, 11, gross of pipes, and two, gross of knives" (Barnes, Lambton).

In 1796, land along the St. Clair River of about 46,000 acres was ceded to be used as Shawnee Loyalist land.

In July of 1827, Chief Joshua Wawanosh and 17 lesser chiefs ceded 2,200,000 acres of land to the Crown. This was called, Treaty Number, 27 ½, or the Amhurstburg Treaty. The treaty was to be paid in trade goods. Four reserves were retained.

In 1825, in the treaty negotiations under Chief Wawanosh, Head Chief of the Sarnia Chippewa, the chiefs and principal men had insisted that four land reserves be kept for the tribe, including Sauble River Reserve, Kettle Point Reserve, Sarnia Reserve, and Walpole Reserve, consisting of about 25,505 acres. (See "Chapter 10: Reserves and Indian Lands" and "Chapter 11: Mounds and Treaties" Chapters.

Elected chiefs replaced hereditary chiefs beginning in 1876, and in 1951, Indian women were given the vote for chiefs and counselors.

In 1954, the Indians were granted voting privileges, and in 1962, they were given federal voting privileges.

Before construction began in 1995, the ancient aboriginal fishing campsites were excavated and salvaged. There were several layers of debris here, including pottery, stone tools, and food remains, representing the middle woodland occupation dating from 200 B.C. to 600 A.D. The Algonquins used this site and the west shore sites opposite on the American side for their great fishing camp.

The Crawford site was discovered in 1947. It was an Iroquois village overlooking the Ausable River and the bog. The Parker Earthworks site is near Corunna; it was an Algonquin Indian site in 1400 to 1600 A.D. The Thedford, site 11, was a Palaeo – first peoples – Indian site. The site covers 700 meters. Barnes points were found here, a fish tail form. Fluted bifaces were also found.

Ipperwash is found in "Chapter 10: Reserves and Indian Lands", as are the other reservations in Lambton County, Ontario.

THE RED RYAN SHOOTOUT

Norman "Red" Ryan, a notorious gangster, spent most of his life in and out of jail and prison. He was known for armed robbery, safecracking, and other major theft. He killed six people in his lifetime. He had conned Prime Minister R.B. Bennett into believing he was a changed man. Shortly after his parole in 1935, he was back at his old line of trouble, robbing stores across the Province. A notorious bandit, Red Ryan – and his partner in crime, Harry Checkly – made a career out of robbing. In 1936, they were in Sarnia where they were going to rob a Christina Street liquor store. Police Officer John Lewis was fatally shot by the two masked men. Ryan and Checkly were shot dead in a liquor store in Sarnia, an officer shooting him three times.

CHAPTER 9
Biographies of Indian Chiefs

The spellings of names are difficult to determine exactly; most chiefs used their totem mark to sign documents, and their names were added by clerks or secretaries. The spelling depended upon how the name sounded to them. Because of this, you will find many variations in spellings of names.

The following chiefs represent mainly the area of Aamjiwnaang – Southern Ontario and Lower Michigan. This list is not all inclusive, but it does record early prominent chiefs who were connected to the area and who signed treaties and appear in other early writings.

AAMJIWNAANG

This is the name of the territory of the Ojibwe which stretched from Toronto, Ontario, Canada to Georgian Bay Ontario to the Saginaw watershed, west of Lansing, Michigan, to Detroit and Alpena, Michigan.

ANIMIKANCE

Variations on names were Animikeence, Animikance, and also Nimekance and Animmikans, meaning "Lightning". A Great Chief, at Lapointe, Wisconsin and then at Boweting (Sault St. Marie), he fought in the Iroquois Wars and later moved his people to the foot of Lake Huron. He was killed at Finley (Findley Ohio) in 1824.

Other names were Nimekans, Annemekins, and Animikans. Animikance was the son of Kioscance, a great chief and warrior of the Oak clan totem. Animikance went with his father as a young man to fight in the Iroquois Wars.

He served with the British under Sinclair, on garrison duty in the old Fort St. Clair at the mouth of Pine River at now St. Clair. He helped build the Fort in 1763 to 1764. He fought with Montcalm in the French and Indian War at Oswego, New York in 1756 and in the Pontiac War. Animikance was a signer on the Treaty of Detroit in 1807, in which one-fourth of southeast Lower Michigan was sold to the U.S.A.

Judge Z.W. Bunce said that when he came to the County of St. Clair, Nimikance was 105 years old, five-and-a-half feet tall, energetic, and capable of tending to his corn field four miles south of Black River and the chase as well.

Every New Year's Day, he was accustomed to sail down the river in his large birchen canoe on the bow of which he would fling the American colors to the breeze. On such an occasion, he would don his gold-laced coat, beaded moccasins, and leggings, and all the ornaments in his possession. Nimekance reached the age of 112. He died in about 1820 and was buried in the Great Mound on Water Street in now Port Huron, Michigan, with his father on Black River. His bones were then moved to the south in Port Huron, Burial Ground at the east side of Military St. near Division. The bodies were finally moved to Sarnia, Ontario across the River. D. Mitts, Adapted from, "As the Wild Goose Flies, Column, The Times Herald, SCC Library, MI Room

As a young man while hunting on the Western Plains for buffalo, Animikance was surprised by viscous bears. He fired his gun at the closest bear's head. The gun misfired. As he re-cocked it and readied to fire again, the bear, with lightning quick movement, struck him down and began pounding and tearing him with her claws, causing great wounds. The cubs followed, throwing themselves against him. Nimikance managed to get his knife and struck out at the Bear wounding her. One of the cubs struck the knife from his hand. The wounded mother bear with added fury pounded him with blows, tearing his abdomen open, tearing flesh from his thighs, chest, and face until the flesh hung in ribbons over his body. He fell back, conquered, and before he lost consciousness, heard them lumber away. Being conquered, the bears ceased to molest him.

When he regained consciousness he was able to stand and bind up his wounds with long grass, weeds, and strips of bark. He finally succeeded in getting back to camp. A surgeon from a nearby fort was brought to attend his wounds. The wounds took two years to heal and left Nimikance disfigured for life (Henry Schoolcraft).

Dr. Zina Pilcher, surgeon at Fort Gratiot and other posts, examined Animikance. He found portions of the cheekbone were gone and *cicatrices* –

*s*cars – of fearful extent upon the face and other parts of his body, wondering how Animikance had even survived.

Nimikance went on to serve as a soldier who helped Patrick Sinclair build Fort Sinclair. He was a friend and frequent visitor of Judge Bunce, Peter Brakeman, the storekeeper and trader, and other early St. Clair County settlers. Nimikance lived between Sarnia and Port Huron.

AU MI CHO AN EWS

The "village was at Port Huron, named for the Ojibwe's chief" (Hindsdale, 1926).

BLACK DUCK

Black Duck – Akockis – was a friend of Americans and lived at Black River. Who at the Great Sundance on the banks near the mouth of Black River near the St. Clair County Community College, near the mouth of Black River murdered a boasting Canadian who had killed his American friends with his hatchet. John Riley intervened to protect him from revenge, he was held in Fort Gratiot for safety, and the family was compensated by Governor Cass with 40 quarts of whiskey drawn from Aura Stewart's store, along with gifts to cover the dead.

The Indians were gathered by the thousands from all over Michigan and Canada. Canoes lined the banks of the Black River and St. Clair River. There were days of speeches, ceremonies, dancing, and feasting at the Sun Dance.

Black Duck, later changed allegiance to the British. Black Duck in an attempt to murder David Macomb near Detroit, was shot by Corporal John B. Jones and later died at Maldon – Amherstburg.

BLACK SNAKE

Black Snake, a chief who lived at Black River Village. He had numerous family and was related to John Riley.

INDIAN DAVE – ISH DON QUIT

Ish Don Quit – "Crossing Cloud", Indian Dave, David Stocker, David Tuscola, Tuscola Dave Davis – was witness of the Treaty of Saginaw in 1819, where 6 million acres of Ojibwe land was ceded to the U.S. Government. He traveled and knew many in the thumb of Michigan, stopping often to share a meal. Black smallpox wiped out his first family. A direct descendent of Chief Pontiac, Dave was the Nitamop - clan leader. Dave lived to 106 years old, and touring his old friends and places in a two-year journey, died in 1909. Dave was born in 1803.

Indian Dave is said to be the man who greeted the first White settlers in the thumb. His father was Chief Nip Mup. He was a man who knew herbs and roots. He knew of coal mines and a copper piece found on the Cass River. Vassar was his home base, but he was around North Branch, Millington, and Tuscola. He had many friends and traveled extensively, visiting all the Indian camps. He never attended schools. He was a Christian in the Methodist Church. He remembered the fires of 1871 and 1881.

John David Davis, son of Indian Dave, traveled with his father throughout the Thumb of Michigan and rarely spoke. He would follow behind his father in the ancient custom. Dave told of his people coming to the petroglyphs area for special meetings, weddings, ceremonies, etc. Ginseng was found near the petroglyphs in the fall. The burial site, of 18 Indians were found in one group here. A man, woman, and child were found in sitting position in a row together. He said Bay City is literally built upon Indian mounds and sites.

He fascinated youngsters and men alike with his tales of Native customs and hunting stories around a campfire. He was an expert bow and arrow maker and canoe builder, which he often sold for his livelihood. He was also a River Guide in Northern Michigan.

Dave would make bows and arrows for the kids and teach them how to bake fish covered in clay in a mud oven and snare trapping. The boys loved to follow Dave, who would teach them and their parents how to use herbs and roots for medicinal purposes. He would often drop off a turkey or fish at their homes. Some were presented with handmade moccasins, bows, or whittled toys. Sometimes they were charged 10 cents for the well-made items.

Nitamop (Netmop), James, and his family, along with Indian Dave were known as the "Tuscola Gathering". This group included Indian Dave's sons, John David – Nesh Kee Zhick, John Davis, and William David Davis, as well as his daughter Nancy Davis, the son's wives, and Frank James and his wife, all relatives. Other family members were Indian Joe, Indian Mary, and Long Tom. The Tuscola Gathering would often paddle into town with hides, baskets, hampers, whittled toys, ginseng, fish, and game to sell. With delight, the local boys would help the aged bent over Dave carry his goods.

JOHN RILEY – BLACK CLOUD

John Riley was the chief of the Black River bands and also the Riley band of the Ojibwe. John built his home beside the Great Burial Mound on Water Street near Military Street in now Port Huron, Michigan, where the Federal

Customs House building now sits. This was the gathering, or rendezvous, place for important council meetings with important chiefs, held on the banks of Black River.

The Allies also stayed at John's home and on his lands while traveling through the area, the place where one of four reservations was established after the 1807 Treaty of Detroit, in which the Ojibwe, Pottawatomie, Ottawa, and Wyandot ceded 5 million acres in southeast Michigan to the U.S. Government. The John Riley Black River band was 200 members.

John was a leading spirit – Holy Man. John was born in 1761 in the Mohawk Valley of New York where his father originated. His mother was a Saginaw Princess, "Menaweamegogua" or "Menawcumegogua", an important Chippewa woman who was daughter of an Indian chief.

John's father was General James Van Slyke Riley, a well-respected Indian trader who served in the Revolutionary War. He was also a federal Indian commissioner, Indian agent, soldier, adventurer, and trader with the Saginaw Indians for 15 years. James Riley served in the Revolutionary War as an Indian commander and interpreter. He held many important occupations in his lifetime. He was Sheriff of Schnechtedy County, New York; interpreter for the U.S. Army; and judge, alderman, and postmaster at Schnechtedy.

James Sr. Riley received commissions negotiating treaties with the Indians. He divorced Mena in 1792 and married again to Janet Swits, having three daughters in New York who loved their brothers. No man was more honored and respected than James Van Slyke Riley, a fearless man of great strength and resolution.

His sons were all well-educated, good looking, well-spoken, and intelligent. The brothers fought with General Cass in 1812 for the American cause. They led raids killing British Indian Allies.

John and his brothers, James and Peter, were employed by the U.S. Government as interpreters, as scouts, and for special assignments. John was a great Indian leader, a Great Spirit. He was indispensable in treaties with the Indians, a faithful and a staunch American. He was sent to secure captives taken in raids and convey information to the Indians and the U.S. Government. John served under General Hull and General Cass. He was away from home much of the time, traveling as a scout and ranger. He was an interpreter, a diplomatic statesman, a peace negotiator for the U.S., and an invaluable aid among the various Indian tribes when securing agreements with them. He received land at the Treaty of Chicago, Maple Groves, Treaty of Saginaw, and many others. John was a liaison and special mission's agent.

John married an Indian woman and had children. He accidently killed Jacob Harson in 1810 or 1811, near Bear Creek in Ontario.

Peter Riley was bribed to be quiet at the Treaty of Saginaw in 1819. Peter lived at Belle River and married a French woman named Delno.

James Sr. at 75 years old returned to Michigan for the Treaty of Saginaw in 1819, held near Caro, Michigan. He was to collect money owed him for 10 years of trading with the Indians. He advised his boys on land deals at St. Clair County and Saginaw. His sons also received land of 640 acres at the mouth of the Saginaw River, John's land being where the present Bay City is now located. The sons were natural leaders and doubly respected as sons of the old Indian trader (Schnechtedy Union Star Newspaper article).

James Jr. was a guide and interpreter for General and Governor Cass on his expedition to the Upper Peninsula in 1820. James worked for Cass until he died in 1829. He served as interpreter to find the source of the Mississippi and the natural resources of the Northwest. Houghton, Schoolcraft, and Douglas were among the entourage.

John and his brothers were scouts for the Americans during the Indian Wars and other wars fought against the British near Detroit and elsewhere. They were honest and faithful, aiding everywhere with loyal fidelity.

A sister, Jane Helen, and Miss Jannet Ryley were gracious and kind to the half-brothers, receiving them as brothers. Jane had accompanied two of the impressive, tall, good looking Ryley boys to the best tailor in town for a complete outfitting. In later years when one of the boys died, he willed his entire estate to his Schnechtedy sister, Jane, who had been so kind to him. She used part of the money to purchase a lot on lower Union Street and build the house where Judge Ryley later died on January 8, 1848.

Graciously entertained by Mrs. Ryley and Jane Helen, the brothers were gentlemanly, handsome, high-toned, and half Ojibwe-Chippewa. They were honorable fellows with the White people, and when with the Indians in the forest, the brothers were perfect Indians in dress, language, hunting, trapping, and mode of living. The boys grew to manhood respected by the Indians as leaders and as sons of James Van Slyke Ryley, who continued to exercise great influence among the Chippewa, even after he returned to the Dorp.

John preferred to live at Black River in now Port Huron, Michigan, where he had a general store and trading post downtown. His fence and gardens reached to 6th Street and south to Pine Street.

John was instrumental in keeping Black Duck safe after he killed a boasting Canadian Indian who talked of killing Americans, who were Black Ducks' friends. John was granted permission from the Fort Gratiot officers to give him protective custody and from Governor Cass to negotiate safe trade of the exchange with the dead man's family, which was liquor and goods to secure his safety.

After the Treaty of Washington ceded the reservations in St. Clair County, Michigan in 1836, John's father bought land on the Belle River northeast of Memphis, Michigan for the band to live on in Riley Center. This land was named Riley Township in 1841, in honor of John Riley. The land was used for hunting and gathering cranberries and maple sugar. John spent his winters there.

The settlement at Riley was called "Knawkechagame". John opened a fine store in Riley Township. John's sister lived at Belle River with him. She gathered cranberries, maple syrup, and candy to trade at Port Huron and the St. Clair River and to stock the store. John built a trading post store there and, because he was trusting and free with credit, in time had extended credit and lost all his goods and money. He was a kind man but went broke, forced out of business and to move to Canada at Bear – Sydenham and Aux Sauble – River.

He was Chief of the Chippewa and Munsees, 25 miles from the Moravian Village in the London District, Ontario, on a 9,000, acre reservation, then at Muncietown on the Thames River. He then lived a White life. John died at Muncietown in 1842. H.P. Chase gave his burial eulogy. One source cites Courtland N.Y. as his burial place.

KIOSKANCE – YOUNG GULL

Son of Animacance, Kioscance was the Principal Chief of the Ojibwe at La Pointe, Wisconsin. At the west end of Lake Superior was the area of the Great Rice Lakes and the main headquarters of the North Western Ojibwe. He was the Great War Chief and Grand Chief of the Ojibwe at Boweting or Sault Ste. Marie. He was a legendary warrior with great Medicine, whose Spirit Guides protected him in battle. He was a war chief over one of the four divisions that went to fight the Iroquois Wars. He came down the east side of Lake Michigan and crossed at St. Joseph River with 400 canoes of eight men each. His flotilla filled the Otissippi River (St Clair River) from the mouth of Lake Huron to Walpole Island in the south. His division represented about 16,000 people.

Kioscance was Chief of the Otchipewas in their wars against the Huron – Wyandotte – and Six Nations Iroquois. He had many dreams of a place with a beautiful river with all manner of good provisions.

On his return to the Upper Peninsula, his men camped on the shore of now Fort Gratiot. The area was beautiful. The beach and rivers were a great fishery. There was plenty of food and game, a perfect place with creeks and rivers, a sheltered place for winter and sugar trees.

In 1690, he moved his people back to the foot of Lake Huron in Southern Ontario and Michigan. It was their favored hunting ground. Kioscance's home was near the old Fort St. Joseph, a strategic position to protect the people. He was Chief over the Ojibwe Rapids tribe at the foot of Lake Huron, called the Kioscanee, also called Saulteurs, the Rapids tribe, and the Detroit Indians, "Detroit" meaning the Strait between Lake Huron and Lake Erie.

Kioscance was born in 1693 and died in 1800; he lived for 107 years.

His Celebration of Life lasted many days as the spirit journey began. It was one of the largest celebrations of life ever seen. He was buried in the Great Burial Mound on the Thames – Horn – River, sight of his great victory over the Seneca 12 miles up-stream (Plain, 1300 Moons).

KISHKOUKAU

Kishkoukau, or Kishkawko, a war chief of the Ojibwe, lived in Saginaw. He was bold and terrible. Kishkoukau was a well-known man in Michigan. Daring and cruel, he was a fierce defender of Ojibwe lands. He was bribed to sign the Treaty of Saginaw, which ceded 6 million acres of land to the U. S. Government. He was a spokesman for the Head Chiefs. He told all gathered near Caro, Michigan for the Treaty, "we didn't ask you to come here. We received our hunting grounds from the Great Spirit and want to keep them for our children's future". Kishkaukau reserved a large parcel of land for his own from the Treaty.

Kishkaukau passed through the St. Clair County area at least twice a year to receive gifts at Sarnia and Walpole island and an annuity at Malden – Ammherstburg, Ontario. He made it a habit to stop at settlers' homes and take whatever he wanted. At Sally Wards home, he and his braves entered the house demanding whiskey. Sally told him there was none. Kiskkaukau, in a rage, turned the faucet of the vinegar barrel on, letting it run out onto the floor. He ordered the braves to take what they could find in bread and foodstuffs. He then pulled the rod from a rifle and whipped Sally Ward with it.

Kishkaukou and his son Chemick terrorized American settlers. They were allies of the British in the War of 1812.

He acted as judge and executioner in an incident with a Delaware Indian who married an Ojibwe woman. The Delaware was on trial for killing a Chippewa in a fight. The offender had made restitution to the relatives of the dead man. By custom, a tribal council would make the arrangements. The Delaware entered the circle of the meeting and, if unmolested by any of the dead man's relatives, the matter was settled, never to be reopened, and he would be restored. He passed all the relatives, but as he passed Kiskaukau, he was struck by one swift stroke of the tomahawk killing him. The whole council was awestruck by this act. When the hereditary Chief Minnoneguotem declared to him that the killing was contrary to Indian law, Kishkaukau replied, "The law is altered".

Kiskaukau was later arrested by White men for breaking their law murdering a Detroit man, and sentenced to hang. While he was in jail awaiting his execution, one of his wives smuggled some poisonous concoction, which he consumed and died in the jail.

MACHONCE

Machonce, Chief Francis, was Chief of the tribes of the Pottawatomies at Lake St. Clair, "The Swan Creek Band", and was bribed into moving with 51 of his people to Kansas in 1837, and became the Osage. He kept a hotel at Swan Creek or Salt River, and he spoke English well. He was civic-minded and helped out, at work Bees and other activities of the community. He often spoke at schools about Native life. His family was an aristocratic Indian family. He became Chief after his Father died from drowning after drinking whiskey.

Tall and well-built, he wore a black frock coat tied around the waist with wampum belt, fringed calico shirt, broadcloth leggings decorated with porcupine quills, and silver ornaments which jingled as he walked. He wore buckskin moccasins and a plug hat ornamented with a broad silver band. He wore a silver ring through his nose and in each ear five or six silver earbobs. He was a Freemason.

Machonce or Macounce – "Small Bear" – or Macoonce, Macaunse, Makonce, Mac Sunse, Machonee, Mascoonse, Cumekumanow. Macompte went to England and shot an apple on the head of a volunteer. He was a Great Brave and a fine specimen of a Native. His family was of the aristocratic Indian. He was much loved by his own people and the pioneers. He was Chief of the tribes on the Reservation at Swan Creek Territory.

He once had Gagette Tremble cook him a bag of venison, and she found it to be the leg of an American Soldier killed at the River Raisen. His nod was the will for the tribes. He was father of Francis Maconce. Francis and his wife kept a hotel and traded at Swan Creek or Salt River. He was a drinker of the White Man's whiskey. One night he drowned after drinking in 1816, and Frances became Chief (MPHC vol. 17, Early History of SCC, Mrs. B.C. Farrand).

MASHEASH

Masheash or Musquash was a prominent chief along the St. Clair River. He was a nephew of Nemekas or Animicance.

Musquesash was a Chippewa chief, who lived in the vicinity of Port Huron. Msqueash died soon after the War of 1812 and was buried on the Indian Reservation north of Mt. Clemons (Askin, vol. 1, 180/Jenks, vol. 1 148, 1912, History of St. Clair County MI).

MINAVAVORA

Minavavora was a Grand Chief, Principal Chief, and War Chief of the Chippewa – Ojibwa. At Michilimackinac, and Mackinac Island, to avenge the murder of Pontiac, he killed two servants of a trading company. He was knifed in his tent in 1770 by a British War Party at Michilimackinac.

MINWEWEH

Minweweh was Principle Ojibwe War Chief.

MITCHIGAMI

Mitchigami was a fortified village on Black River.

NANGE, OJIBWE CHIEF

NAYKEEZHIG

Naykeezhig, grandson of Mesgish, signed the Treaty of 1836, selling the area reservations to the U.S. Government. He was an honored British Army Scout, and one of Bunce's Indians employed by Judge Bunce.

NEGIG

Negig, an Ottawa chief, lived on the River Gervais on Black River. (He was) Chief at St. Clair River (Askin 1) and also a signer of the Treaty at Chenail Escarte.

NEOME

Neome was the Great Chief of the Ojibwe – Chippewa, who lived at the Flint River. He was called a "Lion in the Path" of the Grand Traverse of the Flint, the main trail over the Flint River near Montrose and Lapeer. He was also called Reaume and Nibegon. Neome was the Great Chief of the Ojibwe over the Saginaw Treaty of 1819.

Neome's geographical location and his powerful band stood on the very threshold of the trail leading to the Northwest. The old chief was honest, simple minded, sincere, firm in friendship, and easy to be persuaded by a benefactor who appeased to his sense of gratitude, harmless and kindhearted. He was short and heavy-molded. With his people, he was a Chief of Patriarchal Goodness. His name was never mentioned except with a certain veneration and, after his passing, with a great sorrow (Western Historical Co).

Neome's children began using the surname "Jacobs" after the great friend of Neome, Jacob Smith, Indian Agent at Saginaw.

NICHOLAS PLAIN

Nicholas Plain, Osarskodawa, a descendant of Animikance and Chief of Sarnia Reserve Chippewa, was a Native minister who wrote *The History of the Chippewa of Sarnia* in 1950, and whose descendants were Chiefs at Aamjiwnaang.

O CHIPICAN

O Chipican lived in Ontario and was a signer of many treaties.

OGEMA KEGATOO

Ogema Kegatoo was Head Chief and Orator of the Saginaw Ojibwe during the Treaty Era. At 25 years old, he was Head Chief of the Chippewa Nation and central figure at the Council for the Saginaw Treaty of 1817.

He was over six feet tall, graceful, and handsome with undaunted courage. He lived at the forks of the Tittabawasee River. He wore a superb government medal, five inches long and a quarter inch thick, of pure silver. On one side of the medal was the image of an Indian Chief in full dress; on the other, a representation of the President of the United States with the inscription: "Presented to Ogema Kegato by Thomas Jefferson". Ogema Kegato was reelected Head Chief for 30 consecutive years, ruling the people until 1839 or 1840. Many astounding stories are told regarding his bravery and fortitude, some of which surpass belief. After receiving a knife wound while stopping a fight, his liver protruded; while recovering, he cut a piece of his own liver off and threw the piece on the coals and ate it, saying to those present, "if there is a braver man in the Chippewa Nation than I am, I should like to see him." Many attested to this act (Western Historical Co).

OKEMOS

Chief Okemos, or John Okemos or Ogimaans – "Little Chief", was of the Bear totem of the Ojibwe (Chippewa). Okemos was a well-known traveler and well-respected man, admired and beloved to both the White and Red man. He was a revered warrior and chief of the Grand River band of the Saginaw Chippewa and leader of many Ojibwe bands.

He always played the flute in the morning, and one always knew when he was around. He smoked a pipe that was three feet long. He was five foot, four inches.

He led the French war against the British in 1760, and he was a nephew of Pontiac. He was in the Revolutionary War in 1782. He was a scout against the Americans, taking American scalps. He was second in command to Tecumseh, a bold, daring, skilled warrior.

In the Battle of Sandusky near Cedar Point, Ohio in 1782, Okemos with 16 other warriors were surrounded and severely wounded. Saber scars slashed his body, his skull was cloven, he had dozens of wounds and bullets, and he was left for dead. He remembered a searing pain in his head when everything went black. He and his cousin, Manitocorbway, were found several days later when the women went to the battle site looking for survivors. They found signs of life in Okemos and his cousin. He woke many moons later in the wigwam of a friend. He was nursed for two years and recovered. Manitocorbway was also there and was a crippled man for life.

Okemos fought at the battle in 1790 on the Miami River, defeating the Americans led by General Arthur St. Clair. He fought against General Wayne in 1794 at the Battle on the Maumee River, where the Indians suffered a great defeat, and at Tippecanoe in 1811 (Chaput, MI Archives).

Okemos also fought in some bloody Indian Wars around 1800, of which little is recorded. One against the Shawnees and one against the Chippewa, in both wars the Ottawas and Pottawatomies defeated the invaders.

In 1812, Okemos fought for the British under a colonel's commission. In 1813, Okemos commanded a war party sent to join General Proctor on the Sandusky River at Fort Stephenson, held by Captain Croghan. They met up with American Captain Ball with a strong detachment of dragoons. Okemos saw that they were too strong for his braves to attack and hastily concealed themselves in the brush and would have been secure. But a young warrior fired on the dragoons after they had passed the Indian's hiding spot. A desperate battle took place, and every Indian fell. Okemos with reckless courage was one of the last to fall, with a sabre cut across his skull, his shoulder blade cut through, and gunshot wounds in his side. He later woke and found his brother, "Standing Up Devil".

He fought in the Battle of the Thames in the Fall of 1813 and was severely wounded. He vowed never to fight the Americans again and was ever after a friend. In 1814, he traveled to Detroit and pledged his loyalty to General Cass and the Americans and never fought again. With Governor Cass and the Americans, Okemos signed the Treaty of Saginaw, in which 6 million acres of land were ceded in Lower Michigan.

In the 1830s, he was the leader of many bands. Okemos possessed indomitable courage and was a born fighter, a natural commander and leader, a strategist in battle, and a real military genius. In every way, he was a remarkable man and a typical Indian.

He was born on the Shiawasee River and, when a child, went to live on the Grand River at Shiminicon, twenty-four miles from Lansing on the great trail from Lansing to Grand Rapids. Okemos claims he was born on an island in a lake near Pontiac, Michigan. Okemos became a chief at 20 years old.

The village of Okemos, east of Lansing on the Cedar River, was his home, and many of his tribesmen are buried there. He died December 5, 1858 in a favorite camp on the Looking Glass River, five miles northeast of Dewitt, Clinton County near Lansing. He was buried at Shiminicon on the Grand River in Ionia County the next day. At the time of his death, he was over 100 years old (Chaput).

OLD MOTHER RODD – "WINDY WOMAN" – NAK MAH PUC YHC ZOGMA

Old Mother Rodd was a much-loved Indian woman who was well-known throughout the St. Clair River region. Short and squat of figure, she had a square bronze face with narrow black eyes glittering between the half-closed lids, high cheek bones, long coarse black hair plaited in a thick braid which hung down her back, and great brass hoop rings in her ears. Her broad, flat feet were encased with buckskin moccasins decorated with colored porcupine quills and beads. Above these she wore wide bead-embroidered broadcloth leggings which reached to her ankles and flapped back and forth with a regular movement as she walked. Her narrow skirt was of the same material, elaborately trimmed and fringed with beads, reaching just below the knee. Overlapping this for a short distance below the waist line was a blouse, or short gown as the residents called it, made of gaudy, large-patterned calico. Around her neck were many strings of beads of all colors and sizes, hanging low down the front of her blouse. And outside of all this was a heavy woolen blanket, spread out to its full size over her head and shoulders, drawn tightly across the back and held together in front with her large copper-colored hands. A great bundle of baskets, or corn husk and rush mats, was held in place by a band of bark across her forehead.

Happy were the little children when they were allowed to swap a loaf of quash – *e-gun* (bread) – a piece of *Co Coosh* (pork) or a pan of *Ni Po Nin* (flour) for a bright colored basket. And happier yet when they saw the old dame pitch her camp on the edge of the apple orchard near the beach. Then it was "Hurrah!" for the succotash feast which they knew awaited them.

In front of the camp on the clean, white sand, she built her fire. From a pole resting on two crotched sticks driven into the ground hung the polished brass kettle, containing the savory mess. Old Mother Rodd was scrupulously clean, and when the luscious succotash was dished up with the wooden spoon into bright tin cups, the most fastidious guest could not resist her hospitality.

Hanging from the limb of a nearby apple tree was the bark hammock in which the little papoose, wrapped like a mummy in blankets, was fastened with strips of tanned deerskin. Back from the river, a short distance under one of the largest apple trees, was a little mound which marked the resting place of another papoose who had roamed over the Happy Hunting Grounds for many moons.

With the opening of the apple blossoms each year, Old Mother Rodd made her appearance and celebrated the anniversary over that little mound with the customary Pow Wow, chanting songs, and free indulgence in Santawaba. Two or three days were spent in this manner, until her voice became weak and the firewater gave out. Then she would cover the grave with Indian food and leave it until the apple blossoms came again (The Detroit News Tribune 1896, Dixon).

She carried a long stick with her, a rod or staff; it is said that she used it to pole vault over the streams and sand bars of the St. Clair River at an early date when the river was much shallower. Also, a few boys were corrected with it.

Her father was "Pe Tauch Ne Nouk" or "Touch Ne Nouck", also "Nimence", her grandfather "May Zhe Ke Osh". Her husband was Alexander Rodd, a Metis, part French. His Indian name was "She She Pe Anee" or "Little Duck". They had a nice farm with cattle, horses, and more and a fine log home. She did not drink in her younger days. They were friends with the Americans, and it was for this reason that Alexander was killed by a Saginaw (Nancy Brakeman Papers, SCC Library, MI Room).

Several Indian families were encamped about five miles up the Hauviere Deludes or Black River, for the purpose of making maple sugar. One day, Alexander went out from the camp for a hunt and shot a deer, breaking its leg. The next day, he went out to search for it to bring it to camp, taking with him a cousin of Mother Rodd, named Mass E Nee Ke Zhick or "Mixed Clouds", a son of her uncle, Serpent. Wapoose, Wawanosh, and two other Indians had talked the matter over and decided to kill Rodd and so were on the lookout for him. One shot him in the side, one in the back, and one in the head, the last killing him. A Sarnia said not long ago that it was a Saginaw Indian named *Sha Ne Schaw Pe Nace* or "Greenbird" who was the murderer. They buried him where he fell, on the old Black River Trail near Wadhams. His coat, with a bullet hole in the back, and gun were brought to Mother Rodd. From that time, the poor woman despised the whole tribe of Saginaw Indians.

After this she was twice married but was always known by the name Rodd. Her totem was the Turtle. Upon the corner of her white blanket, which she wrapped about her in cold weather, could often be seen the figure of a small turtle worked with red yarn.

She was strictly honest in all of her dealings. She was also industrious and her work was well done; her brooms, baskets, mats, and more were exchanged for goods with Americans who appreciated the good quality. She would often scold lazy Indians, telling them it was their own fault if they were poor and hungry.

"Granny Rodd" was a friend of the Americans, though she visited her Ontario relatives and her children across the river. She preferred to live on the American side of the river. She stayed near the river in the summer and went to the woods for the winter. She would gather berries and exchange them for provisions, having a full supply for herself and her youngest daughter who remained with her. When she peddled her goods, she always dressed in her best and had her berries in a bright tin pail, saying she made a ready sale for them by doing so. She made good maple sugar and would mold it into cakes to give to the children of her friends, always expecting some present in return. She was a good doctress, using herbs and roots and barks. She even cured the babe Charles Brown of cholera infantium.

She paddled her canoe, traveling to visit friends on Walpole Island. She would receive large presents of corn, always of the white flint variety, which is much the best for hulling purposes, and she hulled it both for soup and for hominy, pounding it in a mortar made by hollowing out a tree trunk of hardwood about three feet long and using a wooden pestle.

She regularly received an annuity from the British Government.

In her later years, she was often under the influence of whiskey and roamed around visiting at her friend's homes, who never refused her their hospitality.

Twenty-two years before her death, she had her grave clothes made and placed them in care of Mrs. Brakeman. The leggings were of bright red cloth, as the British Government furnished the Indians at that time, and were trimmed with ribbons and beads and were very gaudy.

During her last sickness, she wished to be baptized, and Reverend Allen Salt, an Indian preacher, administered to her the Ordinance of Christian Baptism. She lies buried in the Indian cemetery at Sarnia. Her grave is marked by a head board painted white on which in letters of black paint is inscribed her name. Her death occurred in 1870 in Port Huron at 115 years of age.

Two of her children lived with the Moran family at Detroit and spoke the French language. Their names were Mrs. Charlotte Dupre and Antoine Rodd.

A cousin, Andrew Yates, was an interpreter for the British Government. Mrs. Obedig was also a cousin. Both Mother Rodd and Mrs. Obedig retained the use of the Indian blanket and moccasins, as long as they lived.

A portrait of Granny Rodd hung in the State Library at Lansing, a gift from the Honorary D.B. Harrington, former Vice President of the State Pioneer Society (MPHC 1890 Annual Mtg).

PONTIAC

Pontiac – Boon I wuk, Bwon Diac (Boondiac), or Obwandiyag – means "Thunderbirds Landing Upon the Earth". Pontiac was an Ottawa, his mother an Ojibwe. His totem was the Nigig – Otter clan. He was the Ojibwe Chief of the St. Clair region. He was leader of the Mitai or Mide (Grand Medicine Society), he wanted to protect his people from the White men who were taking over all their great lands in the region. He was known everywhere. He had much energy, intelligence, and great oratory skill.

Pontiac was born in the mid 1720's at an Ottawa village along the Maumee River, where the city of Toledo, Ohio now stands. He had a wife named Kantuckegun and two sons, Skegenabe and Hebahkehum, along with other children.

He lived on Peche Island at the mouth of the Detroit River above the fort at the south end of Lake St. Clair. Gouin, a trader, acted as a mediator between the Indians and the English. Pontiac often came to him for advice.

He was the Ottawa War Chief, and he rallied support to evacuate the White men. His plan was to destroy all the British forts west of the Alleghenies in one day. The Allies destroyed 9 of 12 British forts in one day. Detroit, Niagara, and Pittsburgh were the only three that survived. He has been called the greatest Indian military tactician.

George Crogan, British Indian agent, remarked that Pontiac commanded more respect among other nations than most chiefs do among their own tribe. Pontiac was a great hero of the Ottawa and Ojibwe people. Parkman and Peckham, have written outstanding biographies of Pontiac and his times (Chaput).

When Pontiac was killed in Illinois country at Cahokia, the Great Castle, in 1769 when Williamson, an English trader, bribed an Illinois Indian to murder Pontiac. On hearing of his death, the Ojibwe Chief Minavavana, and many others, set out for Cahokia to extract the necessary revenge. The Illinois suffered greatly. Pontiac was buried in Michigan. The Saginaw Ojibwe are his most direct descendants, with many in Canada also. Ottuson, a son of Pontiac, lived on the Upper Huron River (Black River) in Sanilac County, Michigan.

PUTAQUASAMINE

Putaquasamine was born in 1729 and lived until he was well over 100 years old. He lived at Saginaw on an island. Peter Grewitt, a well-known trader, interviewed him in 1834 and he told of the Saginaw history and the Great Sauk War. Who in 1519 and '20, possessed the district from Kawkawlin at Saginaw Bay to the Huron – Clinton River – in Michigan (Indian and Pioneer History of Saginaw County, www).

SANILLAC

Sanillac, famous Wyandotte Chief who was prominent in the Iroquois Wars and was cited for his bravery, Sanilac County was named for him, memorialized in a poem by Colonel Whiting, 1831 (Cass/Col. Whiting/Chaput)

SHABONNA

Shabonna, or Charbonneau, a great Pottawatomi warrior, was born at the KanKaKee River. He joined Tecumseh and became known from Niles to Detroit and Black River. Aid to Tecumseh and, he stood by his side when he fell at the Battle of the Thames. A peace negotiator with the Indians, Black Hawk, the Sac, and Fox, and Big Foot, he was friend of the White man, saving many lives. His land was sold when he was away, and he was broken in spirit and sad. The Ottawa citizens bought him a tract of land, a house and a living.

SHAWANO

Shawano was Aide De Camp for Tecumseh. Shawano, who later was named John Nahdoo, was a hereditary chief who traveled with Tecumseh as his second in command. When Tecumseh fell on the battle field, Shawano secured his body, on the Battle field, and hid it away throughout his life. He daily raised and lowered a flag over his secret grave. The bones were passed to his grandson and other trustworthy men to keep them safe.

In 1846, Shawano came from the Anderdon-Amherstburg Reserve in Essex County, Ontario, Canada, to live on Walpole Island Reserve. He died here in 1861. Shawano received two medals from the British Government: one was a King George VII, the other a Victoria medal, presented by King Edward VII when he came to Canada in 1860. Shawano is commemorated on the Wallaceburg Centennial Coin in 1975.

TECUMSEH

Tecumseh, Tecumtha, or Tekoomse – "Shooting Star" or "Celestial Panther Lying in Wait" – was a great Shawnee chief he was the greatest leader of the Indian Nations and the National President of the Indians, East of the Mississippi (Little Turtle Canada History. www).

He saw the Indian lands being stolen from them and the great degradation of the White man's ways to his peoples. He gathered allies, from all of the Nations East of the Mississippi, even to the Gulf of Mexico. He wanted a great Confederation of the Indians. He did not want war but wanted to resist the White man's ways. He envisioned triumph through passive resistance. He fought with the British to keep the covetous Americans out of the Northwest Territory Indian lands and to keep his people good and healthy.

The Eye of the Panther. He was named "Shooting Star" or Celestial Panther lying in wait. (The Panther Crossing the Sky, Thom). He was named for this phenomenon.

His eyes were the color of the panther. His father, Hard Striker-Pucsinwah, was War Chief of the Kispoko-Panther, Shawnee; his mother was a Creek, Methmtasa-Turtle Mother.

He never signed a treaty as his father before him. (Thom)

Tecumseh was well-respected, by both friend and enemy. A great statesman and leader, who could inspire and motivate his people, he understood early that the White man would not rest until all Native Americans were driven out or eliminated completely.

Tecumseh was born in 1768 in an old village on the Scioto River in Ohio. When he was born, that night a great meteor lit up the sky and burned its way across the heavens. For this phenomenon, he was named "Shooting Star" or "Celestial Panther Lying in Wait".

Ottissippi

As a boy, he saw his tribe fighting the Americans as allies of the British. When he was six, his father was killed in battle. His family fled after being burned out by Americans. He was adopted by the Shawnee Chief Blackfish, and among his foster White brothers was Danial Boone, who had been captured in Kentucky but escaped in a short time.

As a young man, Tecumseh was a great buffalo hunter, killing 16 buffalo with 19 arrows near Piqua, Ohio. It was on a buffalo hunt, using only a knife, when he fell from his horse and the buffalo he had killed rolled over on him. This broke his hip, and he vowed never to drink liquor again. He then walked with a limp the rest of his life.

His eyes were hazel, gentle and understanding or could burn like balls of fire. He was sensitive, thoughtful, and far seeing, proud and brave, a great statesman who understood the greater problems of a whole race and speaks with one tongue. A man of simple dignity, he won the admiration of everyone who conversed with him. He was of light figure, finely proportioned, five foot, nine or ten inches. With light copper skin and an oval face, his eyes were full of cheerfulness, energy, and decision. His face reminded men of Napoleon (Wm. E. Wilson, Shooting Star, 1942).

In Lossing's *Pictorial Field-book of the War of 1812* (1869), he writes,

> *Tecumseh was born near Springfield, Ohio. He was Shawnoese. His name, Tecumtha, meant a Flying Tiger or a wildcat springing on its prey.*
>
> *Tecumseh had three small silver crosses suspended from his lower cartilage on his aquiline nose and a large silver medallion of George III from his ancestor who received it from Lord Dorchester, Governor General of Canada. He wore blue breech cloth, red leggings fringed with buckskin, and buckskin moccasins. He was sagacious (wise) and gallant; he was the admiration of all who conversed with him.*

The story of Pontiac's dream, the American victory over the British, the death and suffering of his people, all moved him to action.

He lived on Peche Island about eight miles north of Detroit on the south end of Lake St. Clair, overlooking Lake St. Clair.

Tecumseh denounced the duplicity of the English, telling General Harrison that he was a liar, upon this statement Harrison said he would speak with him no more.

His plan was to assemble an alliance of all remaining Indian people to unite into a single movement, to defend their culture, lives, and homeland.

The Great Comet of 1811 appeared, and Tecumseh – Tekoomse, told the tribes that the comet signaled his coming. The shooting star across the sky proved that the Great Spirit sent him by a sign. There was also a major earthquake about this time.

While he was away rallying support, Tecumseh's brother, The Prophet, was the Chief of the village at Tippacanoe, Indiana. William Henry Harrison came and burned the village out.

William Henry Harrison, his American enemy, said of him: "If it were not for the vicinity of the United States, Tecumseh would perhaps be the founder of an Empire that would rival in glory Mexico or Peru. No difficulties deter him. For four years, he had been in constant motion. You see him today in the Wabash and in a short time, hear of him on the shores of Lake Erie, or Michigan, or on the banks of the Mississippi, and wherever he goes, he makes an impression favorable to his purpose".

In early 1813, a great meeting was held on Walpole Island to rally the troops for the British defense of Canada. Allies came from near and far to protect the land from the Americans. The Indians hoped to receive justice they had sought in vain from the Americans.

Walpole Island was the Great Council place and rallying point for the Indian Allies before wars, and the celebrations place after victories.

Tecumseh and his warriors were great strategists and brave men. He was not a violent, vengeful man. Tecumseh pledged never to torture weak and helpless prisoners all of his life and his braves were always against any kind of cruel treatment. Tecumseh was a man of honor, kept his word, and could lead his tribesmen. He did not drink Fire Water (liquor) after he was injured in the buffalo hunt.

Tecumseh was a brigadier general in the War of 1812. He led the Ojibways from this area. He was the only North American Indian to hold the position in the British forces during the War of 1812. He was strongly against American Expansion. He came to Canada to help the British. Some of his Allies in the States did not want to be involved in the war as they were on peaceful terms with the Americans.

With the capture of Detroit, Tecumseh held the 4th regiment, the same men who had burned his village at Tippecanoe. Tecumseh would not allow the warriors to scalp and murder prisoners, saying it was cowardly. The braves were in awe of him, and scores of prisoners were saved. Tecumseh invariably showed a humane and merciful attitude toward prisoners. He had a great sense of justice.

Chief Roundhead lived at Fort Malden with Tecumseh.

Tecumseh was at the Raisen, Brownstown, and Magauga – "Walk in the Waters" – Village. Tecumseh was a brigadier general in his Majesty's armed forces (Wilson).

Tecumseh fought many battles in Ohio with his warriors to stop American aggression.

When his men and allies were gathered, the nearby inhabitants were stripped of nearly every means of subsistence. In Ohio, north of Fort Meigs, a lame man had hidden his oxen, whom the son eked out a meager living for the family. The boy met Tecumseh one day on his return from the field, he was plowing with the oxen. Tecumseh walked up to him and said I do not make war on a family, explaining that he had need of his oxen, for his men had nothing to eat and were very hungry. The boy spoke up saying he and his family would go hungry if he took the oxen. Tecumseh reminded the boy that, as British Conquerors, the land was theirs. He insisted on having the oxen so his men would not starve. He told the boy he would pay him $100 for the oxen, which was more than they were worth.

Tecumseh had an order written for the boy's payment by the Indian agent Elliott. The colonel refused to pay it. The troubled boy went to Tecumseh, and he had the boy stay the night with him the warriors enjoyed their feast. In the morning, Tecumseh and the boy went to Elliott. Tecumseh said to him "Do you refuse to pay for the oxen I bought?" The colonel said that he did. Tecumseh remonstrated, saying he had promised the boy to pay for the oxen and insisted that he be paid. The colonel yet refused.

Tecumseh shrugged his shoulders and said that he could do as he pleased, but that before he and his warriors had come "to fight the battles of the Great King", they had food to eat for which they had to thank only the Master of Life and their good rifles. Their hunting grounds supplied them with plenty to eat. And he insinuated that they could return to them.

This answer caused a great change of attitude in the colonel, for if the Indian Allies were to follow the great chief and leave, the British would be very vulnerable on the Frontier. The colonel grudgingly paid, counting out some army bills that the Indians called "Rag Money". Tecumseh said, "give me hard money." The colonel went to his chest and counted out one hundred dollars in coins, which the chief gave to the boy. "Now give me, one more, hard dollar", Tecumseh demanded. He hands this also to the boy, telling him that this was for his trouble in getting his money. "Now come boy, I have young men who will ride you home safe.

The war turned on the British; they were back in Canada in retreat at Moraviantown, near now Chatham, Ontario. On October 5, 1813, when the American troops came and the British troops fled, while Tecumseh and his braves held their ground, he had told British General Proctor to "Go put on a petticoat".

Tecumseh, in the lead of the warriors, was mortally wounded and fell while encouraging his braves. He died at the Thames as in his previous vision. His son and others fought on, but eventually seeing Tecumseh, they sought out the forest. He died on October 5, 1813.

The defeat at the Battle of Moraviantown on the Thames was the last blow to the Indians who returned home defeated. Within 35 years, all American Indians were driven off their land and either killed or placed on reservations.

The words of Tecumseh: "So, live your life that fear of death can never enter your heart. Seek to make your life long, and its purpose in the service of your people. Show respect to all people and grovel to none. When you rise in the morning, give thanks for the joy of living."

Tecumseh's body was hidden and guarded to keep it safe, and moved many times by his faithful friend Shawano. He alone prepared the final rites and kept the secret of his bones. The bones of Tecumseh were passed on to his family, who kept them secret and safe.

On August 23, 1941, after 138 years, the bones of the Great Chief and Commander Tecumseh were placed in a monument in his honor on Walpole Island. Hundreds of Canadians and Americans came from near and far to pay homage. The bones of Tecumseh were sealed in a mahogany box and lowered into the cairn erected in his memory. The Soldiers Club were instrumental in this honor of the greatest chief who ever lived East of the Mississippi.

In June 2003, the Chippewa of Kettle Point and Stoney Point, First Nation Reserve near the foot of Lake Huron, placed a monument with four life-sized bronzed statues honoring First Nation veterans of war, one of which was the Great Chief Tecumseh. The others are a servicewoman, a Canadian soldier, and an American. They are set upon a giant turtle representing the Earth and long life of the Native people.

Tecumseh's dream was sovereign and free Anishinabe Nation. His message was unity and resistance to alcohol, dependence on trade goods, and abandonment of their own traditions and practices.

Before the Battle at Chatham, he sang, "Do not give up, should I fall." The warriors lost their reason to fight for their land and culture. The Ojibwe never again went to war against Americans (Ziibiwing).

His last words after having his leg shot off were "Leave me one or two guns. I am going to have a last shot. Be quick and go."

Many volumes have been written about Tecumseh, whole shelves in libraries. For Indians, he would be compared to President George Washington. Thom is a respected historian. His book, *Panther in the Sky*, is a detailed history of Tecumseh's life and battles.

TIPSECO

Chief Jacob Tipseco, Tuipseco, Tisigo, and Tipsikaw – was from the Shiawasee River Basin, Little Long Lake. Tipsikaw was a super athlete of the band near Romeo. He lived at Tipseco Lake. He was a powerful, well-built man, said to be capable, of running down wolves, bears, and deer, his principal feat being to run to a stake, ten rods away and return before a horse and rider could make a like trip. After leaving the country in 1837 or 1838, he returned in 1874 and was found weeping opposite his former village (Western Historical Co.).

TONEDOKANE

Tonedokane or Tonadogonow made visits to St. Clair County, and he was known for his debating powers, acute understanding, and great prowess in the hunt. He was the successor to Chief Neome, the great Chief of the Ojibwe of Southeast Michigan.

WASSO

Wasso was Ojibwe Chief of the Shiawassee area. The city of Owosso is named after him.

WAUBOJEED

Waubojeed – Waubojeeg or "White Fisher" – of Lapointe, Wisconsin was a chief of the Addick or Reindeer totem. He was the father-in-law of John Johnston, Indian Agent, at Sault Ste. Marie and his wife, Jane.

WAWANOSH

Wawanosh – Trach Bin Mindjl – means "one who sails carefully". Also means Egg Bad. The Great Chief of the Ojibwe of Ontario was born in the District of Michipicoten and had to flee pursuit for some offense. Friendly Indians at the Straits of Mackinaw helped him cross as he was pursued to the

Indian village at Black River in Port Huron. These Indians took him across to the Chippewa of Sarnia, who took pity on him. They hid him in a swamp at a small lake and supplied him with food. The pursuers were told that he went on to Walpole Island and left without a trace. The lake was then called Lake Wawanosh.

He possessed knowledge of the English Language, the people adopted him into their tribe, and he made friends with the settlers.

Oketitchick and Kwaind were chiefs at that time, but Wawanosh was told by his French fisherman friend that when the government representative came to distribute presents to the Indians, and the first question asked was who was the Chief, and if Wawanosh told them that he was, his name would be in the records as the Chief Wawanosh. This is how Wawanosh became Chief of the Chippewa of Sarnia. The generous Chippewas graciously accepted him as Chief, and he became a counsellor and director in their affairs.

Wawanosh was the hereditary Chief of the Saugeen, Lake Simcoe, Coldwater, Credit River, and Munceytown on the Thames, which lands were illegally sold to the Crown Government.

Wawanosh married Elizabeth "Eliza" MacConce, "The Queen", sister of Cheebekun, who came from an aristocratic Indian family. Her brother Francis lived in Michigan and was Chief of the Pottawatomis. They had four sons and one daughter. Wawanosh's son, David Wawanosh, succeeded his father, and in 1860, received a medal awarded to Head Chiefs by Prince Albert of Wales when he visited Sarnia on September 13, 1860.

Wawanosh's Christian name was "Joshua"; his totem was the Caribou. The father of Wawanosh was Chief Pukinans. Joshua Wawanosh was chief for 17 years up until 1827.

Back in the 1860s, Chief Joshua attended the Mission Church on the river front. He had a small black pony and a small democrat wagon, but he never sat on the seat; he always squatted in the bottom of the wagon on some straw while his wife and young grandson, Joshua, sat on the seat with Joshua driving.

The old Chief always wore blue-black broadcloth leggings with wide side flaps all the way down. These flaps were beautifully worked in different colors. He generally wore beaded moccasins and a long blouse or shirt reaching almost to his knees. "Many times, when I was a small boy, his wife would call me in and give me a piece of maple sugar. She was a good old soul" (Frank Thomas, Sarnia/Elford).

Chief Wawanosh died May 26, 1871. The name Wawanosh was anglicized to "Wells".

WENEJEUNS
Wenejeuns was a Huron chief (MPHC 11, 1887, Wm. L. Bancroft).

WEMEKEUNS
Wemekeuns was a Huron chief on the St. Clair when the early French settlers made their locations. He was a prophet of the tribe. He had a trio of noses, one small on each side of the large central nose. Before the Revolutionary War, he was asked to urge his band to join the British Allies; he refused saying, "The new Americans would drive their enemies across the ocean and drive their enemies, friends from their hunting grounds."

OTHER CHIEFS
Below are other chiefs in and near Southeast Michigan and the Bluewater area of Lake Huron and Ontario.

Adams, Telford, Stony Point Chief
Agheezhig, Nabun, also Maobbinnakizhick, "Hazy Cloud", Chief at Grand River near Ada (Ewing)
Ahbettuhwahnuhgund, "Half a Cloud", Chief at Kettle Point (Ipperwash Commission of Inquiry, www)
Aish quay go nay be, Swan Creek and Black River Chief
Aissance, Chief at St. Clair, Ontario (Travers, 2015)
Ajaquanon, a Walpole Island Chief
Aksemepemisawtain, Chief in Southwest Ontario, Beaver totem
Allamina, Fox Peace Chief (Plain, 1300 Moons)
Alleyooue, Wyandotte Chief
Amick Kewetasskum, Odawa Chief (Ipperwash Commission of Inquiry, www)
Anenehinth, Chief at Black River, 1825 (NAMMIR.16:396 – 399)
Angouirat, Wyandotte Chief (Voegelin/Tanner, Ethno History)
Aniquiba, Chief at Detroit (Woolworth, Dearborn H.S.)
Annotowin, Ojibwe Chief, Fish totem (Ipperwash Commission Inquiry, www)
Aquinaga, Miami Chief, father of Little Turtle
Ash a tah ne qua beh, "Almost Touches the Clouds", Daniel Whedon, Wheaton, Methodist missionary and preacher near Saginaw
Ashkeebee, last traditional Pottawatomi chief on Walpole Island
Ash Ton Uk Wut, Chief with Maconse, Osage Territory (NAMMIR.47:719 – 722, 1839)
Assinowa, Detroit River Chief
Askiby, Pottawatomi Chief at Detroit (Askin 1 pg. 212)

Assiginack, War Chief of the Ottawa (Schmaltz, pg. 25)
Atironto, Ouendat or Whyandotte War Chief (D. Plain, 1300 Moons)
Atta wa kie, Ottawa Chief at Detroit (Lajuenesse)
Aubauway, Ottawa Chief
Aumichoanaw, Aumichoanaw's Village at Black River, Port Huron, Michigan (Hindsdale, 1926)
Aw be taw quot, Swan Creek and Black River Chief
Aw taw we go nay be, Swan Creek and Black River Chief
Bald Eagle, Gemoaghpenassee Mississauga and Nipissing War Chief (D. Plain/Schmaltz)
Baemassikeh, Saginaw Chief
Ba Mos Eya, "Dried in the Sun", the pox-marked Chief
Bauzhigeeshigwashekum, Pazhegeezegwahekum, "He who makes footsteps in or steps over the sky", Chief at Walpole Island, born on the Maumee (Travers, 2015)
Bawbeese, Pottawatomi Chief
The Beaver, Shawnee Headman Chief near Amherstburg, Ontario
Big Beaver, Kishkaukau's son
Big Cat, Delaware Chief
Black Snake, Chief of the Black River Indians, father-in-law of Black Duck, related to John Riley
Blackbeard, Shawnee Headman, Chief near Amherstburg, Ontario
Blackfish, Principal Peace Chief of the Shawnee at Chilicothe, adopted Tecumseh and his brothers and sister upon their father's death in war. Thom
Blackhoof – Catahecassa, Shawnee Subchief (Thom)
Blue Jacket, Weyapier Senwaw, Shawnee, lived below Detroit, Great War Chief of the Miami
Breaker in Pieces, Delaware Chief in Ohio (Thom)
Buckongahelas (Wyandottenation.org, www)
Buckwheat, Walpole Island Chief (Travers)
The Buffalo, Shawnee Headman Chief near Amherstburg, Ontario
Buneuairear, Saugeen River Chief
Cam Comme Nania, Chief at Thames River
Camcommenarir, Chief at Chenail Escarte (Travers)
Campanisse, Ottawa Chief at Detroit (Plain, 1300 Moons)
Can E Waup, Saginaw Chief (ARCOIA 1837:532, Clifton Notes)
Captain Ironsides, Meass, "Walk in the water", Supt. of Indian Affairs, a descendent of Tecumseh
Captain Johnny, Shawnee Headman Chief near Amherstburg, Ontario

Ottissippi

Capac, Manco, Chippewa Chief, descended from the old Peruvian line of Emperors, the town of Capac was named for him (Jenks, History of St. Clair County)
Captain Pipe, Chief of the Wolf or Monsey Tribe
Captain Simonton, Saginaw Chief (ARCOIA 1837:532, Clifton Notes)
Catfish (see Taytaymaygasson and Wasson below)
Caw me squaw bay no kay, Swan Creek and Black River Chief
Cha Bou Quai, Chippewa Chief, Detroit River
Chamintawaa, Ottawa Civil Chief
Chaoge Man Shaiowkima, Chief of Southwest Ontario, Beaver totem
Chase, Henry P., Pahtahquahong, "Coming thunder", born 1817 and died at Sarnia in 1900. A Mississauga Ojibwe, interpreter, office holder, minister, and merchant. He was raised by Wm. Case, Superintendent of Methodist Missions in the Canadian conference. Henry was an interpreter at Port Sarnia among the Lake St. Clair Ojibwe and an accountant for 13 years. He was a Methodist preacher in 1856 at the St. Clair Mission, which he served on both sides of the St. Clair River. He served in the Anglican Church from 1887 to 1896. He was president and grand general of the Indian Council in 1874.
He went to London, England in 1876, 1881, and 1885 to gather support for his people.
Chawme, Chawne, Chief and Head Speaker at Bear Creek (Travers/Ipperwash Commission Inquiry, www)
Cheebican, Chief at Sarnia, Caribou totem (Plain/Ipperwash Commission)
Chemick, son of Kishkaukau
Cheneebeesh, Chief Mississauga Ojibwa (Schmaltz)
Chicagau, Agapit, Chief and Leader of the Mitchigamea, Chicago means "garlic"
Chichikateco, War Chief of the Miami at Round Lake or Lake St. Clair (D. Plain, 1300 Moons)
Chikatayan, Eagle totem, Chief (Ipperwash Commission Inquiry, www)
Chimegas, the Wheatons, sons of Chimegas were Nathan, Samuel, and Daniel, who were local preachers on the Flint River
Chiminatawa, Chief near Windsor, Ontario (Lajuenesse)
Chuscom, Chusco, a converted priest of the Ottawa
Cobmoosa, Cub bah moo sa, "The Great Walker", Ottawa Chief at Grand River (Ewing)
Coon, Saginaw Chief at Kinodah, Saginaw Chippewa Village (Eckert)
De Sharemoi, Chief at Moore Reserve
Deyentete, a Huron Chief of Detroit
Dow Yen Tet, Huron Chief, Detroit River

Duyenty, Huron Chief at Detroit (Lajuenesse)
Dutton, Thomas, Sah quh che wa o sa, chief and reverend, Methodist preacher at Taymouth, Michigan
Dutton, America, Luke Hart, born 1777 – 1875, last of the warrior chieftains of the Chippewa
Eastman, Charles, Sioux, raised in Ontario by the Ojibwe. He became a physician and helped his people on the Pine Ridge Reservation. He wrote many books about Indian life and was an inspiration for the Boy Scouts of America with his "Scout Talks". He lived in Ontario, Canada in his later years, and then in Detroit with his son.
Egouchaway, Egouch ae i ouay, Egouch E Ouay, an Ottawa Principal Chief (MPHC #20, pg. 305/lajuenesse)
Ekuschuwe, Agushewa, Augooshaway, Ottawa Chief at Detroit
En Dah In, Ottawa Chief, Detroit River
Endashin, Ottawa Chief at Detroit (Lajuenesse)
Eqcesbawa, Ottawa Chief, Detroit River
E Sha Ha, Detroit River
Essebalc, Chippewa Chief at Detroit (Lajuenesse)
Essebamee, Chippewa Chief, Detroit River
Eskebee, Eshkibie, Pottawatomi Chief at Detroit (Askin, vol. 1, pg. 175)
Fisher, a half blood-Indian, married Francis Macompte's sister, took his own life at Salt River Reserve
Gaiash, Chief at Moore Reserve
Galash, Chief at Detroit (Lajuenesse)
Gayoshk, St. Clair, Ontario; Chief Travers
Gemoaghpenassee, Chief Missisauga Ojjibwe (Schmaltz, pg., 26)
Genway Ku Shook, Chief at Black River, 1835, son of Ogedick (NAMMIR. 36:210 - 212)
Gould, Gerald, Chief of the Swan Creek and Black River Confederated Ojibwe tribes of Michigan at Saginaw
Gould, Harold, Sub Chief of Ojibwe, Swan Creek and Black River
Grand Blanc, Sawanabenase, Pechegabua, Chippewa Chief
Greenbird, Joshua, Ojibwe, first elected Chief of the Walpole Island bands in 1878
Greenskye, Simon Pokagon Greensky, Methodist pastor around the Saginaw Basin for 42 years
Guyash, Chief of Bear Creek (Sydenham) River at Amherstburg (Plain)
Hassaki, Grand Chief of Ottawa (Plain, 1300 Moons)
Hawquosseau, Eagle Tribe Chief at Detroit River

Ottissippi

Hiawatha, the Iroquois name Henry Schoolcraft used in his book; the stories, however, were Chippewa-Ojibwe
Hiquelow, Bear totem, Detroit River
Ishtonaquette, Chief from Lake St. Clair (Schmaltz)
Isononcainen, Chief near Windsor, Ontario (Lajuenesse)
Iyonayotha, Wyandot Chief
Jackson, Andrew, Chief of Black River and Swan Creek people, Saginaw 1893 (LROIA 32393 – 1893)
Jacobs, Burton, Chief in 1964 when self-government replaced the Indian Agent, who had power to overrule the Council
Jacobs, Francis Wilson, Wahbahnoosay, school teacher, Chief of the Ontario Ojibwe for 14 years to 1884, half-brother of Rev. Peter Jones
Johnston, John, Chief at Stony Point (Ipperwash Commission of Inquiry Historical background, www)
Jones, Peter, Kahkewaquonaby, "Sacred Waving Feathers", Desagondensta, "He stands people on their feet", Mohawk, a Metis preacher, translated the Bible and hymns into his Ojibwe Native tongue. He was a well-known preacher at the St. Clair Mission in Sarnia, Ontario, serving on both sides of the river in the Methodist Church to the Native Americans. Peter Jones was taught by and raised by William Case, the Father of Methodism in Canada and Michigan.
Jorihoha, Chief near Windsor Ontario (Lajuenesse)
Kage Kumego, "Otter", Chief at Moore Reserve
Kageskaiua, Chief at Moore Reserve
Kah ka gezhigk, Chief at Sarnia (Ipperwash Commission Inquiry, www)
Kalwahnee, Saginaw Chippewa Chief
Kanobe, Chief of the Swan Creek bands of Indians, from Romeo, Michigan, under Francis Macompte (Maconnce), accused of abducting the Finch child whom he loved
Kaquta, Alexander, Saugeen River Chief
Kawachewan, Ottawa Chief
Kawgagezhic, "Forever Sky", brother of Neome, who spoke in the formal Councils at the Treaty of Saginaw in 1819, Diba Jimooyung, Saginaw Chippewa
Kaw gay ge zhick, Saginaw Chief
Kayask, Bear Creek Chief, Beaver totem (Ipperwash Commission of Inquiry, www)
Kay bay guo um, Swan Creek and Black River Chief
Kay bay yawsigay, Yaw bass, Chief at Bear Creek, Caribou totem (Ipperwash Commission of Inquiry. www)
Kaygegaybe, Payquotuch, Grand River Chief (Ewing)

Kaynotang, War Chief from Bear Creek
Kay Yaskkonse, Chief at Southwest Ontario
Keewaygeeshig, Keewageezhig, signer of the Treaty of 1836, ceding Black River Reservation to the U.S Government
Kee No Chamek, Great Chief of the Chippewa, built a very long raft as a Fire Raft to burn British vessels (Parkman, 1763)
Kenewahbay, Chief near Ipperwash (Ipperwash Commission, www)
Kensauanse, Wolf totem, Detroit River
Keokuk, War Chief, Sax and Fox
Keriay Geezhig, Chief of Swan Creek, Black River, 1836 (NAMMIR.37:116)
Kewadin, "Northwind", Ojibwe Chief and Holy Man
Ke Wayte Nan, Detroit River
Kewayosh, first Chief of the Amalgated Ojibway and Pottawatomi Walpole Band Council in 1940
Kiashke, Chief at Chenail Escarte
Kieuejiwen, Chief at Moore Reserve
Kingewano, Chief of Wolf Tribe at Detroit (Lajuenesse)
Kinisshikapoo, a Southern Ojibwe Chief
Kinonge (Plain 1300 Moons)
Kinousaki, an Ottawa Chief at Detroit (Tanner/Voegelin)
Kiosk, Chippewa Chief
Kishkiwabik, Chief of the Ojibwe (Schmaltz)
Kishko, Chief at the Thames River
Kisis, Ouabimanitou, White Spirit, Mascouten Chief at Detroit (Cleland)
Kitchianaquet, Crane totem, Chief at Chenail Escarte (Ipperwash Commission of Inquiry. www)
Kitchemughgua, Kitchemighqua, Chief at Big Bear Creek and Chenail Escarte (Plain/Travers)
Kitche Ne Gon, "Grand Sable"
Ki wish e ouan, Ottawa Chief at Detroit (Lajuenesse)
Kiwitchiwene, Chief of Eagle Tribe near Windsor, Ontario (Lajuenesse)
Kiyoshk, Chief at St. Clair, Ontario (Travers)
Kondiaronk, Kondorant, "Le Rat" ("The Rat" – Muskrat, Cleland), Wyandotte War Chief, precursor of Pontiac and Tecumseh. His father was Atironto. He had much diplomatic skill in confederating the tribes. A Christian convert, who preached at Michilimackinac, he led the Huron, Petun, and Tionontati against the Iroquois. No Indian had ever possessed greater merit, a finer mind, more valor, prudence, or discernment in understanding to those with whom he had to deal (Parkman).

Ottissippi

Koutache, a Missisauga Chief (Plain, 1300 Moons)
Kowgisawis, Saugeen River Chief
Kuit, Mascouten Chief (Plain, 1300 Moons)
Lago, a Pottowatomi Chief when the Huron were removed by the Iroquois
La Jes, "Big Gate", Northern Chief who at Detroit as a boy shot a soldier at the gate of the fort, later becoming an American captain under George Clark. (Thom, Long Knife)
Lamyma, Fox Peace Chief at Detroit (Cleland)
Langlade, Charles Michel Mouet, Akewaugeketauso, Great Ottawa War Chief from Sault Ste. Marie, leader in many attacks, fought with French, , changed to the British, was interpreter for the King, lived near Malden, Ontario, Canada. He was born at Fort Michilimackinac. Charles was a fur trader in Michilimackinac, Wisconsin territory and the Grand River Valley.
La Pesant, Great Ottawa Chief of Missilimackinac and Detroit (Plain, 1300 Moons)
Laturno, Principal Chief of the Sotu (Saulteur) tribe (Plain)
Leatherlips, Wyandotte Chief, Thom
Le Blanc, Wyandotte Chief
Le Brochet (Plain, 1300 Moons)
La Forest, first Chief of the Wyandotte (Plain, 1300 Moons)
Le Tourneau, "Blackbird"
Little Bear, Okemos, Chief of Chippewa Nations (see below in Okemos)
Little Cedar, Meuetugesheck, Chippewa Chief
Little Elk, Elijah Thomas, champion log burler from Quanicassee, Michigan Thumb, married Betty Pontiac
Little Pine, Chief (Travers)
Little Turtle, (called by white men), really means Great Turtle, (Pokagon, Simon, 1899), Michikinikwa, Michikinakwa, Miami Chief, defeated the U.S. Army with 1,100 men in two major battles St. Clairs, and General Harmars. His father was Chief Aquinaga. Little Turtle did not like to see people enslaved and mistreated. He captured the Blacks and brought them to hide at present Fort Wayne, Indiana. Blacks lived with the Miami Indians, and he wanted to protect them.
Machaba, Jacob, Chief of Black River and Swan Creek People at Saginaw, 1893 (LROIA 32393 – 1893)
Machonce, Machonce's village was at Northwest Lake St. Clair, above the Clinton River (Hindsdale)
Maconse, A She Taw Naw Quot, Muckema, father and son were the Chiefs of the Swan Creek bands of Indians at Salt Point, Salt River, in southeast St. Clair

County, Michigan. Maconse moved 51 of his people to Kansas during the Indian Removal.
Macquettoquett, Macquettequet, "Little Bear", Ojibwe Chief
Madjeckewis, "Bad Bird", Ojibwe Chief
Macquiquiovis, Great Chief of the Saulteaux Ojibwe (Hotchkiss)
Madwayosh, Anishinabe Chief, Saugeen (Travers)
Main Poc, Shiata, Pottawatomi War Chief, fought with Tecumseh at Malden (Eckert). "Withered Hand", Chief of Shawan, Thom
Maishcaw, John, Ottawa Chief, West Michigan (Ewing)
Makatay Kegigo, Catfish, Southwest Ontario Chief
Makouandeby, Head Chief and speaker of the Illinois at Detroit (Plain, 1300 Moons)
Mamaushegauta, "Bad Legs", Chippewa Chief
Maness, Elijah, Stony Point Chief (Travers 2015)
Manitoogeezhiks, Chief at Saginaw Village a large and very prosperous village called Saugenong, Diba Jimooyung, Saginaw Chippewa
Makataykegigo, Catfish, Sarnia Chief (Ipperwash Commission of Inquiry, www)
Manitou, Ottawa Chief
Marass, Elijah, Sarnia Chief (Ipperwash Commission of Inquiry)
Maskeaash, "Falling Snow", also Muskyash, Messkias, Masqyash, Mesik, Miskeass, Mesgish, Megish, signer of the 1807 treaty of Detroit where the southeast quarter of Michigan was ceded to the U.S. Government, signed the 1795 Treaty Deed granting 990-year lease to Harsens Island to Bernardus Harsen, Joseph May, and Jacob Bogart, was killed by Captain Blake in the War of 1812 at Lundy's Lane, grandfather of Granny Rodd and Naykeeshig
Musqueash, Chief who lived in the vicinity, of now Port Huron, Michigan, Musqueash died soon after the War of 1812 and was buried on the Indian Reservation north of Mt. Clemons, Michigan (John Askin Papers vol. 1, 180/Jenks vol. 1, 148, History of St. Clair County MI, 1912)
Makisabi, Great War Chief, Pottawatomi (Plain, 1300 Moons)
Man Do Ao, Huron Chief at Detroit River
Mash Kee Yosh, Chief in Saginaw area
Matchiquis, Chief near Detroit, friend of Colonel De Peyster, near Detroit (Askin, vol. II, pg. 407) Ottawa Chief and British General, legendary Captain in taking Mackinac in 1763. Thom, Long Knife
Maug gich a way, Ottawa Chief at Detroit (Lajuenesse)
Mauk Saub, Cass River Chief (NAMMIR45;147, 148)
Mawbese, Mawbeece, Chief in West Michigan, (Ewing)

Maw che che won, Swan Creek and Black River Chief
May howwain, Chief at Chenail Escarte (Ipperwash Commission of Inquiry. www)
May Tisy, Swan Creek, Black River Chief, 1836 (NAMMIR.37:116)
Mayzin, Chief at Black River (Plain)
Measita, Chippewa Chief
Mechegegoona, "Fish Hawk", Ojibwe War Chief at Sault Ste. Marie, great friend of Young Gull. (Plain, 1300 Moons)
Mejlaquit, Majawqut, Chief at Black River in 1825 (NAMMIR.16:396 – 399)
Men Couts, Chief of Black River and Swan Creek people (Ziibiwing)
Meng Da Hai, Huron Chief, Detroit River
Menoquot, Menoquots Village was on the Cass River in the Thumb of Michigan
Mesass, Chippewa Chief, signer of Treaty of Fort Harmar
Mesackwangie, Pottawatomi Chief at Detroit (Askin, vol. 1, pg. 175)
Meshike waybig, "Red Sky", Mesquahwegezhigk, Missquah wegezhigk, Ojibwe Chief, son of Animikance (Annamakance, "Little Thunder"), War Chief at Black River, Saulteaux, Aamjiwnaang, Oak clan totem (Plain/ Ipperwash Commission, www.; Plain)
Meshkemau, Chief at Miami Bay, Lake Erie
Mesh Qui Ga Boui, Chippewa Chief, Detroit River
Metiewabe, Saugeen River Chief
Metigoob, Chief at Sarnia (Travers)
Mettawansh, Saugeen River Chief
Met Te G Chin, Detroit River
Meuetugesheck, Little Cedar, Chippewa Chief
Mexicinny, Mickseninne, Mixcinninny, "Young Chief" or Wampum Man, Chief at Bowting Village (Grand Rapids), Grand River Ottawas (Ewing)
Michipichy, Ourante Sous, Wyandotte Chief
Michome, "Little Bear", a Chief of the Ojibwe Nation (Moore)
Mikinak, Great Ottawa Chief at Detroit and Saginaw
Miksaba, Pottawatomi Head Chief
Minewe Weh, Ojibwe War Chief of the Lake Indians
Minnonequotm, Minnonequotm, Hereditary Chief (Mitts, D.)
Miniwoa, Pottawatomi Chief at Detroit in 1763 (Woolworth of Dearborn Historical Society)
Miott, Chippewa Chief
Miscocomon, "Red Knife", Ojibwe Chief from the Thames
Mishibizhe, a Chief of the Ontario Ojibwe in 1844

Miskisabet, Pottawatomi Chief at Detroit (Askin, vol. 1, pg. 212)
Miskousouath, Fox Head Chief (Plain, 1300 Moons)
Miskouaki, Ottawa Chief at Detroit (DePeyster, Miscellanies by an Officer, www)
Misquecapowee, Chief at Detroit (Lajuenesse)
Mitchewass, Chief at Thames River and Chenail Escarte
Miz co be na sa, "Red Bird", Saginaw Chippewa Chief
Mokeetchewan, Chief in Southwest Ontario, Eagle totem
Mokegewan, Mokeetchewan, Eagle totem, Chief (Ipperwash Commission Inquiry, www)
Monguagon, Monguagon Village was south of Wyandotte, Michigan
Monimack or Cat Fish, Ojibwe Chief
Monseytown or Munsee Town, Lower Huron River
Moran, a Pottawatomi Chief who lived at the mouth of the Macon – Swan Creek (Fuller)
Mshinikaibek, Chief in West Ontario
Muack Esaub, Chief at River Rouge (NAMMIR. 38:33, 34)
Muckamoot, a Pottawatomi Chief who lived on Muscamoot Bay near Lake St. Clair
Muchatuagie, Chief at Bear Creek/Thames (Travers 2015)
Muck Kuck Cosh, Saginaw Chief (NAMMIR.46:609)
Mushyash Jun, Chief at Belle River and St. Clair River (Askin, vol. 1)
Musquackie, "Yellowhead", Chief of Lake Simcoe Ojibwe (Schmaltz)
Nahnebahwequa, "Standing Upright Woman", Catherine Bunch-Brown, Ojibwe spokeswoman and Christian missionary (Schmaltz)
Nah tachi ke me, Chief of the Saginaw Chippewa (Bentley Library, UOM/Hess family of Saginaw)
Nakatewaquit, Chief at Detroit and Moore Reserve
Nanamakeak, Chippewa Chief, signer of Fort Harmar Treaty
Nangy, Chief at Moore Reserve
Nanck che gaw me, Saginaw Chief
Naow Is E Kan, Chief in Osage Country, 1839 (NAMMIR.47:719 – 722)
Nashan, Chief at Moore Reserve
Natawuato, Huron Chief
Natournee, Chief at Lower St. Clair reserve, Moore. Travers 2015)
Natquato, Nataquato, a Huron Chief well-known on the St. Clair River
Nau bowe, Nabbawe, or Kitschi-Makongs, Beaver totem, Ojibwe Chief at Bear Creek (Ipperwash Commission of Inquiry, www)

Ottissippi

Nau Chi Go Mee San Wan Ban Mo Ca Couch, old Chief Speaker (NAMMIRY2-319,320)
Nawa Cissy Nabe, Chief at Thames River
Nawash, Neywash, Head Chief of the Saugeen Ojibwe, south of Georgian Bay
Naw aug, Peter, Chief at Stony Point (Travers 2015)
Naw Gaw Nee, Peter, Chief at Long Lake
Nawme, Pattawatimas Chief
Naw taw way, Saginaw Chief
Nawwcissy nabe, Chief at Chenail Escarte (Travers 2015)
Naw we ge zhick, Saginaw Chief
Naykeeshig, Naykeezhig, Nay Kee Shick, Nay Gee Zhig, Nay ge zhick, "Young Snake", grandson of Maskeash, cousin of Granny Rodd, an employee of Judge Bunce, one of Bunce's Indians, Black River hereditary Head Chief, Son of the Snake, Chief of the Black River Chippewa
Nayquoscan, Daniel Field, Chief of Eagle tribe at Detroit (Lajuenesse)
Neanigo, Chief at the Fork (Lajuenesse)
Nebanagoshing, Joseph Sayers, Chief
Negawbe, Ottawa Chief West Michigan (Ewing)
Negesi, Snake, Negesick (Ziibiwing), Saginaw Chippewa
Nemekeum, Nemekeum, Huron Chief, had a trio of noses – one small on either side of a large central nose – was well-known of the St. Clair River
Nesowagie, Pottawatomi Chief at Detroit (Askin, vol. 1, pg. 175)
Nesowaghquat, Pottawatomi Chief at Detroit (Askin, vol. 1, pg. 175)
New Corn, a Great Pottawatomi Chief from Detroit to Lake Michigan (Fuller)
Nia ne go, Ottawa Chief at Detroit (Lajuenesse)
Nickeson, Pottawatomi Chief at Detroit (Askin, vol. 1, pg. 175)
Niibaakhom, "Night Thunderer", Ojibwe Chief
Ninevois, Chief of the Chippewa Nation
Ningweegon, "The Wing", leader of the Ojibwe band on the Huron – Clinton – River, who was friendly to Governor Hull
Ninnewa, Pattawatimas Chief
Niquelon, Chief of Ottawa Bear tribe at Detroit (Lajuenesse)
Nisquleawpawn, Detroit River
Nockchegawme, Chief at Shebeon and Sebewaing, Huron County
Nocktschikome, Chief at Shebahyonk, Saginaw
Noname, Pattawatimas Chief
Noonday, Pottawatomi Chief of Ottawas at Grand River District, died in 1855 at almost 100 years old. (Ewing)
Noonday, Amos, preacher from Saganing

Normee, Chippewa Chief, (Eckert 1992, "A sorrow in or heart")
Notaquoto, short, ugly, and powerful, was well-known to early settlers
Notawanee, Chief at St. Clair, Ontario (Travers)
Ocaita, Chief
Oge-bick-in, Ojibwe Chief in Sarnia area, Carribou totem (Ipperwash Commission Inquiry, www)
Ogemaw Ki Keto, Saginaw Chief, signed the 1819 Treaty of Saginaw
Ogontz, Indian Catholic priest at Detroit (Bierce, Historical Reminiscences of Cuyahoga Moravian)
Ogotig, Chief at St. Clair River (Plain)
Ogousse, Ottawa Chief
Ohawwanoo-Chemoke o mon, Kettle Point Chief (Ipperwash Commission of Inquiry)
Ojaouanon, a Chief of Walpole Island
O Kee Tick, Black River Chief (NAMMIR.43:103)
Okeya, Pottawatomi Chief at Detroit (Askin, vol. 1, pg. 175)
Okitchinoyon, Chief near Windsor, Ontario (Lajuenesse)
Omejawennong Que, Black River Chief (NAMMIR.43:103)
Omuhwenahsawn, "He Rushes Upon Him", a Chief of the Bear totem (D. Plain 1300 Moons)
Onabemamtou, Mascouten Chief (Plain, 1300 Moons)
Onanguisse, Pottawatomie Chief (Plain, 1300 Moons)
Old Salt, became a preacher
Old Toga, Chief Tonquish, Pottawatomi of the River Rouge, village named for him, Tonquish's Village (Hindsdale, 1925)
Onagan, Ottawa Chief at Detroit (Lajuenesse)
Onanguisse
Orontony (Nicholas), Detroit Wyandotte Chief, chief in Sandusky Ohio and Indiana
Osawanequat, Pottawatomi Chief at Detroit (Askin vol. 1, pg. 175)
O saw waw bun, Saginaw Chief
Osawweb, Chief at Sarnia, Turtle totem (Ipperwash Commission of Inquiry. www)
O Saw a wip, Chippewa Chief in Southwest Ontario (Ipperwash Commission of Inquiry. www)
Oscawuassanu, "Young Boy", Ojibwe Chief
Otawaun, Chief Speaker Saginaw (ARCOIA 1837:532 Clifton notes)
Ot taw ace, Saginaw Chief
Otter, Daniel (Travers, 2015)

Ottissippi

Oua ouia tenne, Pottawatomi Chief at Detroit (Askin, vol. 1, pg. 212)
Ouenemek, Pottawatomie War Chief (Plain, 1300 Moons)
Ouit A Nis Sa, Chippewa Chief, Detroit River
Oulouigoushquin, Chief and friend of Colonel De Peyster, near Detroit (Askin, vol. II, pg. 407)
Outoutagan, Jean Le Blanc, Ottawa Spokesman (Plain, 1300 Moons)
Pabame, Grand River Ottawa Chief
Pandiac, Chief who signed McKee Treaty 116, south side of the Detroit River and Boise Blanc Island, in 1786, possibly Pontiac
Pasheskiskaquashcum, Bauzhigiezhigwaeshikum, at Springwells, near Detroit.
Paudash, Chief of Missisauga Ojibwe (Schmaltz, pg.26)
Paushquash, Chippewa Chief, signer of Treaty of Fort Harmar
Pawasicko, Chippewa Chief, signer of Treaty of Fort Harmar
Pay baw maw she, Swan Creek and Black River Chief
Pay me quo ung, Swan Creek and Black River Chief
Pay me saw aw, Swan Creek and Black River Chief
Pay Pah Moushee, Chief at River Rouge (NAMMIR.38:33, 34)
Payshawsegay, Ottawa Chief (Ewing)
Pay she nin ne, Swan Creek and Black River Chief
Pazhekezhiquasnkum, Pazhekezkqueshcum, Chief at Walpole Island (Canada West Last Frontier)
Pazhedezhikquashhkum, "He who makes footsteps in the sky", Chief at Walpole
Pebamuchketac, Pottawatomi Chief at Detroit (Askin, vol. 1, pg. 175)
Pecan, Miami Chief (Cleland)
Pee taw waw naw quot, Chippewa, Black River Chief (NAMMIR.43:211, 212 1837)
Pegahmagabow, Francis, Binaaswi, "The Wind that blows off", WWI unsung hero, "Peggy", the most decorated Indigenous soldier in Canada's history, the deadliest sniper, scout, and messenger of WWI, having 378 kills and 300 captures. He rose to the rank of Company Sergeant – Major, several ranks above Corporal. He came home to discrimination. He was Supreme Chief of the Ojibwe Nation of Wasauksing, now Shewanaga First Nation, Caribou totem, and worked for his people. He is honored with a bronze monument at Parry Sound on June 23, 2016, on National Aboriginal Day in Canada.
Pem e quo hung, Pay me quo ung, Chief of the Swan Creek and Black River bands, at Swan Creek on Saginaw Bay
Pemacegis, Chief Saginaw (ARCOIA 1837:532, Clifton Notes)
Pemoussa, Great Fox War Chief (Plain, 1300 Moons)

Pe Nash, Detroit River
Pe nay se waw be, Saginaw Chief
Penayse, Foster, Chief at Grand River, Ottawa (Ewing)
Pendalouan, Great Ottawa Chief in West Michigan (Ewing)
Penence-o-quin, Turtle totem, Chief (Ipperwash Commission Inquiry, www)
Penesewah, Pemuse, Ojibwe Chief at Bear Creek (Ipperwash Commission of Inquiry, www)
Penemou, Pottawatomi Chief at Detroit (Askin, vol. 1, pg. 175)
Petahgegeeshig, "Between Day", Ojibwe, Swan Creek
Petahwegeeshig, Lake St. Clair War Chief (D. Plain)
Petaudig, Chief Black River People, 1825 (NAMMIR.16:396 – 399)
Petawick, Ojibwe Chief at Sarnia, Caribou totem (Ipperwash Commission of Inquiry, www)
Peterwegeshig, "In between Dawn", Walpole Island Chief (Travers, 2015)
Petosee, "The Blackbird"
Pet To E Kie Sic, Petokiesic, "A Middle Cloud", the Great Chief of the Walpole tribe and sole Monarch of Walpole Island
Pet way we tum, Swan Creek and Black River Chief
Pewanakum, Chippewa Chief, signer of the Treaty of Fort Harmer
Peewanshemenogh, Chippewa Chief
Petwegeeshik, Ojibway, last traditional Chief of Walpole Island
Pe Way, "A Hare", Pe Way Ahore, Head Chief of the Pottawatomies
Peyskiky, Chief at Chenail Escarte (Travers, 2015)
Pilcher, Elijah, Chief of the Black River and Swan Creek at Saginaw, 1893 (LROIA 32393 – 1893)
Pinache, Pottawatomi Chief at Detroit (Askin, vol. 1, pg. 212)
Pinessiwagum, Chief in Southwest Ontario, Turtle totem
Pisortim, Turner, Chief at Moore
Plain, David, Native author from Sarnia, Ontario. Author of 6+ award winning books. Descendant of Animikance – "Thunder" – and Kioscance – "Young Gull", "Red Sky", and "On the Plain", great Ojibwe Chiefs at Sault Ste. Marie and Black River at the foot of Lake Huron and Aamjiwnaang Territory.
Plain, Fred, Chief at Sarnia (N. A. Plain)
Plain, Nicholas, "On the Plain", Chippewa Chief at Sarnia, author, preacher, father of David Plain
Pokagon, Simon Leopold, Pottawatomi Chief. Pokagon means "Shield or Defense", or "Club". Pokagon once owned the site where Chicago now stands. He was Catholic and fought for the Pottawatomi lands near the St. Joseph River in Southwest Michigan and Northwest Indiana. A writer and speaker who spoke

four languages. His people kept a small piece of their original lands, and never removed. He was the first Indian, in the White House, visiting President Lincoln.

Pooquigauboawie, Chippewa Chief

Poquaquet, "The Ball", Chippewa Chief

Poquash, Chief near Windsor, Ontario (Lajuenesse)

Poshetonse, Caribou totem, Southwest Ontario Chief (Ipperwash Commission Inquiry, www)

Po Taw Waw Naw Quot, Black River Chippewa Chief (NAMMIR.43:431 – 438)

Pshikie, Chief at Detroit (Lajuenesse)

Pukenai, "The Ball", Ojibwe Chief (Ipperwash Commission, www)

Puckenas, "The Spark of Fire", Pockenaise, Pukinins, Puckenese, Chippewa Chief, Caribou totem, father of Wawanosh (Plain/Ipperwash Commission of Inquiry. www)

Quakegman, "Feather", War Chief of the St. Clair Ontario band

Quakgwan, Quoikeegon, Ojibwe Chief at Stony Point, Beaver dodem (Travers)

Quay kegoin, River Au Sable Chief (Ipperwash Commission of Inquiry, www)

Quakegwon, Wuaikeegon, Beaver totem, Chief at Sarnia, signed the Ontario Treaty of 1827

Quaykigouins, Sauble band Chief

Quaquakebookgk, "Revolution", War Chief, Swan Creek and Salt River bands

Queoonequetwabaw, Ojibwe Chief

Quiconquish, Chippewa Chief

Quinipeno, Mississauga Chief (Schmaltz)

Quinousaki, Ottawa Chief

Quiouigoushquin, Chief (Askin, vol. 1, pg. 407)

Quit a nis a, Chief at Detroit (Lajuenesse)

Quitchonequit, "Big Cloud", Ojibwe Chief

Red Bird, Miz Co Be Na Sa, Saginaw Chippewa Chief

Red Sky, Oak clan totem, son of "Little Thunder" – Animicance Misquahwegezhigk, Black River War Chief, Saulteaux (D. Plain)

Riashke, Chief at Chenail Escarte (Travers)

Richardville, Chief of the Miamis, Thumb of Michigan area.

Rodd, Charles, Ma, Lai, Sha Ban, "Will not go", Chief at Saginaw

Rodd, Peter, Saginaw

Roundhead, Ustaiechta, Wyandotte Chief, war hero who fought with Tecumseh

Rou Nia Hy Ra, Huron Chief, Detroit River

Ruhumatt, "One Can'e", Chief at Moore Reserve
Sahgimah, Sagamah, Grand Chief and great leader of the Ottawa
Saganish, Chief at Chenail Escarte
Sagimaw, Pottawatomi Chief
Saginaw, Chief
Saguina, "Mister Blackbird", Chief of a great band of warriors in the northern region of St. Joseph. (Thom, Long Knife)
Sahenteskon, Chief at Moore Reserve
Sanaban, Chief at Saginaw
Sandusky, Ot San Doos Ke, Otsaandosti, Huron meaning is "Cold Water" (Chaput)
Sasteradzy, Sastaretsi, or Sasterexy, "The Rat", hereditary Chief of the Tobacco-Petun (Huron), Deer clan totem, Chief of the Detroit Wyandotte (Huron) (Parkman)
Sastareche, Sastaretsy, Chief of Hurons at River Cannard (MPHC #20, pg. 305)
Sas Ta Rit Sie, Huron Chief, Detroit River
Sauganash, Billy (Thomas) Caldwell, captain of the Indian Department of Canada. (Ewing, Wallace, Footprints)
Sawgamaw, Ottawa Chief
Saw gaw che way o say, Saginaw Chief
Saw Gee, Head of the tribe, a Walpole warrior
Sca Hou Mat, Huron (Wyandotte) Chief, Detroit River
Skush, Pattawatimas Chief
Segangewan, Chippewa Chief
Seginsavin, Seginsisins, Seginsavin's, Seginsiwin's, on the River Rouge (Treaty 1807), village on south of Clinton River (Hindsdale, 1925)
Sekhas, Sekahas, Head Chief of the Thames, Chippewa War Chief over Mississauga Ojibwa warriors from the Thames River and Kettle Creek Ojibwa
Shaboque, John Clark, Chippeawas Chief at Detroit (Lajuenesse)
Shaboqui, Chippewa Chief at Detroit River
Shaganash, Saganash, Turtle totem, Ojibwe Chief at Chenail Escarte (Ipperwash Commission, www)
Shashawinibisie, Crane totem Chief (Ipperwash Commission Inquiry, www)
Shavehead, Pottawatomi Chief
Shawawanoo, Ashkebahgahnequod, also Chemokomon or John Big Knife, Kettle and Stony Point Chief (Gulewitsch/Plain/Travers)
Shawbequoung, Moses, "Wings", Ottawa Chief at Grand River, son of Penayse (Ewing)
Shaweny-penince, St. Clair, Ontario Chief (Travers, 2015)

Shawnoo, Isaac, Chief at Kettle Point (Ipperwash Commission of Inquiry Historical background, www)
Sha woa ni ssey, Saginaw Chief in 1778, Shiawasee River believed to be named after him
Shawon Epuaysee, Chief at River Rouge (NAMMIR.38:33,34)
Shawshawwanipenisee, Shashawinibisie, Chief at Walpole (Ipperwash Commission of Inquiry. www)
Shaw shaw way nay beece, Saginaw Chief
She Bense, Detroit River
Shebona, Shabonna, Charbonneas, Shebbiona, Shawanoem, descended from Pontiac, Aide De Camp to Tecumseh and, who kept his grave secret and safe. (See "Shawano" above.) Also called Charcoal Burner
She Hou Wa Te Mon, Huron Chief, Detroit River
Shemmendock, Ottawa Chief at Chenail Escarte
Shenabey, Chief of Black River People, 1825 (NAMMIR.16:396 – 399)
Shimindock, Ottawa Chief
Shinekosche, Ottawa Chief, West Michigan (Ewing)
Shingwauk, "Little Pine", Ojibwe War Chief, great leader of the Western bands, comprising all of the Upper Great Lakes Native people, (Three Fires unity)
Shingaba Wossin, leader of the Crane band at Sault Ste. Marie, first Chief of the Chippewa Nation (Schenk), also Singabawossin – "Spirit Stone", shaman and leader of the Crane clan at Sault Ste. Marie (Cleland)
Shoogemah, Chief at Walpole Island (Travers)
Shoppenagon, David, "Lumber Chief", "Old Shopp", a Saginaw lumber baron and river guide, made canoes by hand, born in Indian Fields near Caro, Michigan, told tales to many sitting about a campfire: tales of bear and deer hunts
Siskiboa, Shamon at the St. Clair River, Ontario
Ski Neaque, Detroit River
Small Kettle, Chief of the Ojibwe at Round Lake, villages on Swan Creek and Saline Creek (Plain, 1300 Moons)
Snake or Serpent, "The Snake", Mis She Ke Nay Bick – "The Great Snake" – Chief of the Chippewas at Black River, a brother of Granny Rodd (NAMMIR.43:431 – 438)
Son Din Ou, Huron Chief, Detroit River
Sonis Baw, Saginaw Chief (ARCOIA 1837:532, Clifton notes)
Soskene, Chippewa Chief, signer of Treaty of Fort Harmer
Souskonay, Ojibwe Chief at Chenail Escarte, Bird totem (Ipperwash Commission of Inquiry, www)

Southbird, Tittabawasee (NAMMIR42-319,320)
Squand, Squano, John, "Doc Squano", a medical and expert herb mixing doctor at Sebewaing and Bayport, Michigan for Red and White people
Squashawa, Chief of Ottawa Bear tribe at Detroit (Lajuenesse)
Stevens, General, Nauquachicgawme, Thumb and Saginaw, Michigan
Strong Wind, Missisauga War Chief (Plain, 1300 Moons)
Suk Kew Ge Won, Suck Aingewow, Suck Augewow, Chief at River Rouge Reservation, from Bay Settlement of Toledo (NAMMIR.46:593, 594)
Sumner, John, Chief of the Ontario Ojibwe in 1877
Sunday, John, a well-known missionary convert of the Ojibwes, Canadian, serving in the Upper Peninsula of Michigan and many other places, became a great preacher
Tagannini, Saugeen Chief (Travers)
Ta Hou Ne Ha Wie Tie, Huron Chief at Detroit River
Ta Niom Sa, Osage Country, 1839 (NAMMIR.47:719 – 722)
Tarhe, "The Crane", the Grand Sachem of the Wyandottes
Takay, War Chief of the Detroit Pottawatomi and Wyandotte (Huron)
Tarhe, Wyandotte Chief, Sandusky Ohio
Taychatubm, Taychatin, Wyandotte Chief
Taykaumaw, Caribou totem, Chief in Southwest Ontario
Taytaymaygasson, also Catfish-Sturgeon, Chief at Chenail Escarte (Ipperwash Commission of Inquiry. www)
Tawas, Tawaws, Thous, Tawas, Chippewa Chief at Saginaw
Ted Y A Ta, Huron Chief, Detroit River
Te Ha Tow Renee, Huron Chief, Detroit River
Tharatohat, Chief near Windsor, Ontario (Lajuenesse)
The Fork, Chief of Flint River band (Plain, 1300 Moons)
The Pike, Ottawa War Chief (Plain, 1300 Moons)
Tickamegasson, Chief at Chenail Escarte (Travers)
Tickcome go sson, Chief at Detroit (Lajuenesse)
Tickcouoegossow, Detroit River
Tie cami go se, Chippewa Chief at Detroit (Lajuenesse)
Tihockeres, Chief near Windsor, Ontario (Lajuenesse)
Tiockouanohon, Chief near Windsor, Ontario (Lajuenesse)
Toienthet, Chief near Windsor (Lajuenesse)
Tomago, Chief at Thames River (D. Plain)
Tomego, Chief at Chenail Escarte (Travers)
Tondaganie, "The Dog", Chief at the Miami of Lake Erie

Tonquish, "Old Toga", Ojibwe Chief, village was near River Rouge (Hindsdale, 1925)
Topinbee
Toquish, Chief at Moore Reserve
Tou Geis Ish, Chief at River Rouge Reservation, from Maumee City (NAMMIR.46:593, 594)
Toukwish, Chief at Rouge River
Tren Youmaing, Huron Chief, Detroit River
Tsough Ka Ratsy Wa, Huron Chief, Detroit River
Truckatoe, Sub Chief of the Swan Creek bands of Pottawatomi and Ojibwe, under Chief Francis Maconse
Turkeyfoot, Miami, second in command after Little Turtle
Twisting Vine, Delaware Chief, Thom
Ureaupowannie, "Great Batt", Chief at Moore Reserve
Wa Ban Di Gais, Chippewa Chief, Detroit River
Wabbicommicot
Wabinema
Wagnai, Chief at Moore Reserve
Wahpahgass, Chief at Kettle and Stony Point (Ipperwash Commission of Inquiry, www)
Wah sayguan, Ojibwe, Odawa and Pottawatomi Chief at Chenail Escarte (Ipperwash Commission, www)
Wain ge ge zhick, Saginaw Chief
Wakazoo, Ottawa Chief in West Michigan (Ewing)
Walk in the Water, Walk on the Water, Myeerah or Maera, Turtle totem, "Captain Ironsides", a Huron Chief of the Wyandot tribe, descendent of Tecumseh, who was Superintendent of Indian Affairs, one of the Huron Chief men, persuaded various tribes to remain neutral during the War of 1812, died about 1817 (John Askin Papers vol. 1, pg. 494) (See "Ironsides")
Wapagance, Chief at Sarnia (Plain)
Wapagase, Wapagaee, Johnston, Caribou totem, Chief at Kettle Point (Ipperwash Commission of Inquiry, www)
Wapenousa, Chief at Chenail Escarte (Travers)
Wapishwisbiwininiwak, village on the north side of Lake St. Clair (Hindsdale, 1925)
Wapocmoguth, Great Chief of the Mississaugas (Parkman)
Wapoose, Goerge Menass, a Chippewa Medicine Man, Bear Creek (Thames)
Warpole, a Wyandotte Chief (Wyandottenation.org, www)
Wasagashick, Ottawa Chief

Wasson, Catfish, Win ne meg, Winamek, Old Wasso, Owosso was named for him, Saginaw War Chief who led 250 warriors south of Detroit in the War of Pontiac, a Pottawatomi Head Chief
Waugau, Chief at Miami Bay on Lake Erie
Waupugais, Ojibwe War Chief from Sauble
Wau Wau Som, Walpole Chief
Wawanosh, David, Chief of the Ontario Ojibwe for 15 years to 1867
Wa Watom, "Little Goose", a Chippewa Chief born 1762, lived to 1864
Wawish kuy, Ottawa Chief at Detroit (Lajuenesse)
Wayayachterin, Pottawatomi Chief at Detroit, friend of De Peyster (Askin, vol. II, pg. 407)
Wa waynash, Caribou totem, Chief (Ipperwash Commission, www)
Wa Wish Kuy, Ottawa Chief, Detroit River
Wayweyaghtin, Pottawatomi Chief at Detroit (Askin, vol. 1, pg. 175)
Wetenasa, Chippewa Chief, signer of Fort Harmar Treaty
Whitecloud, Amikoui, Ojibwe Grand Chief at Bawatig, Sault Ste. Marie, Georgian Bay
Whitefeather, famous Chief of the Chippewa
Williams, Lloyd, Stony Point Chief (Travers 2015)
Winamek, Catfish (Cleland)
Windego, Windigo, "Devil", Pottawatomi Chief at Detroit (Askin, vol.1, pg. 175)
Wing, Ottawa Chief, whose son fought with the Americans, annually received two new flags at Detroit and an annuity
Winniwok, Chief and War Chief, Ottawa near Detroit (Eckert)
Wishawas, Chief at Moore Reserve
Wittaniss, a Sub Chief of the Huron Indians, caretaker at Moravian Village when John Askin purchased this land on the Huron – Clinton – River
Wymeegong, Saginaw Chippewa War Chief
Wymnack, Pottawatomi Chief at Detroit (NAMM1105R1)

KETTLE AND STONY POINT CHIEFS – ONTARIO, CANADA

Ashkebahganhequod, John Big Knife, Chemokomon, also Oshawawanoo and Shawawanoo, nephew of Tecumseh, his sons carry the names Shawnoo and Shawkence
Mahwajewong, son of Perwash, son was Wahpahgas
Mamahwegezhego, the oldest known ancestor of the Johnston lineage, born around 1700

Pewash, Ipperwash was named after him, son of the Indian Queen, Quashegn Quakeegwon, signed the Treaty of 1825

Quashegn, the "Indian Queen", second in a long line of Stoney Point Chiefs, beginning with Mamahwegezhego

Shegnobik, "Grindstone", brother of John Big Knife (see above), nephew of Tecumseh

Wahpagas, hereditary line of descendent chiefs which began with Mamahwegezhego, later known as Johnston Mahpahgas, his sons used the surname Johnston

OTHER AREA CHIEFS
Aegakotchis
Angouirot, Wyandotte chief (Tanner /Voegelin)
Ashi Tan Aquit, Esh Ton Oquot, Chief Clear Sky
Aushaw
Beaver, Delaware Chief in Ohio
Blackfoot
Buck ong a helos, leader of the Delawares
Chaminitawaa
Chedig Bedejik
Cracking Noise, Delaware Chief in Ohio
Entatsago, Chief of the Sault
Far-he, Tarhe, King Crane, Grand Chief of the Wyandots, resided at Sandusky (Lossing)
Five Medals, Pottawatomi Chief
Koussidover, Ottawa Chief
Matchekewis, tribal leader of the Ojibwe, Principal Chief of Thunder Bay, fought in many battles, was at the 1795 Treaty of Greenville, ceding Bois Blanc Island on Lake Huron and all his original lands to the U.S.
Madame La Framboise, Madeline, granddaughter of Chief Kewinoquot, an Ottawa on the Grand River, married a fur trader, Joseph, La Framboise. She spoke many languages and was a great help in the fur trade. In 1804, her husband was killed, and she assumed the trade and amassed a great fortune, then built a fine home on Mackinac Island. John Jacob Astor could not compete against her and bought her out in 1818. Her daughter Josette was well-educated and married Benjamin K. Peirce, commandment at Fort Mackinac and brother to the future President of the U.S.
Le Gris, Miami Chief
Le Maigouis, "Trout"

Logan, famous Iroquois War Chief from Ohio, orator of a great speech, Cayuga or Mingo Chief
Machikinaqua, Miami Chief
Mackinac, Chief of L Arbre Croche, Principal Ottawa Chief (Eckert)
Mamongesseda, Ojibwe Chief
Meg Wadisk
Mejlaquit, Meawqut
Minamek
Mineweweh
Montour, Sally, Sara Ainse-Wilson, Metis trader from Detroit
Morning Walker (Plain, 1300 Moons)
Musketta
Nash I Pi Nash I Wish, a Chippewa Chief (Fuller)
Nayquoscan
Ne Bom O Quay, noted Indian sachem
Neewish
Niquelon
Not A Wa Sepe, a Pottawatomi Chief in Southwest Lower Michigan (Fuller)
Ocaita
Omaske
Pacane, Miami Chief
Sabsuitqwa
Shaboque, Chippewa Chief
Sigmabi
Squashawa, Ottawa, Bear tribe
Tenskwatawa – The Open Door, The Prophet, brother of Tecumseh. He was a drunkard who became a changed man and the Great prophet of the Shawnee who gathered many tribes together at Prophetstown in Greenville Ohio and then at the Tippacanoe River and Wabash River in Indiana. Thoms book, *Panther in the Sky*, is a wonderful life history of Tecumseh and Tenskwatawa.
Wabinema
White Cap, Shawnee Principal Chief
Winnemac, Pottawatomi Chief

CHIEFS WHO FOUGHT WITH TECUMSEH
Keyoshka
Manitowanoe, First Lieutenant, devoted and faithful to the Crown, was given a silver medal from the Prince of Wales (later Edward VII), when he visited Sarnia, Ontario in 1860

Minomener
Miskokomon
Nadhee
Paccoos
Shageemah
Shawanoe-Charcoal Burner
Shiata, Main Poc
Thceahyabah
Each of the above, Warriors and their descendants are buried on Walpole Island. They were Pottawatomi, Ottawa, and Ojibwe (Chippewa).
Chiefs and principal men of the Chippewa Nation who signed the British Treaty of 1827 in Southern Ontario. The Western District and the London District, in the province of Upper Canada, bounded in the west by Lake Huron and the River St. Clair, were obtained from the Chippewa Nation of Indians, who inhabited and claimed the tract of land in the area described above.
Wawanosh, Thashawinibisic, Pukinance, Negig, Chiebekun, Makataicijigo, Mishaikinaibik, Animikance, Peetawtick, Shawanipinasie, Sagonosh, Wapagace, Anottawin, Ponessiaugnon, Shaioukima, Chekateyon, Mokeitchwon, Kuakgwon – Eighteen names in all.
This treaty surrendered over two million acres at Amherstburg on July 10, 1827 (Nicholas Plain, The History of Sarnia Reserve, 1950)
The Pottawatomi chiefs of Huron River in 1796 were Bandigalkawa, Cabainse, Chawinabai, Chewenisle, Echawet, Keewaidenenaham, The Little Otter, Mahimak, Mahingan, Nannie ou Kuvainim, Ochichalk, Okia, and Othesneesa. The Chippewa chiefs of land near Lake St. Clair in 1795 were Nangui, Omissass, Ochaisie, Wasson's Son, Withannesse, and Weshebanwi.

OTHER CHIEFS
Aisance
Alleyooue, Whyandotte Chief
Andrew Blackbird, Mackawdebenessy, "Black Hawk", Ottawa and Pottawatomi Chief, wrote *The History of the Ottawa and Chippewa Indians* 1887 was an interpreter and postmaster at Harbor Springs – Little Traverse, was a State Representative. In his whole life he never swore, and lived by the Ten Commandments.
Blackhawk, Black Sparrow Hawk, Maka Tai Me She Kis Kiak, Sauk Chief and War Captain of the Western Indians who fought in the War of 1812. He was of the Thunder Clan of the Sac tribe and was made Chief of the Fox when the Sac and Fox became a confederacy. He moved west of the Mississippi and fought in

the War of 1832, trying to move his people to safety in Canada. His biography was written in 1833, the first Native American biography to be published in the U.S., a best-seller.
Blackhawk, Brigadier General in the British Army (Travers, 2015)
Blackhoof, Principal Chief of the Shawaneese at Wa pah ko netta, Indiana
Joseph Brandt, Mohawk Chief from New York who settled on the Grand River, in Ontario, Canada after the Revolutionary War. He was captain of the Northern Confederate, an able and inspiring leader, and a complete gentleman. He said he believed his people could learn much from the White Man. Brandt came to Detroit to negotiate with and for the Indians. The Indians said England had sold the Indians to Congress, their sacrifice for the British Crown had been in vain.
Charcoal Burner-Shabonna, Sauk Sub Chief at Shabonna, who fought with Tecumseh and kept Tecumseh's body safe, moved the body on Tecumseh's own white horse to a secret burying place near Lake St. Clair, in Ontario. Thom
Chicago-jig, Ottawa Chief at South Shore of Lake Michigan, Chicago named for him
Cornstalk – Hokoleskwah, Shawnee Nation Principal Chief at Chilicothe on the Miamisepe. Thom
Elkswatawa, "The Loud Voice", "The Prophet", brother of Tecumseh, also Pemsquatawah – "Open Door" (Lossing, 1869
Entatsago, Chief of the Sault
Five Medals
Captain Hendrik Aupaumut, Chief of the Stockbridge Indians (Fuller)
Keokuk, War Chief, Sac and Fox, Iowa
Koussidover, Ottawa Chief
LaDemoiselle – Old Britain, Chief of the Piankeshaw in Ohio, also see Memeskia. Thom
Lamehand, a Chief at the Raisen, War of 1812 (Lossing)
Le Peasant, "Heavy Man", Ottawa Chief
Captain Lewis
Mackinac, Chief of L Arbre Croche, Principal Ottawa Chief (Eckert)
Mamongesseda, Ojibwe Chief
Memeskia, La Demoiselle, Le Domoiselle – Old Britian, Miami Chief, pro-British, Old Brittain, fought in the French and Indian Wars in Ohio and Pennsylvania, Pickawillany was Memeskias' village
Ne bom o quay, noted Indian sachem
Nettamop, Otto, Thumb of Michigan, holder of a magnificent war record in WWI

Ottissippi

Nissowaquet, Aukewingeketawso, "Defender of His Country"
Nitarikijk, Nippissing Chief
Nocolas, Nicholas, Orontony, the leading Wyandat Chief at Detroit, then at Sandusky and Indiana, organized a coalition of tribes to remove the French from Detroit in 1747, was of the Turtle clan totem
Old Mackinac, Peekwutinong
Ontonagan or Jean Le Blanc, Ottawa Chief
Osandiah, Miami Chief, fought in Pontiac's battles
Outautagan, Ottawa Chief
Ouilemek, Pottawatomie Chief
Oulouigoushquin, Chief and friend of Colonel De Peyster near Detroit (Askin, vol. II, pg. 407)
General Ely Parker, Donehogaua, born Hasonoanda at Indian Falls New York on the Tonawunda Reservation. A full-blooded Iroquois, born in 1828, who was head of the Indian Bureau, President Grant's Commissioner of Indian Affairs. The first Indian to hold this office. He was the man who made major reforms and restructuring. He had many enemies in Washington.
He had an encyclopedic mind and was keeper of the western door of the Wolf clan. His maternal grandfather was Jimmy Johnson, Sosohawa, grandson of the prophet "Handsome Lake". His father was Seneca Chief William Parker, a veteran of the War of 1812. He was grandson of "Disappearing Smoke" (Old King), a prominent figure in early history of the Seneca. He received the Red Jacket Medal, given to Red Jacket by President George Washington in 1792. The medal was inherited by Jimmy Johnson, Parker's grandfather.
He was Chief of Staff, Military Secretary, and a lifelong friend of Grant's. He was also a Seneca attorney, engineer, tribal diplomat, and brigadier general of volunteers at Appotomax.
Parker was the major informant for the book *League of the Hodenosaunee Iroquois* (1851) by Louis Henry Morgan.
It was Parker who penned the final official document that ended the Civil War. He is interred with Red Jacket and his ancestors in Forest Lawn Cemetery, Buffalo, New York.
Sigennock, "Blackbird", Principal Chief before 1812 at Mantoulin Island, Michigan
Splitlog
Tenskwatawa – The Open Door, The Prophet, brother of Tecumseh. He was born "Loud Noise", a drunkard who became "Open Door", a changed man and the Great prophet of the Shawnee who gathered many tribes together at Prophetstown in Greenville Ohio and then at the Tippacanoe River and

Wabash River in Indiana. Thoms book, *Panther in the Sky*, is a wonderful life history of Tecumseh and Tenskwatawa.

Wabinema

Warrow

The Wolf

Pottawatomi Chiefs of Huron River who sold land to John Askin, John Askin Jr., heirs of Patrick McNiff and John Askwith, Alex Henry, Israel Ruland at River Raisen in 1796. (This grant was declared invalid as lands must be sold through the U.S. Government):

Bandigalkawa, Cabainse, Chawinabai, Chewenisle, Echawet, Keewaidenaham, The Little Otter, Mahimak, Mahingan, Nannie Ou Kuvainim, Ochichalk, Okia, Othesneesa

Chippewa Chiefs of land gifted to John Cornwell, a physician, near Lake St. Clair in 1795 and 1797 were; Nangui, Ochaisie, Omissass, Wasson's son, Weshebanwai, and Withannesse.

CHAPTER 10
Reserves and Indian Lands

The Indians lived on all the waterways of the Bluewater region, including, Lake Huron and Southeast Michigan. They gave gifts of land, rented land, gave grants of land, and ceded land to the French, British, and Americans.

THE ISLANDS

The delta north of Lake St. Clair where the St. Clair River enters the lake is North America's largest freshwater delta. At this delta of the St. Clair River, there are many islands. Upon these Islands, the Ojibwe, Ottawa, and Pottawatomi lived, and other tribes who passed through and camped on their fur trading journeys. They camped on the islands with higher grounds.

The area today is called The Flats; these islands were a special place then, and they are yet today. There are many burial grounds on these islands, some have been raided and disturbed. An old legend tells of a pot of gold. A group of early missionaries with a hoard of gold were passing through, and they met with hostile Indians. They landed upon Harsens Island and buried the gold and never returned for their treasure. Dixon, "Life at the Flats" 1999.

WARPOLE ISLAND – ST. MARY'S ISLAND – WALPOLE ISLAND

The Walpole Island Delta of Lake St. Clair is a large heart-shaped island, known also as Ode Ziibiing – Heart River. Walpole Island was long known as Warpole Island. Michigan State University Libraries scanned maps of Michigan Map Library show many maps depicting Warpole Island.

The largest of all the islands in the St. Clair Delta was later named after Lieutenants Arthur and John Walpole, surveyors for the Royal Engineers, or after Horace Walpole, an Englishman.

Indian tradition says it is named for the Warpoles that once stood at the entrances to the Island, declaring the territory totem. These were long wooden staves planted in the ground, with emblems of First Nations on them. They were seen by early visitors (Patricia Orange)

The Indian Chief Warpole may have been the namesake.

Walpole is one of five Islands included in the Indian lands at the north side of Lake St. Clair. These lands have never been ceded, legislated, founded, established, set apart, or surveyed as a reserve to any government. They are un-ceded territory, now Canadian lands. A very special place with rare flora and fauna (P. Orange).

The other islands of the reserve are St. Anne's, Squirrel, Bassett, and Seaway. With the marshes and waters area, the total reserve lands are about 58,000 acres or 91 square miles. Upper Walpole Island is about 12 feet above mean water level. Lower Walpole is less than 3 feet above water level. About 12,000 acres are habitable, this is the wooded area. The lower marsh lands are covered with cattails, rushes, and other water grasses. The annual variation is about eighteen inches. Lake Huron continues to bring coarse materials to the Delta. The base of the Delta is hard blue clay found at about 15 feet; terrific ice jams occur here in winter and early spring (Hudgins 1933, Wayne University, Detroit).

The *Biodiversity Atlas of Lake Huron to Lake Erie* is a wonderful tool to learn more. It can be found on the www.

The tribes living here are Chippewa-Ojibwe (Ojibway), Ottawa, and Pottawatomi, known as the Three Fires People. The Island is home to over 3,000 people. The Ottawa and Ojibwe were living here in the early 1800s when the Europeans began to settle in the area. The Pottawatomi arrived after the Indian Removal in the United States in the 1830s, most of whom were British Loyalists.

They brought their horses with them, swimming them across the St. Clair River and settled on an island in the middle of Walpole Island, called Pottawatomi Island. The Pottawatomi spread out and ranged most of what is now Lambton County, Ontario.

The horses were of Arabian and Indian pony stock. The competent horses adapted and ran wild, surviving on their own and multiplied. They became known far and wide as "The Wild Ponies of Walpole Island". They became tough, chunky ponies; they were easily managed when captured, easily trained for riding or other work, and were good domestic animals. They were sold to other peoples for farming and travel. In the summer, they fed on grass and, in winter, on twigs. The wild ponies were numerous; in the 1930s, several thousand ponies could be seen roaming on Walpole. The wild ponies were in great demand, supplying the natives with a home-grown industry for many years. They would periodically be rounded up and auctioned off at $1 to $2 per head.

As autos and tractors became popular, the demand for ponies dropped. Eventually they became so numerous and troublesome, damaging crops and gardens, that there were big sales held in the spring. In 1954, the Council organized a huge roundup and most of the ponies were captured and sold to market. A few were transferred to St. Anne's Island by Mr. Johnson to preserve them. They were hunted down and destroyed, being so despised by the majority. A lost treasure, the last of the ponies were seen in the 1970s at the south of Walpole Island around Goose Lake.

When the Americans claimed the United States, some of the Indian Loyalists moved to Canada. The largest number of the Chippewa arrived after the War of 1812, when British Allies were invited to settle there. More came during the Indian Removal of the 1830s and 1840s.

Indian reserves were overrun with squatters and thousands of dollars in Indian trust funds were missing and unaccounted for, the government besieged with Indian complaints (Travers 2015). The settlement was placed under the charge of an Indian superintendent in 1839. Whites had settled on the land and took possession of the islands' fertile lands. The Whites were then evicted.

Many of the Whites had moved from Harsens Island when the British ceded this island to the Americans in 1822, when the International Boundary Commission ruled it American land.

Walpole Island is the final resting place of Chief Tecumseh, the great Shawnee leader.

The islands of the delta are a haven for waterfowl of the Atlantic and Mississippi flyway. There are many private shooting clubs on the islands.

The traditional teachings tell of a small fight with some Spaniards who came up the river in ships. They pitched tents on the Island and buried treasure worth three million dollars. An old Indian saw them bury their Treasure. He dug it up and carried it off to another hiding place. No one has ever found it.

The Chanel Escarte, a channel separating Walpole from the mainland to the east, provided exceptional natural camouflage for rumrunners, who transported illicit booze to the U.S. during the Prohibition from 1920 to 1933 (P. Orange).

In 1846, the first Anglican church was established and remains active. Father DuRanquet built a church building on sacred burial mounds and a cemetery on Walpole Island. The church was burned, and the priest left in 1849 (Travers 2015).

The powerful civil officials controlled the flow of information into the 1850s and beyond (Travers 2015).

In 1863, the first Methodist church was established on Walpole Island.

In 1914, when WWI began, 57 Walpole Island men enlisted in the Canadian Army, and 47 returned.

In 1878, Joshua Greenbird, an Ojibwe, became the first elected chief on the reserve, the Pottawatomi having their own chief. When the two tribes merged, Solomon Kewayosh was elected as the first chief of the Amalgamated Band Council.

In 1939, when WWII began, 69 Walpole Island Natives enlisted in the Canadian Armed Forces. Four were killed in action.

In 1964, under the leadership of Burton Jacobs, the reserve became a self-governing system. Prior to this, the Indian agent had power to overrule the Council. Walpole Island became the first Native band in Canada not to have an Indian agent. Much has been accomplished under self-determination: A bridge was built in 1970 to Wallaceburg, Ontario. A new sports arena and community center were built, along with a highway, a school, fire department, water tower, commercial farming, and more.

The New Year's Feast is a special day to be with friends and share a feast. Entertainment is provided with speeches and a local talent show. A Pow Wow is held on Walpole every summer. It is a time of friendship and celebration. The traditional singing, dancing, and ceremonies are a verification of their love for Gitchi Manito and his people.

There are about 1,800 people living on the Island. A ferry service from Marine City operates to the Island.

A famous baseball pitcher for the Philadelphia Athletics came from Walpole. His name is Ed Pinauce, and they won the World Championship (Patricia Orange 1975).

CANADA AND SARNIA

The Indians of Canada form one of the most diverse populations on Earth. They live much like their neighbors who live close by, farming and working in factories and offices. They are tradespeople, lawyers, doctors, nurses, and teachers. There are those who live in isolated areas closer to the land and water. Some are high steel construction workers, miners, fishers, boat builders, and wood operation. They are caught between two worlds: the old Indian way and the modern life.

SARNIA CHIPPEWA – OJIBWE RESERVE

The Chippewas of Sarnia as of 2000 A.D. prefer to be called Ojibwe. They live on Aamjiwnaang, a portion of what was once a very large territory extending into a large area of Michigan and Ontario.

The Chippewa or Ojibwe of Sarnia are the original occupants of the area known as Lambton County, Ontario. There are about 1,800 members in Aamjiwnaang meaning "At the Spawning Stream". (Sarnia band of Ojibwe). There are over 200 homes on the reserve. The Plain family have been chiefs of the band for a very long time. They have a reservation that is now 3,100 acres. The original reserves were about 10,280 acres, lands that have been ceded and sold. They operate under a Band Council with an elected chief.

The Cameron Lands north of Sarnia are in a court battle; the Aamjiwnaang claim they lost territorial land without proper surrender in 1839. It makes up about 10% of Sarnia.

They have an industrial park for business leasing. They have sold about 1,000 acres of their land to energy-related industrial companies. The area known as Chemical Valley is the largest concentration of chemical companies in Canada.

At the Treaty of 1827, the Chippewa-Ojibwe Indians, the original inhabitants along the shores of the Detroit River, St. Clair River, Lake Huron, Georgian Bay, and as far north as Garden River in the Algoma District at S.S. Marie, were signers. Traces of their campaign grounds and garden plots can be found along this area. At this period, the Indians realized that they were destined to be confined to smaller areas called reserves. The Indians' wishes were respected as regards, to areas they wished to reserve out of the two million acres, namely Aux Sable, Kettle Point, Sarnia Reserve, and Sombra. The reserves were under one chief and five counsellors until Kettle Point and Aux Sable – Stoney Point – demanded separation from Sarnia before 1919. Sombra reserve was sold. There was a small reserve called the lower Saint Clair Reserve which was sold. (Nicholas Plain). The Lower Reserve was 2,575 acres immediately north of Sombra (Travers, 2015).

There was no objection when the first Methodist missionary asked permission to hold preaching services among the Chippewas. The only class of Indians who objected to the intrusion of the Christian missionaries were the "Faker Medicine Men" who practiced witchcraft.

Cheryl Morgan

Through the first camp meeting in Sarnia Reserve was the means of arousing a cooperative spirit in the Chippewas; each answered the question "What is right?" and discussed each problem and applied absolute honesty, purity, unselfishness, and love to its solution.

The missionaries came to look after their spiritual welfare which required, careful handling, for the Indian was already deeply religious and observed all nature, including new settlers and the missionaries. Anyone possessing selfish natures were readily discerned by them were not so easily influenced by such people, be they ever so gifted in eloquence of speech. (Nicholas Plain, 1950, History of Sarnia Reserve, and History of the Chippewa of Sarnia).

Peter Jones, Kahkewaquonaby, "Sacred Waving Feathers", was the first missionary to arrive in 1829. James Evans arrived in 1834, a missionary of the Wesleyan Missionary Authorities in England. These two Missionaries were gifted with being able to speak the Chippewa language. They were led by the Holy Spirit to come and deliver this message to the Indians.

The Indians were pagens of necessity, not by choice, and when they heard the gospel story in their own language from the lips of Reverend Peter Jones and Reverend James Evans, the chiefs and principal men were thrilled to understand that Jesus Christ was the Gift of God – Kechemundo – and through his name they began to pray. In time, they were full of unspeakable joy, and spoke shouts of joy. It affected the whole community; there were camp meetings and mass evangelisms. Nicholas Plain was a preacher and chief at Sarnia Reserve.

The chiefs became Christians, and most of the people followed. Most were of the Methodist Church.

The first government agent was William Jones in 1831, whose records are priceless of the early reserve history. He recommended a man named Harris of Caradoc as a teacher; he is a Methodist and in the habit of preaching occasionally.

A school house was built that also served as the church and community hall. The British Wesleyan Mission to the Chippewa's.

The Land area became common ground for all, small plots selected by one, was carefully respected by the whole tribe. A member could cross the plot without hindrance or objection but not utilize any part of it. The land was very fertile. The wigwams were scattered throughout the 10,280 acres near water and thick bush to protect from wind. Later the government and Chippewas built log and frame homes.

Sarnia 45 Indian Reserve is the official name of the reservation. It lies directly opposite from Marysville Park in Michigan. It was never Crown land.

Ottissippi

Today the reserve is about 3,100 acres. It is bounded by the St. Clair River, Churchill Road and Vidal Street, which curves to the river, LaSalle one mile east past Scott, and back to Churchill Road.

The reserve had an agricultural society and an annual fair, everyone tried to take part bringing whatever animals they had and fowl of every description. The ladies brought preserves, baked goods, sewing, and quilts. Vegetables were of every variety.

There was a good sized, brass band on the reserve. John Maness was the leader. The Walpole Island Brass Band came to the fair. When some of the players went overseas to the first world war, the band gradually dwindled.

The small ship *Hiawatha* brought people from Port Huron to the fair day. People from Detroit came on the big "City of Toledo". Another small ship would pick up passengers for a trip to Tashmoo Park.

Families on the reserve found a good seat along the river bank when the ferry boat, "Omar Conger", was on a moonlight excursion. The music by the orchestra band carried over the water for a long distance. The strains of music came from many other steamers and waves from the passengers. The children jumping into the tremendous wake for fun.

When there was a Bee, neighbor women prepared a bountiful dinner and supper. After the evening meal, there was storytelling, Awt Bo Kawn Un, like Legends. The more absurd and humorous the better.

There were cows on almost every homestead, and each had a bell and could be identified by the sound of their bell clanging. Some put a small bell on their horses, and when on the sleigh or cutter, they made music.

Grain was stood up in sheaves to dry in the fields and was thrashed by hand.

There was unlimited access to the American side of the river. Many would go across to South Park in Michigan to buy supplies and sell fish. Some men kept a light rope and drifted, fishing all day, and in the afternoon, catch a passing freighter and be towed back home.

When Prohibition came into effect in the U.S., there was the exciting practice of supplying nocturnal quiet – traveling motor boats – with cases of Canadian liquor on the shores of the reserve. Some allowed the Indians to hide the liquor in their straw stacks and helped move it to the shore at night, sleeping by day most of the time.

Inter-marriage among those of the same totem sign was strictly forbidden, this gradually changed.

The people went on to build frame homes, and the children went to industrial school at Muncey to learn trades. Fences were built and land cleared;

barns and granaries were built. The operation of lumber mills, flour mills, and general stores in the neighboring village, called Froomfield, was a great convenience.

Froome Talfourd was an Indian agent at Sarnia Reserve who was well-loved. A great feast was made by the Chippewa in honor of his birthday on November 4th, when he was to return to England. He promised to provide a meal for all the Indians of the reserve every year on his birthday, until he came back to Canada. And for many years thereafter, an annual feast was given to the Indians by money given for the celebration from Froome Talfourd, the honored guest, who may not have realized when he made the promise was destined to never return. It was called The Talfourd Feast. Some 400 Indians sat down to a generous Feast that he provided for them. Froome Talfourd died in England in 1902 at the age of 95. To the Indians, he was known as "the Englishman who keeps his word".

A wood yard was at the river dock to supply steamboats with wood fuel. The Indians supplying the wood for supplies in their homes. The reserve was a busy place with everyone working: women making mats, baskets, dresses; men farming, and woodworking, and making tools and many other wooden items. There were all kinds of bees, all happily working to help one another, and the neighboring inhabitants of Sarnia. The area merchants could understand the Indian name for items of merchandise and foodstuffs, so even without the English language, they could buy what they wanted.

When the Chippewas embraced Christianity as their religion, they did not cast off their moral laws but added the Christian principles to their principle of community living and willingly erected a church around 1860. This was supported by all the members of the Methodist church, and they purchased a church bell and hung it in the bell tower, and the ringing of the bell called the congregation to gather for worship. It also gave the death toll, casting an atmosphere of gloom over the whole reserve, the people gathering for a wake and burial, comforting one another.

The Anglican missionaries came early to minister to the Chippewa, and a brick church was built, it was called St. Peters. Henry P. Chase was one of the ministers who served there.

The women sat by themselves on one side of the church, and the men on the opposite side, and the solemnity was observed by silence.

An annual revival meeting, was held in the Methodist Church, a special preacher was called to conduct the preaching services and other speakers from other reserves were always present to take part in the services, a prayer meeting, and a testimony meeting with songs in Chippewa.

The people loved social gatherings, such as teas, New Year, Thanksgiving, picnics. The early churches combined annual picnics, chartering a ferry boat for an excursion to Walpole Island.

The 18-member brass band played for these events. Their entertainment at these gatherings: athletic events were a source of entertainment, foot races, jumping, ball games, and firing fire crackers. Patriotism to the Crown was shown by hoisting the Union Jack at every event.

The last two hereditary chiefs were John Sumner, a descendant of Petawtick, and Nicholas Plain, a descendant of Animikance. F.W. Jacobs was the first to be elected by vote under the Indian Election Act System in 1882. He was the interpreter for the preachers for many years.

Animikeencee was Chief for 30 years, from 1797 to 1827. Wawanosh, Joshua, was Chief for 17 years, from 1827 to 1844. Mishibizhe, David Wawanosh, was Chief for 15 years, from 1844 to 1867. Francis Wilson Jacobs, was Chief for 14 years until 1884. John Sumner was Chief until 1870. Nicholas Plain was then Chief, and his descendants to present.

Many lodges were started: Independent Order of Foresters, Orange Lodge, Temperance Lodge, and one called "The Swamp Club". All of these, have ceased to exist. One sponsored by the Indian Department, "The Homemakers Club", in the 1970s, was well attended.

A baseball team in 1892 attended picnics with the reserve brass band, a favorite for country picnics. A Monster Picnic was held annually in Wilkesport with 2,000 people attending.

William Jones, Indian agent at Sarnia, who was a spy for Tecumseh and General Brock at the Battle of Detroit, was given as a war bounty the settlement of Lord Selkirk, known as Baldoon. He gave a report of the Sarnia Reserve in 1837:

> *there are about 539 Chippewa's. They cultivate small fields of Indian corn, potatoes, and various kinds of pulse (vegetables), and they follow hunting and fishing in summer. In winter, the greater part of them retire to the most favorable situations for hunting and making sugar, where they remain till the season for preparing to plant and sow their spring crop. In the marshes, they kill a great number of muskrats, ducks, and other game, and fish abound. All the expenses of the tribe*

> *are defrayed from the land payments. The agent requisitions for their presents and land payments. (William Jones, Asst. Supt., Indian Dept.)*

Malcolm Cameron bought the timber rights at Sarnia Reserve. Once the land was denuded, much of it was rented to Whites for pasture, and the Indians farmed.

Sarnia became known as Christian Village in the 1860s (Travers, 2015). The government built them log houses, but they preferred the wigwams and used the log structures for barns.

An annual fair was held from 1903 to the late 1930s. It was held on the Council grounds and featured horse races, livestock shows, exhibits of women's handwork, and art. The Pow Wow has taken its place since 1962.

KETTLE POINT – WIIWKWEDONG – AND STONEY POINT RESERVE – AUX SABLE AND IPPERWASH, KNOWN AS SABLE RESERVE

Kettle Point- Wiiwkwedong, mean "By the Bay", or Bosanquet Indians. We have always played a significant role in the development of North American culture, some imposed by others and some by their own innovation.

Between 1776 and 1814, our warriors supported the British cause as loyal allies who fought and died to defend Canadian Territory.

Oshawnoo, one of the founding chiefs, a descendant of Tecumseh, received two medals: a King George III silver Chiefs medallion, dated 1814, and the second presented in 1860 at Sarnia. Oshawnoo and his brother Shignobick were survivors of the Battle of the Longwood's, where Tecumseh died on the Thames near Chatham. They are said to have helped with Tecumseh's burial.

"Our pattern of life depended upon getting to the resources where and when nature made them available to us. During the Iroquois Wars, we lived further to the north and moved south to recolonize our territories. Our technology, medicines, and foods sustained the early explorers and settlers. With our ongoing help and alliance, the establishment and colonization of Canada became possible. Today much of the world's food supply is produced from plant breeds which were developed from our Indigenous crops. Many aspects of modern democracy were inspired from our traditional values. We are a generous people who have surrendered much" (Victor Gulewitsch, 1995).

ANDERDON RESERVE – WINDSOR

Ottissippi

Anderdon Reserve is at now Windsor, Ontario on Canard River near Amherstburg. The Huron Reserve was on the Detroit River in Ontario, Canada. The reserved areas of Moore, Shawanee, and Bear Creek were marshy areas where wild rice was gathered (Travers 2015).

A seven-thousand acre, wetland near Lake Wawanosh contained a two-acre cranberry marsh east of Point Edward and the Sarnia Flats where the Anishinabe camped and planted corn (Travers 2015).

The creation of the international border through our territories cut us off from many resources formerly enjoyed. Independence was limited and our options were few. Our people remained loyal to Britain and had to remove themselves to territory within Canada's borders and give up use of their lands and resources within the U.S.A. Some cross border, access was possible for a few years.

But by 1830, in Michigan, Ohio, Indiana, and Wisconsin, the U.S. calvary was actively hunting down our people. Faced with extermination or forcible removal to the Southwest, many of the families which lived on the American side sought refuge with their friends and allies in Canada. By 1839, a number of related families from Wisconsin, had settled with the few Chippewa families who resided at Kettle and Stony Points. Numerous others from Wisconsin, Indiana, Ohio, and Michigan joined over the course of the last century. Many moved on to other Anishinabek communities.

We were denied the right to vote until 1950 in provincial elections and 1960 in federal elections.

Sarnia, Kettle Point – Wiiwkwedong, and Stony Point – Aazhoodena were classified as a single band until 1919, when Sarnia became separate.

In 1927 and 1928, speculators used unscrupulous tactics to gain 83,000 acres at Kettle and Stoney Point.

IPPERWASH

Ipperwash, meaning "Upper Wash", lies between Kettle Point and Aux Sable – Stoney Point Reserves.

Ipperwash Provincial Park was created in 1932 on land from the front of Stony Point Reserve Beach. It was purchased in 1936 (Ipperwash Commission of Inquiry Historical Background, Attngen.jus.gov.on.ca, www).

> *The government Department of National Defense borrowed our land for an advanced military training facility for troops headed to Hitler's Europe under the War Measures Act in 1942.*
>
> *In February 1942, the government wanted the land, and by March, engineers were drilling test wells without permission, without a vote, and against advice from the Department of Indian Affairs. The surrender vote took place on April 1, 1942 with the land to be returned after the war. By July, the people were moved to swampland at Kettle Point. By the 1960s, Camp Ipperwash was used for cadet training and free camping for military personnel. The lawyer hired to fight for a lease was threatened and stonewalled by federal officials in the Department of Indian Affairs and the Department of Justice. This caused animosity, resentment, and feelings of injustice within the band.*
>
> *The Stoney people were evicted from their 2,440 acres of farm lands, and their homes bulldozed. They were forcibly relocated to Kettle Point. There was much frustration, our sacred burial sites were there. In 1993, we had*

a picnic and occupied the land. There were several altercations with OPP disguised as campers.

In February 1994, the government closed Camp Ipperwash and announced the eventual return of the land to the Chippewas of Kettle and Stony Point after 53 years of unlawful occupation.

We had a peaceful, nonviolent protest on Labor Day of 1995 at Military Camp Ipperwash. In September, a sniper killed unarmed protester, Dudley George, 38 years old, with three shots. He was born in Sarnia in 1957. A riot squad was deployed; a riot ensued.

The Judge ruled that the continued occupancy was 'Spurious and without substance'. After years of waiting, the land was returned in 2007 to the original owners. It was formally signed over in 2009, after numerous attempts to have it returned.

Nearly all the lands and inland waterways in Ontario are subject to treaties between first nations and the British and Canadian governments. These treaties are not relics of the past. They are living agreements, and the understandings on which they are based continue to have the full force of law in Canada today. (Missisauga, Eagle Tribe)

There are 1,000 members on the reserve and 900 off of it.

On September 19, 2015, after 73 years, the land at Ipperwash, the 2,211 acres appropriated by the federal government in 1942 under the War Measures Act, was officially returned. A settlement of 95 million dollars will be made to the families affected, 20 million of which will be for affected families, , compensation and 70 million will be set aside for future development. The land is to be cleaned up of pollutants and debris and all military buildings are to be demolished and removed to finish work begun in 2013.

Kettle Point Reserve is 2,100 acres. There are stones, or concretians, that are perfectly rounded here. Thus, the name Kettle Point. These rare stones are "Thunderbird Eggs". Chert is also found on the shores. There are shale beds here also.

Aux Sable or Stoney Point Reserve – *Aashoodenong*, meaning "the other side of town" – is the sister community of Kettle Point.

> *Our traditions have persisted for millennia, long before Canada existed at all. Our small territories have sustained us through times of change and link us to our colorful past. We have preserved much of our past in oral stories and legends. We have rediscovered details of the past through ongoing archival research.*
>
> *The Kettles are concretions of calcite crystals which literally grow. These boulders are not found at any other Canadian location and have always been a natural wonder.*

Victor Gulewitsch (1995) was the author of the publication The Chippewas of Kettle and Stony Point, Historical Claims Commission Research Office. The above paragraphs are adapted from his writings.

The Flint Bed was a reef; the flint broke from the reef in pieces small enough for a man to carry, them and then it was chipped into smaller articles (Patricia Orange, Lambton Co. Ontario History).

Chief Ashkebahoreguad was War Chief of the Chippewas and a nephew of Tecumseh. He was a signer of the Treaty of 1827. Many of his descendants live at Kettle Point Reserve.

The Chippewa of Kettle and Stony Point were called "Aux Sable" or Sable in the early 1800s during the early post-treaty period on most documents.

SOMBRA RESERVE

Sombra means "shade". The reserve at Sombra was for the Shawnee – Shawanese – British Loyalists to live on after the wars. Sombra was once known as Shawnee Township. This 92,000-acre reserve north of Walpole Island was squatted upon and has been sold. The Shawnee lived on Sombra Reserve after 1812 as British United Empire Loyalists, the land was ceded by a treaty by

Ottissippi

McKee, the Indian agent (P. Orange). Mckee made verbal promises to the Indians that were not kept. By illegal and deceptive means, the land was granted to settlers in the 1840s. This was treaty number six (Adapted from Travers, 2015).

Shawnee means "Southerners", Algonquin-speaking people from Ohio. The Shawnee were driven from Ohio, West Virginia, and Western Pennsylvania. They then moved to Tennessee, South Carolina, Eastern Pennsylvania, and Southern Illinois, then to Indiana. They were neighbors of the Miami, Delaware, Ottawa, and Wyandotte. They had rich hunting grounds. Chilicothe, now Ohio, was the capital and castle of the Shawnee's (Patricia Orange, Ontario 1975). Near Chilicothe are many mound groups of many shapes.

The Sombra lands (the Shawnee Refugee Reserve) were part of the Chenail Escarte. Thomas McKee explained at a council involving thirteen Ojibwa chiefs that "'the King wanted this area not for his own use, but for his Indian children and you yourselves [. . .] will be welcome to come and live therein.' The thirteen Ojibwa Chiefs agreed [. . .] receiving many trade goods, 772 knives, 278 pounds of powder, 2100 pounds of shot and ball, 26 rifles, 3,456 tobacco pipes, 333 kettles, and 1498 blankets."

This kept the Indians loyal to the British. The area was not reserved for the Indians but was opened to White settlers. The Ojibwa were pleased with the goods received and the British concern for the displaced Ojibwa allies. But they were not aware that they were surrendering the land for White settlement. It was this type of Machiavellian diplomacy which permitted the early peaceful settlement of Southern Ontario.

The Lower St. Clair Reserve on the Detroit River was called Huron Christian Reserve or Moore. It was ceded in 1800 in Treaty Number 12 to the British government.

Many treaties were filled with complicated jargon, were ambiguous, incomplete, sloppily conducted, and badly recorded. The land descriptions were often vague or entirely missing. The territory often belonged to other bands. Some of the treaties did not express a single boundary; there were blank deeds. The Indians were cheated in so-called Walking Treaties, the distance a man could travel in a day (Adapted from Schmaltz).

The Upper Canada Legislative Assembly believed the Indian lands that were not in possession of, could be settled. This meant the hunting grounds and fishing grounds. That the pent-up Europeans, were lawfully entitled to take possession and settle thereon. The Indians families had exclusive rights to hunt and fish in specific geographical areas; any Indian encroachment on that land could suffer death as a result (Adapted from, Schmaltz).

Many promises were made to the Indians to protect their lands. The settler squatters were considered by the government as an "uncontrollable force of Natural Law". These false promises then led to more devious land cessions and removal and concentration on reserves. The Indian agents were very ineffective in helping the Indians. This seemed to be the plan to keep them downtrodden and ill informed, secluded and the prey of White officials and their cronies (Travers).

The Indians sold their lands to alleviate suffering of the people and settle accounts with merchants (Travers 2015).

The position of Indian agent was based on patronage; many were given appointments for past military service, very few were farmers. All were Tories; many were members of the Family Compact. Most were corrupt thieves. The Indian agents used many ways to frustrate the Indians attempts to earn income. They created their own rules to oppose any of the Indians' attempts at being self-sufficient. Everything had to have his approval. Supplies could not be bought and products could not be sold without his signature. Band Council meetings could not take place without his authorization, and all minutes needed his approval.

"The Indian agent had complete authority over every aspect of our lives. Permission was necessary to leave the reserve for a short period of time. There were no legal rights" (D. Plain).

Most of the Indian agents were corrupt, keeping Indian funds for themselves. There were a few who had the Indians' interests at heart. Froome Talfourd became Superintendent in 1858 and discovered great abuse and extortion. He was one of the few honest and fair people in government. Since being under self-rule, much had been accomplished. At Walpole, the Snye Bridge, a central school, a highway, a day nursery, a works department, farming, a Council Hall, sports and recreation, parks, and hockey facilities have been built.

Many Indians bought land to stay in their homeland, and many neighbors and friends bought land to help their Indian neighbors and friends stay in their homelands (Tanner).

In 1819, the Treaty of Saginaw ceded six million acres of land, the Saginaw Chippewa-Ojibwe refused to move and sell the land where their ancestors were buried, where they lived and had their homes. They retained 16 band reserves and a large number, of individual lands. Also, the right to hunt, fish, and gather on the ceded lands. The treaty was made by compulsion, threats, bribery, intimidation, and large quantities of liquor, which was illegal under Trade and Intercourse Laws.

A fort was built at Saginaw to control any dissent. The fort was left after two years of mosquitos and swamp fever.

Coal was found and mined in Michigan – 46 million tons – the Saginaw Valley and Jackson being the mining areas. There were 160 coal mines in the Saginaw Valley. Oil and gas were found in Michigan lands; there are over 14,000 oil wells in Michigan and over 13,000 gas wells.

In 1826, water levels swelled and many Anishinabe and settlers were forced to move to places with a higher water table (Travers, 2015).

In 1831, Lewis Cass moved to Washington as Secretary of War. Henry R. Schoolcraft was appointed superintendent of the Indian Agency. Cass and Schoolcraft worked to acquire Indian land and move the Indians out West. Lewis Cass was the man who devised and implemented the Indian Removal Act with Andrew Jackson, President of the U.S.

In 1830, the Graduation Act, a land sale scheme, was passed by Congress. In 1841, the Distribution and Preemption Act made the Graduation Act permanent. This act lowered the price of land the longer the length of time it was on the market. The price of reservation land dropped from $5 per acre to 25 cents an acre. The failure of U.S. banks by 1839 caused land sales to crash, the price drastically reduced.

Speculators purchased large numbers of military warrants for land, which were received as partial payment from veterans.

BLACK RIVER AND SWAN CREEK BANDS OF OJIBWA

After the Treaty of 1807, selling five million acres in Southeast Michigan, the Ojibwe held four reserves in St. Clair County, Michigan, on Lake St. Clair and the St. Clair River. "We kept the right to hunt, fish, and gather on the lands sold. These lands were convenient stopping places when traveling from Canada to Michigan. The border was not recognized between the U.S. and Canada and did not restrict travel back and forth.

The government was to supply a blacksmith on the Saginaw River to mend plows, guns, traps, and kettles. Annuities were to be paid in goods forever. The promised goods were often withheld to reimburse settlers for losses incurred by the Indians. The federal government held the whole tribe responsible for the actions of a few individuals.

The Three Fires Nations heard and endorsed Tecumseh's message of unity and resistance to alcohol, dependence on trade goods, and abandonment of their own traditions and practices. The people fought alongside Tecumseh in the British and Indian War of 1812 against the Americans.

The Indians, being confined to the reservations, did not have the land base to support their traditional way of life. It was impossible to support themselves. The government made it very uncomfortable to stay on Indian homelands. Some people were actually starving to death. The government encouraged all to move west of the Mississippi to uninhabitable lands and unfriendly or enemy tribes" (Diba Jimooyung, Saginaw Chippewa).

On February 16, 1835, Congress passed the Indian Removal Act and began the relocation of thousands of people from their homelands.

At the Treaty of Washington in 1836, to sell the reserve lands in Southeast Michigan, Maconce – Esh Ton Oquot – was the Swan Creek Chief and Speaker. "Clear Sky" – Ashi Tan Aqui – was the Chief of the Black River band. They were being encroached upon; the Whites were stealing their timber (Tanner, The Chippewa of Lower Michigan/Warner, Robert, Economic and History Report on Royce Area 111).

When the Black River and Swan Creek bands moved in 1830 to 1840, they received no reservation and lost federal recognition.

The Black River bands had many chiefs – Chief Naykeezhig, Mayzin, and Keewaykeezhig – and their people moved mostly to Canada at Aamjiwnaang – Sarnia and Bkejwanong – Walpole Island. Some went to the Saginaw and Flint areas. Chief Nangi and Chief Macounce were Ojibwe chiefs. Chief Massas was an Ojibwe leader near Lake St. Clair. Okemos was the Chief of the Ojibwe-Chippewa in 1858 when he died.

After the 1836 Treaty when the Black River and Swan Creek People sold their lands to the United States, John Riley bought land on Belle River, near Memphis Mi. his Band moved there, and traded with settlers at the St. Clair River and Port Huron.

The Swan Creek and Black River Bands were led by, Eshtonoquot (Eshtonaquet), also known as Chief Francis Maconse, "Little Bear". In 1839, Maconse, traders, and U.S. officials worked together to convince 51 of the people to move to Kansas. They arrived with nothing and became part of the Munsee Delaware village, and the group became "The Chippewa and Christian Reserve". Both bands later moved to the Cherokee Nations. In 1838, the Swan Creek and Black River Anishinabe bands numbered 360 people. Chief Francis Maconse, Southbird, and Sprakin explored Kansas, and it did not suit the people.

Many Swan Creek and Black River people refused to move. Those who did not move to Kansas joined a Methodist Mission near the former Black River

Reservation. Others moved to a Wesleyan Mission at Sarnia, Ontario. Two families had bought land near their 1807 reservations. By 1839, 58% of the people had left their Southern Michigan Reservations. In 1841, Indian Agent Robert Stuart counted 108 remaining in Michigan, about 30% of their 1838 population of 360.

The Swan Creek and Black River bands moved several times between 1840 and 1855. The Methodist Church operated a station called the Black River Society during the 1840s. The remnant bands soon left their homes on the lakeshore and moved inland to the mouth of the Flint River in a region surrounded with Saginaw Anishinabe villages and missions. A census by U.S. Indian Agents showed 21 families with a total population of 91 people in 1845.

The small bands moved to Lapeer county in 1850, where they built the Neppesing Mission about twenty miles east of the village of Flint. They acquired 520 acres and farmed 100 acres. The Methodist Church bought another 200 acres to benefit the Anishinabek. The community prospered, and in 1855, numbered 138 persons. Twenty-five church members remained at Belle River.

Other bands lived in their historic homelands but did not own their homes. During the next five years, a few families became members of Methodist churches and bought land near their former reservations and began to farm.

"The Methodist faith helped pull our people from the edge of destruction. People who became converts rebuilt their shattered lives. The church gave them farming tools and animals and helped them build farms" (Kahkewaquonaby – Peter Jones, "Sacredfeathers").

The Black River Mission had 246 members (Al and Dave Eicher, the Indian History of the Michigan Thumb Region).

"Our Methodist spiritual leader demanded that Methodist Anishinabek give up alcohol. Anishinabek responded to the promise of spiritual salvation and also found physical salvation, in their own lifetimes.

Peter Jones visited Michigan on a missionary journey in the 1830s. He also sent missionaries John Sunday, John Taunchy, and Nahgonwawedung – John Kahbeege to teach about the Methodist faith. Madivagivunayaush – Peter Marksman quickly converted and became a missionary preacher to the Anishinabek at Saginaw Valley.

The Methodist Anishinabek built houses, their own church, and schools, including the Nepessing station in Lapeer County on the Flint River at Kopenekahning near Flint and at Pewanegoing, also called Kazier, or Taymouth, in Saginaw County. Reverend Daniel Wheaton, Anishinabe Methodist preacher, served as minister at Taymouth – Kazier, fourteen miles south of Saginaw.

They harvested food to feed themselves, disease came less frequently, and the worst of the whiskey traders left them. The Anishinabe ancestors began to take charge of their political life once again.

> During the time of crisis, the U.S. had done little to give our people the promised help in the 1836, 1837, and 1838 Treaties. By 1837, our people had so little game, money, or property that they were literally starving. Those trying to protect the Anishinabe were ostracized.
>
> Today we attribute our survival to our spiritual strength and faith. Many of our ancestors continued to hold onto and practice Midewiwin and fought diseases. The Methodist Church missionaries and Anishinabek churchmen stood up on our behalf. The Church helped the people in many ways. In their darkest days of pain and rejection, the people found the church a good place.

Camp meetings were held that drew hundreds to camp together for a week or more. They hunted, fished, and gathered wild foods. They met relatives and discussed important political issues. Many found sweethearts who later became spouses.

At one early camp meeting held in 1850, 800 to 1,000 Anishinabek met on the Cass River, at present Bridgeport. Many who came were not Christians; it was not unusual to gather and do things together. Deep respect for one another overcame barriers. The camp meetings provided many opportunities to socialize.

Box Socials were often held at these gatherings. Women made special lunches and decorated boxes. Men would bid for the lunches, eating his meal with the woman who had packed it. The money raised helped pay for travel expenses of those who could not otherwise afford to come. Ministers often became political leaders of the tribe."

The above paragraphs are adapted from, "Diba Jimoouung", Telling our Story, Zibiiwing, Saginaw Chippewa. The book, *Diba Jimooyung*, is excellent reading for more on Ojibwe history in Michigan.

"All that remained of our proud nationhood was our tribal identity, language, clan system, and spiritual connection to the land. Some families held on to our histories, stories, and clans, but these traditions gradually faded away. Few speak the Ojibwe language. But there is now renewed interest in our culture, the young are learning" (Diba Jimooyung).

In 1840, many were hunted down and removed, many fled to Canada and other far-away places.

The Indians who had left Michigan were returning to find their families, and many went to Canada. A deep emotional and economic depression permeated the villages. A lack of understanding of the White ways was the basis for refusing the White ways, to develop the desire to acquire.

An Indian exodus from Detroit never occurred.

The Indian Civilization Act was to remake Indians into a God-fearing New England farm family. Government policy was to convince Indians to forsake their own beliefs and lifeways, to the White man's ways, to take up farming and private property.

The Bureau of Indian Affairs, enlisted Church clergy to act as reservation directors. They were to convert the natives to Christianity, teach only English, emphasize American Government classes, teach farming, and provide blacksmith services, farm implements, and seed.

Mission schools were failures in most cases. A few were successful. Some did not follow the government's standards and were on their own to help the Natives. They upgraded villages following their conscience, with support of their home churches. Catholic Father Baraga was a notable example, coming to the Indians aid (Kah Wam Da Meh, Jean Frazier 1988).

Merriam's scathing report (The Merriam Report) on the reservations of the Northwest in 1928 led to the Wheeler Howard Reorganization Act, returning some power to tribes in Minnesota.

There were many other government programs used to help or control the Indians. The rampant government fraud of the Bureau of Indian Affairs and Congress changed little. The policies were designed to oppress and destroy the Indian, stealing all the resources of the reservations.

The Ojibwe were educated in schools operated by the federal government, our leaders became educated. They became adept at not being taken advantage of by duplicitous government policies.

Government-operated schools helped to bind the scattered Anishinabe community together. In an environment of virulent racism and discrimination, government schools gave Anishinabe children a haven where they could learn, safe from the taunting of White classmates.

In the 1840s, Methodist missionaries built small log buildings where children and adults alike learned to read and write. By 1855, six schools operated at the Anishinabe settlements around Saginaw and Flint. These were day schools. About 220 scholars studied reading, writing, and arithmetic, the books written in the English language.

After the 1855 Treaty, the U.S. built seven new schools, one on the Saganing Reservation and six at Isabella. The children had to leave school to hunt, fish, and gather crops with their parents. They continued to speak the Anishinabe language at home.

The government built Mt. Pleasant Boarding School to separate children from Anishinabe culture and more fully assimilate them to White culture. Children were taken from their homes at a very young age to attend government-run boarding schools.

ISABELLA RESERVATION

The Isabella Saginaw Chippewa Reservation was created after reserves created in the Saginaw Treaty of 1817 and 1819 were ceded to the U.S. government.

BOARDING SCHOOLS

Most students found the systematic eradication of the Ojibwa language a major factor in alienating them not only from their culture, but from their friends on the reserve as well. Students in schools were prohibited from speaking their native language.

Basil Johnston states, "as long as language exists, it enables men to understand and appreciate their ideas and philosophies and to share in their humor, so long do they adhere to their way of life. Once language disappears men forget their former purpose of life and ideas, they could only understand the thoughts of the adopted culture."

The children were comfortable neither in the White man's world nor in the Indian's world, and their self-esteem and self-respect were shattered.

Letters home had to be in English, all appliances supplied except stamps (which many could not afford), and the family could not read.

Sexual abuse of the children by ministers, priests, nuns, and teachers was widespread. Since the abused are inclined to become abusers, reserve life was influenced adversely by these experiences (Schmaltz).

Caleb Atwater wrote,

I am thoroughly convinced that great abuses exist in the Indian Dept. The causes which produced the abuses will continue them, I fear under the pretext of benevolence to the Indians! By the very persons whose duty it is to act very differently from what some of them do. Using all their influence to keep the Indian where they are in ignorance, poverty, and dependence.

Our red brethren will be driven west, until they finally perish on the shore of the Pacific Ocean. The wasteful and villainous expenditures of millions of dollars under the hypocritical pretentions of benevolence and piety, and even charity, toward the Indians, when we all know that not one cent of this money benefits the Indians. It is of no avail against the united efforts of a corrupt set of men, who contrive to plunder the treasury every winter under the solemn sanctions of law.

The power over our fellowman is now pursued by means most selfish and corrupt, and when obtained, abused by the possessor. (Gen. Henry Dodge/Atwater)

"Kings and priests have been in their exercise of power the very worst foes of mankind. One enslaved the body, the other the soul. The perfect union between church and state, the people were always losers. According to the very spirit of our Constitution, our rulers are our servants, not our masters. The people are the only sovereign in this country."

"The greatest gift of God to mankind is great original thinkers – they are the light of the world" (Atwater).

CHAPTER 11
Mounds and Treaties

"I'm choking on the lies and hidden secrets. Balance comes about through divine intervention and human interaction with God's holiness" (Tunkashila).

The 1763 Royal Proclamation brought peace to the region for a short time. There were to be no public land sales. The British gave liberally of presents for the Indians' needs.

The British government made many treaties with the Native Americans in Upper Canada along the waterways of the lakes. Eastern Michigan was part of Upper Canada and Quebec from 1763 until the British evacuated in 1796 after the Revolutionary War (Treaty Texts Upper Canada Land Surrenders. www).

Sir William Johnson from Ireland was the British Indian agent in 1744. He married Molly Brant, sister of Chief Joseph Brant, a very respected chief in New York and Ontario. Johnson was a fair and honest man who worked for peace.

In negotiations with the Indians, much that is important is often concealed. Some obscure person, trader, or adventurer is often the real pilot of events. McKee, Claus, and Elliot, Indian agents, were successful. Early recognized Treaties with American Indian Nations, www).

Colonel Alexander McKee was British Indian agent in Pennsylvania. As a child, he had been adopted by the Shawnee, learning the Indian language and lifeways. He left America and was a British agent in the French and Indian War, the American Revolution, and the Northwest Indian War. He was associated with Matthew Elliot and the Girty brothers, Simon, James, and George. McKee led efforts to promote Indians to British alliance. He guarded Indian interests

Ottissippi

and was an honest friend. He became Deputy Superintendent General of Indian Affairs for the British.

Mckee, Croghan, and others were involved with the Vandalia Colony efforts to start a 14th British Colony. This became the Treaty of Fort Stanwix in 1768, the Indians surrendering land near Lake Erie, Pennsylvania, West Virginia, and the Kentucky portion of the Colony of Virginia, by the Iroquois Six Nations who claimed it (Adapted from Travers 2015).

Hundreds of sales of large tracts of land were made with the Indians, many out of love for good people, many for money, trinkets, vermillion, powder, lead, and rum.

The American Revolution began in 1775 when George Rogers Clark took Vincennes. In 1779, the Americans claimed all the British-held lands in the United States. Detroit and Michigan were not surrendered. The British were nervous and held councils with the Indians of the area, the Pottawatomi, Ottawa, Huron, and Chippewa, to guarantee their alliance. To prove their allegiance, the Pottawatomi gave large pieces of their hunting grounds along the Rouge River and other Eastern Michigan lands to officers, Indian agents, and interpreters stationed at Fort Lernoult. They in turn parceled out this land and sold it to the French Canadian and British families of Detroit.

There were 488 Pottawatomies at this village in Detroit. From this village, the Pottawatomi Trail led North and West; on the north side of the River Rouge, the trail led from Springwells to Oakland County. The south side of the Rouge River went South and West to Ann Arbor Trail (Woolworth, Dearborn Historical Society).

The 1783 Treaty of Paris concluded the American Revolution, the British Crown of England occupying Canada and the American British the Ohio country. Michigan was not immediately turned over; the British held Michigan lands until 1796 when they vacated most of the territory. They wanted to keep the lucrative Fur Trade active, and the boundaries were not clear to the fledgling United States or England. They also wanted reimbursement for the improvements they had made to the Northwest, including homes and buildings.

The British flag flew over forts and posts long after the Revolution ended. Restitution was to be provided for losses of the United Empire Loyalists who were forced out of the U.S. and the cessation of reprisals on Loyalists remaining in the U.S., had not been respected (Early recognized Treaties with American Indian Nations, www).

Large parts of Upper Canada were relieved of Indian title before 1841. In 1790, two million acres in four counties were ceded (under Treaty Number

Two, along Lake Erie). In 1796, 88,000 acres in Lambton County were ceded, more in 1822, and in 1836, the Moravians of the Thames, Township of Zone, ceded their land (History of Canadian Indians 1763 – 1840, Marionopolis College, www).

Treaty Number Seven was the London Treaty. Treaty Number 27 was for 2.2 million acres of Lambton County, called the Huron Tract. This treaty, the Huron Tract, was negotiated over a 10-year span, the Indians reluctant to part with their source of sustenance (Adapted from Travers 2015). Treaty Number 27 ½ involved the four reserves in Lambton County, Ontario. (See "Chapter 10: Reserves and Indian Lands" for more).

Land cessions continued until most of the Canadian Southern Ontario lands were taken by the White men.

TREATIES AND NEGOTIATIONS

The biggest misunderstanding came from the two different cultures' understandings of land rights. The British believed in the right to own land, while the Natives never had such a concept in their culture. No one owns land in their ideology, as no one owns the sky, the air. Territorial rights could be negotiated, but no ownership of land that could be traded to another person or group. The Natives were not selling their land, which the British thought they were buying. They were agreeing to share the land. This is what had led, to the present day, land claims (Canadian Encyclopedia).

The honorable Indians always kept their word when it was given. They believed that the government officials were being honest and true.

The women were always a part of any important decisions; they were always consulted, providing dialogue, influence, and input. Council speakers always reminded the European Americans that their views represented those of the entire community, including women, an important component group whose support was crucial to the consensual decision-making process (Kugel 1998).

Sacred pipes with sacred tobacco were used to seal and make promises and agreements. Smoking the pipe was as swearing on the Bible in a court of law. It was a pledge before God to be honest and pure of heart and speak the truth. Once agreed, the words were law and to be followed. The Indians never called the pipe a "peace pipe". It was called the prayer pipe, ceremonial pipe, or truth pipe.

Europeans wanted only to deal with men in the Fur Trade and treaties. The Anishinabe and laws of humanity were disregarded. The government used every advantage to advance their interests.

Ottissippi

The United States used many conniving ways to deceive the Indians and take their lands. They would prime the people with alcohol well ahead of the treaties and into the treaties. Thousands of gallons of whiskey were given as presents to the Indians, destroying their power and lives.

They would choose Indian leaders who they could influence to sign treaties without the authority of the official tribal leaders. During treaties, those who were not in favor or were influential were often taken to private meetings and kept drunk for days to keep them away from the official signings. They would write the treaties in English, and the people most often found that the final treaties were not as they had been negotiated. Often the treaties were vague in description and were later changed to steal away much more land. The Treaties were often forced at gunpoint, the cessions, were made under duress. Credit was given to the Indians, who would end up owing large sums which had to be paid by land sales.

Preemption Acts promised land titles to squatters who made improvements. The objective of expansion became very clear.

Unauthorized individuals sold land to speculators. Land cessions were used to cover trade debts and annuities and as retribution against military defiance (Sturdevant, 1978).

As more and more settlers illegally moved into Indian territory, the trespassers would abuse Native Americans and promote hostilities, which would be solved by United States troops. After the hostile Natives were subdued, a treaty forced the defeated and harassed Indian Nations to cede more lands to the federal government. Who then sold their lands to speculators and settlers. Treaties avoided costly wars (Sturdevant, 1978).

The White men led by controlling wealth and political machines. (People of the Three Fires).

The Indian title to land in this region was gradually extinguished. The Iroquois conveyed their title in 1784 under protest of neighboring tribes, the Wyandotte, Chippewa, Ottawa, and other tribes by treaties dated 1785, 1795, 1805, and 1807 (Farmer). The Ojibwe Indians signed over 80 treaties ceding the lands, always keeping the right to hunt and fish and gather on the lands ceded.

The 1795 Treaty of Greenville was signed at the St. Mary's River, a branch of the Miami River that runs into Lake Erie. Fort Wayne, St. Mary's River, and St. Joseph's were involved in this treaty, in which the United States agreed to relinquish claim to the remaining Michigan lands. Massas and Mashipinashiwish were outspoken negotiators and influential representatives at Greenville (likely Saginaw's).

The signers of the 1795 Treaty of Greenville were the following:

Cheryl Morgan

- Chippewa: Mashipinashwish – Bad Bird, Nah Shogushe (from Lake Superior), Kathawa Sung, Masass, Nemekass – Little Thunder, Peshawkay – Young Ox, Nan Guey, Meenedohgeesogh, Peewanshemenogh, Weymegwas, Gobmaatick
- The Pottawatomi of Huron: Okia, Chamung, Segugewan, Nanawme, Marchand, Wenameac

The Treaty of Fort Industry was made in 1805, the land ceded being 500,000 acres was in Ohio surrounding Toledo, an area known as the Fire Lands of the Connecticut Western Reserve and Sufferers Land. The signers were; chiefs, sachems, and warriors of the Indian nations of the Ojibwe, Pottawatomi, Ottawa, Wyandot, Munsee and Delaware – Lenape, and Shawnee. Charles Jouett was the commissioner for the U.S. who signed the treaty, the $1,000 to be paid at Detroit or some other convenient place. The Ojibwe, Ottawa, and Pottawatomi living along the Huron River were to receive a payment of $4,000 and six yearly payments of $2,000. The Indians kept their rights to hunt and fish on the land.

The 1785 Treaty of Fort McIntosh ceded six miles deep from the Detroit River from Lake Erie to River Raisen on the Lake St. Clair.

The 1789 Treaty of Fort Harmar, by Arthur St. Clair, was a peace treaty for traders to conduct safe business. It was signed by the following:

- Chippewa: Mesass, Paushquash, Pawasicko, Nanamakeak, Wetnasa, Soskene, Pewanakum
- Delawares: Captain Pipe, Wingenond, Pekelan, Teataway
- Ottawa: We Wiskia, Neagey
- Pottawatomi: Windigo, Wapaskea, Nequea
- Sacs: Tepakee, Kesheyiva,
- Wyandottes: Teyandatontec, Cheyawe, Doueyenteat, Tarhe, Terhataw, Datasay, Maudoronk, Skahomat

In 1799, General Arthur St. Clair sent a letter to the Indians from the Ohio to Sault De St. Marie. The letter was read in every village. Here is a part of the letter: "Believe me, my sons, I wish well to all my Red Children; and the President of the United States will continue to love them and do them good; but there are people who make you uneasy; they love nobody but themselves, and because some of them have prevailed on individuals amongst you to make grants of land to them, contrary to our laws and to all your former practice, that are not approved of, they give you no rest, but are always saying some disagreeable things or other to you. I tell you, and I tell the truth, that it is for your interest the United States do not approve those grants of land. Only consider a little, if every one of you, of yourselves, without the consent of the Nation, may give away the lands that belong to you all, and at times when, perhaps, you have been made drunk on purpose, what will become of your wives and children?

"Do you not see that it is to prevent your being cheated by bad men, who if they can get your lands, do not care if you were all to perish with hunger, that the United States will not allow of their people to buy them but at Public Treaty with the Nation, when you are all sober and know that you are not wronged nor wronging yourselves? Must not war be certain if you find your lands gone and have got nothing of value for them? You would kill some who lived there who perhaps had no hand in cheating you; and some of you would be killed in return, and all the mischief of war would follow.

"I find it to be your wish that some person may be appointed at Detroit to whom you may speak occasionally. Such agents can only be appointed by the President, and when he knows how much you wish for one, I do not doubt that one on whom you may depend will be appointed.

"Without trade in furs, a crisis came, having lost craft skills and dependent on European Americans with little to offer in return other than land for debts run up to live on."

The Ohio Valley and Great Lakes teemed with refugees, and others moved to the Plains and hunted buffalo (Sturdevant, 1978).

The Federalist Administration had opened a general land office at Detroit in 1804 to market, record, and collect payment for parcels sold. Detroit was the great administrative center for Michigan lands that had been ceded in the Michigan Territory. The Michigan Territory was very extensive for a single office.

1807 TREATY OF DETROIT

The 1807 Treaty of Detroit with Governor Hull was signed by the sachems, chiefs, and warriors of the Ottawa, Chippewa, Wyandotte, and Pottawatomie nations of Indians. Money and goods were to be paid for the title. George McDougal, Chief Judge Court D.H. and D., Whitmore Knaggs, and William Walker were the interpreters. The Treaty of Detroit was negotiated at White Rock, the Northern border of the lands ceded for the use of the American government. This treaty gave Southeast Lower Michigan, five million acres, to the U.S. government. It took in most of Southeast Michigan and Northwest Ohio.

Many villages of the tribes were not included in the ceded land, 23 miles square, plus six sections of, one, mile square, were to be chosen by the Indians. The Indians were to have free access to the land for hunting, fishing, and gathering and mineral rights (Indian Affairs: Laws and Treaties, Oklahoma State University, www).

Seventeen Chippewa chiefs signed: Peewanshemenogh, Maraau She Gau Ta or Badlegs, Poo Qui Gau Boa Wie, Kiosk, Poquaquet or The Ball, See Gau Ge Wau, Quit Chon E Quit or Big Cloud, Qui Con Quish, Puck Wnesse or Spark of Fire, Negig or The Otter, Me A Si Ta, Tonquish, Mcquettequet or Little Bear, Miott, Nemekas or Little Thunder, Meu E Tu Ge Shek or Little Cedar, and Sawanabenase or Grand Blanc.

The Wyandots were Ska Ho Mat, Miere or Walk in the Water, and I Yo Na Yo Ta Ha.

The witnesses were George McDougal, C. Rush, Jacob Visger, Joseph Watson, Abijah Hull, Harris H. Hickman, A.B. Hull, Whitmore Knaggs, and William Walker.

The land is described as, "Beginning at the mouth of the Miami river (Maumee River) of the Lakes and running up the middle thereof to the mouth of the Great Au Glaize River, thence due North until it intersects a parallel of latitude to be drawn from the outlet of Lake Huron, which forms the River Sinclair, thence running Northeast, the course that may be found will lead in a direct line to White Rock in Lake Huron, thence due East until it intersects the boundary line between the United States and Upper Canada in said Lake, thence Southerly following the said boundary line down said Lake through the River Sinclair, Lake St. Clair, and the Detroit River into Lake Erie to a point due East of the aforesaid Miami River, thence west to the place of beginning."

The reserved lands of the Indians were one tract three miles square or 5,760 acres on Swan Creek of Lake St. Clair; one section and three-quarters near Salt Creek; one-fourth of a section at the mouth of Riviere Au Vasseau; and one tract of two sections near the mouth of Black River, the aggregate containing about 8,320 acres.

The Indians were promised the net proceeds of the sale of these lands, except the survey and expense of the treaty. The Indians also received 8,320 acres of land west of the Mississippi or in Minnesota (Western Historical Co.).

George McDougal was Chief Judge of Court. Abijah Hull was the surveyor for Michigan Territory.

The 1808 Treaty of Brownstown by William Hull, Governor of Michigan, was signed by Nemekas – Little Thunder, Pukanese – Spark of Fire, Macquettequet – Little Bear, Shimnaraquette, and Miere – Walk in the Water, a Wyandot (Reuben Atwater, Secretary of the Territory of Michigan. OKU, Indian Affairs, www).

The 1815 Treaty of Springwells was a peace treaty with the Ottawa, Pottawatomi, and Ojibwe Indians from all over the Great Lakes and Michigan, ending the Alliance with the British and restoring all possessions, rights, and privileges before the War of 1812.

The Western movement of the agricultural frontier together with the Rush-Bagot Agreement in 1817, the Convention of 1818, and the Adams Onis Treaty in 1819 left the Indians, to be seen as worthless obstacles to "Manifest Destiny". The so-called God-given right to take lands belonging to those who were not Christian nations.

They were no longer needed as allies in the struggle to claim empire in North America. The revised policy was the removal of the Eastern tribes to "The Great American Desert". Andrew Jackson was the man to begin the removal, Lewis Cass his Secretary of War.

TREATY OF SAGINAW

The 1817 treaty negotiations of Saginaw were a long, drawn-out affair. It was signed on the banks of the Cass (Huron) River near Caro, Michigan. At the 1819 Treaty of Saginaw we asked, "where will our children sleep? We will not sell our lands".

Underhanded ways were used to quell dissenters, and special land deals were made. A large quantity of liquor was used before, during, and after the treaty to convince a sale. This treaty gave half of Michigan to the U.S. government, six million acres. There were great oil and coal reserves in this territory. There were 114 signers, chiefs and head chiefs of the Chippewa Nation, their totems affixed to the treaty. Friends all to Jacob Smith, their generous friend and trader.

NEOME

Neome, one of four great chiefs of the Saginaw Treaty, lived at Muscadawain on the Flint River. The English called it the Grand Traverse of the Flint River (Downtown Flint). The present town of Montrose was his "castle", called Neome's Town. The Grand Trail crossed the Flint here. He was called a "Lion in the Path". At the time of the treaty, there was no Flint Village where Flint now is; where Neome lived was called Neome's Village, and where Flint now is, was called Muscadawain. Flint Village in early times was Lapeer, Michigan.

Penazegewezhic or Pewanigowink was another of the four great chiefs, as was Mixauene or Mixadine, brother of Neome (Reaume), and Kish Kau Ko, "The Crow", a Saginaw chief with a violent record.

The tribe of Neome's people were called the Pewongo. The village of Pewonny Go Wingh was the Tribal home of Chief Neome.

Neome was called Reaume on the treaty. He was the principal orator of the treaty, well-loved by his people, good, honest, and kind, short and heavy (some say simple minded and ignorant). Jacob Smith, called Webazince or Wabesins, "Young Swan", his son-in-law and great friend, was an interpreter at the Treaty of Saginaw.

Whitmore Knaggs, a fur trader and a federal agent, scout, and interpreter, was at the Treaty of Saginaw as an interpreter.

Louis Campau worked for the American Fur Company, supplied the government provisions, and erected the buildings for the government treaty men. There was an open-sided council building; it was several hundred feet long, with logs for the Indians to sit on along the shore, a storehouse, and dining room. He went on to trade around the state, founding Saginaw and Grand Rapids. Louis also supplied many useful items to the Indians: spades, shovels, scythes, rings, calico, tobacco, canoes, mats, cotton cloth, a gun delivered to an Indian, and sundry other articles.

Jacob Smith was the unofficial Indian agent at Detroit. He was arrested by the British as a spy. He lost much in the war – goods were seized, fines were given. His brother in Quebec paid his debt.

Ephraim S. Williams, a trader, was also there, as were the Riley boys, James, John and Peter, government employees, the half-Ojibwe sons of James Van Slyke Ryley, Old Indian Trader and Interpreter.

Henry Conner, a trader, attended. J. and A. Wendell, Indian traders, were suppliers for the treaty. Crosses, camp blankets, handkerchiefs, etc. were given to the Indians.

Old Mr. Riley was at the treaty, along with Beaufait, Knaggs, Godfrey, Whipple, Visger, Forsyth, Tucker, Hersey, and Walker (MPHC, vol. 26).

Governor Cass had over ten meetings with the Indians. There were only three formal council meetings with the people. The Saginaw Ojibwe were adamant about not selling the land of their ancestors. There were up to 4,000 Indians present at the council treaty.

There were many private councils with individual leaders of bands or between Anishinabe leaders, traders, and Metis – mixed-blood relatives.

Louis Campau, aid to Governor Cass, wrote a statement: "Going against the law, Governor Cass sent alcohol and gifts ahead of the treaty. He sent 662 gallons of whiskey to keep any opposition away from the negotiations and to help dominate negotiations with those willing to sell."

Many chiefs never signed the treaty; there were scores of chiefs and headmen that would not cede any part of their territory and threatened violence. Only when Smith joined the talks did they move forward to a deal with the U.S.

Chief Neome attended every meeting and made the final decision. He held the balance of Anishinabe power; he represented the majority, of the Saginaw Ojibwe. He spoke for a coalition of large villages throughout the Saginaw Watershed. Neome and Smith desired land for their people and their own families.

There were many traders who had large claims for debts against advanced trade goods.

Governor Cass knew the Anishinabe would not leave their homelands. Without reserved lands, there would be no treaty. The Anishinabe reserved the lands where they lived, played, danced, planted, and buried their dead. The Anishinabe also preserved all their hunting and fishing rights to the whole territory.

After the treaty was signed, and goods and money distributed, all the Indians were drunk. Cass and his party left before daylight the next morning, the troops about ten o'clock.

This treaty sold almost 16 million acres of land – over a quarter of the Lower Peninsula. Very few Anishinabe understood what the treaty meant. The treaty was paid in silver. Neome, Smith, and the Riley's received large land reserves at Flint and Saginaw. The treaty became law on March 25, 1820.

Peter Riley was granted the village on the west bank of the Saginaw River at Carrolton Village, known as Peter Riley Reservation. John Riley's land was on the east bank of the Saginaw River. Each receiving 660 acres. James also received 660 acres at the Saginaw Treaty. Bay City was built on John Riley's land.

To be governed and to be enslaved are ideas which have been confounded by the Indians. The love of independence is so great with these tribes, they have never been willing to load their political system with the forms of a regular government, for fear it might prove oppressive (Henry R. Schoolcraft, 1821, "Travels in Minnesota").

The assimilation to White culture was started. Life went on with little change at first; the land was rich in fish and game, harvested for trade and shipped to Detroit.

Cholera reached Saginaw Valley in 1834. In 1837, smallpox killed nearly one-third of the Saginaw Valley Anishinabe.

The land had valuable timber and other natural resources. The waterways powered mills.

"Flint Village" was what the French called Lapeer – Le Pierre, meaning "The Stone" or "Stone River". The Flint River had a rocky bed. Flint was called "River of Firestones" or "River of the Fire Stone". It was at Peioonnukwing, or Pewonny Go Wingh, another spelling for Neome's Town.

The Pewongo tribe – band of Neome – was succeeded by Tonedogone, or Tonedokane, the war chief.

There are numerous Indian cemeteries in Michigan. The Wajamega Cemetery near Caro is a special place where many grandfathers were buried. On the Thames River in Ontario is a large burial mound sacred to the Indians. Sanilac County has 22 recorded mounds. There are circular enclosures and garden beds, many other sites are not recorded.

In 1818, L. Jouett was the Indian agent for Michigan.

The 1819 Treaty of Saginaw was signed in Caro, Michigan, the Indians being forced to sell. Many fled to Canada, and some were killed for refusing to sell.

Near Caro is a trail that is three feet deep from travel to the area West of Caro, near the old Indian burial ground near Cass river (C. Moore History of Michigan, www).

Trails followed Belle River and Black River and most of the other rivers into the interior.

In 1820, with Lewis Cass at L'Arbre Croche (northwest shore of Lake Michigan) and Michilimackinac, the Ottawa and Chippewa ceded the St. Martin Islands of Lake Huron for goods. They were made of plaster of Paris. The treaty was signed by 11 Ottawa chiefs and 9 Chippewa chiefs, including (Ottawa chiefs) Shawanoe, Oninjuega or Wing, Ceddimalmese or Black Hawk, and (Chippewa chief) Kenojekum or Pike.

The doctrine of "Manifest Destiny" was the rule governments used to say they were doing the right thing, in taking over the lands of the Indians.

Black Hawk, the Sauk Chief, said, "How smooth must be the language of the Whites, when they can make right look like wrong, and wrong look like right."

President Andrew Jackson was a land speculator, merchant, slave trader, and the most aggressive enemy of the Indian in early American history. His army had a high rate of desertion, poor Whites were willing to give their lives and saw the rewards of battle go to the rich. Men were whipped for their first two attempts to desert and executed for the third.

Ottissippi

Gold was discovered in Georgia in 1829 in the Cherokee land. Jackson promised the Indians that, when they moved, they would be free of White government and traders and would possess the land west of the Mississippi, "as long as the grass grows or the water runs" (North American Review, Jan 1830).

Cass, was in charge, of the Indian vaccine of 1832 for smallpox. This was given to all Indians who were involved with the U.S. and were not aggressor Nations or beyond civilization. Many were purposely excluded for economic reasons. In 1837 and 1838, the Upper Missouri tribes who were not vaccinated suffered staggering mortalities. The Mandan, Arikara, Hidatsas, Assiniboine, Cree, Blackfeet and other Northern Missouri River tribes (North American Review).

THE INDIAN REMOVAL

The Indian removal policy of Andrew Jackson and Lewis Cass, his secretary of war, was to remove all the Indians West of the Mississippi to the great desert. The land was inferior, the occupants mostly hostile. Many were forced to walk the "Trail of Tears" or "Trail of Death", where many died along the route in winter. The policy was an extermination of the Indians. The tribes removed did not receive vaccine and were sent into country ablaze with smallpox in 1838.

The farmers who were neighbors of the Indians were friendly with them and did not wish to see them removed. This policy came from industry and capitalists with great influence in government.

In Michigan, the Pottawatomi were forced to move, many on "The Trail of Death", many fled to other places. In the 1830s and 1840s, thousands of refugee Indians from Michigan, Wisconsin, and Minnesota fled to Canada, some stayed on very small reserves in the western portion of Michigan.

The Ojibwe and Ottawa also fled and hid out with others. Some were being fired on as they fled to safety in Canada as British Loyalists. They went underground for a time, many moved back to their homelands.

Solemn treaties were the national honor, made with prayer and mention of God. They were promptly broken, arousing anger and contempt (C. Eastman, Soul of the Indian, www).

The 1836 Treaty of Washington by Henry R. Schoolcraft was signed by the Black River and Swan Creek chiefs and band leaders. It was signed at Washington. This treaty sold the reserved lands from the 1807 Treaty. The Indian chiefs and head chiefs were given the royal treatment, wined and dined.

It was signed by the following: Eton O Quot or Eshtonoquot – Clear Sky, Naygeezhig – Driving Clouds, Mayzin – Checkered, and Keewaygeezhig – Returning Sky.

The officials and witnesses present were Sam Humes Porter, Secretary; Stephen T. Mason, Governor of Michigan; Luscious Lyon; John Holiday; Joseph F. Maisac; and George Moran.

The Treaty of 1837 was for the rest of Michigan. The treaty concerned five-year tracts of land belonging to the Black River people, to trade the land for reservations West of the Mississippi. The removal process was to begin in five years. Abusive tactics were used to restrict and crush: "they made us poor, sick, and shut us up, even to sewing some women's lips together. We never violated or broke our part of any agreement or treaties" (Ziibiwing).

The Ojibwe from Black River migrated to Lapeer County, Michigan, and the Isabella Reserve for the Saginaw. Some remained in Macomb, Wayne, Washtenaw, and St. Clair Counties. Fifty-one went to Kansas; some merged with the Munsee Christian and the Cherokee. Some of the 51 returned to Michigan and Canada.

The 1838 Treaty was a revised version of the 1837 Treaty, to correct errors, in the 1837 Treaty, which was hopelessly flawed.

"We are destroying them off the face of the Earth, may God forgive our tyranny, avarice, ignorance, for it is very terrible to think of" (Schoolcraft 1851).

The better the land was cleared and cropped, the more envious the White settlers became. The finer the timber, the more impatient to possess it. The Indians were cheated, and they sold his timber and, many times, his land; both so unscrupulous were trader and settler (Mrs. Cass Mosher, Isabella County, MI Gen Web).

The Treaty of 1855 was a revised treaty to the Isabella Treaty, which was severely flawed. Lumber and railroad, politicians, and squatters had come in to defraud the people. Organized Christian civilization preyed upon the goodness of the Natives.

The Treaty of 1864 was also a revised Saginaw treaty.

The 1859 Treaty of Kansas was signed by Eshtonquit – Francis McCoonse, Edward McCoonse, William Turner, Antwine Gokey, Henry Donohue, Ignatius Caleb, and John Williams. These were the Black River and Swan Creek people who were part of the Delaware Munsee Christian tribe. This treaty was to settle prior treaty agreements and settle the bands in Kansas (OKU, Indian Affairs, www).

The Ojibwe-Chippewa signed 85 treaties from 1701 to 1867, with various governmental bodies, including 1 with France, 28 with Great Britain, 11 with Canada, and 45 with the United States. Due to distinctly different cultures, it would be another generation before the Ojibwa fully realized that they had not just granted Whites permission to use their lands, but also the right to ownership over it, a concept outside of their known language and historical and cultural understanding (Charles Rivers, History and Culture of the Chippewa).

In 1834, there were 5,347 Chippewa in Michigan in the census, half of whom were near Saginaw.

"All promises and treaties were broken; the boundary lines were never respected or enforced.

We made Wampom belts of shells as a visual reminder of an agreement; it was binding on both parties.

The Anishinabegs highest authority is Gitchi Manido, the Great Spirit, the Creator. Thus, filling the pipe was a solemn act, sealing and binding an agreement before the Creator.

Treaties recognized ownership. In making treaties, we never gave up the right to govern our own people or to worship the Creator as we had for centuries. We reserved the right to hunt and fish, trap, and harvest plants and medicinal food and other resources" Diba Jimooyung, (Ziibiwing).

Charles Eastman said, "We never had anything to count; we valued nothing except having that which cannot be purchased". Never was more ruthless fraud and graft practiced upon a defenseless people by politicians, never more worthless scraps of paper, anywhere in the world than many of the treaties and government documents. They robbed and bullied with troops to suppress them. Wrongs unbelievable of common decency.

Nicholas Plain at Sarnia Reserve: Wampum and the calumet pipe of peace are used in council assemblies as the Bible is used in taking an oath.

Red Cloud: "Which God is our brother praying to now? The same God they have twice deceived when they broke the treaties with us?"

JACOB SMITH

"Jacob Smith has been a useful man in this quarter," Governor Cass wrote. He was a fur trader, interpreter, friend, negotiator, militia, and scout who served the U.S. government in special missions, sometimes the confidential eyes and ears of Cass on the Frontier. Cass wrote, "without Smith, the presence of the Chippewa chiefs could not have been procured in the 1817 Treaty". He was the key figure, "smart as steel". He was influential and controversial and died in obscurity. Smith had advocated a large reserve along the Saginaw and Flint Rivers for Indians from all over the U.S., having self-sufficiency and respect away from negative influence and effects of the White Man.

He redeemed three children taken as captives during the War of 1812. He was translator, courier, and confidential agent among the Saginaw and Ottawa, a spy, scout, and agent of influence. Being in the Fur Trade was excellent for intelligence operatives; they spoke the language and moved freely where no Whites could or would go. He was friend and advisor to the Indians.

He was Lieutenant and Captain of the Michigan militia when Detroit came back into American hands in 1813. He was bold and fearless, warmhearted and generous. He was arrested for helping the Americans when Britain held the Eastern Michigan lands. He had many lawsuits resulting from careless business practices and unpaid debts.

He was a German who came from Quebec. He was born in 1773, slight, strong, and agile. He came to Detroit around 1800. His home was on what is now Woodward Avenue in Detroit, the Wharf's Trail. He had a White family in Detroit.

His Indian wife was Now Wa Be She Koo Qua, who lived at the Huron – Clinton River, called the Upper Huron, "The River Aux Huron", of Lake St. Clair (now Mount Clemons). One of the leaders of this band was "the Wing", Ningweegon, who was friendly to Governor Hull. Smith married Chief Neome's daughter. He had a daughter, Nancy, with his Ojibwe wife. Smith and Chief Neome were as brothers, united in perfect harmony and unity, best friends unto death.

Smith became an Indian farmer, teaching the Indians to farm the American way.

Smith worked in powerful, quiet ways; he was a force for change. He advised the Indians to accept the land cessions to the U.S. This allowed settlers to move into Michigan without attack and confrontation. This promoted American debt and credit for goods they wanted and needed. It also led to more land cessions and saw the passing of the warriors, hunters, and traders.

For the above paragraphs on Jacob Smith, the book; The Daring Trader: Jacob Smith in the Michigan Territory 1802 – 1825, by Kim Crawford, 2012, Michigan State University Press, was a reference.

The Treaty of Washington in 1836 ceded 13 million acres of the remaining Lower Peninsula and half of the Upper Peninsula, the U.S. senate adding that the Indians were to remove within five years West of the Mississippi.

In 1836, the Black River, and Swan Creek, and Saginaw Chippewa bands ceded the four reserves from the 1807 Treaty.

In 1837, on Mackinac Island, the Indians reluctantly signed this Treaty of Washington but utterly refused to leave their Michigan reserves. The Augres and Rifle River reserves were kept by the Chippewa. The Ojibwe continued to live on their reserves and throughout the ceded territory. During the five-year period, the government surveyed and sold the Indian reserves, and their lands were encroached by timber thieves. They were then refugees in their own land and without government protection. (Cleland)

Michigan Indian Affairs were a huge mess. The government effort to remove the Indians was a failure. By 1842, the Indians having no reserves, many had moved to Canada and other places near relatives. A new treaty in 1855 and 1864 created the Isabella Reservation West of Saginaw.

In 1837 and 1838, 75% of the Plains people died, the military massacring all, many were killed trying to flee into Canada. When it was discovered that there was gold in the hills of the West, the White men went crazy to find it, exterminating any who were in the path of progress.

The treaties made between the U.S. government, a sovereign nation, and various Indian nations who were sovereign, are still in existence today, and their existence as legal entities have been tested in courts and affirmed as laws with supremacy over state laws. The treaties affecting Michigan Indian tribes have never been abrogated and are as valid today as when they were written.

The special relationship existing between the federal government and Indian tribes is the result of agreements arrived at and are recognition not of Indian need, but of Indian rights as a sovereign people (Joyce Reid, Treaties affecting Michigan Indian Tribes).

There are many Indian tribes in Michigan today. There are thousands in the U.S.A. and in Canada. They are a sub-culture most Americans know little about.

In 1887, the Dawes Act effectively caused American Indians to lose 90 million acres of reservation land.

COLONIAL OPPRESSION

Historic trauma perpetuates self-oppression. Unresolved anguish felt by individuals, families, and communities in reaction to injustice, such as genocide, disease, land loss, language loss, religious indoctrination, negatively accumulate and is transmitted from generation to generation, compounding the distress (Brave Heart and De Bruyn 1998).

It is impossible to overstate the magnitude of human injustice perpetuated against Indian people in denial of their right to exist on their aboriginal land base as self-determined peoples.

Decolonization is the process of liberation from the state of oppression, reclaiming true freedoms – the freedoms of language, history, values, spiritual systems. These retain identity and rebuild self-esteem and so does the family, community, and nation.

A consensus government with a spiritual value based, egalitarian leadership.

Top Down does not empower the people, a handful holding all power over the people and the top-down system that supports it. Once you start dictating, you are not leading anymore.

Pulling communities together is essential for building healthy communities. When you empower people, for so long downtrodden by Western Colonialism, a whole new energy comes out. They start to see light at the end of the tunnel, respecting people and treating them as family, thanking and worshipping the Creator.

The spiritual component is central to our government – that is the life force. Without it, we self-destruct. We are one with everything. We are connected to all creation; that is who we are (Flocken, UMN 2013).

Democracy and freedom are Native American Indian ideals (Canadian Indian History, www).

The Plains Indians were deprived of their main source of sustenance. The buffalo were all killed, and the people left to wander and steal to avoid starvation. This then caused the military to begin open hostilities. The Gold Rush was the death of many Indian peoples. If they were in the way of progress, they were exterminated. The wars were caused by the aggression of lawless White men. Death by starvation and drunken orgies were the order of the day.

The White people moved into their lands and then expected the federal government to make a new treaty whereby the Indians would relinquish what the White men had no legal right to possess. Many times, the Indians did not receive what was promised in the treaties, or waited many years to see any of it fulfilled. Schools were not built as promised, agricultural assistance did not come, and liquor was not excluded. Indians and their agents were powerless, without redress against the federal government, and the corrupt traders. Indian rings (theft and every evil vise) were everywhere; monopolies of supplies being in remote places, there was no surveillance. The abuses were legion; all but a few, were corrupt and those few were taken care of in many ways. The tribes were vanishing.

Simplicity and fairness cost him his country and his freedom, even extinction as a separate and peculiar people (C. Eastman the Indian Today).

"Noble deeds of man are performed for the good of others. How blasphemous; you give us rum by the thousand barrels, before the presence of God, and charge him as the murderer of the unfortunate Indians. Our fields were coveted, our land. You force us to poor lands we must sell to sustain ourselves; there is no food and no game. We are forced to take cattle, causing war and bloodshed. The dirge of once free and powerful sons of America. The dying fires of his race lie scattered, and the graves of his ancestors desecrated" (George Copeway).

The Indians in acts of kindness were always accommodating, truthful, honest, and punctual to every promise. They helped raise many log homes for the settlers and helped during illness. Also, how Whites used (their) kindness (Frazier/Cameron, Kahwamdameh).

One god man is a lighthouse in a storm to warn and guide the rest (George Copeway).

Pre-contact population of the Native Americans was in the millions. By 1900, 250,000 remained. The tide of White settlers was unstoppable.

At Cahokia, east of St. Louis, Missouri in East St. Louis, Indiana, was a very large magnificent walled city, a 4,000 acre, complex. There lived 30,000 people. There are 120 mounds here. The largest, Monks Mound, is nine stories high. Soils from hundreds of miles away were layered throughout in blue, red, white, black, grey, brown, and orange. This was a huge trading place on the Mississippi. There were town squares and a woodhenge that told the time by the shadow of the sun – a town clock.

Some wanted to spread lies to cover atrocities used to steal riches and land, saying the land was an empty wasteland occupied by a handful of ignorant poor farmers, who were backward and evil. The history and land did not have enormous gaps waiting to be filled by foreigners. It was a complete society that made sense.

The facts are that the Americas were occupied by millions of people who had achieved technological development, similar to contemporaries in Europe, Africa, and Asia. They had excelled in many specific areas. They did have weaknesses like trust, honesty, and kindness that were used to abuse and steal their land, life, and all.

(Adapted from, BC OPEN TEXTBOOKS, opentexcbc.ca, Canadian History, Preconfederacion/Ch. 5-1. Ch. 2 Aboriginal Canada before contact, summary 2.6, John Douglas Belshaw)

MOUNDS

"His land was taken from him, his people all but destroyed by ingenious genocides. The reality of Indian life was cast into romantic myth, lies to cover deceit, they vanished comparatively rapidly" (Steiner).

The State of Michigan was Indian central. In the midst, of the great trade routes between the whole of North America, the Southern Lower half being the most heavily populated (Wm. Hindsdale, UOM, 1931, The Archaeological Atlas of Michigan).

In the Atlas, many sites have been recorded (not the exact locations to protect them), and many more are not recorded. There are 748 village sites, busy centers of aboriginal life accurately made out. Camps and villages were usually surrounded with palisades. There are 265 burial sites known with accuracy in 1931 (Hindsdale). Many more have been identified since then and are yet being found.

There are very extensive corn fields and tool factories. Indian pits or cache pits are so numerous they are not indicated on maps. Pit holes were dug into the ground in dry places. The commonest type of Earthwork in MI. They were 2 – 7 feet deep, the top round and four to eight feet in diameter. Some were very close together.

In the Great Lakes range, there were 1,828 sites in the state, most were in Lower Michigan, 1,707. In Southeast Michigan, there were 819 sites. This is the largest concentration of sites in the state. The Saginaw Valley was a very large concentration of sites, the Clinton River (Huron), also. These two areas were the centers of the greatest mound burial constructions. The largest mounds were on the Grand River and in Wayne County near Detroit.

Interments were at various depths, some below ground, some at ground level, and some above ground level.

Trails and great roadways hundreds of miles in length extended across the country. Our highways and bridges are the same thoroughfares followed by Indians in their transport. The best routes and crossings. A large network over the entire country. One is a 2,000-mile thoroughfare from Montreal to the Mississippi. The great Sauk Trail or Chicago Trail connected to it from Ohio and Detroit to the Mississippi. U.S. 112 follows this route.

The waterways were the places of a great many villages and camps on lakes and navigable rivers and streams (Hindsdale, UOM, 1931).

An abundance of Indian life was left in the soil almost everywhere it was dug up. In the Upper Peninsula, there were hundreds of copper mines, and copper was used in many ways. Some of the Indians spent the summer in the Upper Peninsula of Michigan. There were ancient mining pits where 10 cartloads of ancient hammers were taken, one weighing 39.5 pounds, having a double handle. There were hundreds of mines, tools, wedges, scaffolding, baskets were everywhere (C. Moore, History of Michigan).

Ottissippi

Henry Gillman, in the Smithsonian Report of 1873, declared the Draper Site and mounds in the area as the most interesting archeological find in the state, and some of the best finds were taken from these groups of mounds. There are numerous mounds along streams and lakeshores. Draper Site is near the Blue Water Bridge at Port Huron, Michigan.

The Peabody Museum of Archaeology and Ethnohistory made a report saying there are numerous mounds at the head of the St. Clair River at the foot of Lake Huron. They continue for one and a half miles northward along Lake Huron.

On the west bank of the Black River, there is a great battle mound.

The mound on Water Street, across from the federal building, was a large mound which was used for a very long time and through the 1800s for burials. There were intervals like gates between the mounds. Fires were built within, and the mounds were used as fortifications and hiding places.

Many mounds were terraced on hills near the waterways.

The mound on Water Street near Rural and Tayler Street, Port Huron, had a large number, of human bones, pottery, implements of great length, and a grave lined with pottery which had never been observed before.

In Port Huron at the foot of Griswold Street, there was a burial mound. Another burial site in Port Huron was to the south end. This was originally an old Indian burial ground, north of Dove Street, west of 24th Street, and east of 16th Street, south of Cleveland. West of 32nd Street, farming was done across the tracks.

Most of the bones have been moved to the cemetery at Sarnia Reserve.

On Harsens Island was a burial mound at the south end.

At St. Clair on the Pine River was an Indian cemetery.

The mound builders left innumerable tumuli near the river and lakes. Most are conical or oblong with some cruciform, others resemble birds and animals. The ones on the heights at bends in the river or foot of the lake were perhaps for defense.

St. Clair County was one of the Pagigendamowinaki – "Great Cemeteries" – of the Aborigines. Along the rivers and their tributary creeks, many mounds were found. The number of mounds and character of human remains found in them point out the district as the Necropolis of an extinct race. Stone hatchets, flint arrow heads, unnumbered skeletons. The more valued relics have been here deposited in unusual abundance, greenstone or diorite, seonite, shale, and chert (Andreas).

Much copper was found within tumuli that tells of a civilized and flourishing colony within St. Clair County. Many mounds and garden beds are found in St. Clair County.

The fossils of prehistoric animals have been unearthed from end to end of the county.

The county abounds in these antiquarian puzzles. As late as the 1850s, hundreds of Chippewa and visiting Menominee fared sumptuously on the wild rice and game of the region.

Many mounds have been destroyed, and large amounts of valuable relics have fallen into ignorant hands and have been lost forever.

The great progress of achievement and mighty achievements of industry. All this has been accomplished over ten thousand graves (Andreas).

THE THUMB OF MICHIGAN

The thumb was the great gathering place and was thoroughly littered with artifacts of native occupation. All around the thumb there were roads and trails throughout, as was the whole country.

The West Shores of Lake Huron were called Sanguenaum.

The Saginaw Watershed, *O Sagenon* or *Sag inawe* meaning to flow out, contains 175 inland lakes about 7,000 miles of rivers and streams. It is Americas largest freshwater coastal wetland system! It is like a large web reaching in all directions. Restoration of the Degraded – polluted, environmental conditions, is progressing.

The whole area was called Saginaw it was the great drainage or outlet of half of the state, a rich fishing and hunting place. Sturgeon were thick and lay their eggs all about the waters of Lake Huron and the Ottissippi – the strait. Coal, flint, grindstones, pipestone and lead were all found here. A wealthy and much coveted area.

WHITE ROCK

White Rock is in Lake Huron, near Forestville, Michigan. It has been nearly destroyed by bombing. It was once a very large rock, clearly seen in the Lake. It was on maps as a landmark in the Northwest Territory. It had been used for eons as a meeting place and trading place. What's left of it is three miles north of Forestville and south of Harbor Beach, Michigan. In Sherman Township, it is the Southeast corner of Huron County.

A town was made at White Rock, called White Rock; it was destroyed by fire in 1881. The 1881 fire traveled from Central Michigan to Lake Huron in one day, 125 miles, the wind was ferocious a Great Inferno.

Ottissippi

In Holbrook, the people stayed in the Cass River and kept wet blankets over their heads for many hours. Sandy Cleland buried his money for safety from the fire in the dirt floor of his cabin. When he dug it up he found ashes, the fire had been so hot. (Lynn Spencer)

There are many mounds and burial places in the thumb. There were stone quarries, tool factories and workshops for making weapons, towns and villages. There were Workshops and Factories, Sugar Camps where large Industrial Complexes in Manufacturing occurred. The Ojibwe were master Canoe builders and handlers.

The Thumb of Michigan was thoroughly littered with tools and arrowheads. New finds are constantly made. Truckloads of artifacts have been collected. A pond was filled with artifacts. Many sites are kept secret to protect them from destruction and theft (Joyce Reid, Deckerville, MI, papers). Where there are now towns and villages were the places of the Indian sites and villages. Most parks, government buildings, schools, and cemeteries were once Indian sites.

Frankenmuth, and Birch Run, and Chesaning, Bridgeport, Copeniconing, were Indian villages. Bay City is literally built upon Indian sites and mounds. The Saginaw Watershed was Indian country. Huron County is also rich in Indian sites: Sebewaing, Bayport, Port Austin, Point Aux Barques Harbor Beach, and other points.

Villages and camps were usually surrounded with palisades, tall walls, many times double walls, and a few with three walls.

Koylton Highland Pass is the high point in the center of Michigan's Thumb, the place of the ancient Indian Highland Pass Township at the top of the mound (Juanita Rock).

The Indian fields near Caro, Michigan were Native farm lands; large crops of Indian corn, squash, beans, and potatoes were grown here.

A glacial ridge called Hadley Hills runs from Oakland County into the Southwest of the Thumb through the center to the Northeast.

In Lapeer County, Hadley Township, Pinnacle Point is 1,262 feet above sea level. In Metamora Township is, Mt. Christie at 1,251 feet. In Tuscola County, Fremont Township, a point near Mayville is 1,050 feet above sea level. Petroglyphs Park in Greenleaf Township in Sanilac County, near Cass City, has a 751-foot in southwest Sanilac County is a train of glacial deposited boulders known as, "The Indian Wall", part of the wall can be seen from M-53 south of Cass City Rd. in Greenleaf Twp.

At the Holcomb site in the Thumb, caribou bones were found.

The Saginaw drainage area is a very heavily populated area of history and mounds, as is the center of the Thumb around the petroglyphs.

THE PETROGLYPHS

Petroglyph Park in Sanilac County is the only place in Michigan with rock carvings from Indian culture. The Cass River runs through the area, formerly the Huron River. The Black River - Huron, is also nearby, an easy portage by canoe. The highland of the Thumb along the Cass River.

It is a historic ceremonial site. The area could be easily reached from all directions, being between the Saginaw Bay Watershed on the West and The Lake Huron – Karegnondi, Black River, Huron River, and St. Clair River – Ottissippi (Clear Water) to the East. The grand thoroughfare of commerce.

The historic petroglyphs are a special place, sacred place to the Native Americans. Great meetings and ceremonies were held here.

Cass River passes through a thickly populated Indian district east of Saginaw into the Thumb. The Flint River nearly parallels the Cass River into the Thumb and was used extensively in Indian commerce. Many archaeologists have explored the area; the most well-known are James Fitting, Charles Cleland, and William Hindsdale.

The area is thin soil layered over rocky places, the Cass River having a bedrock bottom.

The high Land of the Thumb along the Cass river was the place of the great meetings of the main chiefs of the tribes, east of the Mississippi river and north of the Ohio river. It is thought that once every 5 years a great meeting was held here. At the time of the great meeting of the tribes, (a super council meeting), a stone carving was made to commemorate the meeting. The large rock of Marshall Sandstone, has 93 aboriginal figures, this would record meetings as far back and 1150 A.D., for about 450 years. As time went by, the older figures would be reamed out to match the newer ones. This explains why the figures were all the same depth. A council circle was nearby. (Dr. Moor/Adapted from History of Petroglyph Park, Lynn Spencer)

The Historic Petroglyphs are a Special Place, a sacred place to the Native Americans. Great Meetings and Ceremonies were held here. It is a place of strong spiritual strength and healing. The Large Rock is called Grandfather by the Anishinabe. Plants with great healing properties are collected here.

There are outlines and figures of men, animals, hand and feet prints, birds, mythical creatures, spirals, cup shapes, animal tracks, clublike glyphs, and rakelike figures. The famous "Bowman", and the, Water Panther or "Great underground wildcat", called "Gitchi-a-nah-mi-e-be-zhew", the spirit ruler of the seasons, having a huge tail.

The Longtailed Copper Bear, is a mythological creation of the Chippewas having a tail of copper. (Schoolcraft/Brown, 1941/The Sanilac Petroglyphs, Richards, Cranbrook Institute of Science, 1958)

Today the Petroglyphs site has a large covered Pavilion made in a round form with a high roof to protect the soft stone carvings and accommodate visitors, for meetings and ceremonial culture. There is a parking area with a path to the Petroglyph site.

Ira Butterfield who documented the area for 30 years and Mark Papworth did much valuable research around the Petroglyphs area.

The Indians living on the reservation at Caro, MI, came to the area to pick and dry berries, and gather Ossier Willow for basket making. (Lynn Spencer)

Ottawa families from, "Indianfields", near Caro MI, came each autumn to trap and gather ginsing roots. (The Sanilac Petroglyphs, Hatt, Cranbrook Institute of Science, 1958/Port Sanilac Museum)

The Holbrook area was named after Mrs. Holbrooks family. She had a trading post on the Cass River from 1836. A Chippewa Indian village was downriver from her. (Spencer)

Before the Fires of 1871 and 1881 in the Thumb. The lumbermen were very wasteful and there was debris, tree tops, bark, stumps everywhere. It was as a very dry and hot summer, grass was parched and ground cracked, it was very windy. Gale winds caused controlled burns to become out of control, the fires started in Lapeer. They were fast moving, going in all directions, in Tuscola and Sanilac, were whirlwinds, the sky turned red, the smoke causing total darkness, blowing balls of fire and huge clouds of smoke, a terrible noise like mighty waters, and tornadoes. People went into wells, dug trenches, went to green corn fields and buried their heads, and ran for water.

In Holbrook, the people stayed in the Cass River and kept wet blankets over their heads for many hours.

Many people moved away after the fires, Indians going in canoes to relatives and Whites moving away. This is where the Red Cross began, the Country wanting to help the homeless who had lost everything.

The Hopewell Complex, centered in South Central Ohio, was the great meeting place with an extensive reach throughout America. Called the Hopewell Interaction Sphere, Chilicothe is the main area of meetings and great mounds culture. The Hopewell Complex was very extensive, reaching into Pennsylvania, West Virginia, Kentucky, and Indiana.

Fort Ancient was in South Ohio, with Cincinnati as the epicenter. The Shawnee and Miami people were driven from these lands.

The New York Hopewell is part of the Ohio Group reaching North to the St. Lawrence Seaway and South into Pennsylvania to meet the Ohio Hopewell. All part of the Hopewell exchange system, Hopewell trading networks were quite extensive, from as far as Yellowstone in now Wyoming to the Gulf Coast.

The Point Peninsula Complex was a large area, including Lake Ontario, Lake Simcoe in Ontario, and far into the Northeast, North of the St. Lawrence Seaway. Part of the Hopewell Group, a serpent mound is at Rice Lake in Ontario near Toronto, the Lower Trent River area.

The many mounds along Lake Huron and in Port Huron along the St. Clair River are believed to be part of these ancient cultures. The Couture Complex was an area covering Southeast Michigan and Northern Ohio, all part of the Hopewell Complex at an early date.

The area of land is called Royce Area 66. These are area maps showing original Indian land cessions in the United States Map Number. This area corresponds with the Treaty of 1807, Land Area of Southeast Michigan.

Lower Michigan was part of the young culture from 1400 to 1600. The Huron Petun in Ontario were also part of the young culture.

The Saugeen Complex is the name for the later inhabitants of Algonquin descent, inhabiting Southwest Ontario and Eastern Michigan.

Southwest Michigan into Indiana and reaching North to Saginaw Bay was part of the Goodall Focus Group.

The pottery found in Lower Michigan into Ontario was part of the Western Basin tradition peoples (Travers 2015 Dissertation, York University, Toronto, Canada).

Garden beds are found, having low earth ridges 18 inches in height. Some are artistic in design, some have a wheel shape and resembled beds in formal gardens, peculiar to Michigan.

DRAPER PARK ARCHAEOLOGY SITE

Draper Park near the foot of the Blue Water Bridge is especially rich in Indian history. Draper Park was part of an area of great activity, the summer camp of many interconnected tribes. The nearby beaches were wonderful for hot summer days and escaping mosquitos. It was on the grand thoroughfare of commerce. The East Shores of the St. Clair River and Lake Huron were also a great gathering place. This was a well-used area of the tribes. The great fishery was at the foot of Lake Huron, the weirs were used to dry fish for many Tribes.

Ottissippi

The tribes camped all along the waters of East Michigan and Southwest Ontario, as well as those of the whole country.

Draper Park is significant, as the land there has never been disturbed by White men. There was an undisturbed garden area, never plowed. McNeil Creek flowed one block away on the east side.

Francis Bonhomme purchased the farm, which included the Draper Site, from his brother, Pierre, in 1800 (Lowrie and Clark 1832). Pierre Bonhomme had purchased the farm from Jacques Lassalle in 1799 (Wayne County Probate Records). Pierre also owned the lower farm South of Francois. The lower farm had been settled in 1792 by Pierre Lovielle. This was the site of Fort Gratiot in 1814. Pierre then built another house fronting on Black River at his upper property (Lowrie and Clark 1832), where he did trading with the Indians. Receiving supplies on credit from Jacques and Francois Lasalle.

In an early day, the area was more like the area of the Flats, with bountiful waterfowl and fish. Before creeks were filled in and lands drained, it was a much more hospitable place for wildlife. The wild rice, fish, and game fed the hundreds who gathered here (Western Historical Co.).

Lt. Col. John McNeil purchased the Bonhomme and Lasalle claims, including the Fort grounds and the Draper Park site. Charles Butler purchased the McNeil lands for the Huron Land Company to develop the North of Fort Gratiot. This, 1,200 acres, was Platted into the, "Village of Huron". Later the Southeast portion became the "Village of Fort Gratiot".

John McNeil yet owned the Draper site in the extreme Southeast of the Village of Fort Gratiot, known as the Steam Mill Lot. It then passed to the Benham family and to Thomas Draper in 1920. This site was never developed upon. Elmwood Street runs across the Draper Park property.

The City of Port Huron purchased the property in 1946. The Draper site is 331 by 200 feet and contains Elmwood Street and a grass-covered plot.

It is clear from archaeological excavations that parts of the park have remained untouched since prehistoric times, before Europeans came. Trash middens of Indian occupation and the filling in of McNeil's Creek from the East and into the center of the lot in the 1900s will be found (Bonhomme/Draper Papers, MI Room, SCC Library).

The mound at Palmer Park in Port Huron was 500 feet long, and 100 to 150 feet wide, and 12 feet high.

In the Township of Springwells, just below Detroit, were nine mounds, one inside the grounds of Fort Wayne. They were circular in form, from 30 to 70 feet in diameter and from 3 to 10 in height. Two parallel embankments led to them, from the East about four feet high. One was opened in 1837 and the one inside the Fort by permission of the War Department in 1876. Both contained numerous skeletons, arrow heads, and vases or pots of earthenware. One contained an iron vessel of two or three gallons and several pounds of a sort of paint. There were 10 villages and two large circular enclosures.

The great mound of the River Rouge, about a half mile below Fort Wayne, was at first probably fully 300 feet long and 200 feet wide. In 1876, it was 20 feet high. A partial investigation by Henry Gillman discovered stone axes, arrow heads, fragments of pottery, and human bones much decayed.

An old Indian said these mounds were erected as Forts at the time the tribes were fighting each other. Indian tradition ascribes these mounds also to the Tueteloes or Tuetle Indians who preceded the Wyandotte. The Tueteloes were supposed to have emigrated from Virginia as far North as the Susquehanna.

Near the Rouge River, there were eight mounds; near Fort Wayne and Great Springwells, there were ten villages, nine mounds, and two circular enclosures. All have been removed and used for building sand.

At Romeo, Michigan are a large concentration of mounds, there were villages and circular enclosures (Hindsdale, Archaeological Atlas of Michigan, 1931).

The Huron (Clinton) River had prehistoric old forts of one to three acres with earth walls about four feet in height, with gateways for openings. These were Indian forts (Cannon 1973).

Macomb County and Sanilac County also had large concentrations of mounds. Lapeer had less mounds and more Indian sites. The whole Southeast of Michigan was filled with Indian sites.

A very large concentration of mounds lies South and West of Saginaw, Michigan and North of Toledo, Ohio.

There are over 1,100 mounds or cemeteries identified in Michigan. Some of the largest were found within the present limits of Port Huron, Michigan, at the head of the St. Clair River, and along Lake Huron, and on Black River. There are 113 other earth constructions and 265 burial sites in the state.

The largest mounds were on the Grand River in Wayne County near Detroit, the Rouge River, and Springwells. Ossuaries are bone heaps near villages and camps (Hindsdale, Archaeological Atlas of Michigan 1931).

On the Ambassador Bridge site near Delray Street, was a large mound, 200 feet high and 300 feet long. The vicinity had 19 mounds in 1841, four on the grounds of Fort Wayne itself. Only one mound remains, being composed of two mounds being bulldozed together (Nailhed www).

Mounds were used as fortifications. Forts were usually in natural areas, enclosed and protected large areas.

Cache pits are so numerous that they are not indicated on maps. Cache Pits were holes dug as a cellar to store food and many other items to have at hand, a very common type of earthwork in Michigan. There are also a great number in Lambton County, Ontario, Canada (Lauriston).

The ancient mounds here at Port Huron are from 10 to 25 feet in height and from 50 to 500 or more feet in length. There are 22 mounds noted by Hindsdale in the University of Michigan Archaeological Map of Michigan at Port Huron, along Lake Huron and tributaries. The exact locations on the map are not noted to prevent looting and protect the sites. It is illegal to disturb and remove Indian artifacts of mounds and burial sites.

Early pottery was also found from 600 B.C. to 2700 B.C. (Greenman, MI Archaeologist 1958).

The Parker prehistoric culture is found in Ontario as well as the young cultures.

INDIAN VILLAGES

There were many named villages in Southeast Michigan. There are many more unnamed. Saginaw County was the most densely populated, trails led in all directions (Hindsdale). Some of the named villages are below:

- Black Elks, Saginaw County
- Kewaonon, the most Easterly village in Michigan; at "Round Point", a bay also called French Aunce Bay, near Detroit
- Peonigenawink, "Plenty of flint"; on the Flint River near Lapeer Michigan; village of Neome (Nibegom Village), the greatly beloved chief of the Ojibwa; also called Reaum's Village after Reaum, a fur trader who had a post here
- Quanicassee, in Tuscola County, means "Little Bear Thumb"
- Menoquet's Village, on the Cass River in the Thumb of Michigan
- Saginaw City, Ke Pay Sho Wink, the great camping ground
- Seginsavin's Village, on the Rouge River
- Teuchsa Grondie, "Place of Many Beavers", the great Indian village at Detroit
- Tonguish's Village, near the Rouge River
- Middle Village, Wagana Kising, at Little Traverse Bay, opposite Petoskey, Michigan

BLUE WATER BRIDGE ARCHAEOLOGICAL SITES

Chippewa oral history tells of groups living in concentrated populations beside the St. Clair River for a long, long time. People came from many tribes and places to meet one another and to fish and exchange exotic goods and materials. This was a rich area; everything was provided for fishing and hunting. Aamjiwnaang means "Where People meet by flowing water" and "At the Spawning Stream".

This area where the bridges are built at the foot of Lake Huron is the narrowest place of the river in this area. The Blue Water Bridge was built over an existing natural trade and transportation corridor. Our people saw the potential first. They weren't wild savages; they were well-organized and well-educated within their system. The Sarnia band is seeking to declare the area a national historic site (Darren Henry/Ray Rogers, Sarnia First Nation).

The Blue Water Bridge site has had major digs made on the Canadian side in Lambton County, Ontario.

In 1993, before the second span of the Blue Water Bridge was built, an archeological search team made two excavations and a series of test pits that produced 410,000 artifacts, including human remains, fish bones, animal bones, tools, fishing equipment, ceramic pottery, net sinkers, projectiles points and arrowheads, hearths, and storage pits.

It is one of the major sites in Ontario and Canada. Bob Mayer, a London archeological consultant, said, "There are very few instances where you have this massive stratification, this overlapping layers of cultural material from different time periods. Nothing like the strata of fish bones has ever been found in Ontario. Campfires and post holes were also found, likely the foundations of fish racks or buildings. This represents less than one percent of the site. Out of respect for the dead, the number of human remains has not been disclosed. The 295,000 fish bones were from sturgeon, walleye, yellow perch, and freshwater drum. Bones were from deer, turtle, and birds."

Many of the artifacts date from 200 A.D. to 500 A.D., with the oldest from about the time of Christ. The mouth of the St. Clair River has long been an important fishing ground and trade corridor.

Some artifacts at the site came from Central Ohio.

The Blue Water Bridge and Aamjiwnaang Ojibwe have created the Souls Memorial sculpture on the riverfront to honor the first peoples' site used for millennia.

ALPENA-AMBERLEY RIDGE – LAKE HURON LAND BRIDGE

Professor John O'Shea from the University of Michigan Anthropological and Archaeological Museum has collaborated with others to research the submerged ancient land bridge called the Alpena-Amberley Ridge, or the Lake

Huron Land Bridge. Since 2009, scuba-trained archaeologists and a remote operated vehicle (ROV) have been charting the Alpena-Amberley Ridge (AAR).

On old nautical charts, the ridge was called Six Fathoms Shoal. A fathom is six feet. They have found the world's oldest caribou-hunting structures below 120 feet of water on Lake Huron, in addition to rock driving lanes and over 60 hunting blinds, tools, and cache sites. The book *Caribou Hunting in the Upper Great Lakes: Archaeological, Ethnographic, and Paleoenvironmental Perspectives*, by John O'Shea, Sonnenburg, and Lemke (2013) of the University of Michigan, details the report about the research.

The AAR is a rocky limestone and dolomite outcrop that runs across the central Lake Huron Basin in the Great Lakes, between Alpena, Michigan, and Amberley-Point Clarke, Ontario. The ridge is 10 miles wide in places and 100 miles long.

Side scan sonar (SSS) was employed to detail the bottom topography, providing detailed information of the lake floor, such as sands and rock, ancient swamps, waterways, and bogs. Scanning sonar was utilized; the sonar head is held in place by a tripod on the lake bottom, the sonar head rotates through 360 degrees, mapping the immediate area. MB, multibeam sonar was used to produce an extremely fine-grained map of depths and to image three-dimensional bottom features and small changes in bottom elevation.

Research has found that the ridge consisted of rocky high land, marshes, shallow lakes, rivers, beaches, sphagnum bogs, fens, and forested wetland areas. Water levels were once much lower, and the exposed AAR was inhabited by plants, spruce and tamarack trees, animals, and humans, an ideal habitat for ranging caribou.

There were once two lakes that made up now Lake Huron. Lake Stanley contained two lakes, and Lake Hough (Georgian Bay), Ontario the other. They have since been covered in deeper water.

Bathymetry techniques for the first time showed the ARR as a continuous feature across the basin, and the discovery of preserved forest remains beneath Southern Lake Huron (Hunter et al. 2006) renewed research to answer the question of whether early archaeological sites might be preserved beneath Lake Huron.

A digital elevation model (DEM) from the National Oceanic and Atmospheric Administration (NOAA) determined the depth of what would have been dry land. Bathymetry then created three-dimensional land surface images using ArcGIS 10. The landscape was evaluated against known caribou behavior and how they are hunted. Three target zones were selected, representing different topographic settings for caribou.

Area 1 is roughly 56 kilometers or 21 miles; it is dominated by a long linear bedrock outcrop and considerable variation in elevation, including the shallowest point of Six Fathom Shoal scarp, and contains upland areas and a portion of the high northeast facing cliffs. This area was the longest distance from shore. This was an area of a large base and rearmament. There were 21 structures in Area 1 at the crossing locality.

The Funnel Drive is located near the high limestone ridge that gave Six Fathom Shoal its name in Area 1. Dragon Drive Line and Blind area contains at least five constructions and one complex structure. Both of these were opportunistic, setting between a large marsh and the high outcropping, of Six Fathom Shoal.

Area 3 is roughly 17 kilometers or 12 miles. It presents an upland setting overlooking a narrow shoreline. Drop 45 Drive Lane was the most complex hunting feature identified on the ARR. It is an overlook locality of Area 3 in 37 meters of water, bounded by a natural raised cobble surface and an area of bog. Two long converging stone lines narrow to a gap, moving herds into narrow channels just below the overlook area. A number, of stone lines and enclosures create its final form. The structures are invisible to animals until they are within the structure. The area was a natural choke point in the annual migrations. The one meter (3.3 feet), drop was similar, to classic bison jumps. There are many structures near the overlook locality of Drop 45: five simple enclosures, V structures, and one rectangular structure. There are 31 structures near the gap locality.

A large group of hunters would have operated here to guide, drive, and kill the animals entering the feature. Open or V-shaped structures were used as blinds, shelter, and to direct the animals' path. Drive lanes were built with boulders, stones, and cobbles to channel movement toward a kill zone.

Area 2 is near shore with the deepest areas of the ridge. It contained a water crossing over a narrow strait. The caribou swimming over it were easily killed from a boat or as they emerged from the water on the shore. It was a choke point where the migrating caribou would have to pass and would have been an excellent ambush point and kill site-processing area.

Area 3 was a region with a narrowed place and a pronounced slope, providing an overlook position, and produced a funneling effect. Between areas 3 and 2, with a bog area to drive caribou into for easy kill, was another ideal area for base camps. Built structures, cairns, and long barricades are constructed to channel the movement of caribou to kill areas.

Numerous other areas do not contain identifiable structures.

Divers collect core and environmental samples, including wood and specimens for analysis. They measure and sketch submerged features for later construction of plan maps. Most diving has been done in 20 to 35 meters (60 to 120 feet).

Spruce poles were used to leverage substantial boulders into a more desirable location, some having smaller stones wedged beneath them to increase height. Wood antler and bone weapons may have been used as well. Stone rings, stone piles, cairns, caches, and shelters were also documented.

Between 2011 and 2013, a total of 171 core sediment and rock samples were collected by divers and Ponar sampler from a surface vessel. One hundred and two sediment grab samples and eleven short cores were obtained for analysis.

Cache sites and camps were nearby; butchering, drying, and hide processing were a large operation.

Archaeologists have divided Michigan Indian pre-history into four major periods: The Paleo Indian period, from the beginning of history, the Archaic Period, the Woodland Period, and the Contact Period. These dates are based on archaeological digs of which there were many.

Deanville is a high hill or small mountain Southwest of Brown City, Michigan. It had a large settlement. They were industrious with crops and produced forged implements for farm work which they traded to other Indians.

Huron County was rich in Indian sites. There are many evidences of Indian camps in Huron County. Near Port Austin was a large Indian factory, making arrowheads and weaponry. Sebewaing River was similar, with mounds and stockades nearby.

In 2006, Hunter at Oakland University wrote of a drowned forest site in Lake Huron at Sanilac County 4.5 kilometers, about 3 miles, off shore of Lexington, Michigan. This discovery was part of a larger area. The forest was of a rich conifer swamp area. The article is on the Internet.

In 2007, in Lake Michigan under 40 feet of water, a Stonehenge was found with a mastodon carving, as well as another Stonehenge on Beaver Island. Indian history says these were calendars.

NATIVE AMERICAN GRAVES PROTECTION AND REPATRIATION ACT (NAGPRA)

The Indian Repatriation Act is a federal law passed in 1990, requiring the return of Native American human remains, funerary objects, and cultural objects to the descendants and tribes. Gradually, the remains are being repatriated and reburied in cemeteries on Indian reserve lands with proper ceremonies. Grants are available to help with the expenses involved.

The Culturally Unidentifiable Database has records from 752 museums and federal agencies. There are 18,097 records describing 131,667 Native American human remains and 1,117,133 associated funerary objects inventoried.

The Culturally-Affiliated Native American Database includes 6,186 records and accounts for 57,159 Native American human remains and 1,232,187 associated funerary objects, inventoried in 569 museums and federal agencies.

For more on treaties, there are many sites on the Internet: Wicki Project Indigenous Peoples of North America/Anishinabe Treaties; Indian Law; Christian Aboriginal Infrastructure Development (CAID), caid.ca; and the Oklahoma University Law and Treaties are very useful.

Cheryl Morgan

CHAPTER 12
Northern Slavery

The role of historians is to discover facts, whatever they may be, and truth as discerned from facts. When the historian is more concerned with presenting a desired conclusion rather than facts and truth, he is a demagogue and a liar (Gay Mathis).

Cultural amnesia is when the truth is being deliberately forgotten or lost.

In 1632, a physician named Hebert was the first settler in New France, now Canada, and received the first slave of the French Colony, a Black boy from the West Indies.

Slavery was common. The Indians also had slaves taken from enemy raids.

Slavery was actively practiced in New France, in the St. Lawrence Valley and in the Louisiana Territory, for two centuries. In the late 1600s, the French took captives from the British Colonies brought from Louisiana Territory and the Caribbean.

The majority of Native American slaves, were given to the French as tokens of friendship. By early 1700, the buying and selling of captives like merchandise was common. (C. Moore, The History of MI)

The hidden history of northern slaves and plantations is ignored or forgotten. Manors, estates, and full-fledged plantations were provisioning operations for owner's properties in the Caribbean. It was a high state of cultivation through forced labor of slaves.

There was slave labor on the plantations near Detroit and in the masters' houses. The traders had slaves to do the work and moving goods (Palmer, Friend, 1906).

The foul stain of African slavery has been blotted out and erased from our constitution and laws by an enlightened public conscience. The Colored man's legal status as human, instead of brutes and cattle, has been established and enforced. This article also deals with religion, slavery, fraud, the elite, and government. (An early Commentary on the United States. D.C, Walker MPHC VOL.28).

Slavery was a gigantic traffic which every family engaged in. The wealthy realized half of the profits. They sold slaves for molasses, sugar, rum, and salt. Rum was manufactured in the colonies, and it was shipped to Africa with other merchandise, and exchanged for slaves (D.C. Walker).

Cotton was king, there were tremendous profits from slavery, without thought for the human misery and degradation it caused. There was unrest and a burning desire to be free from slavery.

The Underground Railroad and Canada permitted them (the slaves) to construct a complete new life. There were strong family units and learning. There were skilled tradesmen, articulate and outspoken (Stanley, From Whence We Came, 1977).

"Injustice anywhere is a threat to justice everywhere." - Martin Luther King

During the many wars between France and England, and England and America, and British Canadians and British Americans, and Indians, and all the others, many slaves were captured and sold as booty. These were of all the nations, including imported Blacks.

Many workers took molasses home and made rum for the Colonists. Ministers of the gospel were often partners in the profits of the distilleries erected in every hamlet. Slavery and intemperance were tolerated and defended from the Sacred Desk (D.C. Walker).

Most residents, who could afford to, owned slaves. Two or three per family was average. Many prominent people fought the idea of freeing slaves in the North (Wm. Macomb owned 26).

Many slaves were brought from Virginia, New York, and Indiana and sold to the inhabitants of Detroit, such as Major Joseph Campau, Judge George McDougal, Jacques Duperon Baby, Indian Agent and Fur Trader Abbott, Finchley, John Askin, John R. Williams, Lewis Cass, Baubien, Alexander McComb, John Hamtramck, Elijah Brush, James Abbott, C. Gouin, James May, and more (Detroit Pioneer Society, 1872, Slavery in the Early 1800s, Detroit, Michigan, J.A. Girardin).

The slaves were well treated by their owners and educated. Many were baptized, but in the old records, the first name was unknown. Several negroes received donation lots, and many spoke French fluently.

American slaves fled to Canada; Canadian slaves fled to Detroit. There were so many ex-Canadian slaves in Detroit in 1805 that Governor Hull formed a Militia of Black Canadian Runaways. Many fought in wars. They were then given freedom.

The Ordinance of 1787 was a clause to prevent slavery Northwest of the Ohio River. The residents paid little attention to it. Most every prominent man had a slave or two, especially merchants.

Detroit and the vicinity was a haven of slave trade with the Indians.

In 1793, there was Abolition of Slavery in Upper Canada. Upper Canada included East Michigan. It was a gradual abolition; children born to slaves were free after age 25. No slaves were to be imported. Slaves could still be exported across borders.

There were a large number, of slaves in and about Detroit, in 1793. More than 300 slaves were in the Detroit District (Palmer, 1922).

Canadian slaves in Michigan (ruled by the British until 1796) began to cross the river in the hope of reaching freedom. There was great dislike of any law that set them free and deprived the owners of their property (Palmer, Friend, 1922, The City of Detroit, 1701 - 1922, www).

In 1807, Detroit Judge Augustus Woodward ruled that all slaves living on May 23, 1793, and in the possession of a Detroiter, must continue to be a slave for the rest of their life. Children of slaves must continue as a slave until their 25th birthday, or be set free immediately, depending on the date of birth.

On one hand, slavery was deplored. But the freedom from slavery, still denied the people, the benefits of the Constitution, and their worth as Human Beings.

Mrs. John Howard, in her diary, wrote:

> *I have seen many young men and young women prisoners of the Indians come into Detroit. The Traders and a few of the Citizens*

> would gather around them and try to buy them from the Indians. They could purchase them for tobacco and whiskey. They succeeded in buying all I ever saw except one. This was a tall young man about sixteen years of age. They would not let him go for anything. They kept him in place of one whom they had lost. Tears rolled down his face but it was all in vain. They seemed to feel sorry and think a great deal of him but were not willing to let him go.
>
> In 1814, I saw a Man by the name of McMillan brought in from the commons, where he had been for his cows, with a hole through his breast and his scalp removed. (Nancy Howard Diary, MI Room, SCC library, P.H. MI).

Many of the older citizens had one or more slaves (Farmer 1884).

Pompey was a well-known property of James Abbott. Judge May had a faithful slave for 25 years to pay a debt owed by Granchin.

Joseph Campau was a large Trader and had 10 slaves. Crow was dressed in scarlet and performed gymnastic tricks. He was purchased at Montreal by Mr. Campau. He was a faithful slave for many years and married Patterson, also a slave. Mnlet was one of the most honest and faithful of all slaves. Mr. Campau employed him as a confidential clerk. He died at an advanced age, respected and esteemed, for his great integrity and fidelity. Tetro, a favorite of Major Campau, was faithful and honest as the day is long. Hector, a faithful and trustworthy slave, was in charge of the newspaper, *The Oakland Chronicle*, owned by Colonel Mack, General John R. Williams, and Major Campau. This paper merged into the *Detroit Free Press*.

Joseph Drouillard of Petite Cote gave two slaves to a daughter as a marriage portion.

Slaves were a *chattel*, possession or property. Several French families on both sides of the Strait had one or more. Slaves were generally liberated after some years or sold out of the territory. Indians said the French keep their slaves to death (Girardin 1872, Detroit Pioneer Society, Slavery in the Early 1800's, Detroit, MI).

Most slave masters were very attached to their *sambo* (slave of African or mixed with Native American heritage) and required a great price to buy him (J.A. Girardin).

Both African and Native Americans were sold at auction. There were southern and northern markets. Sometimes they tore the clothes off women and girls (Metis History, Canadian History a Distinct Viewpoint. www). Young girls were traded.

The West Indian Company had a huge monopoly in slavery.

Slaves were common. In Canadian history, there were 4,092 slaves; 2,692 were Indians and 1,400 were Blacks (Moore, History of MI).

In 1641, Massachusetts, Connecticut, and Virginia permit slavery of Indians, Whites, and Negroes.

Women and children were sold into slavery in the Caribbean.

Seasoning the slaves by taking away their identity breaking them to do what they are told gained a 52% higher profit. Jamaica was notorious. (African Holocaust).

Slaves were denied fundamental freedoms. There were Black Codes (laws restricting and suppressing freedoms and work in labor based on low wages or debt) to preserve slavery. The same tactics were used on Indian reservations.

British slaves fled in 1684 to the Spanish Colony of La Florida, thousands flee for freedom and established St. Augustine, Florida.

The Florida Whites killed 200 Apalaches and sold more than 1,400 captives into slavery.

The Europeans' law (was) "Might is Right" (Metis History, www).

The Church takes in slaves to convert. The Church slaves do not abandon their Holy Spirit God. The Black Robes beg the savages to abandon their Holy Spirit God (Metis History, www).

Indians took captives to adopt for replacing lost loved ones. They also kept slaves who were treated as family members. Children born to slaves were born free.

In 1719, the Louisiana Slave Trade came from Africa.

Slavery began almost with the beginning of settlement. The Indians who gathered near the Fort brought with them captives taken in battle, and some of these were transferred to the French, some as gifts and some were bought in trade. In 1760, there were both Indian and African slaves in Detroit. Most of the slaves were from the Pawnee tribe, a few from the Osage, Choctaw, and other Western tribes who had been captured in war and sold to the French and English residents. The Indians made excellent servants and commanded good prices. At the time of the capitulation, it was stipulated that the French inhabitants should keep their Negroes, but they were to restore those belonging to the English (Farmer 1884).

In 1780, Negro slaves were brought to Montreal by the Indians and sold. They were valuable; there were many Negro slaves in Canada. The Indians also had many Panis or Pawnee slaves. There were also White slaves (The Slave in Canada, Journal of Negro History, 1920).

The Catholic Church was said to be the largest slaveholders in New France. The French kept their slaves until death.

Far from the oppressive life they were forced to live, keeping them uneducated, very poor, and abused in many ways. And the stereotypes perpetrated on the race. Many Blacks were skilled workers when they were brought into slavery by the British and Americans. This is why, they were captured, to do the trade work of silversmithing and growing plants.

In 1775, the British Court ruled that slaves could not be held in the United Kingdom. Fearing the ruling would apply to the American colonies, the ruling government in the south got behind the north in the revolution to leave British aggression (Liberty Law Site, www).

In 1773, there were 96 slaves at the settlement along the Detroit. In 1782, there were 179 slaves along the Detroit.

Slaves of the LaForce family, captured in Kentucky and brought to Detroit in 1779, some of them were Scipo, who was given to Simon Girty; Joseph and Keggy, given to Captain Elliott; Job to Mr. Baby; Candis to Captain Mckee; Ester to Henry Bird; and Hannah to Fisher. The Indians took Bess, Grace, Rachael, and Patrick (Riddell, Life of Wm. Dummer Powell, First Judge of Detroit, 1924).

The promise of freedom was given for Blacks who fought in the Revolutionary War. The Black Loyalist Forces were granted freedom from the British Government. Thousands were taken to Nova Scotia, Jamaica, and Sierra Leone in Africa. In 1783, the U.S. Congress ordered George Washington to retrieve the Americans' property. Slave owners went north to take back their slaves. Many were sent back into slavery and punished severely.

Many Black villages were established in Canada. The main Black settlements are Owen Sound, Amherstburg (Sandwich), Windsor, Chatham, Elgin, Dawn, Dresden, Niagara Peninsula, Toronto, and Hamilton.

In 1807, slavery was abolished in the British Colonies, though it continued under many schemes devised by the owners. Indentured slavery was one of many ways to keep workers in servitude.

Black men also fought in the War of 1812, and many were taken back when the troops evacuated from Charleston and other Ports.

The Book of Negroes, written in late 1780s Canada, records the names of thousands of Blacks who came to Canada for freedom.

Black Loyalists, on the www (world wide web) is the Story of Freed Black Slaves in Canada.

The Ordinance of 1787, had provided that slavery should not exist in the Northwest Territory. The importation of slaves was discontinued after September 17, 1792, the Canadian Parliament by law directing that no slaves should be introduced, and that all born thereafter should be free at the age of 25. Governor Simcoe, an advocate on the side of liberty, but due to opposition from motives of interest, they could carry the subject no further than liberty at 25 to all born after this date (MPHC vol. 17, 1793 Expedition to Detroit, Friends Miscellany).

At that time, this region was not under the control of the American government and there was no barrier to the holding of slaves at Detroit. After the surrender in 1796, of the region to the Americans, slave owners at Detroit yet held their slaves under the Jay Treaty of 1794, which provided that the inhabitants of the territory would be protected in their property. This changed in 1807 when the Northwest Territory was established.

The importation of slaves was abolished in 1808. This led to the rampant abuse of the masters impregnating their slave girls and women to continue breeding their fortunes. The smuggling of slaves continued.

"We were told the Americans were to take our males, young and old, and castrate them, then a horde of Negro men, were to be brought from the South, to whom our wives and sisters and daughters were to be given, for raising a stock of slaves to supply the demand in this country where Negros are scarce" (Taimah, Fox Chief 1832. Indian Oratory 1971, Virginia Irving Armstrong).

In 1830, there were 32 slaves in Michigan; by 1836, all the slaves were either dead or *manumitted* (free). Advertisements for runaway slaves appeared in *The Gazette* as late as 1827.

In 1834, slavery was outlawed in Michigan, and all slaves became free.

The Detroit Antislavery Society was organized in 1837 (Farmer 1884, Slavery and the Colored Race pg. 345, 346, History of Detroit and MI).

The Panis or Pawnee were docile slaves. The French preferred the Panis.

The Pawnees or Punnins were Captives, taken by the Chippewa from the Sioux, or Pawnee Nations. The Pawnees of the Missouri River Basin taken captive were called "Panis". Panis or Pawnee became the generic name for any Aboriginal slave. *Esckave Panis* – Panis or slave" in French. But it is sorrowful to think that in a British Government so famed for liberty, they and a number of the African race, are held in bondage during life (MPHC vol. 17, 1793 Expedition to Detroit, Friends Miscellany).

This human *chattel* created immense fortunes for many prominent Northern families. The British-English settlers and UEL – Loyalists or Tories – brought in their African slaves.

Lord Dunsmore's proclamation in 1775 in Britain led to the Revolution. He ruled slavery illegal in England, and that the land West of the Alleghenies was to be left to the Indians.

This was unacceptable to the colonies, who believed they owned the land as far as the Pacific. It was a great mess, as the Indians were the occupants, The Crown claiming rule over all and the colonies claiming the land by Charters of the King.

There were many Indian Slaves in South Carolina, 1,400.

If the Black men fought with the military, they were to become free. When the Union evacuated the South, they took thousands of freed slaves with them.

Over 4,000 Black men fought in the War of 1812. Upon becoming free, many went to the West Indies and Florida, where they were hunted down by former masters.

Cotton was the national currency. Cotton created New York. There were hundreds of northern cotton mills. Raw cotton made up half of all U.S. exports sent to Liverpool, England. In 1850, there were 75,000 cotton plantations in the South. The North was also profiting from the slave trade (Liberty law site, www).

Some Blacks were free men and did well on their own. Their economic success led to the Ku Klux Klan forming to undermine Black economic interests and force Blacks into sharecropping on unfair terms. Black communities were targeted for acts of terror, whose purpose was to enforce economic apartheid.

Due to "Northern Amnesia", the truth has not been widely known. There was slavery in Detroit for over 120 years. There is a great deal of denial by Whites and others about the whole thing. They don't want to confront it. It's painful to acknowledge what really happened.

Slavery ended in Michigan in the 1830s, yet the law was evaded with indenture laws. Indentured slaves owed the slaver master for some purchase – land, a wife, etc., though not all of the people were against slavery. Lewis Cass, the Irish, and the Free Press all fought the idea of freeing slaves (Liberty Law Site, www).

Slavery in Canada was abolished in 1834, and there was a gradual emancipation over 25 years.

The Dred Scott Decision of the Court in 1857 made the Black people not persons but property. Further, Congress now has no authority to outlaw slavery in any territory.

Slaves left their British Masters and sought freedom in Michigan and Canada. There were many Negro villages near Amherstburg, Ontario.

Sojourner Truth had her headquarters at Battle Creek, Michigan (Moore). She was a former slave in New York, an abolitionist, a preacher, and advocate of women's rights. She traveled the country for 40 years as an advocate of human rights. She had five owners and walked to freedom carrying her baby in 1826. She was illiterate but a fierce speaker for human rights of all kinds. Her grandson could read and write; Sammy Banks traveled with her and was an invaluable companion.

Several people owned slaves at Port Huron, Michigan (MPHC vol. 11, 1887, Wm. l. Bancroft).

"The English came to steal our riches and make slaves of the people as they did in England. Those lacking property at home would have new lands to lord over. Merchants would have exotic products to sell. The clergy could convert the savages to Christianity. The landless poor would have opportunity to rise up from their poverty" (Thomas J. Davis, Arizona State University).

The Northern onslaught on slavery was no more than a cover-up of desire for economic control of Southern states (Charles Dickens 1862). Slavery was about Northern profits, enslaving all Americans. It was a tyrannical government of propaganda. The Kansas and Nebraska Act fueled the formation of the Republican Party. Who were against making new slave states when the U.S. purchased the land west of the Mississippi from the Spanish.

Freedom was national in Federal Territory and on the high seas. Slavery was local with the States having jurisdiction.

Slavery was abolished in the North by 1834, with a gradual emancipation. It did continue, (however), in many creative ways for long after this date.

The slavery system of economics created unimaginable wealth in North America and Europe. Slavery set the framework for the modern global economy (Liberty Law Site, www).

Blacks who were sold into slavery were not ignorant but having desirable skills, such as growing crops, working metals, and many other types of skilled labor. In America, many were kept in ignorance and denied an education to perpetuate the slave economy

Slaves were taken to the Caribbean Islands to be "seasoned", then sold to the mainland for working the plantations and other trades. Fresh slaves could not be trusted.

President Lincoln and the Republicans entered upon the war with no intention of attacking slavery. The Union turned to emancipation reluctantly to advance the war efforts.

They used servile insurrection and Black slaves to kill White Southerners. The slaves themselves were then being killed by local militias – the "kill two birds with one stone" strategy.

Even after slavery was outlawed here in America, it continued in Brazil and Cuba under the U.S. flag. The crops were sugar, cotton, salt, rum, coffee, rice, and tobacco.

It was legal, economic, and social discrimination, the people kept desperately poor, denied equal access to education, and segregated (The Truth about Slavery, www).

In the Virginia Company of London, planters worked for a piece of land in servitude as indentured servants. Servants of the company had no real freedom and were kept by force. They had no choice but to accept any charges the government or Company decided to make, including extension of their contracts. So, many literally were worked to death in very poor conditions. Letters were destroyed to family members, and minor offenses were dealt with severely. There were continual whippings, as well as hangings, shootings, breakings on the wheel, and even people being burnt alive. Some tried to escape to live with the Indians, but they were hunted down and tortured, killed or any other atrocity.

The Indians grew the food, farmed, and sold to and shared. The colonists begged, bullied, or bought corn from the Indians, whom they continually cheated and mistreated.

The English saw vast lands to develop and were rigorous in using raw materials, searching out natural resources wealth, (and) stealing by force huge timber stands (and) teeming rivers. There was a tremendous amount of physical labor involved in pioneer days (Thomas J. Davis, AZSU, Africans in America). They needed labor to strip the land. The people were held captive, labor exploited, then dumped them and went on to lie, cheat, and steal from the next wealthy place.

The English came with a fully developed system of slavery (Charles Jayne). The Royal African Company was an English Crown-owned slave trade company. The great triangle of slavery started with slaves being taken to the Caribbean to make sugar for rum and salt, the rum went to the Colonies and Northwest where it was traded for furs. The furs were then taken to Europe, and the money bought slaves from Africa. Riches were made all around.

Cheryl Morgan

THE UNDERGROUND RAILROAD

Inaction of those who could have acted, indifference of those who should have known better, the silence of the voice of justice when it mattered most, that has made it possible for evil to triumph (Halle Selassie, Jews and African History).

History is suppressed. Zionism is a religious cover for White Supremacy. We are blind to the history of racism and oppression. Balanced respectful critique is a sign of a healthy society. Other opinions are necessary to balance out White Washing (African Holocaust).

In 1805, there were six Colored men and nine Colored women in the town of Detroit. Their numbers increased in 1807 (and) Governor Hull organized a Company of Negro Militia.

In Detroit, a society was formed to aid refugees. Among the most active were Alanson Sheley, Horace Hallock, Samuel Zug, and the Reverend C.C. Foote. They purchased a tract of land ten miles from Windsor, Ontario, and parceled it into farms of ten to fifteen acres each. These were given to refugees, many of whose descendants are still nearby (Historic Michigan, Fuller).

On April 26, 1837, the Detroit Antislavery Society was organized. The Officers were Shubael Conant, President; Edward Brooks, Edwin W. Cowles, and Cullen Brown, Vice Presidents; Henry Stewart, Secretary; George F. Porter, Treasurer; and William Kirkland, Alanson Sheley, and Peter Boughton, Executive Committee. The Society was in existence only a short time, but its spirit remained, and its principles grew increasingly popular.

The Liberty Association was a political organization which sought to promote the election of anti-slavery candidates. Horace Hallock was President, Cullen Brown was Vice President, and S.M. Holmes was Secretary.

In 1850, Congress passed the Fugitive Slave Act. It provided that slaves might be arrested in any state, appointed special officers to secure their arrest and directed that the testimony of fugitives in any trial growing out of their arrest should not be admitted.

This law greatly incensed many citizens and increased the strength of the antislavery sentiment. The proximity of Canada, where the slaves became free men, caused Detroit to become a noted departure, and fugitive slaves were constantly passing through. The attempts to retake fugitive slaves were in the main unsuccessful for the majority of the people were opposed to slavery and thus the slave holders, were foiled and outwitted. Many people helped slaves escaping slavery go to Canada for freedom and safety. There was a complete chain of persons extending to the Southern states, who were organized for the relief and transportation of fugitive slaves.

Ottissippi

The Underground Railroad was a league of men, most of whom were Quakers, who organized a system for spiriting away and conducting runaway slaves from Kentucky, Tennessee, and other Slave States through to Canada. They watched for fleeing bondsmen and ferried them away in rowboats by night over the Ohio river and then started them to the first station to Detroit where they were ferried over the river in rowboats to Canada and Freedom. Everything was kept secret the workings were a great mystery to people. Slaves strangely disappeared and nothing was ever heard of them until reported to have been seen in Canada. None of the methods were known to the public. Levi Coffin was the originator of the Underground Railroad.

The main route, known as the Central Michigan Line, passed through Battle Creek, where the famous old Quaker Erastus Hussey freely assisted with his time and money. Another (passed) through Adrian. The work was done because of a love for mankind, a sense of duty from a moral purpose. Like all Quakers, they would not recognize laws that sanctioned slavery. They were manmade laws; he obeyed only divine laws. Mr. Hussey secreted and fed over 1,000 Colored persons and sent them on to the next station at Marshall. Stations were established every 15 or 16 miles. All traveling was done in the dark, the work done gratuitously and without price. All done out of sympathy and from principal, working for humanity.

A shorter route was started through Ohio by way of Sandusky and thence to Fort Malden and Amherstburg. Stations from Indiana were at Cassopolis, Michigan, (and) Schoolcraft, then Climax. Battle Creek came next. From Marshall the stations were Albion, Parma, one at Jackson, Michigan Center, Leioni, Grass Lake, Francisco, Dexter, Scio, Ann Arbor, Geddes, Ypsilanti, (and) Plymouth; they followed the River Rouge to Swartzburg, then to Detroit, Michigan.

Passwords were used, one being: Can you give shelter and protection to one or more persons?

John Beard, a Quaker minister, and Levi Coffin were sent to Canada to learn how they were succeeding and to see what assistance they may need. Some of the slaves were frightened upon their arrival, while others were full of courage and joy. Usually one to four came together. One time 45 came in a bunch.

Slaves were forced to work in mines. Debt peonage and convict leasing were common, (as well as) coercive labor and human trafficking (The other Slavery, Indian Country Today. www).

Reverend O.C. Thompson ran a station of the Underground Railroad at St. Clair, Michigan. Where he instituted the St. Clair Academy School.

Many ship captains were abolitionists and carried slaves to freedom. Many slaves worked loading ships with goods and later with ore and other resources.

The Federal Fugitive Slave Act of 1850 was to prevent Free States from offering refuge to runaway slaves through Free States and Territories into Canada.

The Underground Railroad formed. The infrastructure was capable of moving, escaping slaves long distances. The Quakers were the primary organizers and operators on the railroad to freedom. Southern Michigan was a very important part of the Underground Railroad and a resettlement place for former slaves.

From 1840 to 1860, the Underground Railroad was underway with slaves from the South escaping to the North. The Detroit Underground Railroad was one of the busiest sectors. There were major stations along the rivers. The Natives were also helping escaped slaves to find freedom in the north.

A paper called *The Voice of the Fugitive* was published, first at Sandwich and then at Windsor, by Henry Bibb. The 1851 issue contained the following:

> *This road is doing better business this fall than usual. The Fugitive Slave Law has given it more vitality, more activity, more passengers, and more opposition which invariably accelerates business. We have been under the necessity of tearing up the old strap rails and putting down T's, so that we can run a lot of slaves through from almost any of the bordering states into Canada within forty-eight hours, and we defy the slaveholders and their abettors to beat that if they can.*
>
> *We have just received a fresh lot today of hearty-looking men and women on the last train from Virginia, and still there is room.*

In 1851, the paper contained this item: "Progress of Escape from Slavery".

> *In enumerating the arrivals of this week, we can count only seventeen, ten of whom came together on the Express Train of the Underground Railroad. This lot consisted of a*

mother with six children and three men. The next day there came four men, the next day two men arrived, and then came one alone. The latter tells of having had a warm combat by the way with two slave catchers, in which he found it necessary to throw a handful of sand in the eyes of one of them; and while he was trying to wash it out, he broke away from the other and effected his escape. (Farmer 1884)

Dresden and the Dawn Settlement, Amherstburg, Malden, Chatham, Windsor, the Elgin Settlement, and Buxton Mission being a few places where the slaves now found freedom and established new lives and towns.

The Indians, Quakers, ship captains, railroads, farmers, families on the river, and small boats were all involved in the Underground Railroad.

A route from Battle Creek ran Northeast through Lansing and Flint to Port Huron, Michigan, where there was an easy transit across the St. Clair River to Canada. There was considerable, pronounced Abolition sentiment in Michigan.

The Strait Detroit River – St. Clair River, was a busy crossing place for escaping slaves to Canada. Many came to work in the Lumber Industry and farming. There were many safe houses with sympathetic whites throughout Southern Lower Michigan.

The census of 1837 counted 228 Negroes in Wayne County and 379 for the State population. Michigan was a haven for slaves fleeing the South (Fuller/ Genealogy Trails, www).

John Brown, the noted Abolitionist, had ties to the area across from Detroit and had rallies for and against slavery here and at Detroit. In 1859, John Brown arrived in Detroit with 14 slaves from Missouri, and John also had five of his own men with him. Frederick Douglas, the Colored Orator, was also present and lecturing on the same evening Brown arrived. After the lecture, a meeting was held to organize the Harper's Ferry Raid. Though John was killed at the Raid, the Emancipation Proclamation was a result of the meeting in Detroit. Ontario has a John Brown Festival every year in Amherstburg.

John Brown, the great Freedom Fighter, had a cabin near Wallaceburg, Ontario. He had many meetings with the Abolitionists near Detroit.

After Emancipation, there were three million free Blacks, a large population. There were Northern Black codes. They received poor care, a form of Black genocide.

Their efforts to obtain citizenship began in 1843.

In 1853, steamers and every boat carried fugitive slaves to freedom in Canada. Any Black residing in Canada since 1819 was free.

In 1861, the Negro population of Detroit was about 500.

The first organization effected to better the condition of Michigan's Afro Americans occurred on October 8th and 9th in 1869. When a convention of Colored men met at Battle Creek, Michigan, for the purpose, of the Right of Suffrage to consider the status of Colored people and devise means to better their condition.

The Fifteenth Amendment to the Constitution of the United States, on March 30, 1870, declared them citizens and voters. The restrictive word "White" was stricken from the Constitution of Michigan on November 8, 1870, and the votes of the Colored citizens were first cast in Detroit on the same day (Farmer 1884).

During the Civil War from 1861 to 1865, 623,000 men died. All slaves were free as of January 1, 1863.

The first celebration in honor of the Emancipation Day was held on January 6, 1863 at the Colored Baptist Church.

Slavery was abolished in 1865. June 19th is now celebrated as "Juneteenth, the actual day slavery ended".

From 1916 to 1970, many African Americans moved North in the Great Migration, for higher wages and shorter work days. Many were attracted to Detroit for the Auto Industry.

WHAT SHALL I TELL MY CHILDREN WHO ARE BLACK – MARGARET BURROUGHS

What shall I tell my children who are black
Of what it means to be a captive in this dark skin?
What shall I tell my dear one, fruit of my womb,
of how beautiful they are when everywhere they turn
they are faced with abhorrence of everything that is black [...]

What shall I tell my dear ones raised in a white world
A place where white has been made to represent
all that is good and pure and fine and decent [...]
white...all, all...white.

Ottissippi

What can I say therefore when my Child
comes home in tears because a playmate
Has called him black, big lipped, flat nosed and nappy headed?
What will he think when I dry his tears and whisper
"Yes, that's true. But no less beautiful and dear."
How, shall I lift up his head get him to square
his shoulders, look his adversaries in the eye,
confident in the knowledge of his worth.
Serene under his own skin and proud of his own beauty?

What can I do, to give him strength
That he may come through life's adversities
As a whole human being unwarped and human, in a world
of biased laws and inhuman practices, that he might
Survive. And survive he must! For who knows?
Perhaps this black child here bears the genius
To discover the cure for. . .cancer
Or to chart the course for exploration of the universe.
So, he must survive for the good of all humanity.

He must and will survive.
I have drunk deeply of late from the fountain
of my black culture, sat at the knee and learned
from mother Africa, discovered the truth of my heritage.
The truth, so often obscured and omitted.
And I find I have much to say to my black children.
I will lift up their heads in proud blackness,
with the story of their fathers and their father's fathers.
And I shall take them into a way back time
of kings and queens who ruled the Nile,
and measured the stars and discovered the laws of mathematics.
I will tell them of a black people upon whose backs have been built
the wealth of two continents.
I will tell him this and more.
And his heritage shall be his weapon and his armor;
It will make him strong enough to win any battle he may face.

*And since this story is often obscured,
I must sacrifice to find it for my children,
even as I sacrificed to feed, clothe and shelter them. [...]
None will do it for me.*

*I must find the truth of heritage for myself and pass it on to them.
In years to come, I believe because I have armed them with the truth,
my children and their children's children will venerate me.
For it is the truth that will make us free!*

(Margaret Dusable Burroughs, Director, Museum of Negro History, Chicago, Illinois)

The Thirteenth Amendment to the U.S. Constitution abolished slavery except for those duly convicted of a crime. Though slavery was abolished, those in bondage were not freed, only their descendants. Another form of slavery was used, called indentured servitude, so the practice of slavery continued into the 1900s.

Selective breeding was practiced; there were restrictions for undesirable ethnic groups, prevention of unfit marriages, and sterilization of defective individuals. Eugenics was in practice in the 1940s. Forty thousand to 70,000 Americans were sterilized against their will; they were the minorities, poor and uneducated (the Heinous Program of Racial Hygiene).

In, *The Lie About When Slavery Ended* (2012), Denise Oliver Velez writes,

> *I hate lies, and History books are still full of them. Lies about the founding of this country, lies about the treatment of Native Americans, lies about the Civil War and slavery. Too many textbooks are yet unrevised. Some have to take it upon themselves to spread some truth."*

> *After 1863, new forms of forced labor emerged in the American South, keeping hundreds of thousands of African Americans in bondage, trapping them in a brutal system that would persist until the onset of WWII. Neo slavery*

began and persisted in 1865-1945. This supported the re-enslavement of Black Americans in prison camps and chain gangs. Evidence has been deliberately suppressed and smoothed over into false face. It has not ended, and we are still being fed lies.

Hillary Crosby, in "When Were Blacks Truly Freed from Slavery", wrote:

Laws were instituted that stripped African Americans of their Rights.

Jail owners profited from hard labor of Black inmates incarcerated for petty crimes like vagrancy, which carried long sentences. Sold workforce to nearby industrial companies to work as coal miners, inmates were often worked to death.

Whites fabricated debts owed by Blacks, forcing them to trade years of free work for their freedom across the Bible Belt. Roosevelt's Anti Peonage Law in 1941 criminalized the practice.

The War on Drugs and Draconian Law created in the 1980s caused mass incarceration in the age of colorblindness. Subjugation through Criminalization.

Jazz Hayden wrote in "The New Form of Slavery" on *Alternet*, www, wrote; "The New Form of Slavery has the same intent and purpose as the old, which is to rob us of our labor and to keep us powerless."

The last slaves in America were freed in the 1900s.

There were slaves in all 50 states of the United States.

February is African American History Month.

Americans are 5% of the world's population and have 25% of the world's prisoners. In some places, the system abuses the fines and surcharges of the court system and community service.

"The Indians were stereotyped, and a racist government created evil against these peoples, as with the Negroes of that day" (Herman Cameron).

QUOTES ABOUT FREEDOM

"Exploitation and humiliation are caused by racism."

"The greatest threat to freedom is the absence of criticism." – Wole Soyika, African Holocaust/Indian Holocaust

"In the classes of oppressed people, there is a relationship between popular education and the politics of oppression. This is called *Second Class Citizenship*. Want people to assume certain positions and never challenge their natural place in Society. Trained in the Industrial Way.

Mental Development, if men can be made to think like his oppressor, then his actions can be determined by remote control on most levels. Opponents of freedom and social justice enslave the mind, not the body." – African Holocaust

"Assured of his superiority, others are made to feel always a failure, subjection of his will is necessary, a freedman was still a slave. When you determine what a man shall think, you do not have to compel him to accept an inferior status; he will seek it himself. If you make a man think he is an outcast, you do not have to order him to the back door." – Motive and Method of the Education System in the U.S. of America

"The European model, traditions, values, hegemony, intellectual imperialism, colonial thinking, cultural thought and behavior are close minded policies. It does not equal intelligence."

"The system colonizer: socialization into accepting the value system, history and culture of the dominant society and education for economic productivity, the public policy to limit, control, and destabilize the life chances and opportunities for children." Lies my teacher told me, Loewen.

CHAPTER 13
Indian Culture And Lifeways, Part I - Religion, Tribal Structure, Roles, And Responsibilities

"Our Native races had often been misinterpreted in the history books, and they are much misunderstood today" (Nicholas Plain, 1950, former Chief of the Sarnia Chippewa).

RELIGION

In the beginning of time, the creator had five sons: A Red son given the gift of taking care of Mother Earth and all our relations on the earth and all it entails. The Yellow son was to give, the gift of patience. The Black son, was to give the gift of strength, to share with the World. The White son was to give the gift of fire to be shared with all. The fifth son had no color because he turned away and called himself God; we don't talk about him, he has no meaning, and he is shunned. (Joe Greaux, Traditional Ojibwe teaching).

"Nature taught of the Supreme Being, all powerful, all wise, his great goodness. Men learned to love and reverence him. They sought him and worshipped him. He was Gitchi Manito, "The Great Spirit" (Handsome Lake). God taught them to hunt, build fire, and the good and evil.

Gezho Monedo means "merciful spirit", revered term for the Great Spirit. Creator – Wazhea'ud, means "Maker", and Universal Father is Waosemigoyan. Matchi Manitou means "evil spirits".

The Indian regards the coming of the White Man as fulfilling the prophesy of their own priests – Holy Men. Indian history is often disguised under symbolic forms. The Sun – Giisis – was a symbol of divine intelligence – The Great Spirit. Even the Dobeka – Moon – reflects that fire at night. Fire was a symbol of purity; it also designated periods of time, or eras, and places where the people lived.

They believe in universal acceptance after death (Schoolcraft, "Travels in Minnesota and Wisconsin", 1821).

"Medicine is the name for everything held sacred and good. No payment was received for it. Later greed led to the demoralizing practice of payment for medical assistance and other good Medicines. The Medicine bag was like an alter; it was carried across the chest.

The Great Spirit was the Supreme Ruler. Upon his will depends everything that happens. Nothing is undertaken without a prayer to the Great Spirit for assistance, his favor sought by prayer, sacrifice, a kindly life, knowledge of him, discipline, fasting, and lonely vigil, and with that knowledge will come his guidance. At times, inspiring or using animals, weather, mountains, men, or things, hence the source of the saying, "The Indian bowed to wood and stone". The chief end of man is to attain manhood, the just development of every part and power, and the full enjoyment of the same. He must achieve manhood in the body way, the knowledge way, the spirit way, and the tribal way. He must then consecrate that manhood to the service of his people, be a good provider, a brave protector, a kind and helpful neighbor, and defend his family, his camp, or his tribe from a foreign foe. When his time comes to die, he should remember he is going to the Next World and should not be afraid to die; he should rest assured, he has done his best with the gifts that were his.

All these beliefs and practices were before the White Man, and the Indian was worshipping the Creator in a religion of spiritual kindness and truth.

The culture is spiritual; the measure of success is; "How much service have I rendered to my people?" His every thought, act, and life are approached with complete realization of the spirit world. The Noble Red man is of lofty character and greatness of mind, sharpened by environment and communion with the Great Spirit by worship, knowledge gained through communion with the Great Spirit in his community.

The Indians believed the Great Spirit was watching from all nature. Their language was free from all swear words. Every day was a holy day. Believing that all life in the whole universe is sustained by God and is given by him to the human race for sustenance. The Indians worked for the good of the tribe. If a member of the tribe was in want, it was because the whole tribe was, all for one and one for all. The land belonged to the whole tribe, not the individual. The

Indian is never known to kill wantonly, for sport (Chief Nicholas Plain, "History of Chippewa of Sarnia". 1950).

The Indian is colorblind – all men are created equal; there is no racism among them." Racial and religious prejudices of others stand in the way of his true understanding. Strange customs and ceremonies are symbolism; they have inner meaning, hidden from the observer. They are then branded as Pagen, and devil-worshippers. Physical worship was wholly symbolic. He no more worshipped the sun than the Christian the cross. He had a reverence and love for plants, the earth, and the sun. The spirit pervades all creation; every creature has a soul in some degree and is an object of reverence. There are miracles in every hand in life.

He is a religious man from his mother's womb, taught silence, love, and reverence. The Trinity of First Lessons, later she adds generosity, courage, and chastity. He is a blood brother to all living creatures of the Great Mystery.

The Indians had a total lack of greed; they were generous, fair, and honest. They are strangers to frugality, sharing everything like the early Christians.

There is one God of the lettered and unlettered. All men were created sons of God. Nature was his cathedral (Charles Eastman, "The Soul of the Indian").

It pleases him to see his people live together in harmony and quiet. All things are the gift of the Great Spirit, and thank must be returned. He alone acknowledged as the Giver. Give thanks for each day, and all things in everything. You are not your own makers, or builders of your future. Speak evil of no one, be given to hospitality, never steal, reverence old age (Handsome Lake). "We have a religion to be thankful, united, to love one another; we never quarrel about religion" (Red Jacket).

THE MIDE - MIDEWIWIN

"The Mide were spiritual leaders. The Midewiniwin or Midewiwin Lodge (the Heartways) was the group of spiritual leaders for the tribe, our spiritual society. The Mide are keepers of the Medicine Lodge secrets. Teaching, guiding, spirituality – traditional values, morals, and ethics.

They record important events, including births, deaths, and marriages. The sacred teachings are passed from generation to generation; oral traditions convey spiritual and timeless meanings of complex content, only completely understood by fluent speakers of the Anishinabe, the English language cannot fully express it.

Anishinabe words are words that have many layers of metaphoric meaning that describe sacred concepts. Our language was a gift from the Creator.

Our healers are well-versed in plants, roots, barks, and other natural materials and all their properties.

Tobacco was used as an incense for meditation, and prayers were sent up with the smoke to the Great Spirit this way. Tobacco was a gift from Gitchi Manito, a sort of offering. Used in council, and solemn agreements, and requests, incense made a binding agreement. It was an essential part of making a treaty. It was used as a thank offering in daily life and asking for blessing and requests. It was used to express thanks and gratitude.

Tobacco was called Kinnickinick and Semaa. It was a blend of sacred plants, dried and ground up for smoking. Sage, cedar, sumac, nicotiana (tobacco), red or spotted willow bark, aster novae, bearberry, pine, rose petals, red clover, and other plant materials were used for tobacco, and dry cedar chips with flint were used to light the pipe. Cedar was used in rituals and ceremonies.

We were to follow the creator's instructions, walk the earth, and name all the animals, plants, hills, and valleys" (Kevin Callahan, UMN).

The spirit world is all of creation, a reciprocal relationship. Tobacco is offered and prayers of Thanksgiving are given to the Spirit of every plant or animal that is taken. A constant dialogue, with tobacco and prayers to the spirits in heaven, earth, water, and fire, is remembered daily and at seasonal ceremonies (Flocken, 2013).

The spirits were never objects of worship. They were unseen assistants and executors of the Great Spirit's will. The power of truth reached some of the most important conclusions of philosophy and drew down from Heaven some of the highest truths of revelation. The people believed in the constant superintending care of the Great Spirit, who ruled and administered the world and affairs of men. The creator, ruler, preserver, all powerful. God reveals himself in nature and is innately written on the minds of men.

In knowledge of the Supreme Being, they rose far above the highest conceptions of ancient philosophy, the foundation of their religion. The Indians' inferior spiritualists fell below the creators of ancient mythology. Faith was enlarged by White ideals in harmony with their creed (beliefs); peace, hospitality, charity, friendship, religious enthusiasm, and domestic affection.

The genius of learning and Christianization changed society and cast an artificial garment over it. The Indian walked the highest virtues of civilized and Christianized man. In the rarest traits of human character surpassed beyond him. All excellences of character are ascribed to faith in the Great Spirit. The one Supreme Being, who created and preserved them" (Lanmar, Red Book).

Native people viewed animals as Helper Beings, having their own spirits and purpose. Dog was sacrificed and eaten on every solemn occasion. They were kept as sheep.

Dreams are very significant and affect the behavior and actions of the Anishinabe. In dreams people are given knowledge to heal the sick, how to teach the children, and for everything. The good knowledge was shared to help others.

There are four types of dreams: a generic meshing of current experiences, a premonition, or a dream of future events. The Traveling Dream is where a person will fly or transport to different places and times to learn about things. And the Power Dream is where you are gifted by an animal or spirit (A. Lossier). All wisdom came to them in dreams (Densmore, 1979).

All the created world, is seen as alive and filled with spiritual power, including each human being. The interrelationship of all creation, is a profound knowledge to science and spirituality in the modern world (George Tinker, Osage School of Theology).

Plant cures were revealed and prescriptions to the Medicine Lodge. Warnings were given to keep the people safe from harm. Sometimes dreams needed to be interpreted.

VISION QUEST

At puberty, the youth are sent on a vision quest to seek their Guardian Spirit. They fast and pray for several days, others are praying for them too. They are seeking Gitchi Manito through their vision, they are many times given a Vision or Dream. Their dream is then interpreted by older men (Medicine Men). the Guardian in the dream given was the grandfather for life to guide and help. Direct communication with the Creator was too powerful for any person. Animal spirits were the intermediaries for the Creator. Like an icon in the Catholic Church.

The Anishinabe may never speak of their guide or vision; it is very personal and very private.

Spirits would give spiritual powers to the Anishinabe, such as medical, spiritual leadership abilities and responsibilities. Gifts were to be used to benefit the community. The spirits share their power with humans, who in turn help each other with these spiritual gifts. The unwritten scripture, a living bible, sowed as precious seed. The whole created universe a sharer of the Great Spirit of the immortal perfection of its Maker. Tobacco is Thanksgiving to the Great Spirit. Flocken, 2013, UMN).

The vision quest calls for fasting and prayer apart from the community over several days. Others pray throughout the time for the individual. By engaging in this ceremony, the person acts on behalf of and for the good of the whole community. The goal is to receive a vision to guide development for life and also a Guardian Spirit, who will be a close supporter for life (George Tinker, Osage School of Theology).

A man's health or sickness were from the spirits; if offended for any reason it was attributed to Illness. Success in hunting, fishing, planting, and war were dependent upon the spirit's good favor. A constant communication was made with the spirits of all creation.

Sweet grass is used in prayer and in a smudge like an incense for cleansing and purifying. It has tons of uses as a medicinal. It is the hair of Mother Earth; we braid it and it is to remind us the earth is our Mother – Sustainer – giving all we live on, given by, Gitchi Manito", The Great Spirit. The waters are the blood of the earth – life-giving, given by The Great Spirit.

"The idea that we have many gods is totally false; it is one of the greatest lies that have been told. The non-Indian never bothered to learn the truth. We worship everything; it is of the spirit of the Creator. There are male and female trees. In the swamp and woods are medicines to heal cancer. There were trees of tremendous size, food and medicine everywhere. The non-Indian has a lot to learn about and from us. We live in peace" (Eddie Benton Benai, Ojibwe History, 2001, www.pbs.org/video/2365039287).

"We look seven generations into the future, what we do in our lives affects the future.

Sacred bundles – Medicine bundles – are used as teaching reminder, tools to teach the Four Directions and other sacred teachings. Medicine bundles are a collection of objects to heal disease and ward off enemies. Which symbolize a spiritual path symbols of power. Sometimes they are herbs, stones, bone, teeth, and feathers" (Ziibiwing).

THE FOUR DIRECTIONS

The Medicine Wheel is a very sacred symbol; it brings all core values and beliefs together into one symbol. In it you can see the Great Spirit, who has no beginning and no end. The Four Directions are represented by the Cross. Very often Eagle feathers are attached to each direction as messengers of the Creator. The circle represents all my family my relatives, the great prayer which expresses the reality of interrelated beings. A simple expression but very profound to those who understand. There is the immediate family, then the wider circle of relatives, and finally, the entire nation, population, and creations. There is great respect for all things created.

The pipe was used as an oath between parties before "The Great Spirit". It was held sacred. No one was to lie; it was like swearing on the Bible at court to tell the truth. To smoke together was to talk, reason, and solve problems. This is what the "Great Spirit" told us to do.

POW WOW

Pow Wow – Bow Wow, also Pau-Wau – was a healing ceremony. It later turned into any Indian gathering. Now there is more of a festival feel with dance, religious ceremonies, arts and crafts, food, and wares (Indians.org www). Pow Wows were family reunions, open to everybody, and everybody comes from all over (Joe Greaux). At most all Indian reservations, Pow Wows are held every summer.

They drew near to God and offered thanks for unnumbered blessings strewn on their path. They asked for protection and continued watch care. Their approaches to the truth rise infinitely above the other races, which originated independently of revelation. They were seekers desiring to fully comprehend the marvelous perfection of the deity, The Great Spirit, simple unpretending scheme of theology of the Children of the Forest, sustaining faith and simple worship (Lanmar, Red Book).

A traditional Pow Wow is rooted in centuries-old beliefs, ceremonials, and religion, unique to Indian culture. Pow Wows vary by tribal custom and the event being celebrated. Each part of a Pow Wow has special meaning and significance: the attire, reverence for life and nature, foods, and all that is said. Gift giveaways are common. Honoring veterans, flags, the disease-ravaged, women, girls, boys, men, elders, hunters, the Great Spirit, and many more thanksgiving celebrations.

The first Blue Water Indian Pow Wow was held in 1995, near the Bluewater Bridge at Port Huron, Michigan. It was a sacred gathering of many nations. The dancing was beautiful. Since that first one in modern times, there have been many held on the grounds North of Black River at the east side of Wadham's Bridge.

Dances are the appropriate mode of worship, the outward ceremony of thanksgiving to the Great Spirit. The belief prevailed that the custom was of divine origin. There is a distinction between their proper religious exercise and their amusements between ancient and modern. The moccasined feet were like soft rain. Some dancers wear feathers, wings, mirrors, shells, beads, fur, teeth, claws, bells, and fringe, all telling stories to celebrate life (Pow Wow www).

Women's jingle dresses are worn as an individual expression. These dresses have tin cones that jingle with short steps. Reverence, pride, and grace are exhibited in all dance competitions.

The drums are the heartbeat, calling up the past, the present, and future. They tell of love, loss, eagle, deer, Mother Sky, Father Sky, days gone by. The eagle represents the Thunderbird, messenger of the Creator. The Flag song is always sung at the start of the ceremonies. We honor many flags.

Some of the dances performed were

- Men's Grass Dance: reminiscent of flowing grasses, an expression of the harmony of the Universe
- Men's Fancy Dance: very elaborate costumes and exuberant dancing
- Men's Traditional: graceful, dignified
- Women's Traditional: beautiful, dance of honor as Givers of Life

The Buffalo Dance is a celebration of the Buffalo. The buffalo was a banquet for the people. It gave up its own flesh and life to feed them. It provided for every need they had. It sheltered them, clothed them, as well as made shoes – moccasins. It gave them tools, utensils, needle, thread, hoes, and fuel, a true relative, God's creation to sustain life and make life possible. The symbol of the buffalo and skill is present in the sacred rituals. A thanksgiving and a reminder of the Great Animal that gives completely of itself for others. A symbol of self-sacrifice, it gives until there is nothing left. It was imitated by the people in their lives. To be generous and give what you have, to others in need or to honor them, is one of the most highly respected ways of acting and being (From the Original Pow Wow Booklet, 1995, Blue Water Pow Wow).

THE DRUM

The drum is a very important symbol to Native people; the circular shape represents unity of Native peoples, a full circle. It is treated with the highest respect for what it represents. Women are not allowed near the drum. Drums are usually large, being three to four feet across. Many men can sit about it and play the music. The drum is like our heartbeat, the essence of Mother Earth and our nations. It tells stories, hymns, prayers, and regulates ceremonies that tie our people together with the Creator and the universe of which we are a part (Joe Greaux, Metis Peace Chief, Black River Woodland Tribe).

The drum music is a spiritual connection to God and the Holy Spirit (Charles Rivers). It sets the tempo and order of songs and dances. The pitch is controlled by warming the hide near a small fire. The elders say that, when the drums are sung, they are heard in the spirit world.

Ottissippi

There is a head singer, who leads the songs. Many songs are requested, the host must be ready. They are chosen because of their skill and reputation in drumming and singing. Singers are held in high regard by the people as keepers of our songs, our history, and our culture.

To blend all the various tribal languages gathered together, vocables (words with certain sounds that enabled all to join and share) were used so all could join in. Some songs are still sung in our Native language, some are very old. Some are newly composed. Many are of a serious nature, such as veterans and honor songs. Some are humorous and make us laugh at ourselves. The 49 and Round Dance songs bemoan the trials of being in love. Songs such as these remind us to not take life so seriously. Bravery, love, and friendship are a few favorite themes.

The songs are carried in the singer's memories and not written down for quick reference. A young boy will usually be sitting in a drum with older singers. Training begins young for learning and remembering songs. Women do not sit at the drum, they do sing with the drum an octave higher than the men.

SUN DANCE

The Sun Dance epitomizes spirituality. The Sun Dance was a thank offering to God for sparing life. It honored women; the cut on the chest was figurative of death. The dance for a day and night. It has lost all meaning in recent times, abused and perverted and became a horrible exhibition and was prohibited by the government. With exaggerated and distorted tortures, the loss of all meaning came under demoralizing additions (C. Eastman).

The Sun Dance was a replay of the original creation; it gave thanks to the Creator. Prayers were made for the renewal of the People and Earth to promote health and honor women (George – John, Copeway).

The Sun Dance is held in June or July during the first full moon closest to summer, when the sun was at its highest. It lasted 16 days, the first eight spent in preparation. The performance is four days. Then 4 days of abstinence. A time for renewal and healing. A sweat lodge was built, purification ceremony was before and after. Participants fasted during the dance around the sun pole. Prayers for life, the world, renewal, and thanksgiving were made. Healing ceremonies were included.

It was a fresh remembrance of our position on Earth and continuous obligation to walk this Earth, in accordance with the sacred ways. There is utmost respect in speaking few words about it, and only Natives are a part of it.

The eagle feather is worn at Pow Wows, only by veterans of combat or by people awarded eagle feathers by combat veterans. A dropped feather is danced over by the veteran who first sees it, then a Brave Man song is sung, he retrieves the feather and returns it to the owner. He then receives a gift of appreciation for the service performed.

The eagle, flies high; the closest creature to the Great Spirit, he is the Thunderbird – messenger – that delivers prayers to God. He is courageous, swift, strong, has great foresight, and knows everything. In an eagle, there is all the wisdom of the world. His feather can cure illnesses (George Tinker, Osage School of Theology).

MEDICINE DANCE

In 1832, Mr. and Mrs. Brakeman, early traders and pioneers at Marine City, attended a Medicine Dance on Harsens Island. A healing ceremony for a sick woman, Mrs. Jacob Harsen, who was an Indian woman. Her bed was set in the center of a large tent for the occasion. It was in the evening. The tent was lighted up by building up places with short pieces of logs and putting earth over the top of them, having fires burning on that. The men were all on one side, and the women on the opposite side, an Indian beating a drum, which was made of a hollow log with a dressed deer skin drawn over the top and down the sides far enough to be tied down. When he began his drumming, the company began their dancing, a sort of shuffling of their feet. The men by themselves and the women alone. A sort of shuffling of the feet moving very slowly around the sick woman. Every man carried a Medicine pouch which are made of a small animal skin filled with medicine, as each man came to her, he would shake it at her, uttering *chugh chugh*. The women did not carry medicine and kept silent. Mrs. Harsen recovered her health and lived many years after (Mrs. Nancy Brakeman, papers, MI Room, St. Clair County Library, Port Huron, MI).

They won first prize in the world. The first night at a competition recently. They didn't even know there was a contest. They won the "Best and most Unusual Performance in the World". The group grew up and moved away and went to college or are working. Brian and I started this, were the only ones left of the original group" (Joe Greaux, Peace Chief, Woodland Metis, 2014).

The White Cloud Singers – Drummers – are local men who play Indian music together. The Black River Pow Wow Natives are our ancestors they were all here in Michigan and Ontario, the Anishinabe. Song – Creator – I will not leave your path. "Way I Ya, Way I Ya Way, Yah Way, I Ya Ho."

THE SWEAT LODGE

The Pokagon – Bodewadmi or Pottawatomie – are featured on a great website that explains many cultural ways. The following sweat lodge information is from this site – Pokagon Bodewadmi.

The sweat lodge is to re-purify and find the way back to the Great Red Road, the Right Road, The Good Way, traditional ways of living. Without corruption of evil vices, to repair damage done to the spirits, minds and bodies. It is a place of spiritual refuge and mental and physical healing. A place to get answers and guidance from spiritual leaders, counselors, the Creator, and Mother Earth for needed wisdom and power. A new spiritual beginning day. It is also used when meditating on an important future event, feeling depressed or negative about your surroundings, or having been around sickness.

There is an alter to place sacred items upon. Anything unnatural is not allowed in the sweat lodge. A smudge of sage, sweet grass, or cedar smoke is used for a ritual cleanse - purification. The dried plant materials were bound together and laid in a shell to smudge, a feather is used to fan the medicines. Mshkwadewashk, common sage, is used in smudging rituals; it is antibiotic, astringent, antifungal, and antispasmoid. Kishig, white cedar, is sacred and has many uses. Pine and lavender are also used. Sweet grass, a sweet, holy-smelling grass was used in many ways.

Houses were also cleansed by smudging usually before a meeting or Grand Entry to a ceremonial. It is a symbol to help, bring peace and prosperity to the users.

Medicine – Mshkiki – is strength from the Earth, plants, song, story, and art. The Anishinabe were given these gifts of medicine from the Creator. Tobacco – Asayma – given as a gift, we gain knowledge and grow spiritually. Pokagon, Bodewadmi – Pottawatomie.

A sweat lodge purifies the participants and readies them for the lengthy fasting, and dancing. It generates hot moist air like a sauna, hot rocks are splashed with water to create steam. It is used for renewal and healing education of youth. All Indians use sweat lodges.

A sacred peace pipe is used in prayer, that the participant may know and speak the truth in their supplication. The smoke from the tobacco carrying your requests to the Great Spirit, asking guidance or forgiveness.

Healing begins here for disease, physical, emotional, directional, and spiritual needs.

A sweat is typically four rounds or sessions, each lasting 30 to 45 minutes. Prayers are made, meditation, learning, and healing (Bodewadmi).

"We need to unite all of the races and both sexes, if we are going to be strong and the Sacred Hoop is to be mended. Turning towards each other, instead of away from one another" (Barefoot Wind Walker).

"There were no buses, there was a path to the neighbors. People watched out for each other. The path was worn smooth. Now all weeds grown over. We always shared. *Pamape* – Someday we will meet again" (Frank Bush 1992).

Indian spirituality is private and entirely cultural. It is not evangelistic; it is not sold. It is misunderstood, maligned, it is very complex socially and philosophically, not easily described or represented. The whole culture is and was infused with spirituality that cannot be separated from the rest of the community life at any point. All things were accompanied by prayer and ceremony, hunting, war, birth, death, and marriage.

Respect for life and the decision to go to war required ceremony lasting days, allowing time to reconsider and consecrate lives that may be lost as a result.

Offerings of tobacco, furs, etc. were used, often individually.

Gift-giving was an important part of every important ceremony to honor any person or event. The gesture is more important than the value of the gift. It is an honor to both give and receive a gift. It was common to give to utter impoverishment, in simplicity gives all he has especially to the poor and aged. Orphans and aged were cared for by the whole clan. Natives believe there is little merit in amassing material wealth. Far more prestige comes to those who shared surplus property.

Gift giving was also a ritual to build alliance and obligations between families, communities, and nations.

Lying was a great offense. The deliberate liar is capable of any crime, cowardly untruth, and double dealing (C. Eastman).

THE PROPHESIES

Seven powerful spiritual prophets were given prophesies for our people, The Anishinabek. Seven Fires, eras of time, were prophesied. The Seven Fires, were also Prophesied seven places we lived recorded on sacred scrolls and in oral history. There were seven nations, allied by seven prophesies.

THE MIGRATION – SEVEN FIRES PLACES WE STOPPED

In 600 to 900 A.D., many Eastern North Atlantic peoples allied in a Great Confederacy. All the Algonquin-speaking tribes or nations were part of this Great Confederacy. Great Gatherings and debates took place, centered on the Seven Prophecies delivered to the people at that time.

Ottissippi

We lived on the Eastern Seaboard, near the Great Salt Water. We migrated to the West, as our prophets told we were to follow the setting sun for our survival. There were seven stops on the Great Walk. It took many generations. The megis (cowry) shell cloud led them to seven stopping places on the way to the "place where food grows on water". There were seven places we stopped at along the migration route.

The seven places we stopped were:

The first stopping place, the St. Lawrence River near Montreal, Canada. We were to camp by a certain large body of water.

Here they would build a lodge, lighting the first Fire. At a Turtle, shaped Island. The Three Fires Confederacy formed here. As prophesied, there were many battles with our Enemies, the Nandawe – Snake People, the Iroquois.

The Turtle is prominent and very important to both the beginning and the end of the long migration. The Turtle Nation Anishinabe tradition tells the first stop, the turtle shape linked to purification of the Earth.

The second stopping place.

We continued moving slowly West to "The Great Falls", Niagra Falls "Place of Thunder Waters", called Gitchi Ga Be Gong. We continued to battle the Enemies, the Naadaawe – Iroquois.

The Anishinabek would camp by a large body of water, the path of the megis shell cloud and the spiritual strength of the people will become lost. A special boy will be born to lead the people on the Great Walk. They stayed for some time.

Then we moved to a third stopping place. The Turtle Nation Anishinabe traditional teaching says the Council of Three Fires, a unified alliance, moved to Round Lake (Lake St. Clair), near Detroit.

We continued to the place where the water slices through the land like a knife. The Third Fire stopping place was the Detroit – the Strait – area, including Michigan and Ontario, Canada.

The third stopping place was where two great bodies of water are connected by a thin narrow river, a river deep and fast, a ribbon of water that slices through the land like a knife. We did not immediately cross the river but established a neutral territory in what is now Detroit, Michigan. Here the migration stalled for a long time. We found and congregated on a beautiful island, Anwaatin, or Minising ("Peaceful Place Island"), teeming with waterfowl, beaver, muskrat, and medicines in abundance. Bakyiwang Ziibi – "river flowing off" – or Walpole Island was the third stopping place.

The Anishinabe also established Aazhoogayaming – "The Crossing Waters Place", at now, Sarnia, Ontario. Here the St. Clair and Detroit Rivers drain Lake Huron and Lake St. Clair into Lake Erie. The people lived in several villages along the Detroit and St. Clair River.

We were the Misi Zaagiing – "Those at the Great River Mouth". Between Lake Erie and Lake Huron. This area became a stronghold, the Midewiwin Lodge and our People flourished.

Walpole Island – Bakyiwangziibi, meaning River flowing off to Sarnia – Aazhoogayaming, "The crossing waters place", we were here a long time uniting with the Shawnee, Miami, Huron, and Ouendat – Wyandottes.

It was here that we established a stronghold of the Confederacy and the Midewiwin lodge. We became strong and grew and united with other nations, the Shawnee, Miami, and Huron. We realized the sense of being a Great Nation, our resolve and covenants were kept through the Lodge teachings. The third prophecy would begin, following the Stepping Stones to a great island.

We remembered the prophets' words to "Find Stepping Stones to a Great Island". We followed to the fourth stopping place, Mantoulin Island, east of Mackinac Island, Michigan. A Sacred Island, the Midewiwin Lodge grew in strength. It became the homeland of the Odaawaa – Ottawa people. The migration stopped here for a long time, then moved to Baawaating or Baawaatingamii – Sault Saint Marie.

The fifth Stopping place was Baawaatingamii, Baawaating – Sault Saint Marie, a land of plenty; there the people grew large. The river was later named St. Mary's by the Black Robes. The land between Lake Superior and Lake Huron was called Baawaatingami.

The sixth stopping place was Spirit Island near Duluth, Minnesota, "where food grows on water" *manomin*, wild rice, a highly nutritious grain. The light-skinned came to the East. We divided into two groups, one north along Lake Superior and one along the south shore. On the southern route at the west end of Lake Superior, we saw a turtle-shaped island in the center of the beautiful bay. Nearby was found, wild rice in great quantity, the "food that grows on water".

The seventh and final stopping place was at Madeline Island in Lake Superior, north of Lapointe, Wisconsin. At Spirit Mountain was a turtle-shaped island in the center of a beautiful bay, Madeline Island, La Pointe, Wisconsin. Here the Midewiwin grew into its fullest strength. Some of the people continued west to Minnesota, Dakota, Montana, Northern Ontario, Manitoba, and the Canadian Rockies.

After 500 years and seven generations, the migration was complete. This was during the Fourth Fire era of time. The prophets warned of the Fourth Fire time; the light skinned, by their hearts, it became clear that coexistence, peace and brotherhood were not to be. Soon Gitchi Mookmaan – Long Knives – brought death and disease, whole villages were dying by the thousands daily.

We were pushed out to the mainland by settlers and developers.

America was known as "Turtle Island".

News of White explorers arrived in 1540 A.D. Many families of the people stayed to live along the migration way. They maintained and cared for the towns and lodges where migrants passed.

For centuries, our people traveled widely throughout the Great Lakes, gathering at specific places to hunt, fish, gather plants, socialize in unhurried fashion.

Hundreds of our people gathered at Baawaating – Sault Ste. Marie – each summer to harvest the abundant whitefish in the rapids of the Saint Mary's River. They would stay for several months. They built dome shaped homes of bent saplings covered with cattail mats and birch bark.

Thanksgiving feasts are given at the beginning of each harvest, sugar, berries, garden, etc.

Gifts were offered to people and spirits when requesting their assistance. The spirits share their power with men who in turn help one another with these spiritual gifts. Gift-giving built an ongoing shared kinship relationship between humans, animals, spirits. Gift-giving was a way to build alliances and shared resources between families, communities, and nations.

There was 100 years of war with other tribes, the Iroquois and Sioux increasing our Territory during the 1700s and 1800s. We separated into four divisions that are separate even now.

The Mississaugas or "River Men of Many Outlets" lived in a large area of Southeast Ontario and Michigan. The Mississaugas are ancestors of the Saginaw Chippewa, "The Lakes People".

The occupants now in East Michigan and Ontario are part of the Southwest Chippewa-Ojibwe who came from Lake Superior in Michigan's Upper Peninsula, Wisconsin and Minnesota, the "Saulteaux people". The Northern Chippewa-Ojibwe are in Northern Ontario; they are the Cree people. The Western most Chippewa-Ojibwe are also Saulteaux of the Western Plains.

The Native population by the 1900s was reduced to one million. Disease, warfare, and alcohol took their toll. By 1950, there were only 0.9 million.

THE FIRES, ERAS OF TIME

In the beginning, seven nations were allied by the Seven Prophesies, later our people were known as the Three Fires.

The Seven Great Fires are seven great historical eras. Prophesized by seven powerful prophets, there were seven periods of time called "Fires". There were Seven Fires or stopping places where we lived. These events were recorded on sacred scrolls and in oral history maintained by the Mide Lodge – Holy Men.

A light-skinned race of people would arrive over the Great Salt Water. Great changes were described, threatening our lifeways. Our elders and leaders urged us to move West or be destroyed. We were to migrate West where food grows on water.

In the time of the Third Fire, great hope and anticipation will arrive. The megis shell cloud will lead the Anishinabek to their new home to the place where food grows on water.

THE FOURTH FIRE TIME ERA

The prophets warned of the Fourth Fire time: the words of the Prophet "By their hearts, shall you know them". The Light Skin Hearts became known as "Gitchi – Mookmaan" – Big Knives – who brought death and diseases that destroyed thousands daily. Our medicines and healing ceremonies were ineffective against the new scourge.

The Turtle Nation Anishinabe traditional Fourth Fire told of the light-skin race coming over the Great Salt Water: The faces of the light-skin people will tell the future. If the face of brotherhood, a time of wonderful changes for generations to come. They will bring new knowledge and articles that can be joined with the knowledge of this country. In this way, two nations will join to make a mighty nation. Their hearts may be filled with greed for the riches of this land. If they are indeed your brother, let them show it. You shall know the face is one of death if the rivers run with poison and fish become unfit to eat.

THE FIFTH FIRE ERA

The Fifth Fire Time, was a time of intertribal warfare for control of the land, fur, and waterways. The prophets foretold of a difficult choice and a great struggle with the choice. We suffered increasing hardships, social and cultural distress, from our choices.

It was predicted in the Fifth Fire time that a difficult choice would come to keep our ancestral teachings and traditions or leave the old way for the European ways.

We embraced the French and the metal tools making our lives easier. They also brought guns, whiskey, missionaries, land thieves, and corruption, during the time of the next three Fires.

Ottissippi

The fifth prophet foresaw a world of increasing difficulty. Intertribal warfare took place for control of the land swarming with fur-bearing animals, the waterways, lakes, and rivers (highways).

The Turtle Nation Anishinabe traditional Fifth Fire time told of great struggle. Come one who hold a promise of great joy and salvation. False promises nearly destroy the people. All those who accept this promise will cause the near destruction of the people.

THE SIXTH FIRE ERA

The sixth prophet predicted social and cultural turmoil. Most Anishinabek will accept the promises that were made in the time of the Fifth Fire. Turning their backs on the old ways and discouraging their children from listening to the elders' teachings, the language, and the traditions. The false faces brought greed and harm to the earth, the rivers run with poison and the fish are unfit to eat. Suffering was the result of our decision to embrace Gitchi Mookmaan ways, values, laws, and religion. Many left the traditional teaching of the elders. Elders would lose their reason for living, a sickness, would come over the people. Our great leaders, Pontiac and Tecumseh, warned of the devastation and sickness of alcohol, disillusionment, loss of language and identity. Our Good Medicine, teachings, to heal our people were left behind.

Some good leaders hid the sacred bundles and scrolls, holding the teachings in memory and shared the teachings, waiting for the Seventh Prophecy. The people are reconnecting with our God, honoring cultural and spiritual lifeways.

The Turtle Nation Anishinabe traditional Sixth Fire time told they would take children away from the old teachings of the elders. Grandson and granddaughter would turn against the elders, elders lose reason for living and their purpose in life. New sickness, the balance of many disturbed. Cup of Life, a Cup of Grief.

THE SEVENTH FIRE ERA

Though Native religion was forbidden by laws and schools, the language and ceremonies continued in secret. This is the time of the beginning of the Seventh Fire. The time is now come to be reborn, a time of renewal and blessing. The prophets told of hope reborn and a future filled with blessings and promise. The Last Great Fire is a time when new people will emerge and the Anishinabe will be reborn (Wm. W. Warren).

The Turtle Nation Anishinabe traditional Seventh Fire told, new people emerge, retrace their steps, find what was left by the trail, rekindle the old ways.

Return to the elders and seeking knowledge, ask them to guide them on their journey. Many will have fallen asleep, awaken with nothing to offer. Water drum will again sound its voice, Rebirth of the Anishinabe Nation and rekindling of Old Flames. The Sacred Fire will again be lit.

In the Seventh Fire, all people must choose between two paths – Destruction or Compassion. It will light the Eighth and Final Fire, the light-skin race given the choice between two roads.

The Eighth Fire is an eternal fire of peace, love, brotherhood, and sisterhood. The wrong choice of the roads then the destruction which they brought with them in coming to this country, will come back at them and cause much suffering and death to all the Earth's people.

When the world has been befouled and the waters turned bitter by disrespect, human beings will have two options to choose from: Materialism or Spirituality. If they choose spirituality, they will survive, but if they choose materialism, it will be the end of it. Turn from materialism, choose path of respect all colors and faiths, for all these things and people, wisdom and spirituality. Environmental and social catastrophe can be avoided and an era of Spiritual Illumination will unfold with peace and respect and Love for one another. The elders say major Earth changes are due to occur soon.

MIDEWIWIN OR GRAND MEDICINE SOCIETY

The Midewiwin is a religious society, for the purpose, of curing the sick and extending life. Members must pay to enter the different levels of the society. Each level has different types and amounts of medical and spiritual knowledge. Sickness was thought to be of evil spirits, so medical practice was associated with the supernatural.

Leadership was not hereditary; it was chosen at each gathering.

The history of the Anishinabe was preserved and recited during Midewiwin ceremonies: The Creation, the Great Flood, the Spiritual Migration of the Aanishinibek, behavior ethics. The Mide taught its members herbal knowledge for a price, honored the Manitos (or Manitous, the spirits and essence of power, the most powerful being the Four Winds) and Kitchi Manito in order to restore health and emphasize ethical behavior.

Membership was limited. Initiates underwent long periods of study in medicines, history, spiritual knowledge, and behavioral ethics. Every person of the Mide, from the first to eighth degrees, were obliged to be present at every meeting. They were the repositories of this knowledge for their communities.

It was the responsibility of everyone to look after the needs of orphans and widows and the overall community.

As a young person, each Native American receives a private name, a sacred name, for prayer; this is how the Spirit knows him. The young person learned by their dreams to live moral lives, to be industrious and moderate in tobacco use.

For the Anishinabe, the spiritual world is not separated from the physical world and the physical world is not separated from the spiritual world. All things were treated as being alive, having a spirit just like people. They were brothers and sisters and were respected (Jenness, 1954). All political, spiritual, economic, and social life depended on and incorporated the spirits.

The Jusikid had higher occult knowledge, with access to the spirits. The Shaking Tent Ceremony answered peoples' questions.

These were the Faker Medicine Men who practiced witchcraft. These persons obtained their knowledge of incantations to produce spells, on other people and also knowledge of herbs to produce poison from contact with these evil spirits in their fasts, and only people that came under the sway of witchcraft were very superstitious people. In Alarm and I believe that from these people came the origin of hair-raising, haunted stories. Some such stories are entertaining and were used to entertain the Indians at their tea meetings and feasts (Chief, Nicholas Plain, 1950, "History of the Chippewa of Sarnia").

The Moral Laws in every phase of life were rigidly adhered to. The code of Laws of which there are many. Especially laws, similar to uncleanness of issues and their cleansing found in the Bible (Nicholas Plain, Chief Sarnia Reserve, 1950).

CREATION STORY – NANABOZHO

Nanabozho is the great cultural hero of the Ojibwe Indians. There are many stories about him for entertainment. He was a man of miraculous birth. He was often humorous. He is the patron saint of the Algonquins. In the story, he was on a raft of logs floating on the vast sea of water in company with all kinds of animals and fowl of the air. He could talk to all these creatures. His mission was to devise ways and means to solve their problems. Their need was to devise ways and means to secure land.

Nanabozho chose the Otter – Ojeeg – to dive down to the bottom of the waters to bring up a quantity of earth. Ojeeg jumped off the raft and dove down to the bottom and became exhausted. Without reaching the bottom, after a while the body of Ojeeg surfaced. Nanabozho could find no trace of earth on his paws.

Ahmik – Beaver – volunteered to go down and get the earth. Nanabozho accepted his offer and Amnik, like Ojeeg, became exhausted, and his body came floating to the surface of the waters. Nanabozho examined its paws and, finding no trace of earth on them, he called the creatures to get themselves to him and asked them, if any among them could swim and dive better than Ojeeg and Ahmik, to present themselves to him.

Whazhugk, the Muskrat, steps out to volunteer. Nanabozho looked at the tiny creature and says to him, "How can you, being so small, have the courage to say that you can do what the swiftest of swimmers, Ojeeg, and the strongest of swimmers, Ahmik, could not do? But nevertheless, I will give you my permission to go ahead and dive down and get the earth." So Whazhugk dove down and down, till he was just about exhausted. He reached the bottom and with his paws he scratched the earth and passed out like Ojeeg and Ahmik before him. When his body floated to the surface, Nanabozho examined his paws and, greatly rejoicing, greeted this discovery of a little bit of Earth upon his little paws. Nanabozho uttered his incantations, causing this little bit of earth to grow and grow till it became a vast country – North America (Nicholas Plain, 1950).

Nanabozho was the creator of the earth, man, and the animals. It was he who had invented nets and taught the Anishinabe how to catch fish. It was he who was the founder of Midewiwin who taught the men medical knowledge. The inventor of hieroglyphs (writing pictures).

Tobacco is cast on the water to ask for a good catch of fish. Offerings were made as presents to the spirits, asking for assistance to catch fish. If nothing was received, the Indians became angry with the spirit who had received a gift and given nothing in return. The Indian believed in many spirits, some good and some evil.

In Peter Jones' book on Ojibwe history, he tells the same story, but each animal has the breath of life blew back into them. And the Muskrat, is blessed with never becoming extinct.

The Indians also have a Jonah story. The great fish would follow and swallow up people, with their canoe and all. Nanabozho decided to be swallowed up, and he was. While he then worked with his weapons against the fish, which ran to the shore and died. Nanabozho was happy to save many people from the Great Monster (Andrew Blackbird).

We're all connected and responsible for each other, to enrich all people. Red, Yellow, Black, White – people of all colors (Ziibiwing).

FAIRIES – LITTLE PEOPLE

There is a belief in these little people or fairies (Wiindgookwe) who live around rocks and streams. Myth of Fairy Stories, about men and women beasts who do wonderful things that ordinary people cannot do at all. They partake of the nature of men and beasts or of men and gods. They were about streams whose clear waters went laughing and singing on their way. (Charles Eastman, 1902) Little people, or fairies, love to dwell on rocks (Schoolcraft).

INDIAN FEAST

Mr. Peter and Mrs. Nancy Brakeman attended an Indian feast in 1832 on Walpole Island. An Indian named Ogaw Pickeral came over some time previous and invited she and Mr. Brakeman to attend. Mr. Brakeman gave an invitation to his friend John K. Smith, ESQ to accompany them, which he accepted. When the time arrived for the party, O Gaw came after them with a large canoe, had a nice mat spread on the bottom for the company to sit upon, he, paddling the canoe, when about halfway across the river, he gave a very loud war whoop as much as to say, "we are coming", his friends on land answered him in the same way with several loud whoops. When they landed, the Chief leading men met them at the river, after shaking hands with them, Mr. Brakeman took his presents of pipes and tobacco for the Chief and Head Men. They had a large tent put up for the occasion with rush mats spread over the ground floor, had a drummer beating the drum, but not during their principal refreshments consisting of pigeons, nicely dressed and boiled whole. They were served in a very peculiar manner, they had long poles arranged up over the top of the tent, one on each side. The pigeons were tied by the legs, two together, and strung on the pole from one end to the other. After drumming, chanting, and visiting for a while, some of the women took down the pigeons and passed to the company, each two in their hands; no plate, no knife or fork was used. They sat and picked the meat from the bones. Had a very pleasant time until late in the evening when Ogaw conveyed them home.

The sound of the drums took time to become accustomed to, having them at Point Du Chein (Algonac), they held feasts and dances often (Nancy Brakeman Papers).

The Indian had harmless amusement, council about the campfire, peaceful industry, useful precept. They had tragedy, struggle, old graves, sterile garden farms, wild apple trees, buried relics gave a hint of the glory before the White Man. This was his home and rightful kingdom, taken up by the sponge of greed in the name of progress (Ivan Swift, Harbor Springs, Paper, The MI Room SCC Library). "We treat them quite wrongly because we understand them so little. The Indian suffered these losses, not because he was bad but because he was humble, honest, and too kind to his alien guest" (Ivan Swift).

"They are mild considerate men, not interfering and non-scolding the guest of his wife. A man of few words, when he was displeased, he walked away, his actions acknowledged her right to rule. His pride and manliness exalt him above the folly of altercation" (Schoolcraft).

Anishinaabemowin was the language of the Ojibwe. It is a pictorial language: you see it at the same time you speak it. Some words have different meanings for men and for women (Joe Greaux).

Our language is our spirit, our soul, our identity; it's everything about us. Every word had great meaning.

We are connected to Mother Earth. We have a relationship to Mother Earth. We are a thankful people. The Western world has a separate Church and State. For the Anishinabe, the spirit world and the physical world are always together. It is all one. Without that, we are nothing but a shell. We are circular thinkers. Without the spiritual, the system self-destructs.

The Anishinabe Constitution cannot be written because it could not be accurately described. You would mess it up trying to define something that was never meant to be defined. It is of the heart and soul, the role of the Creator.

The Ojibwe were the most populous important and widespread branch of the Algonquin (means friend" or Allies) race. The Ojibwe were the government leaders and warriors – protectors of The Three Fires, who were the Original Men – Annishinibek – who migrated to Ontario and Michigan. The Anishinaabe had originally migrated to the Upper Peninsula of Michigan where they grew and became "The Three Fires" or the Fire Nation.

The Ottawa were their brothers of The Three Fires, who were the Traders. The Pottawatomi, brothers of The Three Fires, were keepers of the Fires, they were great farmers and were responsible for the hospitality and fires at the yearly or every other year council gatherings.

Horses were acquired in 1730 to 1740.

The people lived in longhouses and other dwellings, there were pits in the floors where baskets of food were stored. There were fires, built in the center aisle of the longhouses, where families did their cooking. There were rooms on either side of the buildings for bedrooms or apartments. Longhouses were usually about 24 feet wide and up to 200 feet long. They had thick bark roofs with a space about two feet wide in the center for the smoke to escape from their fires. The fires were built on a bed of sand, and rocks were used to cook with and retain warmth. The walls were of bark either slabs or rolled from Birch Bark, in the summer, woven mats were used to give a cooler shelter. Sticks were added to the bark to seal it up and fill holes against the weather.

Dome-shaped wigwams covered with birch bark sheets, sometimes over 20 feet long, were carried to each campsite for the seasonal collecting of foodstuffs and planting of garden fields. The women built the houses. A 14 by

20-foot wigwam with comfortable lodging for eight persons could be built and ready for occupancy in less than a day. Sometimes there were more people sleeping snugly in the shelter. In the winter, the Wigwams were banked with pine bows (boughs) and snow for insulation (Quimby, 1960).

The foot of Lake Huron was a great fishing area called Northport before becoming Ft. Gratiot, as were all the waterways. The people tell of having the fish stacked as high as a man stands. The area was a great trading area: all the Native tribes came to this area. To trade for tobacco, fish, canoes, maple sugar, and many other products. Port Sanilac was one of the main stopping areas before the Natives continued to Fort Detroit – Ft. St. Joseph – at the foote of Lake Huron.

Canoes for the trade of furs and other goods were gigantic, some being up to 75 feet long, typically they were 60 feet long and about five feet wide. Dugouts made of a single log were 30 to 40 feet long and about four feet wide. Basswood, cottonwood, or soft maple were used for dugouts they are light, porous, and very buoyant.

Trees were so large people actually lived inside of trees.

The Indian flute has a beautiful, sweet sound.

The drum is held sacred, its music is the heartbeat of the people. The drum chases bad spirits away. It is a peacemaker. Tobacco, drums, and prayer are all an intricate part of Bimoodiziwin – The Good Way – asking the spirits to protect and aid in the well-being of the Anishinabe. The spirits take our thanks and prayers to "The Great Spirit". The drum was also used for a code language.

In many Indian cultures, the women made the decisions. They chose the chiefs, having an innate knowledge, a women's intuition of each one's qualities, and what was best for the clan's welfare. Elder women were called Minimayo – "the one who keeps everything together".

From a child, we are taught to exhibit patient endurance of human suffering. With stoical indifference to pain and hunger and the love of a wild forest independence. Children are taught by the elders to obey parents never scoff at the decrepit or deformed. To be modest in their conduct. To be charitable and hospitable (Mason, 1997).

Every act was a religious act. Prayer and daily devotion was more necessary than daily food. All days are God's days.

The Indian reverenced game and freed with honor the spirit of his brother. Whose body his need compelled him to take to sustain his own life. Gratitude prayer was made for all food and offering of gratitude were made(Eastman). Animals have a sinless purity. They are innocent, and we paid homage to their spirit with prayers and offerings.

There was great hospitality among the people, unless there was war. To have a friend and be true under any and all trials is the mark of a man (Eastman).

The Indian had a certain innate power and self-poise, wholly independent of circumstances. There is a spiritual mind a physical mind; the body is subdued by fasting and hardship. We had a reverence and love for all nature, plants, earth, and sun. We believed the spirit pervades all creation and is an object of reverence.

There are miracles on every hand in life.

The Indian did not envy or desire the achievements of the White man. He rose superior to them; he scorned them. Virtue and happiness are independent of things if not incompatible with them (C. Eastman).

INDIAN PRAYER

"When you rise in the morning, give thanks for the light, for your life, for your strength. Give thanks for your food and the joy of living. If you see no reason to give thanks, the fault lies in yourself" (Tecumseh).

Henry Schoolcraft:

Indian history is often disguised under symbolic form (Schoolcraft). They followed a spirit who deceived and made miserable, not the Spirit of Truth (Schoolcraft, "Travels in Minnesota, and Wisconsin, 1821).

They are a widespread race (Chippewa). All had the common language (Schoolcraft).

There was oral literature on long winter evenings for the amusement of the Lodge (Schoolcraft).

CHIEFS

Chiefs were not what most of us think they were. They were many times the most poorly dressed in their village. The Chiefs, having given their substance to the needy. They were the voice of the people; although they were very influential and respected, a chief was a servant of the people. A chief was many times a son of a previous chief, brought up to learn to care for the needs of the clan family. Learning everything, he needed to know about being a good Chief. Often chosen from the last Chiefs Son's They were many times also the spiritual leaders of the tribes, bands, and clan families. At times, men were chosen to be chief for a specific task or for a period of time. There were war chiefs, peace chiefs, and head chiefs. They were usually very good orators and were persuasive and kind; they held great influence with the people and were usually good providers and hunters. They did not rule the people, but rather, they were ruled by consensus, much like a jury of today one talks, listens, and votes to make decisions.

The real power is in the people in Clans in Council. There was one mind and one mouth it is the decision of all. Fusion and fission were choices of freedom and independence. Hunting groups had a spokesman in clans. There are spiritual, warrior groups. War chiefs had tremendous influence, always used to support the civil chief. The elder civil chief was given final authority. Ogimas – civil chief – could also serve as war chief. This was a common practice throughout North America.

Chiefs, elders, and grandmothers were reverenced and highly respected. When they came to the meetings and councils, not a word was said as a path was made for the elder to walk up to speak.

The chief was treated as any regular citizen when not engaged in chieftain duties. A chief was a servant who had proved he was a generous, sensible, caring man. His traits were emergent, seen as he grew to manhood, being taught the chief's role from a child. He was an eloquent orator, a spiritual leader, a teacher. His role was to be the voice of the people and to resolve conflict. He was chosen by consensus from the people, based on his virtues, not a position of power or wealth. He was generous to the poor, needy, and elderly. Leadership was exercised upon need and circumstances, neither constant or permanent.

He was only the Chief, as long as the community and the Elders chose to respect and follow his lead. A chief could only suggest, they did not demand. All members were part of a consensus, Clan Groups sat together in councils. Women were honored and recognized for their intuitiveness. The women's support was crucial to the decision-making process (Kugel 1998, Harry Flocken, UMN, Dissertation, 2013). And Sometimes decisions took days, weeks, months or never. The fluidity was a strength that allowed leaders to interface and reestablish common ground between them as change occurred. If some did not accept the decision, they were free to leave and become part of other related groups or start a new settlement.

The councils gathered together to share their thoughts, advise, and make potential plans. The act of passing the pipe was central to any important meeting. Councils usually lasted several days. Carefully considering all aspects before acting. Debate was no part of it.

When they gave their word on a decision, it was final, a binding pledge, irrevocable. It was a test of being true. Keeping their word was the measure of a person's integrity.

The system is spiritual, holistic, consensual, and egalitarian. People first, familial and spiritual – it empowers people.

The chiefs are now chosen by vote; a man or woman can be Chief.

Each tribe was independent, each clan independent, each individual independent. Having great latitude to do whatever he pleased.

Leadership was not something contended for, it Is a burden. Leaders emerged, chiefs took a vow of poverty when they came into office. Chiefs were relied upon to steer the community through trial and tribulation, and successfully lead the people to a larger place. The chief preserves and protects. This required spiritual assistance. Almost all leaders are Midewiwin members. Leaders were very spiritual. They were also the leaders in the ceremonies for the tribe, teaching Bimaadiziwin – The Good Way – healthy ways of living, for the good and blessing of the people.

Spiritual leaders were the most prominent people in the village to cure, guide in hunting, war, and lead the ceremonies. Hunting was very spiritual with ceremonies before and after the hunt. War was the same: ceremonies were conducted before and after the war parties left and returned. A war chief was an influential man whose achievements grew and so did his followers, spreading through the bands.

Poor behavior resulted in negative spiritual consequences. Behavior was governed through inner control rather than outward coercion. Children were taught by example and encouragement, not by ridicule.

The chief always sought the benefit of the whole nation. The chief always reminded the European Americans that their views shared represented those of the whole community. The choices were of freedom and independence. The elder was the head of the family.

The related villages sometimes worked together and had a head chief over all (Smith, 1973). At councils with area chiefs, a leader was chosen from the chief's present. He was the head chief. A head chief would preside over the council chief. Greater Area councils had a tribal chief over a territory. He was Gitchi Ogema – Big Chief – for the council meeting. This was a position situational only for important problems. The great council met every, one to two years. If issues impacted larger regions, grand councils were called, and the head chief would attend. At various levels of council, the most articulate and charismatic chief was chosen to preside over the rest of the chiefs (Roufs, 2006).

The best listeners and persuasive speakers were chosen as chiefs. The people were free to replace him. This empowered the people and their voice.

At the national level, the chief was called Grand Chief – Nitom – meaning "foremost".

The Crane and Loon clan were chosen by default as the traditional leadership clans.

Ottissippi

Principal chiefs, carried out the head chiefs of council's edicts.

Band chiefs were over a clan family of villages. A convention of district chiefs formed the Band Council. An Ogima was selected to lead. There were Ogima for each major area in Anishinabe country.

The local council was called "Smoking". There was much talking, listening, and dealing with problems. Great Smoking was called the district council. A sacred fire was kept for the duration of the meeting.

The pipe bearer was responsible for keeping and presenting of the sacred pipe, used in council before Gitchi Manito. He officiated in all public councils, making known the wishes of his chief to gain his goodwill.

During Great Councils, the pipe was passed, the Pipe having an ax on one side and a peace pipe on the other. With the ax up when passed, it meant War, pipe up meant peace. The pipe was called the sacred pipe, prayer pipe, ceremonial pipe, or truth pipe. It was to be smoked in truth and brotherly love, seeking God's will, with God as witness to all that transpired.

Councils drew all together, furnished excitement, recreation, recounted exploits, offered tributes of respect to the deceased, listened to laws and regulations by sages, athletic games with Olympic zeal, national dances, rattle and drum, pleasure and amusement, trade, and the opportunity to meet a future spouse. (Lanmar, Redbook). Councils usually met annually for warfare and resource allocation.

No laws restricted individual freedom – this was true freedom! Major crimes were usually amended through restitution. There were no written laws that bound the liberties of individuals. Gossiping and politics were considered evil.

All wisdom came to them in dreams, and knowledge was shared with others. These were gifts from the creator. Including medical, spiritual, leadership abilities and responsibilities.

Direct communication to the Creator was too powerful for any person. Animal spirits were the intermediaries for the Creator (Warren 1885). This belief was Biblical, too, as animal sacrifices were used extensively in the Old Testament of the Bible (Flocken). Dogs were kept as sheep, they were a delicacy at feasts, they were used for sacrifice. Each man had a dog, they were also used for hunting. The villages had many dogs.

Gifts were offered to people and spirits when requesting their assistance. Tobacco was mostly used. Every request came with a gift. Every gift came with a reciprocal obligation of some kind.

Manido, Manito, or Muneedog means "spirit". The Anishinabe believe in a Supreme Being, but intervention and assistance come from the spirits. All things and beings have a spirit, even emotions have a spirit. The physical world is not separated from the spiritual world. All political, religious, economic, and social life depended on and incorporated the spirits (Flocken). The Manido interacted with the people; some were helpers, some mischievous, and a few were evil. They had human-like qualities and could change depending on circumstances. Life was an illusion, an imitation of the real world, which was the spiritual realm. Dreams were messages and direction (D. Plain).

Every village was a temple, every forest a school (Henry Schoolcraft, 1848).

The Anishinabe Constitution is not a written document. It is from the Great Spirit and is written on the heart, mind, and soul. Without the spiritual – the life force – the system self-destructs. The only way to survive is to return to the Creator (Flocken, 2013).

We are one with everything; we are connected to all creation. That is who we are. Unity was very important; bickering and pettiness was not the Anishinabe way. Complaining was not a virtue. Giving helping, sharing, are our way of life. We are not accumulating or materialistic. Bimaadiziwin – The Good Way. It is Life Flow, life is good, healthy, and flowing smoothly. The good way - God's way. Good conduct led to good life. It is the good blessing of the people. Values for the good way were love, respect, honesty, truth, bravery, giving, and humility.

Warriors were the Ojibwe policemen (Flocken, 2013). Clan families are responsible for the behavior and actions of all clan members. They are responsible for justice and retribution among each other.

TOTEMS

Totems – *ododem* – were clan symbols of family names, going back to ancient ancestors. The word "band" is now used for the totem clan family. Traced back to the beginning, there were five totems: theCatfish, Crane, Loon, Moose, and Bear groups. These groups were subdivided and given other totem names. The Marten clan was the Metis, or mixed-blood.

The mother always had a different Dodem than the father. Marrying within the same Doodem, was forbidden. Cousins are considered as brother and sisters. Paternal uncles and their wives had complete disciplinary privileges.

Many tribes are represented within a band through intermarriage and migration. Band leadership is by the dominant tribe (Herman Cameron 1988).

Totems were represented by badges of identification worn by clan members; they were a source of religious power and spiritual clout in complex social relationships of the root or familial stock. The people consider themselves blood relatives of every Indian sharing the same totem. Within every tribe, a member could approach any totem relation and expect assistance. Each totem word sign, defines a blood-related extended Indian family. The totem practiced communal living. Nothing was owned by an individual.

Totem poles were a family crest depicting the totems of the clan family and their territory. Before the White men, Indians did not have a last name, the totem sign was their last name. A very large family. Many Indians used the name of a respected White friend as their last name.

When dissension arose, the elders in the totem settled the dispute. Each generation and sex had a well- defined place and responsibilities in the tribal structure. Infants and children were held in high esteem, with little discipline. There was never hitting involved in correcting of any children; they learned through example, encouraged with positive conversation, and were indulged with love.

By the late 1800s, there were 21 Ojibwe totems. Due to the repeated division and relocation of the people. They are now the most widely dispersed peoples in the North American continent (Wm. W. Warren).

Phratries are divisions of clan groups within tribes. A tribe includes all the Indians within one nation. bands are members living within a designated area.

Elders were revered. Their knowledge gained through experience was respected and sought. They were the totem's historians, teachers of nature's methods, and religious leaders.

Responsibilities were not seen as work or chores. They were contributing to a joyous life.

WOMEN

Women were the head of the household and made everyday decisions. She was the boss of the home for internal daily leadership. Women serve as Mideiwikwe (female ceremonial leaders), and Ogichidoakwe (Medicine women), as warriors – protectors and chiefs.

Women are gifted with the power of creation to bring children into the world. This is the greatest power in the universe.

Some girls were married at 13 years old, and ceremonies and customs varied widely. Sometimes the parents chose the spouse, sometimes the woman did. If a woman wants a divorce, she sets his belongings outside the door. He is divorced – that simple.

Women wore loose-fitting dresses and skirts reaching the knees, of soft cured deerskin, fringed or painted to decorate them. The women wore leggings in cold weather and their moccasins were decorated with dyed porcupine quills. Necklaces and earrings of shell or beads and copper amulets were worn for decoration.

The women tended the fires, the family center. Every woman knew which plants, roots, or other medicinal elements were needed for medicine, whether for snake bite or injury. Their work was endless: sewing, cooking, preserving foods, tanning hides, gardening, weaving, milling; women served many roles. The women were the gardeners, working the soil, planting, gathering, keeping their seed.

Fields were burned to kill insects and weed seeds and for encouraging new growth of plants for gathering medicinal resources. A feast was made to ask the Great Spirit to bless the gardens. The gardens were never watered. A straw scarecrow helped keep pests away. The wild pigeons came by the thousands, fertilizing the ground, and were caught in long nets for delicious meals (Densmore).

The totem clans were matrilineal, through the mother's line and totem. Bands were separated by the woman's totem. After the White customs came, it was changed to the male totem being the dominate clan family.

The women were the leaders and decision maker. Though men were the chiefs who carried out their wishes. The sign for woman is to sweep your hands down both sides of your hair.

The women often built the home they would live in (Joyce Reid). Women had a separate living area they went to during their monthly cycle; no one, was allowed to be with them during this time, but food was brought to the abode.

"The position of women is the test of civilization. Our women were secure. All property was held by the woman. Modesty was her chief adornment. She ruled undisputed within her own domain, a tower of moral and spiritual strength. She created a happy home. There was nothing artificial about her person; she had a strength and poise not to be overcome by any ordinary misfortune. Young women were usually silent and retiring" (Eastman).

INFANTS AND CHILDHOOD

THE CRADLE BOARD

Babies were strapped to a cradle board – *tickenagun*. This was an ingenious item with soft (sterile) moss, the fuzz of cattails placed around them for warmth and diapering. They were made with soft deer skin or birch bark, there was a catch drawer at the bottom to empty the soiled moss. It had a band across the top to hang some interesting items for play and protective covering. There was a leather strap at the back where mom could carry the baby on her back. The strap was handy to hang on a low branch, nearby a work area and the baby lulled by a gentle breeze. It was also stood up for the baby to see. Babies were frequently unwrapped and moved around freely. Children were coddled and dearly loved. The cradle boards were often very decorative.

The mothers make use of a certain little boards stuffed with cotton upon which the children lye as if their back were glued to them, being swaddled in linen and kept on with swathbands run through the sides of the boards. To these boards, they hang their children upon branches of trees when they are about anything in the Woods (Lahonton).

When the child grew, they could stand in the cradle board. In cold weather, the babie's feet were wrapped in a rabbit skin fur inside of soft down of cattails placed around them. The cradle board was warm and protective.

It was placed horizontally across the waist with a shawl for travel. It could be rocked with the feet, as a hammock or a swing. The mothers sing lullaby. A duck bone or bill with maple sugar was used to keep it quiet.

A cap of leather was used to protect the baby's head and eyes, a bill used for shade. Diapering materials were of absorbent dried moss (sterile), cattail down, and rabbit fur skins. The babes were greased and sooted, wrapt in beaver skin (Schoolcraft).

Breast feeding for three or four years was proper. The world average is 4.2 years.

Children were cared for by the whole village. They were received as a gift to the people with much ceremony, festivities, and feasting.

Childbirth was viewed as very natural, and the women were physically fit. Most women gave birth without help, there were mid-wives who assisted women in their birthing.

Children were never hit or spanked; the good behaviors were encouraged and rewarded. Foolish behaviors were usually ignored until the child grew to understand and was taught to behave properly. Childhood was a time to play and explore. Though older children did help with any chores that needed help doing.

Francis Dunsmore wrote in "Ojibwe Culture" that playthings and toys were for the children: stuffed birds, stringing berries, miniature snowshoes, bows, musical instruments, songs, races, sand drawings, wood drawings, stories, clay animals, dolls of grass, willow needles, single hollyhock and cloth dolls stuffed with moss, sticks, marbles, stones, and playing "camp", "build a wigwam or fire", or fishing.

Rib bones with a cross stick were bound tightly together like a cutter, they were lined with buffalo hide; the people coasted standing erect with a lariat tied to the curved end. Narrow ones were used as skis with a pole to balance. They sped like lightning down hills. Other skis were made of basswood or elm bark.

A kind of skate was made of bones and tusks in the very old days of peculiar workmanship. The young ones rode a tame buffalo calf or a big dog. Birds were taught to talk. They played field hockey, water lacrosse, or canoe ball (C. Eastman, "Indian Boyhood"). They also played badminton, field hockey, cat's cradle, darts, lacrosse, and spinning tops (Red Road, Terri).

MEN

Men were the protectors and providers. Anything outside the household or village, the external, was relegated to men. The eldest or wisest male of the family served as sub-chiefs at Council. Traditionally chief selection was hereditary, a Chief would name his heir.

Men are associated with external futuristic leadership and destruction.

Family groups could split off from the bands and clans when the population grew too large to support the area they were living in or for political differences.

The Chippewa's men did most of the heavy work and were considerate of their women.

In the summer, men only wore moccasins and breechcloth. When at war, they had full movement of their bodies and nothing to get caught on. In winter, they wore leggings of deer skin and skin coat. The men wore a bandolier bag over their shoulder to the thigh. In it they carried necessities for travel and hunting.

Blankets were made of warm skins of bear and buffalo or smaller skins sewn together. Villages averaged between 100 to 300 people. Large bands of 600 used land areas of up to 1,200 square miles. Having up to 30 hunting groups of about 20 members each (Quimby, 1960).

God taught them to hunt and build fire (Schoolcraft, Travels in MInn. and Wisc. 1821).

STORYTELLING

Sacred stories were passed down orally from generation to generation. They told us our history and how to ensure a long life on the Good Way. Teaching a truth or value. Some stories were very amusing and embellished for laughter.

These stories never failed to draw the attention of whole assemblies of Indians, particularly the children. The boys especially absorbed the stories of creatures into their minds, and the memory of them kept them interested in all animals, birds, fishes and reptiles they came in contact with, on their hunting trips with bow and arrows and spears for fish. There is a story connected with each of these creatures.

For example, "Once upon a time, a little Indian boy was left an orphan, and the grandmother took him in, and unfortunately, the grandmother was of a wicked nature and started to torment the little Indian boy. The little boy wished that Nanabozo would turn him into a bird, and Nanabozo granted the little boy's wish. And he flew up into the limb of the tree that was standing near the wigwam of his grandmother and started to laugh, and his grandmother begged him to come back, and the little Indian boy would not, and so we have the Robin Redbreast, still hanging around near a dwelling house."

There are absorbing stories attached to almost every creature found in North America and to the Indian when he enters the forest or the grassy plain. There is never any lack of interest as he is a part of nature, and he talks to the creatures as brothers (Plain, 1950).

Stories were told truthfully with a touch of humorous or dramatic exaggeration (Eastman). Lodge stories are oral fictitious lore, tales, and legends for amusement to convey instruction and impress examples of courage, daring, or right action. There are always spiritual notions of the wild forest that reveal hopes and fears, notions of deity, belief in the future state (Schoolcraft, "30 years among the Indians").

The Anishinabe society was an oral culture; speaking the history and teachings were always kept up. This way it would be known and remembered. The art of public speaking and storytelling was much respected. The people memorized the teachings and stories. The Anishinabek language is very descriptive and was easily recalled using strong images with words. This way it would be known and remembered. The Anishinabe were very good listeners; no one spoke as the messages were conveyed in story and history. The speeches were eloquent and persuasive, conveying the exact meaning of the news or information.

There was very little conflict among the people; any serious crimes were very unusual. Arguments, criticism, and complaining were not acceptable behaviors. If some could not live together, they moved to another area or a new village among other family members or totem family.

WIGWAM AND CLAN ETIQUETTE

The strongest band was on the right of the entrance, the next on the left. Opposite was the post of honor, the Head Chief of a large camp. The circle is symbolic of life; women rule the lodge, on the right of the entrance is the grandmother, the mother on the left side of her husband, then the sons, father, and grandfather. Young children were between the grandparents. The grandfather was the Master of Ceremonies, at all times.

The people were quiet and never stared. No women used the greeting "How." Emergencies were met with calmness and decision. The other man is regarded more than self. Duty is sweeter and more inspiring. Patriotism more sacred, friendship was a true and eternal bond.

The Indian was conscious of his relations to all life. The spiritual world was real to him. The splendor of life stands out preeminently, and beyond all dwells the Great Mystery.

All exertion seems play rather than painful toil for possessions' sake. He was public spirited, always ready to undertake the impossible or to impoverish himself to please his friend. He takes his pay in the recognition of the community and the consciousness of unselfish service.

Love of possessions allowed its way will disturb the spiritual balance. The child must learn early the beauty of generosity, to give what he prizes most by tasting the happiness of giving. Grasping for and clinging to possessions, our legends tell of contempt and disgrace falling on the ungenerous man (C. Eastman).

Totemic bands occupied the same hunting and gathering areas every year.

In summer, the men fished intently and hunted little. The catch was mainly whitefish, trout, and sturgeon. The nets were brought up in the morning for breakfast. Then the women dried and processed the fish. During the summer, the people often slept in the open near the lakeshore (Nodinens/Dunsmore). The people went barefoot in the summer. They left their crops after the potatoes were hilled.

MAPLE SUGAR

The maple tree was called *Ninautik* and the sugar *Sinzibuckwud*. Maple sugar was a main staple of the Anishinabe; it was produced in abundance in the early spring. The people made enough for the trading for other goods. At the sugar camp, up to 900 taps were made, up to three per tree. A slash was made into the tree and a piece of wood used to direct the flow of the sap was driven into the opening. Spiles were made of sumac and other types of hollowed wood. The sap begins to run when daytime temperatures are warming up above freezing and the night remains cold.

Little troughs from felled and hollowed out trees were used to gather sap. Basswood and birch basins were made to collect sap. They were stored until the next season in sheds of bark along with the utensils used nearby the sugar camp (C. Eastman).

Legends said an Indian woman cooking venison in sap figured out the maple syrup process when she tasted the change in flavor. The Indians placed heated rocks into the vessels of sap to boil it up and evaporate it to a thick consistency. It takes 40 gallons of sap to make one gallon of syrup. A gallon of syrup weighs 22 pounds. For the sugar, the syrup is reduced more, then worked into crystals with the hands or a paddle in a trough until it is cool or poured out into containers for sugar cakes (Dr. Koelling, MSU). Wax sugar is poured into containers and not stirred (Pierre Girard, Native Tec).

Maple sugar was produced in huge quantity for trade. Thousands of pounds were packaged up in makuks, or mococks, large birchen bark container boxes weighing 50 pounds; some were 80 to 100 pounds and some 20 to 30 pounds. Containers of all sizes were used to store the sugar. Duck bills filled with maple sugar were a favorite for infants.

In the early spring, the troughs or vats and containers of sap would freeze overnight, the ice being removed. Sugar does not freeze. This repeated freezing was another way of reducing. By removing water from the sap. The sweetest and clearest syrup was made using this method. If sap could be evaporated without heat, the sugar would be white as snow. Freezing sap leaves the finest syrup ever tasted (Vermont Agricultural Report).

Sugar maples are almost always found on high ground. Other trees were also tapped: birch was used, also walnut, hickory, box elder, butternut, sycamore, and basswood. Maple sap contains 2% sugar and is boiled down to 66% sugar for syrup. Some trees carry more sugar content than others.

A crude way to tap a tree is to break off the ends of limbs and let the sap drip into a vessel. Also, a deep gash with the tomahawk with a rude container to collect the sap.

Bark was stripped off the elm trees and hundreds of buckets were made. The buckets held about four gallons each. Sap was drawn from trees when water was not available in the wilderness.

The sap was reduced down by cooking, the water vapor removed from the sap. About 40 gallons equals one gallon of syrup

Spiles were made from sumac, the pith removed to make a hollow tube. Then they are pounded into the slash made into the tree with a hatchet or a wood chip was pounded to make into a V shape. The sap was boiled in the grove, close to the trees being tapped. The sap can also be tapped from the tree roots.

The children love to help and make candy by pouring the hot syrup on the snow to cool. It was stored in underground pits called cache pits.

Maple sap is drawn by cutting the tree two inches deep in the wood, sloping to ten to twelve inches. A knife is thrust into the tree, sloping so the water runs along the cut as through a gutter and runs out on the knife with vessels underneath to receive it. Some trees yield five to six bottles of this water a day. The hole does no damage to the tree (Lahonton).

Sap buckets were made of white birch bark, about four gallons each. Reservoirs were vats of moose skin, holding 100 gallons which was then put into boilers holding 12 to 20 gallons each.

The last run sap was thick and dark. The first run sap was considered the best.

The large copper kettles, some 15 gallons, were kept boiling all night. The sap was boiled to a thick syrup, strained and then heated slowly to proper consistency. In very old days, hot rocks were put into the troughs to boil the syrup down, the rocks replaced to keep the syrup boiling.

The sugar was used to season fruit, vegetables, cereals, fish, and meat. It also made a delicious drink and was mixed with medicines to make them palatable. The sugar was mixed with bear's fat and used as a dip for meat. It was mixed with corn and flour and eaten in travel. It was eaten by itself at times, in small amounts. The children ate sugar by the handfuls. It was made into all sorts of shapes: flowers, stars, small animals – all kinds of shapes. The molds were greased before pouring the sugar.

An offering of First Fruits Feast was held to ask the Great Spirit – Gitchi Manido – for safety, health, and long life, with speeches, ceremonies, prayers, dancing, and feasting. Some of the special food, the first fruits, was shared, with all of the people, and some put on the graves of our people (Densmore).

The sugar camp was a time of renewal, to reunite with family and friends like a festival.

Vessels and kettles were stored nearby the sugar camps in cache pits or bark storage buildings (Nearing, "The Maple Sugar Book", 1950. Reprinted from The Maple Sugar Book, copyright 2000 by The Good Life Center, used with permission from Chelsea Green Publishing (www.chelseagreen.com)).

The annual spring spawn runs for fishing were shortly after the sugar time. After the fish runs, the people moved to summer encampment areas.

CACHE PITS

Cache pits were used to store food that was processed for winter or future use. The Indians had cache pits nearby their hunting, gathering, fishing, sugar camps and fields where corn, other grains, and vegetables grew. They had cache pits to store weapons, ammunition, and many other items.

Some pits were near the village, others were secretive. The food kept perfectly. Sugar, vegetables, meat seeds etc. The food cache was about six feet deep and was lined with birch bark or elm bark.

Makuks were used for storing many food items. They were made from birch bark, in all sizes, large and small, (storage boxes and containers). Skins were used as bags, along with woven bags worked from yarn, grasses, strips of rabbit hide, and other materials. There were many other types of containers. Baskets made of grasses, rushes, twigs and wood strips; pottery made with sand, clay, and glue (made from boiling hooves from the hunt, or sturgeon parts); clay vessels were made for cooking; buckets and shallow containers made of bark and wood; gourds used for storage vessels; wooden pails and boxes; and later glass jars. All of these were used to store useful items. Twigs, grasses, bark, and rushes were also used to make mats, baskets and other containers. They were gathered in their season to be stored in a sheltered building and used them as allowed. Bark sheets were used to bundle dried fish which were tied with cording made from basswood strips. When the pit was nearly filled, a layer of hay or grass was placed over the containers. A covering of birch or other bark or pine boughs was added. Then beams or planks of wood were laid across and covered with a mound of soil.

It was a simple efficient storage and preservation method. Well-drained locations were chosen to protect the cached items from decay. Food caches held all kinds of nice things stored in the fall. Strings of dried cranberries, potatoes and apples.

The cache was well hidden by building a fire over it or covering with rocks, brush, dry leaves or sand.

Francis Densmore, "Chippewa Customs", was the main source for the above paragraphs.

TANNING HIDES

The women did most of this work while the men were out hunting. The hides were stretched out on a frame, scraped of fat, and tanned with the brain or smoked. The smoked hides were made soft and never shrunk. Hides were smoked over a low fire, the smoke giving it a golden-yellow color. The hide is almost white before being colored this way. The smoked hides were made soft and never shrunk. The women sometimes chewed the skin to soften it, wearing their teeth down.

Fresh skins were rolled up moist and kept warm for a time; this treatment caused the hair to easily slip out from the skin. They were then washed and scraped with a large flat piece of stone, bone, metal, or wood (Calvin Thorpe, Vol. 28, MPHC).

Deer hide was sheared then soaked for two days in clean water, then the rest of the hair was scraped off. The fleshy tissue was removed on the inside using a scraper, a bone implement called a flesher. The brains, fat, and liver of the deer were rubbed on the hide to soften it.

The skinning of otter and other small hides were started at the hind legs; the hide was then drawn forward and the head left on. It was then stretched on a frame. Rabbit skins were not tanned but hung on bushes to dry.

Furs were dried and packed, the largest on the bottom, stacking and folding the sides and securing the bundle with cords. Bear or wolf skin was placed over the top of each bale. Each bale was numbered and its contents listed.

Whether with pottery, clothing, or moccasins, every tribe had its own distinctive designs, and one could tell instantly which tribe had made it.

TWINE

Twine was made of basswood fiber or bark. It was a very useful article. Fiber was taken from between the bark and the wood of the tree. It was pulled and cut away, then soaked in the water. It was secured to grass or reeds and left to soak for 10 days, making it soft and slippery. The fibers easily separated. It was made into narrower strips, wound into coils, then hung to dry. It was stored with the other bark supplies until needed. There were many layers to the fiber, some were of thinner strings, others of thicker cording and ropes for many uses. It was boiled, making it tough and stronger. Slippery elm was also used this way. It was very useful for tying bundles, as thread, fish line, clothesline, towing, hinges – you name it. Twisted twine and cord was also made by rolling the fibers on one's leg with the palm until it twisted.

Nettle fiber was fine and strong; it was used in weaving cloth for bags, undergarments, fish nets, and snares. Sinew from game was also used as a string or thread.

Nets are woven with a wood shuttle to about 60 arm-spreads long. Pieces of light wood act as floats, and stones are used as sinkers. Nets are soaked in tubs with sumac leaves to destroy the fish odor, then are spread out to dry over a long pole on tall stakes.

Rushes and grasses were gathered and made into mats. Mats were very useful items for floors, walls, seating, bedding, bags, and more. The mats were used to cover the wigwam in summer, as well as the floor of the wigwam. A separate building was used to keep the rushes shaded and moist, keeping them pliable. When moving with the seasons, the blankets were rolled inside the mats;

the baby could also be placed in the rolled mats to carry on the women's back. Dried moss and cattail down were gathered in quantity for baby diapers, and rabbit skins were also used.

BIRCH BARK

Birch bark was cut in early spring when it was most easily removed from the trees. The bark was very thick, up to one inch thick on large trees. Birch bark was used for many home crafts: boxes, containers, dishes, molds, walls for the tepee or wigwam. It was used for messages, like paper. Canoes were made from it. The bark had natural antiseptic properties for storing food supplies. Frances Densmore, "Chippewa Customs", was the main source for this information.

On the birch tree, the bark would be the last part of a tree to decay, keeping its form after the wood had disintegrated. It has little thunderbirds that decorate the bark; this was more distinct in some locals.

The bark had six to nine distinct layers. The thinnest like tissue paper, tough and used to wrap packages. The birch bark keeps from decay any contents stored in it. It is used as tinder for fire, for torches, and as a cooking vessel. The inner surface exposed to the fire. With water or liquid in the bark, it did not burn (Densmore, Chippewa Customs).

There is a short window out of the year when a birch tree can be peeled without injuring the tree. After the bark is removed, the tree regenerates new bark in 10 or 12 years, which can then again be removed (Lois Beardslee, 1995/Modern Indian).

Basswood is also known as tilia or linden tree. It has very little graining, it is used in carving and intricate woodworking for windows, its fiber is called bast. It is used as a diffuser for aquariums. So, it has breathing qualities, holding air in the wood. The leaves are heart-shaped. The wood is soft and easily worked and very buoyant. It is used to make instruments, having wonderful acoustic properties.

The flowers of basswood have many medicinal uses, the double-flower type used in making perfume. It is an elm in Greek, or black poplar.

TOOLS

Indian men made many tools, jewelry, weapons, and more. The aze was a hammer: a stone was fastened to a wooden handle by splitting the stick and binding it tightly with leather. Smaller types were used to pound meat and berries.

The men made knives, spearheads, axes, clubs, arrowheads and many other tools and useful items. Scrapers were made of stone. Truckloads have been found and removed from throughout the thumb of Michigan, Ontario, and the whole continent.

Wooden articles were made with knives – a crooked knife was the most useful. Ash was used for light articles; witch hazel, elder, birch, spruce, cedar, oak, ironwood, maple, and hickory all had their special uses. Bowls were made from knots. For clubs, spoons, snowshoes, and sleds, wood was bent by placing it in hot water or near a fire. Snow shovels, pack frames, paddles were of all kinds and sizes, from spatulas to canoe paddles, from troughs to work sugar to wood implements for gardening. Fire coloration was made by smoking using black mud fumes.

The Indians made use of copper which was mined in the Upper Peninsula of Michigan and other places. It was often exposed, and pits were dug to mine the copper. Fire was built and heated the rock, then cold water was poured on the hot rocks, and they cracked and the copper was extracted. There were thousands of mining pits. Copper from the Upper Peninsula was traded extensively throughout America, Mexico, and Central America (Nishnawbe, Deur). The Anishinabe are renowned for their ability to locate copper ore (Wm. W. Warren).

MOCCASIN – MAKIZIN

Moccasins were the footwear used by the Indians. In moccasins, the feet have full play: they bend and grasp like an acrobat when crossing slender and slippery logs or passing along dizzying trails. They do not stick in the mud. They are warm when stuffed with fur. A person can move swiftly, as they are lightweight. They prevent corns and cure them (C. Thorpe, MPHC vol. 28). They are also silent. Moccasins are very warm, they do not chafe the skin, cause corns, cut off circulation, or cause other problems with the feet.

The Ojibwe moccasin had a puckered seam up the front. Other tribes used a tongue-shaped piece to make the front of their moccasins. The moccasins were sewed up with sinew thread.

In cold weather, the moccasins were lined with rabbit fur. The comfort and practicality was unsurpassed. The lowest temperatures were without discomfort.

At night, the moccasins were not dried by the fire, but were simply wrung out and put on wet in the morning. In cold weather, the feet were wrapped in one or more layers or pieces of blankets called *nepes*. Sometimes wisps of hay were placed inside the moccasins (Emmert, MHC vol. 47).

Hides were used to make soft clothing and blankets. Strips of rabbit fur were woven into a soft, warm blanket (Francis Densmore, "Chippewa Customs").

Summer villages were groups of individual autonomous hunting groups linked by kinship, marriage, and totemic – Doodem, affiliations. The people, lived in great peace; all were allowed to do as they wished. All were equal. The Indian cherishes patience and understanding. They respect age as wisdom. It was more important to give than receive.

The Ojibwe would never be seen walking side by side with his wife. He always walks ahead, and in the assemblies, the women were in one place, the men occupying the prominent place. This was in observance of cleanliness laws.

Grandparents told our history, repeating the time-hallowed tales with dignity and authority to lead into his inheritance in the stored-up wisdom and experience of the race. The old were dedicated to service of the young; they were the teachers and advisors. The young regarded them with love and reverence. Old age gave much freedom.

We are a polite people, the warrior a man of gentleness among family and friends. A soft low voice is an excellent thing in men. They have unfailing respect for the established place and possessions of every other member of the family circle.

They are not demonstrative of affection at any time. Two who love should be united in secret before the public act of their union.

The family social unit was also the government unit. The larger clan family was made up of several clans by intermarriage and voluntary connection; this constitutes the tribe. Marriage was forbidden within the clan family (Eastman).

Textiles and clothing were made of leaf, nettle fibers, and animal hides. Sinew and nettle fiber were used for sewing thread (Densmore, 1979). Turkey feathers were sometimes woven into a coat (Schoolcraft). Bone or thorns were used as needles.

At the age of seven, boys were instructed by the men and taught to hunt and fish.

When the hunters went to the forest for the winter camps. The old men and women remained at the main village, some of the women and children stayed also. Some families went to the hunting camp to help with the work, cooking, gathering wood, tanning hides, and drying meat.

Torches were made from rolled bark and pitch. In the crotch of a pine tree is found a bunch of dry needles with pitch on them: they make a fine torch.

Wood was used for many things: homes, fuel, canoes, furniture, arrows, bowls, utensils, boxes, paddles, rattles, shuttles for weaving, fish nets, and war clubs. Scoop shovels were also made from wood. The birch bark was used for writing, scrolls, and making maps.

We had runners, messengers who would deliver important information. They were endurance runners, messengers, who would deliver important information. They were endurance champions, running up to 50 miles a day. Called "runners of the woods", or curriers.

WAMPUM AND BELTS

Wampum, strings of shells, are usually referred to as "Indian money". Wampum was a charm to protect the one who surrendered goods from evil influence that might be incident to the transfer. The handing over of the property was a gift, and the wampum received in return was accepted as a protective medicine. The term "value received" had no meaning to the Indians.

Wampum belts were made and given to record significant events. They told of transactions made between parties; they were used as written legal documents and kept as evidence to prove what was agreed to between parties involved.

Wampum and the calumet pipe were very important items. Belts or strings of wampum were made of strung shell on deerskin that were pictorial documents. They were used in making solemn agreements, and the belts were kept for records. White and black or purple beads were used to tell the story, being perfectly understood by the parties. War belts were painted red. When a belt was received, a council was held by the chiefs and principal men. If the message was accepted, the bearer was invited to the council house to smoke the pipe. The promise to observe the terms of the agreement being pledged in the smoke rising to Gitchi Manito – The Great Spirit. The pipe bearer was the keeper of the pipe to care for and provide it as needed.

Belts of white and purple shells were given at treaties as seals of their friendship. The art of making them obtained from the Dutch. They were a hand width by two feet, some much longer. Strings or belts could be interpreted, or talked, laws enacted, the exact law or transaction of which it was made at the time, the sole evidence. The only visible record, a secret record. The promise or assurance of a foreign power was of little importance unless the belt or strings were given to preserve it in recollection. Sachems were keepers of wampum and versed in the interpretation. It was a letter or bond (Lanmar, Red Book).

Michigan Indians never wore the tall bonnets of feathers portrayed in movies. Those were the ceremonial headdress of the Sioux and others West of Michigan.

FOOD, PLANTS, AND GATHERING

Every tree, bush, and plant was a gift from Gitchi Manito and had a use for mankind. Many leaves, fruits, and roots were used for foods and medicine.

The tribal members were nomadic with the seasons: the beach in summer, the forest in winter, the planting ground, sugar camp, the hunting ground, the best fishing spring and fall. They were frequently found in various places within 100 miles of the St. Clair River. The Ojibwe planted, hunted, fished, and gathered each season in different places.

The people worked cooperatively , together, to store food for the winter, many hands making the work enjoyable. The whole community contributed to the well-being of the whole. Conflict and arguments were detracting from the well-being of the people, these activities were always avoided.

Water was carried in bags of tripe or pericardium, bladders of game, or birch bark pails.

Akeeks were clay cooking vessels.

All of the Indians were farmers to some extent, growing corn, beans, squash, pumpkins, sunflowers, and tobacco. Each family had a plot used by consent, all sharing the land.

Hills were made about four feet apart, or raised beds were made. The Indians had great fields cleared for growing corn, their mainstay.

Pemmican is pounded dried meat; fresh chokecherries were pounded, pits and all, and mixed with the jerky, then melted suet was poured over all and mixed into balls or stored in cases of bladder or rawhide with melted suet poured over to seal completely. This was travel food.

Vitamin-rich teas were favorite drinks, juniper, sassafras, and wintergreen and many more.

Salt was unknown to the Indian in cooking. The Indians had a no-salt added diet. They were less bothered by mosquitoes.

CORN – MAIZE

Mundahmin, corn, is the most valued and useful food of the Indian fields.

The legend is told by Chief Netahgawinene of Coldwater: "Many winters ago, the Great Spirit appeared to one of our wise forefathers and showed him a plant of the *mundahmin* or Indian corn on which grew two ears. The Great Spirit then told him to preserve the two ears until the next spring when he was to plant them. He was further commanded to preserve the whole crop and send two ears to each of the surrounding nations with the injunction that they were not to eat of it until the third crop. The wise Indian did as he was commanded. His corn grew and brought forth much. The next summer, he planted all his seed, which yielded bountifully. He then sent two ears to each surrounding nation of tribes with proper directions, which they observed, and by this means that the corn was distributed among all American Indians." It is considered by them the best grain in the world because the Great Spirit gave it to them for their bread.

Pounded parched corn and pemegun is the celebrated food for warriors and travelers in the Western and Northern countries (Peter Jones, The History of the Ojibwa). Pemekun is made of dried berries. Usually the choke cherry, is pounded up, seeds and all, then mixed with fat and dried meat. This is very nutritious sustenance for long travels. It is stuffed into casings of cleaned intestinal tubes. It will keep a very long time. Cornmeal was mixed with meat or fish and cooked for meals; it was called *sagamite*.

Much time was spent grinding corn, it was done on a flat stone, or *metate*, and a grinding stone called *mano*. The Indians also used a mill made of a piece of log which was burned and hollowed out, a wooden tamper was used to crush the kernels.

The Great Spirit about this time also gave the Indians the tobacco plant. That he might smoke the Pipe of Peace with his fellows to cause the smoke of the calumet to ascend to the Great Spirit as a sweet incense.

There are more than 60 types of corn, all have different uses. There are many beautiful colors: pink, blue, green, white, multicolor, popcorn, dent corn, pod corn, with each kernel having a husk. The large kernel field corn was pounded very fine and was called *nokeg* and *hokeg*. The English called it hoe cake, being the pronunciation of the Indian name, though surely people have cooked a corn cake on a metal hoe. Corn flour was carried in a pouch for travel and was mixed with water in the hand and eaten or mixed and cooked on a hot stone. This was "fast food".

The hominy corn is used by soaking the kernels in a lye solution made from wood ash until the hull loosens and is washed off. The Indian soup called corn soup is made using this type of corn. It is eaten at almost every gathering and is simply made with a piece of smoked meat to flavor it. It was also served with maple syrup or maple sugar. The hominy is used in soups and stews and is served with meat broth.

Green corn was cooked for fresh roasting ears, simply dipped in water and placed on the fire or buried in hot sand and cooked.

Ottissippi

Parched corn was always a quick snack and easy travel food.

Corn for meal made fresh had a rich flavor, with the germ still in it being even more nutritious. Corn meal mush was made by boiling the meal in water or sap; it was served with marrow fat, maple syrup, or both.

Succotash was made with corn, beans, herbs, and other vegetables sometimes. It was flavored with meat or salt pork. The cobs were added for flavor and removed later. The beans were used fresh or dried.

Corn was dried off and on the cob. The silk was saved and dried to use as a thickener in many dishes. Sometimes wood ash was used for flavoring. Maple sugar was also used freely to season foods, including meat. Herbs were used extensively for flavor.

Squash and pumpkins were sliced into a long string-like form, being cut in a circular way. They were then hung on a pole to dry. Sometimes the strips were woven and dried looped on a stick. The fruit was used in stews and soups and many other ways. Squash and pumpkins were also baked whole in the ground oven.

Many berries were collected and dried: blueberries, whortleberries, huckleberries, service berries, chokecherries, rose hips, wild plums, apples, pears, elderberries, strawberries, gooseberries, blackberries, and raspberries.

When first traded frying pans, some young and old used them for sleds, sliding down hills on them.

Indian *Fry* bread is a new phenomenon. It is delicious, light, and tasty. The bread is mixed up with baking powder, made into a flattened ball, and fried in hot fat or oil. Indian tacos are made with the fry bread, using a sort of thick chili and toppings over whole or torn up bread. The bread is served with honey or maple syrup. Yummy.

Reginald and Glady's Laubin, the Indian Tipi, was the reference for the paragraphs on corn.

A coarse bread from corn was called *semp*.

Peter Jones writes in *The History of the Ojibewa* about more fruits that were gathered: black currents, wild grapes, and marsh cranberries. He also mentions other plants used for food: the ground nut root and the swan potato found in bogs or marshy soil. It is boiled and eaten in extreme cases of hunger. Another root, called *oduhpin*, is long, white, and tender and has a warm, pungent taste.

Corn husks made good bedding material. Corn cobs were used to make pegs and pipes.

Cornmeal must be fresh ground or kept refrigerated.

A recipe for corn bread would be: 1 quart of meal, 1 tsp. salt, 1 pint, warm water. Stir together until light. A couple eggs may be added. Some people use milk instead of water. This batter can be baked as one flat loaf on a greased shallow pan in a reflector oven or in a Dutch oven. Use moderate heat and bake 45 minutes. Indians sometimes added nut meal to this batter. Pumpkin or sunflower seed meal could also be used.

This bread can be baked in hot ashes and is called ash cake. It can also be baked on a hot flat rock. If the dough is rolled into little cylinders and fried, it is called corn dodgers.

WILD RICE

Wild rice is not a true rice: it is "Zizania Aquatica" or *manomin*, meaning "good fruit" or "good berry". It is called *psina* by the Sioux. It is a choice food for people and waterfowl. It is found in Lake St. Clair and countless small lakes, ponds, and streams. It grows in mud bottom waters, not sand.

The stalks are one inch in diameter. The plant grows from four to twelve feet tall, four feet above the water. It is an annual and grows in water depths of between one and eight feet. It is gathered in the autumn (Albert Ernest Jenks, 1901, "Wild rice Gatherers", www and in William Warrens, "History of the Ojibwe").

Wild rice keeps indefinitely.

Many of the small lakes yield plentiful supplies of wild rice, which the Indians gather in great abundance in the autumn and made into soup (Jones). Many wild foods were gathered in the field, forest, and swamp.

The cattail was a very useful plant; the white shoots in early spring were cooked and eaten. The young green spikes were also eaten. Fresh roots were used to treat burns or wounds. The dried root was good for stomachaches. The yellow pollen on the tails was used as flour, as was young tails. The cattails were collected and dried for diapering infants in their cradle boards. The long flat leaves were very useful in making mats and baskets. The mats served as rugs in their home and as a covering in the summer on the walls. This allowed cool breezes to flow into the structure.

Acorns and hickory nuts were collected and used like flour, some were roasted, ground, and dried to be used as a drink like coffee. Walnuts and chestnuts and many other types of nuts were collected, even trading with the chipmunks and squirrels for their supply. Mushrooms and other fungi were known and eaten.

Milkweed was collected when it blossomed and eaten like asparagus. It was used in soups or mixed with cornmeal. A tea was made from milkweed roots and was used in medicine. Plantain was a useful plant; it was used as an antiseptic band-aid wrapped around a cut and tied with a piece of grass – medicine and band-aid all in one (Jackie Praeter). White sage is an effective remedy when bandaged over bed sores (Joe Greaux). Cattail was a very useful plant for diapering, tinder, food source, mats, and arrows from the stalk. Sweet grass was used in prayer for smoke smudge cleansing; it has many uses, such as to treat gall stones, kidney stones, urinary tract infections, and for tea. Other grasses had many uses, such as for tying and fastening items, making toys, making roof and wall materials, making mats and baskets, cleaning whisks, tinder, and many more uses.

Each season was anticipated with joy for the harvest of good things from Mother Earth.

The Mide Medical Society had their own powerful formulas used as medicinals. They were highly effective when other methods failed. Today over 1,000 medicines are from Indian pharmaceuticals. Roots, barks, seeds, leaves, corms – every nuance was known to the Mide.

Herbalists were trusted healers. There were medicine men and women.

In the wigwam, there were hidden pits in the floor covered with mats where food was stored in baskets along with other items. Nuts, seeds, sugar, rice, corn, beans, dried apples and potatoes, carrots, and rutabaga were stored for cooking meals.

Blankets, a stock item in trade and annuities, was an important article of dress. Men wore their blanket over one shoulder and under the other arm, the lower part of the blanket being drawn closely around the waist. They took much pride in the arrangement of the blanket to a graceful folding across the arm. The blanket was usually worn over the left shoulder, leaving the right arm free, but if a man were left-handed, he wore the blanket over his right shoulder. The women usually wrapped the blanket around the limbs like a tight skirt and fastened with a belt; the upper part of the blanket was then thrown loosely around the arms and shoulders, affording warmth and yet leaving the arms free for work. A woman could put her babe in the blanket between her shoulders or, if desired, she could drop the upper part of the blanket entirely, drawing it around the waist. The blanket also served as a portable bed, for whenever night fell, he could roll up in it, preferably before a fire, and sleep (Emmert, MHC vol. 47).

Dog stew was made in every way imaginable. It was a delicacy and was served for ceremonial feasts and other gatherings. The village had many dogs they kept as sheep and were also used as a sacrifice offering to the Great Spirit. Every man had a dog for hunting. Dogs were a great protection from wolves and other wildlife. The dog was akin to the sacrificial lamb (Kevin Callahan, UMN).

Pit ovens were used as a secret concealment place.

Garden beds were often made in raised ridges eighteen inches high. The fields were often very large and many acres. Sometimes the beds were in mounded circles. With the poor drainage in the area, this was the reason to raise the planting beds. It also warmed the soil much earlier for planting.

When the soil became depleted of nutrients, a new area was chosen, and the trees were burned off, the fertile soil planted. This was one reason to move occasionally, about every 10 or 20 years. Fish entrails were used as fertilizer, as were many other plant and animal refuse. Fertilizer literally fell from the sky in the excrement of the thousands of pigeons and other birds and water fowl of the air, which were thickly populated.

The passenger pigeon dwindled; the females laid only one egg per year, the last disappeared in 1906.

Women worked hard in her accepted role. They were strong and healthy from a very active life.

Meal times varied with each clan. Some ate early, others late or whenever hungry or convenient.

WIGWAMS, LONGHOUSES, TEPEES, AND OTHER SHELTER

Before the 1730 - 1740s, it was women's work to erect and dismantle the wigwam when moving to the other seasonal camps. Dogs were used with a travois, two saplings laid across with a covering to carry the household items, bark rolls for the wigwam, and other necessities. Sometimes the babies were piled on with the loads. The travois was attached to the dogs, and the end of the two poles dragged behind.

Women have been the vital link, holding tradition and keeping the family together. The Indian people are very family-oriented (Joyce Reid, Indian Women 2014, Deckerville, MI). The home was the woman's; she was boss at home. Her husband was a guest in the wigwam. The women preserved man from soul-killing materialism by owning what few possessions they had, branding possession as feminine. The moral salvation of the race (C. Eastman).

Tepees were used mainly for a temporary lodge in the Great Lakes by travelers. A large tipi was 24 feet across. They often had a lining inside the outside covering which was made of skins, rolled bark, or mats made of rushes. There was a ground cloth for the floor, or mats were used as a rug. In cold weather, the lining would be stuffed with straw or dried grass, making it very snug and warm with a fire in the center of the structure. The space between the lining was also used for storage. Warm furs and robes were used to make a bed upon. Guests were always welcome. The families slept with their feet toward the fire. The fire was made on a raised hearth to cook upon and in. Three or four large stones were used to set cooking vessels on so that the coals might be pushed beneath and around them. A strip of hard dry ground surrounded the fire in the center of the dwelling. It was swept clean with a broom of cedar boughs.

Mats were used in the summer to allow cool breezes; they could be rolled up as a window vent. In the winter, boughs and snow were packed against the outside wall to keep cold and wind away.

Tepees were easily put up and taken down quickly; light poles are used, they are fastened together at the top, the poles set into the ground for stability.

The bags stored along the walls were used as pillows.

A big fire was kept in the middle of the camp at times and was shared for cooking. Smaller fires were made in the wigwam at night for warmth. A big rack for drying meat was over the fire. At night, the rack was moved and the men dried their clothing, smoked, and talked (Densmore, Chippewa Customs).

Each member of the family had a particular place, in the wigwam. The bedding consisted of blankets and hides and was placed at night upon a base of cedar boughs and rush mats. During the day, it was rolled up and placed along the walls (Emmert, MHC, vol. 47).

Wigwams – *Nuh Gak O Gumigk*, or a dome-shaped bark dwelling. They are built of basswood and other available species of wood. The roof was made of strips seven to eight feet wide and tied down with pliable inner bark made into thin strips. Saplings were driven into the earth, and bent to the center, and secured with strips of bark. The logs were split into slabs two or three inches thick and laid horizontally, lapping over to seal the gap and to make it weatherproof. In the center was an opening for the smoke to exit, following the sloped walls. The floor was covered in fur rugs or mats of wide grasses and other plant materials. A stone fireplace was in the center for heating and cooking. The entrance always faced east. The size was made to accommodate the number of people to live within. The Ojibwe were expert builders, knowing the precise pitch of the roof for the draft to draw the smoke out at the center of the dwelling.

Birch bark was also used to cover the structures. In the spring, it was easy to cut a long sheet to strip the trees' one-inch thick bark and roll it up. The bark was sewed together and attached to the poles. Pitch was used to seal the seams. The birch bark was durable, lasting about 10 years. When the people moved, they rolled up the bark and carried it to the new site for the seasonal harvests. In the winter, snow was banked on the walls to insulate the dwelling.

In hunting or traveling in winter, men made a bank of snow on the windward side and a fire on the other side to sleep between. A fire where he wished to sleep was made, and the embers were scraped away, then he wrapped in a blanket on the warm ground.

Furniture was made of small limbs tied with gut (Ziibiwing).

Torches of rolled bark and pitch were used as lights at night for errands, work, and in hunting. Deer were attracted by the light. Deer tallow was also used. Sticks were pounded to crush the fibers and dipped in tallow, wrapped in cloth, and dipped again. Hazel brush made this way would burn all night.

Signal fires were used for messages across wide expanses of water.

Pipe stems were made of any wood with a pith; it was split open, the pith removed, and glued back together. Glue from sturgeon was commonly used. Sometimes pitch was used. The mouth end was slightly flattened. The bowl was of many types of materials. They were made of stone, wood, corncob, etc. Two types of stone were found on the Cass River in the thumb of Michigan.

THE SEASONS

The people worked night and day, making the best use of materials at hand. A stick was used to count the days, a long stick to last a year. A new stick was begun in the fall. A big notch for the first day of a new moon, a small notch for the other days.

The blossoms of pumpkins and squash were dried along with corn silk used to season and thickening for stews. The grained sugar was used as a seasoning. Wild ginger, bearberry, mountain mint, and wood ash were used as well.

Water was boiled and leaves or twigs were added to flavor it, and was drank hot or cold. Some additions were wintergreen, raspberry, spruce, snowberry, twigs of wild cherry, labrador tea leaves, and choke cherry.

Acorns were gathered and cooked in several ways. Sometimes the flower of the milkweed, root of bulrushes, sap of aspen, birch, basswood, and moss from white pine were eaten.

Apples and grapes were gathered and stored.

Dyes were of vegetable substance for color and a mineral substance to set it. Items were dipped, boiled, or painted on. Some of the colors came from plum, alder, sumac, butternut, oak, dogwood, and bloodroot. Minerals were grindstone dust, red substance (vermillion) near certain springs, and black earth near certain springs (Nodinens/Dunsmore).

A FEW INDIAN RECIPES

These recipes are shared from the *Booklet of Recipes Past and Present*, Deckerville, Historical Museum/Reid, J.

SUNFLOWER SEED OIL

Extracted by bruising and boiling the seeds, then skimming the oily residue off the broth.

SUNFLOWER SEED BUTTER

The ground paste is made by bruising and boiling the seeds and retaining the natural oils for a fine butter.

ACORN FLOUR

Boil the acorns with wood ashes, dry the acorn meats, and grind into flour after removing from the shell or hull.

NUT OIL

Pound the nuts into flour, then boil in water with maple wood ashes, then skim the oil off. The flour is retained and used in baking breads and cereals.

NUT MILK

Pound the dried meats, then boil in water and strain, reserving the oily part of the liquid, which is rich like fresh cream.

WOOD ASHES

Wood ashes of distinctive woods, such as cedar, juniper, hickory, etc. were used as flavorings and cleansing agents. Spoon fresh ashes out of a fireplace, stove, or campfire for use in the recipes.

BUTTERED NETTLES

1 scallion, 2 quarts young nettle* tops, ½ cup boiling water, sunflower oil or butter. Saute scallion, add nettles and water, simmer covered 20 min. Serve with broth.

*Cooking destroys the nettles' stinging properties.

FRIED SQUASH BLOSSOMS

½ cup flour, 1 cup milk, salt, ½ tsp. chili powder, oil, 1 quart, squash blossoms. Heat oil, mix the 4 ingredients and dip the blossoms in the batter, fry until crisp.

DAYLILY BLOSSOMS

Daylily blossoms are used in stews.

WILD SPRING GREENS

Dandelion, milkweed, lamb's quarters, or wild lettuce.

CORN DUMPLINGS

2 cups cornmeal, fine. 1 cup nut milk, 1 tsp. crushed dried mint leaves, 2 tbsp. nut oil. Blend all together and drop by spoonful onto steaming stew broth. Cover and steam 15–20 min.

CLOVER SOUP

2 cups clover blossoms and leaves (fresh or dried), 2 small wild onions, chopped. 4 tbsp. sunflower seed butter, 1 quart, water, 3 medium potatoes, chopped dill weed to taste, spicebush berries, dried and grated to taste. Saute clover and onions in butter. Add water, potatoes and seasonings. Simmer covered 20 min.

HICKORY NUT CORN PUDDING

1 ½ cup cooked corn, 2 beaten eggs, ½ cup chopped dried hickory nuts, 2 tbsp. honey, 2 tbsp. nut butter, 2 tbsp. fine cornmeal, ¼ cup goldenrod blossoms. Combine all and pour into a well-greased dish, sprinkle top with additional nut meats. Bake in 350° oven 1 hr. Seeds, raisins, other edible blossoms may be substituted for goldenrod blossoms.

ACORN BREAD

1 cup, acorn meal, ½ cup cornmeal, ½ cup whole wheat flour, 3 tbsp. oil, 1 tsp. salt, 1 tbsp. baking powder, ¼ cup honey, 1 egg, 1 cup milk. Grind acorn meats, mix dry ingredients. Combine honey, egg and milk, add to dry ingredients. Mix and pour into greased 8x8 pan, bake 350° for 20-30 min. Makes 1 loaf. For a sweet loaf, add sugar and nutmeg.

INDIAN FRY BREAD

A favorite at Pow Wows and family meals.

3 cups flour, 1 tsp. salt, 3 tsp. baking powder, 1 cup milk, ¼ cup warm water, hot oil in deep fryer or pan. Combine dry ingredients, slowly add milk and warm water as needed to moisten dry ingredients. Cover and let dough rest for 15 to 30 min. Pinch off fist-size pieces and flatten with the hand or a rolling pin. Fry in hot oil about 5 min. until golden brown on both sides. Drain on paper towels.

Fry Bread Dinner Favorites: use as a taco shell; cut up and serve with your favorite dip; roll warm fry bread in sugar, add cinnamon; break up and serve with chili and taco toppings; top with honey, peanut butter, cream cheese, jelly (Terri Jean, *365 Days of Walking the Red Road*)

ROSE HIP TEA

Dry rose hips, grind to a powder, use 1 tsp. to a cup of boiling water, let steep 1-2 min.

BLACKBERRY WINE

6 quarts, berries, 6 cups water, 2 cups sugar to each qt. of juice, 1 cake yeast, 1 slice rye bread. Mix berries and water, boil gently 15 min., press out juice. Add 2 cups sugar to each qt. Pour into large jar or crock. Spread toasted bread with yeast cake and float on top of juice. Cover for one week. Carefully pour off wine into gallon jug and stuff opening with a wad of cotton. Keep in a cool place until wine clears and shows no sign of fermentation. Carefully decanter into sterilized bottles and tightly cap. Let it age at least until the weather gets cold.

CHAPTER 14
Indian Culture And Lifeways, Part II - Hunting, Fishing, And War

BEAVER – CASTOR CANADENSIS

"They find a rivulet – small creek – across a meadow and make banks and ramparts with trees, which they cut down with four great sharp teeth and drag them as they swim in the water. They arrange the trees they load themselves with grass and fat earth, which they transport upon their great tails and throw it between the wood as a skilled bricklayer does. They make banks 400 to 500 paces in length, 20 feet in width, and seven to eight feet thick. Their cottages are made by skill and strength with six posts exactly in the middle of the made lake. Upon these posts, they build their house in the form of an oven made up of fat earth, herbs, and branches of trees, having three stories that they may mount up from one to the other when the water rises by rain or thaw.

Each beaver has an apartment to himself. They enter under water through a hole in the first floor, which is encompassed with asp wood cut in pieces to easily drag it to their cells to eat. As their common food, they lay up great heaps of it during autumn, foreseeing the cold weather will freeze up their lakes and keep them shut up two to three months in their cabins. They have no predators, but men. Their sharp cutting teeth defend them, and they never go farther than 20 paces from the edge of their lake and always set sentinels to watch who cry out when they hear the least noise.

Of beavers: they have so much wit, capacity, and judgment. They join in a society, of an hundred; they seem to talk and reason with one another. The savages and Couriers De Bois say they have an intelligible jargon, whereof they communicate to one another, consulting about what they must do to maintain their cottages, banks, lakes and about everything that concerns them.

You cannot go four to five leagues, three miles, in the woods of Canada but you meet a little beaver lake. All this vast continent is a country for beaver hunting.

About the end of autumn, the savages set out from their village in a canoe to go and post themselves in the place for hunting. They argue among themselves to allot each family certain grounds. Each fires his house in the middle of that ground. There are eight to ten hunters in each cottage who have four to five lakes for their share. They lay traps with bait for otter, fox, bears, land beavers, and martins, checking them every day. They are very just and do not go out of the bounds allotted them.

They feed well and make merry during this hunting season of four months. They find their trout, hares, wood, fowl, bears, and deer and roebucks.

They make a great hole under their banks and drain the water off, leaving the beaver on dry ground. All are killed except a dozen females and half a dozen males. The hole is made sure to fill up with water as before. In winter, nets are laid by the holes, and the kennels are laid open with an ax. They slaughter the beasts and stretch out their skins in the air or on the ice to dry them. This imployment lasts until the great thaw, then they bundle their skins and carry them to the canoes" (Lahonton II, 1703).

"There are old bachelor beavers who live by themselves, build no houses, work at no dams, but live in holes. Traps of iron or logs are used to take these and baited with popular branches. The tail is a luxurious morsel" (Alexander Henry and Schoolcraft, Project Gutenberg, the American Indians).

"The winter was the time of beaver hunting; the furs were in their best condition, thick and glossy with new winter growth. Beaver skins were valuable for the trade and for clothing. They were used as money. The meat was eaten. Front paws and the tail were delicacies.

Beavers are quite large: they are three feet long and weigh more than 70 pounds. They have a flat paddle-like tail and large front teeth.

Beavers eat twigs, leaves, roots, stems, and bushes.

They are capable of felling tall trees six inches in diameter in 15 minutes. They can remain under water for 20 minutes. They are construction experts and create dams and homes from logs, branches, and mud. In winter, their coats are thick and glossy" (Eastman).

"There is a land beaver who makes a hole or den in the earth like a rabbit or fox and never go near the water but to drink.

The beaver carries upon its tail the clay, earth, or other materials to make their banks and kennels or huts by a wonderful instinct. Its paws are three and a half inches long, formed much like a man's hand. The five toes are joined like those of a duck, with a membrane. Its eyes are like a rat's eyes. Before its muzzle are four teeth or cutters, two in each jaw and it has 16 grinders. The cutters are above an inch long, ½ a half-inch broad, very strong and sharp like a cutlass and cuts down trees as big as a hogshead. A beaver has two layers of hair: one is long and of a shining black color, with a grain as big as that of a man's hair, the other is fine and smooth and, in the winter, very long. In a word, the finest down in the world. But the price varies according to the goodness. In winter and autumn, the flesh of a beaver eats very well if it be roasted.

There are white beavers, but they are very scarce.

The most valued are the fat winter beavers, called Muscovy beavers. They are made into robes by the savages and worn long enough to be thoroughly greased by contact with their bodies" (Lahonton, "Travels through Louisiana").

"There were giant beavers at 2.5 metres length and weight of 100 kilograms" (Canadian History, Open Text Books, Pays d'en Haut, www).

OTHER ANIMALS

"The Michibichi is a sort of tyger. Only less than the common tyger, the puma, American tiger cat.

The reddish bears are mischievous creatures, for they fall upon the huntsman, whereas the black one's fly from us.

The Natives hunt elk with dogs and sometimes beaver with dogs" (Lahonton).

Bears were fat in the fall before their hibernation. Their hides were used for robes and blankets. Bear grease had many uses for cooking and the skin. It was mixed with clay or dyes to be used as war paint. Colors and symbols told the story. Red was for life. Black for mourning. Generous use on the body kept the warrior warm and waterproof.

Deer were caught by snares, shot with arrows, or driven into an enclosed area or into the water where they were easily killed by hunters waiting in canoes with axe or spear. Deadfall traps were used, swing door pits, fire enclosures, and other enclosures.

Deadfall and nets were used to trap otter, muskrats, and mink.

"Buffalo – *pisikious* – had been in the area prior to 1800. Called oxen or wild cattle by the French.

Sibola or *cibola* (was the) Spanish name for buffalo" (Kellogg).

"Moose the French called *la biche*. They love to eat succulent water plants; they are found in swampy areas of which we had many. Moose were also called *eland* and *oriniack*" (Kellogg).

Wildcats, lynx, panthers, and bobcats were native to the Bluewater area of East Michigan. Harts were the common deer.

Elk – *wapiti* (Cervus Canadensis) – were once plentiful.

Fishers – Fisher Cat – though not a feline, are forest dwellers. Males weigh eight to thirteen pounds and are 35 to 47 inches long, females four to six pounds and 30 to 37 inches. It feeds on small animals, fruits, nuts, mast, birds, and fungi. It is a member of the weasel family.

Coyote – their howling was always a scary thought. Foxes were grey and red. Mink and ermine are found along the water's edge.

A muskrat was often passed off as a young beaver; they are two to five pounds and 20 inches long. They make holes in banks or make a dome house of mud and plant materials. They eat cattail and other aquatic plants, fish, and clams.

River otters grow up to four feet long; they weigh over 30 pounds at maturity. Porcupine quills were much used for decoration of textiles and moccasins. Racoons are mostly out at night. Wolves were plenteous and a nuisance.

WAR

"Women were in the winter camp. There was much work to do tanning skins, drying meat, preparing meals, making and repairing clothing. Children helped in many ways. They hauled wood, scraped hides, brought water from the creek.

Every nation is perfectly well-acquainted with the boundary of their own country. At the age of 15, they begin to bear arms and lay them down at 50.

Each village has its Great Head of Warriors – Ogitchidaw – who by valor, capacity, and experience is proclaimed such by a unanimous consent. This title invests him with no power over the warrior. These people are strangers to a military, as well as civil subordination. Though invested with power and authority, yet they acquiesce entirely, doing what he proposes. There are other leaders that head a certain number of warriors who follow them out of friendship and respect.

The war party meets for ceremonies addressing "The Great Spirit", sacrificing, singing, and feasting until they march. Each man carries Indian corn in a bag of 10 pounds weight; they feed each man on this mixed with a little water without boiling. They march one after another; the last takes care to throw the ground with leaves to cover their footsteps.

They run all night and, in the day, lay upon their bellies in the copses and thickets. These warriors show no mercy – not to women and children. There is refuge taken in the little French forts. There are some of the defeated parties who choose rather to kill themselves than to be taken prisoner. As soon as a savage is fettered, he sings his death song" (Lahonton, II, 1703).

Captives are called *Panis* or *Pawnee*. Some are kept as slaves, some tortured to death in horrible ways.

WAUBOJEEDS DEATH SONG
My friends, when my spirit is fled – is fled
Ah, put me not bound in the dark and cold ground
Where light shall no longer be shed – be shed
But lay me up, scaffolded high – all high
Where my tribe shall say, as they point to my clay,
He never from foe sought to fly – to fly
He never from foe sought to fly.
And children who play on the shore – the shore
And children who play on the shore
As the War Dance they beat, my name shall repeat,
And the fate of their Chieftain Deplore – Deplore
And the fate of their Chieftain Deplore.

This death song was shared by Ed Baldwin, friend and speaker, near Lansing, Michigan. He loves to research and share Indian artifacts and history.

COUNTING COUP
"To the Indian, it was deeds that counted, not conquest and annihilation. To strike an enemy with the hand, or an object held in the hand, was one of his greatest achievements.

The war club, or tomahawk, was a symbol of bravery and personal hand-to-hand combat. Those Natives who served in the U.S. armed forces were denied admission to the Old Time Warriors Club, the reason being the White man's war is just shooting, and there was no chance to be close to the enemy and earn real honors" (Richard A. Pohrt, Michigan Archaeologist, vol. 3, #2, 6 – 15 – 1957).

Getting close enough to touch an enemy without harming, touching a live enemy and getting away unharmed, this was counting coup. The warrior earned an eagle feather for this brave act.

Bravery was a high moral virtue, absolute self-control. The truly brave man yields neither to fear nor anger, desires nor agony. He is at all times master of himself.

"Let neither cold, hunger, pain, fear of them, nor danger, nor death itself prevent you from doing a good deed," said an old chief to a scout sent out to relieve a starving people.

The slayer of a man in battle mourned 30 days, blackening his face and loosening his hair. A sign of reverence for the departed spirit. It was no sin to take the life of an enemy. The killing of women and children, without a husband or protector, was a pitiable case. The warrior's spirit was content if no widow or orphan was left to suffer, want, and weep.

Wanton cruelties, and more barbarous customs of war, greatly increased by the coming of the White man. Fiery liquid and deadly weapons aroused the Indians' worst, provoking revenge and cupidity – greed and bounties for scalps of the innocent men, women and children.

The boys at seven years old were taught by the men to fish and hunt.

The men had tool factories and workshops.

Bows are made of many types of wood: ironwood, red cedar, or hickory were the best choices, along with bone, etc.

Arrowheads are made of quartz, flint, chert, and other types of stone of an imperishable nature. Bone, copper, and other metals were also used. Flint is of many colors: white, black, red, and mottled. The shaft is made from wild rose and other long strait wood types. Heat and bear grease are used to straighten it, the head is split, the arrowhead inserted into the shaft and tied on with leather.

The ammunition was hidden away for future use in cache holes. Slings with stones were also used.

Shields were made of wood covered with moose or deer hide. The shields were often decorated and used to ward off arrows in war.

In Charles Eastman's book, *Indian Boyhood*, he talks about "buffalo skin boats as round as tubs". Charles Eastman (Ohiyesa), born in Minnesota in 1858, lived on Lake Huron in Canada at Desdarats. He died in Detroit, Michigan, where his son lived. He is buried there in Evergreen Cemetery. His grave was unmarked until 1984. Raymond Wilson and the Dartmouth Club Indian University placed the stone there.

"Ohiyesa", his mother and father believed dead at Wounded Knee, was raised in Canada by an uncle and went to Dartmouth College in New York. He was the first Indian writer to write from an Indian perspective. A teacher, writer, and physician for the government at Wounded Knee in Dakota, he wrote for *Boy's Life*, the magazine of the Boy Scouts of America. He gave Scout Talks at his camp to teach boys about Native American ways. He wrote the *Boy Scout Guide*, teaching wilderness survival. In 1925, he became the U.S. government Indian inspector of Indian reservations. He made two trips to England to speak to their people about Indians.

Charles Eastman was an educated man; he went East for his college education and became a medical doctor, a full-blooded Sioux. He was a wonderful man who, with his Scout Talks, was an inspiration and a founder of The Boy Scouts, teaching the Native American lifeways to many. He was also an early worker who helped establish the YMCA. He has written several superior books on Indian culture. *Indian Boyhood* (1902) is especially fitting for this section on hunting. The following are from his work.

"In hunting songs, the animals are introduced; they come to offer their bodies for the sustenance of his tribe.

The side of the tree with lighter colored bark and most regular branches is the South. It is also, more rough and not weathered.

The leaves of trees are more vertical on the North side, reaching for the light. Moss color and thickness also tells the secret of the North side.

Know exactly where you are before starting out. Look for natural landmarks, check the wind.

The Big Dipper handle points West and North in summer. The Milky Way lies North and South.

Never approach a grizzly's den from the front; go behind and throw your blanket or a stone in front of the hole. He comes out and sits before any attack; aim at his heart then. Taught to outwit savage beasts.

Most large game moves continually about, except the doe in spring. Call with a birchen doe caller. Be very watchful; a large wildcat understands the call of the doe perfectly well. If you are not equipped for a pitched battle, the only way to make him retreat is to take a long sharp-pointed pole for a spear and rush toward him. No wild beast will face this, unless he is cornered and already wounded. The fierce beasts are generally afraid of the common weapon of the larger animals – the horns, long and sharp – they dare not risk an open fight. There is one exception: the grey wolf will attack fiercely when hungry. But their courage depends upon their numbers; they will stampede a herd of buffalo to get the calves or rush upon a herd of antelope, but they are always careful about attacking a man.

Ottissippi

Young men are expected to endure hardship without complaint and must be an athlete used to undergoing all sorts of privations, able to go without food and water two to three days without displaying any weakness. Or run a day and a night without any rest. Traverse a pathless and wild country without losing his way, day or night. He must do these things if he aspires to be a warrior. Must fast all day and blacken our faces with charcoal.

A sudden war whoop over my head in the morning, sound asleep, I am expected to leap up with perfect presence of mind. Always ready to grasp a weapon and give a shrill whoop in reply or shoot off his gun, giving blood curdling yells. I became used to this. I wished to be a brave man, as much as a White boy desires to be a great lawyer or president.

Our manners and morals were not neglected. Adults were respected; we were not allowed to speak in their presence.

We were taught to be strong of heart, be patient. No tobacco use, in any form until a warrior of record.

A wife before 22 or 23 years and a brave man was sneered at; he must also be a skillful hunter. He cannot be a good husband unless he brings home plenty of game.

Boys were a prince of the wilderness with little work to do but practice simple arts in warfare and the chase. He was master of his time, games and plays, keen competition; he strove to excel all others, practicing what we expected to do when grown up. Feats of bow and arrow, foot and pony races, wrestling, swimming, imitation of our fathers, customs, and habits. We enjoyed our sports to the fullest extent molded by the life and customs of our people. A precarious life, full of dreadful catastrophes.

A born hunter with inborn depth of native caution, noiseless like a cat, scanned every object, the hunting instinct to chase and kill. Bow, arrow, knife, hatchet of bone, or sharp stones were used to kill small birds, rabbits, squirrel, and grouse.

Boys would imitate calls with or without birch bark, horn or other adjunct. They would offer food and rove in their domain without doing them harm.

A slingshot and bow and arrow were the favorite weapons. A leather pouch with a dozen small rounded stones, a buckskin thong 18 inches long with a piece of rawhide two inches square, was a long-distance gun. Boys learned to throw stones accurately by hand with coordination and strength. We hunted with stones. We would deceive by daubing our bodies with mud and lay motionless on the shore, using mudballs to only stun then quickly gather.

Bows of four to five feet long were made from a modest young elm, oak, hickory, ash, dogwood, or ironwood, or elk horn, sheep horn, and buffalo ribs, worked to a perfect shape by steam. A boy's ordinary bow was made from any kind of wood, a sapling to get elasticity.

We would find new and strange things in the woods, examined for the slightest sign of life. Climb large trees, trapping, putting sharp burrs in the rabbit's path. Nooses of twisted horse hair and slip knot on, limb down to the track. Chipmunk hunt, imitate call with wild oat straws. We prepared meals of game on a stick. A large tripe, washed and tied, suspended between four stakes, filled with cold water; meat is boiled by adding red hot stones.

A doe was called with a thin piece of birch bark between two flattened sticks.

The sex of deer is determined by the footprint: the female's is sharper and narrower, the male has rounded points to the hoofs, the toes widely spread – playing close run for life. At the end of the trail, they make two loops and conceal themselves to catch the pursuer or to escape. Displacement of leaves, grass, broken sticks, dew marks with the reflection of the sun all tell the direction. The Indian is a close reader of character with insight and great powers of observation.

'The Stone Boy' story: he was turned to stone; he abused his strength and destroyed for mere amusement the lives of creatures given to him for sustenance use only" (C. Eastman, Indian Boyhood, 1902).

THE EAGLE AND FEATHERS

"The eagle is the most war-like bird, the most Kingly, of all birds, his feathers unlike any others. This is the reason why they are used to signify deeds of bravery.

For coup, the after stroke or touching of, after he has fallen is much more difficult to accomplish than shooting one from a distance (an enemy). It requires a strong heart to face the whole body of the enemy in order to count, the coup on the fallen one who lies under the cover of his kinsman's fire. When a warrior approaches his foe, dead or alive, he calls upon the other warriors to witness. Upon return, the heralds announce all deeds of valor which then become a part of the man's war record. Any brave who wears the eagle feathers must give proof of his right to do so. Wounded in some battle, he counted his coup, he wears the feather hanging downward. When wounded but no count, he trims his feather, and it need not be an eagle feather. All other feathers are merely ornamental.

A feather with a round mark means he slew his enemy. When the mark is cut into the feather and painted red, it meant he took a scalp.

Ottissippi

A brave successful in 10 battles is entitled to a war bonnet and if a recognized leader, he was allowed to wear one with long trailing plumes. The Plains Indians wore bonnets, the Woodland Indians did not.

Those who counted many coups may tip the ends of the feathers with bits of white or colored down. Sometimes the eagle feather is tipped with a strip of weasel skin; this means the wearer had the honor of killing, scalping, and counting the first coup upon the enemy all at the same time.

All feathers worn by common Indians mean nothing; they have never gone on the war path, they may wear any other kind of feather but not an eagle's. Sometimes one is worn of a great occasion by the child of a noted man to indicate the father's dignity and position" (C. Eastman).

"Dogs are taken hunting; every man had a dog. The dogs' barking scared bear or wolf away. They also helped in the hunt.

Only old Medicine Men wear bear claws regularly. The son of a great warrior who kills a grizzly may wear them upon a public occasion. It is always better to earn them yourself.

White ermine was given for all achievements at home and at war. Buffalo hair trim, for taken many scalps.

The buffalo tail was only used on the pole of the chief. No one else may do so without the authority of the tribe.

The highest degree conferred only on men tried, again and again, by every conceivable ordeal. Heroism is common; the universal spirit of gallantry and chivalry requires it.

The honors were shared with the war horse; the horse wears the eagle plume in its forelock as proudly as his master, the tail and mane trimmed and dyed according to the rider's war record, or to mourn by having it cut quite short.

Sometimes a long pipe or war club is adorned with honors.

A man may wear none, not awarded in council of his tribe" (Eastman).

"There are two kinds of scouts: hunting scouts and war scouts. Scouts were much in demand for the White man, their tracking skills legendary, their mapping skills unparalleled.

The person of an envoy, currier, or messenger was sacred among the Indian tribes. To maltreat one was the worst possible of insults.

Snares were used in hunting. This allowed men to be in several places at the same time. A snare was made of long fibrous bass wood or nettle fiber or other materials. It was placed along paths used by the animals. When the animal came along and was caught in the snare, it quickly tightened the snare as it struggled to be free. Calls were used for hunting; the voice, twigs, grass, etc. were used to make calls.

Women and children used snares near camp to catch rabbits for meat. The snares were checked daily or frequently for the catch.

The men in canoes, by torchlight, hunted deer along the shore of the lake.

The animals were considered people in those days. The Indians always made an offering to the Great Spirit for taking their sustenance. They asked forgiveness of the animal.

Indians traded with the animals; finding their cache of nuts stored for winter, would replace what they took with other food for the animals. The Indian knew he was only a part of the Great Spirit's creation and had a reverence for all things. The animals were his brothers in creation.

A hunting bonfire was made, every man went out at daybreak. The first to return with a deer was to be envied. The deer was thrown down at the door of his wife's mother's home, according to custom.

Hunting with snoeshoes in the winter, sleds of buffalo ribs and hickory saplings, runners were bound with rawhide, hair side down. Used to haul game or furs back to camp.

We hunt and trap alone or with a companion, a knife, hatchet, bow and arrows, maybe a canoe. Build a shelter of whatever material is most abundant. A lean-to is two trees close together a pole in the forks. The poles were then covered with evergreen boughs or grass or rushes. Fire is the best protector. A wickiup is poles set in the ground with willow wands tying the tops. Any mat for covering, protection from the cold, wind, rain, a canoe to crawl under a great hollow tree. All trapped animals were cooked and eaten, except the marten.

It takes a trained mind to reach the height and physical system of endurance, long building produces results.

Conscious of his relations to all life. The spiritual world is real to him. The splendor of life stands out preeminently. Beyond all and in all dwells the Great Mystery, the Great Spirit, or Master of Life" (Eastman).

"They always ask for the pardon of an animal killed" (Schoolcraft, "Travels in Minnesota and Wisconsin").

"Lichen and the inner bark of certain trees are famine foods; we familiarize ourselves with the edible roots, herbs, fruits, and fungi – mushrooms. Jerking meat in thin strips and drying on poles in the sun. Berries and wild fruits are easily dried for future use.

For fires, cattail down, dry punk wood, shredded birch bark, or dry pine needles. A drill and bow. A spit to roast meat, planked, against a flat rock toward a hot fire. Tripe or rawhide to boil in, or case food in wet clay and bury deep in ashes or sand under a good fire. With birds, only wet the feathers before burying them; they are juicy and delicious under a black coat that peels off like the skin of an onion.

Fish, potatoes, green fresh corn, shellfish – almost anything is done in two or three hours or leave all day if necessary without harm.

A cache is well-hidden by building a fire over it or covering it with rocks, brush, dry leaves, or sand" (C. Eastman, Indian Boyhood).

SIGNS AND SIGNALS

"A blaze trail is made to the meat killed and hung up and a direct road home. A slash or mark three inches long and three feet from the ground is made on trees. At every turn, a sapling is felled at the same height as the blaze, the felled top pointing in the desired direction.

Game trail blazes are smaller and five feet high on the tree and farther apart. At each turn, the jack is deeper on the left or right of the tree to give direction.

A trapper trail is even higher on the tree, opposite the first trap, a double hack or twig clipped. Along the lake shore or river, a stick marks traps, broken off two feet from the ground and bent over until it touches the water, for a trap in the water that cannot be reached on shore designates a birch bark twig trap in a hole.

When hiking, a bunch of grass tied to a low branch on the right side of the road he takes. If off the path, a stick with a knot of grass on top is bending in the right direction.

For 'return and meet others', break two opposite twigs toward one another. If 'to camp', he draws a circle on the ground.

In a group of trees, a right-angled gash pointing straight to the next blaze.

Above the blaze, two hacks and arrowhead mark – follow blaze 200 paces in direction of arrow, then search for another mark. Diagonally arrow mark leads to the lake of camp.

A small blaze and figure of an animal is for found game.

Stone piles to give information, a pointing arrow in the direction with a trail of others behind the main pile.

'Enemy' is made with a small stone on either side of a bigger control stone.

An 'obstacle' is made with two stones in front of the control one.

The stones are used again and again on the prairie-blazed trail" (C. Eastman, Indian Boyhood).

"Being constantly in motion and covering a large area each year, the people communicated from a distance by using signals: smoke and mirrors, blankets, drum, yodels, or musical shouts. Imitation calls were used to convey messages.

A fire keeper's bag was a man's role. It held flint, tinder, and needles to start a fire. A fire was smothered with coarse green grass and earth around it to make smoke signals using a blanket to regulate the message" (Eastman).

During the WWII Theater, Indian Code Talkers from 18 tribes were very instrumental in sending messages for the U.S. government. Their codes were never cracked by the enemy.

"Sign language and secret codes are used. We are taught to be silent, to listen to nature. Our wireless was the gesture language. The whole body speaks. All oratory is accompanied by graceful and significant gestures, charm, rapidity, and movement.

The shadow of the sun tells the time. Hunger is a good guide, as is distance traveled. Weather and animals give signs. The wolf, give the storm call the evening before. Horses kick and stomp. Buffalo low nervously. Waterfowl have a strange agitation. The wind in the leaves, the color of the grass and leaves. Waves whisper, a ring around the sun. Opacity and disk of the moon. Old wounds ache and swell with a change in the atmosphere. Birds give sign in the morning and evening skies" (Eastman).

WARFARE

"Vengeance in the field of battle was a lofty virtue. In some ways, we despised the White race, whose powers bordered on the supernatural.

How gentle is the wild man when at peace, how quick and masterful in action. A sound and efficient body is what he must be to overcome difficulties, to resist pain and hardship and win the object of his quest" (Eastman).

"Warfare is an institution of the Great Mystery. In Indian culture, it was an organized tournament, with elaborate rules and counts for the coveted honor of the eagle feather, to develop manliness, and it was patriotic. It was never for the overthrow of a brotherly nation or territorial aggrandizement. It was a great display of daring and horsemanship. Those wounded and killed were scarcely more than a football game" (C. Eastman, The Soul of the Indian).

"Gather in summer, scatter in winter for trapping and hunting, hugging the river bottoms. Trained for all around natural life and all emergencies, manful, honest, unhampered existence. My horse and dog my closest companions, they were regarded as brothers. I went out to seek inspiration and store up strength for coming manhood" (C. Eastwood, From the Deep Woods to Civilization).

"When they route their enemies, they pull the bark off the trees, for five to six feet everywhere they stop and paint a totem of victory with coal painted with jot and ayl. These pictures explain to passersby what exploits they have done, who they are" (Lahonton II, 1703).

TORTURE

"The Iroquois that are caught expect a fearful torture. The least punishment is obliging the poor wretchs to put their fingers into the mouth of a lighted pipe. Some burn their prisoners, others keep them in slavery.

Approaching their own villages, they make a cry for as many dead as they have lost men. And when it is accompanied with a musket shot repeat, it is for the number of slain enemies. The youth 12 to 15 years old make a lane, and armed with sticks, beat the prisoners as they enter, the warriors carrying the hair of those they have slain upon the end of their bows. The next day, the old men distribute prisoners commonly to women or maids who have lost relations in the expedition and to those that want slaves. The women then chose to keep them as family or make them slaves to work or sell or torture. The women prisoners are distributed among the men who are sure to grant them their lives" (Lahonton II, 1703).

"Prisoners have their nails torn from their hands, fingers are put into the smoke pipe. Burning fire brands are applied to burn to the bone. A necklace of glowing hatchets is placed and not removed until cold. They cut off flesh and broil it and eat at once. They pour boiling water over wounds, pierce the neck and armpits with red hot irons, burn genitals with birch bark. Every nerve and artery is set with fire or knife. Then they are scalped, and hot ashes and sand are put on the bleeding flesh. The blow of the hatchet on the head, or stab in the heart, or cut off the head. The Iroquois burn by inches for five or six days. Humanity is regarded as cowardice" (Cadillac).

THE FOREST

"The forest was a cathedral; it was home, it was protection. Mother Earth was very fruitful, providing everything the indigenous people needed. The Great Spirit was worshipped and adored in his magnificent creation.

Bark and trees for home building, canoes for travel – many, many useful items were made from the forest. Sap for sugar, pitch for glue, fiber for bags and clothing, wildlife for sustenance. Roots for sewing and medicine. The Native was very thankful for the Great Spirit's benevolence. The forest floor was park-like, the towering trees, the wildflowers, the wildlife paths, the Native traveling through the trails which led in all directions.

In the winter, the forest was much warmer than out in the open, winds were blocked by the trees, firewood was readily available. A nearby stream provided water.

To fell trees, a fire was used to burn the wood at the bottom, mud was applied on the upper portion to keep the whole tree from burning.

When new planting fields were needed, fire was used to clear the land in preparation.

The virgin soil was very fertile. Planting fields were used for about 20 years before moving to a new section. The healthy bird and waterfowl population applied natural fertilizer, fish entrails were buried in planting rows to decay and add fertility.

Michigan and Ontario had a great variety of trees. Some of them are alders, apple, ash, basswood (tilia americana or tilia canadensis), or whitewood, beech, birch, blue beech, bush cranberry, buttonwood (sycamore), bush cranberry, butternut, cedars, cherry, crabapple, dogwood, elder, elm, hazel, hemlock, hickory, ironwood, larch, maples, mountain ash, oaks, pear, pine, poplar, plums, sassafras, slippery elm, spruce, tamarack, walnut, and willows. This list is not exhaustive; there are probably more Native trees these are the most well-known" (Plain/Jones).

"Black ash was used for splint to make baskets and was plentiful. Hickory made bows and arrows. White ash for paddles and spear poles and many other useful articles. Pounding mills were made of black birch, about a foot in diameter, the center of which was burnt out with live coals and finished with sandstone to make it smooth, and when it was completed, it made a good pounding mill to make corn flour for the community.

They made their kneading bowls out of soft maple and ladles for every purpose also rolling pins" (Nicholas plain, "History of the Chippewa of Sarnia", 1950).

"Snowshoes were made many ways: the round snowshoe, the snowshoe with a tail, and the, turned up toe snowshoe. All had a wooden frame with a net across the opening. A wooden sort was used with a thong across the toes. They are usually made of Ash the wood being bent by heating it. Rawhide strips were often used for the netting. Horsehide was a favorite, as it does not shrink or stretch when wet. Intestines and sinew were also used. The round shoe was like a bear print. Emergency snowshoes were made of unpeeled branches laced with basswood fiber" (Densmore, Chippewa Customs).

CANOES

The Algonquins were the experts of canoe men on the continent, in both building and using them. Villages had large numbers of canoes, especially those who were traders.

Some were designed for speed and others for safety. Nanabozho had taught them, to make canoes as well as bows, arrows, and all other useful things.

Ojibwe canoes were of many kinds and sizes, some small, others massive.

"Indian canoes were 15 feet long and used for visiting between villages. The north canoe was 25 feet long and was the canoe used in long distance travel and for warriors. This canoe held eight men, plus supplies and weaponry. The Montreal canoe was 36 feet; it was used for trading freight. It held 3,000 to 4,000 pounds of furs" (David Plain).

"Dugout canoes were made of a single tree, a very large tree. They were made of basswood, cottonwood, and soft maple. The wood is soft, porous, and very buoyant. The average dugout was 12 to 16 feet long. To dig it out, crosswise cuts are made a foot apart, and the wood is split off lengthwise between the cuts. Then a small pick axe is used to carve out the interior, leaving a four to six inch, outer wall; a chisel was used to smooth the walls. On the outside, a draw knife or ordinary knife was used to shape the bow, and stern, keel, and the top edge. In primitive times, bone knives and sharp clam shells were used. Fire may be used to dry and polish the wood.

For bark canoes, the bark is cut away in one long strip. In early spring is the best time when the sap is flowing to gather bark. The bark is thick, about a thumb's width, and very durable. Though rolled patch materials and pine tar pitch are carried for repairs. A man sits on the bottom of the canoe, not on the cross bracing, or a seat is slung across with a braided rope to sit on.

Another way to seal the canoe and make it waterproof is by using glue made of sturgeon blubber, horn or hooves, or rawhide boiled down to a glue. Charcoal is added to make it set up" (C. Eastman, Indian Boyhood, main reference).

In 1950, Nicholas Plain, Chief of Sarnia Chippewa, gives this description on canoe-making:

"First was to find a white birch tree large enough to provide a sheet of bark large enough to cover the widest part of the framework of the canoe to be built – that is, from rim to rim. When the tree is found, a scaffold is put up against the tree, and one of the men goes up with a sharp tool and cuts the bark straight down, and the bark is peeled off the tree and rolled in a bundle to be carried to the camping ground where it is unrolled on a level ground with the inside of the bark under, and the framework which is built by thin pieces of cedar is put on the bark which is stretched on the ground, and the bark is brought up to the frame and sewed on with cedar rootlets. And when the canoe is finished, it is made waterproof by a formula composed of pitch and other gummy substances of herbs. The lightness of the canoe makes it more suitable to carry heavy loads on the water than the dugout canoes made of basswood".

Toboggans were very useful.

FISHING

Amaug was a fishing place.

"We had fish lines made of hemp, sinew, or horsehair. Fish were caught with lines, snared, speared, or shot with a bow and arrow. We tickled them with a stick in fall and quickly threw them out. We dammed brooks, and they were driven into a willow basket made for that purpose" (Eastman).

"Hatchet, nettle fiber, basswood strips, and horsehair were also used in fishing. Hooks were made of bone, shaped twigs, and other materials.

Fishing was carried on all through the year. Nets, seine, hook, hatchets, spears, and weirs were used. Weirs are a kind of dam that leaves a channel for the fish to go through, and they are easily caught. Weirs were made with stone, sand, and logs.

Weirs – *kagun yoke* – are built of logs, saplings, cord, rocks and sand, or mud. The weir is like a funnel, sometimes made to angle to a very narrow opening. Usually a person could walk along the top of the weir to use nets and spears to collect the catch.

During the runs of spring and fall, the men would go out into the rapids – *Sauk or Sohk*, meaning the outlet of a river or lake – and float down in canoes with long poles with a net on the end and scoop large quantities. This required great dexterity, standing in the canoes. The fish was then dried on racks and sometimes powdered by the women and children and stored for later use" (D. Plain).

In the fall, the fish came near the shore in great numbers in November. Sein nets, spearing at night, with a torch, traps, bait and hook, and by trolling were the methods used to harvest the fish.

The nets were thoroughly washed and sometimes dipped in a concoction of sumac in water to disinfect them.

For ice fishing, a hole was chopped in the ice to the water, a hole was made. Sometimes a man would cover his head and short spear with a blanket to keep the light out. A frame was used like a large basket, which was covered with a blanket, decoy fish were near the surface of the water. The spear when thrown or shot loosened itself from the handle but was attached to a strong line which was drawn out. Covering the hole caused it to be illumined and, like an aquarium, the quiet water under the ice is very clear and the fish are easily seen as they swim into the baited hole.

Nets were also used in ice fishing.

"Spearing by torchlight, *flambeau*, was done at night along the shorelines of the waterways. A rolled bark torch was held over the bow – front of the boat – on a pole, the light lured the fish to be seen and speared by a long-pronged harpoon spear.

The canoe was navigated by two Indians, usually a man and a boy, the darkest nights being the most successful. The man in front directs the boy to steer from the rear – stern. The catch of catfish, pike, and perch was plenteous, fifty or more lights moving upon the smooth lake in every direction" (John Rutherford, Indian captive, narrative at what is now Pine Grove Park and Lake Huron, Port Huron, MI. 1763).

Lake trout were also ice-fished or any other species that appeared in the hole.

WHITEFISH – ADDIKUMAIG OR ATTICAMEG – THE DEER OF THE WATER

Whitefish were the main catch. They were abundant at Aamjiwnaang – "The Spawning Stream", St. Clair River, Sarnia, Port Huron, Fort Gratiot on Lake Huron, and throughout the Strait. The people dried tons of fish. They would gather in great numbers during the spring runs and through the summer and fall runs. The drying racks were stacked eight feet tall near the beach at the foot of Lake Huron.

Michilimackinac was also a wonderful place to catch whitefish. Sault Ste. Marie, on the St. Mary's River at the foot of the falls, was fish central for the Northern tribes.

The fish was dried and packed for storing in cache pits for later use. When used, it was usually finely crumbled and cooked with corn and in many other ways.

A scoop net was used to catch whitefish. They averaged three pounds; some were six to nine pounds. They had the mouth of a sucker with firm white flesh. There were very few bones when boiled, they were also grilled, battered and fried in butter, or chowder or in a pie (Schoolcraft 30 years Among the Indians).

STURGEON – NAMAI OR KABASSAK

Lake sturgeon are bottom feeders. Most adults weigh 200 pounds and are about seven feet long. The females are the larger. They like a warm water temperature and return to spawn in streams. The males live to about 55 years, and females can live to 100 years. They spawn every four to five years.

White men considered them "trash fish" and killed them when they damaged nets.

Sturgeon, were plentiful. They were huge, sometimes weighing 100 to 300 pounds and were six to eight feet long at maturity.

In 1889, four million pounds of fish were harvested with 4,000 pounds of caviar. Detroit was the center for sturgeon buying and selling.

Lake trout commonly weighed 50 pounds.

The Ottissippi (St. Clair River) was the spawning stream where the sturgeon and many other kinds of fish laid their eggs, and spawn.

In Saginaw Bay every spring, they swam in large numbers to lay their eggs in shallow water near shore. They were easy prey. Wading into the water, the fisherman speared them, stunned them with a club, or picking them up, threw them on shore to be killed with knives by the women and children.

There are over 70 varieties of fish in the waters of the Strait – Detroit, St. Clair River, and Detroit River. Sturgeon, whitefish, pickerel, quansig or walleye, perch, bass, catfish, sunfish, smelt, crappie, herring, salmon, trout, pike, bullhead, and blue gill, to name a few.

FOWL

Turkeys, partridges, grouse, pheasants, and pigeons were plentiful.

All the fowl flying about created natural fertilizer over the land, creating a very fertile growing place. The great Mississippi and Atlantic flyway passing through the area made for lots of fertilizer without cost. Many birds could be a nuisance to crops, but a great harvest was still collected and stored.

The passenger pigeon was in such great numbers that it would be in flock's miles long and wide, the great numbers creating a shadow upon the ground as they passed. The pigeons were caught in nets in great numbers and eaten, cooked in myriad ways. These pigeons persisted into the 1900s.

As a child, I remember seeing many pigeons. Many of the boys in those days were encouraged to shoot the birds, like blackbirds, as being a nuisance.

WATER FOWL

Ducks were killed in countless numbers, their noise like the roar of heavy thunder. They were so thick, they had to part for the canoe to make a path through them.

Ottissippi

This area is part of the great Atlantic and Mississippi flyway. Untold thousands of waterfowl pass through the area, the marshes and waterways supplying food in abundance for them. They follow the lakes' and rivers' paths on to their winter grounds.

The Indians used decoys to lure fowl in close at times. Decoys were made of the skins of ducks and geese; they were dried and stuffed with hay, the feet attached to a plank which floats around the hut of grass. They drew wonderful numbers.

Swans were once very plentiful in the area waterways.

Canadian geese are abundant, and some, make the area their home year round.

The feathers and other parts of fowl were not wasted; the bills were used for maple sugar molds for pacifiers.

The loon is a waterfowl of the penguin species, the size of a goose. It is black and white; having a white ring around its neck, the back and neck are spotted black on white. Their skins are used by the Natives as pouches. The loon lives on small fish. When pursued, it will dive under water for a long time.

WILD RICE

Wild rice was also known as "Zizania Aquatica, or *mano min*, meaning good fruit or berry. *Psina* is the Sioux name. *Folle avoine*, the French name. Wild, mad, or false oat or wild kick were other names for it.

Wild rice – wild oats – is the choice for waterfowl, fish, and Indians, who harvest great quantities of it for consumption. It is used in soups and stews and parched for travel.

Stalks are one inch in diameter, it grows four to twelve feet above the surface of the water, and it is an annual, the rice falling to the bottom of a muddy water and producing every year. It was once abundant in Lake St. Clair, Georgian Bay, Lake Erie, and throughout the Bluewater area and North America. It grew in countless small ponds and streams.

It is harvested in autumn, when the sugar trees are as red as the robin breast. It is narrow, a quarter by one inch long, and is gathered by canoe after having been tied in bundles to prevent the flocks from eating it. It is then bent over and left to ripen for two to three weeks, making collecting it easier and marking out the territory to others. It also protects it from rain and wind. There is a one-month harvest; the women pound out the rice into the canoe with a stick. The rice is then dried in the sun or a slow fire, the hull then rubbed off by shaking it in a blanket or treading on it, winnowing by the wind, or fanning by trays of birch bark, in the old way. There is great celebration of this harvest with festivities and ceremony.

Minnesota is the large production area for wild rice. It takes a bit longer to cook than other rice. It is not a true rice. It is highly nutritious, having much protein in it. The rice swells to 3 or 4 times its size. It is eaten extensively among Indians and was a cause for many wars over the rice beds" (Albert Ernest Jenks, "Wild Rice Gatherers", was the main source).

Wild Rice can also be popped (like popcorn) and is delicious. Barb Barton

Rice fields in many lakes are threatened by homeowners wanting to eradicate it. Wild rice is a protected species. There are people, who are reintroducing wild rice in Michigan and other places.

All wildlife, were respected as members of the Great Spirit – God's creation; they had a spirit and purpose in creation and were never killed for sport, but a necessary sustenance. It was always accompanied with ritualistic ceremony, offerings, fasting, and prayer. It was very serious to take and use something from Mother Earth. Thanksgiving offerings were always made to the spirit (essence or life power) of any harvest, a part of the creation family. They were part of the universal relatedness of all things.

Careful consideration of the effect of their actions was always in the forefront of hunting, fishing, and gathering practices. All were gifts given by the Great Spirit; they were not seen as being entitled to the gifts of Mother Earth, and they were thankful for everything given to them by Gitchi Manito – The Great Spirit.

Conservation has always been the way for Anishinabe to live. They always left animals to repopulate what was taken and used for food, for the future wellbeing of the animals or plants and the people themselves.

The social life of the Anishinabe included games played by the family or larger groups. Games of chance and those of skill were the favorites.

The moccasin game was popular and widespread. Some small object, a stone or piece of bone was hidden under one of a number of moccasins, by a player. The other contestant was to choose the correct placement. Bets were laid on the outcome. It was not unusual to discover, losing a gun, tobacco, pipe, and clothing.

A sort of dice game was played with marked wood; these were tossed up into the air and matching the pieces of marked wood.

Wrestling and other athletic contest running, racing, catching an object with a bag or hoop, shooting, and throwing for accuracy or distance, were common. Water games and canoe games were always fun, small family groups played for fun.

In larger groups, a spirit of rivalry was strong. In the game of lacrosse, large teams played a sort of soccer. It was a great contest, like a football game: village against village.

CHAPTER 15
Blue Water Indians Then and Now

"It was thought by many that the Indian was the vanishing American. He was thought to be culturally extinct, to have unhappily vanished from the face of the land" (Stan Steiner, The New Indians, 1968).

The country was heavily populated before the White man came (Iroquois www). European diseases reached the Northeast with such devastating effects, even prior to European exploration. We know little about the Indians of the Upper Ohio Valley in this period. Some scholars suggest a Native population decline of 90 to 95% within a century after contact, loosening the Natives' grip on land more than any other factor.

The Indians didn't accumulate material wealth or develop stratified classes, they were a very thankful people (Sturdevant, Handbook of North American Indians, 1978).

There was a delta at the mouth of the St. Clair River at the foot of Lake Huron. It was shallow with large rocks for our fish weir. There were three mouths, the main mouth went east to where Point Edward, Ontario is now. A part of the channel is now a lake at Canatara Park in Point Edward, Ontario (Lake Chipican). We could walk most of the way across the Ottissippi (St. Clair River) on sand gravel bars. Some used poles to vault over deeper areas, or canoes, swimming, and rafting to cross. Horses swam across also.

"We welcomed the French and the metal tools to make our lives easier. They also brought guns, whiskey, missionaries, land thieves, and self-seeking exploiters. As predicted, we were faced with a difficult choice. To keep, our own traditions or abandon the old way for European ways. A world of increasing hardships as the fur trade brought whiskey, religion, dishonest traders, opportunists, and missionaries.

Ottissippi

Increasing tribal warfare took place for control of the land teeming with fur-bearing animals and the waterways, lakes, and rivers (highways). Social and cultural distress were suffered as the result of the decision to embrace the Gitchi Mookmaan ways, values, law, and religion, many leaving the teaching of the elders behind. Pontiac and Tecumseh, our spiritual leaders and seers, tried to warn us of the devastation and sickness of alcohol, disillusionment, loss of language and identity, but in vain.

Europeans saw our seeming infinite resources, forests, waters, grasslands, and wonderful food supply, as ripe for the taking, never with respect, appreciation, or as a gift from the Creator, Gitchi Manido. Disaster was brought on by the headlong insensitive flight of progress.

More and more, the Native concept of living in harmony is being understood. We saw the world as a place full of living beings with a spirit and character to be respected. This is essential to understanding who we are. All beings come from one supreme creator, and we are part of creation. Ethics demand that humans treat all of creation with respect.

We believe in one creator, a Supreme Being, Gitchi Manido. He created the universe and put it in motion, revolving around the sun. He created Earth and all in it – mountains, plains, and waters. He gave each its direction and purpose to flourish and lend order. He then made every species of animal, and much time passed.

God made man in four colors, each in different parts of the world.

The Anishinabe on Turtle Island – America. Universal order was made; He made laws that govern natural laws. When humans defy or alter this natural order, all beings suffer, but humans the most – pollution of water, air, land, animals, fish, bodies, and ozone.

There are four layers to the world: The earth, the sky, beyond the sky realm, and beyond that, the spirit realm, the abode of the Creator, Gitchi Manido. The earth has four layers; human and animals dwell on earth, water is the lifeblood upon it, the surface veins, all earth life depends upon water to live. Thus, Mother Earth nurtures and sustains. The fiery center, the fourth layer, is underground, as the center of the universe is the sun. There is the rock layer, the soil layer, the water and humans.

The universe in its vast realms follow the Creator's will and natural law to carry out the sacred design and order of creation. Anishinabe theology ascribes the Creator's essence or spirit to all of creation. Thus, all of creation is of the spirit, the Great Spirit.

The majority of Anishinabe have embraced Christianity and belong to churches.

Our Dodem, Clan Signs Totems, originally, there were seven clans given to the people after the cleansing of the earth by the Great Flood. Each had a special purpose within the greater tribal system. We are now the Three Fires Midewiwin Lodge. The conference fosters intertribal cooperation on many issues, treaty rights, and education.

During the Sixth Fire Time Era, we faced many difficulties. A glimpse of our past, our story, our leaders, warriors, and families faced great odds and survived to save some land, our customs, spirituality, and heritage over nearly overwhelming adversity. We are telling our story to help people understand the past and educate others about where we have been and where we are going.

The Seventh Prophecy is still unfolding today. The flames of the Seventh Fire are preparing us for a bright and promising future" (Diba Jimooyung, Saginaw Chippewa, Ziibiwing, 2005).

Expansion brought short term wealth, but the price was very high. This became clear during the 1800s as hard times and disease took their toll. Disease came, and we neglected the teachings of grandparents; illness and death came, virulent diseases that we had no resistance to. Very few were given vaccinations against these diseases when sought out. Acculturation brought loss of identity, language, pride, and self-esteem. Contact brought racism and denial of basic human rights by the dominant society. Alcohol was the biggest and most devastating scourge.

We have survived all the tragedies of the Sixth Fire Prophecy. We are now the fastest growing ethnic population in North America. Our birthrate is the highest among Non-White minorities. The life span is increasing and is now at 59.5, after being 47.5 and 37, although the Western and Northern peoples are suffering from alcohol addiction and suicide at alarming rates.

The Black River and Swan Creek people lived between the Saginaw Bay Watershed and Lake St. Clair Watershed. Pottawatomies and Wyandots were also living in the area (Ron Satz, Chippewa Tribal Rights). They were labeled as a notoriously turbulent band of Chippewa, staunchly loyal to the British. They leased and rented their lands to White settlers with whom they were friendly. To three families who were helpful to them, annual payment was made in trade goods.

In the beginning of the 1800s, there were 20 distinct villages in St. Clair County, Michigan (Tanner, Atlas of Great Lakes Indians, 1987).

During the War of 1812 to 1814, a party of half-breeds and Indians, crossing from the Marine City area of Michigan to attack the Canadian Indians, met at Baby's Creek, south of Mooretown, a battle took place. For many years after, the banks and bottom of the creek were strewn with unburied Indian bones and skulls.

The following is from Charles Eastman's "The Indian Today and as He Was":

The Indian is free born, a free thinker, their government pure democracy. An intrinsic right and justice which governs his conception and play of life. Naked and upright before the Great Mystery, he does not excuse himself or lie to save his miserable body. He allows others the same freedom.

Spiritual life is paramount. Daily he meets with the "Great Mystery", morning and evening, from the highest hilltop in the regions of his home. He has respect for all. The only laws as necessary are to guard personal and tribal purity and honor. There is respect for all. No undue advantage was sought by any individual. With us the individual is supreme. There is no national wealth, no taxation for government. Chiefs were natural born leaders, with much influence but little authority.

There were no fermented drinks; no salt was used in the Indian diet. They were God-fearing, clean, honorable people. Women do not associate with men outside the family. The women have one child every three years to, five children.

He will not be forced to accept materialism, as the basic principle of his life. He is fearless of hunger, suffering and death.

The Indian will not be forced to accept Materialism as the basic principle of his life. He preferred to reduce existence to its simplest terms.

The Indians were peaceful, kind, patient, and reasonable, offering resistance only when faced with irresistible provocation (C. Eastman, The Indian Today). In religious zeal to gain honor and converts, the Black Coats and others represented them as godless and murderous savages. Otherwise there was no one to convert (C. Eastman the Indian Today).

There is not one instance of a Scout betraying the cause he served. Once his honor is pledged to a public trust, he must sustain it at any cost.

The Indian value system placed importance on respect for Mother Earth fellow man, having no prejudice, respect for the Great Spirit – God, the aged and family tradition, generosity, and sharing. There were no tranquilizers, drugs, alcohol, or ulcers. There was, thousands of years of peace before 1492. There are no taxes, borders or boundaries, no insane asylums, jails or prisons, no orphanages. There was honest leadership selection, bravery, and courage. There was no religious animosity, no poor and no rich (Will Antell, Ed McGaa, DSS Publication, St. Paul Minn).

Strength in the sense of endurance and vitality underlies all genuine beauty. He is prepared at any time to volunteer his services on behalf of his fellow people at any cost or inconvenience and real hardship, and thus to grow in personality and soul culture. Generous to the last mouthful of food. Fearless of hunger, suffering, and death.

"A hero is not to have, but to be" is his national motto. No politics and no money in it for anyone. His conscience is never at war with the mind. No undue advantage was sought by any individual. Justice must be impartial; if the accused alone knew the facts, it was common to surrender himself.

Indian warfare was mainly rivalry in patriotism, bravery, and self-sacrifice. The willingness to risk life for the welfare or honor of the people was the highest test of character. A system of decorations evolved to preserve an example to the young. This was of feathers and skins.

In duels and small skirmishes, a small scalp lock was worn by the leader, mourning for dead enemies. Only after bounties were made by colonial governments were scalps and murder for pay.

Weaknesses are very apparent with the complicated system of civilization.

There was no fermented drink; liquor was the ruin of our race. Cholera, venereal disease, immoralities of Whites, indoor life, bronchitis and pneumonia, tuberculosis, consumption, unsanitary crowded space, and unwholesome food were our sickness.

Scouts, guides, and allies were of great value to the early history of this country. There is not one instance of a scout betraying the cause he served, even against his own tribe and relatives. Once his honor is pledged to a public trust he must sustain it at any cost.

Often the means to bring neighboring tribes into subjection was cruel warfare. Relentless, demoralizing, based on a desire to conquer and despoil of possessions – a motive unknown to the Primitive American. With weapons more effective and deadly, spiritual and moral loss was great. The Indian came to believe that the White man alone has a real God. And things he thought Sacred are inventions of the devil. This teaching undermined the foundations of his philosophy. The inconsistency of its advocates made it difficult to accept or understand.

Whiskey and gunpowder were the two great civilizers. The Indian sold his birthright; his manhood began to crumble. White officers deserted wives and children after, as if there was no binding obligation. The demoralizing was gradual but certain, culminating in the final loss of his freedom and confinement to reservations under the most depressing conditions. The last surrender was in 1886.

OTTISSIPPI

Wars were incited by the insolence and aggressiveness of Americans. Algonquins and Iroquois were used as allies in the long struggle and conflict between the French and the English, and thus were initiated into the motives and methods of the White man's warfare. The Pontiac War was caused by a few self-seeking men, gross overcharging and use of liquor to debauch the Natives. He accumulates much tainted wealth, buys land, then much stock or a mill on Indian water power, and becomes a man of influence in his home state. From the vantage point of a rough border town peopled largely with gamblers, saloon keepers, and horse thieves, this man and his kind plot, the removal of the Indian from his fertile acres. They harass him in every way and at last forced resistance upon him. Then he loudly cries, "Indian outbreak! Send us troops! Annihilate the Savages!" Many went our way.

The Indian was hospitable; he was willing to shelter fugitive slaves.

The Seminole tribe in the Florida Everglades is the only unconquered band in the U.S. today.

The Great Lakes Indians are scattered far and wide in fragments.

The 1836 Blackhawk War was the end of Algonquin resistance.

The Southwest Frontiers were occupied by remnants of the Eastern tribes. Starving Indians were promised support that never came; they sought sustenance, revolted, and were massacred. 15,000 people in the Black Hills were massacred for the railroad and gold. Over 120,000 were massacred in California for gold. It was impossible to conquer the Plains Indians without destroying the buffalo. Vast herds were destroyed ruthlessly by the U.S. Army. By 1880, they were practically extinct. The reservations were concentration camps. Serving time, a beggarly apathetic way of life, and then many died a broken heart. Called incorrigible savages, the Indians was defrauded of the finest country in the world.

Christian men and women came tardily to the conclusion that these brave people had lost everything in the face of Herculean advance of the dominant race. Reflection upon the sordid history of their country's dealings with Red men taught them to think clearly above the clamor of the self-seeking mob. Under Churches and missionary organizations, they try to put an end to official corruption.

"My father was one of 260 pardoned by President Lincoln" (Charles Eastman, The Indian Today and as he was).

THE INDIAN AT SCHOOL

In "From the Deep Woods to Civilization", Charles Eastwood wrote of his experience when his father chose to educate him in the White way.

I asked few questions. New ideas didn't fit with the cardinal principles of Eternal Justice. I saw a false life, a treacherous life. My father converted and gave a totally new vision of White men as a religious and kindly man. A race which learned to weigh and measure everything including time and labor. We learned to accumulate and preserve wealth and records for future generations. We never had anything to count. We valued nothing except honor that cannot be purchased.

Taught to commune alone with the Great Spirit, I heard for the first time him addressed openly in a house full of men and women.

I was given a big bag to fill with straw, a small one for a pillow, sheets and blankets. We filled our own water and wood.

A painted globe was placed before us, and the teacher said that our world was like that, that upon such a thing our forefathers had roamed and hunted for untold ages as it whirled and danced around the sun in space. I felt that my foothold was deserting me. All my Savage training and philosophy was in the air, as if these things were true. Dr. Riggs explained the industries of White man, his thrift and forethought; we could see the reasonableness of it all. Economy is the able assistant of labor and the two together produce great results. Systems and methods of business, especially the medium of exchange, was of deep interest.

Dr. Riggs' personality, words of counsel, and daily prayers found root. He did more than any other next to my father to make it possible for me to grasp the principles of true civilization, teaching me to stick with whatever I might undertake. The world gradually unfolded before me and the desire to know all that the White man knows was my total desire.

My father said to me, "I find the White Man has a well-grounded religion and teaches his children the same virtues that our people taught to theirs. The great mystery has shown to Red and White men alike the good and the evil from which to choose. Then you must be careful; success lies in the choice of the right road. Be doubly careful, for traps will be laid out for you. The most dangerous is the spirit – water, that causes a man to forget his self-respect."

Grandmother said, "always remember the Great Mystery is good; evil can only come from ourselves." I parted from my first teacher, the woman who taught me to pray.

Reverend Doctor John P. Williamson influenced me powerfully toward Christian living. My father wrote to say an Indian can learn all that is in the books of a White man, so he may be equal to them in the way of the mind. I studied hard. Missionaries were poor and government policy of education for Indians was not developed. In two years, I caught up and could translate every word into the Native tongue. I was now studying algebra and geometry.

Ottissippi

Cities were crowded, and everyone was in a greatest hurry.

I absorbed knowledge through every pore. The more I got, the larger my capacity grew, and my appetite increased in proportion.

I discovered my theory of this new life was all wrong and was confronted with problems entirely foreign to my experience. English was almost beyond my grasp. History and geography to me were legends and traditions. I soon learned the logic of mathematics. I then went on to Dartmouth N.H. college to become a physician to my people, to serve my race.

I had been accustomed to broad, fertile prairies and tribal ways. Here I had my savage gentleness and Native refinement knocked out of me. I gained more than their equivalent (C. Eastman).

"European colonial powers competition undermined our economic stability. Wars came as British ships seized French merchant ships and disrupted fur and tobacco shipments to Europe.

The British treated us as inferior savages. In the French and British wars, the Indians had some on each side and some neutral. We fought for those who gave us the best prices on our furs and would treat us with a degree of respect.

The Saginaw Chippewa lived in a huge beautiful village at the north end of Lake St. Clair in the 1730s. There were 1,500 people there in 1736, in one village in Ontario and Michigan. We grew between 1740 and 1760 and flourished. We gained material wealth, but the cost was irreparable to our culture and peaceful way of life. Death and warfare became the major parts of Anishinabe life" (Diba Jimooyung, Ziibiwing, Saginaw Chippewa).

"Metis Fur Trade warriors, with Charles Langlade, led war parties to attack the British. In 1758, at Pittsburgh – Ft. Dusquesne, we had overwhelming victory and received much valuable prizes: gold, silver, cloth, weapons, 1,000 rifles, 100 oxen, and 400 to 500 horses. We used horses much after this battle for some time.

The decisive war began in 1756, the Seven-Year War. Famine and disease weakened us at home and on the battlegrounds. Smallpox claimed many more than bullets ever could. From Niagara to Mackinac, European biological warfare (disease), chemical warfare (alcohol), and psychological warfare – the destruction of our culture – devastated all Anishinabe people.

In 1760, the French surrendered to the British, ending the war and French Canada. The British also claimed the Mississippi Valley, the Ohio Valley, and Florida. The British moved to the heart of our territory, occupying the fort at Detroit. The Anishinabe had not lost a single battle. Our great leader Pontiac, an Ottawa with an Ojibwe mother, led the way, taking 9 of 11 forts West of the Appalachians.

Cheryl Morgan

Booniwuk (Pontiac) means "Thunderbirds Landing Upon the Earth". He was a warrior, statesman, and father. His clan totem was the Otter. We wanted to return to Anishinabe life uncomplicated by the European influence of alcohol, fur trade, competition, and war. We were preeminent, courageous defenders – warriors, patriots – of the people and the land. We had not been defeated in War. We would not sell our land and would not surrender. Pontiac was murdered at Cahokia (the large castle opposite St. Louis) by a Peoria Illinois.

The British assumed ownership and domination over our people. They did not give gifts, a tribute for our friendship and use of our land, as the French had. The British showed no respect. Whiskey and rum were rampant, traders charged outrageously high prices for supplies and limited the powder and lead. The same tactics used the world over to build the British Empire.

The British wanted to punish us for the War. Rum was used very effectively to destroy our people and tribes. We were tested daily to protect our hunting lands and territory. The Whites came as locusts to the feast. As unending waves of the ocean. The Family Compact and patroons were given power by the English king.

In the War for Independence in 1776, we were urged to remain neutral, the government promising not to move North of the Ohio River. Despite the wampum belts as visual reminders of an agreement binding on both parties, all such promises and treaties were broken. The U.S. claimed to defeat the British and all Anishinabe allies as well, claiming our territory by right of conquest. We yet held our western boundary. We traveled south to protect our borders in the 1780s and 1790s, attacking settlements and taking captives who were often adopted by our families and the tribe. Peace treaties followed as the U.S. government built its treasury and strengthened its army.

The U.S. behaves as though we were defeated enemies, dictating boundary lines, offering no compensation for lands taken in the process. They never enforced the treaty lines ever. In 1786, the Northwest Ordinance promised to stay behind their boundaries to never take our land without consent and to never invade or disturb us unless in just and lawful wars authorized by Congress. But laws founded in justice and humanity shall from time to time be made for preventing wrongs being done to them, for preserving peace and friendship. Noble words, outright lies, and lots of whiskey.

The U.S. adopted the new policy in hopes of averting all-out war. They were never satisfied, continuing to cross into our territory with immunity. We continued to resist incursions onto our Native soil. The Three Fires and Lakes People held long meetings at Walpole Island and Saginaw Valley. The Bear clan leaders urged all-out war.

Ottissippi

Harmer was badly defeated in 1790. St. Clair in 1791 had huge losses of 700 men. Mad Anthony Wayne trained his army in our tactics for two years. The British at Fort Miami would not help us, and the Americans prevailed. Many Whites were adopted to replace those who died. The new American government was weak; the Northwest Territory was up for grabs. No nation controlled them. France, Britain, and Spain had a covetous eye on it. In our pain, heartbreak, and loss, we prayed for the coming generations.

At the 1819 Treaty of Saginaw, we refused, saying "We will not sell our lands." After 640 gallons of whiskey, over ten council meetings and endless private meetings with Chief Neome, Jacob Smith, Kishkahko, Ogemaw – Ogemagigido, the Riley's, and other traders and chiefs, 114 Anishinabe signed their totems, giving up a very large portion of Michigan – over five million acres. Some Anishinabe moved to Canada, others to the reserved lands. Cholera and smallpox from 1832 to 1837 killed over one-third of the Anishinabe in the Saginaw Valley. It took many of our leaders and whole villages.

None of these treaties were by the people's consent. We do not know which leaders went or why. We have a democracy government of consensus by all. We never gave up the right to govern our people, to worship the creator, to hunt, fish, trap, and harvest plants and medical foods and other resources.

The Anishinabe never left their homelands. Most still live on their homelands. Only two small groups did not stay.

The Chippewa-Ojibwe signed over 80 treaties with the U.S. government, more than any other tribe. After 1804, the treaty negotiations were in a foreign language; we couldn't understand what was said or written, we couldn't defend ourselves" (Diba Jimooyung, Telling Our Story, 2005, Ziibiwing, Saginaw Chippewa).

The Anishinabe placed land in the care of the Indian Department employees, merchants, former soldiers, and officers to protect them from being taken by the government, squatters, and unscrupulous trade and speculators. The Indian alliance were to protect them for Indian use to hunt fish and fowl, plant corn, and make maple sugar on any unsettled lands. This was the purpose of making these agreements (Adapted, Travers, 2015).

The Lake Indians suffered an extraordinary loss of numbers by the late War of 1812, not so much from those who fell in battle as from camp diseases and hunger and misery, consequent upon their return to their distant villages. Whole villages in the North were depopulated or reduced to but a few souls, and I have passed over sites of towns populous in 1802, which are now overrun with grass and bramble and where not a single soul dwells to repeat the tale of their sufferings. The furs diminished very rapidly, and this trade was completely prostrated in Michigan in about 1837. The Indians had been plied freely with ardent spirits during this time, and they were deteriorated in their tone and independence of mind and left sadly in debt. Several tribes began to think of disposing of their surplus lands to clothe their families and pay their debts. Everything in the condition of the state communities is adverse, to their prosperity, as whole tribes and their emigration has therefore naturally forced itself upon the attention of the public as the only practicable mode of rescuing them and preserving them as a distinct race (H. Schoolcraft, 1838).

If an Indian had the audacity to stand up for his peoples being defrauded, repressed, and oppressed, he was quickly put down. Leonard Peltier has been serving a 40-year sentence for bringing to light the injustice being done to the reservation Indians at Pine Ridge, South Dakota. Dennis Banks, Russel Means, Clyde Bellecourt, Lee Brightman, Leonard Peltier, and many others were given time in prisons for seeking help with deplorable conditions on the reservations.

Stereotypes eroded the status of Indians as real human beings, making them seem as beasts. Descriptions given for wild animals (in) propaganda implied racial defects. They were depicted as cruel and war-like with limited potential, or exploited and despoiled, saying it would serve all to have them removed West of the Mississippi, where they would be free to roam and hunt.

Andrew Jackson, Louis Cass, and Christian missionaries were sending them to an unwelcome West already settled by other tribes. With goodwill and utter righteousness, they set out to save the Indian by destroying their economy, language, social systems, and religions. Imperial aggression took their rich lands, the Indians were exploited as unskilled labor. It brought on the total collapse of all they treasured. Military force was used, presents, liquor, land grants, traders, and debt. The Indians only source of money was their land.

The government officials having a vested interest, dictated to the men they used as representatives of the tribes, what to say. Governor Cass, Indian Agent Henry Schoolcraft, and Stuart, a fur trader for John Jacob Astor's American Fur Company, used the illusion of progress for removal, greed, and opportunism (Cleland, Rites of Conquest).

The Indian agents controlled all aspects of life on the reserves. The dictatorial power of the Indian Department and its agents through patronage appointments did much to prevent economic progress on the reserves. Farming was the only acceptable occupation, retarding improvements on reserve lands that were in most cases not suitable for farming. Fishing and lumbering were taken over by Whites as were other Indian industries. The loss of fisheries was especially decisive; fishing formed the traditional backbone of Ojibwe economic survival (Schmaltz, The Ojibwe of Southern Ontario).

Ottissippi

The necessary seed and supplies for farming were often detained for weeks and months, too late to sow them. Most Anishinabe spent any money on provisions, tools, housing, and to settle accounts. Laws and acts were made to protect indigenous people from criminal behavior of the Upper Canada Colonists. Property was swindled and whittled away to acquire what was formerly given as presents (Travers 2015).

The Indians were hemmed in and lost their freedom of movement. Filth, disease, starvation, and crushing poverty afflicted life in almost every Indian settlement. Economic and cultural racism prevailed. For survival, interracial couples and their children concealed their identities (Travers 2015).

Written records of the period are sparse, careless, inaccurate, and often highly biased. Their history is fragmentary, full of gaps. Much of the evidence is sketchy, oral and undocumented. Some of the printed sources are unreliable (Darlene Gay Emmert, "The Indians of Shiawassee County", Michigan Historical Commission, vol. 47).

Records and numbers were a story of decline and degeneration, as if they were a vanishing people, and they were treated as if they were. The system was designed for eventual elimination. This was a false accounting, for although the people were suffering, they had their traditional values and cultural life designed to survive (Adapted from Travers 2015).

The French commandment at Detroit from 1714 to 1718, Jacques Charles Sabrevois De Blury, describes the "Saguinan" as the "most unruly and unmanageable in the whole region".

In 1823, Territorial Governor Lewis Cass wrote a missionary group: "with respect to the establishment of a Mission at Saginaw, I will state the facts: the Chippeways who live there were the most troublesome Indians in this quarter. They are in the lowest state of moral degradation. Heretofore they have not been favorably disposed; in one instance, the attempt has failed. But so much depends on the experience and personal character of those appointed to conduct such a work".

The Methodists appear to have been the primary influence in the St. Clair and Shiawasee area. They were quite important in the entire Saginaw Basin.

Joseph T. Marsaac, overseer of farming for the Saginaw Indians, wrote,

"I am requested, by the majority, of the principal chiefs of the Saginaw Indians, to enter a complaint about the Methodist Indians toward them.

"Firstly, the M. Indians have and do urge them to join the Church of the Methodists by threats of the Department at Detroit as well as by the President of the United States, saying that in case the Indians should not join their

Church, they would be sent West of the Mississippi. They confirm their report by saying that their ministers at different times received letters from the President of the United States which letter-authorized them to use such language among the Indians.

"Secondly: whenever the Methodists have succeeded by using the authority of the government to make one or more proselytes, the chiefs say that there are among such a band of Indians so no more peace and farming in the band, but discords and discussion separates friendship.

"Thirdly: it appears by the report of the chiefs that the M. Indians also commit predations among the other Indians; they have already killed one horse and threatened to kill oxen likewise."

White men in general and government officials in particular tended to look with greater favor on Indians who were Christian and who were more ready to grant their wishes.

When the Indians became poorer, their hunting and fishing grounds taken up by settlers, relations between the races changed. The settlers gradually dominated the old hunting grounds and became increasingly disturbed by the begging of the Indians. Large quantities were never taken, just enough for the food that they needed. The visitors were usually not dangerous, though alcohol sometimes added spirit to their demands.

Whenever a White man found himself in need of Indian hospitality, there is no record of his having been turned away. Problems were created by the difference between White and Indian concepts of hospitality.

Liquor introduced by the White man became a major problem for the Indian who rarely could control his desire. The insatiable appetite for liquor led the Indian to give anything he had to obtain it. The influence of this beverage often made otherwise harmless Indians both frightening and dangerous (MHC. vol. 47 Emmert).

Between 1837 and 1840, cross border meetings gradually disappeared between Michigan and Canada. The U.S. people were cut off. The U.S. policy of British gifts given annually was that they must reside in Canada to receive the gifts. Grand Councils continued, runners carried messages between the border.

In 1862, in Mankato, Minnesota, Abraham Lincoln orders the largest mass execution in history. Thirty-eight Santee Dakota Sioux were hanged because they dared to protect the rights to their lands in the Sacred Black Hills. The ink was hardly dry on the Black Hills when the government wanted timber rights, they really wanted gold to cover the cost of war. This led to Custer's gold-finding mission; any who resisted were deposed (Metis Timeline, www).

Ottissippi

Major Richard Dodge at the Arkansas River saw a great herd of bison cross the river. It took five days for the herd to pass a given point, and the herd was not less than 50 miles wide, viewed from a high vantage point in 1868 (Metis Timeline, www). Over 50 million buffalo were killed, the bones used for fertilizer, the hides and tongues shipped east for sale in the Fur Trade. By 1888, the U.S. Game Report only six buffalo exist. The last buffalo drives were cattle hunts; old, stringy steers were let loose to be run after by old men who had grown up in the presence of endless herds of sacred buffalo. It was over, and even the dream of what it once had been was dying (Tunkashila).

Buffalo weighed up to 5,000 pounds with horns six feet across. Today they weigh about 2,000 pounds and are about 12 feet long and six feet tall at the shoulders. The hump on their back stores fat.

There were 80 million buffalo. Now there are 130,000 (PBS American Buffalo, Spirit of a Nation. www).

(The Natives) facing starvation, the government respond with minimal rations and used them to force land concessions and subjugation (Metis Timeline, www).

"The Indian lived a life of liberty, simplicity, and innocence. Critical of traditional religious and political beliefs. The New Enlightenment, a belief in the power of human understanding, unaided by divine revelation, (rose up). A substituting the natural for the supernatural explanation of the workings of plants and animals and human beings. The ever increasing, multiplicity of (each).

The Indian was declared equal by Thomas Jefferson, but his actions implied something else, a buffoon - lies.

Human progress, expansion, and conquest seemed to justify history as progressive and superior to other peoples. This led to White Supremacy and the belief in discovery and a conjectural history regardless of geography or history. This gave life and social sciences a larger scape, using the European standard and idea of progress to measure the direction and amount of development. Assumptions in the new guise of cultural and social evolution. A classification scheme embracing all people and made it into a sequential relationship of a time series. With newly emerging discipline and social evolution, a race of progress and a dying race. Ranking all societies in a hierarchical order according to ethnocentric criteria, confusing culture and biology.

Racism is an invention of European peoples: the moral qualities of a certain group are correlated with their physical characteristics, and all humankind is divisible into superior and inferior stocks based on the first assumption. The inherent racial differences and the moral judgments thereon are the explanation of diversity, entirely of, mainly in terms of racial inheritance.

Race replaced the word "nation" to designate a major division of humankind: civilized and primitive peoples, primordial origin, rather than subsequent history. Types of (Categorizing) humankind as separate species, rather than tracing cultural history of mankind as a whole as the key to understanding human diversity.

Changing the religious atmosphere and divorce between religion and scientific study of human origins, the division of a few races instead of many nations or peoples, biased gross comparisons, and prejudice.

A spectrum of variation, instead of hard and fast differences among races. So, search for fast proof switched to another index, head measurements, part of the pro-slavery argument for inherent inferiority. The range of sizes to them proved conclusively the superiority of Whites over all other races. All attempts to civilize have failed, also every endeavor to enslave them. Violent racism was given the Pettina of Science through craineology (head measurements). It was used to rationalize White American policy toward Indians and Blacks. The cultural hierarchy fused with racial hierarchy and evolution progress. Lower races possessed darker skin and bad manners, and organic equipment was inferior as well. Racial selection for the history of mankind. A racial psychology, stereotypes of various peoples in confusion of race, physical structures and culture, and ethnic psychology, rather than cultural pluralism – many varieties.

Racism is discredited in science and considered merely political and social ideology by those who would dominate other peoples for political or economic reasons, repudiating raceology and evolution, espousing the idea of culture as the way of understanding human diversity in lifestyles as the foundation concept of their discipline. We need to replace the conjectural approach with actual history.

The comparative method – superficial research – that ripped the cultural element out of its context to fit a preconceived scheme - the Postulative Stage Theory, the wholeness of a single culture rather than comparisons across cultures. There is diversity of cultures with no morally absolute ranking in favor of variety, a total entity not in relation to other cultures.

The appreciating of Native American cultures in their variety, and understanding Indians and their achievements in terms of themselves. The Indians have played a role in American history and still have a role to play, not as museum pieces, nor as individuals lost in the melting pot. The Indian ways and traditions, we grow and change. A unified way of life with values being superior to fragmented modern industrial life. The wholeness of man, humanity of interpersonal relationships, and integrity of unity.

Ottissippi

The White men studied other cultures according to the premise of their own stereotyped and racial biases. In White eyes, the Indian was bad, without history. The White Man chose racism and ethnic cleansing to cover the taking of the Indian lands and rich resources. This ignorance is yet perpetuated (The White Man's Indian, Robert F. Berkhofer Jr. 1979). The records of most of the early Indian and White history and White dealings have been lost, hidden, or destroyed.

I found Yankees of the uneducated class very Indian-like in their views and habits. Strong character, plain spoken and opinionated, very frugal and saving. Counting barrels of potatoes and apples before they were grown, and every brooklet forced to do a river's work in mills and factories (C. Eastman "From the Deep Woods to Civilization").

I became the government physician to Pine Ridge S.D., a bleak and desolate place. There was no medical equipment, no sanitation or preventive work; my people were groping blindly for spiritual relief in bewilderment and misery. They had many grievances and causes for profound discontent. Sickness was prevalent and the death rate alarming, especially in children. Trouble had been developing, and humane conciliatory measures may have checked this.

Rations were cut from time to time, protests disregarded. Never was more ruthless fraud and graft practiced upon a defenseless people than these poor Natives by politicians. Never more worthless scraps of paper anywhere in the world than many of the treaties and government documents.

Dishonest politicians robbed, bullied, then in a panic, called troops to suppress them – wrongs unbelievable of common decency.

I believed a great government like ours would never condone or permit such practices while administering a large trust fund and being guardian to a race made helpless by lack of education and legal safeguards. I had not dreamed what American politics really is. The people were starving. Those who had testified for the Indians or tried to bring about an honest investigation were punished. In the face of official opposition, the usual method is to deprive them of various privileges, imprison on trivial pretexts, ordered off as disturbers of the peace, slandered, or make (their) position intolerable and force a resignation. Harassed, (with) fake charges, government employees were usually dismissed from service or transferred. Many were forced to leave.

I had faith in everyone and accepted civilization and Christianity at face value – a great mistake. I was struck with the loss of manliness and independence in these reservation Indians. I longed to help them regain their self-respect.

A gross fraud had been committed. I determined to secure justice; in my inexperience, I believed that it had only to be exposed to be corrected. The farces were Whitewashed. The White man is a man of business and has no use for a heart. Some imagine we are still wild savages living on the hunt, but we are now fully entrenched in the battle of civilized life (1916, C. Eastman, From the Deep Woods to Civilization).

Dishonor and abuse of their trust has brought them to mistrust even friends.

The barbarous and atrocious character commonly attributed to him have dated from the transition period when strong drink, powerful temptations, and commercialism of the White man led to deep demoralization.

In the simple condition, morality and spirituality thrive better than organized society. The struggle for existence with the forces of nature and not with one's fellow man.

C. Eastman – Ohiyesa, or Always Wins – was the acknowledged hero of the Boy Scouts and Camp Fire Girls, teaching that there is no superior race and no inferior. He was a founder of the YMCA. He was associated with the YMCA preaching Jesus; he established 32 Indian groups of the YMCA. He served as BSA National Councilman for many years and under many U.S. presidents in many capacities.

One old battle-scarred warrior said, "Why, we have followed this law you speak of for untold ages. We owned nothing because everything is from Him. Food was free, land free as sunshine and rain. Who has changed all this? The White Man: and yet he says he is a believer in God! He does not seem to inherit any of the traits of his Father, nor does he follow the example set by his Brother Christ."

Another older man said, "I have come to the conclusion that this Jesus was an Indian. He was opposed to material acquirement and great possessions. He was inclined to peace. He was unpractical as any Indian and set no price upon his labor of love. These are not the principles upon which the White Man has founded his civilization. It is strange that he could not rise to these simple principles which were commonly observed among our people. He was glad we had selected such an unusual character for our model. Another old chief of the Sac and Fox tribe in Iowa was glad I was satisfied with the White Man's religion and his civilization. As for them, neither had seemed good to them. The White Man had showed neither respect for nature nor reverence toward God, but tried to buy God with the by-products of nature, tried to buy his way into heaven but did not even know where Heaven is. As for us, we still follow the Old Trail. I said Christianity is not at fault for the White Man's sins, but rather the lack of it. I knew many good men, Christians; had I not, I would have long ago returned to the woods" (C. Eastman, "From the Deep Woods to Civilization").

Ottissippi

Why do we find so much evil and wickedness practiced by the nation's Christian? Behind the material and intellectual splendor of our civilization, a primitive savagery and cruelty and lust hold sway, undiminished and unheeded. A system of life based on trade, the dollar the measure of value, and might still spells right. Otherwise, why war? Never lose the Indian sense of right and justice for development along social and spiritual lines, rather than commerce and nationalism or material efficiency. I am an American.

All other means failing these men will not hesitate to manufacture evidence against a man's or a woman's personal reputation, in order to attain their ends (C. Eastman).

The word-by-word reliving of the past by the Indians was extraordinary; it still is. They told history you won't find in the library, nowhere known in written history. It is recited from tribal memory, a necessity, a time machine with no written language. Every man had to be his own history book, his own walking archive, history, geography, nature study, and ethics, stories that would create in me the desire to become brave, good, strong, to become a good speaker, a good Leader.

Deceitfulness was a crime. Absolute honesty toward each other was the basis of character. The Indian code was so deeply ingrained that when they met the cunning and deception of the White Man, these were ways of behavior for which the Indian had no name. Justice was human; human needs were the measure of wrong and right.

The values that industrial societies place on property, money, status, and manufacturing of products for market were non-existent in tribal societies. Every little thing was cherished: human beings, all people. Every living thing is cherished. Every living thing was to be shared. The culture of mass media is fed to us, choked down our throats (The New Indian).

Roy Rogers said, "The slogan is honor; the object is land."

When I think of our condition, my heart is heavy. I see men of my race treated as outlaws and driven from country to country or shot down like animals. Whenever the White Man treats the Indian as they treat each other, then we will have no more wars. We shall all be alike – brothers of one father and one mother with one sky above us and one country around us and one government for all. Then the Great Spirit Chief who rules above will smile upon this land and send rain to wash out the bloody spots made by brother's hands from the face of the earth. For this time, the Indian race are waiting and praying. I hope that no more groans of wounded men and women will ever go to the ear of the Great Spirit Chief above and that all people may be one people (Chief Joseph, Nez Perce).

It does not require many words to speak the truth (Chief Joseph, Nez Perce).

European values and beliefs were imposed upon the people. The English are socially retarded, their politeness restricted. It is the issue of imported cultural failings. They have little regard or respect for people who lived on the land for thousands of years (Ojibwe History and Migration to the Great Lakes, www).

Benjamin Franklin cites the Iroquois people's governing traditions as a model for his Albany plan (being, of the people, by the people, for the people). The League of Nations – United Nations – was modeled after the system used by the Native Savages, Americans (Concensus).

Indian women were not allowed to vote in American elections until 1960.

JOE GREAUX, METIS WOODLAND PEACE CHIEF OF THE BLACK RIVER BANDS, 2014 INTERVIEW

Joe Greaux – Minnwaasenieta – Joseph O. Bennett Greaux, was a "tunnel rat" in Vietnam, rising in rank to Lance Corporal in the U.S. Marines. His health was affected by Agent Orange. He worked for and retired from the Port Huron Area School District in maintenance, plumbing, and repairing audio visual equipment. He also repaired technical equipment as a side line.

Joe wants to have an all culture get-together to share common bonds, promote goodwill, and exchange cultural traditions. God bless you, Joe, and thanks for serving our country and being a proud and patriotic American and Marine.

Joe was born October 23, 1950 and passed to eternity on February 5, 2017. He was honored with a celebration of life at the Pow Wow grounds on Black River, near Wadhams Michigan, on August 12, 2017. An Eagle soared over the Black River nearby. He was an elder and spiritual leader, Peace Chief and a Medicine Man, of the Woodlands Ojibwe. He loved to share with and teach younger people the Ojibwe language and culture. Joe headed the Black River Pow Wow for many years; he was a singer-drummer with other local men who won awards for their drumming. Joe was of Ojibwe and Seneca ancestry.

The first Blue Water Pow Wow Celebration was held in 1995. Joe, was instrumental in organizing it. Sharon Kota, taught the culture and language also, and was a founding Pow Wow member.

"We need to stop disrespecting ourselves and one another. People need to have respect for themselves and others, being kind, courteous, helping one

Ottissippi

another. Like any culture, there are good and bad. There are those that are polite and those that are not polite.

We are still here. There were many battles and important meetings on Black River. Many of our kids went to Indian schools. This almost destroyed our culture. We were to be annihilated. Our lifestyle, customs, language, and religion were nearly destroyed. But the people survived. We went underground; together we overcame the cloak of darkness.

The records of atrocity were burned, hiding the truth. The rich man had to get rid of the people to fill their pockets. Most wars are based around money, oil—wherever you look, everything is based on money.

In the 1920s and 1930s, we were a mixed people. After the first child the government tied [the] tubes. The truth is hidden. Before 2006, it was against the law to speak our language off-reserve. In 2006, George Bush restored Indian American rights to freedom of religion and other traditions.

At one time, the St. Clair River was much shallower. Our people dried fish at the lake. The racks were stacked eight feet high. At lakeside, the shoreline was another 150 feet out. Dams from hydro companies and dredging has made it deep. At Pine Grove Park, the shore was 75 to 100 feet farther out. The stumps of trees that were cut are still there in the original bank of the St. Clair River.

General Custer was a bad sicko.

Our language is pictorial; you see it at the same time you speak it. Some words have different meanings for men and women.

In a lot of Indian cultures, the women made the decisions.

Pow Wows are family reunions open to everybody; everyone comes – they come from all over.

The Boy Scouts started with Indians.

This was a great trading area; all Native tribes came to trade in this area.

The Tobacco and Neutral nations are totally extinct.

Some of our people helped the slaves from the south; Natives were a part of the Underground Railroad. This was one of the biggest points, a lot came through for freedom.

Our people, we worked as loggers.

We were soldiers for the best-paying country at war.

The Indians thought they were suckering Europeans into giving them money because the Earth belongs to all, the Earth is the Lord's. It belongs to God and cannot be bought, as the sky, water, [and] sun also belong to God.

There were four races in the same boat: eight people.

In the beginning of time, the Creator had five sons: A Black son to give the gift of strength to share with all the world, a Red son given the gift of taking care of Mother Earth and all our relations, the Earth and all it entails. The Yellow son was given the gift of patience, the White son the gift of fire. The fifth son had no color because he turned away and called himself God.

An old man said this at the Fire Teaching, the Elder said: "The Black is strong but didn't share his gift, or he would teach all the people to be strong inside. The Yellow didn't share, or you wouldn't have suicide, because people would have patience. (The Lodge got more quiet.) The Red man, if he kept his word, you wouldn't have pollution or sickness. The White brother kept his word – light on in the morning, electricity for cooking food, heat, cars, everything, has to do with fire. Even the *giisis* – sun. Dobeka, even the moon reflects that fire at night. No Color was cast out; we don't talk about him, he has no meaning – shunned."

White sage bandaged over a cut and it will heal, bed sores are healed this way. The Sarnia Ojibwe are a quiet people; they keep to themselves.

Sweet Grass has tons of uses, as a smoke or smudge, in teas, for gall stones, kidney stones, urinary tract infections.

This is Mount Pleasant Territory, Mt. Pleasant Reserve Territory."

The Canadian Truth Commission was an act to search out the reasons for Indian discontent following the Camp Ipperwash Protest Picnic. In 1995, the Truth Commission issued their report which outlined the abuse inflicted upon Indians since the 1800s and reservation era and boarding school experience of atrocious abuse.

"For 500 years, our people's spirituality and way of life have been recorded from the Eurocentric point of view. The Europeans who came to our country had no comprehension of our lifeways. Our people have suffered greatly during the past 500 years. Our elders and ancestors have made many sacrifices for us. Despite all the new resources, our people are still haunted by the oppression and colonization endured at the hands of American society. Many more generations will pass before our people recover from the traumas of boarding schools, substance abuse, racism, and prejudice. Many have overcome debilitating social scourges" (Ziibiwing).

The Indian population of Michigan in 1980 was 40,038 by census figures. The Michigan Department of Education school count was 60,374.

Indians have a destiny: to save the Earth from the evil that would attempt to destroy it. We are all children of the Universe with a responsibility to save it, each other, and all that is in it (Frazier/Cameron).

White government ignored centuries of acquired skills, values, spiritual beliefs, and lifestyles practiced by the tribes. Cultural genocide destroyed the Anishinabe trade, social, political, and economic systems. There is cultural amnesia, a void. The people are reintroducing traditional models of leadership. This builds ownership, self-identity, and self-esteem.

Colonial oppression has transformed what was a bottom-up structure to Western top-down structure, often filled with nepotism, favorites, and corrupt and coercive leadership. This system perpetuates disempowerment of the Anishinabe. Coupled with historic trauma, this engenders self-oppression and social dysfunction. Youth are starving spiritually (Flocken, UMN. 2013).

The Ojibwe of Southeast Michigan and Southern Ontario were never removed, as so many other tribes have been, but by successive treaty sales were restricted to reservations within this territory with the exception of a few families who moved to Kansas.

The Black River Reservation was sold in 1836. Three hundred and sixty of the people stayed on the land until after 1838. A few went to the Wesleyan Mission near Port Sarnia.

"Port Huron has been the place for paying the annuity to the Swan Creek and Black River Chippewa's.

The Black River Indian place of residence are nearly the same that they ever have been since the ancestors of the present chiefs, the brave Mashkeos at the head of the Algonquin, drove the Iroquois Confederacy from the Peninsula now called Michigan.

In the sugar-making season, most of them may be found at their old sugar camp in what is now called Lexington and Burchville. They plant upon Mill Creek in Clyde Township and in Burchville. In the hunting season, they and many more are scattered through the forests of this and the adjoining counties. At other seasons, they may be found at Port Sarnia, just opposite this place in Canada, where they have friends (and) relations and where they receive religious instruction. Most of them are professing Christians of the Methodist persuasion. Many give satisfactory evidence of being truly pious and enlightened Christians. I have often preached to them on both sides of the River St. Clair and have baptized a few. They attended my school while I had the means to continue it, and their progress in learning at that time was rapid.

Under the supervision of Colonel Bunce in Clyde, several have become tolerable farmers. There also I have often preached to them by the help of their Chief Nagezhik, Andrew Yates, who will hear me speak rapidly for more than half an hour, then rise and interpret the whole discourse faithfully and in a beautiful stile of language. Something less than a half a dozen of this kind are still unconverted to Christianity" (Norman Nash Port Huron to Robert Stuart, 1844 NAMIR.56; 145-147. Ziibiwing).

In the 1840s, the Black River Society Methodist Church was a great help to the Ojibwe peoples.

Many bought land and homes to stay on the original indigenous homelands. They are our neighbors, working, school, college, and church, living, loving and raising families.

As of the year 2000, there are 2.45 million Native Americans in the U.S. with 58,479 in Michigan. We survived and are hungry to reconnect with our cultural and spiritual heritage.

Modern day pirates on the border smuggle goods across to Canada. Tobacco is the main product in a very lucrative trade, (along with) whiskey and illegal immigrants. The St. Clair River is a smuggler's paradise (Belfy).

A prayer to Gitchi Manito, the Great Spirit: "Teach us honor, humility, love, and respect, so that we may heal the Earth and heal each other" (Ziibiwing, Saginaw Chippewa).

In 1924, all Indians were made full American citizens. There was also a law against identifying one's self as an Indian in Virginia; this law was overturned in 1967.

In 1940, hundreds of Indian tribes were eliminated as political entities when the termination policy began. The U.S. terminated numerous tribal rights and Indian treaties.

In 1941 to 1978, Whites adopted 35% of American Indian children in the U.S., and 67% in the Western States.

In 1979, the Indian Religious Freedom Act was passed as law.

Incest is a European tradition (Metis Timeline, www).

Exploitation by large corporations often in collusion with politicians at local, state, and federal levels with Indian governments continues today. To prevent general public outrage and demand, Indian history is written out of existence and the people kept ignorant. To be honest, the people are required to know their history and assume responsibility. The Indian heritage is hidden by those who seek to obscure it (The New Indian).

The Canadian Constitution was amended in 1982 as part of the process of completing the evolution of Canada as a self-governing nation, recognizing and affirming Aboriginal and treaty rights, including the right of Aboriginal self-government within the Canadian Constitution.

NATIONAL AMERICAN INDIAN HERITAGE MONTH

On August 3, 1990, November was officially declared National American Indian Heritage Month in the United States of America.

In 2009, June was declared National Aboriginal History Month in Canada.

Indian Day, an act established in 1974, is set aside on the fourth Friday in September to honor and celebrate Native Americans in Michigan.

NAGPRA

The Native American Graves and Protection Repatriation Act was passed by Congress on November 16, 1990 and signed into law by President George Bush. Hundreds of thousands of pieces of Native American human remains, cultural pieces, and funeral objects are being returned to tribal lands. The remains are held in museums and universities across the country. The return is ongoing at government expense.

INDIAN SCHOOLS

In 1879, the Carlisle Indian Boarding School opened in Pennsylvania. By 1884, there were 200 Indian schools operating in the U.S. and many more in Canada. Indian schools were built to civilize the people. Children were forced to attend; they were taken away from their families, kidnapped to live at boarding schools. The teachers at most of the schools were former rejects who were unwanted elsewhere. The Catholic Church was a large holder of Boarding Schools. One school had 62 sex offenders out of 63 employees.

The Federal Government operated 48 Indian schools in the country. Of all the nation's Mission and boarding schools for Indians, Michigan had 21 Indian schools. These schools were notorious for abuse. The children were not allowed to speak their own language and were punished for using it. Their culture was stripped away from them. They were not well cared for or fed. Physical, mental, and spiritual abuse was rampant at these schools.

The heinous abuse and genocide perpetrated on Native Americans by the U.S. lasted until the late 1900s. Violent methods of educating Native American children included murder, with no repercussions. The Isolation Policy of the BIA gave Carte Blanche Authority. The most extreme forms of child abuse resulted in permanent psychological and emotional injuries. (Isolated on reservations away from white society, and scrutiny of the public, who were kept ignorant of the illegal activities)

MISSION SCHOOLS

The Mission schools did teach many trades and provided a place where the children didn't face virulent racism and discrimination, a haven where they could learn. Indian agents complained that the children did not learn much at school because they had to leave school to hunt, fish, and gather crops with their parents and the language at home slowed their education. Some went on to public schools but had difficulty and were ridiculed by White students. Many grew up without any education. Being scattered over a large territory, the government could not afford to build a school at every settlement. By 1884, the Federal Government operated 81 boarding schools and six industrial or manual labor schools. All of the Mission schools, were closed in 1889.

BOARDING SCHOOLS

Mount Pleasant, Michigan Indian Boarding School children endured school policies, and a sense of brotherhood and solidarity was created. The children learned trades, mechanics, farming, nursing, and home economics. They did most of the work at the schools and farms to support them.

Thousands of children attended Mt. Pleasant Boarding School, having 300 to 375 students at a time. It had eleven brick buildings. Many children never saw their families while they attended school; there was great culture shock both going to school and returning home. There was great heartache and homesickness. Many students ran away, attempting to return home. It was a military school: the students marched, wore uniforms, had a strict schedule and rules. They woke at 4:00 AM. School employees were quick to punish students who broke the rules. Discipline and work were the curriculum. The school prepared them for low-paying, menial jobs.

Many people believed they received a good education, had fond memories; the band and football teams were favorites, friendships made were treasured. Other schools had horror stories; sexual abuse was rampant. Rejects were sent to teach at the Catholic Schools, and many children were beat to death, heads were slammed into the walls. The children were rented out to farmers and others during the summer. One young woman in Ontario was slapped every day for speaking her own language, and when she grew older, she finally stopped the teacher, holding her arms, and asked how would you like to be slapped for speaking your own language. The slapping stopped.

Basil Johnson (Ojibwe author) said, "As long as language exists, it enables men to understand and appreciate their ideas and philosophies and to share in their humor, so long do they adhere to their way of life. Once language disappeared, men began to forget their former purpose of life and ideas; they could only understand the thoughts of the adopted culture" (Schmaltz).

Letters home had to be in English as well, as all appliances supplied, except stamps (which many could not afford), and the family could not read.

Ottissippi

The children were comfortable neither in the White Man's world nor in the Indian's world, and their self-esteem and self-respect were shattered.

Sexual abuse of the children by ministers, priests, nuns, and teachers was widespread. Since the abused are inclined to become abusers, reserve life was influenced adversely by these experiences (Schmaltz).

Some were sterilized at the school's hospital. Many were not treated for ailments and died from disease or the flu and common cold. It was a hell for many. Many will not speak about their time at boarding school. In Ontario and other places, the truth is coming out. The Catholic Church was known for great abuse at their schools. Many lawsuits are still ongoing. Many have been paid something for their abuse; many never did, as they are now dying off. The latest is the Catholic Church is claiming bankruptcy in their lawsuits and not paying anything.

In 1928, Merriman's scathing report led to the Wheeler Howard Reorganization Act which returned some of the power back to the Indians, more self- government and responsibility.

The Wheeler Howard Act created Red Apartheid in America; it was passed by corruption and fraud. 80% of billions of dollars were used for administrative costs (Means).

Secularization was used as a tool to cover great theft and genocide (Means).

Schools whipped, kicked, beat, raped, and sexually abused, many students were made to eat their own vomit, used the electric chair, a funny sight for missionaries, laughing as a child was given the treatment with legs waving. Violence and intimidation to silence those who complained. The last boarding school closed in 1978. Some had a 50% death rate, and some students were beaten every day for speaking their own language (Metis Timeline, www).

"The children were told that their language was the Devil's tongue, a sinful way to talk, that their cultural practices and teachings were wrong. They were told they were dirty Indians and stripped, then disinfected by alcohol, kerosene, or DDT poured on them. They were renamed, their hair cut, personal belongings taken and never returned" (Ziibiiwing, Saginaw Chippewa). The people were chronically, desperately sick after over 100 years of reserve life. The medical profession was well aware, but consider it normal for the race (Metis Timeline, www).

There was a boarding school at Sault St. Marie, one in Carlyle, Pennsylvania; and at Haskell in Kansas, where many Michigan children were taken. Ontario also had boarding schools. Disease, poor housing, poor food, sexual abuse, and beatings were the norm. The children were not allowed to speak their own language and were beaten if they did. Most of the schools were operated to destroy Indian culture in the children who were the future Indians. So, the schools also destroyed the tribal culture and home. Many schools, it seemed, were there to destroy the Indians as a people. The abuse suffered has caused generational trauma, along with the historic trauma of the Indian people. There is great abuse of alcohol and drugs, physical abuse, drug abuse, and hopelessness. On the Rez (reservations), there are not many jobs; there is yet great abuse by Whites who come to sell alcohol and take women. Sex abuse, kidnapping, and murder are rampant in Canada.

The Mount Pleasant Indian School, a manual labor boarding school, was home to many Anishinabe children from across the Great Lakes region from 1893 to 1933. The children were taken from their parents, often at a very young age, to attend government-run boarding schools intending to separate children from Anishinabe culture and assimilate them into White culture.

Some of the schools did better at teaching the kids life skills than others. Mostly they were used to do the work for the school, upkeep and growing crops. Some were boarded out for summer work. The death rate at some Indian schools in the U.S. and Canada was 50%. Medical care was insufficient, food was poor, and abuse was much.

Canada has formally apologized for the abuse of Native Children in their provinces. They are trying to change the educational system to have respect for the Natives. There have been major lawsuits settled on behalf of abused boys and girls.

Apology to the Native American Indian, by Dr. Mary Harmer M.D. (2009), is a long letter written to a Walpole Indian detailing abuses to Natives. It is found at Countercurrents.org/harmar081209.htn.

The Canadian Truth Commission had a report about boarding schools. They have issued a public apology to Native Canadians for the atrocities committed against them. There are many reverberations in Canada with abuse in Indian communities: there are many suicide epidemics in Canada, the North and West particularly. Many Native women disappear; many are raped and abused. Human trafficking is rampant in Michigan, Ontario, and on reservations. One in three Native Women will be raped. Eighty-eight percent of rapes are by non-native perpetrators.

The website *Students on Site* is a good resource for learning about boarding schools and Mission schools. There are many others across the Internet. The Canadian Truth Council's website is also a great source for further information.

CANADIAN TRUTH AND RECONCILIATION REPORT

The Canadian Truth and Reconciliation Council Commission sought out the truth of the Indian situation for six years, from 2008 to 2015. The idea was modeled after a study in South Africa.

In Canada, 150,000 children were removed from their communities to residential schools. There were 139 schools in Canada; 60 of these were run by the Catholic Church. More than 6,000 children died at these schools. The record-keeping of these horrors was very poor.

In 2002, nuns in Canada received eight months prison time for beating children. Indians never raised a hand to any child.

The schools operated from 1883 to 1996, the children were dying like flies. Sexual assaults were rampant by dormitory supervisors and others. There are 80,000 former students living today. 2.8 billion dollars have been paid in claims to victims of abuse to 36,000 people or 48% of the children at these schools. The number does not include former students who died prior to 2005 (Students on Site, Native American Missions and Schools).

The Royal Commission on Aboriginal Peoples in 1996 recommended ethical principles respecting aboriginal cultures and values, the historical origins of aboriginal nationhood and inherent right to Aboriginal self-determination, health and healing strategies, and public education to promote understanding.

The Catholic Sexual Abuse Survivor network of those abused by priests and others was first publicized in 1985. In 2002, minors came forward. A cover-up pattern was exposed. It became a crisis for the Catholic Church globally. There were hundreds of millions of settlements with 80% of the sex abuse of minors in the United States. It was about 4% of the priests, 4,392 men during 1950 to 2002. Many schools and parishes closed. It was a huge cover-up involving other churches and Protestant-run schools; there was over 25 billion awarded in lawsuits. 166.1 million dollars was awarded to Native Americans in the Pacific Northwest, 660 million in Los Angeles, and 198 million in San Diego.

The denial of the problem is over the reluctance to deal openly with the public about the nature and extent of the problem. Pressuring students into silence, the schools were the dumping grounds for problem priests and teachers. Children were beaten at home and school by paddle and fist.

Half of all Natives suffer abuse. It is not *if* raped, but *when*. The murder rate is 10 times the national average. There is no law enforcement at the federal level. 86% of crimes by White people against Natives go unpunished (Students on Site, Native American Missions and Schools).

The trauma of child abuse, brutalizing emotionally, physically, psychologically and spiritually, has been manifested in rampant suicide, alcoholism, drug abuse, and domestic violence that plague Indian country. The unrelenting tragedy of suffering, the ruin of lives, shame, despair, and violent death, poverty, ignorance, and disease have been the products of the BIA agencies work.

In the United States, the rampant abuse of the Natives by the authorities of the BIA, by schools, and by medical systems instituted by the government to abuse and destroy Native culture and people is atrocious, from outright theft to huge bribes to stealing resources belonging to the Natives. To sterilization of women to exterminate their unborn. Every evil tactic and vice has been allowed to perpetuate the extermination policy of the United States against the indigenous peoples. The continued exploitation is an evil that is just now being addressed; there are major lawsuits against the BIA and their exploitation of the Natives from its inception.

In the West, there is finally coming an accounting of the BIA and the great fraud and abuse against Indians and their land. Billions of dollars have been stolen from Indian land resources, and there are many lawsuits ongoing to regain land, resources and reimbursement for untold abuse.

There is hope in returning to the Indian values which are a great asset to humanity. The truth is finally coming out about the lies, racism, disease, alcohol, and propaganda used against Natives to take their great riches, their religion, and loving culture.

President Obama has made an apology in 2009 that has been kept quiet. This is an outrage. The American people are being kept dumb and uninformed.

Enos Whiteye of Walpole Island wrote a book about his experience in boarding school in Ontario. In *A Dark Legacy*, he tells his story: many were repeatedly raped, many were beaten daily.

Our Seventh Prophecy gave us new reason for hope; it told us we could become a New People. Many are returning to our culture and traditions, restarting clan relationships. Our nation is being reborn. The sacred fire is being revived through diversity, acceptance, and equality in our own communities.

The Bureau of Indian Affairs has issued an apology. It can be found on the Internet at *Tuhtonka, World Future Feed*. The BIA has had a covert policy toward Indians; a policy of ethnic cleansing has been in effect since the 1830s. A less than human stereotyping that leads to shallow and ignorant beliefs. A policy of grand theft of resources designated for Indian benefit and use. A policy of hate and violence, destruction and annihilation. Their language, religion, and tribal ways were taken from them for a long time. Their children were seized and taken from them; they were taught to be ashamed of who they are.

Hitler used North American Indian policy as his model of holocaust. The 500 Year War against the Indians has been called "The American Indian Holocaust". The world's longest holocaust in the history of mankind and loss of human lives—500 years of hate crimes. It was mass death and mass evil. The bodies were used for dog food. Sterilization and poor medical care had been used into the 1970s.

The time of dying is at its end. Shame and fear are over. We are replacing anger with hope and love. There is a rebirth of joy, freedom, and progress.

Most young people with Indian Metis (mixed-blood) or full Indian-blooded were taught that the Indians were bad. Many were not told that they had Indian blood to keep them from the stymie and racism that was rampant in White schools. Their parents did not claim their heritage to protect their children from boarding schools and other traumatic ways. They were told a lot of nasty things about Indians, mostly lies. Many adults will not talk about their experiences at these boarding schools, as they were a horror to live and witness, nor will they share much about the Indians' history. They were brought up to be ashamed of being an Indian. There were actual laws made that a person could not say they were Indian. Many, many people were Metis in Ontario and along the waterway borders. Many Indians were threatened by authorities and other figures to never talk about being an Indian, speak the language, or practice any traditional ways.

On the reserves, they were not allowed to earn a living as they wished, but often were dictated to as to what they could do and were opposed in every way in doing it. They were not to be tradespeople. Many were soldiers for the U.S. and Canadian governments, for it is a privilege and honor to the Indian to do difficult assignments without complaint.

The Indians were erased from modern society; they were invisible, excluded, silenced. In fact, most people hardly knew they were living amongst them. There has been a revisionist history by the Europeans and has been perpetuated as a nostalgic past. It has hidden the brutal and genocidal legacy of U.S. history. The Indians were reduced to tenants on their ancestral homelands. Congress was given absolute power over Indian lands and lives without their consent, and in opposition to the purpose of hundreds of treaties, under the rhetoric of benevolence and civilization (Decolonization, www).

The Natives are reclaiming their culture with self-determination, taking control of their own schools and communities. The Indian agents are losing their grip over Native lives.

Here are some Internet sites for further study: MIIBS, Attiwapiskat, NABS; National healing coalition, Russel Means; Indian Boarding Schools, Auschwitz in Canada and the U.S, Newsvine, Grisham; White Bison, WKAR survivor stories, Detroit, and 10 lies about Indians, K Porterfield; Counter currents.org, *Apology to The Native American Indians*, by Dr. Mary Harmer, M.D. dedicated to Onikwit, Ojibwe from Walpole Island, Ont. Canada; an apology from the BIA at Tuhtonka, World Future Feed; Ancestry free page, School Records.

There are 1,500 projects across the country, a healing movement of 100 years of forced institutionalization. It was not until 1965 that Michigan, under special Federal and State legislation, had legal rights for any dealing with its Native Americans. Congress and the War Department were over the Bureau of Indian Affairs. One of the Bureau's responsibilities was to direct procedures for Indian treaties. In 1849, the Bureau was moved to the newly established Department of the Interior where it has remained.

Tens of millions of dollars were spent on anthropologists to make reports, to reduce the people they study to objects, instead of treating them as human beings. This is scientific racism (Russell Means, Where White Men Fear to Tread).

A huge hoax was perpetrated upon Michigan and the nation when men, Scotford and Soper, tampered with original artifacts, adding a cuneiform style and mystic symbol. They made claim that these were relics unearthed, when in fact many were manufactured. These relics were sold as artifacts. Some were crowns said to be lifted from the heads of ancient kings and copies of Noah's diary. In 1911, they were determined to be a hoax of the lowest order. Their aim was to convince people that the Phoenicians had in fact been in America thousands of years before Columbus was born. Many priests believed the ruse, lending credence to the hoax (Nailhed, www).

The problem of stereotyping is not so much a racial problem as it is a problem of limited knowledge and perspective. "And who, down to the lowest idiot, will not think blind and downright malicious those who dare to spread this belief and defame so many people, saying Indians need tutors because they are incapable of organization, when in reality they have kings and governors, villages, houses, and property rights" (Fray Bartolome De Las Casas, Spanish Missionary, 1511).

The Indians contributed much to our modern life, (the following is a) a partial list of products: corn, popcorn, wild rice, squash, pumpkins, peanuts, cranberries, chewing gum, chocolate – cacao, tapioca, beans, maple syrup, potatoes, tomatoes, pineapples, avocado, turkey, clam bakes, pemmican, jerky, vanilla, cotton, rubber, quinine, and tobacco, to name a few. In addition, over 1,000 types of pharmaceuticals, freeze dried food, syringes, root beer, rubberized clothing, peppers, strawberries, many tenants of the Constitution, the number zero, and interstate highways over Indian trails (K. Porterfield, "10 lies about Indigenous Science).

The indigenous people were experts in plant breeding and genetics. Over half the world's present food supply comes from the American Indians' agriculture, primarily corn and potatoes (Antell/MCGAA DSS, Publication 137, St. Paul Minn. /Library of MI).

What cannot be obtained by moral right is being achieved by legal right (Metis Timeline, www). The journey for Forgiveness Marches begin the healing process in 2009; the White Bison Group lead a local march at the Mount Pleasant Boarding School (Ziibiiwing).

The Indians survived. They were determined to save their race and their nations. They held their treaty documents, and the Federal Government was forced to explain, justify, or rescind their actions (Herman Cameron).

SAGINAW CHIPPEWA

The Ziibiwing Cultural Center, is in Mount Pleasant, Michigan. Ziibiwing Center of Anishinabe Culture and Lifeways and Tribal Museum is the Midwest's premier American Indian Museum. There is a permanent display and a changing display of history and artifacts, art and archival documents. The Nindakenjigewinoong Research Center, is a wonderful place for research, it is located, in the Ziibiwing Cultural Center. There is a Gift Shop with books, and much more. It is located east of Mount Pleasant Michigan, adjacent to the Soaring Eagle Casino, and the Tribal Offices.

The Saginaw Chippewa operate, Soaring Eagle Casino for entertainment. It is east of Mount Pleasant, Michigan on tribal land. There is a hotel on the property and many others nearby. The Saganing Eagles Landing Casino in Standish, Michigan is also a Saginaw Chippewa Casino.

The Saginaw Chippewa currently maintain and utilize 6 cemeteries throughout the Central Michigan area. They also work with the State of Michigan to care for the Sanilac Petroglyphs, where cultural teachings and ceremonies are conducted.

INDIAN QUOTES

"Not to know is bad; not to want to know is worse" (Metis Timeline, www).

BLACK ELK

"It is from understanding that power comes. Nothing can live well except in a manner suited to the way the Sacred Power of the world lives and moves."

"Whenever the truth comes upon the world, it is like rain. The world is happier after the terror of the storm."

"Truth comes with two faces: one sad and suffering, the other laughs."

"Give me strength to walk the soft earth, a relative to all that is. Give me eyes to see and strength to understand, that I may be like you. With your power only can I face the winds."

"Once we were happy on our own country and seldom hungry. The many came, dirty with lies and greed."

"The fighting was about the yellow metal that they worship and that makes them crazy."

"My father is with me, and there is no great father between me and the Great Spirit."

OTHERS

"Men get fat by being bad and starve by being good" (Crazy Horse).

"Understanding – with this on Earth, you shall undertake anything and do it" (Sacred Flames).

"Whosoever controls the education of our children controls the future" (Chief, Wilma Mankiller).

"Almost always the creative dedicated minority has made the world better" (Martin Luther King).

"True power does not amass through the pain and suffering of others" (Jay Harjo).

"The Indian was despised for his poverty and simplicity; our culture forbade accumulation of wealth and enjoyment of luxury. It was considered a snare and burden, a needless peril and temptation. The Indian kept his spirit free from the clog of pride, cupidity, or envy and carried out the Divine Decree, a matter of profound importance to him" (Charles Eastman, The Soul of the Indian).

The first effects of Whites, was an increase of cruelty and barbarity. Even the Sun Dance was perverted and abused; it became a horrible exhibition and was prohibited by the government.

The Church spoke of the spiritual, seeking only the material, bought and sold everything. The lust for money and power and conquest was in contrast with the spirit of the meek and lowly Jesus, the unwritten scripture, a living Bible sowed as precious seed, as Jesus told the parables to each as necessary. The whole created universe is a sharer of God's Spirit, of the immortal perfection of its Maker (C. Eastman).

The Church, education, and the government colluded to wipe out the Anishinabe Constitution, to assimilate and erase our language, spirituality, and world views. We became a magnet for predators in a vortex of sexual, economic, land, and resource exploitation. The ongoing historical trauma has created self-oppression and social sickness and dysfunction (Flocken, UMN, 2013).

The last of the Mohican is alive and well, West of Green Bay Wisconsin (Iroquois Whoa, www).

"Don't knock a man down and ask why he lives in the dirt. Don't strip a man of clothing then ask why he is naked. Don't filch him of authority and the right to rule his home, his dignity as a man, and then ask why his culture is substandard" (Chief Dan George 1966).

"No European language has more sweetness and greatness than the Indian. There are 147 sounds in the whole language God gave to them" (William Penn 1900. Metis Timeline, www).

"The False Faces brought greed and destruction of the Earth; the rivers run with poison, the fish are unfit to eat" (Ziibiwing).

The seven teachings that the Creator gave us (are) love, respect, bravery, honesty, humility, wisdom, and truth. The Creator gave us the Seventh Fire, seven teachings - values to the world. The Creator has given great healing, courage, strength, and protection of our beautiful way of life.

"Fly like a butterfly and stand firm like a bear" (Ziibiwing).

"The principle of direct action is the defiant insistence on acting as if one is already free!" (David Graeber, The Guardian).

From the Democracy Project: "the democracy of riot squads, corrupt politicians, magnate-controlled newspapers, a surveillance state is as phony and fragile as East Germany 30 years ago."

"As long as you fear you cannot experience true freedom" (Russel Means).

"Black means cleanliness and purity, as the thunder clouds are black and bring the cleansing, purifying, and life-giving rain. One of the holy paint colors" (Means).

"Silence is a sign of respect" (Means).

"Christopher Columbus, the exterminator, said, 'they are a people so peace-loving and generous as if to a fault. Therefore, they would make excellent slaves'" (Means).

"We, in endeavoring to assist you, it seems we have wrought our own ruin." – A Wea Indian after the 1783 British surrender of U.S. lands.

THE NATIVE INDIAN PRAYER

"Oh, Great Spirit, whose voice I hear in the winds and whose breath gives life to all the world – hear me – I come before you, one of your children. I am small and weak. I need Your strength and wisdom. Let me walk in beauty and make my eyes ever behold the red and purple sunset. Make my hands respect the things You have made, my ears sharp to hear your voice. Make me wise, so that I may know the things you have taught my people, the lesson You have hidden in every leaf and rock. I seek strength not to be superior to my brothers, but to be able to fight my greatest enemy, myself. Make me ever ready to come to you, with clean hand and straight eyes, so when life fades as a fading sunset, my spirit may come to you without shame" (Yellow Hawk, Sioux Chief).

"Great Maker pity us, your two-legged creation" (Tunkashila).

"The world is one; we are all connected" (Tunkashila).

CHAPTER 16
Early St. Clair County Pioneers

British Lieutenant Patrick Sinclair in 1765 was the first permanent British-English settler along the St. Clair River, and the only one until 1772. Sinclair purchased 3,759 acres from the Chippewa Indians, and the fort post was active from 1765 to 1782. It was a pinery with a mill and fields for crops. Sinclair supplied posts in the Upper Great Lakes and sent lumber to Detroit.

Nimekance, or "Lightening", served under St. Clair, helping to build Fort Sinclair Trading Post and working there for Sinclair, and lived near Judge Bunce. He grew corn nearby the judge's home, still attending his fields at 105 years old. Nimikance lived to 112 years old.

The British engaged the Hessians Aux. Reg. from Germany to fight the Americans during the Revolutionary War. Many of these men settled in Upper Canada, now Southern Ontario. After the Revolutionary War, many Pennsylvania German, Plain Folk, Mennonites, Dunkards, Moravians, Amish, and Hutterite emigrated to Canada.

Bouvier and LaSalle came in 1785, North of the fort, and claimed land.

Denis Causlet, a Frenchman, was the first White settler in now Port Huron, settling near the mouth of Black River before 1790. Causlet and Peter Brandamour were couriers in the service of the French traders who deserted and came to live among the Indians at Black River. Brandamour, also a Frenchman, located on land in now Port Huron two years after Causlet. Peter Jr. was born at Port Huron in 1802, being one of the oldest settler families in St. Clair County. James, Peter's son, was a raftsman in the lumber business. Rufus, another son, as a boy played with the bow and arrow and canoe with the Indian boys and ran errands for the officers at Fort Gratiot. He, too, was in the lumber business. Frank Brandamour was the first White child born in St. Clair County.

Peter Bonhomme, or Burnham, built a log house at Fort Gratiot. Racine had a house at the foot of Butler Street. The other French families who had come to live on Black River – Riviere Dulude – were Francois Laviere, Baptiste Levais, J.B. Duchesne, Michel Jervais, J.B. Corneais, Peter Moreaux, M. Duprey, and the two brothers Burnham. They were permitted to build shanties and cultivate small patches of land on the flats.

The name "Delude" was after a man who was drowned in the river. They called this place Desmond (St. Clair County).

Jacob Hill owned land on the St. Clair River previous to 1796 near Algonac. Ignace Champagne owned land on the St. Clair River previous to 1796 near Algonac. Pierre and Joseph Mini and Joseph Bassinet were also land claimants prior to 1796 near Algonac on the St. Clair River. McNiff, James Robertson, and Rowe were also early land claimants. Also, Antoine Nicholas Petit, Jean Marie Beaubien, Fontenoy, Toussaint Chovin, James Cartwright, John Wright, and McDonald.

"George Cottrell was born in Detroit and came up the river about 1781. The Cottrell family were the earliest settlers on the River St. Clair. He married Archangel Minnie Cottrell. She was born on the river. He built a store and trading post with a palisade around it and hired Frenchmen to guard it" (Fuller). Captain George Cottrell had three sons and one daughter. Henry was the sheriff, and David the associate judge.

The Negro, Harry, a faithful worker of Meldrum and Park, was given a farm near St. Clair.

Cotton Point was in the South of St. Clair County on the St. Clair River. Francois Marsac bought the land in 1808.

Jacob Harsen from Holland came from New York during the American Revolution. A gunsmith and fur trader, in 1778 he received a grant of 3,000 acres of land from the Indians. It was then called Harsens Island. In 1783, he bought Jacobs, or James, Island from the Indians. He had three sons: Jacob, George, and Frank. Jacob came to Michigan on horseback from New York. He was an associate of John Jacob Astor in the Fur Trade. His daughter and son-in-law, Isaac Graveraet, a silversmith, came with him and worked with him. A grandson, James Harsen, was accidently shot by John Riley, the Black River Chief in 1810 or 1811.

Henry Robertson was born in Cottrellville about 1790. He was a captain on the lakes, sailing the *Gratiot*, one of the first steamers on the River St. Clair.

Ottissippi

In 1780, James Thompson received a deed to the island, Pakassanecayank, of five Chippewa chiefs. It was also called Laughtons, Dickinsons, Stromness, St. Clair, and Thompsons Island. Asa C. Dickinson received a deed from the Indians in 1780.

"Antoine Morass worked at James Baby's Mill at Baby Creek, now Bunce Creek, in Marysville, Michigan, on the St. Clair River. Negig, an Indian chief, lived on this land. Morass then worked for Judge Abbott at Abbottsford, running his mill called Morass mill. The Abbottsford Mill was on Mill Creek – Gorse Creek, near Black River.

Bonhomme, or Burnham, bought land on the south side of Black River, known as the Campau Tract. He also bought land where Fort Gratiot was to be built" (Adapted from, Jenks, 1912).

"Other early settlers of the township include James Gill, B. Sturgis, S. Hueling, James Young, and A.F. Ashley. When they arrived, it was covered in forest and was Indian country. After the U.S. took possession of this land from the British in 1796, soldiers received bounty lands for part of their pay for their service to the country. Many sold their bounties to men who would buy up many lands for huge parcels of land ownership.

Thomas Knapp built the first settlers store on Quay Street at Black River in now Port Huron.

George McDougal was the keeper of the Fort Gratiot lighthouse built in 1822. He was also a territorial general, officer of the militia, postmaster, and a lawyer. George and his brother, John, sold their inheritance, Belle Isle, to William Macomb, a slaveholder. Their father, George McDougal Sr. of the Royal Navy, obtained a grant of land from King George III, who obtained the deed from the Chippewa and Ottawa Indians with goods. George had a negro boy valet who combed, oiled, and brushed out his voluminous wig.

Jonathan Burtch built a store on the north side of Black River near 7th Street. It was the first frame store in Desmond. He operated a lumber business and farmed. Daniel Harrington worked in his store and later bought out his employer" (Adapted from, Jenks). Burtch came in October 1828, he built and owned the Central Hotel in 1834. He later went into lumbering at Lakeport and Alpena.

"Joseph B. Comstock and his brother, Alfred, opened a General Store in Desmond – Port Huron – in 1835" (Jenks).

"John Riley, the half-breed Ojibwe chief, lived at the Black River near Military Street and the St. Clair River. He operated a trading post and was very important to the U.S. Government and the Ojibwe Indians. Riley Township is named after John Riley. He built two houses, one on the west side of Black River.

A road was called for by the Board in 1824 to run from John Riley's to Morass's mills on Black River.

Jacob Kendall came in 1825 and purchased land near Algonac. He held every township office in Clay Township, except constable. John B. Kendall, his son, was once sheriff of St. Clair.

Edward Petit was a fur trader who lived near John Riley in Port Huron. His family was the earliest family living in Port Huron, Michigan in 1788 along with the Natives. Anselm Petit (his father) was the only resident on the assessment roll of 1821 for Port Huron" (Adapted from, Jenks 1912). "Edward Petit was born in 1813 in a log house built by his father near the present foot of Court Street in Port Huron. A sister married McDougal who kept slaves, two of them named Jo and Callette. Anselm helped build Fort Gratiot. Edward attended the missionary school at Fort Gratiot. The teachers were John Hudson and Mr. Hart, who taught there for three years before removing to Mackinaw. These were Edward's only lessons, learned in a box of sand. Edward hunted and fished with the Indian boys. He learned their language, his parents' French, and English from the new settlers, all spoken fluently. He was well equipped for the fur trade being employed from boyhood. He told of Old Father Badin visiting at his father's house, and at St. Ann's Church in Detroit, he received the sacraments of the Roman Catholic Church from Pere Richard" (History of St. Clair County, Michigan, Western Historical Co.).

"Edward platted land where the homestead farm of 19 acres was at Court Street. The village was called Peru. These lots were the beginning of Port Huron, Michigan.

The bears were very plenteous and disputed with the inhabitants the right to fresh meats which were not under lock and key" (History of SCCMI, Western Historical Co. p. 144).

"Baubien settled in 1781. Westbrook later bought his claim in St. Clair" (Fuller).

Captain Robertson lived south of Marine City. He caught large quantities of whitefish on the St. Clair River.

Captain Thorn came West before 1770. He was a ship pilot in the fur trade and the military for both the British and Americans. He lived in Detroit for a time and then settled at Cottrellville, North of Algonac, in 1783. His sons were William and John. John owned and plotted the first village lots in Port Huron. He had three daughters: one married James Fulton, the Founder of St. Clair, one married Andrew Westbrook. Captain Thorn was famous for being the first captain to pass through the St. Mary's River at Sault. Saint Marie between Lake Huron and Lake Superior. He was arrested as a British spy after having sailed for the British for 20 years. He also named Put In Bay, Ohio. When his crew ran out of provisions, he and his crew were reduced to eating a flour and water mixture called putin or pudding, which later became Put In Bay.

William Thorn of the River Sinclair in 1789 sold land to Meldrum and Park of Detroit. Meldrum and Park purchased a large tract of land by deed, with 27 Indian chiefs confirming the purchase in 1788 made to Patrick Sinclair. One Vatiren, a Canadian, received the lands to dispose of as he wished when Patrick Sinclair left the country in 1782. The land was sold at auction in 1784; it was four miles deep, and the survey indicated 33,759 acres. Five families settled on the land as squatters in 1800, one as a tenant of Meldrum and Park, and nineteen farmers claim, under Indian deeds in 1780 and 1782. George Knaggs was a tenant.

George Meldrum had sons: John, James, William, and David.

In 1790, Jarvais, or Gervais, settled on Indian Creek, it was renamed Jarvais Creek.

In 1796, when the Americans claimed the eastern shore of Michigan, Captain William Thorn, Captain Paschal, Robertson, William Brown, Joseph Minne, Captain John Cottrell, and Captain Alexander Harrow claimed lands near Algonac as war bounties.

Mr. Chortier, Shirkey, Minne, Basney, and William Hill were early residents of Pt. Aux Tremble, near now New Baltimore.

William Macomb purchased Grosse Isle and Stoney Island, an area some 6,000, acres. He established 10 tenants on them. He supplied the military fort with trade goods. He had 26 slaves. He also bought Belle Isle from George McDougal and his brother, John, who had inherited it from their father, George Sr.

William Brown and his wife, Martha Thorn Brown, purchased land in 1806 from the Indians on the St. Clair River opposite St. Clair City, living here until 1814. Choosing to be Americans, they removed to Cherry Beach two miles South of Marine City in St. Clair County. Captain William Brown resided in Canada on the St. Clair River. He was the father of Nancy Brakeman. He took the Oath of American Citizenship and moved in 1814 to the other side of the river in Macomb, then near Cherry Beach in Algonac. William Brown was born in British Detroit in 1774. His playmates were the French and Indian boys. He spoke three languages fluently: French, English, and Indian. His parents settled at Cottrellville. He went sailing for Judge Abbott. He married the daughter of Old Captain Thorn. He worked for the government as a carpenter and sutler. He kept a public house for 30 years. He was known as "Uncle Billy Brown". He was appointed the first coroner of St. Clair County and served twelve years and was elected three times. He was postmaster of the township. He built the first dock between Detroit and Marine City and sold wood for boats and vessels running between Buffalo and Chicago. He kept a fur trading post and farmed. He was the first subscriber to the *Detroit Free Press* from this county. His daughter, Anna, married Peter Brakeman.

Morttenger came in 1814.

The Brakemans first lived in the township of Moore, County of Kent, Upper Canada. In the summer, travel was by sail boats and canoes; in the winter, carioles and French trains on the ice. There were no roads in those days.

Peter F. Brakeman was a fur trader who did extensive trade with the Indians at Cottrellville, buying up grain and flint corn to sell at Mackinac. The grain was grown on Harsens Island and Walpole Island. He built the first dock and warehouse in Port Huron built on the river. He was a farmer, supplying the Fort Gratiot. He moved to Willow Creek in then Sanilac County, now Huron City in Huron County, where he engaged in lumbering in 1847. He and his partner owned a steam mill, one of the first between Saginaw and Lexington, Michigan. See "Peter Brakeman" in "Chapter 6: Trade and Traders".

Joseph Campau and Robert Abbott were large business owners operating out of Detroit.

Captain Francoise Marsac came around 1798 to Tremble Creek near New Baltimore, Michigan and, prior to 1790, to Swan Creek four miles from New Baltimore.

Cartright owned Cartright Island near Algonac. Chartier, or Chortier, lived near Algonac. He was a trapper and raised ponies, feeding them on the prairie at Duchene.

Harvey Stewart operated a small distillery on Harsens Island. He married Mr. Graveraet's daughter. Graveraet came to Harsens Island and worked in the silversmith business. He married Jacob Harsen's daughter.

Alexander Harrone, or Harrow, owned a large tract of 14,400 acres, deeded by the Indians. He was a ship captain and lieutenant and commander of the Naval Armament in the wars along with Captain Thorn, as both a British and American lake pilot. He transported the officers of the wars. He built a distillery on his land North of Algonac. Captain Harrow's plantation was called "Newburgh".

Peter Yax lived near St. Clair. Recorr was an early settler near Marine City.

Alexander St. Bernard furnished lumber for St. Anne's Church in Detroit, and the rebuilding of Detroit in 1805, from his father Louis St. Bernard's timber. He piloted the *Grand Turk*, the first boat built at St. Clair,

Ottissippi

and worked carrying supplies for the government to Chicago at Fort Dearborn. He also piloted the first iron warship in America, if not the first in the world. For the next quarter of a century, he remained in government service.

James Fulton bought land of Meldrum and Park's and laid out the village of St. Clair. He sold his interest to Thomas Palmer of Detroit. This was the first village on the St. Clair River.

In St. Clair County in 1807, there were 51 land claims. The remaining land was Indian land until the Treaty of 1807, which ceded Southeast Michigan to the U.S. Government.

In 1809, *The Michigan Essay* and *The Impartial Observer* were the State's first newspapers by James M. Miller.

John Riley, the half-breed, owned the site of Port Huron until 1836. He was a Great Spirit and chief of the bands near Port Huron and across the river in Ontario. His home was on Military and 6th Street next to the great burial mound on Water Street where now stands the federal building. This was the Indian reservation set aside for the Indians' use in the 1807 Treaty of Detroit.

In 1816, numerous families of Indians resided on Black River: Old Black Snake, numerous family related to John Riley, and a strong-built Indian called Black Duck.

John Riley accidently shot Mr. James Harsen, who died 6 months later. "All inhabitants were accustomed to bear arms for protection and hunting. There was a well-organized militia. George Cottrel was Lieutenant Colonel" (Jenks 1912).

"Louis Facer owned a farm at Quay Street, and in his house, he inaugurated inn keeping in 1821" (Western Historical Co.).

"Daniel B. Harrington was a civic promoter of Port Huron, possessed with great executive energy. He made pencils and clerked in Z.W. Bunce's store at Fort Gratiot. He was a fur trader and founded the first newspaper, founding two newspapers in total. He was also a lumberman, banker, railroad man, and lawyer and built the Lapeer Plank Road, 80 miles west into the wilderness to Brockway, opening up the West for development. He helped organize the city government of Port Huron in 1857. He was the first president of the First National Bank and the Port Huron Savings Bank. He was postmaster of Port Huron and a state senator. Early voting was done at his farm on Black River. His biography is found in "Chapter 6: Trade and Traders".

Jeremiah Harrington bought land at Black River.

Lambert Minnie lived at Algonac; his father came in 1790.

John Oakes engaged in lumbering on Black River. He built mills on the river and then moved to St. Clair and farmed. He held many offices in the township.

Sam Ward came in 1818 to the mouth of Belle River and laid out the village of Marine City – Newport. This was the second village on the St. Clair River. He operated a tavern there and then proceeded in shipbuilding. Sam was appointed associate judge of the County Seat. Z.W. Bunce was the Chief Justice, and David Oaks was associate judge" (Adapted from, Jenks, 1912). He became a very prosperous man. More steamboats and sail vessels have been built in these shipyards than anywhere else in the State.

Eber Ward was the wealthiest man in the State of Michigan.

Crocket McElroy was a shipbuilder, merchant, manufacturer of staves and salt, timber ranger, and mayor of St. Clair. As State Senator, he was a great reformer of early Frontier life, changing railroad laws, roadway laws, village and city laws, and protection laws. He was the man who first used hydraulic water in the mining of salt. Due to his judgment, ingenuity, and persistence, the Salt Industry was established in St. Clair County.

Henry Whiting lived at St. Clair, Michigan.

John Swartout came with his sons; they settled near Algonac.

"Joseph Watson owned land east of Military Street. In 1817, the town of Montgats was Joseph Watson's town on the south side of Black River at the mouth. He sold a parcel to Michel Kelly, who built a house which was used for a store and tavern for many years. The street called Water Street was barely 24 feet wide, very narrow, and then called Mill Street" (Mitts, D., The Times Herald, SCC Library, MI Room). Mill Street led to the water mill of Monsieur Gervais at the outlet of Indian Creek – Riviere Gervais – on the south bank of Black River, just east of 7th Street" (Mitts, D.).

"John K. Smith came to Detroit with the army and settled at Stromness Island as a potter in 1818. He then began a store and went on to become probate judge and chief justice of the county under Governor Louis Cass. He was appointed deputy collector of customs and was the first postmaster in the county. As justice of the peace at Point Office and Algonac, he heard cases from all over the county, and his business exceeded that of the county court for many years. He was a great peacemaker, and he had a greater record of marriages than any of the justices in St. Clair County. He had great judgment and was straightforward and conscientious to duty.

John M. Robertson was a captain on the lakes and enlisted in Co. 1 First Michigan Engineers during the Civil War. He became a lawyer and lighthouse keeper at the Upper Light on the St. Clair Flats ship canal.

Ottissippi

Abram Smith, son of John K., carried mail as a young man. He engaged in lumbering and built ships. He held various offices of the county and school.

At Pte. Aux Tremble were four families: Chartier, Minnie, Basney, and Hill.

Shortly after John K. Smith settled in Point Office and Algonac, Ira Marks, Ebenezer Westbrook, and Silas Miller bought land south of him to the Point.

Other men from near St. Clair and Marine City were William Gallagher, Amasa Memmenger, Hamilton, John Fish, Carleton, Charles Larned, Bassenet, Charles Phillips, Everett Beardsley, and Stephen Rose.

At Marine City, an immense ship building trade ensued. There was a large tannery at St. Clair and at Port Huron called English and Walker, and D. Sheldon was superintendent at both. He also had a large brickyard at St. Clair.

Zephaniah W. Bunce's grandfathers, Bunce and Drake, were sea captains, owning their own vessels in the East. They dealt in foreign commerce, the West Indies Trade, privateering prisoners of the British pirates who escaped. Zephaniah learned the Hatter Trade and was a fur buyer for his uncle. He was also a great horseman who had many near-death experiences on the icy rivers.

Judge Bunce headed to Michigan with a one-horse wagon with 8,000 dollars-worth of ready-made clothing and other goods for Detroit. He came on a ship from Buffalo to Detroit in 1817. Judge Bunce arrived in St. Clair County in the fall of 1817. He sold his goods at Detroit for one year and then lived as a bachelor, later marrying his wife, Laura Ann Duryea. He traveled extensively throughout the territory and knew every man in Michigan. He built the only house in the area at Bunce Creek, formerly Baby Creek, now in Marysville, Michigan. Bunce owned land on the St. Clair River, four miles in length and a half a mile back. There were no houses in Port Huron then. The land became known as Bunceville.

General Cass, Territorial Governor of Michigan, was a frequent visitor at the Bunce Homestead. He appointed Joseph Bunce, Zephaniah's brother, as territorial judge. Joseph returned East and Zephaniah was appointed.

The Bunce Mill site was built in 1828 at Bunce Creek, where the judge was a trader and supplier to the military and settlers. At this site, there were mills built in 1697 and 1738. The lumber was sent to the Detroit dock built by Mr. Baby. Judge Bunce also kept a store at Fort Gratiot. Daniel Harrington worked for him for a time in 1828.

He built the road from his home to Fort Gratiot at Lake Huron in 1827 and a road, 20 miles south of his place toward Swan Creek in the now Southern part of St. Clair County. The roads were nearly impassible in spring and fall. He operated two sawmills for Judge Abbott, then bought one for himself in Clyde Township and then in Burtchville. Judge Bunce employed many Indians called 'Bunce's Indians'. Z.W. Bunce was justice of the peace and colonel of the 3rd Michigan Militia. He then became the chief justice of the county courts along with Sam Ward and David Oaks Associates. Then Bunce became probate judge, then worked in the Michigan Legislature. He lived to 102 years old.

He with his brother, Horace, who came in 1825, were in the lumbering and trading businesses. He built a gristmill in the town of Abbottsford in Clyde Township, also lumbering and farming. Judge Bunce moved to Abbottsford in 1833, where he kept a boarding house for his people working the Lumber Trade at Abbottsford. Smith Humphrey kept the boarding house for Judge Bunce. Judge Bunce lived here until 1846, moving back to Bunceville at Bunce Creek on the St. Clair River" (Adapted from, Jenks 1912).

"Judge Bunce employed many Indians at his businesses; they were called 'Bunce's Indians'. They were lumberman and loggers in his mills and trade post. Some came across the river to work for him. He had many great friends, both Red and White. The Indians camped at Abbottsford and at Bunce Creek when working for the judge in the logging and trading businesses.

At Abbottsford in now Clyde Township, Ignace Morass built a sawmill in 1816. James Abbot purchased and rebuilt this mill and also purchased a gristmill built by Z.W. Bunce. A post office operated here from 1892 to 1942. There were over eight hotels in the area and many boarding houses for the men who worked in the lumber camps along Black River and Mill Creek.

The area around Ruby and along Black River into Grant Township is a state game area. Most of this land was formerly owned by the Beards and Glyshaws, comprising over 7,000 acres. Before Black River was obstructed with dams, sturgeon, pike, and mullet went far up this stream to deposit eggs at the spawning streams. During the logging era, often the sturgeon were late in getting down and would be in deep holes, waiting for a flood, and the Indians would capture them.

Judge Bunce had many trials by travel in water, ice, and mud. He seemed to have nine lives. A great birthday celebration was made for Judge Bunce at his 100th year. He was much-loved and memorialized. Judge Bunce died in 1889. He was known throughout the Northwest Territory. He had two sons, Mumford and Lefferts, and one daughter, Louise Ann. Of the Pioneer Sunday School, the Judge was a member. He was bright, witty and kind, loved and respected.

Horace Bunce, brother of Zephaniah, arrived in 1825 and lumbered with his brother and farmed. He was a member of the State Legislature in 1860. He married Martha J. Westbrook. He also built a gristmill at Abbottsford.

Ottissippi

General Cass was a frequent visitor to Judge Bunce's place, many times conducting government business at his home on the St. Clair River" (Adapted from, MPHC, vol. 1, O.C. Thompson).

The Dorsey House Restaurant and Tavern was built in 1847, serving travelers and lumbermen. It was formerly called the Halfway House, being halfway between Port Huron and Brockway Center – Yale. It was then called the Wildcat Hotel. The Dorsey House was on the Wildcat Road at Port Huron to Lapeer Plank Road, now Beard Road – M136 at Wildcat Rd. in Clyde Township, St. Clair County. There were five or six rooms above the tavern and a blacksmith shop in back where people had their horses shoed. They would stay the night. It was known for its great meals and dancing was, a big draw on the weekends. A gun fight – duel – was said to have taken place in the back yard at the hotel. The original building has been replaced with a modern building.

The Handy Brothers Railroad used rails for their sugar factory. They built the trestle over Mill Creek at Ruby. This huge trestle no longer exists, though it was a great feat in its day.

"The first minister of the Gospel in 1818 was Mr. Dickson at the Methodist Episcopal Church on Harsens Island" (Brakeman/Jenks 1912).

Land was not open for sale to the public domain until 1818. The price was $2.00 per acre, one-fourth down and the remainder the second, third, and fourth year with 6% interest. Few purchases were made under those terms. In 1820, the price was amended and reduced to $1.25 per acre, cash, all credit being abolished. There were no sales until 1823 and very few until Hartford Tingley from Providence R.I. purchased speculation land of 3,500 acres in 18 sections. Almost half the county was purchased in speculation between 1830 and 1836.

Section 16 of every township was granted to the State for schools, and all salt springs within the State, up to 12, with 6 sections of land adjoining were to be State land, selected by 1840. "Local government was often conducted in homes and the local taverns, the one place large enough to accommodate large gatherings" (Lauriston). "Railroad lands were also set aside, including 3,568 acres in St. Clair County. W.R. Bowes, Augustus D. Griswold, and Amos Gould were the men authorized to administer these lands. Railroad lands were given to railroad companies to build a railroad within 10 years.

All swamp land belonged to the State, including 29,552 acres in St. Clair County. The legislation of the nation and the state were negligent in carrying out this law. Nearly six million acres were patented to the state as swamp land, and much of the land was not swamp but high and well-timbered with pine and other valuable wood. Much was sold at greatly discounted costs. Many fortunes were made this way, buying timber land worth 10 to 30 dollars per acre, at a dollar per acre in cash: 'Frittered away by neglect and reckless donations of the legislature until nothing of value is now left to the people. A few have been enriched with no benefit to the great mass of our citizens. Wasted to the lasting injury of its sons and daughters'" (Jenks, History of St. Clair County Michigan, 1912, vol. 1).

"In 1821, the only taxpayers living in Algonac were Silas Miller, Ira Marks, and Angus McDonald.

In 1824, Catholic Point – near Marine City – was purchased for a Mission by Reverend Father Gabriel Richard of Detroit. In 1826, Rev. Pierre DeJean built Saint Felicite here, the first Catholic church in the county. When the St. Mary's River and St. Clair River were dredged for shipping, Lake St. Clair became deeper and the church was rebuilt on higher ground. The first foundation and cemetery are flooded over and under preservation. Also in 1826, Ira Marks and Ebenezer Westbrook bought land in section 10, now Ira Township, and built the Methodist Episcopal Church, the first Protestant church building in the county" (Jenks, 1912).

"Henry Baird and his son, William Baird, Scotch Colonists from the Jones Colony, came to Port Huron in 1828. The town was a mere struggling Hamlet skirting the river bank. They settled in China Township in the blacksmith trade and later went into the lumber business. William Baird worked at Andrew Westbrook's shop, a pioneer workman at the forge. His brother was Dr. Robert E. Baird, living at Marine City. William served as a lieutenant of Co. K, the U.S. Red Colored Unit famous as sharpshooters, in the Civil War. He was taken prisoner and suffered horribly. He went into the lumbering business at St. Clair and was a lawyer, postmaster, and a salt manufacturing with his brother, Robert. He was president of the Soldier and Sailor Association of Macomb, St. Clair, and Sanilac Counties" (Jenks, Biographical Memoirs of St. Clair County).

Other early settlers in the Lower St. Clair River were David Robertson, Chester Rankin, and Richard Allington.

In 1825, the lighthouse was built at the mouth of the St. Clair River, the first on the Upper Lakes. Port Huron was the third village on the St. Clair River. John Thorn Plat was on the north side of Black River. James H. Cook, a representative of Thomas S. Knapp, came in 1825 and built a store and trading post on the north bank of Black River.

"In 1827, a mail route was established from Pontiac to Port Huron, stopping at Washington Village, this being the only office between the former place and Mt. Clemons. It necessarily served a very large extent of country, the mail bag originally carried on foot and, afterward, on horseback for ten or twelve years. The mail carrier always remaining at Washington overnight. Shortly after 1836, the mail was brought by stage from Detroit until the completion of the Grand Trunk Railroad and a regular line of easy coaches, lumbering stages, or dilapidated buggies were alternately the means of transit" (History of Macomb County).

"Captain John Clarke came in 1833 to Port Huron to run the steam mill for Dr. Rice. He then lived at China Township on the St. Clair River. He built a store and dock and traded in furs, etc. He was the Indian commissioner for the State of Michigan, a senator, a postmaster, and was a representative elected to the Territorial Convention which framed the first Constitution of this State. John Clark was called upon to help those in difficult circumstances: a vessel had a great gaping hole in it and was having difficulty staying afloat; he went to his cellar and wrapped a large slab of pork, which he took to the vessel and had the men shove into the hole. Then he piloted the boat to Detroit as the exhausted men took a rest. He was captain of the *General Gratiot* steamboat for two years.

He was the first senator from the fifth district of the new State of Michigan. He served, a number of years as chair of important committees. He was the highest degree mason in the State, having gone to Europe to receive two more. He was the third highest in the United States, the vice eminent grand captain general. He named China and Casco Townships after his hometown and township in Maine.

The St. Clair Academy School and Church near Algonac was established by Rev. O.C. Thompson, a Presbyterian minister, who was instrumental in educating many people. Many young men went on to serve the people. He was a conductor on the Underground Railroad, helping escaped slaves to freedom across the river in Canada.

In 1830, there were 14 families with 50 people on both sides of the Black River.

Ai Beard came to Desmond in 1830, settling at Abbottsford in the now village of Ruby in Clyde Township, where he built a sawmill. His sons David, John, and James went into lumbering. Lumber from the Beard Mill was said to have built Milwaukee, Wisconsin at an early day.

There were 80 men at Fort Gratiot, a few French families along Black River, and the Indians. These were all the inhabitants of Port Huron in 1830" (Jenks History of St. Clair County 1912).

"In 1835, whiskey was .50 cents a gallon at the Comstock Store, which was painted red, on the south side of Black River. Powder was .50 cents a pound, eggs were .19 cents a dozen, sugar and pork were one shilling per pound, and butter was .20 cents. Potatoes were $1.00 per bushel, flour was $6.00 per barrel. Shingles were $1.50 per thousand" (Jenks, 1912).

In 1835, the first village plat was made by Edward Petit, north of Court Street, now Port Huron, and called Peru Village. Edward Petit was a fur trader for the Williams Brothers.

Joseph Watson was at one time, secretary of the territory under Governor Hull. He bought 80 acres south of Black River from 7th Street to Griswold Street; his village was called Montgats. The land was then considerably higher and was often referred to as "the Hill". Black River and the St. Clair River were once much shallower, the banks much higher, before the canal was dug and the shipping channel was dredged, allowing more water from Lake Huron.

Harrington and White, platted Port Huron Village the same year as Edward Petit. They then bought Joseph Watson's plat, and this was then known as White's Plat and went west to 10th Street. The village was then called Desmond.

Major John Thorn laid out the village of Paris, which then became known as the village of Gratiot. John Thorn Jr., his son, along with Thomas S. Knapp, owned the Thorn Plat or the village of Gratiot in 1837.

In 1837, St. Clair County had one gristmill and 40 sawmills. In 1854, St. Clair County had four gristmills and 39 sawmills. A woolen mill was operated in Yale, St. Clair County. Chicory, a coffee substitute, was produced in Port Huron. The Indians living in the area liked to trade venison for farm goods, especially homemade bread. A sturdy peg on the outside of the cabin was used to hang the meat from time to time in exchange for bread. The Indians were seen along the creeks and rivers, camping and gathering items to make baskets to sell, into the early 1900s.

Port Huron was the transportation hub for the Eastern Thumb Region. Lumbering was the area's largest industry. Port Huron was also the central market for the produce of the interior settlement, playing a central role in trade, steam mills, and the attraction of manufacturing activities. St. Clair County developed as an industrial center, producing heavy machinery and equipment.

"Thomas S. Knapp was sheriff of Wayne County and owned a mill on Black River, half a mile south of Jeddo, and also had a trading post on the north side of Black River near its mouth. He also owned, along with John Thorn Jr., the Thorn Plat or the village of Gratiot, one of four plats that made up the town of Port Huron in 1837" (Jenks/ Clark Papers, MI Room SCC Library).

Bartlett Luce came to Port Huron early and was one of the early lumbermen.

Ottissippi

Charles Butler was a famous railroad owner and promoter and the largest stockholder in the Huron Land Company. He platted the Butler Plat and the town of Huron north of Black River. The men were the leading business men in New York and Boston. The Huron Land Co. bought the old LaSalle and Bonhomme claims. The land between the military reserve and Holland Road and the McNeil Tract became the town of Huron.

William L. Bancroft was a leader who did much to promote Port Huron's civic projects. He came to Port Huron in 1844, became a lawyer and partner with Omar Conger, and was a newspaper owner, banker, lumberman, State Senator, and Port Huron's first mayor, who helped organize the city government of Port Huron. He was also into railroad building to Chicago, which was the Grand Trunk Western, and became part of the Grand Trunk System. He joined the John Johnston & Co. Bankers to form the First National Bank.

Three road districts were established, dividing the township of St. Clair, and Plainfield – Clay – and Cottrellville were added.

James Abbott laid out the village of Abbottsford near the Morass Mill, which he bought, in what is now known as Ruby, Michigan. Judge Abbott was a large trader and American Fur Company representative from Detroit; he was a partner with Z.W. Bunce in the fur trade. The town of Abbottsford was named after him. He owned the Morass Mill at Abbottsford, and Antoine Morass ran it. Abbott also had a mill at Lakeport in Burtchville Township.

District 2 included the dwellers on Black River above Riley's fence corner to the extremity of the settlements. This included the Morass Mill people at Abbottsford. In 1827, this district was known as Desmond, and Martin Peckins was the supervisor. The other two districts were St. Clair and Plainfield – Clay. Wolf scalps were $4.00 each. Clyde Township, was set off of Desmond in 1827, greatly reducing the township of Desmond.

Ralph Wadhams built a gristmill in 1830 on Black River in Clyde Township, the second one in the county. In 1834, Wadhams was supervisor of Desmond, then of Clyde Township. He was the postmaster at Clyde Mills, now Wadhams, in Kimball, Township, as well as a lumberman and cattleman. The mail ran twice a week. He was a delegate to the First Commission of the Constitution of the State of Michigan.

By 1836, the small canoe ferry gave way to the bridge over Black River. In the same year, a village plat of Algonac was made, the land bought from Silas Miller and Ebenezer Westbrook. There was a frame house on the north side of Black River near the mouth.

"A great many Indians were visiting Port Huron, traveling in birchen canoes from the Saginaw country and the Ausable. Mr. Brakeman was an extensive trader with the French and Indians. He spoke their language fluently and was a great favorite of theirs. They were frequent visitors at our house and never left hungry or cold.

There were many friends, Mother Rodd was a frequent visitor, Chief Okemos and his family. His Totem was the Bear. The Settlers used flint and punk in starting fires. Cooking was done by fireplaces. We were given gifts of maple sugar, venison, berries, baskets, etc. Cranberries from Riley, near Memphis on Belle River, were brought to Port Huron to exchange for store goods" (Nancy Brakeman Papers, SCC Library, MI Room).

In 1838, the mail route from Mt. Clemons to Fort Gratiot was weekly. There were Indian trails in every direction and the rivers for transportation, and a few roads.

"The Indian burial mound on Water Street on the site of the federal building at the end of 6th Street and Black River. Scaffolds seven to eight feet high and small low houses made of wood were built over graves. Early pioneers saw numerous ancient burial rites. The deceased were buried in a sitting position, placed that way after death. Dressed in his best and wrapped in a most brightly-colored blanket, with ornaments, weapons, jewelry, and foodstuff, he was buried facing West toward Indian Heaven. Foods, weapons, and other necessities for the journey of four days were buried with the body" (Mitts, D., As the Wild Goose Flies, The Times Herald, SCC Library, MI Room).

"In 1838, Oliver Hazard Perry (not the famous general) from Cleveland came to St. Clair County to hunt elk in the forests of Clyde Township with two other men. Their camp being near the Great Indian Trail, Abbottsford and Beard Road, Perry became lost near an old Indian camp near Mill Creek or Pine River. In his diary, he wrote that the Indians were not numerous, but occasionally a band would go by their camp, which was in a pine grove in a swail: 'Their wigwams were scattered all through the woods, and the Chippeweas from Canada were in the habit of hunting on these grounds every fall. We found great numbers of elk horns hung up in their camps. Peter Non E Quit, a Saginaw Indian, killed while we were hunting two elk in one day some three miles from our camp, but the fall being too dry for good hunting, the Indians all left for Belle River where the hunting was better'. After passing the forks of the Black River, we came to where a man lived by the name of Beard. He gave us something to eat and some first-rate whiskey to drink. He showed us an extraordinary, large pair of elk horns that the Indians had given him'.

The men stayed at Mr. Wadhams' home the following night on the return to Port Huron. Mrs. Wadhams made them comfortable. She said that the old buck elk they kept in a fence with some deer had broken out and ran through the window after her, and she had sprung up the ladder into the garret of the log house, screaming and halloed most lustily, when Mr. Wadhams, finding out the trouble, got his rifle and shot the elk in the house" (Larry Wakefield, 1999 Michigan Out of Doors).

"In 1849, Gold Fever broke out in the West and California; the horde of immigrants drifted by sea and land to California" (Jenks, Biographical Memoirs of SCCMI).

Jane M. Kinney (vol. 29. MPHC. 1899 p. 170) wrote of Clyde, Wadhams, and Abbottsford. She wrote of the sawmills in the area, Farrand Mills at Lakeport, Brockway Center, Wadhams, Howard Mills, Beards, Bunce, Abbott, Chase, and Miller, of the Sanborns, Whites, Williams, and Rust and Co.

"Wolves, bears, and wild cats roamed the woods. A log schoolhouse was made at Abbottsford, a Corduroy Road followed the old Indian trails from the St. Clair River. She tells of the area being the favorite camping ground of the Indians traveling from Saginaw, Michigan and Sarnia and Walpole Island in Ontario. How they heard the Christian Indians singing hymns on sweet summer evenings.

She wrote, 'They always came to our home for flour and meat, tea, sugar, straw for their beds. Mother spoke their tongue; her father was a storekeeper at Bear Creek (now Sydenham) on the east side of St. Clair River, Harsens Island, and Baby's Point. Uncle Sampson and Henry Ward traded among them.

Settlers started with an axe, a pot, blankets, and a gun, a month or two of provisions, energy, and self- denial. There was much hard work to make a home in the woods. Often starting with a lean-to to live in, then a bigger shelter of saplings and posts, then a log home chinked with mud and sand. Large bark slabs were laid over saplings like a trough for the rain to run. Paper was dipped in oil to make a transparent window. Fireplaces were stones filled with sand with a stick and mud chimney and packed with clay as mortar. Pots were suspended and could be swung over the fire. A Dutch oven was often used for baking".

"Robert Durling came to Marine City and was sheriff, constable, and village marshal. In the mid-1800s, he captured a major crime gang of river pirates, which infested the shore from Port Huron to Detroit. Stealing from warehouses, boats, and dwellings, they were a desperate gang, shrewd and daring. Officers and citizens were afraid to hunt them out, but Mr. Durling, with determination in performance of his duties, followed them to their lair on the St. Clair Flats, surrounded them, and bagged his game, breaking up the gang of thieves that had become the terror to the people of the river" (Wisc. Historical Co.).

"The use of intoxicants upon all noted occasions and upon most common events of pioneer life was held to be a necessity. Liquor was used as a cure for all diseases that assailed the system. At births, weddings, and deaths, its inspiring aid was sought.

Prominent in the history of each new settlement were the bees when extra help was needed to accomplish some task, such as loggings and raisings. At these bees, whiskey was free and was often the secret which attracted them to the place. The timber used was much larger than used now, (so) a large force was called together. Problems and accidents led to the Temperance Laws" (History of Macomb County).

"The Temperance Societies were organized to bring sobriety to the land. Perhaps in no city in the world had more earnest workers than that at Port Huron. The lessons which it then taught and the earnest manner of the teachers rescued numbers of people from the ruin which strong drink was bringing or had already brought upon them" (Western Historical Co.). "Whiskey was the main money crop of the Frontier farmer" (Lexington Michigan History, www).

"Port Huron north of Black River was known as Frenchtown and south of Black River was Dutchtown, as there were many Germans" (Mitts).

"Supplies dwindled in the winter, and spring brought great rejoicing when supplies came in. Flour barrels were pricey in the spring. Women had sewing circles for friendly company.

Fires caused a great loss of property and ruination of homes and businesses. Many were rendered homeless and penniless by the great disasters. Bucket brigades tried to save structures.

There were no free schools in Michigan until 1842 in Detroit; around 1870, the system extended throughout the State. Sand trays and slate boards were used. There were few textbooks. Schools were open only about three to six months of the year" (Bald, MI in 4 Centuries).

THE CANADIAN EARLY SETTLERS

The Traitor Campau lived on the Canadian side of the river, directly opposite the city of St. Clair. The government gave him this farm, and it has since been known as the Sutherland Farm. John Courtney, a Dutch farmer, lived above Campau on the Canadian side of the St. Clair River. He is said to be the first White settler in Lambton County. Sampson Ward was North of Courtney back of Elk Island. Frank Bartrow, the blacksmith, lived near Ward.

Mary Bean was the first White female child born on Black River. She married Richard Bean, a soldier under General Harrison. He was at the Battle of Tippecanoe and was discharged in 1815. He drew a pension, as long as he

Ottissippi

lived. In 1824, he moved near Judge Bunce and then to Black River above Wadhams, making shingles and farming. Richard Jr. as a child was a frequent companion with the Indian boys. He went on to be highway commissioner and held other township and school offices.

David Lockwood was born at the fort. His parents were here when the fort was built in 1814.

Dr. Justin Rice, a prominent Detroit physician, was one of the owners of the Black River Steam Saw Mill Company and a staunch democrat.

John Miller was the bookkeeper and manager for the Black River Steam Mill Co. who became Port Huron's first banker. He was born at Sugar Lake, Ontario in 1818. He was also village president and mayor, then representative to the State Legislature.

Ezra Rust called St. Clair home as a child. He went on to become one of the very wealthy timber barons of the Northwest. He had brothers and a sister.

John Wells opened roads through the forests for lumbering along Black River.

Other early St. Clair County pioneers were the Smiths, Browns, Caswells, Phillips, Cooke, Wards, Westbrooks, Witmans, Wordens, Clarkes, and Beards, John, Ai, and James. Other men of honor were Fulton, Harrington, Hartsuff, Kimball, Griswold, William Bancroft, and Henry Howard.

Newport was Yankee Point and, later, Marine City.

Omar Conger was a lawyer, lumberman, and politician. He was also a United States Senator. He was the man responsible for the Harbor of Refuge at Harbor Beach. He was influential in the building of the Lake St. Clair Ship Canal and the Port Huron Customs House.

Mark Hopkins was the first postmaster of St. Clair. He was a hotelier and went on to railroad fame.

Henry McMorran owned McMorran and Co. and Michigan Mills. They loaded huge vessels with ground flours. He was also a large chicory coffee producer, among other achievements. He was a philanthropist who built the McMorran Auditorium for the people of Port Huron.

James W. Sanborn, merchant and seafarer to the West Indies and the Atlantic, came to Port Huron with Abner Coburn, since Governor of Maine, Charles Merrill, and Joseph Kelsey. They located 25,000 acres of land in St. Clair and Sanilac Counties. He went to Lapeer and became a legislative representative. He had large lumber interest on the Saginaw, Muskegon, Ausable, Thunder Bay, Rivers, Pine River in the Upper Peninsula of Michigan, and Cheboygan, Michigan. He had a quick perception and was far-seeing. He was among the foremost organizers of the Republican Party under the Oak Tree at Jackson,

Michigan, making history. He was elected to the House of Representatives, then Commissioner of the State Land Office.

"Aura Stewart's father, Henry, a distiller, came to Michigan on foot with his brother from New York. He worked at the Distillery of Mack and Miller on Harsens Island, turning grain into whiskey. He had worked in the lumber business and as a farmer and distiller on the Thames in Ontario.

The Strait of St. Clair and Detroit Rivers was a very rich region. Transportation facilities greatly improved the potential; there was great growth in population in the 1830s and 1840s. Steamers greatly improved transportation on Lake Erie. The opening of the Erie Canal in 1825 to circumvent Niagara Falls opened up the West to settlement and reasonable transportation costs". Aura Stewart

"Enos Goodrich came to Michigan in 1834. His recollection of the journey was in the MPHC, vol. 26, 1896: 'It was a chill morning in November when our staunch Lake Steamer came up at the dock and disgorged its human freight upon the muddy streets of what then was Detroit, Michigan. The aspect was neither romantic nor inviting. The heavy rains of November had saturated the black mud along the low banks of the river, and it was churned to a thin paste by contact with wheels and hoofs of everything capable of locomotion, for a paved street was what the Michigan of that period had never known.

About every second man I saw was a Frenchman, and every third man a Negro. The French generally bore indisputable marks of a mingling of Indian blood.

But to me there was one thing cheering: I had got rid of the seething, nauseating fumes of the greasy sick engine and the deathly sickness produced by the ceaseless rock of the boat, and my number ten Stoga boots were once more planted upon *Terra Firma*. Passing the rest of that chill November day sizing up the Detroit of 1834 and settling my system from the unpleasant sensations of my first trip across Lake Erie, I took my first night's slumber on Michigan soil and early the following morning struck out for the still more remote west. I found nothing of that miserable starvation fare at back woods taverns, which so many emigrants complained of. On the contrary, we found the rude tables of the Frontier hostelries bountifully supplied with the necessities of life and what to me were real luxuries, venison and wild honey found in abundance at nearly every meal in the territory.

I was always an ardent admirer of the works of nature; the Lordly woods, the green fields, the blue skies, the fleecy floating clouds, and the running waters always possessed charms for me which I never found in dusty towns and crowded cities. I have spent some lonesome days in cities, but I never yet saw a lonesome day where I could go out and read in Nature, Nature's God'".

A.M. Beardsley, born in 1815 in the Wooly West, wrote of early life: "A log cabin was 20 feet square with three little seven-by-nine inch, windows, one and a half stories high and roofed with wood shingles. The cabin was furnished with homemade furniture.

Chills and fever came every spring and fall. Mosquitos, fleas, and bedbug pests, millions without number annoyed and sucked the life blood out of us every night. Ponds and lakes then held pestilence and poisons, causing sickness and death.

The celebration of the completion of the Erie Canal and first public improvements were of great consequence in the New Country. Whiskey was free and gunpowder filled the air over the country.

Free speech, free press, and free schools make this the Paradise Age of the world. The day of superstition, witchery and omens, signs of the moon and woodchucks are fast fading away.

Trains cross every township in the country, bringing to our very doors the comfort and luxuries not only of our own state, but from every section of the Union, purchased for a trifle compared to the early days. Travel was by ox team to the Lake to haul salt to preserve bacon.

We rejoiced that those early days are but a memory, and we live in this Golden Age to see the wonderful things man has wrought" (MPHC vol. 5, 28).

"The first County Court was held at St. Clair Village on January 28, 1822. The first question presented to the court was the application of Andrew Westbrook for a tavern license. James and David Robertson were his bondsmen. The court granted the application provided the tavern be conducted at the Westbrook Dwelling House. William Brown, Moses Birdsal, Zephaniah W. Bunce, and James Robertson were granted a similar license the same day to conduct taverns. On January 30, licenses to keep taverns were granted to Oliver Record and James Fulton. In January 1823, licenses to keep taverns were granted to Reuben Hamilton and Charles Chortier (Western Historical Co.). James Fulton was granted a license to maintain a ferry across Pine River. James Wolverton was granted a like permission to keep a ferry on Belle River.

When the Erie Canal opened in 1825 to circumvent Niagara Falls, the steamships came in great numbers with hordes of people looking for freedom and cheap land to build farms on. It was a great melting pot of people. The settlement and development of St. Clair County followed slowly, and the population of 327 which had been in the Census of 1820 increased during the decade of 1830 to 1840 from 1,114 to 4,606" (W.L. Jenks SCC Centennial & Home Coming Celebration 1921).

John Farmer's maps were potent in bringing emigrants to Michigan. They were sold in the Eastern states in 1830. 15,000 emigrants arrived in 1830, and the steamboats were crowded through 1837 with passengers for Michigan and the West, to say nothing of those who arrived by land and sail vessel. In 1831, in one week 2,000 arrived by steamboat. They came to Michigan to purchase land and settle in Michigan. Steam and sail vessels were crowded to the utmost capacity. On October 7, 1834, four steamboats brought nearly 900 passengers. In 1836, three boats arrived each day with over 700 passengers. On one day in May, 2,400 arrived. The roads to the interior were literally thronged with wagons. One citizen observed a wagon leaving the city every five minutes during the 12 daylight hours. Most of the people were coming from New York and New England. Most of the immigrants were hardy, honest small farmers.

"There were no records kept of early migrations. Hundreds of thousands of immigrants arrived at 'The Ellis Island of the Midwest' in the two decades after the Civil War. Port Huron became the first stop for many immigrants from and through Canada, who crossed at Sarnia in Upper Canada to Port Huron, Michigan, USA. Few roads were available; many stayed in St. Clair County, some went on to Flint and other places in Southern Michigan and the West. Hamilton, Ontario was the checkpoint for immigration by water. St. Albans Border Crossing Records at Vermont, where records include entries from all ports along the Canada and United States border.

The National Archives has microfilm records of passengers. The LDS Church also has records on microfilm. The Port of Detroit, Michigan recorded land crossings and vessel crossings from Ontario. Manifest records recorded the contents of vessels. The National Archives and LDS offer films of passenger lists of those entering through the Port of Detroit from 1906 to 1954; they include other Michigan ports of entry, Bay City, Detroit, Port Huron, and Sault Sainte Marie. These records are also at other repositories, including the Library of Michigan in Lansing. Another good resource is a book by Jan Steven Zalewski (1993), *Guide to Records of Border Crossings between the United States and Canada, 1895 to 1954.*

Half of the immigrants came from Canada. Port Huron, next to New York, receives the largest number of any ports in the United States. Between 1860 and 1900, more than 700,000 immigrants came to Michigan, and nearly 400,000 of these new arrivals were born in foreign countries" (Michigan Manual 2001-2002, the Legislative Service Bureau, Michigan 2002/ Marilyn and Diana Hebner).

Ottissippi

There are six official ports along the Michigan-Ontario border:

- Wallaceburg, Ontario (ON) to Algonac, Michigan (MI)
- Windsor, ON to Detroit, MI
- Sombra, ON to Marine City, MI
- Sarnia/Point Edward, ON to Port Huron, MI
- Port Lambton, ON to Roberts Landing, MI
- Sault Ste. Marie, ON to Sault Ste. Marie, MI

"These are the official ports. It was very common for people to cross by boat, canoe, horse, or walk across when the river froze. Only a few records exist for the majority of the crossings from Ontario to Michigan" (Marilyn Hebner, President, SCC Family History Group/MI Genealogical Council. Diana Hebner, Research, SCCFHG and MGC).

"The long, exposed border was a drawback, the forest and swamps and the Indians who lived there.

This was the area of greatest immigration next to New York's Ellis Island. The immigrants came from the world over; there was immense diversity. Many military men came to claim their war bounty lands. Many others sold their land bounties to speculators. Many Germans and Irish came to America and this region beginning in 1670. Dutch, Finns, and Scandinavians came. Later the Italians, Poles, Greeks, Hungarians, and others" (Clever Bald, MI in Four Centuries).

"The great wave of settlers began coming in the 1830 to 1840s. By 1834, there were 87,278 non-Indians in Michigan, 85,856 living in the Southern Lower Peninsula. In 1837, when Michigan became a State, there were 174,543 people living in Michigan. By 1840, there were 212,267 people living in Michigan. These were mostly farmers from the Eastern states.

Immigrants sailing across the Atlantic on returning timber vessels carried their own food and bedding and lived huddled below decks for the duration of the trip, taking from 6 to 10 weeks depending on the weather. There was no difficulty, whether the wind was favorable or calm, in distinguishing by odour alone a crowded immigrant ship. The passengers suffered from the ills that crowding brings about and from the ravages of the cholera epidemics of 1832 and 1834. All were detained at the quarantine stations on Grosse Ile. Many a pioneer family left a grave there and arrived with fewer members than it had on leaving Britain" (Canada West Last Frontier).

In 1837, Mr. Trowbridge wrote to Governor Cass in Paris as the U.S. Minister to France: "The opening of navigation has brought us immense crowds of old-fashioned immigrants with their wives and babies and wagons and spinning wheels and a hundred dollars to buy an eighty-acre lot for each of the boys. I never saw so many crowded boats. Yesterday May 28, 1837, our arrivals were eight steamboats, one ship, three large brigs, and nineteen schooners. The day before, seven steamboats arrived. One the preceding day, the *James Madison* took up the lake upwards of one thousand passengers and the *Pennsylvania* followed with as many as she could carry. There is as much bustle in our streets as ever, and although money is so very scarce, nobody has failed here and all wear cheerful faces."

At Detroit, Mrs. Jameson stated, "there are some excellent shops in the town, a theatre, and a great number of taverns and gaming houses. There is also a great number of bookseller shops.

One of the local diversions was riding back and forth on the ferry which ran to the Canadian shore. The passengers she described as English emigrants and French Canadians; brisk Americans; dark, sad-looking Indians folded in their blankets; farmers; storekeepers; speculators in wheat; artisans; and trim girls with black eyes and short petticoats, speaking a Norman Patois and bringing baskets of fruit to the Detroit market.

Captain Marryat said that Windsor had fine stores stocked with choice English goods, sent there "entirely for the supply of Americans by smugglers. There is also a row of tailor shops, for cloth is a very dear article in America and costs nearly double the price it does in the English Provinces. The Americans go over there and are measured for a suit of clothes which, when ready, they put on and cross back to Detroit with their old clothes in a bundle."

Mrs. Martineau tells of one settler who three years before had purchased his eighty acres of land for a dollar an acre: "He could now sell it for twenty dollars an acre. He shot last year a hundred deer and sold them for three dollars apiece..."

She tells of coming upon an immigrant party near Ypsilanti, consisting of a woman and her eight children: "She had brought them in a wagon, four hundred miles, and if they could only live through the one hundred miles that remained before they reached her husband's lot of land, she hoped they might thrive."

"This was the raw material of which Detroit and Michigan were wrought – the raw material of strong hands and fearless hearts of devotion and stubborn determination" (Frank Woodford, "Yankees in Wonderland". Michigan Room SCC Library).

"The Orphan Train immigrants were homeless and orphaned children from New York and Boston who came on trains to the West. There were 150,000 children who went West for adoption and a home between 1854 to

1929. The children were accompanied with an official who made the arrangements with families who would care for them" (Al and Dave Eicher).

La Riviere Noire – Black River – was an open sewer; residents kept their windows shut.

"Records were not kept in the early migrations; the people just kept coming. They came on steamers and sailing vessels by the hundreds every day. The population nearly doubled between 1837 and 1845. There was huge economic significance of the railroads to Chicago. This greatly reduced transportation costs. There was now a speedy, reliable service route to the East.

The traveler of modern days can scarcely appreciate the difficulty of the opening of the Gratiot Turnpike Highway. From Detroit to Port Huron was one vast stretch of forest with slough holes, pit falls, swails, and mud at such frequent intervals as would appall the traveler of today. Four of five miles above Mt. Clemons, the road passed through a swamp which, in the wet season, furnished the wild duck and swan with a swimming place and the Indian with a splendid hunting ground for bird game" (History of St. Clair County MI, Wisc. Hist. Co. p. 150).

"Reverend Oren Cook Thompson was a well-loved man who did much to provide for education and spiritual needs among the early settlers at St. Clair and among the county residents. He started a school which was to teach many leading men. His home was also a station on the Underground Railroad.

Sam Edison, father of the famous Thomas Edison, was a supplier to Fort Gratiot. He kept a garden and small dairy on the fort grounds near the North end of Pine Grove Park. Tom's brother, William, ran an early rail service and transportation service in the city of Port Huron.

Great highways were planned from Detroit to Lake Michigan and Black River to Grand Rapids. Father Ricard, our Third Territorial Judge, was instrumental in establishing four roads: Fort Gratiot, Pontiac, Grand River, and Detroit and Chicago.

The churches in each village were the primary social functions and religious renewal. The banding of hopes and dreams, the comfort found in togetherness against a hostile society.

The children went to school for three months in the winter and farmed all summer. A sand box was used for lessons. Teachers were not trained, but those who were educated were sought out.

In 1837, there was a severe famine; all suffered from it. Everything was recycled: clothes, buildings, bath water, and flour sacks. Bootleggers or kitchen operators were too numerous to mention. Bathtub gin was popular.

St. Clair County was progressive on building roads. It became the leading road building companies home, they were leading the way to good roads. Road building equipment was made and sold here. Farming equipment was also built here.

Michigan was the great lever opening up fountains of wealth and civilization. In 1834, many pioneers came to Michigan, it being the West at that time, the Old West. Michigan by nature was the very lap of wealth and power.

In 1855, wheat, corn, grain, potatoes, and lumber were being shipped in great quantities. In 1856, the great tide of emigration from every part of Europe came" (MPHC vol. 38, p. 589). "Most of our great grandparents were among them. The Detroit Port Huron region was the next most important immigration center in the New World next to New York and New Jersey. There was no point of immigration; they just freely came West through Michigan. Many went onward to other points West. There was no written documentation of these early crossings.

Port Huron, owing to its central location for the important producing and shipping interests, it has become the point from which the major part of these are managed. Being at the end of a road by the rapids at the foot of a long stretch of smooth water, Port Huron naturally became a depot and entrepot for supplies, and so the town grew" (Western Historical Co. History of St. Clair County, MI).

"In 1857, the Agricultural College of Michigan was established in Lansing, the first of its kind in the nation.

The Panic of 1857 was a trying time for the citizens of Michigan and St. Clair County. Lumber was not bought, and the people suffered. The value of farm products depreciated and prices of commodities increased. The effect was perceptively visible. Impoverishment and ruin stared many in the face, and escape there from was only accomplished after trials no pen can adequately describe" (Western Historical Co.).

In 1872, the Michigan Grange was organized to help Michigan farmers. In 1879, the streets of Port Huron were a mess, mainly due to cattle, hogs, and geese wandering through the streets. It was said to be the filthiest American city. Notices were given to owners of cattle or other livestock that they would be impounded if found running at large at night.

In 1882, Marine City had a major salt company on Catholic Point.

The country experienced another financial panic in 1890.

William Bard was the founder of life insurance in America. He was the President of New York Life Insurance and Trust Company. His father was physician to George Washington and his family in New York. His grandfather was the first physician to dissect the human body.

Aura Stewart wrote of the New Country coming in 1815:

"Coming as I did from an inland and thickly settled district, I had seen no flowing water save brooks and rivulets. I had seen no forests but in the distance and, though a boy of twelve, I could not but feel impressed with the beauty of my new home. The dense and almost impenetrable forests, the magnificent River St. Clair, the countless number of every variety of water fowls flying over my head or resting and sporting on the bosom of the beautiful waters, the howling of wolves at night, the constantly passing and repassing canoes of the strange looking Indians, their stealthy tread through the woods and their unintelligible shouts as they passed each other, and last but not least, the merry songs of the French voyageurs toiling at the oar and propelling their boats swiftly over the blue waters – these were new scenes to me and called forth my wonder and delight.

Nearly sixty years of my life having been spent in Michigan, I have witnessed the improvements made in the county of St. Clair; flourishing towns have sprung up and a large portion of our older settlers have become wealthy. All have shared in the conveniences of modern improvements and comforts. But yet for my own part, I could enjoy no greater pleasure than for a short time to see Michigan as I saw it in 1815, wild and romantic as it then was. Fancy ofttimes leads me back to the dear old primitive days, and then I am a boy again.

"Alas, the vision lingers not; I am an old man with increasing infirmities and nothing is left me but the memory of the past" (Marine City Gazette 1876/Wisconsin Historical Co.).

"After the Fur Trade had moved to other areas, there were sawmills and ship building and repair, mining and manufacturing of salt and innumerable other industries, some of which were fisheries, tanneries, cooper shops – barrels, dry docks, ship chandleries and sail makers, breweries and boiler works, carriage and wagon manufacturing, auto plants, manufactured agriculture implements and road making equipment, mule power, street railway, electricity, and street cars.

The first electrified street railroad in America was in Windsor, Ontario, Canada. Port Huron was the first city in the world to have electric cars cross a movable bridge and the first to have street cars lighted with incandescent lamps.

The whining and screeching of the planing mills mingled with the caulkers' mallets on the hundreds of boats in Black and St. Clair Rivers. The clang and bang of riveters in the boiler works and shrieks of whistles from tugs working the St. Clair River all made for a mechanical symphony. The vibrant pulsating industries gave the area continued life and economic stability to transition from Lumber Central to a progressive community.

Michigan, was an empire in itself with the world's most important inland waterway for transportation. The St. Clair River region led the way both as shipbuilders and masters of ships. There were sloops, schooners, barques, brigs, steamers, barges, and cargo ships" (Mitts, D., As the Wild Goose Flies, The Times Herald, SCC Library, MI Room).

"James Edward O'Sullivan, a contractor-engineer who envisioned the Grand Coulee Dam, and after untold hardship and ridicule saw it through, had his start in Port Huron.

Miciah Walker was a self-taught hydraulic engineer who in 1873 established Port Huron Waterworks. He helped in saving millions of dollars of property in Chicago with two fire trucks he was delivering to the area. He built hydraulic engines in Fenton, Michigan at his factory, and became the Walker System of Water Works. He went on to build Waterworks in 15 cities and villages. Michael Walsh was his engineer" (Mitts, That Noble Country).

Thomas Edison spent his boyhood in Port Huron and learned his craft here. There is not space to elaborate on him. There are many other works written about him, and the Internet is a great source. Henry Ford history can also be found on the Internet. Thomas Edison and Henry Ford were lifelong friends. The Port Huron Engine and Thresher Company was one of the manufacturing concerns Henry Ford worked with in development of Ford farm equipment. Trying all types to test and study them, he acquired some of their tractors and every other tractor available, which led to the 1916 Fordson Tractor, which became a famous household word and made Henry a wealthy man.

Port Huron was the leader in the country for road building equipment. The first mile of macadamized road was birthed here by the Port Huron Engine and Thresher Co. on 24th Street. Port Huron Engine and Thresher Co. was known far and wide as the most complete macadamizing outfit in the world. The first Convention of Road Builders was held in Port Huron.

The Railroad Tunnel was completed in 1891. Joseph Hobson, Canada's greatest engineer, was responsible for this great feat, making him world famous for building the first under-river tunnel. He, having worked on the bridges at Niagra and was chief engineer of the Great Western Railroad. In later years, he was chief engineer of the Grand Trunk Railroad, rebuilding Victoria Bridge at Montreal, Ontario over the St. Lawrence River.

The tunnel between Port Huron and Sarnia was built of solid cast iron plates bolted together. The length of the tunnel is 6,026 feet. A thousand tons of nuts and bolts were used in the construction. The lining of the tunnel weighed 28,000 tons.

The Detroit Edison Power Plant in Marysville, Michigan was built in 1914. It imploded in 2015, its usefulness over. C. Harold Wills and Henry Ford worked for Detroit Edison Co. They met at night to create the Auto Industry. Wills was the chief engineer for Ford from its inception in 1903. Wills left the company in 1919 and began his own auto co. manufacturing plant in Marysville. He worked for Walter Chrysler, selling patents to him in the 1920s. Francis Malane was the plant manager for, Wills St. Clair. Wills was the founder of Marysville, creating a village for his employees. He produced 14,000 vehicles and closed the plant in 1926.

The "Northern" automobile was manufactured in Port Huron in 1907, Willian E. Metzger organized the company. The EMF Co. was merged with the Studebaker Brothers and became Studebaker Corp. Studebaker cars were manufactured in Port Huron until 1912 and were discontinued in 1964. Harold S. Vance became president. Studebaker later merged with Packard Motor Co.

Havers Motor Car Company was a Port Huron manufacturing company. Cass Motor Truck began in 1910, as did the Havers Motor Co.

Buhl Aircraft had a Marysville factory and airstrip at what is now Busha Highway, along the St. Clair River.

William Pitt Edison had a carriage and transit business that became a train service: The Rapid Transit Service from Port Huron to Detroit, the Electric Interurban Railway, and the Detroit Urban Railway.

In 1918, snow removal starts on Michigan roads. The automobile was beginning to be used by more people around the 1920s. The passenger train was done in 1926. By 1932, street cars were done. Automobiles and trucks had replaced the horse, boat, and train for passenger transportation and the transport of many goods.

Women were allowed to vote in 1920.

Small villages and small towns sprung up everywhere, in large measure they were self-sufficient, grouped about the mill. The coming of the railroads changed small town life. Many small towns vanished, leaving not even a trace of the activities of pioneer days. Ghost towns, buildings converted to other uses, or merely a name that is left in some obscure map or paper, or the old folks who remain to remind the next generation of the old days.

In 1938, the Blue Water Bridge opens.

The Great Depression came, and all suffered, using up, making do and wearing out whatever they had. Depending on others for kindness to survive.

In 1941, Michigan was the Arsenal of Democracy for WWII. By 1945, when the War ended, 673,000 Michigan men and women had served.

In 1957, the Mackinac Bridge was complete, linking the Lower Peninsula of Michigan to the Upper Peninsula. In 1959, the St. Lawrence Seaway opens.

In 1967, the Michigan State Income Tax was enacted.

In 1973, the Vietnam War ended, and 400,000 Michigan men and women had served.

Other great men came to and from St. Clair County. These lists are not all inclusive. Jenks (1912) has written three volumes, and Andreas (1884) has written the history and biographical memoirs of St. Clair County. These works are a more complete history of St. Clair County and its men, people and government of the early history as an American Country, the United States of America.

GLOSSARY
Indian Names and Places

INDIAN NAMES

The Ojibwe Indians were known by over 70 different names in the past (Inex Hilger). We can see the difficulty in sorting out the who, what, and where of these people. In early writings, there are a great number of different spellings and much confusion in using totem clan names, place names, or landmarks, rather than tribe names, not knowing they were part of a much larger group (Warren).

This chapter will help to understand their variations in other historical writings, for without these sources of information, there can be no correct or accurate knowledge of the past.

ALGONQUIN is the language group that many of the Northeastern tribes were originally a part of. Algonquin means "friends" or "allies".

ANISHINABE are the "First men" or Original Men. The Ojibwe spelling is A-Nich-In-Aub-Ay or Nish-Nah-Bay (Warren/Chaput).

Anishinabeg, Ahnishenahbek, or Anishinabek is plural for Anishinabe. Ahnishenahbi is the masculine singular. Anishenahbikwe or Ahnishenahbikwe is the feminine singular (Plain).

Anishinabag, is another spelling. Name used to describe ourselves as a People, to describe our Nation, A Band, or to describe any Member of the, Three Fires Confederacy, and sometimes to describe any Aboriginal People. David D. Plain, Ojibwe Author, Sarnia, Ont.

Nishnob is commonly used among Indians for Anishinabe.

Asistagueronon is the name of the **Three Fires**, also Gens De Few, "The Fire Nation", or "The Fire People", the name the French used for all Michigan tribes. This nation alone was more populous than all the Neutral nations, all the

Huron's, and all the Iroquois enemies of the Huron put together. It consisted of a large number of villages, wherein was spoken the Algonquin language (Jenks 1912)

Atsistaehronons means "The Fire Nation", a very large group.

Assisternonon is the spelling for The Fire Nation in Michigan, Fox, Sauk, Mascoutin, and Pottawatomie (Ojibwe Whoa, www).

OJIBWE, OJIBWA, CHIPPEWA

The **Ojibwe** are the Older Brother of the Three Fires. They came from the ancient Crane clan, Ojibwauk or Ojebik, meaning "the root or stem of the people". As the Ojibwe grew in numbers, other totems intermarried and adopted the name for the whole nation of Ojibwe peoples. The Ojibwe were the government leaders, keepers of records, and protectors and hunters. "The Ojibwe were extremely prosperous due to the high demand for copper. The people were cold hammering and annealing copper for many uses as tools and decoration" (NA of the Clinton Water Shed. www).

Ojibweg or Ojibwag is the plural of Ojibwe.

The name **Chippewa** became the common English name for the Ojibwe. If we put an "O" in front of "Chippewa", we can see the similarity – OChippewa. The people prefer to use the traditional name, Ojibwe.

See "Ojibwe" in the Appendix for more variations on names and spellings.

OTTAWA

The **Ottawa** were the Second Younger Brother, the middlemen and traders for their kindred tribes. The Ottawa dealt chiefly in cornmeal, sunflower oil, furs, skins, rugs, mats, tobacco, medicinal roots, and herbs.

Ottawa were called Outaoues, Odahwah, Adawa, and Tawas. It was the name given to all who went to trade with the French, though they were of widely different nations (Thwaites, 1959).

POTTAWATOMI

The **Pottawatomi** – Bodawatomi, were the Third Younger Brother, who were the farmers and Keepers of the Fire for councils and hosted, with hospitality for great meetings of the people, which were held every year or every other year.

Pottawatomi were called Pou Kunahayanu – "The Watermelon People".

Originally, there were five totem groups among the Three Fires people who were all interrelated. The Crane, Bear, Fish, Loon, and Moose. Marten was added for the mixed blood peoples. The Bear totem was always in the forefront in warfare. Warriors were like policemen or protectors.

Ottissippi

Later there were 15 major divisions of Ojibwe peoples. Nations are Tribes or Totems. Tribes were over the many Bands. Bands were over Clan Families, and Clans over Villages, Towns, or "Castles".

AAMJIWNAANG, or Aajomwnaang, means "Place by the Rapid Water". It is pronounced Am-Jin-Nun (Askin Papers vol. 1).

After the Great Purge and Refugee Movement following the Iroquois Wars, the people migrated to the Upper Peninsula for safety, and after the Ojibwe obtained guns and pushed the Iroquois back to New York. Kioscance "Young Gull", the war and principal chief from Boweeting at Ste. St. Marie, moved his people to the foot of Lake Huron, they were called the Kioscanee tribe. Kioscance had 16,000 acres at the foot of the Rapids, which is now Port Huron, Michigan. The people grew large in number and expanded far and wide.

The territory was called Aamjiwnaang. It stretched from Toronto to Georgian Bay, from Alpena to Detroit, and west to the Saginaw watershed and west of Lansing.

The **Bawiitigwakinini** band, the people living along the Strait, the Bluewater Area Indians, were also called Saulteurs, Sauteurs, or Saultex, "People of the Falls". *Saut* meaning "falls" or "rapids". At the St. Mary's River at Ste. Saint Marie, the name moved with the people from Boweting to Aamjiwnaang.

Saulteurs - Sauteurs, as the name moved with them from the Sault Ste. Marie. The name given as the Expert Navigators canoes were wont to bounce through the rapids, lifting the canoes over sandbars, and rushing, turbulent waters.

Saulteurs was the French Name for the Ojibwe. The term comes from Sault, a type of Rapids in which waters appeared to tumble or roll. The French term for the entire Ojibwe Nation at S.S, Marie and elsewhere. Lahonton

The Ojibwe or Sauteurs are seen as the Original Crane People of the Algonquins. The Leadership and Record Keepers, Hunters and Protectors.

The Crane – a loud and far sounding cry, gathered Clans to the Sound of his Voice. The Noblest and Greatest among the Ojibway. *Bwa*, means Voice, thereby denoting, "The Voice of the Crane". The Crane goes back to the Flood. The lofty Crane Totem of Ancient Bands. Bus in aus e – Echo Maker or Crane. Warren 1984/Schenk 1997

Saultex band of 3,000 warriors (this represents 15,000 people) led by Chief Laturno.

The Saulteurs were, "The Lake Indians, the, Back Country Indians, The Detret, De Troit or Detroit Indians, meaning the Strait. The "Foot of the Rapids Tribe".

SAULK

The Ojibwe were also called Sauk, or Sohk, Sawk, Saulk, meaning "outlet of a river". Sauk or Sac – Asakiwaki – the Saginaw area, means "People of the Outlet".

Sotu, Souters, or Sotoes, also Jumpers or Leapers. Souters – Missisauga, Jumpers, to jump up & down on a river, experts in navigating numerous rapids, in the river, canoes were wont to jump its channels.

Sac – Ozaagii Wag, meaning Yellow Earth, Those at the Outlet.

The Black River, Swan Creek, and Saginaw bands were subtribes. Bands are clan families living nearby one another, they are of mixed *phratries* (totems). They did not marry within their own family totem clan.

Black River Band – Makade Ziibii

"Blackwater River People" - Mekadewagamitigweyawinniwak, Living on Black River. Access Geneology www

MISSISSAUGAS

Missisaugas, or Messesauui, means "River People" and "many outlets", a settlement by the fork of a stream. The Ojibwe tribe who inhabited the Bluewater area for the last 300 years, and before the Iroquois invasion. The principal totem of the people is the Crane. They were Neutrals who were Ojibwe who grew to a great number in Southern Ontario and Northern Ontario. They were of the Eagle subtribe. Charlevoix wrote that they have darker skin than any other tribe in North America. They had flint beds, the sources of which were kept secret, as trading materials to be made into weaponry for hunting and protection from enemies.

Massissuaguays (Ojibways) came from Me sey-sah gieng at the head of Lake Huron (George Copway).

Neuters – Missisaugas, Ojibwe – Chippewa (Jenks, "History of St. Clair County", 1912, www).

Sagamum

Sageeny - easternmost shore of Lake Huron.

Sahgeeng means "river".

Saugeen, river on South end of Lake Huron, in southwest, Ontario.

Sauganaw, or Saginaw, Sauk town, or Saginaw

Sauguinan - peninsula of upper Canada in 1686.

Zaginau Ziibii – Saginaw band.

Nez Perces – Amikwa Ottawas, from the eastern waters of Lake Huron, north of Georgian Bay. They became great horsemen and supplied the people with many horses and ponies. They bred horses for endurance and other desirable traits. They moved to Northern Canada after the Iroquois Wars.

Folle Avoine – Sauteurs, were the **"Rice" Ojibwe** from Wisconsin.

Ottissippi

Neutre Nation De Truite – French name for the Missisauga, Ojibwe.

Nipissings, meaning, at the small lake Northeast of the Greater Lake (Huron). They were the Sorcerers, or a Nation of Sorcerers.

Nipissiriniens were the true Algonkin's.

HURON

The HURON – Onoontatearonons – were Iroquois traders who lived among the Ojibwe and traded with them. They became part of the Ojibwe after the Iroquois Wars. Huron Tobacco – Petun, and Iroquoin Neutrals were wiped out in the Iroquois Wars. Survivors became part of the Six Nations Iroquois.

The **Neutrals** were great farmers, growing at least 15 varieties of corn, 60 types of beans, and 6 kinds of squash and produced large quantities of Sunflower Oil

Huron traders became wealthy, having a monopoly on trade with the French at Montreal Quebec for a long time. They knew the Algonquin language of their friendly neighbors and did much trading. This caused other tribes to be covetous of their trading.

Tobacco Petun were the Huron people of Southern Ontario and were friendly with the Neutrals. They were called Wenro – Wenrohronon.

Tionontati were the Tobacco Huron who became part of the **Wendat**, meaning islanders or dwellers on a peninsula The Tionontati invaded East Michigan after 1630 in search of furs and battled with the Fire Nation.

Wyandotte or Wyandot, and Ouendat and Wendat, were the Huron Petun – Tobacco Nation – who became the Wyandotte after the Iroquois Wars. After 1649, the Wendat became Wyandat.

IROQUOIS – Ho Da Shone, "People of the Long House", the Senaca, Mohawk, Oneida, Onondaga, and Cayuga. The Iroquois were from New York. These Long Houses often had 12 fires in them with 24 family firesides. The Iroquois were doing a great trade, with the Dutch traders at Albany, New York.

Seneca Iroquois were from the St. Lawrence and New York.

Mohawk – Mahican, Mohegan – were called "Wolves" – "Loupes" – by the French. They were wealthy from the flint trade.

Oneida – Onyotaa:ka – "People of the Stone Set Up" were from New York.

The **Covenant Chain** was with the Iroquois and other nations for trade and military alliance.

The **Five Nations Confederacy** - League of the Tree of Peace and Power, the original of the Onondaaga's, Cayuga's, Seneca's, Oneidas, and Mohawks.

The **Six Nations**, the Tuscarora's of North Carolina who were Iroquoian-speaking, united with the Iroquois Five Nations.

Tuscarora, who were from North Carolina and were Algonquin's, who then lived on the east bank of Niagara. The Seneca Iroquois adopted them into the Six Nations in 1722.

Tuetelo, Tuetelos, or Tuetle from Virginia went to Susquanan and were absorbed by the Six Nations Iroquois.

Mingo were Iroquois mixed with adopted people of the Neutral, Huron, and Erie from the War of 1650. The Delaware – Lenape – and the Shawnee were also mixed with the Iroquois in 1700. These groups lived in Eastern Ohio, Virginia, and Western Pennsylvania, wanting to be free of League control and political power (Iroquois Whoa, www).

Mahican or Mohican of Ohio were absorbed by the Delaware at Stockbridge. They were invaluable to the British and Rogers Rangers in 1756. They were negotiators with the Western Alliance in Ohio at war with the U.S. and the War of 1812 American Army. Iroquois Whoa, www

The Neutrals – Attioundaronk, meaning those who speak a little differently, were Iroquois of a large number who lived in Southern Ontario and near the St. Lawrence. They stayed Neutral between the Huron and Iroquois in war. Most of those who stayed Neutral were Huron Iroquoian subtribes.

ERIE – Cat People, Erieehronon, living north of Lake Erie, were destroyed by the Seneca Iroquois and their allies, some were absorbed into the tribe.

SHAWNEE – Shawaneese or Shawanoe – means the (Algonquin-speaking) Southerners from Ohio. Their capital or castle was at Chilicothe, Ohio. They extended into West Virginia, Western Pennsylvania, Illinois, and Indiana. They were driven to Tennessee, South Carolina, Eastern Pennsylvania, and Southern Illinois, then Indiana. They were neighbors to the Miami and Delaware (Patricia Orange, Ontario 1975).

Shawnee was "Chaouanon" in French. The Shawnee were the Youngest Brother to the Ojibwe. (Schoolcraft, Travels in Minn. And Wisc. 1821).

KICKAPOO, or Kickabeaux, were part of the Shawnee tribe (Lee Stultzman, Tolatsga, www).

FOX – Masquackie, (Masquackie is now the preferred name) lived near the St. Lawrence, then in Southern Michigan as close neighbors and allies with the Sauk, and were dispersed to the West of Lake Michigan after the Iroquois Wars. They controlled the Fox River leading to the Mississippi. The Fox were one of the largest Great Lake tribes prior to contact, in 1737, there were 500.

Outagami - Fox", brothers to the Chippewa (Schoolcraft, 1821).

Ottissippi

Musquakee, Masquackie, or Meshkwahkihaki means "Red Earth People", "Red Earth Men", or "The Red Earths". "Renards" is the French name for the Fox, meaning "Red". The Fox is the original and preferred name.

MIAMI – Piankashaw, Wea, and Mascouten – lived in the southern third of the Lower Peninsula of Michigan.

Weas – Aouitanons – is the branch of the Miami's, southwest of Michigan and Northern Ohio and west of Lake St. Clair (Jenks).

Miami - Aouittanons was the Miami chief, "Little Turtle", (Great Turtle) who told of his forefathers who kindled the first Fire at Detroit – The Strait region. The Miami moved South and occupied the Northern Ohio lands into Indiana and Illinois. The Maumee – Miami River area was their homeland. It was the great route of travel from Lake Erie to the Mississippi for trading.

Piankashaw, Miami people living in western Ohio and Indiana.

Mascoutin – means "Little Prairie People", who lived in Southwest Michigan.

SIOUX – DAKOTA (Dakota Sioux) at one time lived near the East Coast of Virginia and North and South Carolina. They were called Sioux, Naudowaewug or Naudowaig, meaning "Like unto Adders" or "Snake People". They were in the Central U.S. from the Mississippi to nearly the Atlantic. They were cut up and exterminated by the Algonquin and Iroquois.

Dacota – Sioux – Soos

Bwanag-Sioux people had an alliance with the Ojibwe-Sauteurs. They gave their daughters in marriage.

Nakota or **Nakoda** means "the allies", related to the Lakota and Dakota. They are Asiniibwoan – Stone Sioux or Stoney Indians – so named because they used stones to boil food.

Assiniboine Wah Kah Towah (Ojibwe Whoa, www). Assiniboine-Sioux means "to cook by stones". They were separated from the Yankton tribe of Dakota, they moved North and West. (Lahonton)

CREE, closely related to the Ojibwe, living in the North Canadian Provinces. The Sauteurs gave aid to the Cree who were at war with the Sioux, and 40 had been killed. Then both were at war with the Sioux.

DELAWARE– LENAPE, meaning "Original Men" or "common people", moved to Pennsylvania, Ohio, and then Michigan and Ontario, Canada.

Lenape or Lenappi were originally on the Atlantic Coast in the Manhatten Island area of New York.

MENOMINEE – Malouminek or Maroumine, meaning The People of Great Chief Okosh in Green Bay, Wisconsin, also means Oumalouminek –

Wild Rice People or "Wild Rice Indians", Par Excellence, The Nation of Oats. (wild oats were Wild rice). They were the Algonquin group who lived with the Winnebago.

Noquet – Nocke, were the Algonquin of the Bear totem, allies of the Saulteurs.

WINNEBAGO – Hotchungara or Hochuk, and Hochunk – were of two *phratries*, Air and Earth. Living in Wisconsin.

ILLINOIS, or Illiniwek, means "The Men"; they had 80 villages and 120 mounds. A magnificent walled city of 30,000 people, it was a great trading center. It was an Algonquin-speaking tribe West of the Miami.

Cahokia was the Great Castle City, opposite of St. Louis on the Mississippi. They were destroyed by Ojibwe allies after a Cahokia killed the Great Chief Pontiac.

Kaskaskia was the principle tribe of the Illinois Indians, on the Mississippi River.

Alligewi was the name for the Cherokee, Iroquoin-speaking people.

Talligwei was the name for Cherokee.

WOODLAND INDIANS

The Algonquin-speaking people were called the **Woodlands Indians**. They included Ojibwe, Ottawa, Pottawatomi, Huron, Winnebago, Menominee, Illinois, Wisconsin, Nipissings, Cree, Sauk, Fox, Miami, Kickapoo, Wea, Piankashaw, Mascoutin, and Shawnee.

There are Black Indians in some tribes.

INDIAN PLACES

CANADA means "From the Heart" (Joe Greaux). It also means "cabin", and the Spanish called it "A Canada" – "There is Nothing" (Gold).

Mackinaw Island was "Turtle Island" and Michigan was "Turtle Island". The now U.S. was "Turtle Island". Maine was the head of Turtle Island; the head faces East where we came from, where the Creator brought us through. Michigan, Florida, Texas, and Alaska are the feet of the Turtle. Baja California is the tail (Greaux).

At an early date, the area of Southeast Michigan was occupied by the Great Saulk Nation. The Fox – Masquackie – were neighbors to the South and West. West of the Fox were the Mascoutin and Kickapoo peoples.

The Three Fires peoples lived in Michigan and Ontario, the Northern areas of Canada, into Wisconsin and Minnesota.

Ottissippi

The Ojibwe were in Northern Michigan, the Upper Peninsula around Lake Superior, and into Wisconsin and Minnesota. Lapointe, Minnesota was their castle of government. Madeline Island was their Midiwiwin lodge. They were also around Lake Huron and Georgian Bay.

The Neutrals, who were Missisauga Ojibwes, lived in Ontario also around Georgian Bay, about the Missagi River. They were called Neutrals because they did not take sides in the disagreements between the Huron and Erie tribes. The Missisauga had the secret flint beds used as trading materials to be made into weaponry for hunting and protection from enemies. The Erie also had flint beds for trading.

The Huron were to the North and the Erie tribes to the South in Ontario. The tribes were friendly to each other and carried on great trading relationships. Their territories were bounded by lakes, rivers, and streams.

The Huron-Petun (Tobacco) and Tionontati Huron were great farmers. They were part of the Neutrals Confederacy, along with many other Iroquoian peoples and were wiped out along with the Huron and Erie (Cat People) in the Iroquois Wars.

The Pottawatomi were in South and West Michigan and around Chicago in now Illinois.

The Iroquois slaughtered the Huron tribes in 1649. The Neutrals took the Huron as prisoners. The Iroquois from New York destroyed them all. The Neutral survivors became Seneca Iroquois. Between 1648 and 1656, the Iroquois league grew from 10,000 to more than 25,000, due to the absorption of other tribes from warfare with fire sticks (firearms).

Many Seneca Iroquois towns were entirely conquered enemies.

APPENDIX
Peoples, Places, and Waterways

PEOPLES

Tribes associated with the Great Lakes and Bluewater Indian history.

THE OJIBWE were known by over 70 names. The following are some of them:

Amikouai: lived at French River; they became part of the Bawitig Ojibwe at Sault Ste. Marie, Michigan

Asistagueronon: Gens De Feu, The Fire Nation, or The Fire People; was the name the French used for all Michigan tribes

Attikamek (Lahonton)

Baouichtigouin: Bawa Tigowinini Wug, "People of the Falls"; the name moved with the band to Aamjiwnaang (Plain)

Bawichtigowek: by the Jesuits' relations

Bawitigwakinini: band called Saulteurs or Saulteux, "People of the Falls"; *Saut* meaning "falls" or "rapids"; the name moved with the people to the foot of Lake Huron

Bungees: Bangii (Yaad) by the Hudson's Bay traders

The Lake Indians

Cabellos Realzados: Spanish translation

Chippewa: Chepawa, English; Schipuwe, German name for Ojibwe

Chippeway

Cree: Kilistinon, Northern Ojibwe (Schmaltz)

Eskiaeronnon: "People of the Falls"; Huron name for band from Bawitigwakinini; the Ojibwe. (Plain)

Fies (Lahonton)

Ottissippi

Folle Avoine Sauteurs: Rice Ojibwe from Wisconsin

Gens du sauts du lac: "People of the falls from the lake"; are the Saulteux from St. Clair (David Plain, The Plains of Aamjiwnaang)

Ha Ha Ton Wan: Dakota name for Ojibwe

Iche Poyes

Itchinwo (Chaput)

Jumpers (or Leapers) (Hennepin 1698, New Discoveries)

Makade Ziibii: Black River band

Messesaga: Massasauga; also, Tisagechroamis, Zisaugeghroanu, and many other spelling variations

Mickinac: "Turtle People"

Mikikouets: Mississsakis; Saulteurs (Ojibwe) (Metis History, www)

Missisaking Dachirinouek: Misi Zaaging Dash Ininweg; regular speakers of the Great River Mouth; living at the Missisauga River near Georgian Bay to Kawartha Lakes region in Ontario and the Credit River west of Toronto

Nakota: "allies" or "confederates"

Nikikouek: associated with the Missisauga; east of North Shore of Lake Huron

Nockes: Bear (Lahonton)

Noquet: Bear Foot, Bear Gens totem; from south of Lake Superior; allies of the Saulteurs

Ojeejok: Crane, ancient totem, leaders of the Three Fires; *Bwa* means "voice"; Ojibwe means "Voice of the Crane"; A loud and far sounding cry, as he called gathering his clans to the sound of his voice.

The Cranes go back to the Flood; the Lofty Crane totem of ancient bands; the ancient band of Red Men whose totem is the Lofty Crane (Schenk, The Voice of the Crane Echoes Afar, 1997); the Crane clan were the Ojibwe leadership, and the people took on the totemic name, Bus in aus e – Echo Maker or Crane (Warren 1984)

Ojibois: Saulteurs or Jumpers or Leapers (Jones)

Od Jib Wag: plural of Odjibwa (Chaput)

Ojibwag: *wag* means "man"; the plural of Ojibwa

Ojibwas (Jones)

Ojibwauk or Ojebik: means "root or stem of peoples" (Schenk 1997)

Ojibwe: preferred spelling; Ojibwe or Saulteurs were originally "The Crane People" of the Algonquins, "the stem or root of peoples", the leadership over the tribes.

Warren says the meaning of the word Ojibwe is "to roast till puckered up" and came from the old custom of torturing prisoners of war by fire

(Chaput). Further research has put to rest this tale. Ojibwe means "the Crane", who were the original Ojibwe government and elders.

Ojibweg: plural, many; also means "pictograph" (Anishinabe used a written language to keep records, based on pictures or symbols); French meaning (Andreas)

Oochepoys

Osage: group of Missisauga Ojibwe who moved to Arkansas and Oklahoma during the Iroquois wars, to escape the wars and live a peaceable life. Part of the Stockbridge Munsee Delaware Christian Indians and the Black River Chippewa, of whom a very small group moved to Kansas during the 1836 era, removal and Trail of Tears.

Osaugee: Osage; the Black River Chippewa

Otchichak: originally the Crane People of the Algonquins, the noblest and greatest among the Ojibway (Schenk)

Oucabipoues: Sauteurs; "Good Warriors" (Lahonton)

Ouichibo: Chippewa; associated with the Marameg; North of Lake Superior

Outchibous: (Kinietz), as above

Otchipwes

Oucabipoues: Saulteurs; the Eagle tribe; the Missisauga Ojibwe (Lahonton II, 1703)

Outchibouee: derived from Crane (Schenk)

Ouchipoe

Oumisagia: Missisauga Eagle Gens, Eagle people

Ozauke: Sauks

Ozhibiiwe: "Those who keep records"; the Midewiwin Rites kept by the Mide – Holy Men (Andreas)

Pahouitingqach Irini: "People of the Falls"; Saulteur Michinac (Turtle People and Noquet – Bear)

Pahouitingwach: Irini (Kienetz), as above

Panoestigons: Chippewas (Kellogg)

Panoitigoveienhac: Sauteurs of St. Mary's River; Ojibwe or Chippewa (Metis History. info/metis.aspx)

Paouichtigouin: in Jesuit relations books

Poueouatami

Ronans or Noanu: means "people" or "tribe" (Lahonton)

Sac or Sauk: Asakiwaki; Saginaw area; means "People of the Outlet"

Sac: Osaagii Wag, meaning "Yellow Earth" and "Those at the Outlet"

Sagamum

Ottissippi

Saheeny: Easternmost Shore of Lake Huron
Sahgeeng: means "river"; River Indians
Saginaw: Saganawm, also Saganawe
Saki: Ojibwe (Kellogg)
Salt: Panoestigonce (Kellog)
Sauganaw: Sauk town or Saginaw
Saugeen, foot of Lake Huron, Ontario
Saugeeng: means "river"
Sauguinan: Peninsula of Upper Canada, 1686
Saulteurs: French name for the entire Ojibwe nation at S.S. Marie and elsewhere; the term comes from Sault, a type of rapids in which waters appeared to tumble or roll (Lahonton)
Saulteux: band of 3,000 warriors lead by Chief Laturno
Sauk or Sohk: Sawk, Saulk; means "outlet of a river"
Soto: Sotu and Sotoes
Sotties (Chaput)
Souters: Missisauga Jumpers; "to jump up and down on a river"; experts in navigating numerous rapids; in the river canoes were want to jump its channels
Tisage Chroanu: the Missisaugas from Lake Huron; lived on much of Southern Ontario into Michigan (Tanner)
Wabisiwisibiwiniiniwak: "Men of Swan River"; lived at Swan Creek at the southern tip of St. Clair County, Michigan, now known as Anchorville (Access Geneology, www); on northwest side of Lake St. Clair
Wah Kah To Wah: Assiniboin name for Ojibwe (Tanner)
Wapiswam Ziibii: Swan Creek band
Wapisiwibiwininiwak: "Men of Swan Creek" (Access Geneology, www)
Zaginau Ziibii: Saginaw band
Zisaugeghroanu: Aghsiesage chrone, another name for the Missisauga from Lake Huron, who had eight big castles (towns) (Schmaltz)

The original five totems were Crane, Bear, Fish, Loon – Ahahwuk, and Moose – Monsone.

THE OTTAWA

The Ottawa were the second elder brother of the Three Fires. The traders were called Ottawas. They were mainly Ojibwe (Schmaltz).

Adawa

Cheveux releves: "High Hairs"; French name for the Ottawa (Rogers/Smith, 1995)

Nez Perce: Amikwa Ottawas; from the Eastern waters of Lake Huron, north of Georgian Bay. They became great horsemen and developed breeding programs to improve endurance and other desirable qualities, breeding appaloosas with Arabian and others. They supplied the people with many horses and ponies. They moved to Northern Canada after the Great Iroquois Wars.

Odahwah

Odahwaug

Outaoues

Tawas (Chaput)

THE POTTAWATOMI

Ariatoeronon (Jenks)

Assisternonon: The Fire Nation; in Michigan, Fox, Sauk, Mascoutin, and Pottawatomie (Ojibwe Whoa, www)

Assistoius (Jenks)

Atsistarhonon: Huron name for them

Couacronon (Jenks)

Kunahayanu: "The Watermelon People"

Ondataouius (Jenks)

Poux

Teoronius (Jenks)

THE HURONS

Attiwandaron: Indians at Sarnia in 1627; called by the French Neutrals

Dionondadies

Hyroquois: Iroquois (Kellogg)

Kionontatehronen: Tobacco Petun, Huron

Onoontateronons: Iroquois traders who lived among the Ojibwe and traded with them. They became part of the Ojibwe after the Iroquois Wars.

Quatoghies

Roundheads: Huron (Snowowl.com. Where have all the Flowers Gone.)

Tionontaties

Tobacco Petun: Huron people of Southern Ontario; friendly with the Neutrals

Wyandot: Ouendat, Wendat; the Huron Petun-Tobacco nation; became the Wyandotte after the Iroquois Wars

NEUTRALS

The Neutrals: Attiouendaronk; people of central Southern Ontario; some were Huron, Petun, or Tobacco Huron; Iroquois and many other Iroquois groups were wiped out, and the survivors became part of the Six Nations Iroquois; stayed neutral between the Huron and Iroquois Wars. The Erie and Cat people were destroyed. Some Missisauga Ojibwe were also neutral.

The Neutre Nation De Truite: French name for the Missisauga Ojibwe

Nipissiriniens: the true Algonkins

The Nippissings: at a small lake northeast of Lake Huron; the great Sorcerers (Nation of Sorcerers)

THE ERIES

The Eries were Iroquoin, called the Cat People. They were destroyed by the Seneca Iroquois and their allies, and some were absorbed into the tribe.

SIOUX

Assiniboine: Wah Kah Towah; Sioux (Ojibwe Whoa, www)

Assiniboine: means "to cook by stones"; separated from the Yankton tribe of Dakota, they moved North and West. (Lahonton)

Nadouke or Nago: Sioux (Kellogg)

Nikikouek: associated with the Missisauga; east of the North Shore of Lake Huron

THE FOX - MESQUACKIE

The Fox: one of the largest Great Lakes tribes prior to contact in 1737; after the Fox Wars, there were 500.

Kandechiondius (Jenks)

Kutaki (Ojibwe Whoa, www.)

Masquackie: Meshkwahkihaki; Algonquin; the original, preferred name for the Fox Nation; means "Red Earth Men" or "The

Red Earths"

Musquawkee: means "Red Earth People"

Outagami

Renards: French name meaning "red"

Schenkioctontius (Jenks)

Wagoosh or Wagosh

Wakeshi or Wakoshe: Miami name for Fox (Chaput)

Miami

Kickapoo: Kikabou; Lower Michigan; related to Mascoutin and Shawnee

Mascoutan

Mazcoutin or Mackkouteng: Iskousogos (Kellogg)

THE IROQUOIS

The Iroquois were from New York.

The Five Nations Iroquois Confederacy: Ho Da Shone, People of the Long House, The Seneca, Oneida, Mohawk, Onondaga, Cayuga

The Six Nations, the Tuscaroras, united with the Five Nations Iroquois.

The Covenant Chain was with the Iroquois and other nations for trade and military alliance.

Mingo: mixed with adopted people of the Neutral, Huron, and Erie from the war of 1650. The Delaware and Shawnee were also mixed with the Iroquois in 1700. These groups lived in Eastern Ohio and Western Pennsylvania, wanting to be free of league control and political power (Iroquois Whoa, www).

Mahican or Mohican: of Ohio; absorbed by the Delaware at Stockbridge. They were invaluable to the British and Rogers Rangers in 1756. They were negotiators with the Western Alliance in Ohio, at war with the U.S., and in the War of 1812 with the American Army (Iroquois Whoa, www).

Mohawk: Mahican, Mohegan; the French called them Loupes – Wolves.

Onondaga

Oneida: Onyotaa Ka; "people of the stone set up"

Seneca: from the St. Lawrence and New York

Tuscaroras: from North Carolina; Algonquins who were Iroquoin-speaking and lived on the east bank of Niagara; the Seneca Iroquois adopted them into the Six Nations in 1722.

Tuetelo: Tuetelos or Tuetle; from Virginia; went to Susquanan and were absorbed by the Six Nations Iroquois

CHEROKEE

Allegewi: Cherokee, Talligewi: Cherokee

Oppenago: Wolves; at Detroit (Cadillac/Lajeunesse)

WINNEBAGO

Winnebago: also called Hochuk, Hoatchungara, from Wisconsin

PLACES

MICHIGAN

Mitchi Sagaigan: means "very large lake" (Gagnieur, Chaput, MI Archives)

Mitchi Asugyegan: means "Lake Country"

Bawatig: Sault Ste. Marie, Upper Michigan and Canada, on the St. Mary's River that flows between Lake Huron and Lake Superior

Pawating: means "cascade" or "rapids"; early spellings are Pawateer, Pawating, Bawateeg, Pauwating, Bawitig, Pau, Paw or Pou; means "falls"; Ing, Ig, and Eeg mean "at" or "by" (Chaput, MI Archives)

Junundat or Chenuda: southwest end of Lake Erie (Voegelin/Tanner, Indian of Northern Ohio and Southeast Michigan Ethno History)

La Pointe de Montreal: changed to L Assomption at Da Troit; Mission of Assomption founded in 1728 by Father de la Richardie (Lejuenesse)

MICHIGAN TOWNS

Algonac: known as Point Du Chene, Oak Point, Manchester, and Clay

Anchorville: first known as Swan Creek

Big Salt Lick or Grand Saline: known as Knagg's Place at Kitchewandanguonink in Burns Township; Whitmore Knaggs established a trading post here in 1820 on the Shiawasee River; Ozhaw wash kway se be, meaning "Green River", part of the Saginaw Watershed; a chief called Sha woa ni ssey is believed to have given his name to the River (Chaput).

Catholic Point: south of Belle River at now Marine City

Cholera Point: Port Huron at Pine Grove Park, where land once jutted out into the St. Clair River, near the now Port Huron Waterworks, below Fort Gratiot; where soldiers in 1832 were taken off the ship, *Henry Clay*, and left at the fort grounds, where many died of cholera and were buried at the fort cemetery. The soldiers are now in Lakeside Cemetery, near the west entrance with a marker to honor them.

Cheboyganing Creek: the place of the great rice gathering

Fair Haven: Swan Creek, Riviere Des Sygnes

Fairfield: the Delaware Moravian Indian settlement on the Huron River; later moved to the Thames River in Southern Ontario, west of Lake St. Clair

Fort Detret: Tieugsachrondio, meaning "Place of Many Beavers"; in St. Clair County, Fort Gratiot area (Jenks)

Manchester: Algonac

Michilimacina: called Isle of Orleans (Wm. Clements Library, U of M/Mitts)

New Milwaulkee: now Lakeport

Newport: now Marine city

Palmer: now St. Clair

Peach Island: Peche; fishing Island; also Isle du Large (Lejuenesse)

Point Aux Chenes: Nemitigomisking, meaning "Oak Point"; now Algonac, Michigan (Chaput)

Point Du Chene: now Algonac

Pinconning: means "Place of Potatoes" and "potato"

Red River Basin: large river east of the foot of Lake Huron (Huron Tract Treaty # 29, 1827)

Shigemaskin: means "Soft Maple Place"; now Shiawasee Town or Shi town

Washington City: now in Oakland County at the Northeast section

Windmill Point: was on the Detroit River near Lake St. Clair

Wywyaehtonock

Yankee Point: north of Belle River at what is now Marine City

WATERWAYS AND ISLANDS
THE DETROIT
Chanontian: "Place of Many Beavers"

Ka Ron Taen: the coast of the Strait (Farmer)

Cataroqui: in 1689 (Fuller)

Wa We A Tun Org: means "a circuitous approach", being located on the bend of the river (Farmer)

Wa Wea Wtonong (Lanmar, Redbook, www)

Yondatia: Detroit, the Strait, meaning "water shallow on the rocks"

Yon do tiga: Yon Clotia; a great village (Farmer 1884)

LAKE ST. CLAIR
Tziketo: means on the "Lake De La Chandiere"

Wahahehyahtahnoong: Missisauga name for Lake St. Clair (Dorothy Mitts, "That Noble Country")

Wahwehpyahtahnoong: "The Round Lake"; Missauga Ojibwe (Jenks 1912)

Lake De Ste. Claire: on De L'islles map of 1700

Lac Ganatchio on the Ste. Claire: on De L'Islles map, 1703 to 1718

Wakashan: Iroquois name for the Southern Great Lakes

ISLANDS IN THE DETROIT RIVER
Belle Isle: also known as Isle Aux Cochons or Hog Island – Kouishkouishki

CANADIAN ISLANDS IN THE DETROIT RIVER

Bois Blanc: We Go Bee Min Is, or Whitewood Island and Bass Tree Island; occupied by the Huron in 1742, a village of several hundred people. In 1796, the British built a blockhouse here and later erected a fort at Malden. Tecumseh camped here before the 1813 Battle of the Thames, where he died. The Patriots were in possession of the Island in 1838.

Isle La Peche: or Isle of the Fishes, then Peach Island in 1810; at the head of the Detroit River and above Belle Isle; home of Pontiac during the summer months

Ottissippi

Fighting Island: also, Turkey Island in 1796; originally occupied by the Wyandots, then sold to the Canadian government in 1810; Indian intrenchments were plainly visible on the Northeast end of the Island, and from these warlike appearances the island took its name. It lies across the river from Ecorse, Michigan.

Canatarra: now a park, the East Channel of the St. Clair River once flowed through here; Lake Chipican remains to mark the place.

Drummond Island: Isle of Detour, also Pontaganipy; named in honor of Sir Gordon Drummond, then Lt. Governor of Canada.

Grand Bend: Aux Coches, meaning "riverbend"; where the Aux Sable River takes an abrupt turn from flowing North to flowing South. It lies on the Southeast Shore of Lake Huron, about 45 minutes north of Sarnia, Ontario. It was called Port Franks at one time.

LAKES

Lake Burwell: in North Lambton County; drained in 1892 for farm land

Lake Chipican: "Lake of Roots"; in Canatarra Park; was once part of the East Channel of the St. Clair River, one of three channels which flowed into the St. Clair River from Lake Huron.

Lake George: North Lambton County; drained for farming, and a cut was made through it to change the course of the Ausable River to Lake Huron at Port Franks Harbor.

Lake Nipissing: in Northern Ontario; means "small lake"

Lake Ontario: Lake of St. Louys

Lake Smith: a resting place for tundra swans, geese, and other migratory birds; drained in 1955 for farmland. The birds still migrate here every spring. There is a "Return of the Swans" celebration at the Lambton Heritage Museum in early April (Ontario Encyclopedia, www).

Lake St. Clair: Lac des Eaux de Mer; salt water lake (Lejuenesse)

Lake Wawanosh: named for Chief Wawanosh, who was chief over the three reservations of Sarnia, Stoney Point, and Kettle Point; Wawanosh means "One Who Sails Carefully", also Egg Bad.

RIVERS

Au Chaudiere Riviere: Catfish Creek at Northwest Lake Erie

Duluth Riviere: Black River

La Rivere Aux Dindes: Turkey Creek on the Detroit River, south of Detroit, north of River Canards

La Vielille Reine: on the Detroit River, south of Windsor

Rifle River: Mishowusk; flows into Lake Huron at Au Grey, Michigan

OTHER WATERWAYS ASSOCIATED WITH THE BLUEWATER AND GREAT LAKES INDIANS

Muskingum: Moose King Goom, Moose Eye
River Aux Peches
Puces
Ruscom: Rochester Township
Wye: east of the town of Midland, Ontario
Black River: Skoo Taw Gur Mish (Johnson and Browning Map)
Ottissippi: Waikai Go Sing
Chis So Wee: Big River

AFTERWORD

"Who speaks for the Indian? Amazingly, his cause is almost without truth." John Keats wrote this in 1964.

"Under the assumed inevitable defeat and triumph of White man. The Indian was crushed, broken, disorganized, externally and internally, they gave up the fight. He knew no one would listen to him. Break the silence imposed on him and us and our children: 'Let freedom ring, the truth be known'" (Steiner).

"We need to unite all the races and both of the sexes if we are going to be strong and the Sacred Hoop is to be mended, turning towards each other, instead of away from one another" (Barefoot Windwalker, Bodawadmi, www).

"The rights of man come not from the generosity of the State, but from the hand of God" (John F. Kennedy).

"The present events with counsels leave observations and conclusions to the liberty and faculty of every man's judgement" (Francis Bacon, Advancement of Learning).

"A morsel of genuine history is a thing so rare as to always be valuable. It only informs of what bad government is" (Thomas Jefferson).

"This book tells a part of the Indian history of the Great Lakes, laying the groundwork for further study. One can delve further into every area of culture and history and gain a more complete picture of these peoples. Due to time and space constraints, I have not been able to include a more detailed history. Each source will further enhance this study if one will search it out.

This book is a starting point to gathering more indigenous history and early St. Clair County history. Many of you have information within your own studies, libraries, public records, family records, and oral history that tells another piece of the puzzle of the Great Lakes Indians History". I would appreciate any input to fill in the missing pieces. Together we can create understanding where there is great ignorance. *American Holocaust* by David E. Stannard, written in 1992, is a real eye-opener, and I recommend reading it for the serious study of history" (Morgan).

"To learn the true story of America, we must search for it in our own backyards. Nowhere in the country is this more clearly shown than in the St. Clair River District, for its story is the story of Michigan, and the great Northwest Territory is, in fact, the story of America" (Mitts).

"The Indians survived our open intention of wiping them out, and since the tide turned, they have even weathered our good intentions toward them, which can be much more deadly" (John Steinbeck America and Americans).

"The Native American experience continues to evolve. It is a story that has not ended. The Colonial Era is still here alive and well, and so are the Indians" (Morgan).

"Concealment of the historical truth is a crime against the people" (Gen. Petro G. Grigorenko. Samizdat letter to a History Journal, 1975 USSR).

"He that cannot reason is a fool. He that will not is a bigot. He that dare not is a slave" (Andrew Carnegie).

It has been a very emotional and shocking journey through the early history of the indigenous people of St. Clair County, Michigan and the Northwest Territory. I have survived the torturous trail through it all and will be forever changed by these people and the light of truth now exposed. May we be kind to one another and honest. May we, too, catch a vision of a United Nation with love for our brother. May we appreciate and learn from one another, gleaning the good for all mankind, learning from the past and its flaws, to see a new future where love and goodness flourish.

Cheryl Morgan, 2015

END NOTES

"True patriotism is based on knowledge and understanding rather than on ignorant prejudice. By learning how far we have come during the preceding centuries. We should be able better to chart our course for the future. Recognition for past mistakes can help us to avoid making the same ones a second or a third time" (Clever Bald, Michigan in 4 Centuries, 1954).

November is Native American Heritage Month.

Natives know that optimism is the key to good health. Worry makes you sick, as do bad thoughts. Replace them with happiness and optimism, and you shall live a long and healthy life (Terri Jean, 365 days of Walking the Red Road).

"Without freedom of thought, there can be no such thing as wisdom, and no such thing as public liberty without freedom of speech" (Benjamin Franklin).

"Lethargy is the forerunner of death to public liberty" (Thomas Jefferson Letters).

Humankind has not woven the web of life; we are but one thread within it. Whatever we do to the web, we do to ourselves. All things are bound together, all things connect (Chief Seattle).

RECOMMENDED READING

The most helpful books on Ojibwe history are the following:

The Archaeological Atlas of Michigan, Hindsdale (1928), Michigan Room SCC Library, Clark Historical Library, Mt. Pleasant Mi., Ziibiwing Cultural Center, Mt. Pleasant, MI. Many other places also have this book.

The Atlas of Great Lakes Indians, Tanner, Helen H. This is a great history of the Great Lakes tribes. Helen was an authority to the government and courts on locations of the Tribes, and their histories.

Diba Jimooyung, Telling our Story, Saginaw Chippewa history. This is an excellent source of Ojibway history.

The Plains of Aamjiwnang by David Plain, descendant of Little Thunder, who made his home at the foot of Lake Huron and Black River. Plain has written six books about Native culture and history.

The Ojibwe of Southern Ontario, Schmaltz, Peter. This book answers many questions and corrects many false ideas. It is taken from historical facts and oral tradition.

The Soul of the Indian, Indian Boyhood, and *From the Deep Woods to Civilization*, Charles Eastman's writings, are a wonderful source of Ojibwe culture. He was a prolific writer who lived in Southern Ontario and Detroit.

Ojibwe Culture. Francis Densmore was an expert on Ojibwe culture.

Panther in the Sky, Thom, James A., NY: Ballantine Books. Early History of the Northwest Territory, Ohio and British Indian wars, excellent history of Tecumseh's life.

MSU, MSU Libraries, Map Library, scanned maps of Michigan. These old maps give a lot of history of town and place names.

BIBLIOGRAPHY

Andreas. *History of St. Clair County, Michigan*. University of Michigan, 1884. Quod.lib.umich.edu

Armstrong, Virginia Irving. *I Have Spoken: Indian Oratory*. Swallow Press, 1971. ISBN – 10: 0804005303, 13: 978-0804005302

Askin, John. Papers Vol. 1, 1747-1795, 1928; Vol. 2, 1796-1820, 1931, includes Father Dennison, Biographies of Early Detroit and Canada. Milo Quaife/Burton Historical Collection.

Bald, Clever. *Michigan in Four Centuries*. Brown, 1954. www

Banai, Edward Benton. *The Seven Fires, The Mishomis Book*, and *The Voice of the Ojibway*. UMN Press, 1988. 9780816673827

Barnes, John T., honorary Chippewa Chief. Lambton, 1967.

Beardslee, Lois. *The Modern Indian*. 1995.

Belfy, Phil. *Three Fires Unity: The Anishinabeg of the Lake Huron Borderlands*. University of Nebraska Press, 2011.

Benz, Williamson, and Ekdahl. *Diba Jimooyung, Telling Our Story: A History of the Saginaw Ojibwe Anishinabek*. Mt. Pleasant, MI: Ziibiwing Cultural Society, 2005. 978-0-9672331-1-6

Berkhoffer, Robert F., Jr. *The White Man's Indian*. NY: Vintage Books, Random House, 1979.

Blackbird, Andrew. *The History of the Ojibwe Indian.* www

Bonhomme, Draper. *Papers.* Michigan Room, St. Clair County Library, Port Huron, MI.

Brakeman, Nancy. *Remembrances of Mrs. Peter Brakeman.* Michigan Room, St. Clair County Library, Port Huron, MI.

Burton Historical Library. Detroit, Michigan.

Burton, Clarence. 1896, Cadillac Village or Detroit under Cadillac, 1853-1932. Hathi Trust. Burton, Clarence. *Beginnings of Michigan, Hathi Trust, and the City of Detroit, 1701-1922.* S. J. Clark Publishing Co., 1922. www

Cameron, Herman E. Memorial Foundation, "Kah Wam Da Meh" ("We See Each Other"). 1988. Jean Frazier.

Chaput Collection, Papers, Indian Place Names, Michigan Archives, Library of Michigan, Lansing, MI.

Cleland, Charles E. *Rites of Conquest.* University of Michigan Press, 1992.

Clifton, James A., George L. Cornell, and James McClurken. *People of the Three Fires: The Ottawa, Potawatomi, and Ojibway of Michigan.* Grand Rapids Intertribal Council, 1986.

Copeway, George (John). *The Traditional History and Characteristic Sketches of the Ojibwa Nation, 1850.* Indian Life and Indian History, 1860. www

Crawford, Kim. *The Daring Trader: Jacob Smith in the Michigan Territory 1802-1825.* Michigan State University Press, 2012.

Densmore, Francis. *Chippewa Customs.* 1979.

Deur, Nishnawbe. 1981.

Diba Jimoojung, *Telling Our Story: A History of the Saginaw Ojibwe Anishinabek,* Mtl. Pleasant, MI: Ziibiwing Cultural Society, 2005. 978-0-9672331-1-6

Dixson. *Life at the Flats, 1999, St. Clair Memories.* Mt. Clemons, MI. 586-242-2222

Eastman, Charles. *The Soul of the Indian, The Indian Today and as He Was, From the Deep Woods to Civilization,* and *Indian Boyhood.* 1902. www

Echert, Allan W. *A Sorrow in Our Heart: The Life of Tecumseh.* Wilderness Empire, 1992. Little Brown & Co.

Eicher, Al and Dave. *The Indian History of Michigan's Thumb, The Orphan Train.* Program Source. Com.

Elford, Jean Turnbull. *Canada, West's Last Frontier: A History of Lambton.* Ontario: Lambton County Historical Society, 1982.

Emmert. Michigan Historical Collection, Vol. 47.

Ewing, Wallace K. Ph. D, *Footprints: Stories of Native Americans in West Central Michigan,* 2016

Farmer, Silas. *History of Detroit and Michigan,* Vol 2. 1884. www

Farrand, Mrs. B.C. *The Indians at Sarnia, Wyoming, Ontario,* Lambton Archives.

Farrel, David. *The Detroit Fur Trade,* Dissertation, 1865, U of W, Milwaukee, Michigan Archives, Lansing, MI.

Flocken. *Chiefs.* University of Minnesota, 2013. www

Fowle. "Sault Ste. Marie and Michigan". G.P. Putnam's and Sons, 1925. www

Frazier, Jean. *Kah Wam Da Heh*. Herman E. Cameron Foundation, 1988.

Fuller, George N. *Historic Michigan: Land of the Great Lakes, 1917-1941,* Vol. 1. MPHC, MHC, 1944, National Historic Assoc., 1924. Dayton, OH: University of Michigan. www

Fuller, George N. *Local History and Personal Sketches of St. Clair and Shiawassee Counties; Historic Michigan, 1873; A Centennial History of the State and Its People, 1939*. The Lewis Publishing Co. Hathi Trust. Michigan Pioneer and Historical Society. www

Greaux, Joe. Woodland Metis Ojibwe Peace Chief. 2014 Author Interview.

Hatt, Richards. *The Sanilac Petroglyphs*. Cranbrook Institute of Science, 1958. Bulletin No. 36. Papworth, Butterfield/Port Sanilac Museum.

Hebner, Marilyn and Diana. SCCFHG, MIGC, Immigration Papers.

Helbig, Althea K. *Nanabozhoo, Giver of Life*. Brighton, MI: Green Oak Press, 1987. 0931600065/9780931600067

Hennepin, Louis. *A New Discovery*. Description of Louisiana, 1683. www

Hinsdale, Wilbert B. *The Archaeological Atlas of Michigan*. Ann Arbor, Michigan: University of Michigan Library, 1928. www

Hodgins, Bruce W. *Canoeing Fur Trade, 1994*. Toronto Heritage. www

Hodgins. Ontario Genealogical Society.

Hotchkiss, George W. *History of the Lumber and Forest Industry of the Northwest.* 1898. SCC Library, Michigan Room.

Howard, Nancy. *Diary, 1813.* Michigan Room, St. Clair County Library.

Hudgins. Detroit Papers. Wayne University.

Hudgins. *The Biodiversity Atlas of Lake Huron to Lake Erie.* EPA, 2002. www

Jenks and Clark Papers, Michigan Room, St. Clair County Library, Port Huron, MI.

Jenks, William L. *St. Clair County Centennial and Homecoming Celebration.* 1921. www

Jenks, William L. *The History of St. Clair County, Michigan: Biographical Memoirs of St. Clair County.* Vol. 2. Chicago and NY: University of Michigan, The Lewis Publishing Co., 1912. quod.lib.umich.edu

Jenness. *Culture Change and the Personality of Ojibwe Children.* 1954. www

Johnson, Ida A. *The Michigan Fur Trade.* Lansing MI Historical Commission, 1919.

Johnston, A.J. Lambton County Place Names. Sarnia, ON: Lambton County Council, 1925. Revised 1942, 2nd Edition. Wyoming, ON: Lambton Archives, 2008.

Jones, Rev. Peter. *The History of the Ojibwe Indians.* 1861. www

Kellogg, Louise P. "Early Narratives of the Northwest, 1634-1699". 1897. NY: Barnes and Noble, 1953. www

Kienietz. *Traditional Ojibwa Religion*. Library of Michigan.

Lahonton, Louis A. "Voyages to New France". 1703. www; "Voyages to North America II" with Thwaites. www; and "Travels Through Louisiana". www

Lambton Archives. Wyoming, Ontario.

Landon, Fred. *Lake Huron, 1944*. Bobbs-Merrill Co., Quaife, WHS.

Lanman, Charles. *The Red Book of Michigan 1819-1895, 1855*. E. B. Smith & Co. Philip Solomons, 1871. quod.lib.umich.edu

Laubin, Reginald and Gladys. *The Indian Tipi*. University of Oklahoma Press, 1957.

Lauriston, Victor. *Lambton's 100 Years, 1849-1949*. Beers Book, 1906. Our Roots, 2006. U of Calgary.

Levy-Bruhl, Lucien. *How Natives Think*. Lilian A. Clare. 1910, 1927. 9781614277866

Lewis, Kenneth E. *West to Far Michigan*. MSU Press, 2002.

Loewen, James W. *Lies My Teacher Told Me*. The New Press, 1995, 2007. 9780743296281

Lossing, Benton J. *Pictorial Field Book of the War of 1812*. 1869/Bill Carr, 2001, Free Pages History, Roots Web, Ancestry.com

Lowrie and Clark. *American State Papers and Military Affairs*. 1832.

Marantette Papers, Fur Trade, Michigan Archives.

Mason. Culture. 1997.

Mayhew, Eugene J. *Fort Sinclair: The British Roots of St. Clair, Michigan*. St. Clair Historical Commission, 2003.

McArthur, Patsy and Farrand, B.C. *Historic Saugeen Metis.* Southampton, ON: Inverhuron Learning Center, 2013. www

McKenny. Native Advocate. 1959.

Means, Russell. *Where White Men Fear to Tread.* St. Martin's Press, 1996.

Michigan Archives, Lansing, MI.

Michigan Pioneer and Historical Collection. www

Mitts, Dorothy Marie. *That Noble Country: The Romance of the St. Clair River Region.* Philadelphia: Dorrance & Co., 1968. Dorothy Mitts was a newspaper columnist for the *Port Huron Times Herald* in the mid-1900s.

Moore, Charles. *History of Michigan*, Vol. 4. The Lewis Publishing Co., 1915. www

MPHC, 1890, Annual Meeting, Granny Rodd, Harrington.

MPHC, Vol. 1, O.C. Thompson, Early St. Clair County History.

MPHC, Vol. 8, Wm. T. Mitchell, Early St. Clair County History.

MPHC, Vol. 4, Mack and Miller Distillery, Harsens Island. "Recollections of Aura Stewart", 1881, pg. 346.

MPHC, Vol. 6, 1883, Autobiography of Eber Ward.

MPHC, Vol. 8, Wm. T. Mitchell, Early St. Clair County History.

MPHC, Vol. 11, 1887, Wm. L. Bancroft, Duperon Baby, Slavery.

MPHC, Vol. 17, 1793, Friends Micellany, Gage, Trade, 1762, Early History of St. Clair County, Mrs. B.C. Farrand.

Vol. 20, List of Indian Locations and Numbers.

Vol. 26, Treaty of Saginaw, 1817, 1819. Enos Goodrich, 1896, Early Detroit.

Vol. 28, Calvin J. Thorpe, Trade, Harrington, D.C. Walker, Northern Slavery.

Vol. 29, 1899, Jane M. Kinney, Clyde Twp.

Vol. 38, Emigration.

Vol. 47, Prescott, Emmert, Religion, Williams, Disease.

Vol. 52, David Farrel, Settlement along the Detroit Frontier, 1860-1796.

Methodist Ministries in Michigan, Dorothy Reuter, 1993, Library of Michigan, Lansing, Michigan. www

Munson, John. Michigan Historical Commission, British History, MI Room, St. Clair County Library, Port Huron, MI.

Nearing, Scott. *The Maple Sugar Book*. 1950. 9781890132637. Chelsea Green, 2000.

Nelson, Larry L. *A Man of Distinction Among Them, Alexander McKee*. Kent State UP, 1999.

Niehardt, John G. *Black Elk Speaks, 1932*. State University of New York Press, 2008.

Orange, Patricia. *Lambton County, Ontario Ojibwe History*. Wyoming, ON: Lambton Archives, 1975.

Parkins, Almon E. *The Historical Geography of Detroit, 1879 – 1940*. Lansing MI Historical Commission, 1918. www

Parkman. *The Conspiracy of Pontiac*. 1763. www

Plain, Alymer N. *History of Sarnia Reserve*. 1950, Lambton Archives.

Plain, Aylmer N. Osarkodawa in Retrospect, 1975. Sarnia Reserve and Ojibwe History. G. Smith.

Plain, David D. *The Plains of Aamjiwnaang: Our History*. Trafford Publishing, 2007.

Plain, David. *1300 Moons*. Trafford Publishing, 2011.

Plain, David. *From Quisconson to Caughnowaga*. Trafford Publishing, 2015.

Plain, Nicholas. *Sarnia Reserve History of*, and *History of the Chippewa of Sarnia*. 1950, 1951.

Playter, George F. *The History of Methodism in Canada*. Canadian Methodist Historical Society, 1862. www

Prescott, William. *A History of Michigan Methodism, The Father Still Speaks, Worldcat*. 1941. www

Quimby. Culture. 1960.

Reid, Joyce. Papers. Deckerville, MI: 2014. (Joyce has devoted her life to education in the spiritual, music, and Indian history. She has received many honors for her work. She has hosted an annual Indian Day in Deckerville for 30 years, never forgetting her own heritage once she found that she had Native blood as a young woman.)

River, Charles. *The Chippewa Native American Tribes: The History and Culture of.* Editor. 2014.

Roufs, Chiefs, Culture, 2006, U. O. Oklahoma.

Schenk, Theresa M. *The Voice of the Crane Echoes Afar: The Sociopolitical Organization of the Lake Superior Ojibwe, 1640-1855.* Garland Pub. Inc., 1997.

Schmaltz, Peter S. *The Ojibwa of Southern Ontario.* University of Toronto Press, 1991.

Schoolcraft, Henry. *30 Years among the Indians*, 1848, 1851, Travels in Minnesota and Wisc. 1821. www

Smith, Donald B. and Rogers, Edward S. *Aboriginal Ontario: Historical Perspectives on the First Nations.* Dundurn, 1994/2012.

Smith, Donald B. Kahkewaquonaby, Peter Jones, "Sacred Feathers" (Sacred Waving Feathers). University of Toronto. www

Smith, Donald B. *Missisauga Portraits: Ojibwe Voices from Nineteenth Century Canada.* University of Toronto, 2013. www

Sonnenberg, Lemke, and John M. O'Shea. "Caribou Hunting in the Upper Great Lakes". University of Michigan, Museum of Anthropology Memoir 57, Anthropological Archaeology.

Speck, Gordon. *Breeds and Halfbreeds.* C. N. Potter, 1969. ASIN B00R1ZLG8M

Spencer, Lynn. *History of Petroglyph Park.* M.913.87 – Michigan Printing Co., Bad Axe, MI/Port Sanilac Museum.

Stanley, Margueritte. *From Whence We Came.* 1977. Port Huron Library.

Ottissippi

Stannard, David E. *American Holocaust.* Oxford, 1992. 0 – 19 507581 – 1, 0 – 19 – 508557 – 4, PBK

Tanner, Helen H. and Voegelin, Ermine W. *Indians of Northern Ohio and Southeastern Michigan: An ethnohistorical report (American Indian Ethnohistory: North Central and North Eastern).* Garland Publishing, 1975. Copyright Creative Commons.

Tanner, Helen H. *Atlas of Great Lakes Indian History.* Newberry Library, University of Oklahoma Press, 1987.

Tanner, Helen H. *The Chippewa of Lower Michigan.*

Tanner, Helen H. *The Ojibwe.* Newberry Library: Chelsea House Publishers, NY, Philadelphia, 1992.

The Clark Library of Western History, CMU, Mt. Pleasant, MI.

The History of Macomb County, Michigan. www

The History of Saginaw County, Michigan. www

The History of Warren, Michigan. www

The History of Wayne County, Michigan. www

The Indian and Pioneer History of Saginaw County. www

The Indians at Sarnia. Mrs. B. C. Farrand, Wyoming, Ontario: Lambton Archives.

The Library of Michigan, Lansing, MI.

Thom, James A. *Panther in the Sky.* NY: Ballantine Books, 1989.

Thom, James A. *Long Knife.* NY: Ballantine Books, 1979.

Tunkashila, Gerald H. *Indian Mythology and History*. NY: St. Martin's Press, 1994.

Utley, Henry M. *Michigan as a Province, Territory and State*. Vol. 4. 1906. www

Vecsey, Christopher. *Traditional Ojibwe Religion*. www

Warner, Robert. *Economic and History Report on Royce Area 111*.

Warren, William W. *History of the Ojibwe People*. 1885. www

We See Each Other. Frazier/Herman Cameron Foundation.

Western Historical Co. *The History of St. Clair County, Michigan*. www

Wilson, William E. *Shooting Star – The Story of Tecumseh*. NY: J.J. Little and Ives Co., 1942.

Woolworth, Dearborn Historical Society, Detroit Indians, Michigan Room, St. Clair County Library.

Zinn, Howard. *A People's History of the United States, 1492-Present*. 20th Anniversary Edition. Harper Collins, 1999.

ONLINE SITES

African Holocaust, Indian Holocaust, Wole Soyika, www

Andreas, History of St. Clair County, MI. 1884, www

Angel Fire, Native History, www

Archaeological Atlas of Michigan, Hindsdale, 1928, University of Michigan www

Bureau of Indian Affairs Apology to Native Americans, Tuhtonka, World Future Feed, www

Ottissippi

Blackwater River People, www

Black Elk, www

Blackhawk, www

Bodewatomi History and Culture, www

Burton, Clarence, Beginnings of Michigan, Cadillac, www

Canadian Indian History, www

Cannon, Mounds, 1973, www

Chippewa History, E How, www

City Data, Michigan History, Indian Allies, www

Constantin, Phil, Ojibwe Calendar, www

Davis, Thomas J., African, Indian Americans, Arizona State University, www

Decolonization, www

Detroit Historical Society, 1872, Slavery in the Early 1800s, Detroit Michigan, J.S. Girardin, www

dickshovel.com, www

Ehow, www

Flocken, University of Minnesota, 2013, Chiefs, www

From the Deep Woods to Civilization, The Soul of the Indian,
Charles Eastman, www

    Genealogy Trails, Fuller, Slavery, www

    Gulewitsch, Victor, 1995, Chippewa of Kettle and Stoney Point, Historical Claims Commission Research Office, www

    Hathi Trust, wonderful source of historical writings, www

Cheryl Morgan

Hennepin, *A New Discovery*, Description of Louisiana, 1683, www

Ottissippi

Historic Saugeen Metis, Patsy McArthur/B.C. Farrand, Upper Detroit to Saugeen, Lower Lake Huron's Metis and Trade, Upper Region of the Detroit River, Lake Huron Watersheds, Bruce Peninsula, Inverhuron Learning Center, Southampton, Ontario, 2013, www

History of Canada and Canada West, www

History of Canadian Indians, 1763-1840, Marionopolis College, www

History of Macomb County, Michigan, www

History of Methodism in Canada, George Frederick Playter, 1862, www

History of Michigan, www

History of the Ojibwe Indians, Andrew Blackbird, www

History of the Ojibwe Indians, Rev. Peter Jones, 1861, www

History of Saginaw County, MI, www

History of St. Clair County, MI, Western Historical Co., www

History of Warren, MI, www

History of Wayne County, MI, www

Hodgins, Bruce W., Canoeing Fur Trade, 1994, Toronto Heritage, www

Hudgins, Wayne University, Detroit, Papers, www

Indian Affairs: Law and Treaties, Oklahoma State University, OSU, www

Indian and Pioneer History of Saginaw County, MI, www

Indian Boyhood, Charles Eastman, www

Indian History Timeline, www

Indian Law, www

Indians. Org. Culture, www

Ipperwash Commission of Inquiry historical background, Attngen.jus.gov.on.ca

Iroquois, www

Isabella County, MI, Gen. Web, www

Jenks, A. E., Wild Rice Gatherers, 1900, www

Jenks, Wm. L., History of St. Clair County, MI, 1912, Biographical Memoirs of St. Clair County, Vol. 2, St. Clair County Centennial and Homecoming Celebration, 1921, www

Jews and African History, Halle, Selassie, www

Kugel, 1998, Treaties, www

Lahonton, Louis Armand, De Lom D'Arce, Baron De La Honton, Voyages to New France, 1703, Voyages to North America II/Thwaites, Travels through Louisiana, www

Lanman, History of MI from Its Earliest Colonization, www

Lejeunesse, E. J., The Windsor Border Region: Canada's Southernmost Frontier, www

Lexington MI history, www

Liberty Law Site, www

Lincoln Quotes, www

Little Turtle, Canada History, www

Losser, A., Ojibwe Culture, www

Early Recognized Treaties with American Indian Nations, www

Macomb, William, Memoir, www

Ottissippi

Methodist Ministry in Michigan, Dorothy Reuter, 1993, Library of Michigan, Lansing, MI

Metis History Timeline, Canadian History, a Distinct Viewpoint, www

Metis History, www

Michigan Pioneer and Historical Collection, MPHC, Vol. 40, www

Mills, James Cooke, History of the Saginaw Chippewa, 1918, www

Missisauga Eagle Tribe, www

Moore, Charles, History of MI, Vol. 4, The Lewis Publishing Co., 1915, www

MSU, MSU Libraries, Map Library, Scanned Maps of MI, www

Mystic Detroit, Patriot War, www

Native American Apology, Canada, www

Native Tec. Pierre Girard, www

Ojibwe Culture, Kevin Callahan, UMN, www

Ojibwe History, Migration to the Great Lakes, www

Ojibwe Indian History Timeline, www

Ojibwe Whoa, , www

Ontario Encyclopedia, www

Papal Bulls, www

Parkins, Almon Ernest, *The Historical Geography of Detroit*, 1918, www

Parkman, *The Conspiracy of Pontiac*, 1763, www

Porterfield, Kay, *10 Lies about Indigenous Science*, www

Prescott, Wm., *Native Religion*, 1941, Worldcat, www

Project Gutenberg, the American Indian, Alexander Henry, and Henry Schoolcraft, www

Sarnia, Wikipedia, www

Schoolcraft, Henry, *30 Years among the Indians*, 1848, 1851, Travels in Minnesota and Wisc., 1821, www

Smith, Donald B., *Missisauga Portraits: Ojibwe Voices from Nineteenth Century Canada*, 2013, U.O. Toronto, www

Students on Site, Native American Missions and Schools, www

Sturdevant, Treaties, 1978, www

The Canadian Truth Commission Report, www

The History of County Creation, CMU, excellent site, www

The History of the County of Middlesex, Canada, Godspeed Publishing, 1889, www

The Indian and Pioneer History of Saginaw County, www

The Indian Today and as He Was, Charles Eastman, www

The Lies about when Slavery Ended, Denise Oliver Velez, 2012, www

The Plains of Aamjiwnaang, David D. Plain, Sarnia, Ont. Ojibwe History, and five other books, www

The Pokagon Bodewadmi, Pottawatomi, www

The Soul of the Indian, Charles Eastman, www

The Truth about Slavery, www

The Westbrooks Ontario, www

Ottissippi

The Writings of Cadillac, www

Tinker, George, Osage School of Theology, www

Tolatsga, Tolatsga.org, Coral Painter Magazine, www

Travers, Karen Jean, Dissertation, Seeing with Two Eyes, Colonial Policy, The Huron Tract and Change 1780-1863, York University, 2015, Toronto, Canada

Treaty Texts, Upper Canada Land Surrenders, www

Turtle Nation Indians, www

Tutonka, World Future Feed, www

University of Oklahoma, Indian Affairs Law and Treaties, www

Upper Canada History, Early Canadian History Narrative, www

Vecsey, Christopher, Traditional Ojibwe Religion, www

War Bounty Lands, Ancestry, www

Western Historical Society, 1883, French History, Northwest and Indian History, www

When were Blacks Truly Freed from Slavery, Hillary Crosby, www

Whoa, dickshovel.com site map, First Nations Histories, Lee Stultzman, www

Wisconsin State Historical Society, Great Lakes Indian History, www

Wisconsin State Historical Society, Vol. 6, The Northwest 1817, Storrow Letters, www

WSHS, Collection of, Vol. 10, Blackhawk, www

Wyandottenation.org

PERIODICALS

Blue Water Indian Pow Wow, 1995, booklet

Friends of the St. Clair River Watershed, Brochure

Harpers Magazine, Vol. 98, Pokagon, Simon, The massacre of Fort Dearborn at Chicago, 1899, www

Marine City Gazette, 1876, Western Historical Co., Aura Stewart, Early St. Clair County

Michigan Archeology, Vol. 3, 1957, Richard A. Pohrt, War Club

North American Review, 1830, Jackson Treaties

Sarnia Observer, Shirley Brownlee, 1857, Lumbering, Barnes, Ojibwe, 1967

Saturday Evening Post, 1947, Robert Murphy, Mother Rodd

The Detroit News Tribune, 1896, Dixon, Mother Rodd

The Penny Magazine, April 29, 1837, Ontario, Canada

The Smithsonian, 2014, Amanda Foreman, The Birth of American Freedom and the Founding of the Union

ACKNOWLEDGEMENTS

Marilyn Hebner, President of the St. Clair County Family History Group, was a great help to me in researching. Her friendship and encouragement are much appreciated. Marilyn and Diana Hebner's research on immigration was very helpful. I would also like to thank others at SCC Family History Group for their encouragement.

My family: son, Tom, and daughter-in-law, and my grandkids who helped a low-tech grandma with the Technical World. My Husband Tom, who was supportive. My sisters-in-laws for their encouragement.

Friends: Pat Walker, Lynn Kamendat, Gail Terpening, Bob and Margie Archer, and others who were there to encourage.

The many people at libraries and archives, and Anita Herd, at Ziibiwing Cultural Center. Thank you for all your help in accessing research publications.

Joyce Reid, for all her kindness and support. Joe Greaux for the 2014 interview. David Plain for his help and work in making known the local history. Mike Connel for his review of Chapter 7, French, British, English and Americans.

My Editor Sara Constantino for her wise work in making the book professional.

Thank you all for your part in bringing this work to fruition.

Cheryl Morgan

AUTHOR BIOGRAPHY

This book came about after a visit to the library where I could not find local Indian History. I grew up in the St. Clair and Black River area of Michigan, fishing on all the area waters with my father and brothers. I loved books, libraries, horses and puzzles; I was not a tech person. I love to cook, garden, travel, and camp. I determined to find and share the truth. This has been a difficult journey in every way. I give you, the reader, the truth and blessings I also reaped.

Cheryl Morgan

Cheryl Morgan lives near Port Huron, Michigan with her husband, Tom, and dog, Fred.

INDEX

A

Aamjiwnaang, 14, 15, 23, 41, 48, 253, 305, 315, 337, 342, 359, 372, 406, 407, 501, 573, 580, 581, 602, 611
Abbott, James, 149, 158-160, 167, 178, 220, 237, 267, 414, 415, 555
Abbottsford, 167, 168, 178, 180, 181, 186, 272, 543, 550, 553, 555, 556, 557
Alcohol, 68, 118, 139, 140, 166, 214, 238, 250, 253, 326, 371, 373, 381, 387, 445, 447, 507, 508, 509, 513, 514, 518, 531, 532, 534
Algonac, 17, 48, 110, 119, 153, 182, 451, 542, 544-549, 552, 553, 555, 563, 587
Algonquin, 1, 5, 34-36, 42, 44, 45, 47, 69-71, 81, 82, 83, 101, 200, 292, 304, 369, 402, 442, 452, 511, 527, 571, 572, 575- 578, 585
Allegheny, 28, 162, 204, 205, 215, 216, 226, 248
American Fur Co.,38, 134, 149, 155, 157, 165, 251, 386, 516, 555
American, 20, 28, 38, 49, 82, 92, 96, 102, 103, 109, 114, 115, 122, 126, 129, 131, 134, 142, 149, 151-157, 159-167, 170, 179, 186, 187, 193, 198, 211, 212, 215-224, 226, 228, 230, 232, 233, 234-240, 242-244, 246, 247, 250, 251, 254, 256, 258-263, 265, 267, 269, 271, 272, 273, 274, 275, 276, 280, 284, 286, 292, 293, 301, 303, 304, 306, 307, 309, 312, 313, 316, 319, 323-326, 335, 352, 357, 361, 364, 365, 375, 378, 379, 383, 385, 386, 389, 392, 393, 394, 410, 412, 414, 416 -418, 428, 429, 449, 459, 474, 485, 486, 490, 506, 510, 515, 516, 519-521, 523-526, 528, 529, 532-537, 542, 545, 546, 555, 566, 570, 576, 586, 592, 593, 600, 603, 604, 609-612
Amherstburg, 28, 160, 172, 200, 220, 233, 242, 255, 268, 282, 284, 297, 307, 322, 330, 332, 351, 365, 417, 420, 423, 425
Anishinabe, 1, 3-5, 7, 36, 41, 47- 49, 50, 63, 67, 80, 82, 97, 105, 127, 130, 139, 208-210, 212, 218, 238, 250, 255, 326, 336, 365, 371-376, 381, 386-388, 401, 410, 433-435, 440, 441, 443, 446-450, 452, 453, 457, 458, 463, 464, 470, 504, 507, 513-515, 517, 527, 532, 537, 539, 571, 582
Arrowheads, 489
Askin, John, 150, 151, 152, 156, 158, 159, 232, 293, 336, 347, 348, 354, 414
Astor, John Jacob 155, 157, 164, 165, 349, 516, 542
Automobiles, 569

B

Baby, Duperon, 150, 167, 179, 220, 221, 274, 414, 601
Bear Creek, 28, 29, 112, 310, 331, 332, 333, 334, 338, 342, 347, 365, 557
Beard, Ai, 180, 182, 553

Bears, 56, 63, 75, 76, 86, 170, 192, 306, 327, 485, 486, 544, 557
Beaver, 26, 29, 46, 47, 139, 182, 329, 330, 331, 333, 338, 343, 349, 410, 449, 485
Belle River, 17, 26, 51, 173, 189, 310, 311, 338, 372, 373, 388, 548, 556, 561, 587, 588
Black Duck, 307, 310, 330, 547
Black River, 1, 13, 14-16, 18, 23, 24, 26, 29, 40, 41, 43, 45, 47-51, 107, 112, 117, 118, 125, 130, 145, 150, 153, 155, 166-168, 171-182, 186-189, 220, 252, 254, 257, 264, 267, 270, 274, 278, 306-310, 314, 318, 321, 328-335, 337, 339-343, 345, 372, 373, 384, 388, 390, 391, 393, 397, 400, 403, 405, 437, 438, 440, 508, 524, 525, 527, 528, 541-544, 547, 548, 550, 552-556, 558, 559, 565, 574, 581, 582, 589, 590, 594, 614
Black Robes, 37, 67, 68, 79, 80, 81, 97, 130, 416, 444
Black Snake, 307, 330, 547
Blackhawk War, 266, 511
Blackwater River People, 16, 574, 606
Blacksmiths, 135, 180, 186, 187, 201, 240, 265, 371, 375, 551, 552, 558
Bloody Run, 26, 179, 211, 285
Bluewater Bridge, 302, 437
Boarding Schools, 376, 526, 529, 530, 532, 533, 535, 536
Bois Blanc Island, 18, 73, 255, 349, 588
Boone, Daniel, 148, 205, 218, 222, 248, 269
Boundaries, 8, 12, 15, 151, 270, 293, 294, 379, 509, 514
Bow, 437, 491
Boweting, 5, 24, 48, 305, 311, 573
Brakeman, 16, 153, 240, 307, 318, 320, 440, 451, 545, 546, 551, 555, 556, 596
British, 12, 13, 18, 21, 25, 30, 31, 44, 69, 70, 102-104, 112, 114, 115, 120, 133, 141-143, 146, 147, 149-153, 155-157, 159-164, 166-168, 172, 179, 189, 191, 193, 194, 202, 204-227, 230-232, 234, 236-252, 254, 255, 259, 261, 262, 264, 266, 268, 270, 272, 274, 275, 280, 281, 283, 284, 292-296, 298, 303, 306, 307, 309, 310, 312, 314, 316, 319-326, 329, 334-336, 351, 352, 355-357, 360, 364, 367-369, 372, 378-380, 385, 386, 389, 412-420, 508, 513-515, 518, 540, 541, 543-546, 549, 576, 586, 588, 594, 600, 602, 613
Brockway Center, 168, 181, 551, 557
Brockway, 111, 168, 181, 188, 547, 551, 557
Buffalo, 30, 41, 78, 174, 253, 330, 353, 438, 486, 493, 496, 519, 546, 549
Bunce Creek, 29, 150, 178, 182, 186, 274, 543, 549, 550
Bunce Z. W., 167, 179, 187, 306, 547, 548, 550, 555
Bunyan, Paul, 177
Bureau of Indian Affairs, 375, 534, 536, 606

C

Cadillac, 38, 63, 64, 94, 96, 107, 141, 144, 154, 192, 198, 199, 200, 201, 202, 261, 268, 274, 279, 292, 497, 586, 596, 606, 611
Cahokia, 158, 215, 220, 247, 281, 321, 395, 514, 578
Calendar, 6, 7, 281, 410, 607
Camp Meeting, 111, 113, 117, 120, 123, 125, 360, 374
Campau, Joseph, 154, 159, 161, 166, 188, 414, 415, 546
Canada, 9, 10, 13, 15, 21, 23-25, 29, 30, 35, 38, 43, 47, 48, 51, 56, 69, 73, 74, 81, 83, 90, 91, 93, 102-104, 109, 111, 116, 118, 119, 120, 121, 123, 129, 130, 133, 137, 139, 145, 150-153, 156-159, 160, 163, 164, 172, 175, 177, 178, 184, 186, 191, 193, 194, 196, 198, 202, 205, 208, 214, 217, 218, 220, 222, 224, 225, 227, 229-234, 236, 237, 239, 240, 242-245, 248-250, 253-255, 261, 273, 275, 278, 281-284, 290, 292-303, 305, 307, 311, 321-324, 326, 332, 333, 335, 341, 344, 352, 357, 358, 359, 362, 364, 365, 367, 368, 369,

371, 372, 375, 378, 379, 384, 388, 389, 390, 391, 393, 396, 402, 405, 406, 412-414, 417-420, 422-426, 443, 485, 489, 513, 515, 517, 518, 527-529, 532, 533, 536, 541, 545, 546, 553, 556, 562, 563, 567, 568, 574, 577, 578, 584, 586, 589, 595, 597, 603, 604, 607, 609-612
Canadian Truth Commission, 526, 532, 611
Canal, 253, 559, 560, 561
Captives, 10, 37, 45, 98, 102, 203, 233, 260, 269, 270, 309, 392, 412, 416, 418, 488, 514
Cass, Lewis, 241, 243, 245, 371, 385, 388, 389, 414, 419, 517
Castles, 44, 47, 49, 52, 573, 583
Cat People, 37, 576, 579, 585
Catholic Point, 17, 108, 552, 566, 587
Catholic, 17, 66, 68, 70, 76, 96, 97, 98, 103, 104, 106-108, 154, 162, 172, 183, 198, 208, 217, 247, 254, 284, 291, 298, 299, 340, 342, 375, 417, 435, 529, 530, 531, 533, 544, 552, 566, 587
Chemical Valley, 301, 302, 359
Chenail Escarte, 20, 28, 231, 274, 299, 314, 330, 334, 337, 338, 339, 342, 343, 344, 345, 346, 347, 369
Chicago, 63, 148, 149, 158, 167, 182, 188, 239, 240, 262, 263, 266, 284, 289, 291, 300, 302, 309, 331, 342, 352, 396, 428, 546, 547, 555, 565, 568, 579, 599
Chiefs, 153, 222, 224, 241, 252, 305, 312, 315, 328, 335, 342, 349, 354, 364, 369, 454-456, 509, 597, 603, 607
Chilicothe, 29, 240, 269, 330, 352, 369, 402, 576
Cholera, 16, 108, 128, 266, 388, 510, 515, 587
Clans, 5, 33, 42, 375, 455, 456, 460, 462, 471, 508, 573, 581
Clark, George Rogers 219, 220, 221, 226, 237, 247, 379
Clinton River, 15, 17, 25, 26, 99, 189, 270, 321, 335, 344, 392, 396
Clyde Mills, 175, 182, 188, 555

Coal, 371, 398
Company K, 257
Copper, 31, 51, 52, 84, 101, 401, 470
Corn, 38, 43, 49, 50, 52, 56, 62, 70, 75, 77, 91, 95, 96, 121, 123, 134, 135, 147, 150, 156, 157, 168, 188, 196, 221, 225, 228, 230, 253, 260, 275, 278, 280, 282, 287, 306, 318, 319, 363, 365, 396, 399, 401, 421, 466, 467, 473, 474, 475, 476, 477, 480, 482, 487, 495, 498, 501, 515, 537, 541, 546, 566, 575
Counting Coup, 488, 489
Coureur Des Bois, 139
Cradle Board, 460, 461, 476
Crane, 5, 34, 334, 344, 345, 346, 349, 456, 458, 572, 573, 574, 581, 582, 583, 603
Creation, 5, 41, 448, 610
Cree, 111, 139, 298, 389, 445, 577, 578, 580
Croghan, George, 237, 265
Cumberland Gap, 162, 215
Custer, 518, 525

D

Dakota Sioux, 138, 518, 577
Delaware, 129, 207, 227, 235, 273, 369
Delaware, 17, 21, 28, 129, 158, 205, 207, 221, 222, 227, 235, 250, 272, 273, 275, 312, 330, 347, 349, 369, 372, 382, 391, 576, 582, 586, 587
Delta, 18, 20, 22, 48, 231, 355, 356
Depeyster, 157, 220, 221, 223
Detroit River, 7, 13, 14, 17, 18, 21, 40, 48, 73, 78, 146, 149, 157, 159, 160, 167, 179, 189, 190, 199, 200, 213, 219, 220, 227, 229, 231, 233, 240, 241, 243, 261, 262, 268, 283, 284, 285, 286, 287, 288, 290, 296, 299, 320, 329, 331-334, 336, 337, 339, 341, 342, 343, 344, 345, 346, 347, 348, 359, 365, 369, 382, 384, 425, 443, 502, 560, 587, 588, 589, 607
Detroit, 278, too numerous
Disease, 43, 45, 67, 91, 92, 97, 103, 127, 128, 129, 130, 224, 226, 228, 253, 284, 374, 394, 436, 437, 441,

445, 508, 510, 513, 517, 531, 532, 534, 602
District of Hesse, 158, 159, 227, 248, 249, 294
Dog, 52, 53, 104, 110, 157, 270, 346, 457, 462, 478, 493, 496, 535, 614
Draper Park, 403, 404
Dulhut, 16, 76, 79, 84, 194, 195, 196, 246
Duluth, 16, 78, 79, 84, 90, 96, 194, 195, 196, 260, 261, 444, 589

E

Eastman, Charles, 57, 58, 233, 391, 433, 451, 489, 490, 509, 511, 538, 594, 607, 608, 611
Elliot, 160, 378
English, 23, 66, 68, 71, 72, 79, 91, 96, 103, 107, 113, 117, 121, 124, 126, 137-139, 141, 142, 144, 148-153, 155, 158-164, 170, 191, 194-200, 202-212, 215-217, 219-222, 225, 231, 233, 234, 237, 243, 246, 248-250, 252, 254, 255, 261, 262, 268-270, 280, 281, 283, 286, 295, 313, 320, 321, 324, 328, 362, 375, 376, 381, 385, 416, 419- 421, 433, 474, 511, 513, 514, 524, 531, 541, 544, 545, 549, 564, 572, 580, 613
Epidemics, 37, 82, 108, 127, 128, 253, 266, 532, 563
Erie tribe, 579
Ewing, Wallace K., 597
Explorers, vii, 66, 71, 202, 261

F

Family Compact, 154, 254, 274, 293, 295, 296, 370, 514
Father Ricard, Richard, 108, 565
Feathers, 117, 122, 333, 360, 604
Ferry, 175, 290, 425
Fire Raft, 334
Fire Water, 169, 324
Fishing, 73, 484, 500, 516
Flint River, 26, 125, 314, 331, 346, 373, 385, 388, 392, 400, 405
Flood, 6, 53, 64, 448, 508, 573, 581

Fort Detroit, Detret, 14, 16, 23, 26, 78, 83, 195, 211, 220, 224, 233, 453, 587
Fort Edward, 22, 251, 262, 264, 268, 299
Fort Gratiot, 14-17, 29, 47, 69, 90, 107, 166, 167, 246, 247, 252, 255, 261-265, 267, 268, 275, 292, 306, 307, 310, 311, 403, 501, 542-544, 546, 547, 549, 553, 556, 565, 587
Fort Malden, 160, 233, 246, 268, 325, 423
Fort Ponchetrain, 96, 141, 204, 206, 249, 261, 268
Fort Sinclair, 147, 148, 214, 235, 262, 307, 541, 600
Fort St. Joseph, 14, 16, 23, 79, 84, 89, 96, 98, 143, 195, 196, 197, 198, 203, 221, 240, 260, 261, 292, 312
Fossil Trees, 15
Fox-Mesquackie, 27, 38, 39, 43, 44, 96, 143, 202, 203, 321, 329, 338, 351, 352, 576-578, 585
French and Indian War, 89, 205, 216, 248, 306, 352, 378
French, 9, 10, 13, 14, 16, 20-22, 27, 28, 30, 34, 35, 36, 38, 43- 45, 63, 66-72, 74, 76, 78-83, 85, 89, 91, 93-98, 100-104, 107, 108, 114, 120, 122, 124, 128, 132, 133, 135, 137-146, 149, 154, 155, 158, 159, 161-164, 170, 172, 177, 191-199, 202-217, 219-221, 231, 233-235, 237, 240, 246-252, 254, 255, 260, 261, 263-65, 267-269, 272, 274, 276, 279-281, 286, 287, 289, 292, 293, 296-299, 306, 310, 316, 318, 320, 328, 329, 335, 352, 353, 355, 378, 379, 388, 405, 412, 414-418, 446, 486-488, 503, 506, 511, 513, 514, 517, 541, 542, 544-546, 553, 556, 560, 564, 567, 571-573, 575-577, 580, 582, 583, 584, 585, 586, 612, 613
Fur Trade, 30, 38, 43-45, 78, 79, 97, 102-104, 107, 114, 132-136, 139, 140-143, 145, 146, 151, 152, 154, 156, 161-163, 165, 166, 195, 196, 197, 207, 216, 225, 232, 236, 379,

381, 392, 414, 513, 519, 542, 567, 597, 598, 599, 600, 608
Furs, 120, 147, 157, 468

G

Garden, 359, 403, 478
Georgian Bay, 10, 14, 29, 36, 47, 49, 71, 73, 82, 138, 145, 154, 183, 305, 339, 348, 359, 408, 503, 573, 574, 579, 581, 584
Gitchi Manito, 1, 2, 32, 42, 54, 57, 358, 431, 434, 435, 436, 457, 472, 473, 504, 528
Gnadenhutten, 30, 221
God, 12, 81, 88, 113, 237, 259, 395, 447, 509, 522
God, 1, 4, 12, 41, 42, 53-55, 57, 62, 64, 66, 72, 81, 84, 87, 88, 93, 104, 109, 113, 117, 126, 200, 237, 259, 272, 273, 360, 375, 377, 378, 380, 385, 390, 391, 395, 416, 431, 432, 433, 434, 437, 438, 439, 440, 447, 453, 457, 458, 462, 504, 507, 509,510, 522, 524, 526, 539, 561, 591
Great Lakes, 3, 5, 7, 8, 9, 10, 11, 15, 25, 28, 35, 42- 45, 48, 49, 52, 67, 69, 71, 76, 82, 84, 103, 128, 129, 136, 139, 146, 147, 151, 152, 156, 162-164, 189, 206, 207, 209, 212, 214, 217, 222, 225, 230, 246, 250, 251, 302, 345, 383, 385, 396, 407, 445, 479, 508, 511, 524, 532, 541, 580, 585, 588, 591, 594, 598, 604, 610, 612
Great Spirit, 1, 3, 6, 32, 36, 53, 54, 57, 80, 82, 87, 97, 99, 100, 109, 207, 238, 244, 259, 309, 312, 324, 391, 431-437, 440, 441, 453, 458, 460, 466, 472, 474, 478, 487, 494, 497, 504, 507, 509, 512, 523, 528, 538, 540, 547
Greaux, Joe, 14, 24, 186, 431, 437, 438, 440, 452, 477, 524, 578, 613
Griffon, 76, 77, 78, 140, 189, 268

H

Hamilton, 117, 151, 162, 163, 172, 218, 219, 220, 228, 273, 282, 300, 417, 549, 561, 562
Harmar, General, 228, 335
Harrington, Daniel, 166, 175, 180, 187, 320, 543, 549, 554
Harrison, 31, 238, 239, 244, 245, 324, 558
Harsens Island, 19, 20, 24, 69, 154, 168, 190, 336, 355, 357, 397, 440, 542, 546, 551, 557, 560, 601
Hessians, 218, 541
Hides, 157, 468, 471
Holy Men, 3, 35, 61, 431, 446, 582
Horses, 19, 40, 51, 143, 177, 181, 183-186, 201, 205, 214, 227, 228, 245, 248, 253, 272, 275, 280, 282, 298, 318, 356, 361, 452, 496, 506, 513, 551, 574, 584, 614
Howard, Henry, 173, 174, 175, 179, 188, 559
Hull, General, 237, 240, 243, 268, 309, Governor 235, 242, 243, 246, 251, 275, 286, 339, 383, 392, 414, 422, 554
Hunting, 11, 39, 82, 219, 318, 407, 455, 456, 484, 494, 604
Huron Land Co., 264, 555
Huron River, 17, 21, 26, 98, 158, 189, 222, 250, 321, 338, 351, 354, 382, 400, 587
Huron tribe, 70, 579
Huron, entries are too numerous

I

Illinois, 13, 38, 63, 74, 96, 144, 150, 164, 188, 194, 197, 200, 203, 215, 219, 220, 223, 237, 239, 276, 281, 291, 294, 302, 321, 336, 369, 428, 514, 576, 577, 578, 579
Immigration, 127, 129, 133, 179, 223, 283, 289, 296, 562, 563, 566, 598, 613
Indian Agents, 105, 220, 226, 235, 254, 370, 373, 378, 379, 516, 530, 536
Indian Dave, 307, 308

Indian Village, 14, 67, 141, 204, 328, 401, 406
Indian, entries are too numerous
Indiana, 28, 30, 150, 159, 168, 220, 238, 239, 246, 247, 252, 276, 324, 335, 340, 342, 350, 352, 353, 354, 365, 369, 395, 402, 414, 423, 576, 577
Indians entries are too numerous
Interpreters, 67, 68, 71, 96, 121, 133, 135, 138, 155, 157, 165, 220, 241, 309, 379, 383
Ipperwash, 21, 304, 329, 331, 333, 334, 336-338, 340, 342-349, 366, 367, 526, 608
Iroquois War, 44, 47, 48, 82, 305, 311, 321, 350, 364, 573, 574, 575, 576, 579, 584, 585
Iroquois, 5, 6, 10, 24, 35-38, 42-49, 67-73, 76, 77, 79, 82- 84, 90, 91, 93, 94, 96, 98, 100, 103, 129, 133, 138, 139, 143-145, 191, 194-197, 199, 202, 205, 206, 208, 218, 221, 225, 226, 239, 260, 261, 268, 304, 305, 311, 321, 333-335, 350, 353, 364, 379, 381, 443, 445, 497, 506, 511, 524, 527, 539, 572-577, 579, 582, 584-586, 588, 608

J

Jesuits, 9, 45, 68, 69, 72, 73, 80, 81-84, 97, 98, 100-103, 107, 114, 135, 140, 141, 190, 198, 199, 208, 580
Johnson, John, 216
Johnston, 327, 333, 347, 348, 349, 376, 555, 599
Jones, Peter, 32, 109, 112, 113, 114, 116, 117, 119, 126, 333, 360, 373, 450, 474, 476, 604, 608

K

Karegnondi, 10, 40, 41, 46, 48, 400
Kaskaskia, 158, 164, 194, 215, 220, 247, 578
Kent County, 13, 147, 206, 255, 293, 294
Kentucky, 30, 148, 162, 171, 172, 208, 215, 216, 218, 219, 222, 223, 224, 226, 229, 237, 239, 240, 247, 248, 270, 276, 323, 379, 402, 417, 423
Kettle Point, 21, 43, 303, 326, 329, 340, 345, 347, 359, 364, 365, 366, 368, 589
Kickapoo, 37, 38, 43, 578, 583
Kimball, 117, 177, 182, 555, 559
Kioscance, 24, 46, 305, 311, 312, 342, 573
Kioscanee, 24, 312, 573
Kitchi Manito, 448 see Gitchi Manito

L

Lahonton, 10, 44, 64, 82, 84, 85, 88, 89, 90-94, 99, 101, 137, 196, 197, 260, 261, 461, 466, 485, 486, 488, 497, 573, 577, 580-583, 585, 599, 609
Lake Erie, 9, 13, 17, 20, 26, 27, 28, 29, 30, 47, 49, 56, 71, 77, 145, 160, 173, 196, 199, 204, 231, 234, 244, 278, 312, 324, 337, 346, 348, 356, 379, 380, 381, 382, 384, 444, 503, 560, 576, 577, 586, 589, 599
Lake Huron Land Bridge, 10, 407
Lake Huron, too numeros
Lake Michigan, 9, 10, 26, 27, 37, 38, 39, 46, 72, 197, 222, 311, 339, 352, 388, 410, 565, 576
Lake Ontario, 9, 10, 28, 71, 77, 78, 145, 151, 402, 589
Lake St. Clair, too numeros
Lake Superior, 1, 4, 5, 9, 10, 13, 17, 23, 24, 25, 30, 39, 72, 73, 74, 79, 83, 107, 108, 138, 139, 143, 150, 156, 188, 194, 218, 245, 276, 311, 382, 444, 445, 544, 579, 581, 582, 586, 603
Lambton, 14, 20, 22, 28, 29, 31, 120, 254, 274, 292, 293, 294, 296, 298, 299, 302, 303, 304, 356, 359, 368, 380, 405, 406, 558, 563, 589, 595, 597, 599, 600, 602, 605
Langlade, Charles, 204, 205, 248, 513
Lansing, 14, 26, 43, 47, 49, 126, 130, 138, 161, 231, 256, 259, 305, 317,

320, 425, 488, 562, 566, 573, 596, 597, 599, 601, 602, 605, 609
Lasalle, 77, 78, 292, 403
Lenape, 221, 382, 576, 577
Lifeways, 3, 431, 484, 537
Louisiana, 9, 43, 64, 76, 78, 102, 103, 132, 141, 191, 196, 197, 202, 206, 234, 281, 292, 412, 416, 486, 598, 599, 607, 609
Lumber, 29, 176, 185, 266, 275, 345, 390, 425, 550, 553, 566, 568, 598
Lumbering, 554, 612

M

Maconse, 329, 335, 347, 372
Madeline Island, 25, 34, 444, 579
magician, 40
Maiden, 21, 220, 233, 242, 244, 255, 268
Malden, 18, 21, 28, 109, 156, 231, 242, 244, 246, 253, 254, 268, 284, 297, 312, 335, 336, 425, 588*see Fort Malden
Manitos, 53, 116, 448 see Kitchi Manito
Manoomin, 1, 7, 11
Maple Sugar, 57, 146, 147, 155, 165, 251, 287, 311, 318, 319, 328, 453, 461, 465, 466, 475, 503, 515, 556, 602
Mascoutin, 43, 202, 572, 577, 578, 583, 584
Master of Life, 1, 32, 87, 99, 207, 325, 494
Maumee, 27, 28, 30, 158, 159, 204, 210, 230, 231, 316, 320, 330, 347, 384, 577
McDougal, George, 160, 268, 383, 384, 414, 543, 545
McKee, Alexander, 31, 219, 222, 227, 231, 378, 602
Medicine, 3, 53, 54, 64, 123, 127, 268, 278, 311, 320, 347, 359, 432, 433, 435, 436, 440, 441, 447, 449, 459, 493, 524
Megis Shell, 2, 3, 4
Menominee, 34, 39, 398, 578

Methodist, 105, 106, 107, 109, 113, 116, 117, 118, 120-126, 180, 253, 298, 308, 329, 331-333, 358, 359, 360, 362, 372-374, 376, 517, 527, 528, 551, 552, 603, 609
Metis, 4, 5, 14, 72, 73, 77-79, 80-83, 96, 97, 98, 101, 128, 130, 131, 133, 137-139, 145, 146, 153, 166, 176, 186, 190, 191, 194, 206, 216, 233, 261, 269, 318, 333, 350, 386, 416, 438, 440, 458, 513, 518, 519, 528, 531, 535, 537-539, 581, 582, 598, 600, 607, 609
Miami River, 27, 28, 226, 316, 381, 384, 577
Miami, 27, 28, 30, 34, 35, 63, 77, 154, 158, 159, 197, 200, 203, 204, 207, 210, 226-228, 239, 261, 268, 316, 329, 330, 331, 335, 337, 341, 346-350, 352, 353, 369, 381, 384, 402, 444, 515, 576, 577, 578, 585
Michigan, too numeros
Michilimackinac, 5, 25, 39, 63, 74, 78, 79, 135, 140, 141, 143, 145, 156, 157, 162, 164, 194, 195, 196, 198-200, 203, 204, 207, 210, 211, 214, 221, 227, 230, 232, 248, 314, 334, 335, 388, 501
Mide, 3, 4, 53, 54, 82, 320, 433, 446, 448, 477, 582, see Holy men
Midiwiwin, 54, 579
Migration, 4, 5, 34, 209, 294, 426, 448, 524, 610
Mills, 19, 29, 38, 174, 175, 182, 188, 289, 555, 557, 559, 609
Mission schools, 375, 530, 533
Missionaries, 9, 66, 82, 202, 261, 264, 360, 512
Missions, 105, 108, 113, 117, 120, 122, 125, 126, 136, 198, 298, 331, 533, 534, 610
Mississauga, 29, 47, 48, 116, 121, 226, 231, 248, 300, 303, 330, 331, 343, 344
Mississippi, 9, 11, 13, 27, 28, 30, 35, 38, 39, 43, 51, 74, 77, 78, 144, 151, 152, 157, 158, 161, 162, 190, 196, 197, 203, 208, 210, 211, 215-218, 221, 223, 234, 238, 239, 240, 241, 247,

249, 250, 253, 255, 276, 292, 310, 322, 324, 326, 351, 357, 372, 384,389, 390, 393, 395, 396, 400, 420, 502, 503, 513, 516, 518, 576, 577, 578
Money, 85, 86, 92, 95, 101, 111, 117, 136, 146, 165, 168, 170, 180, 185, 188, 225, 229, 234, 250, 288, 310, 311, 325, 362, 374, 377, 379, 383, 387, 399, 401, 422, 423, 472, 485, 510, 516, 517, 523, 525, 526, 539, 558, 564
Montreal, 9, 21, 30, 35, 37, 38, 43-45, 49, 51, 69, 70, 73, 76, 77, 78, 79, 82, 83, 91, 93, 94, 97, 98, 102-104, 120, 133, 134, 138-141, 143-145, 150-152, 155-158, 166, 172, 178, 194, 197, 198, 201, 202, 217, 224, 243, 287, 302, 396, 415, 417, 443, 499, 568, 575, 586
Moravians, 147, 234, 380, 541
Mother (Granny) Rodd, 319, 320, 336, 339, 345, 601
Mounds, 39, 60, 252, 253, 264, 281, 304, 308, 358, 378, 388, 395, 396, 397, 398, 399, 400, 402, 404, 405, 409, 578, 606
Mrs. John Howard, 414
Musqueash, 336

N

Nations, 14, 20, 24, 33, 37, 44, 66, 93, 95, 101, 135, 210, 213, 216, 218, 226, 227, 242, 248, 251, 302, 311, 322, 335, 356, 371, 372, 378, 379, 381, 389, 418, 524, 573, 575, 576, 585, 586, 604, 611
Negroes, 224, 416, 417, 418, 425, 430
Neutrals, 35, 37, 42, 43, 44, 45, 68, 79, 130, 574, 575, 576, 579, 584, 585
New France, 13, 30, 43, 65, 67, 68, 69, 71, 72, 73, 74, 75, 78, 82, 88, 91, 96, 101, 102, 103, 128, 129, 133, 137, 143, 172, 178, 191, 193, 194, 196, 197, 199, 202, 208, 225, 412, 417, 599, 609
Norsemen, 4, 66, 127
Northwest Co., 114, 166

Northwest Territory, 28, 35, 67, 168, 175, 210, 214, 215, 222, 223, 225, 227, 228, 230, 234, 245, 247, 248, 252, 254, 274, 285, 286, 322, 399, 418, 515, 550, 592, 594

O

Ohio Company, (The), 223, 247
Ohio River, 13, 28, 30, 43, 152, 162, 163, 205, 206, 210, 215, 217, 218, 222, 223, 225, 226, 227, 234, 238, 248, 269, 414, 514
Ohio, 9, 13, 21, 27-31, 43-45, 83, 109, 118, 128, 144, 150-152, 158, 159, 162, 163, 166, 174, 177, 187, 188, 200, 203-206, 208-210, 212, 215-219, 221-223, 225-232, 234, 237-240, 243, 247, 248, 249, 252, 254, 260, 265, 269, 272, 273, 276, 284, 287, 292, 299, 305, 316, 320, 322, 323, 325, 330, 340, 346, 349, 350, 352, 353, 365, 369, 379, 382, 383, 384, 396, 400, 402, 405, 407, 414, 423, 506, 513, 514, 545, 576, 577, 586, 594, 604
Ojibwa, 24, 34, 43, 44, 47, 54, 72, 116-118, 204, 205, 226, 232, 248, 250, 251, 295, 296, 303, 314, 331, 344, 369, 376, 391, 406, 474, 581, 596, 599, 603
Ojibwe, 1, 3-8, 12, 17, 18, 22, 24, 25, 27, 32-39, 41-52, 54, 55, 69, 72, 94, 96-98, 103, 113-118, 120, 122, 125, 128, 129, 132, 138, 139, 146, 153, 158, 165, 186, 193, 194, 200, 208-210, 212, 213, 221, 226, 231, 232, 235, 241, 245, 248, 250, 251, 252, 258, 261, 293, 302, 305, 307- 312, 314-316, 320, 321, 327, 329, 331-334, 336-352, 355, 356, 358, 359, 370-372, 374, 375, 381, 382, 385-387, 389-393, 399, 407, 431, 436, 445, 449, 450, 452, 458, 459, 461, 471, 473, 476, 480, 499, 513, 515, 516, 524, 526-528, 530, 536, 543, 571-585, 588, 594-596, 598, 599, 602--605, 607-612

Ottissippi

Okemos, 222, 259, 316, 317, 335, 372, 556
Ontario, 1, 6, 7, 9-11, 14, 20-22, 24, 25, 28-31, 34, 35, 37, 38, 40-44, 46-50, 68-73, 77, 78, 82, 97, 102, 105, 113, 114, 117, 120, 121, 130, 138-140, 145, 146, 151, 158, 159, 171, 175, 183, 193, 200, 206, 208, 214, 220, 221, 224-226, 231, 239, 242, 245, 248, 251, 255, 257, 259, 261, 262, 268, 274, 275, 282, 292-295, 297, 298, 300-306, 310-312, 315, 319, 322, 326, 327, 329-338, 340, 342-346, 348, 350-352, 356, 358, 359, 365, 367-369, 373, 378, 380, 388, 402, 403, 405-408, 420, 422, 425, 440, 443-445, 452, 470, 498, 506, 513, 516, 527, 530, 531, 532, 534, 535, 541, 547, 557, 559, 560, 562, 563, 567, 568, 574-579, 581, 583-585, 587, 589, 590, 594, 597, 598, 600, 602-605, 607, 610, 611, 612
Otchipwes, 24, 47, 582
Ottawa River, 38, 46, 71, 76, 144, 145
Ottawa, 4, 5, 10, 24, 25, 34, 35, 37-39, 42, 43, 45- 47, 71, 74, 76, 84, 91, 98, 102, 129, 139, 144, 145, 147, 148, 158, 196, 200, 202, 204, 206, 209, 210, 213, 220, 227, 230, 231, 235, 249, 261, 303, 309, 314, 320, 321, 330-353, 355, 356, 369, 379, 381--383, 385, 388, 389, 392, 401, 444, 452, 513, 543, 572, 578, 583, 584, 596
Ottissippi, 7, 17, 40, 41, 46, 48, 71, 107, 398, 400, 502, 506, 590

P

Panis, 102, 224, 417, 418, 488
Patriot War, 254, 255, 265, 267, 295, 609
Pawnee, 102, 224, 416, 417, 418, 488
Pennsylvania, 9, 21, 30, 144, 158, 203, 205, 208, 212, 217, 218, 221, 222, 223, 225, 233, 237, 239, 248, 273, 352, 369, 378, 379, 402, 529, 532, 541, 564, 576, 577, 586
Petroglyphs, 400, 401, 537, 598

Pine Grove Park, 16, 18, 19, 22, 41, 209, 261, 264, 266, 270, 501, 525, 565, 587
Pipe, 136, 173, 179, 191, 200, 207, 218, 277, 296, 316, 331, 380, 382, 391, 434, 437, 441, 455, 457, 472, 474, 480, 493, 497, 504
Piqua, 29, 204, 221, 323
Pirates, 157
Point Edward, 22, 41, 175, 251, 292, 299, 300, 302, 365, 506, 563
Pontiac War, 209, 306, 511
Pontiac, 18, 26, 114, 146, 149, 155, 161, 169, 197, 205, 209, 210, 211, 212, 213, 214, 215, 240, 262, 270, 306, 307, 314, 316, 317, 320, 321, 323, 334, 335, 341, 345, 348, 353, 447, 507, 511, 513, 514, 552, 565, 578, 588, 602, 610
Port Huron, Michigan, 22, 29, 48, 69, 108, 125, 153, 154, 155, 173-175, 193, 261, 302, 306, 308, 310, 330, 336, 397, 405, 420, 425, 437, 544, 562, 573, 614
Pottawatomi, 4, 19, 20, 27, 34, 35, 38, 46, 103, 149, 158, 160, 161, 197, 200, 202, 203, 220, 221, 227, 231, 235, 240, 250, 261, 278, 280, 321, 329, 330, 332, 334, 336, 337, 338, 339, 340, 341, 342, 344, 346, 347, 348, 349, 350, 351, 354, 355, 356, 358, 379, 382, 385, 389, 452, 572, 578, 579, 611
Pow Wow, 41, 60, 318, 358, 364, 437, 438, 439, 440, 483, 524, 525, 612
Presents, 63, 232, 269
Proctor, 237, 239, 242, 243, 244, 316, 326
Prohibition, 176, 291, 299, 357, 361

Q

Quebec, 9, 13, 37, 43, 45, 68, 69, 71, 72, 73, 82, 101-104, 107, 141, 143, 146, 149, 162, 192, 193, 197, 199, 200, 204, 206, 214, 215, 217, 220, 225, 247, 261, 272, 274, 281, 292-294, 378, 386, 392, 575

R

Racism, 115, 122, 375, 422, 430, 433, 508, 517, 519, 520, 521, 526, 530, 534, 535, 536
Recipes, 481
Recollects, 68, 69, 77, 83, 84
Religion, 25, 32, 55, 65, 67, 73, 82, 92, 98-100, 110, 114, 116, 120, 137, 139, 144, 162, 192, 214, 282, 362, 413, 431-434, 437, 447, 506, 507, 512, 520, 522, 525, 534, 535, 599, 602, 605, 610, 611
Reservations, 20, 21, 105, 117, 119, 126, 304, 309, 311, 314, 326, 372, 373, 375, 390, 416, 437, 490, 510, 511, 516, 527, 529, 532, 589
Revolutionary War, 216, 217, 218, 222, 228, 229, 259, 273, 293, 309, 316, 329, 352, 378, 417, 541
Riley, John, 51, 153, 166, 307, 308, 309, 311, 330, 372, 387, 542, 543, 544, 547
Rivers, 27, 31, 47, 158, 190, 205, 217, 292, 299, 391, 438, 443, 559, 560
Ruby, 117, 167, 168, 180, 181, 186, 188, 189, 550, 551, 553, 555

S

Saginaw Bay, 27, 38, 41, 50, 56, 126, 153, 184, 321, 341, 400, 402, 502, 508
Saginaw Chippewa, 8, 14, 22, 37, 45, 47, 79, 82, 130, 176, 256, 259, 316, 331, 333, 336, 338, 339, 343, 348, 370, 372, 374, 376, 393, 445, 508, 513, 515, 528, 531, 537, 594, 609
Saint Clare, 12
Saint Felicite, 108, 552
Sandwich, 21, 29, 159, 160, 172, 246, 254, 255, 274, 282, 297, 299, 417, 424
Sarnia Chippewa, 14, 303, 431, 499
Sarnia, 8, 14, 20-24, 28, 31, 47, 80, 114, 117, 120, 121, 130, 171, 173, 175, 180, 184, 218, 253, 254, 262, 292, 295, 297, 298, 299, 300-304, 306, 307, 312, 315, 319, 320, 328, 331, 333, 336, 337, 340, 342, 343, 347, 350, 351, 359, 360, 362-365, 367, 372, 373, 391, 397, 406, 431, 433, 443, 444, 449, 498, 499, 501, 526, 527, 557, 562, 563, 568, 571, 584, 589, 599, 602, 603, 605, 610, 611, 612
Saulk, 27, 38, 39, 574, 578, 583
Sault St. Marie, 48, 165, 193, 305, 532
Saulteurs, 36, 73, 76, 133, 312, 573, 578, 580, 581, 582, 583
Schoolcraft, Henry, 252, 269, 458, 516, 610
Scouts, scout, 153, 269, 309, 316, 341, 386, 392, 489, 490, 510
scutes, 6, 35
Shawnee, 29, 31, 37, 45, 158, 200, 205, 207, 216, 217, 221, 225-228, 235, 237, 239, 244, 269, 296, 303, 322, 323, 330, 350, 352, 353, 357, 368, 369, 378, 382, 402, 444, 576, 578, 583, 586
Slavery, 64, 65, 102, 103, 172, 294, 412, 413, 414, 415, 416, 418, 419, 420, 421, 423, 424, 426, 428, 429, 601, 607, 611, 612
Smallpox, 97, 127, 128, 129, 130, 206, 214, 513
Smith, Jacob, 315, 385, 386, 392, 393, 515, 596
Snake, 26, 42, 307, 330, 339, 345, 443, 547, 577
Sombra, 20, 31, 255, 274, 296, 297, 299, 359, 368, 369, 563
Spanish, 66, 76, 97, 103, 130, 132, 151, 170, 194, 221, 232, 238, 247, 416, 420, 486, 536, 578, 580
St. Clair Flats, 19, 174, 548, 557
St. Clair River, 12-20, 22-24, 26, 27, 29, 31, 37, 40, 41, 46, 48, 71, 98, 110, 119, 143, 150, 153-155, 167, 168, 173-175, 177, 178, 181, 183, 189, 190, 209, 214, 220, 221, 231, 241, 246, 250, 261, 262, 264, 266, 268, 270, 275, 279, 281, 295, 296, 297, 298, 301-303, 307, 311, 314, 317, 318, 331, 338, 339, 340, 345, 355, 356, 359, 361, 371, 372, 397, 400, 402, 403, 405-407, 425, 444, 473,

Ottissippi

501, 502, 506, 525, 528, 541-545, 547- 554, 557, 558, 567, 568, 569, 587, 589, 592, 601, 612
Stewart, Aura, 190, 242, 307, 560, 567, 601, 612
Stony Point, 329, 333, 336, 339, 343, 344, 347, 348, 365, 366, 367, 368
Sturgeon, 27, 346, 398, 502
Swan Creek, 1, 13, 15, 27, 48, 50, 107, 189, 230, 254, 278, 313, 329, 330, 331, 332, 333, 334, 335, 337, 338, 341, 342, 343, 345, 347, 372, 373, 384, 390, 391, 393, 508, 527, 546, 549, 574, 583, 587

T

Tecumseh, 18, 20, 114, 155, 197, 236-245, 269, 295, 316, 321-327, 330, 334, 336, 343, 345, 347-350, 352, 353, 357, 363, 364, 368, 371, 447, 454, 507, 588, 594, 597, 606
Teuscha Grondie, 14
Thames River, 28, 29, 145, 311, 330, 334, 338, 339, 344, 346, 388, 587
The Ohio Company, 223
The Rapids, 21, 22, 23, 24, 40, 71
The Three Fires, 4, 6, 37, 371, 443, 452, 514, 578
Tippacanoe, 31, 238, 324, 350, 353
Tobacco, 35-37, 43, 45, 53, 57, 62, 65, 84, 98, 110, 131, 132, 138, 147, 169, 172, 184, 186, 196, 201, 215, 247, 248, 271, 284, 289, 303, 344, 369, 380, 386, 415, 421, 434, 435, 441, 442, 449-451, 453, 457, 473, 474, 491, 504, 513, 525, 528, 537, 572, 575, 579, 584, 585
Toronto, 14, 21, 47, 49, 69, 114, 145, 146, 172, 212, 275, 294, 297, 305, 402, 417, 573, 581, 598, 603, 604, 608, 610, 611
Totem, 32, 33, 79, 459, 556, 573
Traders, 74, 83, 84, 103, 114, 132, 148, 157, 158, 161, 163, 169, 171, 185, 232, 235, 414, 452, 546, 547
Trails, 49, 50, 51, 52, 68, 108, 148, 167, 180, 202, 233, 388, 289, 396, 398,

405, 425, 470, 497, 537, 556, 557, 607
Treaties, 105, 115, 144, 153, 194, 208, 225, 226, 228, 232, 233, 234, 235, 245, 250, 252, 253, 264, 293, 304, 305, 309, 315, 367, 369, 374, 378, 379, 381, 384, 390, 391, 393, 394, 410, 473, 514, 515, 521, 528, 535, 536, 608, 610, 611, 612
Tribes, too numerous
Tunnel, 174, 176, 291, 294, 302, 524, 568, 569
Turtle Island, 5, 7, 445, 507, 578

U

UEL, United Empire Loyalists, 224, 254, 293, 295, 419
Underground Railroad, 413, 423, 424, 425, 525, 553, 565
Upper Canada, 23, 102, 116-118, 212, 218, 224, 234, 242, 243, 245, 248, 249, 274, 293, 294, 351, 369, 378, 379, 384, 414, 517, 541, 546, 562, 583, 611

V

Vincennes, 149, 219, 220, 247, 379
Virginia, 163, 171, 172, 175, 205, 206, 208, 209, 215-217, 219, 220, 222, 223, 229, 247-249, 270-272, 369, 379, 402, 404, 414, 416, 418, 421, 424, 528, 576, 577, 586, 595

W

Wadhams, 43, 117, 175, 177, 179, 182, 188, 319, 524, 555, 556, 557, 559
Walpole Island, 15, 19, 20, 28, 46, 107, 112, 119, 154, 231, 311, 319, 322, 324, 326, 328, 329, 330, 332, 340-342, 345, 351, 355-358, 361, 363, 368, 372, 443, 444, 451, 514, 534, 536, 546, 557
Walpole, 8, 15, 19, 20, 28, 40, 46, 56, 107, 112, 119, 120, 154, 168, 231, 304, 311, 312, 319, 322, 324, 326, 328-330, 332, 334, 340-342, 344,

345, 348, 351, 355-358, 361, 363, 368, 370, 372, 443, 444, 451, 514, 532, 534, 536, 546, 557
Wampum, 191, 201, 218, 337, 391, 472
War of 1812, 31, 106, 155, 156, 161, 162, 187, 236, 240, 241, 245, 250, 254, 263, 287, 312, 314, 323, 324, 336, 347, 351, 352, 353, 357, 372, 385, 392, 417, 419, 508, 515, 576, 586, 600
Ward, Sam, 188, 189, 548, 550
Washington, George, 152, 163, 204, 205, 215, 216, 219, 221, 222, 224, 228, 234, 237, 248, 271, 272, 327, 353, 417, 567
Waubojeed, 327, death song, 488
Wawanosh, 113, 303, 319, 327, 328, 343, 348, 351, 363, 365, 589
Wayne, Anthony, 229, 230, 515
Westbrook, Andrew, 240, 271, 275, 544, 552, 561
Western District, 160, 231, 248, 249, 294, 351

White Rock, 14, 67, 171, 383, 384, 398, 399
Whitefish, 9, 24, 41, 64, 73, 284, 445, 287, 501
Wild Rice, 11, 72, 504, 578, 608
William Case, 105, 106, 109, 112, 113, 116, 117, 119, 333
Windsor, 21, 29, 159, 172, 183, 255, 274, 282, 291, 296-, 298, 331, 333, 334, 340, 343, 346, 365, 417, 422, 424, 425, 563, 564, 567, 589, 609

Y

Young Gull, 24, 46, 47, 48, 311, 337, 342, 573

Z

Ziibiwing Cultural Center, 537, 594, 613

Made in the USA
Middletown, DE
12 May 2025